Contents

Rover 820i Saloon

Rover 820Se Fastback

Rover 820 Owners Workshop Manual

John S Mead

Models covered
Rover 820 Saloon and Fastback with 1994 cc 16-valve
fuel injection engine

*Does not cover Rover 825 or 827 models, or base model 820 with
8-valve carburettor engine*

ABCDE
FGHIJ
KLMNO
PQRST

THE
BOOK
®

Haynes Publishing Group
Sparkford Nr Yeovil
Somerset BA22 7JJ England

Haynes Publications, Inc
861 Lawrence Drive
Newbury Park
California 91320 USA

Acknowledgements

Thanks are due to the Champion Sparking Plug Company Limited who supplied the illustrations showing the various spark plug conditions, and to Duckhams Oils, who provided lubrication data. Certain illustrations are the copyright of the Austin Rover Group Limited, and are used with their permission. Thanks are also due to Sykes-Pickavant Limited who provided a selection of workshop tools, and to all those people at Sparkford who helped in the production of this manual.

© **Haynes Publishing Group 1989**

A book in the **Haynes Owners Workshop Manual Series**

Printed by J. H. Haynes & Co. Ltd, Sparkford, Nr Yeovil, Somerset BA22 7JJ, England

ISBN 1 85010 380 1

British Library Cataloguing in Publication Data
Mead, John S. *1950-*
    Rover 820 owners workshop manual
    1. Cars. Maintenance & repair. Amateurs' manual
    I. Title   II. Series
    629.28'722
    ISBN 1-85010-380-1

About this manual

Its aim

The aim of this manual is to help you get the best value from your vehicle. It can do so in several ways. It can help you decide what work must be done (even should you choose to get it done by a garage), provide information on routine maintenance and servicing, and give a logical course of action and diagnosis when random faults occur. However, it is hoped that you will use the manual by tackling the work yourself. On simpler jobs it may even be quicker than booking the car into a garage and going there twice, to leave and collect it. Perhaps most important, a lot of money can be saved by avoiding the costs a garage must charge to cover its labour and overheads.

The manual has drawings and descriptions to show the function of the various components so that their layout can be understood. Then the tasks are described and photographed in a step-by-step sequence so that even a novice can do the work.

Its arrangement

The manual is divided into 12 Chapters, each covering a logical sub-division of the vehicle. The Chapters are each divided into Sections, numbered with single figures, eg 5; and the Sections into paragraphs (or sub-sections), with decimal numbers following on from the Section they are in, eg 5.1, 5.2, 5.3 etc.

It is freely illustrated, especially in those parts where there is a detailed sequence of operations to be carried out. There are two forms of illustration: figures and photographs. The figures are numbered in sequence with decimal numbers, according to their position in the Chapter – eg Fig. 6.4 is the fourth drawing/illustration in Chapter 6. Photographs carry the same number (either individually or in related groups) as the Section or sub-section to which they relate.

There is an alphabetical index at the back of the manual as well as a contents list at the front. Each Chapter is also preceded by its own individual contents list.

References to the 'left' or 'right' of the vehicle are in the sense of a person in the driver's seat facing forwards.

Unless otherwise stated, nuts and bolts are removed by turning anti-clockwise, and tightened by turning clockwise.

Vehicle manufacturers continually make changes to specifications and recommendations, and these, when notified, are incorporated into our manuals at the earliest opportunity.

Whilst every care is taken to ensure that the information in this manual is correct, no liability can be accepted by the authors or publishers for loss, damage or injury caused by any errors in, or omissions from, the information given.

Project vehicles

The main project vehicle used in the preparation of this manual, and appearing in the majority of the photographic sequences, was a 1986 Rover 820 Se Saloon. Additional work was carried out and photographed on a 1988 Rover 820 Si Fastback.

Introduction to the Rover 820 Series

Designed in conjunction with the Honda Motor Company of Japan, the Rover 820 series was launched in the UK in July 1986 as a replacement for the ageing Rover SD1. Initially available in four-door Saloon guise, a Fastback version was added to the range in mid-1988.

The cars covered by this manual are all powered by a 2.0 litre twin overhead camshaft, sixteen valve engine with single-point or multi-point fuel injection. The engines are based on the proven Austin Rover O-series engine used in the Montego and other Austin Rover vehicles, but with an all-new cylinder head and valve train. The engine is mounted transversely, and drives the front wheels through a five-speed manual gearbox or four-speed automatic transmission.

Suspension is independent at the front by double wishbones and coil springs, and at the rear by transverse trailing links and coil springs. Power-assisted steering is standard on all models.

A comprehensive range of electrical and interior features are offered as standard equipment, including electric front windows, central locking and stereo radio cassette player. Optional equipment is also extensive, including ABS braking system, air conditioning, headlamp wash, and electric rear windows available on most models.

General dimensions, weights and capacities

Dimensions
Overall length .... 4690.0 mm (184.6 in)
Overall width (including door mirrors) .... 1970.0 mm (77.6 in)
Overall height .... 1400.0 mm (55.0 in)
Wheelbase .... 2760.0 mm (108.7 in)
Front track .... 1490.0 mm (58.7 in)
Rear track .... 1450.0 mm (57.1 in)
Ground clearance .... 145.0 mm (5.7 in)
Turning circle .... 11.1 m (36.5 ft)

Weights
Kerb weight:
  820 e Saloon .... 1305 kg (2870 lb)
  820 i Saloon .... 1300 kg (2860 lb)
  820 Se Saloon .... 1325 kg (2915 lb)
  820 Si Saloon .... 1320 kg (2905 lb)
  820 e Fastback .... 1335 kg (2935 lb)
  820 i Fastback .... 1330 kg (2925 lb)
  820 Se Fastback .... 1355 kg (2980 lb)
  820 Si Fastback .... 1350 kg (2970 lb)
Maximum gross vehicle weight:
  Saloon models .... 1785 kg (3935 lb)
  Fastback models .... 1850 kg (4079 lb)
Maximum roof rack load .... 70 kg (154 lb)
Maximum towing weight:
  Braked trailer .... 1550 kg (3417 lb)
  Unbraked trailer .... 500 kg (1102 lb)
Maximum towing hitch downward load .... 50 kg (110 lb)

Capacities
Engine oil (including filter) .... 4.5 litres (8.0 Imp pts)
Cooling system .... 10.0 litres (17.6 Imp pts)
Fuel tank .... 68.0 litres (15.0 Imp gals)
Manual gearbox .... 2.3 litres (4.0 Imp pts)
Automatic transmission:
  Total capacity .... 6.0 litres (10.5 Imp pts)
  Service refill .... 2.0 litres (3.5 Imp pts)
Power steering reservoir .... 1.5 litres (3.0 Imp pts)

Jacking, towing and wheel changing

Jacking and wheel changing

To change a roadwheel, first remove the spare wheel and jack, which are located under the luggage compartment floor. Firmly apply the handbrake and engage first gear on manual gearbox models, or PARK on automatic transmission models. Place chocks at the front and rear of the wheel diagonally opposite the one to be changed.

Remove the wheel trim and slacken the wheel nuts with the tools provided in the tool kit. Position the jack head in the reinforced jacking point, at the base of the sill nearest to the wheel to be changed. Raise the jack to just take the weight of the car. If the tyre is flat, position the base of the jack so that it is flat on the ground. If the tyre is not flat, position the jack so that the base elbow is resting on the ground and the base is just clear. Raise the car until the wheel is clear of the ground, then remove the wheel nuts and the wheel. Fit the spare wheel, and screw on the wheel nuts. Lower the jack until the tyre is just touching the ground, and tighten the wheel nuts moderately tight. Now lower the jack fully and tighten the wheel nuts securely in a diagonal sequence. Refit the wheel trim, then remove the jack and stow it together with the wheel and tools in the luggage compartment.

When jacking up the car with a trolley jack, position the jack head under the front towing eye if the front is to be raised, or under the rear towing eye if the rear is to be raised. If the side of the car is to be raised, position the jack head under the reinforced areas at the front or rear of the side sills. Do not jack up the car by means of the sump, or any of the suspension or steering components. Supplement the jack using axle stands or sturdy blocks. The jacking points and axle stand positions are shown in the accompanying illustrations. **Never** *work under, around, or near a raised car, unless it is adequately supported in at least two places.*

Towing

Towing eyes are fitted to the front and rear of the vehicle for attachment of a tow rope. The front towing eye is situated under the centre of the front bumper, and the rear towing eye is located under the centre of the rear bumper behind a detachable trim plate. Always turn the ignition key to position one when the vehicle is being towed to prevent the steering lock operating. Note that if the engine is not running, greater effort will be required to apply the brakes and steer the car.

Before being towed, release the handbrake and place the gear lever in neutral. Do not tow at a speed greater than 30 mph (50 kph). On no account may the car be towed with the front wheels on the ground if the transmission is faulty, if the gearbox oil or transmission fluid is low, or if the towing distance is greater than 30 miles (50 km).

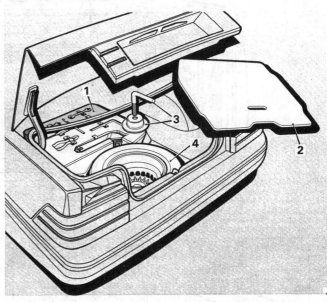

Spare wheel and tool locations

1 *Tool kit*
2 *Floor panel*
3 *Spare wheel clamp*
4 *Spare wheel*

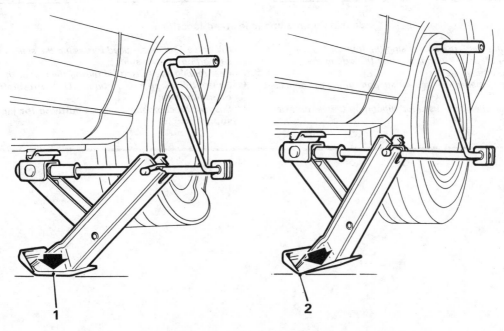

Using the vehicle tool kit jack

1 *Jack base positioned flat on the ground (deflated tyre)*
2 *Jack positioned with base elbow on the ground, and base just clear (inflated tyre)*

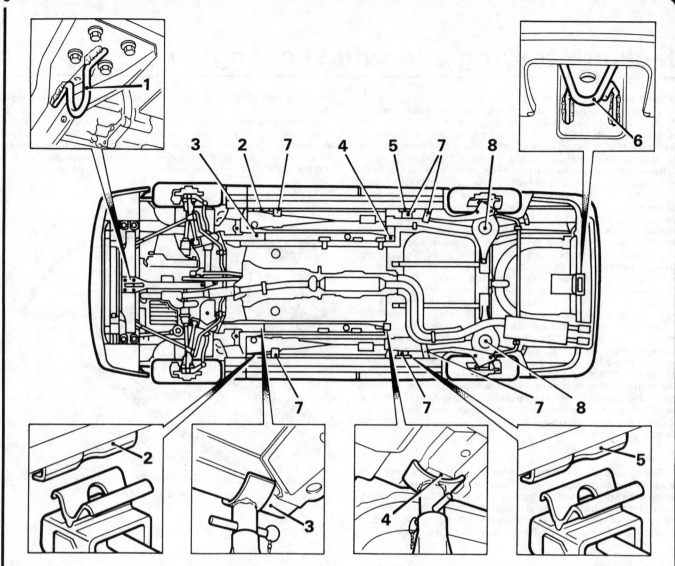

Jacking points and axle stand locations

1 Front towing eye – used for raising the front of the car
2 Reinforced sill area – used for raising the side of the car, or supporting on axle stands
3 Front chassis member – used for supporting the car on axle stands
4 Rear chassis member – used for supporting the car on axle stands

5 Reinforced sill area – used for raising the side of the car, or supporting on axle stands
6 Rear towing eye – used for raising the rear of the car
7 Square tubular chassis sections – **Not suitable for jacking or supporting**
8 Suspension components – **Not suitable for jacking or supporting**

Buying spare parts and vehicle identification numbers

Buying spare parts

Spare parts are available from many sources, for example: Rover garages, other garages and accessory shops, and motor factors. Our advice regarding spare part sources is as follows.

Officially appointed Rover garages – This is the best source for parts which are peculiar to your car, and are not generally available (eg complete cylinder heads, internal gearbox components, badges, interior trim etc). It is also the only place at which you should buy parts if the vehicle is still under warranty – non-Rover components may invalidate the warranty. To be sure of obtaining the correct parts, it will be necessary to give the storeman your car's vehicle identification number, and if possible, take the old part along for positive identification. Many parts are available under a factory exchange scheme – any parts returned should always be clean. It obviously makes good sense to go straight to the specialists on your car for this type of part, as they are best equipped to supply you.

Other garages and accessory shops – These are often very good places to buy materials and components needed for the maintenance of your car (eg oil filters, spark plugs, bulbs, drivebelts, oils and greases, touch-up paint, filler paste, etc). They also sell general accessories, usually have convenient opening hours, charge lower prices and can often be found not far from home.

Motor factors – Good factors will stock all the more important components which wear out comparatively quickly (eg exhaust systems, brake pads, seals and hydraulic parts, clutch components, bearing shells, pistons, valves etc). Motor factors will often provide new or reconditioned components on a part exchange basis – this can save a considerable amount of money.

Vehicle identification numbers

Modifications are a continuing and unpublicised process in vehicle manufacture, quite apart from major model changes. Spare parts manuals and lists are compiled upon a numerical basis, the individual vehicle identification numbers being essential to correct identification of the component concerned.

When ordering spare parts, always give as much information as possible. Quote the car model, year of manufacture, body and engine numbers as appropriate.

The vehicle identification number is stamped on a plate attached to the front body panel.

The body number is stamped on a plate attached to the front right-hand inner wing valance.

The engine number is stamped on the rear face of the cylinder block, below the cylinder head.

General repair procedures

Whenever servicing, repair or overhaul work is carried out on the car or its components, it is necessary to observe the following procedures and instructions. This will assist in carrying out the operation efficiently and to a professional standard of workmanship.

Joint mating faces and gaskets

Where a gasket is used between the mating faces of two components, ensure that it is renewed on reassembly, and fit it dry unless otherwise stated in the repair procedure. Make sure that the mating faces are clean and dry with all traces of old gasket removed. When cleaning a joint face, use a tool which is not likely to score or damage the face, and remove any burrs or nicks with an oilstone or fine file.

Make sure that tapped holes are cleaned with a pipe cleaner, and keep them free of jointing compound if this is being used unless specifically instructed otherwise.

Ensure that all orifices, channels or pipes are clear and blow through them, preferably using compressed air.

Oil seals

Whenever an oil seal is removed from its working location, either individually or as part of an assembly, it should be renewed.

The very fine sealing lip of the seal is easily damaged and will not seal if the surface it contacts is not completely clean and free from scratches, nicks or grooves. If the original sealing surface of the component cannot be restored, the component should be renewed.

Protect the lips of the seal from any surface which may damage them in the course of fitting. Use tape or a conical sleeve where possible. Lubricate the seal lips with oil before fitting and, on dual lipped seals, fill the space between the lips with grease.

Unless otherwise stated, oil seals must be fitted with their sealing lips toward the lubricant to be sealed.

Use a tubular drift or block of wood of the appropriate size to install the seal and, if the seal housing is shouldered, drive the seal down to the shoulder. If the seal housing is unshouldered, the seal should be fitted with its face flush with the housing top face.

Screw threads and fastenings

Always ensure that a blind tapped hole is completely free from oil, grease, water or other fluid before installing the bolt or stud. Failure to do this could cause the housing to crack due to the hydraulic action of the bolt or stud as it is screwed in.

When tightening a castellated nut to accept a split pin, tighten the nut to the specified torque, where applicable, and then tighten further to the next split pin hole. Never slacken the nut to align a split pin hole unless stated in the repair procedure.

When checking or retightening a nut or bolt to a specified torque setting, slacken the nut or bolt by a quarter of a turn, and then retighten to the specified setting.

Locknuts, locktabs and washers

Any fastening which will rotate against a component or housing in the course of tightening should always have a washer between it and the relevant component or housing.

Spring or split washers should always be renewed when they are used to lock a critical component such as a big-end bearing retaining nut or bolt.

Locktabs which are folded over to retain a nut or bolt should always be renewed.

Self-locking nuts can be reused in non-critical areas, providing resistance can be felt when the locking portion passes over the bolt or stud thread.

Split pins must always be replaced with new ones of the correct size for the hole.

Special tools

Some repair procedures in this manual entail the use of special tools such as a press, two or three-legged pullers, spring compressors etc. Wherever possible, suitable readily available alternatives to the manufacturer's special tools are described, and are shown in use. In some instances, where no alternative is possible, it has been necessary to resort to the use of a manufacturer's tool and this has been done for reasons of safety as well as the efficient completion of the repair operation. Unless you are highly skilled and have a thorough understanding of the procedure described, never attempt to bypass the use of any special tool when the procedure described specifies its use. Not only is there a very great risk of personal injury, but expensive damage could be caused to the components involved.

Tools and working facilities

Introduction

A selection of good tools is a fundamental requirement for anyone contemplating the maintenance and repair of a motor vehicle. For the owner who does not possess any, their purchase will prove a considerable expense, offsetting some of the savings made by doing-it-yourself. However, provided that the tools purchased are of good quality, they will last for many years and prove an extremely worthwhile investment.

To help the average owner to decide which tools are needed to carry out the various tasks detailed in this manual, we have compiled three lists of tools under the following headings: *Maintenance and minor repair, Repair and overhaul*, and *Special*. The newcomer to practical mechanics should start off with the *Maintenance and minor repair* tool kit and confine himself to the simpler jobs around the vehicle. Then, as his confidence and experience grow, he can undertake more difficult tasks, buying extra tools as, and when, they are needed. In this way, a *Maintenance and minor repair* tool kit can be built-up into a *Repair and overhaul* tool kit over a considerable period of time without any major cash outlays. The experienced do-it-yourselfer will have a tool kit good enough for most repair and overhaul procedures and will add tools from the *Special* category when he feels the expense is justified by the amount of use to which these tools will be put.

It is obviously not possible to cover the subject of tools fully here. For those who wish to learn more about tools and their use there is a book entitled *How to Choose and Use Car Tools* available from the publishers of this manual.

Maintenance and minor repair tool kit

The tools given in this list should be considered as a minimum requirement if routine maintenance, servicing and minor repair operations are to be undertaken. We recommend the purchase of combination spanners (ring one end, open-ended the other); although more expensive than open-ended ones, they do give the advantages of both types of spanner.

Combination spanners - 10, 11, 12, 13, 14 & 17 mm, and $7/16$, $1/2$, $9/16$, $5/8$, $11/16$, $3/4$, $13/16$, $7/8$, and $15/16$ in
Adjustable spanner - 9 inch
Gearbox drain plug key
Spark plug spanner (with rubber insert)
Spark plug gap adjustment tool
Set of feeler gauges
Brake adjuster spanner
Brake bleed nipple spanner
Screwdriver - 4 in long x $1/4$ in dia (flat blade)
Screwdriver - 4 in long x $1/4$ in dia (cross blade)
Combination pliers - 6 inch
Hacksaw (junior)
Tyre pump

Tyre pressure gauge
Oil can
Fine emery cloth (1 sheet)
Wire brush (small)
Funnel (medium size)

Repair and overhaul tool kit

These tools are virtually essential for anyone undertaking any major repairs to a motor vehicle, and are additional to those given in the *Maintenance and minor repair* list. Included in this list is a comprehensive set of sockets. Although these are expensive they will be found invaluable as they are so versatile - particularly if various drives are included in the set. We recommend the ½ in square-drive type, as this can be used with most proprietary torque wrenches. If you cannot afford a socket set, even bought piecemeal, then inexpensive tubular box spanners are a useful alternative.

The tools in this list will occasionally need to be supplemented by tools from the *Special* list.

Sockets (or box spanners) to cover range in previous list
Selection of Torx type socket bits
Reversible ratchet drive (for use with sockets)
Extension piece, 10 inch (for use with sockets)
Universal joint (for use with sockets)
Torque wrench (for use with sockets)
'Mole' wrench - 8 inch
Ball pein hammer
Soft-faced hammer, plastic or rubber
Screwdriver - 6 in long x $5/16$ in dia (flat blade)
Screwdriver - 2 in long x $5/16$ in square (flat blade)
Screwdriver - $11/2$ in long x $1/4$ in dia (cross blade)
Screwdriver - 3 in long x $1/8$ in dia (electricians)
Pliers - electricians side cutters
Pliers - needle nosed
Pliers - circlip (internal and external)
Cold chisel - $1/2$ inch
Scriber
Scraper
Centre punch
Pin punch
Hacksaw
Valve grinding tool
Steel rule/straight-edge
Allen keys (inc. splined/Torx type if necessary)
Selection of files
Wire brush (large)
Axle-stands
Jack (strong trolley or hydraulic type)

Special tools

The tools in this list are those which are not used regularly, are expensive to buy, or which need to be used in accordance with their manufacturers' instructions. Unless relatively difficult mechanical jobs are undertaken frequently, it will not be economic to buy many of these tools. Where this is the case, you could consider clubbing together with friends (or joining a motorists' club) to make a joint purchase, or borrowing the tools against a deposit from a local garage or tool hire specialist.

The following list contains only those tools and instruments freely available to the public, and not those special tools produced by the vehicle manufacturer specifically for its dealer network. You will find occasional references to these manufacturers' special tools in the text of this manual. Generally, an alternative method of doing the job without the vehicle manufacturers' special tool is given. However, sometimes, there is no alternative to using them. Where this is the case and the relevant tool cannot be bought or borrowed, you will have to entrust the work to a franchised garage.

> Valve spring compressor (where applicable)
> Piston ring compressor
> Balljoint separator
> Universal hub/bearing puller
> Impact screwdriver
> Micrometer and/or vernier gauge
> Dial gauge
> Stroboscopic timing light
> Dwell angle meter/tachometer
> Universal electrical multi-meter
> Cylinder compression gauge
> Lifting tackle
> Trolley jack
> Light with extension lead

Buying tools

For practically all tools, a tool factor is the best source since he will have a very comprehensive range compared with the average garage or accessory shop. Having said that, accessory shops often offer excellent quality tools at discount prices, so it pays to shop around.

Remember, you don't have to buy the most expensive items on the shelf, but it is always advisable to steer clear of the very cheap tools. There are plenty of good tools around at reasonable prices, so ask the proprietor or manager of the shop for advice before making a purchase.

Care and maintenance of tools

Having purchased a reasonable tool kit, it is necessary to keep the tools in a clean serviceable condition. After use, always wipe off any dirt, grease and metal particles using a clean, dry cloth, before putting the tools away. Never leave them lying around after they have been used. A simple tool rack on the garage or workshop wall, for items such as screwdrivers and pliers is a good idea. Store all normal wrenches and sockets in a metal box. Any measuring instruments, gauges, meters, etc, must be carefully stored where they cannot be damaged or become rusty.

Take a little care when tools are used. Hammer heads inevitably become marked and screwdrivers lose the keen edge on their blades from time to time. A little timely attention with emery cloth or a file will soon restore items like this to a good serviceable finish.

Working facilities

Not to be forgotten when discussing tools, is the workshop itself. If anything more than routine maintenance is to be carried out, some form of suitable working area becomes essential.

It is appreciated that many an owner mechanic is forced by circumstances to remove an engine or similar item, without the benefit of a garage or workshop. Having done this, any repairs should always be done under the cover of a roof.

Wherever possible, any dismantling should be done on a clean, flat workbench or table at a suitable working height.

Any workbench needs a vice: one with a jaw opening of 4 in (100 mm) is suitable for most jobs. As mentioned previously, some clean dry storage space is also required for tools, as well as for lubricants, cleaning fluids, touch-up paints and so on, which become necessary.

Another item which may be required, and which has a much more general usage, is an electric drill with a chuck capacity of at least $5/16$ in (8 mm). This, together with a good range of twist drills, is virtually essential for fitting accessories such as mirrors and reversing lights.

Last, but not least, always keep a supply of old newspapers and clean, lint-free rags available, and try to keep any working area as clean as possible.

Spanner jaw gap comparison table

Jaw gap (in)	Spanner size
0.250	1/4 in AF
0.276	7 mm
0.313	5/16 in AF
0.315	8 mm
0.344	11/32 in AF; 1/8 in Whitworth
0.354	9 mm
0.375	3/8 in AF
0.394	10 mm
0.433	11 mm
0.438	7/16 in AF
0.445	3/16 in Whitworth; 1/4 in BSF
0.472	12 mm
0.500	1/2 in AF
0.512	13 mm
0.525	1/4 in Whitworth; 5/16 in BSF
0.551	14 mm
0.563	9/16 in AF
0.591	15 mm
0.600	5/16 in Whitworth; 3/8 in BSF
0.625	5/8 in AF
0.630	16 mm
0.669	17 mm
0.686	11/16 in AF
0.709	18 mm
0.710	3/8 in Whitworth; 7/16 in BSF
0.748	19 mm
0.750	3/4 in AF
0.813	13/16 in AF
0.820	7/16 in Whitworth; 1/2 in BSF
0.866	22 mm
0.875	7/8 in AF
0.920	1/2 in Whitworth; 9/16 in BSF
0.938	15/16 in AF
0.945	24 mm
1.000	1 in AF
1.010	9/16 in Whitworth; 5/8 in BSF
1.024	26 mm
1.063	11/16 in AF; 27 mm
1.100	5/8 in Whitworth; 11/16 in BSF
1.125	1 1/8 in AF
1.181	30 mm
1.200	11/16 in Whitworth; 3/4 in BSF
1.250	1 1/4 in AF
1.260	32 mm
1.300	3/4 in Whitworth; 7/8 in BSF
1.313	1 5/16 in AF
1.390	13/16 in Whitworth; 15/16 in BSF
1.417	36 mm
1.438	1 7/16 in AF
1.480	7/8 in Whitworth; 1 in BSF
1.500	1 1/2 in AF
1.575	40 mm; 15/16 in Whitworth
1.614	41 mm
1.625	1 5/8 in AF
1.670	1 in Whitworth; 1 1/8 in BSF
1.688	1 11/16 in AF
1.811	46 mm
1.813	1 13/16 in AF
1.860	1 1/8 in Whitworth; 1 1/4 in BSF
1.875	1 7/8 in AF
1.969	50 mm
2.000	2 in AF
2.050	1 1/4 in Whitworth; 1 3/8 in BSF
2.165	55 mm
2.362	60 mm

Conversion factors

Length (distance)

Inches (in)	X	25.4	= Millimetres (mm)	X 0.0394	= Inches (in)
Feet (ft)	X	0.305	= Metres (m)	X 3.281	= Feet (ft)
Miles	X	1.609	= Kilometres (km)	X 0.621	= Miles

Volume (capacity)

Cubic inches (cu in; in³)	X	16.387	= Cubic centimetres (cc; cm³)	X 0.061	= Cubic inches (cu in; in³)
Imperial pints (Imp pt)	X	0.568	= Litres (l)	X 1.76	= Imperial pints (Imp pt)
Imperial quarts (Imp qt)	X	1.137	= Litres (l)	X 0.88	= Imperial quarts (Imp qt)
Imperial quarts (Imp qt)	X	1.201	= US quarts (US qt)	X 0.833	= Imperial quarts (Imp qt)
US quarts (US qt)	X	0.946	= Litres (l)	X 1.057	= US quarts (US qt)
Imperial gallons (Imp gal)	X	4.546	= Litres (l)	X 0.22	= Imperial gallons (Imp gal)
Imperial gallons (Imp gal)	X	1.201	= US gallons (US gal)	X 0.833	= Imperial gallons (Imp gal)
US gallons (US gal)	X	3.785	= Litres (l)	X 0.264	= US gallons (US gal)

Mass (weight)

Ounces (oz)	X	28.35	= Grams (g)	X 0.035	= Ounces (oz)
Pounds (lb)	X	0.454	= Kilograms (kg)	X 2.205	= Pounds (lb)

Force

Ounces-force (ozf; oz)	X	0.278	= Newtons (N)	X 3.6	= Ounces-force (ozf; oz)
Pounds-force (lbf; lb)	X	4.448	= Newtons (N)	X 0.225	= Pounds-force (lbf; lb)
Newtons (N)	X	0.1	= Kilograms-force (kgf; kg)	X 9.81	= Newtons (N)

Pressure

Pounds-force per square inch (psi; lbf/in²; lb/in²)	X	0.070	= Kilograms-force per square centimetre (kgf/cm²; kg/cm²)	X 14.223	= Pounds-force per square inch (psi; lbf/in²; lb/in²)
Pounds-force per square inch (psi; lbf/in²; lb/in²)	X	0.068	= Atmospheres (atm)	X 14.696	= Pounds-force per square inch (psi; lbf/in²; lb/in²)
Pounds-force per square inch (psi; lbf/in²; lb/in²)	X	0.069	= Bars	X 14.5	= Pounds-force per square inch (psi; lbf/in²; lb/in²)
Pounds-force per square inch (psi; lbf/in²; lb/in²)	X	6.895	= Kilopascals (kPa)	X 0.145	= Pounds-force per square inch (psi; lbf/in²; lb/in²)
Kilopascals (kPa)	X	0.01	= Kilograms-force per square centimetre (kgf/cm²; kg/cm²)	X 98.1	= Kilopascals (kPa)
Millibar (mbar)	X	100	= Pascals (Pa)	X 0.01	= Millibar (mbar)
Millibar (mbar)	X	0.0145	= Pounds-force per square inch (psi; lbf/in²; lb/in²)	X 68.947	= Millibar (mbar)
Millibar (mbar)	X	0.75	= Millimetres of mercury (mmHg)	X 1.333	= Millibar (mbar)
Millibar (mbar)	X	0.401	= Inches of water (inH₂O)	X 2.491	= Millibar (mbar)
Millimetres of mercury (mmHg)	X	0.535	= Inches of water (inH₂O)	X 1.868	= Millimetres of mercury (mmHg)
Inches of water (inH₂O)	X	0.036	= Pounds-force per square inch (psi; lbf/in²; lb/in²)	X 27.68	= Inches of water (inH₂O)

Torque (moment of force)

Pounds-force inches (lbf in; lb in)	X	1.152	= Kilograms-force centimetre (kgf cm; kg cm)	X 0.868	= Pounds-force inches (lbf in; lb in)
Pounds-force inches (lbf in; lb in)	X	0.113	= Newton metres (Nm)	X 8.85	= Pounds-force inches (lbf in; lb in)
Pounds-force inches (lbf in; lb in)	X	0.083	= Pounds-force feet (lbf ft; lb ft)	X 12	= Pounds-force inches (lbf in; lb in)
Pounds-force feet (lbf ft; lb ft)	X	0.138	= Kilograms-force metres (kgf m; kg m)	X 7.233	= Pounds-force feet (lbf ft; lb ft)
Pounds-force feet (lbf ft; lb ft)	X	1.356	= Newton metres (Nm)	X 0.738	= Pounds-force feet (lbf ft; lb ft)
Newton metres (Nm)	X	0.102	= Kilograms-force metres (kgf m; kg m)	X 9.804	= Newton metres (Nm)

Power

Horsepower (hp)	X	745.7	= Watts (W)	X 0.0013	= Horsepower (hp)

Velocity (speed)

Miles per hour (miles/hr; mph)	X	1.609	= Kilometres per hour (km/hr; kph)	X 0.621	= Miles per hour (miles/hr; mph)

Fuel consumption*

Miles per gallon, Imperial (mpg)	X	0.354	= Kilometres per litre (km/l)	X 2.825	= Miles per gallon, Imperial (mpg)
Miles per gallon, US (mpg)	X	0.425	= Kilometres per litre (km/l)	X 2.352	= Miles per gallon, US (mpg)

Temperature

Degrees Fahrenheit = ($°C$ x 1.8) + 32   Degrees Celsius (Degrees Centigrade; °C) = (°F − 32) x 0.56

*It is common practice to convert from miles per gallon (mpg) to litres/100 kilometres (l/100km), where mpg (Imperial) x l/100 km = 282 and mpg (US) x l/100 km = 235

Safety first!

Professional motor mechanics are trained in safe working procedures. However enthusiastic you may be about getting on with the job in hand, do take the time to ensure that your safety is not put at risk. A moment's lack of attention can result in an accident, as can failure to observe certain elementary precautions.

There will always be new ways of having accidents, and the following points do not pretend to be a comprehensive list of all dangers; they are intended rather to make you aware of the risks and to encourage a safety-conscious approach to all work you carry out on your vehicle.

Essential DOs and DON'Ts

DON'T rely on a single jack when working underneath the vehicle. Always use reliable additional means of support, such as axle stands, securely placed under a part of the vehicle that you know will not give way.

DON'T attempt to loosen or tighten high-torque nuts (e.g. wheel hub nuts) while the vehicle is on a jack; it may be pulled off.

DON'T start the engine without first ascertaining that the transmission is in neutral (or 'Park' where applicable) and the parking brake applied.

DON'T suddenly remove the filler cap from a hot cooling system – cover it with a cloth and release the pressure gradually first, or you may get scalded by escaping coolant.

DON'T attempt to drain oil until you are sure it has cooled sufficiently to avoid scalding you.

DON'T grasp any part of the engine, exhaust or catalytic converter without first ascertaining that it is sufficiently cool to avoid burning you.

DON'T allow brake fluid or antifreeze to contact vehicle paintwork.

DON'T syphon toxic liquids such as fuel, brake fluid or antifreeze by mouth, or allow them to remain on your skin.

DON'T inhale dust – it may be injurious to health (see *Asbestos* below).

DON'T allow any spilt oil or grease to remain on the floor – wipe it up straight away, before someone slips on it.

DON'T use ill-fitting spanners or other tools which may slip and cause injury.

DON'T attempt to lift a heavy component which may be beyond your capability – get assistance.

DON'T rush to finish a job, or take unverified short cuts.

DON'T allow children or animals in or around an unattended vehicle.

DO wear eye protection when using power tools such as drill, sander, bench grinder etc, and when working under the vehicle.

DO use a barrier cream on your hands prior to undertaking dirty jobs – it will protect your skin from infection as well as making the dirt easier to remove afterwards; but make sure your hands aren't left slippery. Note that long-term contact with used engine oil can be a health hazard.

DO keep loose clothing (cuffs, tie etc) and long hair well out of the way of moving mechanical parts.

DO remove rings, wristwatch etc, before working on the vehicle – especially the electrical system.

DO ensure that any lifting tackle used has a safe working load rating adequate for the job.

DO keep your work area tidy – it is only too easy to fall over articles left lying around.

DO get someone to check periodically that all is well, when working alone on the vehicle.

DO carry out work in a logical sequence and check that everything is correctly assembled and tightened afterwards.

DO remember that your vehicle's safety affects that of yourself and others. If in doubt on any point, get specialist advice.

IF, in spite of following these precautions, you are unfortunate enough to injure yourself, seek medical attention as soon as possible.

Asbestos

Certain friction, insulating, sealing, and other products – such as brake linings, brake bands, clutch linings, torque converters, gaskets, etc – contain asbestos. *Extreme care must be taken to avoid inhalation of dust from such products since it is hazardous to health.* If in doubt, assume that they *do* contain asbestos.

Fire

Remember at all times that petrol (gasoline) is highly flammable. Never smoke, or have any kind of naked flame around, when working on the vehicle. But the risk does not end there – a spark caused by an electrical short-circuit, by two metal surfaces contacting each other, by careless use of tools, or even by static electricity built up in your body under certain conditions, can ignite petrol vapour, which in a confined space is highly explosive.

Always disconnect the battery earth (ground) terminal before working on any part of the fuel or electrical system, and never risk spilling fuel on to a hot engine or exhaust.

It is recommended that a fire extinguisher of a type suitable for fuel and electrical fires is kept handy in the garage or workplace at all times. Never try to extinguish a fuel or electrical fire with water.

Fumes

Certain fumes are highly toxic and can quickly cause unconsciousness and even death if inhaled to any extent. Petrol (gasoline) vapour comes into this category, as do the vapours from certain solvents such as trichloroethylene. Any draining or pouring of such volatile fluids should be done in a well ventilated area.

When using cleaning fluids and solvents, read the instructions carefully. Never use materials from unmarked containers – they may give off poisonous vapours.

Never run the engine of a motor vehicle in an enclosed space such as a garage. Exhaust fumes contain carbon monoxide which is extremely poisonous; if you need to run the engine, always do so in the open air or at least have the rear of the vehicle outside the workplace.

If you are fortunate enough to have the use of an inspection pit, never drain or pour petrol, and never run the engine, while the vehicle is standing over it; the fumes, being heavier than air, will concentrate in the pit with possibly lethal results.

The battery

Never cause a spark, or allow a naked light, near the vehicle's battery. It will normally be giving off a certain amount of hydrogen gas, which is highly explosive.

Always disconnect the battery earth (ground) terminal before working on the fuel or electrical systems.

If possible, loosen the filler plugs or cover when charging the battery from an external source. Do not charge at an excessive rate or the battery may burst.

Take care when topping up and when carrying the battery. The acid electrolyte, even when diluted, is very corrosive and should not be allowed to contact the eyes or skin.

If you ever need to prepare electrolyte yourself, always add the acid slowly to the water, and never the other way round. Protect against splashes by wearing rubber gloves and goggles.

When jump starting a car using a booster battery, for negative earth (ground) vehicles, connect the jump leads in the following sequence: First connect one jump lead between the positive (+) terminals of the two batteries. Then connect the other jump lead first to the negative (–) terminal of the booster battery, and then to a good earthing (ground) point on the vehicle to be started, at least 18 in (45 cm) from the battery if possible. Ensure that hands and jump leads are clear of any moving parts, and that the two vehicles do not touch. Disconnect the leads in the reverse order.

Mains electricity

When using an electric power tool, inspection light etc, which works from the mains, always ensure that the appliance is correctly connected to its plug and that, where necessary, it is properly earthed (grounded). Do not use such appliances in damp conditions and, again, beware of creating a spark or applying excessive heat in the vicinity of fuel or fuel vapour.

Ignition HT voltage

A severe electric shock can result from touching certain parts of the ignition system, such as the HT leads, when the engine is running or being cranked, particularly if components are damp or the insulation is defective. Where an electronic ignition system is fitted, the HT voltage is much higher and could prove fatal.

Routine maintenance

Maintenance is essential for ensuring safety, and desirable for the purpose of getting the best in terms of performance and economy from your car. Over the years, the need for periodic lubrication has been greatly reduced, if not totally eliminated. This has unfortunately tended to lead some owners to think that because no such action is required, the items either no longer exist, or will last forever. This is certainly not the case; it is essential to carry out regular visual examination as comprehensively as possible, in order to spot any potential defects at an early stage before they develop into major expensive repairs.

The following service schedules are a list of the maintenance requirements, and the intervals at which they should be carried out, as recommended by the manufacturers. Where applicable, these procedures are covered in greater detail throughout this manual, near the beginning of each Chapter.

Every 250 miles (400 km) or weekly – whichever occurs first

Engine, cooling system, steering and brakes

Check the oil level and top up if necessary
Check the coolant level and top up if necessary
Check the brake fluid level in the master cylinder, and top up if necessary
Check the fluid level in the power steering reservoir, and top up if necessary

Lights and wipers

Check the operation of all interior and exterior lamps, wipers and washers
Check and if necessary top up the washer reservoir

Tyres

Check the tyre pressures
Visually examine the tyres for wear or damage

Every 6000 miles (10 000 km) or 6 months – whichever occurs first

Engine (Chapter 1)

Renew the engine oil and filter
Visually check the engine for oil leaks

Cooling system (Chapter 2)

Check the coolant level and top up if necessary
Check the hoses, hose clips and visible joint gaskets for leaks, and any signs of corrosion or deterioration

Fuel and exhaust system (Chapter 3)

Check the operation of the accelerator cable and linkage
Visually check the fuel pipes and hoses for security, chafing, leaks and corrosion
Check the fuel tank for leaks, and any sign of damage or corrosion
Check the exhaust system for corrosion, leaks and security

Braking system (Chapter 9)

Check visually all brake pipes, hoses and unions for corrosion, chafing, leakage and security
Check and if necessary top up the brake fluid level in the master cylinder
Check the operation of the footbrake and handbrake

Suspension and steering (Chapter 10)

Check the fluid level in the power steering reservoir, and top up if necessary
Check and if necessary adjust the tyre pressures
Check the tyres for damage, tread depth, and uneven wear
Check the tightness of the wheel nuts
Check the condition and tension of the power steering pump drivebelt

Electrical system (Chapter 10)

Check the function of all electrical equipment and accessories (lights, indicators, horn, wipers etc)
Check the condition and tension of the alternator drivebelt
Check and if necessary top up the washer reservoir
Check the condition of the wiper blades

Bodywork (Chapter 11)

Lubricate all hinges and locks with a few drops of light oil (do not lubricate the steering lock)
Where applicable, check the condition and tension of the air conditioning compressor drivebelt

Road test

Check the function of all instruments and warning lamps
Check the performance of the engine, transmission, brakes, clutch, steering and suspension, paying attention to any abnormalities or noises
Check the operation of the seat belt inertia reels
Check the operation and hold of the handbrake ratchet

Every 12 000 miles (20 000 km) or 12 months – whichever occurs first

In addition to all the items in the 6-monthly service, carry out the following:

Engine (Chapter 1)

Visually check the engine for oil leaks, and for the security and condition of all related components and attachments

Fuel and exhaust system (Chapter 3)

Renew the air cleaner element
Check the base idle speed and mixture settings, and adjust if necessary

Ignition system (Chapter 4)

Renew the spark plugs
Clean the distributor cap, coil tower and HT leads, and check for 'tracking'

Clutch (Chapter 5)

Check the clutch hydraulic pipes and hoses for chafing, leaks, and security

Manual gearbox (Chapter 6)

Visually check for oil leaks around the gearbox joint faces and oil seals
Check and if necessary top up the gearbox oil

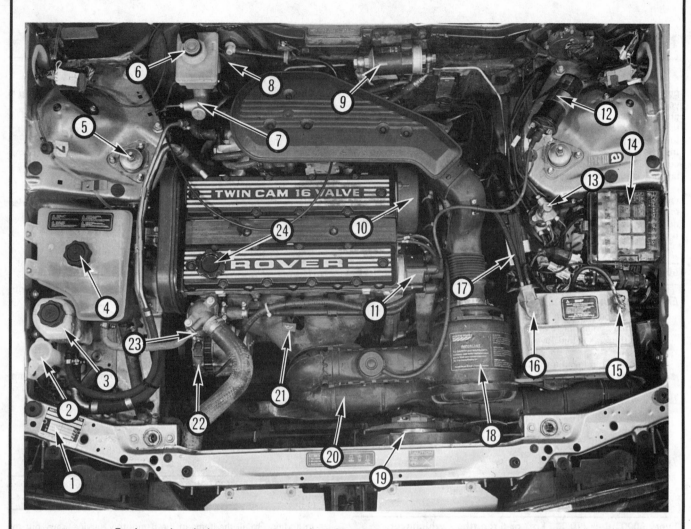

Engine and underbonnet component locations (models with single-point fuel injection)

1 Vehicle identification plate
2 Screen washer reservoir filler
3 Power steering fluid reservoir filler
4 Cooling system expansion tank filler
5 Front shock absorber top mounting

6 Brake and clutch fluid reservoir filler
7 Brake master cylinder
8 Brake vacuum servo unit
9 Fuel filter
10 Power steering pump drivebelt (models with rear-mounted pump)

11 Distributor cap
12 Ignition coil
13 Brake pressure reducing valve
14 Fuse and relay box
15 Battery negative terminal
16 Battery positive terminal
17 Ignition/fuel ECU

18 Air cleaner assembly
19 Radiator cooling fan
20 Air cleaner intake trunking
21 Engine oil dipstick
22 Alternator
23 Thermostat housing
24 Engine oil filler cap

Engine and underbonnet component locations (models with multi-point fuel injection)

1 Vehicle identification plate
2 Screen washer reservoir filler
3 Power steering fluid reservoir filler
4 Cooling system expansion tank filler
5 Front shock absorber top mounting

6 Brake and clutch fluid reservoir filler
7 Brake master cylinder
8 Brake vacuum servo unit
9 Fuel filter
10 Fuel system ECU
11 Ignition coil
12 Brake pressure reducing valve

13 Fuse and relay box
14 Battery negative terminal
15 Battery positive terminal
16 Air cleaner assembly
17 Radiator cooling fan
18 Air cleaner intake trunking
19 Engine oil dipstick
20 Airflow meter

21 Throttle housing
22 Plenum chamber
23 Engine oil filler cap
24 Alternator
25 Power steering pump (models with front-mounted pump)

Front underbody view

1	Engine undertray	6	Front tie-bar	11	Gearchange rod	17	Front lower suspension arm
2	Front towing eye	7	Gearbox drain plug	12	Gearbox steady rod	18	Brake caliper
3	Longitudinal support member	8	Driveshaft inner constant velocity joint	13	Fuel pipes	19	Oil filter
4	Clutch slave cylinder	9	Gearbox filler plug	14	Exhaust section flange joint	20	Driveshaft damper
5	Reversing lamp switch	10	Front anti-roll bar	15	Power steering gear	21	Engine oil drain plug
				16	Steering tie-rod		

Rear underbody view

1	Exhaust intermediate section	4	Handbrake cable
2	Fuel tank	5	Fuel pipes
3	Exhaust rear heat shield	6	Trailing link

7	Fuel filler neck connection	10	Rear anti-roll bar
8	Transverse link	11	Rear silencer
9	Fuel tank retaining straps	12	Brake caliper

Automatic transmission (Chapter 7)

Visually check for fluid leaks around the transmission joint faces and oil seals
Check and if necessary top up the automatic transmission fluid

Driveshafts (Chapter 8)

Check the driveshaft constant velocity joints for wear or damage, and check the rubber gaiters for condition

Braking system (Chapter 9)

Check the operation of the brake pad and fluid warning indicators
Check the front and rear brake pads for wear, and the discs for condition

Suspension and steering (Chapter 10)

Check the front and rear shock absorbers for fluid leaks, damage or corrosion
Check the condition and security of the steering gear, steering and suspension joints and rubber gaiters
Check the condition of the roadwheels
Check the front and rear wheel alignment if there is any sign of abnormal tyre wear

Bodywork (Chapter 11)

Carefully inspect the paintwork for damage, and the bodywork for corrosion
Check the condition of the underseal

Electrical system (Chapter 12)

Check the condition and security of all accessible wiring connectors, harnesses and retaining clips
Check the screen washer jets, and adjust their position if necessary
Clean the battery terminals and smear with petroleum jelly
Check and if necessary adjust the headlamp aim

Every 24 000 miles (40 000 km) or 24 months – whichever occurs first

In addition to all the items in the previous services, carry out the following:

Engine (Chapter 1)

Check the condition and tension of the timing belt

Cooling system (Chapter 2)

Drain and flush the cooling system, and renew the antifreeze mixture

Fuel and exhaust system (Chapter 3)

Renew the fuel filter

Manual gearbox (Chapter 6)

Renew the gearbox oil

Automatic transmission (Chapter 7)

Renew the automatic transmission fluid

Braking system (Chapter 9)

Renew the brake fluid

Every 48 000 miles (80 000 km) or 48 months – whichever comes first

In addition to the items in the 6 and 12-monthly services, carry out the following:

Engine (Chapter 1)

Renew the timing belt

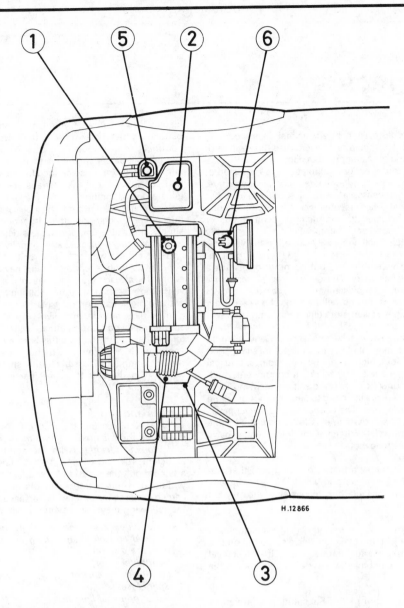

H.12 866

Recommended lubricants and fluids

Component or system	Lubricant type/specification	Duckhams recommendation
Engine (1)*	Multigrade engine oil, viscosity SAE 10W/40 to API SF or SF/CD	Duckhams QXR, Hypergrade, or 10W/40 Motor Oil
Cooling system (2)	Ethylene glycol based antifreeze	Duckhams Universal Antifreeze and Summer Coolant
Manual gearbox (3)*	Multigrade engine oil, viscosity SAE 10W/40, to API SF or SF/CD	Duckhams QXR, Hypergrade, or 10W/40 Motor Oil
Automatic transmission (4)	Dexron IID type ATF	Duckhams D-Matic
Power steering reservoir (5)	Dexron IID type ATF	Duckhams D-Matic
Brake and clutch fluid reservoir (6)	Hydraulic fluid to FMVSS 116 DOT 4	Duckhams Universal Brake and Clutch Fluid
General greasing	Multipurpose lithium based grease	Duckhams LB 10

*Note: *Austin Rover specify a 10W/40 oil to meet warranty requirements. Duckhams QXR and 10W/40 Motor Oil are available to meet these requirements.*

Fault diagnosis

Introduction

The vehicle owner who does his or her own maintenance according to the recommended schedules should not have to use this section of the manual very often. Modern component reliability is such that, provided those items subject to wear or deterioration are inspected or renewed at the specified intervals, sudden failure is comparatively rare. Faults do not usually just happen as a result of sudden failure, but develop over a period of time. Major mechanical failures in particular are usually preceded by characteristic symptoms over hundreds or even thousands of miles. Those components which do occasionally fail without warning are often small and easily carried in the vehicle.

With any fault finding, the first step is to decide where to begin investigations. Sometimes this is obvious, but on other occasions a little detective work will be necessary. The owner who makes half a dozen haphazard adjustments or replacements may be successful in curing a fault (or its symptoms), but he will be none the wiser if the fault recurs and he may well have spent more time and money than was necessary. A calm and logical approach will be found to be more satisfactory in the long run. Always take into account any warning signs or abnormalities that may have been noticed in the period preceding the fault – power loss, high or low gauge readings, unusual noises or smells, etc – and remember that failure of components such as fuses or spark plugs may only be pointers to some underlying fault.

The pages which follow here are intended to help in cases of failure to start or breakdown on the road. There is also a Fault Diagnosis Section at the end of each Chapter which should be consulted if the preliminary checks prove unfruitful. Whatever the fault, certain basic principles apply. These are as follows:

Verify the fault. This is simply a matter of being sure that you know what the symptoms are before starting work. This is particularly important if you are investigating a fault for someone else who may not have described it very accurately.

Don't overlook the obvious. For example, if the vehicle won't start, is there petrol in the tank? (Don't take anyone else's word on this particular point, and don't trust the fuel gauge either!) If an electrical fault is indicated, look for loose or broken wires before digging out the test gear.

Cure the disease, not the symptom. Substituting a flat battery with a fully charged one will get you off the hard shoulder, but if the underlying cause is not attended to, the new battery will go the same way. Similarly, changing oil-fouled spark plugs for a new set will get you moving again, but remember that the reason for the fouling (if it wasn't simply an incorrect grade of plug) will have to be established and corrected.

Don't take anything for granted. Particularly, don't forget that a 'new' component may itself be defective (especially if it's been rattling round in the boot for months), and don't leave components out of a fault diagnosis sequence just because they are new or recently fitted. When you do finally diagnose a difficult fault, you'll probably realise that all the evidence was there from the start.

Electrical faults

Electrical faults can be more puzzling than straightforward mechanical failures, but they are no less susceptible to logical analysis if the basic principles of operation are understood. Vehicle electrical wiring exists in extremely unfavourable conditions – heat, vibration and chemical attack – and the first things to look for are loose or corroded connections and broken or chafed wires, especially where the wires pass through holes in the bodywork or are subject to vibration.

All metal-bodied vehicles in current production have one pole of the battery 'earthed', ie connected to the vehicle bodywork, and in nearly all modern vehicles it is the negative (–) terminal. The various electrical components – motors, bulb holders etc – are also connected to earth, either by means of a lead or directly by their mountings.

Electric current flows through the component and then back to the battery via the bodywork. If the component mounting is loose or corroded, or if a good path back to the battery is not available, the circuit will be incomplete and malfunction will result. The engine and/or gearbox are also earthed by means of flexible metal straps to the body or subframe; if these straps are loose or missing, starter motor, generator and ignition trouble may result.

Assuming the earth return to be satisfactory, electrical faults will be due either to component malfunction or to defects in the current supply. Individual components are dealt with in Chapter 12. If supply wires are broken or cracked internally this results in an open-circuit, and the easiest way to check for this is to bypass the suspect wire temporarily with a length of wire having a crocodile clip or suitable connector at each end. Alternatively, a 12V test lamp can be used to verify the presence of supply voltage at various points along the wire and the break can be thus isolated.

If a bare portion of a live wire touches the bodywork or other earthed metal part, the electricity will take the low-resistance path thus formed back to the battery: this is known as a short-circuit. Hopefully a short-circuit will blow a fuse, but otherwise it may cause burning of the insulation (and possibly further short-circuits) or even a fire. This is why it is inadvisable to bypass persistently blowing fuses with silver foil or wire.

Spares and tool kit

Most vehicles are supplied only with sufficient tools for wheel changing; the *Maintenance and minor repair* tool kit detailed in *Tools and working facilities*, with the addition of a hammer, is probably sufficient for those repairs that most motorists would consider attempting at the roadside. In addition a few items which can be fitted without too much trouble in the event of a breakdown should be carried. Experience and available space will modify the list below, but the following may save having to call on professional assistance:

Spark plugs, clean and correctly gapped
HT lead and plug cap – long enough to reach the plug furthest from the distributor
Distributor rotor
Drivebelt(s) – emergency type may suffice
Spare fuses
Set of principal light bulbs
Tin of radiator sealer and hose bandage
Exhaust bandage
Roll of insulating tape
Length of soft iron wire
Length of electrical flex
Torch or inspection lamp (can double as test lamp)
Battery jump leads
Tow-rope
Ignition waterproofing aerosol
Litre of engine oil
Sealed can of hydraulic fluid
Emergency windscreen
Worm drive clips
Tube of filler paste

If spare fuel is carried, a can designed for the purpose should be used to minimise risks of leakage and collision damage. A first aid kit and a warning triangle, whilst not at present compulsory in the UK, are obviously sensible items to carry in addition to the above.

When touring abroad it may be advisable to carry additional spares which, even if you cannot fit them yourself, could save having to wait while parts are obtained. The items below may be worth considering:

Throttle cable
Cylinder head gasket
Alternator brushes
Tyre valve core

One of the motoring organisations will be able to advise on availability of fuel etc in foreign countries.

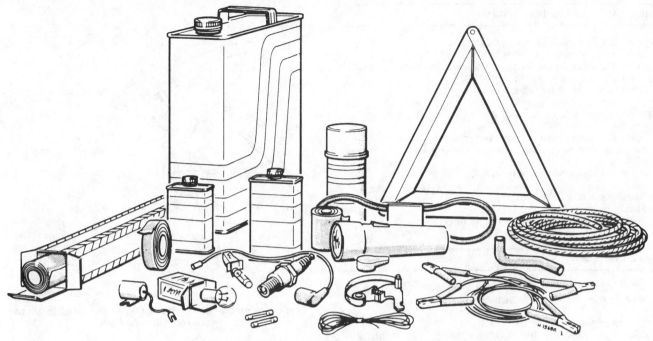

Carrying a few spares may save a long walk!

Engine will not start

Engine fails to turn when starter operated
Flat battery (recharge, use jump leads, or push start)
Battery terminals loose or corroded
Battery earth to body defective
Engine earth strap loose or broken
Starter motor (or solenoid) wiring loose or broken
Automatic transmission selector in wrong position, or inhibitor switch faulty
Ignition/starter switch faulty
Major mechanical failure (seizure)
Starter or solenoid internal fault (see Chapter 12)

Starter motor turns engine slowly
Partially discharged battery (recharge, use jump leads, or push start)
Battery terminals loose or corroded
Battery earth to body defective
Engine earth strap loose
Starter motor (or solenoid) wiring loose
Starter motor internal fault (see Chapter 12)

Starter motor spins without turning engine
Flat battery
Starter motor pinion sticking on sleeve
Flywheel gear teeth damaged or worn
Starter motor mounting bolts loose

Engine turns normally but fails to start
Damp or dirty HT leads and distributor cap (crank engine and check for spark)
No fuel in tank
Fouled or incorrectly gapped spark plugs (remove, clean and regap)
Other ignition system fault (see Chapter 4)
Other fuel system fault (see Chapter 3)
Poor compression (see Chapter 1)
Major mechanical failure (eg camshaft drive)

Engine fires but will not run
Air leaks at inlet manifold
Fuel starvation (see Chapter 3)
Other ignition fault (see Chapter 4)

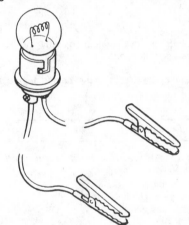

A simple test lamp is useful for tracing electrical faults

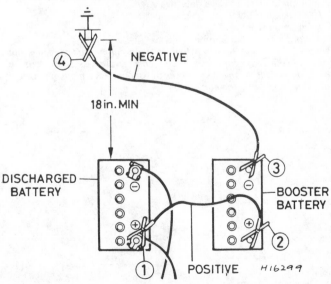

Jump start lead connections for negative earth vehicles - connect leads in order shown

Engine cuts out and will not restart

Engine cuts out suddenly – ignition fault
　Loose or disconnected LT wires
　Wet HT leads or distributor cap (after traversing water splash)
　Coil failure (check for spark)
　Other ignition fault (see Chapter 4)

Engine misfires before cutting out – fuel fault
　Fuel tank empty
　Fuel pump defective or filter blocked (check for delivery)
　Fuel tank filler vent blocked (suction will be evident on releasing cap)
　Other fuel system fault (see Chapter 3)

Engine cuts out – other causes
　Serious overheating
　Major mechanical failure (eg camshaft drive)

Engine overheats

Ignition (no-charge) warning light illuminated
　Slack or broken drivebelt – retension or renew (Chapter 12)

Ignition warning light not illuminated
　Coolant loss due to internal or external leakage (see Chapter 2)
　Thermostat defective
　Low oil level
　Brakes binding
　Radiator clogged externally or internally
　Electric cooling fan not operating correctly
　Engine waterways clogged

Note: *Do not add cold water to an overheated engine or damage may result*

Low engine oil pressure

Gauge reads low or warning light illuminated with engine running
　Oil level low or incorrect grade
　Defective gauge or sender unit
　Wire to sender unit earthed
　Engine overheating
　Oil filter clogged or bypass valve defective
　Oil pressure relief valve defective
　Oil pick-up strainer clogged
　Oil pump worn
　Worn main or big-end bearings
Note: *Low oil pressure in a high-mileage engine at tickover is not necessarily a cause for concern. Sudden pressure loss at speed is far more significant. In any event, check the gauge or warning light sender before condemning the engine.*

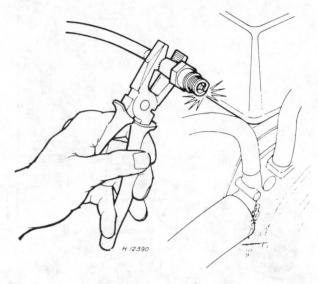

H 12390

Crank engine and check for spark. Note use of insulated tool to hold plug lead

Engine noises

Pre-ignition (pinking) on acceleration
　Incorrect grade of fuel
　Ignition ECU fault
　Excessive carbon build-up in engine

Whistling or wheezing noises
　Leaking vacuum hose
　Leaking manifold gasket
　Blowing head gasket

Tapping or rattling
　Worn valve gear
　Worn timing belt
　Broken piston ring (ticking noise)

Knocking or thumping
　Unintentional mechanical contact (eg fan blades)
　Worn drivebelt
　Peripheral component fault (alternator, water pump etc)
　Worn big-end bearings (regular heavy knocking, perhaps less under load)
　Worn main bearings (rumbling and knocking, perhaps worsening under load)
　Piston slap (most noticeable when cold)

Chapter 1 Engine

Contents

Specifications

General

Type	M16 twin overhead camshaft
Designation	20 HD
Number of cylinders	4
Bore	84.45 mm (3.327 in)
Stroke	89.00 mm (3.506 in)
Capacity	1994 cc
Firing order	1-3-4-2 (No 1 at timing belt end)
Direction of crankshaft rotation	Clockwise
Valve operation	Overhead camshaft/ hydraulic tappets
Compression ratio	10.0:1

Cylinder block

Material	Cast iron
Block height	294.07 mm (11.192 in)
Bore diameter	84.456 to 84.469 mm (3.3275 to 3.3280 in)
Maximum cylinder bore taper	0.15 mm (0.006 in)
Maximum cylinder bore ovality	0.15 mm (0.006 in)
Maximum gasket face distortion	0.10 mm (0.004 in)

Crankshaft

Main bearing journal diameter	54.005 to 54.026 mm (2.1277 to 2.1286 in)
Crankpin journal diameter	47.635 to 47.647 mm (1.8768 to 1.8772 in)
Main bearing journal running clearance	0.03 to 0.38 mm (0.001 to 0.014 in)
Crankpin journal running clearance	0.04 to 0.08 mm (0.001 to 0.003 in)
Crankshaft endfloat	0.03 to 0.14 mm (0.001 to 0.005 in)

Pistons and piston rings

Piston-to-bore clearance:	
Top of skirt	0.08 to 0.10 mm (0.003 to 0.004 in)
Bottom of skirt	0.04 to 0.05 mm (0.001 to 0.002 in)
Piston ring fitted gap:	
Compression rings	0.30 to 0.50 mm (0.011 to 0.020 in)
Oil control rails	0.25 to 0.50 mm (0.010 to 0.020 in)

Gudgeon pin

Type	Fully floating
Diameter	23.810 to 23.815 mm (0.9381 to 0.9383 in)
Clearance in connecting rod	0.003 to 0.025 mm (0.0001 to 0.0010 in)
Clearance in piston	Hand push fit at 20°C (68°F)

Connecting rod

Small end bush reamed diameter	23.818 to 23.825 mm (0.9384 to 0.0387 in)

Camshafts

Drive .... Toothed belt
Number of bearings .... 5 per shaft
Camshaft bearing clearance:
    New .... 0.043 to 0.094 mm (0.0016 to 0.0037 in)
    Used .... 0.10 mm (0.039 in) maximum

Valves

Face angle .... 45° 30'
Head diameter:
    Inlet .... 31.70 to 32.00 mm (1.24 to 1.26 in)
    Exhaust .... 29.20 to 29.40 mm (1.15 to 1.16 in)
Stem diameter:
    Inlet .... 7.09 to 7.10 mm (0.279 to 0.280 in)
    Exhaust .... 7.07 to 7.09 mm (0.278 to 0.279 in)
Seat width .... 1.5 to 2.0 mm (0.060 to 0.078 in)
Installed height .... 44.00 mm (1.733 in) maximum
Valve spring free length .... 41.00 mm (1.615 in)

Cylinder head

Maximum gasket face distortion .... 0.20 mm (0.007 in)
Valve seat angle .... 45°
Valve seat width .... 1.50 to 2.00 mm (0.059 to 0.078 in)
Valve guide protrusion .... 12.00 mm (0.472 in) above head face

Lubrication system

System pressure:
    Idling .... 0.7 bar (10.15 lbf/ in) minimum
    Running .... 3.8 bar (55.10 lbf/ in) minimum
Engine oil type/ specification* .... Multigrade engine oil, viscosity SAE 10W/ 40, to API SF or SF/ CD (Duckhams QXR, Hypergrade, or 10W/ 40 Motor Oil)
Engine oil capacity (including filter) .... 4.5 litres (8.0 Imp pints)
Difference between MAX and MIN marks on dipstick .... 0.5 litre (0.9 Imp pint)

* **Note:** *Austin Rover specify a 10W/40 oil to meet warranty requirements. Duckhams QXR or 10W/40 Motor Oil is available to meet these requirements.*

Torque wrench settings

	Nm	lbf ft
Timing belt upper cover bolts	3	2
Timing belt lower cover bolts	6	4
Timing belt bottom cover bracket bolts	6	4
Timing belt tensioner retaining bolt	25	18
Timing belt idler pulley bolt	25	18
Camshaft sprocket retaining bolt	65	48
Cylinder head backplate	6	4
Crankshaft pulley retaining bolt	85	63
Camshaft cover bolts	10	7
Camshaft housing to cylinder head	25	18
Cylinder head bolts:		
Stage 1	45	33
Stage 2	80	59
Stage 3	Further 60°, or to 108 Nm (80 lbf ft) – whichever comes first	
Oil pump retaining bolts	6	4
Flywheel retaining bolts	85	63
Torque converter driveplate bolts	110	81
Starter ring gear to driveplate	32	23
Adaptor plate to engine:		
Bolts below crankshaft centre-line	25	18
Bolts above crankshaft centre-line	45	33
Sump drain plug	35	26
Sump pan bolts	8	6
Oil pick-up pipe bolts	6	4
Main bearing cap bolts	105	77
Big-end bearing cap nuts	55	40
Front and rear engine mounting-to-mounting bracket nuts	80	59
Front engine mounting bracket bolts	40	30
Rear engine mounting bracket to engine	90	66
Rear engine mounting bracket to body	25	18
Right-hand engine mounting through-bolt	45	33
Right-hand engine mounting to engine bracket	60	44
Right-hand engine mounting bracket to engine	25	18
Engine tie-bar through-bolts	45	33
Snubber to longitudinal support member	55	40
Snubber bracket to adaptor plate	80	59
Longitudinal support member bolts	45	33

1 General description

The M16 engine fitted to Rover 820 models is a water-cooled, four-cylinder, four-stroke petrol engine, of double overhead camshaft configuration, and 1994 cc capacity.

The combined crankcase and cylinder block is of cast iron construction, and houses the pistons, connecting rods and crankshaft. The solid skirt cast aluminium alloy pistons have two compression rings and an oil control ring, and are retained on the connecting rods by fully floating gudgeon pins. To reduce frictional drag and piston slap, the gudgeon pin is offset to the thrust side of the piston. The forged steel connecting rods are attached to the crankshaft by renewable shell type big-end bearings. The crankshaft is carried in five main bearings, also of the renewable shell type. Crankshaft endfloat is controlled by thrust washers which are located on either side of the centre main bearing.

The twin overhead camshafts are located in the cylinder head, and each is retained in position by a housing bolted to the cylinder head upper face. The camshafts are supported by five bearing journals machined directly into the head and housings. Drive to the camshafts is by an internally-toothed rubber timing belt, from a sprocket on the front end of the crankshaft. An idler pulley and adjustable tensioner pulley are fitted to eliminate backlash and prevent slackness of the belt. The distributor rotor arm is attached to the rear of the exhaust camshaft, and on early models, the power steering pump is belt-driven from a sprocket attached to the rear of the inlet camshaft. On later models, the power steering is located at the front of the engine, and is belt-driven from a sprocket on the crankshaft.

The M16 engine utilizes four valves per cylinder, mounted at an inclined angle, and running in guides which are pressed into the cylinder head. The valves are of small diameter, to improve breathing efficiency and reduce valve mass. Each valve is opened by a hydraulic tappet, acted upon directly by the lobe of the camshaft, and closed by a single valve spring.

Blow-by gases from the crankcase are vented by a positive crankcase ventilation system back into the intake air stream for combustion. The system incorporates an oil separator, to return oil droplets to the sump, and a diverter valve, which channels the vapour to inlets on either side of the throttle valve, depending on manifold depression.

Engine lubrication is by a conventional forced-feed system, and a detailed description of its operation will be found in Section 24.

2 Maintenance and inspection

1 At the intervals given in *Routine maintenance* at the beginning of this manual, carry out the following operations on the engine.
2 Visually inspect the engine joint faces, gaskets and seals for any signs of oil or water leaks. Pay particular attention to the areas around the camshaft covers, cylinder head, crankshaft front oil seal and sump joint faces. Rectify any leaks by referring to the appropriate Sections of this Chapter.
3 Place a suitable container beneath the oil drain plug, located on the rear-facing side of the sump (photo). Unscrew the plug using a spanner or socket, and allow the oil to drain. Inspect the condition of the drain plug sealing washer, and renew it if necessary. Refit and tighten the plug after draining.
4 Reposition the bowl to the side of the engine, under the oil filter.
5 Using a strap wrench or filter removal tool, slacken the filter initially, then unscrew it from the engine and discard (photo).
6 Wipe the filter housing mating face with a rag, then lubricate the seal of a new filter using clean engine oil.
7 Screw the filter into position, and tighten it by hand only – do not use any tools.
8 Unscrew the filler cap on the camshaft cover and fill the engine, using the correct grade of oil, until the level reaches the MAX mark on the dipstick (photo). Refit the filler cap, then start the engine and check for leaks around the filter seal. Switch off, wait for a few minutes for the oil to return to the sump, then check the level on the dipstick once more. Top up if necessary to bring the level back up to the MAX mark, and maintain the level between the MAX and MIN marks at all times. Approximately 0.5 litres (0.8 pts) will raise the level from MIN to MAX on the dipstick.

2.3 Engine oil drain plug location

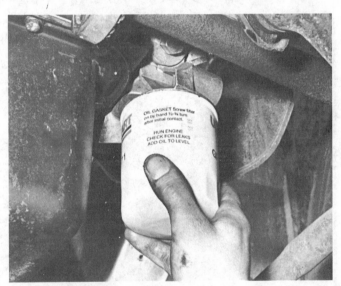

2.5 Removing the oil filter

2.8 Fill the engine with oil through the filler orifice on the camshaft cover

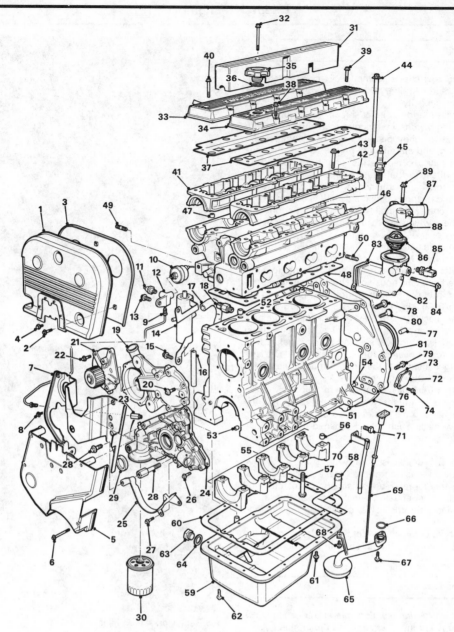

Fig. 1.1 Exploded view of the engine external components (Sec 1)

1 Timing belt upper cover	24 Oil pump housing	47 Camshaft housing dowels	69 Oil dipstick
2 Upper cover bolt	25 Timing belt bottom cover	48 Cylinder head gasket	70 Dipstick tube
3 Backplate	26 Bottom cover bolt	49 Inlet manifold stud	71 Dipstick tube bolt
4 Backplate bolt	27 Bottom cover bolt	50 Exhaust manifold stud	72 Crankcase cover plate
5 Timing belt lower cover	28 Bolt adaptor	51 Cylinder block	73 Gasket
6 Lower cover bolt	29 Crankshaft front oil seal	52 Cylinder head dowel	74 Cover plate bolt
7 Backplate	30 Oil filter cartridge	53 Oil pump housing dowel	75 Gearbox adaptor plate
8 Backplate bolt	31 Spark plug cover	54 Adaptor plate dowel	76 Adaptor plate gasket
9 Oil pipe	32 Spark plug cover bolt	55 Main bearing caps	77 Gearbox locating dowel
10 Oil pressure transducer	33 Inlet camshaft cover	56 Bearing cap dowel	78 Adaptor plate bolt
11 Oil pressure switch	34 Exhaust camshaft cover	57 Main bearing cap bolt	79 Adaptor plate bolt
12 Adaptor	35 Oil filler cap	58 Crankcase breather	80 Adaptor plate Torx bolt
13 Adaptor bolt	36 Filler cap seal	extension tube	81 Crankshaft rear oil seal
14 Oil separator	37 Baffle plates	59 Sump	82 Thermostat housing
15 Oil separator bolt	38 Camshaft cover bolt	60 Sump gasket	83 Gasket
16 Breather hose	39 Camshaft cover bolt	61 Sump bolt	84 Thermostat housing bolt
17 Breather hose	40 Camshaft cover bolt	62 Sump bolt	85 Coolant temperature
18 Knock sensor	41 Inlet camshaft housing	63 Drain plug	thermistor
19 Water pump housing	42 Exhaust camshaft housing	64 Drain plug washer	86 Thermostat
20 Water pump housing bolt	43 Camshaft housing bolt	65 Oil pick-up pipe strainer	87 Water outlet elbow
21 Water pump	44 Cylinder head bolt	66 O-ring seal	88 Gasket
22 Water pump bolt	45 Spark plug	67 Pick-up pipe bolt	89 Outlet elbow bolt
23 Oil pipe adaptor	46 Cylinder head	68 Pick-up pipe bracket bolt	

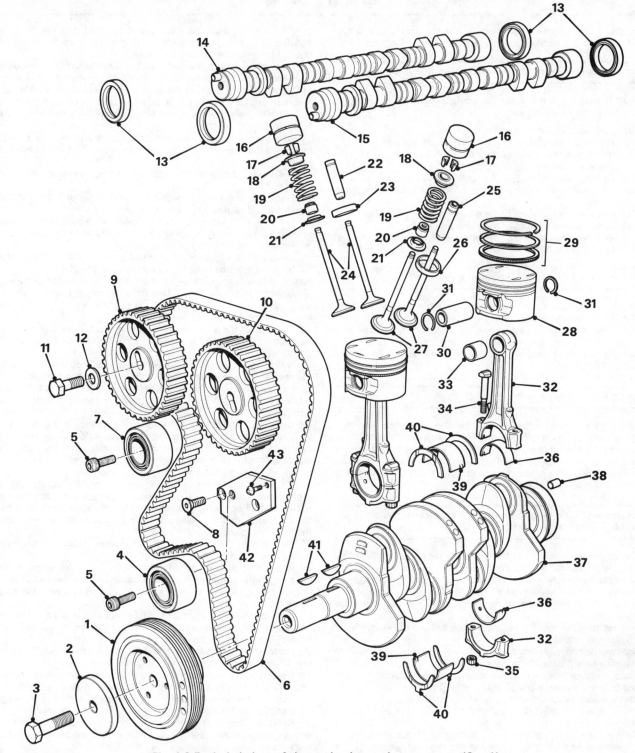

Fig. 1.2 Exploded view of the engine internal components (Sec 1)

1 Crankshaft pulley and sprocket
2 Flat washer
3 Crankshaft pulley bolt
4 Timing belt tensioner pulley
5 Pulley retaining bolt
6 Timing belt
7 Timing belt idler pulley
8 Mounting plate countersunk screw
9 Inlet camshaft sprocket
10 Exhaust camshaft sprocket

11 Sprocket retaining bolt
12 Washer
13 Camshaft front oil seals
14 Inlet camshaft
15 Exhaust camshaft
16 Hydraulic tappet
17 Valve collets
18 Valve spring top cup
19 Valve spring
20 Valve stem oil deal
21 Valve spring seat
22 Inlet valve guide

23 Inlet valve seat
24 Inlet valves
25 Exhaust valve guide
26 Exhaust valve seat
27 Exhaust valves
28 Piston
29 Piston rings
30 Gudgeon pin
31 Circlips
32 Connecting rod and cap
33 Connecting rod small end bush

34 Connecting rod bolt
35 Connecting rod cap nut
36 Big-end bearing shells
37 Crankshaft
38 Dowel
39 Main bearing shells
40 Crankshaft thrustwashers
41 Woodruff keys
42 Timing belt tensioner mounting plate
43 Mounting plate bolt

9   At the service intervals specified, renew the timing belt and/or adjust the belt tension, using the procedures described in Section 10.

3 Major operations possible with the engine in the car

The following operations can be carried out without having to remove the engine from the car:

(a) *Removal and refitting of the timing belt*
(b) *Removal and refitting of the camshaft and tappets*
(c) *Removal and refitting of the cylinder head*
(d) *Removal and refitting of the sump*
(e) *Removal and refitting of the big-end bearings*
(f) *Removal and refitting of the piston and connecting rod assemblies*
(g) *Removal and refitting of the oil pump*
(h) *Removal and refitting of the engine mountings*
(i) *Removal and refitting of the flywheel or driveplate (after first removing the transmission)*

4 Major operations requiring engine removal

Strictly speaking, it is only necessary to remove the engine if the crankshaft or main bearings require attention. However, owing to the possibility of dirt entry, and to allow greater working access, it is preferable to remove the engine if working on the piston and connecting rod assemblies, or when carrying out any major engine overhaul or repair.

5 Methods of engine removal

The engine and transmission can be lifted from the car as a complete unit, as described later in this Chapter, or the gearbox or automatic transmission may be first removed, as described in Chapters 6 and 7 respectively. It is not possible to remove the engine on its own, leaving the gearbox or transmission in the car, owing to space restrictions in the engine bay.

6 Engine and manual gearbox/automatic transmission assembly – removal and refitting

1   Extract the retaining clips and release the support struts from the bonnet. Tie the bonnet back in the fully-open position.
2   Drain the cooling system as described in Chapter 2, the gearbox oil or automatic transmission fluid as described in Chapters 6 and 7 respectively, and the engine oil as described in Section 2 of this Chapter.
3   Remove the complete air cleaner and intake trunking assembly, as described in Chapter 3.
4   Remove the battery as described in Chapter 12, then undo the three bolts and remove the battery tray (photo).
5   Undo the three bolts and remove the air cleaner support bracket, located below the battery tray (photo).
6   On cars with single-point fuel injection, undo the three ignition/fuel ECU mounting bracket bolts, and move the ECU and bracket aside.
7   Slacken the clips and remove the radiator top hose, then disconnect the expansion tank hose at the thermostat housing. On single-point injection models, disconnect the two heater outlet hoses at the inlet manifold.
8   Disconnect the remaining vacuum hose at the inlet manifold.
9   Undo the bolt securing the engine rear tie-bar support bracket to the inlet manifold (photo).
10 Undo the two through-bolts securing the engine rear tie-bar to the engine and body brackets, and recover the special forked nut (photo). Note that the forked end of the nut engages with a bracket projection to prevent the nut turning.
11 Withdraw the rear tie-bar from its brackets, noting that it is stamped with the word TOP on the upper face of the larger end, which must be refitted accordingly (photo).
12 Slacken the clips and disconnect the radiator bottom hose at the radiator and main coolant pipe (photo), the bottom hose take-off at the expansion tank pipe, the two heater hoses at the heater matrix

(photo), and the heater outlet hose at the inlet manifold or throttle housing. On automatic transmission models, disconnect the two coolant hoses at the transmission oil cooler.
13 Place absorbent rags around the fuel filter outlet banjo union bolt on the left-hand side of the filter, then slowly unscrew the bleed screw in the centre of the bolt, or the bolt itself as applicable, to release the fuel system pressure. When the pressure is released, remove the bolt and recover the two copper washers. Tighten the bleed screw where fitted.
14 Release the clip and disconnect the fuel return hose from the pipe below the fuel filter. Plug or tape over the disconnected fuel hoses and unions.
15 Disconnect the accelerator cable at the throttle end, as described in Chapter 3.
16 Undo the brake servo vacuum hose banjo union bolt at the inlet manifold, and recover the two copper washers.
17 On cars with single-point fuel injection, disconnect the wiring multi-plug from the ignition/fuel ECU, and remove the relay from its holder behind the ECU location (photo).
18 Separate the engine wiring harness from the main wiring harness by disconnecting the large round wiring multi-plug located behind the battery (photo). Additionally, on cars with single-point fuel injection, disconnect the adjacent large flat multi-plug (photo), and on cars with multi-point fuel injection, the multi-plugs at the rear right-hand side of the engine compartment (photo).
19 Disconnect the two sensing leads at the battery clamps, noting their locations, and also the main positive lead to the starter motor at the battery clamp.
20 Remove the cover from the fuse and relay box on the left-hand side of the engine compartment, then lift off the cover over the fusible links.
21 Lift out the engine harness cable retaining clip (photo), undo the cable retaining screw, and remove the cable from the fuse and relay box (photos).
22 Disconnect the HT and LT leads at the ignition coil (photos).
23 Disconnect the single cable at the starter solenoid (photo).
24 Undo the bolt and disconnect the earth lead on the side of the gearbox (photo) or automatic transmission, then slide up the rubber boot and disconnect the reversing light switch wires.
25 On automatic transmission models, extract the spring clip and withdraw the steel and rubber washers securing the selector cable end to the transmission selector lever. Undo the outer cable retaining nut at the abutment bracket, release the inner and outer cables, and recover the inner cable spacer.
26 Disconnect the speedometer transducer cable at the wiring multi-plug .
27 Check that all electrical connections between the engine and the car main wiring harness have been disconnected and moved clear. The engine wiring harness stays *in situ*, and is removed with the engine assembly.
28 Slacken the hose clips and disconnect the two power steering hoses at the fluid reservoir (photos). Plug the hoses and the outlets immediately to reduce fluid loss.
29 Undo the two power steering pipe support bracket bolts, and release the pipes from the brackets (photo).
30 On cars with a rear-mounted power steering pump, slacken the clip and disconnect the power steering fluid return hose from the pipe (photo), then remove the pipe and hose assembly clear of the engine.
31 Jack up the front of the car and support it on axle stands.
32 Refer to Chapter 3 if necessary, and separate the exhaust front section at the manifold and intermediate pipe flange joints. Remove the exhaust front section from the car.
33 On manual gearbox models, extract the spring clip and withdraw the clevis pin securing the clutch slave cylinder pushrod to the gearbox release arm. Undo the two slave cylinder retaining bolts and move the cylinder aside.
34 On manual gearbox models, undo the bolt in the centre of the gearbox steady rod. Remove the dished washer, slide off the steady rod and remove the inner flat washer. Remove the spring clip to expose the gearchange rod-to-gearchange shaft retaining roll pin. Using a parallel pin punch, tap out the roll pin and slide the gearchange rod rearwards off the shaft (photo).
35 Undo the eight bolts and remove the longitudinal support member from beneath the engine (photo).
36 On cars with a front-mounted power steering pump, undo the pipe union and remove the fluid pipe from the rear of the pump. Plug the unions to prevent fluid loss.

6.4 Undo the three bolts and remove the battery tray

6.5 Undo the three bolts and remove the air cleaner support bracket

6.9 Undo the engine tie-bar-to-inlet manifold bolt (arrowed)

6.10 Remove the tie-bar through-bolt (A), and recover the forked nut (B)

6.11 The tie-bar must be refitted with the word TOP (arrowed) uppermost

6.12A Disconnect the radiator hose (arrowed) at the main coolant pipe ...

6.12B ... and the heater hoses at the heater matrix (arrowed)

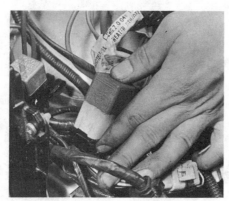

6.17 Remove the relay behind the ignition/fuel ECU

6.18A Disconnect the large round wiring multi-plug (arrowed) ...

6.18B ... and the adjacent flat multi-plug

6.18C Disconnect the appropriate multi-plugs at the rear of the engine compartment

6.21A Lift out the engine harness cable retaining clip ...

6.21B ... undo the cable retaining screw ...

6.21C ... and remove the cable from the fuse and relay box

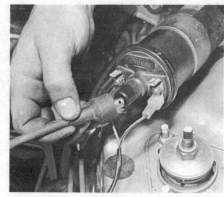

6.22A Disconnect the HT lead ...

6.22B .. and LT leads at the ignition coil

6.23 Disconnect the starter solenoid cable

6.24 Disconnect the gearbox earth lead (A) and reversing light switch wires (B)

6.28A Slacken the power steering hose clips (arrowed) ...

6.28B ... and disconnect the hoses

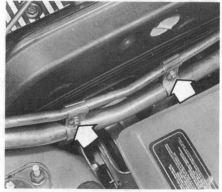

6.29 Undo the power steering pipe support bracket bolts (arrowed)

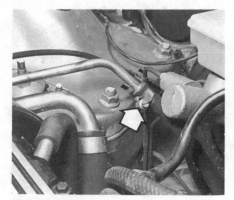

6.30 Disconnect the power steering fluid return hose (arrowed)

6.34 Separate the gearchange rod from the shaft after removing the roll pin

6.35 Undo the bolts and remove the longitudinal support member (arrowed)

37 Undo the nut securing the right-hand steering knuckle balljoint to the lower suspension arm (photo), then release the balljoint from the arm using a universal balljoint separator tool or two-legged puller.

38 Pull the steering knuckle outwards, then using a suitable flat bar or large screwdriver, lever between the driveshaft inner constant velocity joint and the differential housing to release the joint.

39 Move the driveshaft clear, then repeat these operations on the left-hand driveshaft.

40 Attach a suitable hoist to the engine using rope slings, or chains attached to brackets secured to the cylinder head. Adjust the ropes or chains so that the engine will hang at approximately 30° to the horizontal, with the timing cover end uppermost, when it is lifted out.

41 On automatic transmission models, undo the mounting bracket bolts and remove the engine lower tie-bar from under the front of the car, complete with mounting brackets.

42 Undo the right-hand engine mounting through-bolt, and recover the special nut. Note that the forked end of the nut plate locates over a stud on the body bracket.

43 Undo the two bolts securing the engine mounting to its mounting bracket, and remove the mounting (photo).

44 Undo the two bolts securing the air cleaner trunking support bracket to the front chassis member, and remove the bracket (photo).

45 Undo the nut securing the front engine mounting to its gearbox or transmission bracket (photo).

46 Undo the nut securing the rear engine mounting to its gearbox or transmission bracket.

47 Raise the engine slightly, then on cars with a rear-mounted power steering pump, undo the power steering pipe union nut at the rear of the pump, and remove the pipe. Plug the unions to prevent loss of fluid.

48 Make a final check that everything connecting the engine and gearbox or transmission to the car has been disconnected and moved well clear.

49 Carefully lift the power unit upwards, whilst moving and twisting it slightly to clear the various projections (photo). When the unit has been raised sufficiently, draw the hoist forwards to bring the engine assembly over the front body panel, then lower the assembly to the floor.

50 Refitting is a straightforward reverse of the removal sequence, bearing in mind the following points:

   (a) Refit all the engine mounting bolts loosely, then tighten them in the sequence shown in Fig. 1.3 or 1.4 as applicable
   (b) Refill the cooling system as described in Chapter 2
   (c) Refill the gearbox or automatic transmission as described in Chapters 6 or 7 respectively
   (d) Fill the engine with oil as described in Section 2
   (e) Refill and bleed the power steering system as described in Chapter 10
   (f) Adjust the accelerator cable as described in Chapter 3, and where applicable, the automatic transmission kickdown cable as described in Chapter 7

7 Engine – separation from, and attachment to, manual gearbox/ automatic transmission

Separation – manual gearbox models

1 With the engine and gearbox removed from the car, undo the starter motor retaining bolts, and remove the unit from the gearbox bellhousing (photo).

2 Undo the three bolts and remove the engine snubber bracket from the gearbox adaptor plate beneath the engine sump.

3 Undo the two bolts securing the front engine mounting bracket to the gearbox, and remove the bracket (photo).

4 Undo the boits securing the rear engine mounting bracket to the gearbox, noting the location of the crankshaft sensor bracket (photo). Move the sensor aside and remove the bracket.

5 Undo all the remaining bolts securing the gearbox to the engine.

6 With the gearbox well supported, release the locating dowels and draw the unit squarely away from the engine (photo).

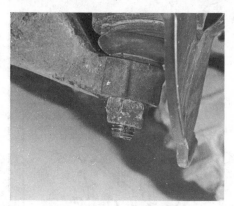

6.37 Undo the nut and separate the steering knuckle balljoint

6.43 Remove the right-hand engine mounting

6.44 Undo the bolts (arrowed) and remove the air cleaner trunking support bracket

6.45 Undo the nut securing the front engine mounting

6.49 Removing the engine and gearbox from the car

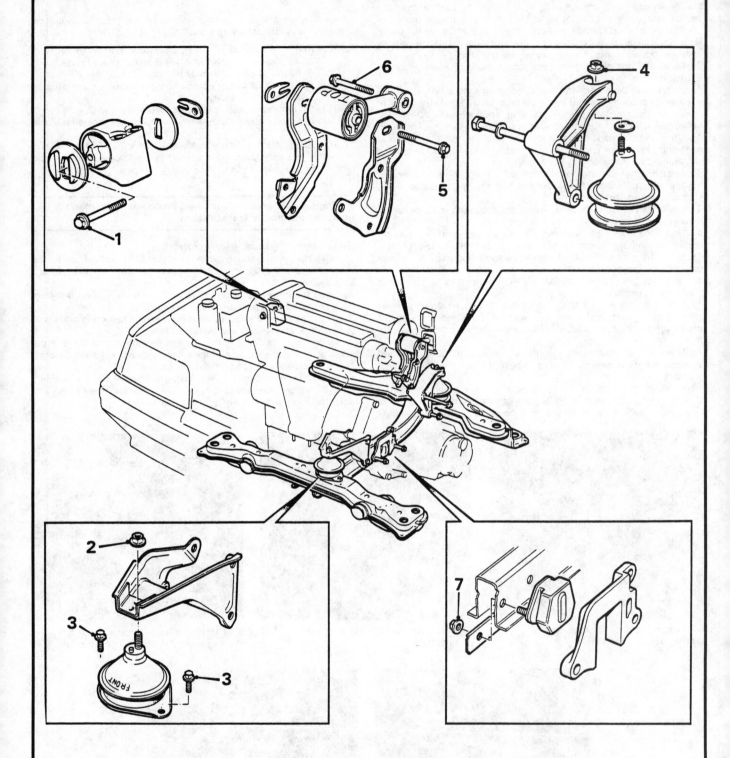

Fig. 1.3 Engine mounting tightening sequence – manual gearbox models (Sec 6)

Tighten the mountings in the numerical sequence shown

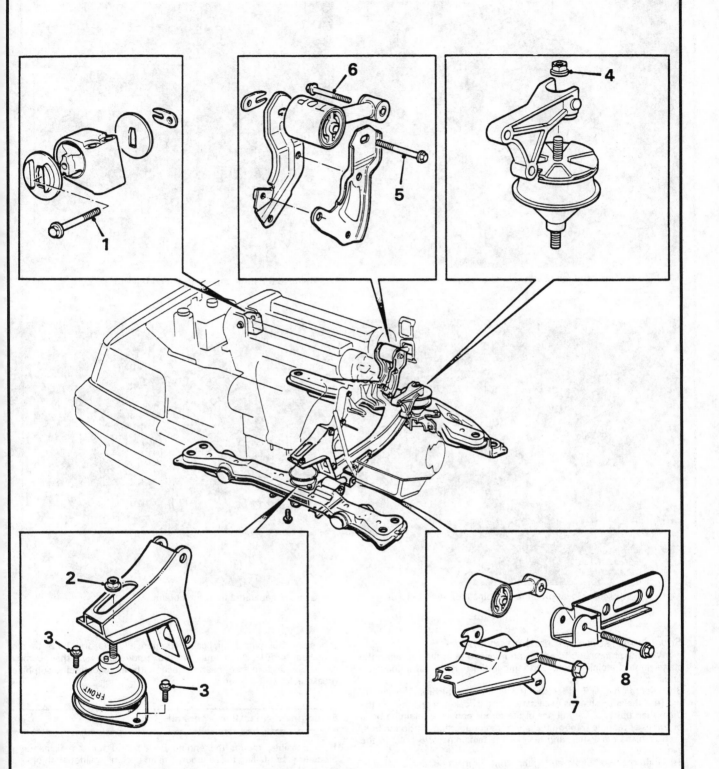

Fig. 1.4 Engine mounting tightening sequence – automatic transmission models (Sec 6)

Tighten the mountings in the numerical sequence shown

7.1 Undo the bolts and remove the starter motor

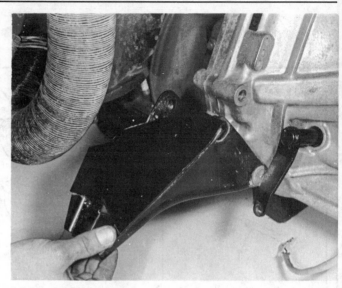

7.3 Remove the front engine mounting bracket

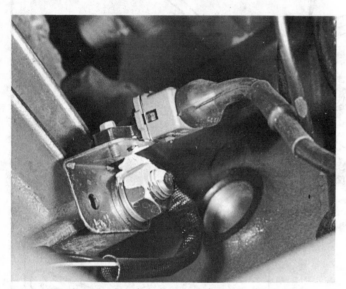

7.4 Crankshaft sensor location on rear engine mounting bracket

7.6 Gearbox separated from the engine

Separation – automatic transmission models

7   With the engine and transmission removed from the car, undo the starter motor retaining bolts and remove the unit from the converter housing.

8   Refer to Chapter 7 and release the kickdown cable from the engine.

9   Turn the crankshaft as necessary, using a socket or spanner on the crankshaft pulley bolt, until one of the torque converter retaining bolts becomes accessible through the starter motor aperture. Undo the bolt, then turn the crankshaft and remove the remaining two bolts in the same way

10   Undo the two bolts securing the front engine mounting bracket to the transmission, and remove the bracket.

11   Undo the bolts securing the rear engine mounting bracket to the gearbox, noting the location of the crankshaft sensor bracket. Move the sensor aside and remove the bracket.

12   Undo the remaining bolts securing the transmission to the engine.

13   With the transmission well supported, release the locating dowels and draw the unit squarely away from the engine. Ensure that the torque converter stays in place on the transmission.

Attachment – all models

14   Attachment is the straightforward reverse of the separation sequence, but where applicable, tighten all nuts and bolts to the specified torque. On manual gearbox models, smear the gearbox mainshaft and release bearing face with molybdenum disulphide grease before attachment.

8   Engine dismantling – general

1   If possible, mount the engine on a stand for the dismantling procedure, but failing this, support it in an upright position with blocks of wood placed under the sump or crankcase.

2   Drain the oil into a suitable container before cleaning the engine or commencing dismantling, if this has not already been done.

3   Cleanliness is most important, and if the engine is dirty, it should be cleaned with paraffin or a suitable solvent, while keeping it in an upright position.

4   Avoid working with the engine directly on a concrete floor, as grit presents a real source of trouble.

5   As parts are removed, clean them in a paraffin bath. However, do not immerse parts with internal oilways in paraffin, as it is difficult to remove, usually requiring a high pressure hose. Clean oilways with nylon pipe cleaners.

6 It is advisable to have suitable containers to hold small items, as this will help when reassembling the engine, and also prevent possible losses.

7 Always obtain complete sets of new gaskets, but retain the old ones with a view to using them as a pattern to make a replacement if a new one is not available.

8 When possible, refit nuts, bolts and washers in their location after being removed, as this helps to protect the threads, and will also be helpful when reassembling the engine.

9 Retain unserviceable components, in order to compare them with the new parts supplied.

9 Ancillary components – removal and refitting

1 If the engine has been removed from the car for major overhaul or repair, the following externally-mounted ancillary components can now be removed. The removal sequence need not necessarily follow the order given, nor will it always be necessary to remove all the components listed. This will depend on the extent of the work to be carried out, and the operations involved.

Thermostat housing and heater pipes (Chapter 2)
Water pump and housing (Chapter 2)
Inlet and exhaust manifolds (Chapter 3)
Distributor cap, spark plugs and HT leads (Chapter 4)
Knock sensor (Chapter 4)
Crankshaft sensor (Chapter 4)
Clutch assembly (Chapter 5)
Power steering pump (Chapter 10)
Alternator (Chapter 12)
Oil filter cartridge (Section 2 of this Chapter)
Engine mountings (Section 25 of this Chapter)
Dipstick tube (photo)
Alternator mounting bracket (photo)
Alternator adjustment arm or front mounted power steering pump bracket (photo)
Oil separator and oil pressure switch bracket (photo)

2 Refitting is essentially the reverse of the removal sequence, with reference to the Sections and Chapters indicated.

9.1A Remove the dipstick tube ...

9.1B ... the alternator mounting bracket ...

9.1C ... the alternator adjustment arm and bracket ...

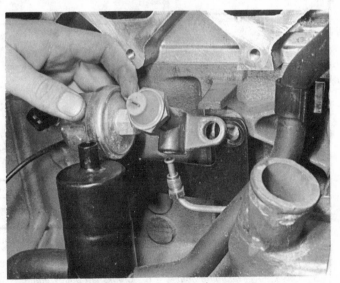

9.1D ... and oil pressure switch bracket

10 Timing belt – removal, refitting and adjustment

Note: *Accurate adjustment of the timing belt entails the use of a tension checking gauge, which is a Rover special tool. An approximate setting can be achieved using the method described in this Section, but the tension should be checked by a Rover dealer on completion.*

1   Disconnect the battery negative terminal. (Refer to Chapter 12, Section 1, before doing this).

2   Slacken the right-hand front wheel nuts, jack up the front of the car and support it on axle stands. Remove the roadwheel.

3   Undo the three bolts and remove the access panel under the wheel arch.

4   Position a jack and interposed block of wood under the sump, and just take the weight of the engine.

5   Undo the bolts securing the power steering pipe support brackets, and move the pipes slightly to gain access to the right-hand engine mounting (photo).

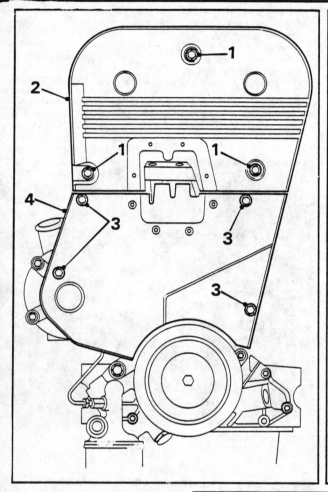
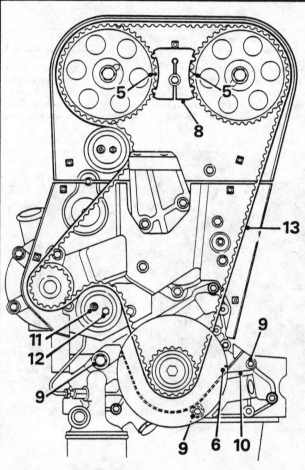
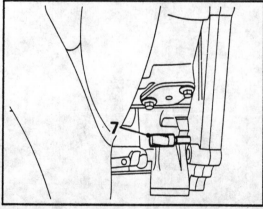

Fig. 1.5 Timing belt component details (Sec 10)

1	Upper cover retaining bolts	5	Camshaft sprocket timing marks	7	Locking the crankshaft through the hole in the adaptor plate	9	Bottom cover retaining bolts
2	Upper cover	6	Crankshaft pulley timing mark	8	Special tool for locking camshaft sprockets	10	Bottom cover
3	Lower cover retaining bolts					11	Tensioner retaining bolt
4	Lower cover					12	Tensioner adjusting hole
						13	Timing belt

6 Undo the engine mounting through-bolt (photo), and recover the special nut. Note that the forked end of the nut plate locates over a stud on the body bracket.

7 Undo the two bolts securing the engine mounting to its mounting bracket, and remove the mounting.

8 Raise the engine slightly, then undo the three bolts (photo) and lift off the timing belt upper cover.

9 Undo the four bolts (photo) and remove the timing belt lower cover.

10 Refer to Chapter 12 and remove the alternator drivebelt.

11 Using a socket or spanner on the crankshaft pulley, turn the crankshaft in an anti-clockwise direction until the timing notches on the camshaft sprockets are facing each other and aligned horizontally (photos). The notch on the crankshaft pulley should also be aligned with the edge of the metal bracket which forms the timing belt bottom cover (photo). In this position, the crankshaft is at 90° BTDC, with No 1 piston on its compression stroke.

12 If required, the crankshaft can be locked in this position, by inserting a dowel rod or drill of suitable diameter through the hole in the gearbox adaptor plate, near to the lower edge of the cylinder block on the front-facing side of the engine (Fig. 1.5). The dowel or drill will then engage with a corresponding hole in the flywheel.

13 Undo the three bolts and remove the timing belt bottom cover (photo).

14 Using a suitable Allen key, undo the timing belt tensioner retaining bolt, and remove the tensioner (photo).

15 Slip the belt off the sprockets, and remove it from the engine (photo).

16 If the timing belt is to be re-used, mark it in chalk with an arrow to indicate its running direction, and store it on its edge while it is off the engine.

17 Check the condition of the timing belt and the various sprockets, with reference to Section 23.

18 Before refitting the belt, check that the crankshaft is still at the 90° BTDC position, and that the timing marks on the two sprockets are still aligned.

19 Engage the timing belt with the teeth of the crankshaft sprocket, and then pull the belt vertically upright on its straight, right-hand run. Keep it taut, and engage it over the exhaust camshaft sprocket, then the inlet camshaft sprocket.

20 Check that none of the sprockets have moved, then feed the belt around the idler pulley and engage it with the teeth of the water pump sprocket.

21 Fit the timing belt tensioner and secure with the retaining bolt, tightened finger-tight only at this stage.

22 Engage an Allen key with the hexagonal adjusting hole in the tensioner (photo), and turn the tensioner body until there is moderate tension on the belt. Hold the tensioner in this position, and tighten the retaining bolt.

23 Remove the locking pin (if used) from the gearbox adaptor plate, and turn the crankshaft one complete turn clockwise, followed by one complete turn anti-clockwise, and re-align the timing marks.

24 Check that it is just possible to deflect the belt, using moderate hand pressure, by 19.0 mm (0.75 in) at a point midway between the crankshaft and exhaust camshaft sprockets. Re-adjust the tension if necessary by slackening the tensioner retaining bolt, and repositioning the tensioner body with the Allen key. Recheck the tension again after turning the crankshaft one turn clockwise, then one turn anti-clockwise. It must be emphasised that this is only an approximate setting, and the tension should be checked by a dealer, using the Rover tension gauge, at the earliest opportunity.

25 Refit the timing belt bottom cover, turn the crankshaft to align the pulley timing mark with the edge of the bottom cover, and make a final check that the camshaft sprocket timing marks are still aligned.

26 Refer to Chapter 12 and refit the alternator drivebelt.

27 Refit the timing belt upper and lower covers.

28 Refit the engine mounting to its mounting bracket, lower the engine and secure the mounting to the body with the through-bolt and special nut.

29 Refit the power steering pipe support brackets, the wheel arch access panel, and the roadwheel.

30 Lower the car to the ground, tighten the wheel nuts fully, and reconnect the battery.

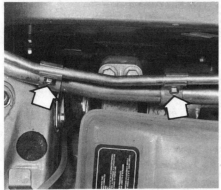
10.5 Undo the power steering pipe support bracket bolts (arrowed) and move the pipes

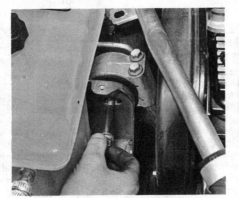
10.6 Undo the right-hand mounting through-bolt

10.8 Timing belt upper cover retaining bolt locations (arrowed)

10.9 Timing belt lower cover retaining bolt locations (arrowed)

10.11A Turn the crankshaft to align the sprocket timing marks (arrowed) ...

10.11B ... then check their horizontal alignment with a straight edge

10.11C Crankshaft pulley timing notch (arrowed) aligned with timing belt bottom cover edge

10.13 Removing the timing belt bottom cover

10.14 Removing the timing belt tensioner

10.15 Slip the timing belt off the sprockets

10.22 Tensioner hexagonal adjusting hole (arrowed)

11 Camshafts and tappets – removal and refitting

1 Remove the timing belt as described in the previous Section.
2 Using a suitable Allen key, undo the bolt securing the timing belt idler pulley to the cylinder head (photo). WIthdraw the pulley, noting that there is a spacing washer fitted between the pulley and cylinder head backplate (photo).
3 Undo the retaining bolt securing each sprocket to its respective camshaft (photo). To prevent the sprockets turning as the bolts are undone, either insert a large screwdriver through one of the sprocket holes and engage it with one of the backplate bolts behind, or make up a holding tool from scrap metal, as shown in photo 11.35, which is of a scissor shape, with a bolts at each end to engage with the holes in the sprocket.
4 Withdraw the two sprockets from the camshafts, noting that they are not identical, and are marked INLET and EXHAUST on their front faces to avoid confusion (photos).
5 Undo the four bolts and remove the cylinder head backplate (photos).
6 Undo the two retaining bolts, withdraw the distributor cap, and place it to one side.
7 Undo the retaining Allen screw, and remove the distributor rotor arm (photo).
8 Undo the two screws and remove the distributor adaptor plate from the cylinder head (photos).
9 On cars fitted with a rear-mounted power steering pump driven off the inlet camshaft, remove the power steering pump drivebelt as described in Chapter 10, then withdraw the spacer behind the camshaft pulley (photo). Undo the two nuts and two bolts, and remove the power steering pulley backplate (photos).
10 On cars fitted with a front-mounted power steering pump, undo the two bolts and remove the blanking plate from the cylinder head (photo).
11 Detach the breather hose from the rear of the inlet camshaft cover.
12 On cars with multi-point fuel injection, release the plastic covers

then undo the two bolts securing the plenum chamber support brackets to the plenum chamber.
13 Undo the two bolts and lift off the spark plug cover from the centre of the cylinder head. Note that the spark plug HT lead grommet engages with the end of the cover, and on certain models, an accelerator cable support bracket is also retained by the right-hand cover bolt.
14 Undo the ten bolts securing each camshaft cover to its respective camshaft housing, and lift off the two covers (photos).
15 Withdraw the baffle plates, taking care not to damage the sealing edges on both sides of the plates (photo).
16 Slacken the ten bolts securing each camshaft housing to the cylinder head, then remove all the bolts except two on each housing at diagonally opposite corners. Make sure that the heads of the bolts left in position are at least 5.0 mm (0.2 in) clear of the housing face. Note that two types of retaining bolts are used to secure the camshaft housings. The three bolts on the inner edge of each housing nearest to the spark plugs are plain bolts, while all the rest are patch bolts (photo). All the bolts are of the micro-encapsulated type, having their threads filled with a locking and sealing compound, and new bolts must be obtained prior to reassembly.
17 Using a plastic or hide mallet, carefully tap up each housing to release it from the locating dowels. When the housings are free, remove the remaining bolts and lift off the two housings (photo).
18 Carefully lift out the camshafts, and remove the oil seals at each end. Identify each camshaft, inlet or exhaust, with a label after removal.
19 Have a box ready with sixteen internal compartments, marked Inlet 1 to 8, and Exhaust 1 to 8, or alternatively mark a sheet of card in a similar way.
20 Lift out each tappet in turn (photo), and place it upside down in its respective position in the box or on the card. If the tappets are difficult to remove by hand, use the rubber sucker end of a valve grinding tool to lift them out.
21 Carry out a careful inspection of the components with reference to Section 23, and renew any parts as necessary. Prior to reassembly, obtain new camshaft oil seals, a complete set of camshaft housing

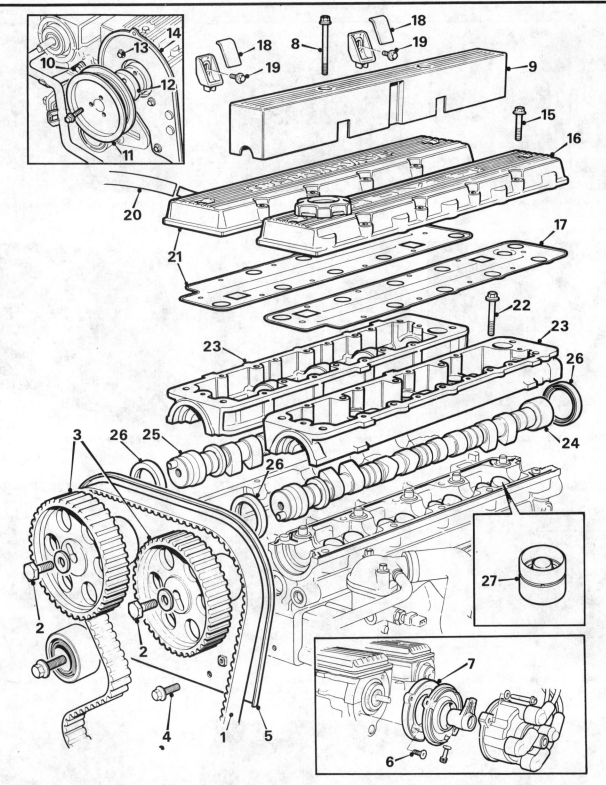

Fig. 1.6 Exploded view of the camshaft and tappet components (Sec 11)

1 Timing belt
2 Camshaft sprocket retaining bolts
3 Camshaft sprockets
4 Backplate retaining bolt
5 Backplate
6 Distributor adaptor plate retaining screw
7 Distributor adaptor plate

8 Spark plug cover retaining bolt
9 Spark plug cover
10 Heater bypass pipe bracket
11 Power steering pump pulley
12 Pulley spacer
13 Pulley backplate retaining bolt
14 Pulley backplate

15 Camshaft cover retaining bolt
16 Exhaust camshaft cover
17 Baffle plate
18 Plastic covers (multi-point fuel injection models)
19 Plenum chamber support bracket bolts (multi-point fuel injection models)

20 Breather hose
21 Inlet camshaft cover and baffle plate
22 Camshaft housing retaining bolt
23 Camshaft housings
24 Exhaust camshaft
25 Inlet camshaft
26 Oil seals
27 Hydraulic tappets

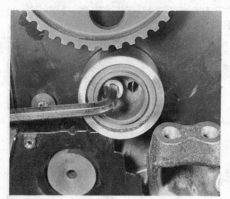

11.2A Undo the timing belt idler pulley bolt ...

11.2B ... and remove the pulley, noting the spacer behind (arrowed)

11.3 Undo the camshaft sprocket retaining bolts

11.4A Withdraw the sprockets from the camshafts ...

11.4B ... noting they are marked INLET and EXHAUST on their front faces (arrowed)

11.5A Undo the four bolts (arrowed) ...

11.5B ... and remove the cylinder head backplate

11.7 Remove the rotor arm

11.8A Undo the two screws (arrowed) ...

11.8B ... and remove the distributor adaptor plate

11.9A Withdraw the spacer behind the power steering pulley ...

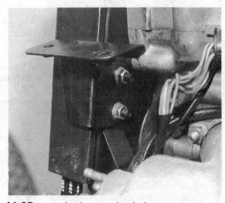

11.9B ... undo the two backplate nuts ...

11.9C ... and the two bolts, then remove the backplate

11.10 Undo the bolts (arrowed) and remove the blanking plate

11.14A Undo the camshaft cover retaining bolts ...

11.14B ... and remove the covers

11.15 Remove the baffle plates over the camshafts

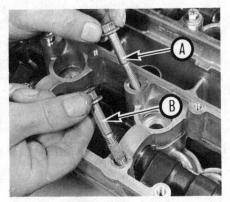

11.16 Camshaft housing plain bolts (A) and patch bolts (B)

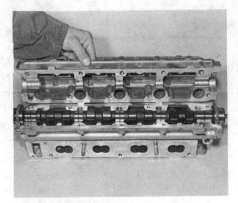

11.17 Removing the exhaust camshaft housing

11.20 Lift out the tappets and keep them in order

retaining bolts, and a tube of Loctite sealant 574.

22 Remove all traces of old sealant from the camshaft housing retaining bolt holes in the cylinder head, preferably using an M8 x 1.25 mm tap, but alternatively, using one of the old bolts with two file grooves cut into its threads. Also ensure that there is no oil remaining at the bottom of the bolt holes.

23 Thoroughly lubricate the tappet bores in the cylinder head, and refit the tappets in their original positions.

24 Lubricate the camshaft journals and lobes, then place the camshafts in position (photo). Set the camshafts so that when viewed head-on, the locating roll pin for the exhaust camshaft sprocket is in the 8 o'clock position, and the pin for the inlet camshaft sprocket is in the 2 o'clock position.

25 Lubricate the sealing lips of the new oil seals, carefully ease them over the camshaft journals, and position them against the shoulder in the cylinder head (photo),

26 Apply a thin bead of Loctite sealant 574 to the camshaft housing-to-cylinder head mating face (photo), then place both housings in position on the cylinder head.

27 Refit the housing retaining bolts, noting the location of the two different bolt types with reference to Fig. 1.7. Tighten the bolts progressively, and in a diagonal sequence, to the specified torque (photo).

28 Place the baffle plates in position over each housing.

29 Refit the camshaft covers, and tighten the bolts in a diagonal sequence to the specified torque. Refit the breather hose.

30 Refit the spark plug cover.

31 Where applicable, refit the two bolts securing the plenum chamber brackets to the plenum chamber, followed by the plastic covers.

32 On cars fitted with a rear-mounted power steering pump, refit the power steering pulley backplate, followed by the pulley spacer, then refit the pump drivebelt as described in Chapter 10.

33 On cars fitted with a front-mounted power steering pump, refit the blanking plate to the cylinder head.
34 Refit the distributor adaptor plate, followed by the rotor arm and distributor cap.
35 Refit the cylinder head backplate, then place the two sprockets in position on their respective camshafts. Fit the sprocket retaining bolts, then tighten the bolts to the specified torque while holding the sprockets to prevent them turning (photo).
36 Turn the sprockets as necessary to align the timing marks (photo).
37 Refit the timing belt idler pulley, noting that the hole in the pulley

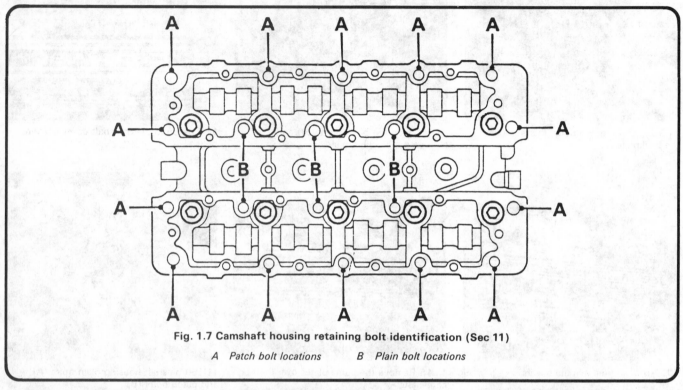

Fig. 1.7 Camshaft housing retaining bolt identification (Sec 11)

A Patch bolt locations   B Plain bolt locations

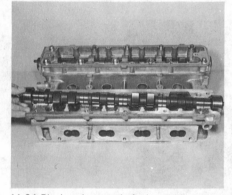

11.24 Placing the camshafts in position

11.25 Fitting the camshaft oil seals

11.26 Apply sealant to the camshaft housing mating face

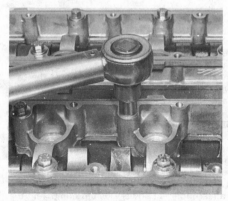

11.27 Tighten the housing retaining bolts to the specified torque

11.35 Home-made tool to prevent camshaft rotation

11.36 Align the sprocket timing marks (arrowed)

body engages over the peg in the backplate (photo).
38 Refer to Section 10 and refit the timing belt.
39 When the engine is started on completion of the work, be prepared for a considerable rattle from the tappets until they completely fill with oil. This may take a few minutes, and will be more pronounced if any of the tappets have been renewed.

12 Cylinder head (single-point fuel injection models) – removal and refitting

1   Drain the cooling system as described in Chapter 2.
2   Remove the air cleaner, air box and intake trunking as described in Chapter 3.
3   Remove the timing belt as described in Section 10 of this Chapter.
4   Undo the four nuts and separate the exhaust front pipe from the manifold flange. Recover the gasket.
5   Slacken the clips and disconnect the radiator top hose, and the expansion tank hose at the thermostat housing.
6   Disconnect the wiring multi-plug at the coolant temperature thermistor (photo).
7   Undo the brake servo vacuum hose banjo union bolt on the right-hand side of the inlet manifold, and recover the two copper washers.
8   Slacken the clip and disconnect the heater hose at the inlet manifold, behind the brake servo vacuum hose.
9   Undo the bolt securing the stay bar to the inlet manifold, below the heater hose.
10 Slacken the clips and disconnect the heater bypass hose at the thermostat housing (photo).
11 Slacken the clip and disconnect the heater hose at the other end of the bypass pipe.
12 Undo the bolts securing the bypass pipe to the exhaust manifold, cylinder head and main coolant pipe, release the clips securing the wiring harness (photo), and remove the bypass pipe from the engine.
13 Slacken the clip and disconnect the coolant hose at the left-hand end of the inlet manifold.
14 Disconnect the vacuum hoses from the inlet manifold, adjacent to the coolant hose. Mark the location of each vacuum hose as it is disconnected.
15 Undo the bolt securing the support bracket to the inlet manifold, below the vacuum hoses.
16 At the rear of the engine below the inlet manifold, release the wire clip and detach the breather hose from the top of the oil separator. Also detach the hose from the crankcase ventilation system diverter valve (photo).
17 Disconnect the two wires to the inlet manifold heater temperature sensor, on the underside of the manifold, and the single lead to the manifold heater at the wiring connector.
18 Slacken the accelerator cable locknuts, and unscrew the lower locknut off the outer cable end (photo). Open the throttle at the throttle cam, slip the cable end out of the cam slot, and remove the cable from the support bracket. Release the cable from the camshaft cover support bracket, and place it clear of the engine.
19 On automatic transmission models, disconnect the kickdown cable, using the same procedure as for the accelerator cable.
20 Disconnect the wiring multi-plugs at the idle speed stepper motor, the fuel injector, and the throttle potentiometer (photo). Move the wiring harness clear of the cylinder head.
21 Place absorbent rags around the fuel filter outlet union banjo bolt on the left-hand side of the filter, then slowly unscrew the bolt to release the fuel system pressure. Remove the bolt and recover the two copper washers after the pressure has been released. Tape over the filter orifice and banjo union to prevent fuel loss and dirt ingress.
22 Disconnect the fuel return hose at the pipe below the fuel filter.
23 Remove the dipstick from the dipstick tube.
24 Refer to Section 10, and carry out the operations described in paragraphs 6 to 15 inclusive, with the exception of paragraph 12.
25 On cars fitted with a rear-mounted power steering pump, extract the circlip from the end of the power steering pump drivebelt tension adjuster bolt (photo). Slide the adjuster rearwards, and undo all the accessible bolts securing the adjuster bracket to the cylinder head (photo). Now move the adjuster the other way, and undo the remaining bolts (photo), then remove the adjuster assembly complete.
26 Progressively slacken all the cylinder head retaining bolts, in the reverse sequence to that shown in Fig. 1.8. Remove the bolts when all

11.37 Timing belt idler pulley locating peg (arrowed)

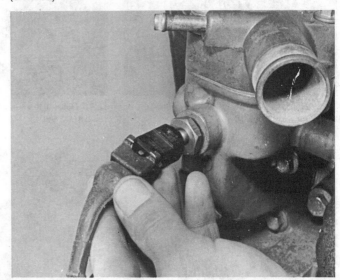

12.6 Disconnect the coolant temperature thermistor multi-plug

12.10 Disconnect the heater bypass hose at the thermostat housing

have been slackened.

27 With the help of an assistant, lift the cylinder head, complete with manifolds, off the engine. If the head is stuck, it can be carefully levered up using a large screwdriver between the cylinder block and the protruding cylinder head flanges. Do not insert the screwdriver under the head-to-block mating face. Place the head on blocks on the bench to protect the valves.

28 Remove the cylinder head gasket from the block.

29 If further dismantling is to be undertaken, refer to Section 14. Inspect the cylinder head and its related components, with reference to Section 23.

30 Prior to refitting, ensure that the cylinder block and head mating faces are thoroughly clean and dry, with all traces of old gasket removed. Clean the threads of the retaining bolts, and remove any oil, water and thread sealer from the bolt holes.

31 Locate a new gasket over the dowels on the cylinder block

(photo). *Do not use any jointing compound on the cylinder head gasket.*

32 Check that the crankshaft is still positioned at 90° BTDC position, and that the timing marks on the camshaft sprockets are aligned (see Section 10).

33 Lower the cylinder head assembly onto the gasket, and refit the retaining bolts. Working in the sequence shown in Fig. 1.8, initially tighten the bolts to the Stage 1 torque setting given in the Specifications (photo), then to the Stage 2 setting. Finally tighten through a further 60° (one sixth of a turn), or to the Stage 3 setting – whichever comes first. If possible, use an angular torque gauge (photo) to determine accurately the 60° movement. These are readily available from motor factors at modest cost, or it may be possible to hire one from larger DIY outlets. Using the gauge in conjunction with a torque wrench, the bolt is tightened until either the pointer moves through 60°, or the torque wrench reaches the Stage 3 setting (photo).

12.12 Release the wiring harness clips from the bypass pipe

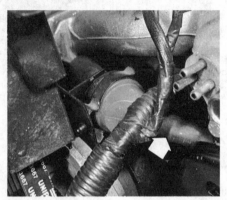

12.16 Detach the hose from the diverter valve (arrowed)

12.18 Disconnect the accelerator cable

12.20 Disconnect the throttle potentiometer wiring multi-plug (arrowed)

12.25A Extract the circlip from the adjuster bolt ...

12.25B ... move the adjuster one way and undo the accessible bolts ...

12.25C .. then move the adjuster the other way, and remove the remaining bolts

12.31 Locate a new cylinder head gasket over the dowels

12.33A Tighten the cylinder head bolts to the specified torque ...

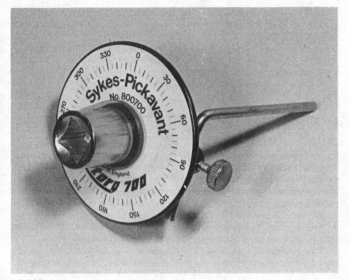

12.33B ... then using an angular torque gauge ...

12.33C ... tighten the bolts to the specified angular torque setting

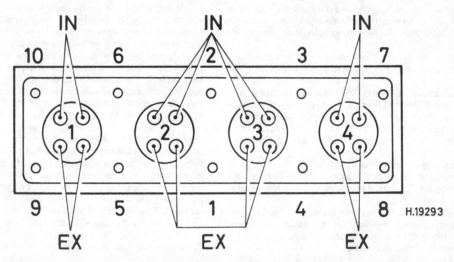

Fig. 1.8 Cylinder head bolt tightening sequence (Secs 12 and 13)

If an angular torque gauge is not available, an alternative is to draw two lines at 60° to each other on a piece of card, with a hole large enough to fit over the bolt head at the intersection of the two lines. Place the card over the bolt head, followed by the socket bit of the torque wrench, then align the torque wrench handle with the first line. Hold the card to prevent it moving, and torque the bolt until either the torque wrench handle is aligned with the other line on the card, or the Stage 3 setting is reached. Repeat this procedure for the other bolts in sequence.

34 Refit all the wiring, pipes, hoses and components to the cylinder head, using the reverse sequence to removal.

35 Refit the timing belt and adjust its tension, as described in Section 10.

36 Refit the power steering pump drivebelt and adjust its tension, as described in Chapter 10.

37 Refit the accelerator cable as described in Chapter 3, and the automatic transmission kickdown cable (where applicable) as described in Chapter 7.

38 Refit the air cleaner components as described in Chapter 3, and refill the cooling system as described in Chapter 2.

13 Cylinder head (multi-point fuel injection models) – removal and refitting

1 Drain the cooling system as described in Chapter 2.

2 Remove complete air cleaner assembly as described in Chapter 3.

3 Remove the timing belt as described in Section 10 of this Chapter.

4 Undo the four nuts and separate the exhaust front pipe from the manifold flange. Recover the gasket.

5 Slacken the clips and disconnect the radiator top hose, and the expansion tank hose at the thermostat housing.

6 Disconnect the wiring multi-plug at the coolant temperature thermistor on the side of the thermostat housing.

7 Undo the brake servo vacuum hose banjo union bolt on the right-hand side of the inlet manifold, and recover the two copper washers.

8 Slacken the clips and disconnect the heater bypass hose at the thermostat housing.

9 Slacken the clip and disconnect the heater hose at the other end of the bypass pipe.

10 Undo the bolts securing the bypass pipe to the exhaust manifold, cylinder head and main coolant pipe, and remove the bypass pipe from the engine.

11 Slacken the clips and disconnect the two coolant hoses from the underside of the throttle housing.

12 At the rear of the engine, disconnect the wiring multi-plugs and leads at the crankshaft sensor, knock sensor, oil pressure switch and oil pressure transducer.

13 Disconnect the main engine wiring loom multi-plug(s) on the right-hand side valance as necessary, to enable part of the loom to be removed with the cylinder head – see photo 6.18C.

14 Check that all the wiring likely to impede removal of the cylinder head and its ancillaries has been disconnected, and the harness moved clear. It may be necessary to disconnect additional wiring, depending on options or additional equipment fitted.

15 Disconnect the breather hoses from the oil separator.

16 Open the throttle fully by hand, and slip the accelerator inner cable end out of the slot on the throttle lever.

17 Slacken the outer cable locknuts, and unscrew the outer locknut, nearest to the cable end, fully. Remove the washer and rubber bush, then withdraw the cable from the support bracket.

18 On automatic transmission models, disconnect the kickdown cable, using the same procedure as for the accelerator cable.

19 Place absorbent rags around the fuel filter outlet union banjo bolt on the left-hand side of the filter, then slowly unscrew the bleed screw in the centre of the bolt to release the fuel system pressure. Tighten the bleed screw when the pressure has been released. Undo the outlet union banjo bolt, and recover the two copper washers. Tape over the filter orifice, and banjo union to prevent fuel loss and dirt entry.

20 Unscrew the union nut and disconnect the fuel return hose at the fuel pressure regulator, on the left-hand side of the inlet manifold.

21 Remove the dipstick from the dipstick tube.

22 Refer to Section 10, and carry out the operations described in paragraphs 6 to 15 inclusive.

23 On cars fitted with a rear-mounted power steering pump, extract the circlip from the end of the power steering pump drivebelt tension adjuster bolt. Slide the adjuster rearwards, and undo all the accessible bolts securing the adjuster bracket to the cylinder head. Now move the adjuster the other way, and undo the remaining bolts, then remove the adjuster assembly complete.

24 Progressively slacken all the cylinder head retaining bolts, in the reverse sequence to that shown in Fig. 1.8. Remove the bolts when all have been slackened.

25 With the help of an assistant, lift the cylinder head, complete with manifolds, off the engine. If the head is stuck, it can be carefully levered up using a large screwdriver between the cylinder block and the protruding cylinder head flanges. Do not insert the screwdriver under the head-to-block mating face. Place the head on blocks on the bench to protect the valves.

26 Remove the cylinder head gasket from the block.

27 If further dismantling is to be undertaken, refer to Section 14. Inspect the cylinder head and its related components, with reference to Section 23.

28 Prior to refitting, ensure that the cylinder block and head mating faces are thoroughly clean and dry, with all traces of old gasket removed. Clean the threads of the retaining bolts, and remove any oil, water and thread sealer from the bolt holes.

29 Locate a new gasket over the dowels on the cylinder block. *Do not use any jointing compound on the cylinder head gasket.*

30 Check that the crankshaft is still positioned at the 90° BTDC position, and that the timing marks on the camshaft sprockets are aligned (see Section 10).

31 Lower the cylinder head assembly onto the gasket, and refit the retaining bolts. Working in the sequence shown in Fig. 1.8, initially tighten the bolts to the Stage 1 torque setting given in the Specifications, then to the Stage 2 setting. Finally tighten through a further 60° (one sixth of a turn), or to the Stage 3 setting – whichever comes first. If possible, use an angular torque gauge (see photo 12.33B) to determine accurately the 60° movement. These are readily available from motor factors at modest cost, or it may be possible to hire one from larger DIY outlets. Using the gauge in conjunction with a torque wrench, the bolt is tightened until either the pointer moves through 60°, or the torque wrench reaches the Stage 3 setting. If an angular torque gauge is not available, an alternative is to draw two lines at 60° to each other on a piece of card, with a hole large enough to fit over the bolt head at the intersection of the two lines, Place the card over the bolt head, followed by the socket bit of the torque wrench, then align the torque wrench handle with the first line. Hold the card to prevent it moving, and torque the bolt until either the torque wrench handle is aligned with the other line on the card, or the Stage 3 setting is reached. Repeat this procedure for the other bolts in sequence.

32 Refit all the wiring, pipes, hoses and components to the cylinder head, using the reverse sequence to removal.

33 Refit the timing belt and adjust as described in Section 10.

34 Refit the power steering pump drivebelt and adjust its tension, as described in Chapter 10.

35 Refit the accelerator cable as described in Chapter 3, and the automatic transmission kickdown cable (where applicable) as described in Chapter 7.

36 Refit the air cleaner components as described in Chapter 3, and refill the cooling system as described in Chapter 2.

14 Cylinder head – overhaul

1 With the cylinder head on the bench, remove the camshafts and tappets (Section 11), thermostat housing (Chapter 2), inlet and exhaust manifolds (Chapter 3), and the spark plugs (Chapter 4).

2 To remove the valves, compress each spring in turn with a universal valve spring compressor, until the two retaining collets can be removed (photo).

3 Release the compressor, and lift off the spring top cup, valve spring, oil seal, valve spring seat and the valve (photos).

4 It is essential that the valves are kept in their correct order, unless they are so badly worn or burnt that they are to be renewed. If they are going to be refitted, place them in their correct sequence, along with the camshaft tappets removed previously. Also keep the valve springs, cups, seats and collets in the same order.

5 With the valves removed, scrape away all traces of carbon from the valves, and the combustion chambers and ports in the cylinder head, using a knife and suitable scraper, and with reference to Section 23.

6 Examine the heads of the valves for signs of cracking, burring away or pitting of the valve face, or the edge of the valve head. The valve seats in the cylinder head should also be examined for the same signs. Usually it is the valve that deteriorates first, but if a bad valve is not rectified, the seat will suffer, and this is more difficult to repair. If the valve face and seat are deeply pitted, or if the valve face is concave where it contacts the seat, it will be necessary to renew the valve, or have the valve refaced and the seat recut by a dealer or motor engineering specialist. It is worth considering having this work done in any case, particularly if the engine has covered a high mileage. A little extra time and money spent ensuring that the cylinder head and valve gear are in first-class condition will make a tremendous difference to the performance and economy of the engine after overhaul. If any of the valves are cracked or burnt away, it is essential that they are renewed. Any similar damage that may have occurred to the valve seats can be repaired by renewing the seat. However, this is a job that can only be carried out by a specialist.

7 Another form of valve wear can occur on the stem, where it runs in the guide in the cylinder head. This can be detected by trying to rock the valve from side to side. If there is anything but the slightest movement at all, it is an indication that the stem or guide is worn. Check the valve stem first, with a micrometer, at points along and around its length. If it is not within the specified size, a new valve will probably solve the problem. If the guide is worn, however, it will need renewing. This work should be carried out by a Rover dealer or motor engineering specialist.

8 Check the valve installed height by fitting each valve into its respective guide, and measuring the distance from the spring seat location in the cylinder head to the top of the valve stem. If the figure exceeds the installed height dimension given in the Specifications, the valve, or additionally the valve seat, must be renewed.

9 Assuming that the valve faces and seats are only lightly pitted, or that new valves are to be fitted, the valves should be lapped into their seats. This is done by placing a smear of fine carborundum on the valve seat, and using a suction-type valve holder, lapping the valve *in situ*. Using a semi-rotary action, rotate the handle of the valve holder between your hands, lifting it occasionally to redistribute the paste. As soon as a matt grey, unbroken line appears on both the valve face and cylinder head seat, the valve is 'ground in'.

10 When all work on the cylinder head and valves is complete, it is essential that all traces of carbon dust and grinding paste are removed. This should be done by thoroughly washing the components in paraffin or a suitable solvent, and blowing out with a jet of air.

11 With the valves and valve seats suitably prepared, and with the valves in their correct order, commence reassembly, starting with the first valve of No 1 cylinder as follows.

12 Place the valve spring seat in position, then fit a new oil seal over the valve guide, pushing it fully into position.

14.2 Compress the valve spring with a spring compressor, and remove the collets

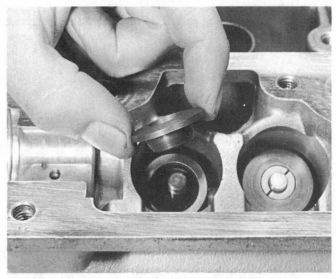

14.3A Release the compressor, and remove the spring top cup ...

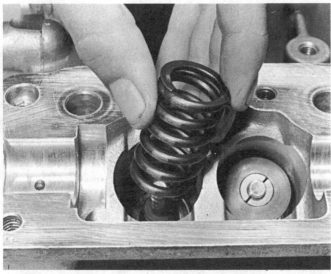

14.3B ... valve spring ...

14.3C ... oil seal ...

14.3D .., spring seat ...

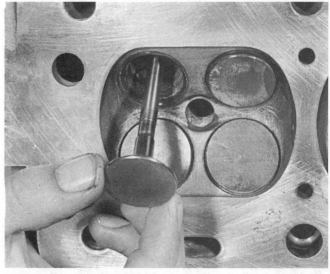

14.3E ... and the valve

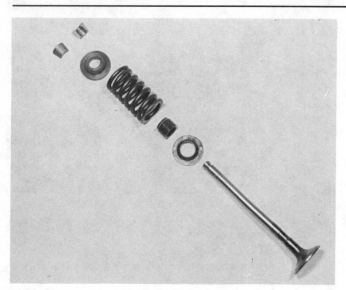

14.3F Valve components ready for inspection

15.7 Sump special retaining bolt location

13 Lubricate the valve stem with engine oil, then insert the valve into its guide.

14 Fit the valve spring, and place the top cup over the spring and valve.

15 Using the compressor tool, compress the valve spring until the two collets can be slid into position. Release the compressor carefully, in order not to displace the collets.

16 Refit the remaining valves in the same way. When they are all fitted, tap the end of each valve stem with a plastic mallet to settle the components.

17 Refit the components listed in paragraph 1, using the reverse sequence to removal, and with reference to the applicable Sections and Chapters of this manual.

15 Sump – removal and refitting

1 Disconnect the battery negative terminal. (Refer to Chapter 12, Section 1, before doing this).

2 Apply the handbrake, jack up the front of the car and support it on axle stands.

3 Drain the engine oil as described in Section 2.

4 Remove the exhaust front section as described in Chapter 3.

5 Undo the bolts securing the longitudinal support member to the underbody beneath the engine, and remove the member.

6 Disconnect the crankcase breather hose from the pipe stub on the side of the sump.

7 Slacken, then remove, the eighteen sump retaining bolts, noting that the corner bolt on the drain plug side at the flywheel end is longer than the rest, and has a flat washer and elongated washer in addition to the normal spring washer (photo).

8 Withdraw the sump from the crankcase, tapping it from side to side with a hide or plastic mallet if it is stuck. Recover the sump gasket.

9 If the oil pick-up tube and strainer are to be removed, undo the two bolts securing the tube flange to the crankcase, and the single bolt securing the support bracket to the main bearing cap (photos).

10 Slide the support bracket from under the crankcase breather oil return pipe, and remove the pick-up pipe and tube from the crankcase. Recover the O-ring from the pick-up pipe flange.

11 Clean the sump thoroughly, and remove all traces of old gasket and sealant from the mating faces of the sump and crankcase.

12 If removed, clean the pick-up pipe, and the filter gauze in the strainer.

13 Place a new O-ring seal on the pick-up pipe flange (photo), fit the pipe and strainer assembly, and secure with the retaining bolts, tightened to the specified torque.

14 Apply a bead of RTV sealant to the joint between Nos 1 and 5 main bearing caps and the edge of the crankcase (photo). Apply gasket sealant to the sump and crankcase mating faces, then place a new gasket in position (photos).

15.9A Undo the two pick-up pipe-to-crankcase bolts ...

15.9B ... and the support bracket bolt (arrowed)

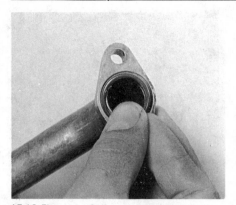

15.13 Fit a new O-ring to the pick-up pipe flange

15.14A Apply sealant to the main bearing cap joints ...

15.14B ... then place the sump gasket in position

15.15A Fit the sump ...

15.15B ... and tighten the bolts in sequence to the specified torque

15 Refit the sump, and tighten the retaining bolts progressively, and in the sequence shown in Fig. 1.9, to the specified torque (photos).
16 Refit the crankcase breather hose.
17 Refit the exhaust front section as described in Chapter 3.
18 Refit the longitudinal support member.
19 Lower the car to the ground, reconnect the battery and fill the engine with oil as described in Section 2.

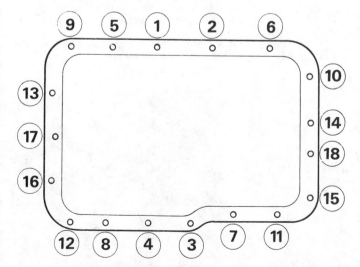

Fig. 1.9 Sump retaining bolt tightening sequence (Sec 15)

16 Oil pump and housing – removal and refitting

1 Using a socket and long handle, slacken the crankshaft pulley retaining bolt. To prevent the crankshaft turning, engage 1st gear and firmly apply the handbrake. On automatic transmission models, it will be necessary to remove the starter motor (Chapter 12) and lock the driveplate ring gear, through the starter motor aperture, using a large screwdriver or similar tool. If the engine is not in the car, engage a small strip of angle iron between the ring gear teeth and one of the adaptor plate dowels, to prevent rotation of the crankshaft.
2 Remove the timing belt as described in Section 10.
3 Drain the engine oil and remove oil filter as described in Section 2.
4 Unscrew the crankshaft pulley bolt and withdraw the pulley (photo). Carefully lever it off using two screwdrivers if it is tight.
5 Remove the Woodruff key from the slot in the crankshaft (photo).
6 Unscrew the oil pipe union on the side of the filter housing, then undo the bolt securing the oil pipe retaining clip and timing belt backplate to the crankcase (photo).
7 Undo the pump housing retaining bolts, and withdraw the assembly from the crankshaft and crankcase (photo). Recover the gasket.
8 Ensure that the pump housing and crankcase mating faces are thoroughly clean, with all traces of old gasket and sealer removed.
9 Apply a bead of RTV sealant to the vertical joint between the main bearing cap and the crankcase, and smear jointing compound to both faces of a new gasket. Place the gasket in position on the crankcase (photo).
10 Lubricate the lip of the oil seal, then locate the pump housing in place.
11 Fit the retaining bolts, and tighten them to the specified torque.
12 Refit the timing belt bottom cover.
13 Reconnect the oil pipe union, and refit the pipe support clip retaining bolt.

16.4 Removing the crankshaft pulley

16.5 Removing the Woodruff key

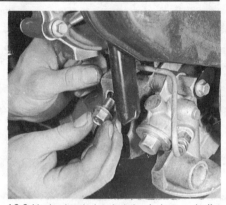

16.6 Undo the timing belt backplate and oil pipe clip retaining bolt

16.7 Undo the retaining bolts (arrowed) and remove the oil pump housing

16.9 Use a new gasket when refitting the housing

14 Place the Woodruff key in its crankshaft groove, then refit the crankshaft pulley, retaining bolt and washer.

15 Tighten the pulley retaining bolt to the specified torque.

16 Refit the timing belt as described in Section 10.

17 Fit a new oil filter, and fill the engine with oil as described in Section 2.

17 Oil pump and housing – dismantling and reassembly

1 With the pump housing removed from the engine, undo the four Torx retaining bolts on the housing rear face, and lift off the pump cover (photo). Inspect the condition of the inner and outer rotors for visual signs of scoring or wear ridges. Note that the pump internal parts

are not available separately, and if there is any sign of wear, a complete new oil pump and housing assembly must be obtained. Refit the pump cover.

2 To remove the pressure relief valve components, extract the split pin and withdraw the plug cap, spring and relief valve plunger (photo).

3 Check the plunger for scoring or wear ridges, and renew if necessary. Also renew the plug cap O-ring if it shows signs of deterioration.

4 Lubricate the relief valve components with engine oil, then refit the plunger, spring and plug cap. Secure the cap with a new split pin.

5 Using a screwdriver, prise out the crankshaft front oil seal from the oil pump housing (photo).

6 Place a new oil seal in position, and carefully tap it home with the aid of a mallet, block of wood and the old oil seal.

17.1 Oil pump cover retaining bolts (arrowed)

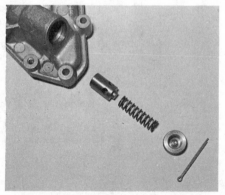

17.2 Oil pressure relief valve components

17.5 Using a screwdriver to remove the crankshaft front oil seal

18 Pistons and connecting rods – removal and refitting

1 Remove the cylinder head, the sump, and the oil pick-up pipe as described in earlier Sections of this Chapter.
2 Turn the crankshaft by means of the pulley bolt, until No 1 and No 4 pistons are at the bottom of their stroke.
3 Using a knife or scraper, clean the carbon ridge from the top of the cylinder bore, to facilitate removal of the piston.
4 Mark the No 1 cylinder connecting rod and cap on their sides, using a centre-punch and hammer, to indicate the cylinder the assembly is fitted to, and also the fitted relationship of the cap to the rod.
5 Undo the big-end cap nuts on No 1 connecting rod, then remove the cap, complete with the lower bearing shell (photo). If the cap is difficult to remove, tap it from side to side with a plastic mallet.
6 Push the piston/connecting rod upwards with the aid of the wooden handle of a hammer or similar tool, then withdraw the assembly from the top of the cylinder bore (photo).
7 Refit the bearing cap and shell to the connecting rod after removal.
8 Repeat paragraphs 3 to 7 for No 4 connecting rod.
9 Turn the crankshaft back through half a turn, until No 2 and No 3 pistons are at the bottom of their stroke.
10 Repeat paragraphs 3 to 6 for No 2 and No 3 connecting rods.
11 To remove the pistons from the connecting rods, extract the two gudgeon pin retaining circlips, using a small screwdriver (photo), then push out the gudgeon pin. If the pin is tight, warm the piston in hot water, which will expand the piston slightly, enabling the gudgeon pin to be pushed out. As each piston is removed, mark it on the inside with a punch, as before, indicating its cylinder number.
12 To remove the piston rings, slide them carefully over the top of the piston, taking care not to scratch the aluminium alloy of the piston. It is very easy to break piston rings if they are pulled off roughly, so this operation should be done with extreme caution. It is helpful to use an old feeler blade to facilitate their removal, as follows.
13 Turn the feeler blade slowly around the piston; as the ring comes out of its groove it rests on the land above. It can then be eased off the piston, with the feeler blade stopping it from slipping into empty grooves. If the old rings are to be re-used, identify each as it is removed using a label, marked No 1 top, No 1 second, etc.
14 Clean and examine the dismantled components, with reference to Section 23.
15 Check that the piston ring grooves and oilways are thoroughly clean and unblocked. Piston rings must always be fitted over the head of the piston, and never from the bottom.
16 The easiest method to use when fitting rings is to position two feeler blades on either side of the piston, and slide the rings down over the blades. This will stop the rings from dropping into a vacant ring groove. When the ring is adjacent to its correct groove, slide out the feeler blades, and the ring will drop in.
17 The procedure for fitting the rings is as follows. Start by sliding the bottom rail of the oil control ring down the piston, and position it below the bottom ring groove. Fit the oil control expander into the bottom ring groove, then slip the bottom rail into the bottom groove. Now fit the top rail of the oil control ring into the bottom groove. Make sure that the ends of the expander are butting together, and not overlapping. Position the gaps of the two rails and the expander at 90°

to each other.
18 Fit the second compression ring to its groove, with the step towards the gudgeon pin, and the word TOP or the letter T facing the top of the piston.
19 Fit the top compression ring to its groove, with the word TOP or the letter T facing the top of the piston.
20 When all the piston rings are in place, set the ring gaps of the compression rings at 90° to each other, and away from the thrust side of the piston.
21 To refit the pistons to their connecting rods, start with No 1 and insert the connecting rod into the piston, so that the offset at the gudgeon pin end of the rod is towards the side of the piston marked FRONT on its top face (Fig. 1.10 and photo). Insert the gudgeon pin, and refit the retaining circlips. Ensure that the circlips fully enter their grooves.

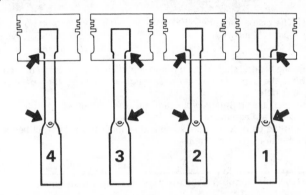

Fig. 1.10 Connecting rod offset and oil squirt hole relationship (Sec 18)

22 Assemble the No 3 piston and connecting rod in the same way.
23 Assemble the No 2 and No 4 pistons and connecting rods in the same way, but with the offset at the gudgeon pin end of the rod away from the side of the piston marked FRONT.
24 Wipe the cylinder bores clean with a cloth, then lubricate the bores and pistons with clean engine oil.
25 Starting with No 1 piston/connecting rod assembly, fit a universal piston ring compressor over the piston, and tighten it fully to compress the rings. Remove the bearing cap and shell from the connecting rod.
26 Insert the piston into its bore, making sure the word FRONT on the piston crown is towards the crankshaft pulley end of the engine.
27 Slide the assembly down the bore until the bottom of the piston ring compressor rests on the cylinder block face. Now gently, but firmly, tap the piston through the compressor, using the wooden handle of a hammer (photo).
28 As soon as the rings have entered the bore, remove the compressor, and continue pushing the piston down until the connecting rod approaches its crankshaft journal.
29 Wipe the connecting rod, crankshaft journal and bearing shell, then fit the shell to the rod, with its tag engaged with the notch in the rod.
30 Lubricate the crankshaft journal with engine oil, then draw the rod down onto the journal.

18.5 Removing the connecting rod big-end cap and bearing shell

18.6 Removing the piston and connecting rod assembly

18.11 Using a small screwdriver to extract the gudgeon pin circlip

18.21 The pistons are marked FRONT on their top face (arrowed)

18.27 Refitting the piston and connecting rod assemblies, with the aid of a ring compressor

18.32 Tighten the bearing cap nuts to the specified torque

31 Fit the bearing shell to the big-end cap, then refit the cap to the rod.
32 Refit the cap retaining nuts, and tighten them to the specified torque (photo).
33 Repeat the refitting procedure for the remaining piston and connecting rod assemblies.
34 Refit the oil pick-up pipe, sump and cylinder head, as described in earlier Sections of this Chapter.

19 Flywheel (manual gearbox models) – removal and refitting

1 With the engine removed from the car and separated from the gearbox, or with the gearbox removed as described in Chapter 6,
remove the clutch assembly as described in Chapter 5.
2 Knock back the tabs of the locking plate, using a screwdriver or small chisel, and undo the six flywheel retaining bolts. To prevent the flywheel turning, lock the ring gear teeth using a small strip of angle iron engaged in the teeth and against the adaptor plate dowel. Note that the flywheel retaining bolts are of the encapsulated type, incorporating a locking compound in their threads, and new bolts must be obtained for reassembly.
3 Lift off the locking plate, then withdraw the flywheel from the crankshaft (photos).
4 Examine the flywheel and the ring gear teeth with reference to Section 23, and renew any components as required.
5 Refitting is the reverse sequence to removal. Tighten the bolts to the specified torque, then bend over the tabs of a new locking plate (photos).

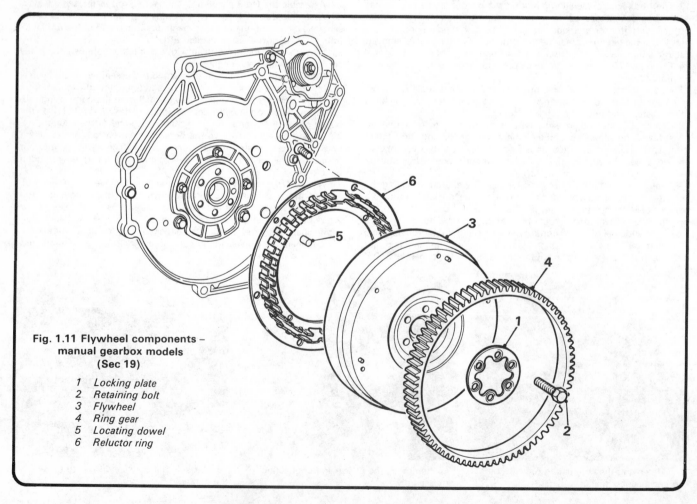

Fig. 1.11 Flywheel components – manual gearbox models (Sec 19)

1 *Locking plate*
2 *Retaining bolt*
3 *Flywheel*
4 *Ring gear*
5 *Locating dowel*
6 *Reluctor ring*

19.3A Lift off the locking plate ...

19.3B ... then withdraw the flywheel

19.5A Tighten the flywheel bolts to the specified torque ...

19.5B ... then bend over the locking plate tabs

20 Torque converter driveplate (automatic transmission models) – removal and refitting

1 With the engine removed from the car and separated from the transmission, or with the transmission removed as described in Chapter 7, undo the six bolts securing the driveplate to the crankshaft. To prevent the driveplate turning, lock the ring gear teeth using a small strip of angle iron engaged in the teeth and against the adaptor plate dowel. Note that the driveplate retaining bolts are of the encapsulated type, incorporating a locking compound in their threads, and new bolts must be obtained for reassembly.
2 Remove the reinforcing plate, then withdraw the driveplate from the crankshaft. Recover the spacer between the driveplate and crankshaft.
3 Examine the driveplate and the ring gear teeth with reference to Section 23, and renew any components as required.
4 Refitting is the reverse sequence to removal, but tighten the bolts to the specified torque.

21 Gearbox/transmission adaptor plate – removal and refitting

1 Remove the flywheel or torque converter driveplate as described in Sections 19 and 20 respectively.
2 On cars equipped with a rear-mounted power steering pump, refer to Chapter 10 and remove the power steering pump.
3 Undo the two bolts securing the crankshaft sensor to the adaptor plate, remove the sensor, and recover the spacer (photo).
4 Undo the bolts securing the adaptor plate to the cylinder block, noting the various bolt lengths and their locations. Note also that the four Torx type bolts are of the encapsulated type, incorporating a sealer in their threads, and new bolts must be obtained for reassembly (photo).
5 Remove the adaptor plate from the cylinder block, and recover the gasket.
6 The crankshaft rear oil seal should be renewed as a matter of course. Tap out the old seal, and fit a new one with its open side

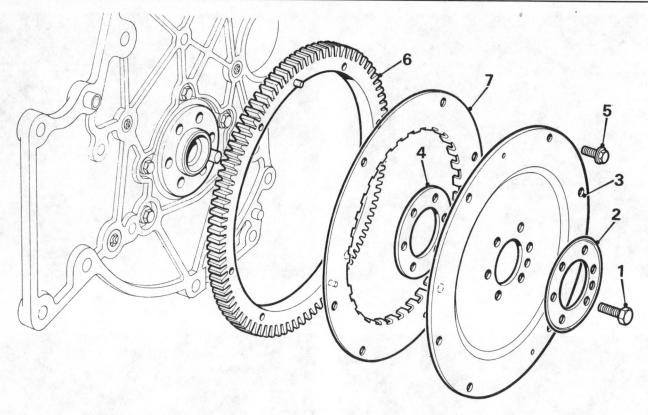

Fig. 1.12 Torque converter driveplate components – automatic transmission models (Sec 20)

1	Driveplate retaining bolt	3	Driveplate
2	Reinforcing plate	4	Spacer

5	Ring gear retaining bolt	7	Reluctor ring
6	Ring gear		

towards the engine. Tap the seal into place using a block of wood or the old seal.

7   Ensure that all traces of old gasket are removed from the adaptor plate and block mating faces.

8   Apply a bead of RTV jointing compound to the vertical joint of the rear main bearing cap, and lubricate the oil seal in the adaptor plate with engine oil.

9   Place a new gasket in position (photo), then fit the adaptor plate, taking care as the oil seal locates over the crankshaft.

10 Fit the retaining bolts, and tighten them progressively to the specified torque.

11 Refit the crankshaft sensor and spacer.

12 Refit the power steering pump as described in Chapter 10.

13 Refit the flywheel or torque converter driveplate.

22 Crankshaft and main bearings – removal and refitting

1   With the engine removed from the car, as described in Section 6, and with all the components removed from it, as described in earlier Sections, the crankshaft and main bearings can be removed as follows.

2   Withdraw the crankcase breather tube elbow from the outside of the cylinder block (photo).

3   From within the crankcase, remove the crankcase breather extension tube (photo). To do this, move the tube from side to side to release the sealing compound, then tap it out using a dowel rod inserted through the elbow aperture.

4   Note that the main bearing caps have their numbers cast on the face of each cap, and in addition, Nos 2, 3 and 4 have arrows

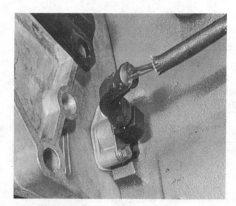

21.3 Crankshaft sensor location on gearbox adaptor plate

21.4 Adaptor plate Torx type retaining bolt locations (arrowed)

21.9 Place a new gasket in position, then refit the adaptor plate

indicating their fitted direction (photo).

5 Undo the main bearing cap retaining bolts, one turn at a time, then when all are slack, remove the bolts.

6 Lift away each main bearing cap and the bottom half of each bearing shell, taking care to keep the bearing shell with the right cap. If the caps are tight, tap them on their sides with a plastic mallet to release them from the locating dowels.

7 When removing the centre main bearing cap, note the bottom semi-circular halves of the thrustwashers, one located on each side of the cap. Lay them, with the centre bearing cap, along the correct side.

8 Lift out the crankshaft, followed by the bearing shell upper halves and the thrustwashers. Keep the bearing shells and thrustwashers with their correct caps.

9 Carry out a careful inspection of the crankshaft and main bearings, with reference to Section 23.

10 Prior to refitting, ensure that the crankshaft and crankcase are thoroughly clean, and that all oilways are clear. If possible, blow the drillings out with compressed air, then inject clean engine oil through them to ensure they are clear.

11 If new bearing shells are being fitted, carefully clean away all traces of the protective grease with which they are coated.

12 Fit the five upper halves of the main bearing shells to their location in the crankcase, after wiping the location clean (photo). Note that on the back of each bearing is a tab, which engages in locating grooves in either the crankcase or main bearing cap.

13 Wipe the bearing shell locations in the bearing caps, and fit the five lower bearing shells to their caps.

14 Wipe the recesses either side of the centre main bearing which locate the upper halves of the thrustwashers.

15 Place the upper halves of the thrustwashers (the halves without tabs) in position on either side of the centre main bearing, with their oil grooves facing outwards (photo). Use a little grease to retain them in place.

16 Generously lubricate the upper halves of the bearing shells, and carefully lower the crankshaft into position (photo).

17 Using a screwdriver between the crankcase and one crankshaft web, lever the crankshaft forwards, and check the endfloat using feeler gauges (photo). This should be as given in the Specifications. If excessive, new thrustwashers must be fitted.

18 Lubricate the crankshaft journals (photo), and fit Nos 2, 3 and 4 main bearing caps into their respective locations.

19 When fitting the centre main bearing cap, ensure that the thrustwashers, generously lubricated, are fitted with their oil grooves facing outwards, and the locating tab of each is engaged with the slot in the main bearing cap (photo).

20 Apply RTV sealant into the vertical grooves on the edges of Nos 1 and 5 main bearing caps, then fit these caps to their locations.

21 Fit the main bearing cap retaining bolts, and tighten them moderately tightly at this stage, starting with the centre cap bolts, then working outwards to the others in turn. As each cap is tightened, test the crankshaft for freedom of rotation. Should it be very stiff to turn, or possess high spots, a most careful inspection must be made, preferably by a skilled mechanic with a micrometer, to trace the cause. It is very seldom that any trouble of this nature occurs, unless the bearing caps or shells have been fitted to the wrong locations.

22 Tighten the main bearing cap bolts to the specified torque (photo), and recheck the crankshaft for freedom of rotation.

23 Apply sealer to the crankcase breather tube extension, then fit the tube to its location. Apply sealant to the breather tube elbow, and fit the elbow, ensuring that it is tapped down until the shoulder contacts the crankcase.

23 Engine components – examination and renovation

Crankshaft

Inspect the main bearing journals and crankpins. If there are any scratches or score marks, then the shaft will need regrinding. Such

22.2 Withdraw the crankcase breather tube elbow

22.3 Remove the crankcase breather extension tube

22.4 Main bearing cap identification number and direction arrow

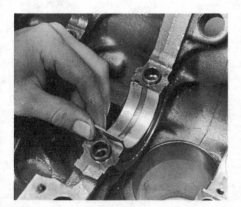
22.12 Fitting the main bearing shell upper halves

22.15 Fitting the crankshaft thrustwasher upper halves

22.16 Crankshaft installation

22.17 Checking crankshaft endfloat

22.18 Thoroughly lubricate the crankshaft journals

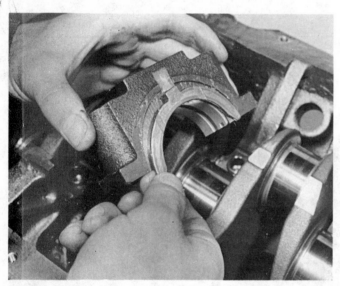

22.19 Fitting the crankshaft thrustwasher lower halves to the centre bearing cap

22.22 Tighten the bearing cap bolts to the specified torque

conditions will nearly always be accompanied by similar deterioration in the matching bearing shells.

Each bearing journal should also be round, and can be checked with a micrometer or caliper gauge around the periphery at several points. If there is more than 0.001 in (0.025 mm) of ovality, regrinding is necessary.

A Rover dealer or motor engineering specialist will be able to decide to what extent regrinding is necessary, and also supply the special undersize shell bearing to match whatever may need grinding off.

Before taking the crankshaft for grinding, also check the cylinder bores and pistons, as it may be advantageous to have the whole engine done at the same time.

Main and big-end bearings

With careful servicing and regular oil and filter changes, bearings will last for a very long time, but they can still fail for unforeseen reasons. With big-end bearings, the indication is a regular rhythmic loud knocking from the crankcase. The frequency depends on engine speed and is particularly noticeable when the engine is under load. This symptom is accompanied by a fall in oil pressure, although this is not normally noticeable unless an oil pressure gauge is fitted. Main bearing failure is usually indicated by serious vibration, particularly at

higher engine revolutions, accompanied by a more significant drop in oil pressure and a rumbling noise.

Bearing shells in good condition have bearing surfaces with a smooth, even matt silver/grey colour all over. Worn bearings will show patches of a different colour, where the bearing metal has worn away and exposed the underlay. Damaged bearings will be pitted or scored. It is always well worthwhile fitting new shells, as their cost is relatively low. If the crankshaft is in good condition, it is merely a question of obtaining another set of standard size. A reground crankshaft will need new bearing shells as a matter of course.

Cylinder bores

A new cylinder is perfectly round, and the walls parallel throughout its length. The action of the piston tends to wear the walls at right-angles to the gudgeon pin, due to side thrust. This wear takes place principally on that section of the cylinder swept by the piston rings.

It is possible to get an indication of bore wear by removing the cylinder head with the engine still in the car. With the piston down in the bore, first signs of wear can be seen and felt just below the top of the bore where the top piston ring reaches, and there will be a noticeable lip. If there is no lip, it is fairly reasonable to assume that bore wear is not severe, and any lack of compression or excessive oil consumption is due to worn or broken piston rings or pistons.

If it is possible to obtain a bore-measuring micrometer, measure the bore in the thrust plane below the lip, and again at the bottom of the cylinder in the same plane. If the difference is more than 0.006 in (0.15 mm), a rebore is necessary. Similarly, a difference of 0.006 in (0.15 mm) or more between two measurements of the bore diameter taken at right-angles to each other is a sign of excessive ovality, calling for a rebore.

Any bore which is significantly scratched or scored will need reboring. This symptom usually indicates that the piston or rings are also damaged. Even in the event of only one cylinder in need of reboring, it will still be necessary for all four to be bored, and fitted with new oversize pistons and rings. A motor engineering specialist will be able to rebore the cylinders and supply the necessary matched pistons. If the crankshaft is also undergoing regrinding, it is a good idea to let the same firm renovate and reassemble the crankshaft and pistons to the block. A reputable firm normally gives a guarantee for such work.

Pistons and piston rings

If the old pistons are to be refitted, carefully remove the piston rings, and then thoroughly clean them. Take particular care to clean out the piston ring grooves. Do not scratch the aluminum in any way. If new rings are to be fitted to the old pistons, then the top ring should be of the stepped type, so as to clear the ridge left above the previous top ring. If a normal but oversize new ring is fitted, it will hit the ridge and break, because the new ring will not have worn in the same way as the old.

Before fitting the rings on the pistons, each should be inserted approximately 75 mm (3 in) down the cylinder bore, and the gap measured with a feeler gauge. This should be between the limits given in the Specifications at the beginning of this Chapter. It is essential that the gap is measured at the bottom of the ring travel, for if it is measured at the top of a worn bore and gives a perfect fit, it could easily seize at the bottom. If the ring gap is too small, rub down the ends of the ring with a very fine file until the gap is correct when fitted. To keep the rings square in the bore for measurement, line each one up in turn with an old piston inserted in the bore upside down, and use the piston to push the ring down about 75 mm (3 in). Remove the piston and measure the piston ring gap.

The groove clearance of the new rings in old pistons should be checked with the rings in place. If it is not enough, the rings could stick in the piston grooves, causing loss of compression. The ring grooves in the piston in this case will need machining out to accept the new rings.

Before fitting new rings onto an old piston, clean out the grooves with a piece of broken ring.

If new pistons are obtained, the rings will be included, so it must be emphasised that the top ring be stepped if fitted to a cylinder bore that has not been rebored, or has not had the top ridge removed.

Camshafts and tappets

Check the camshaft journals and lobes for scoring and wear. If there are very slight scoring marks, these can be removed with emery cloth or a fine oil stone. The greatest care must be taken to keep the cam profiles smooth.

Examine the camshaft bearing surfaces in the cylinder head and camshaft housings – if they are scored and worn it means a new cylinder head and camshaft housings will be required.

Check for scoring or pitting of the tappets, and check the fit of the tappets in their respective bores. Renew any that show signs of wear.

Timing belt and tensioner

Check the belt for any sign of cracks or splits in the belt, particularly around the roots of the teeth. Renew the belt if wear is obvious, if there are signs of oil contamination, or if the belt has exceeded its service life (see Routine maintenance). Also renew the sprockets if they show any signs of wear or chipping of the teeth.

Spin the tensioner, and ensure that there is no roughness or harshness in the bearing. Also check that the endfloat is not excessive. Renew the tensioner if worn.

Cylinder head and pistons – decarbonising

This can be carried out with the engine either in or out of the car. With the cylinder head removed, carefully use a wire brush and blunt scraper to clean all traces of carbon deposits from the combustion spaces and the ports. The valve head stems and valve guides should also be freed from any carbon deposits. Wash the combustion spaces and ports down with petrol, and scrape the cylinder head surface free of any foreign matter with the side of a steel rule or similar article.

If the engine is installed in the car, clean the pistons and the top of the cylinder bores. If the pistons are still in the block, then it is essential that great care is taken to ensure that no carbon gets into the cylinder bores, as this could scratch the cylinder walls or cause damage to the piston and rings. To ensure this does not happen, first turn the crankshaft so that two of the pistons are at the top of their bores. Stuff rag into the other two bores or seal them off with paper and masking tape. The waterways should also be covered with small pieces of masking tape, to prevent particles of carbon entering the cooling system and damaging the water pump.

Press a little grease into the gap between the cylinder walls and the two pistons which are to be worked on. With a blunt scraper carefully scrape away the carbon from the piston crown, taking great care not to scratch the aluminium. Also scrape away the carbon from the surrounding lip of the cylinder wall. When all carbon has been removed, scrape away the grease which will now be contaminated with carbon particles, taking care not to press any into the bores. To assist prevention of carbon build-up, the piston crown can be polished with a metal polish. Remove the rags or masking tape from the other two cylinders, and turn the crankshaft so that the two pistons which were at the bottom are now at the top. Place rag or masking tape in the cylinders which have now been decarbonised, and proceed as just described. Decarbonising is now complete.

Flywheel or torque converter driveplate

Inspect the starter ring gear on the flywheel or driveplate for wear or broken teeth. If evident, the ring gear should be renewed. On automatic transmission models, the ring gear is bolted to the driveplate, and renewal is straightforward. On manual gearbox models however, the ring gear is a shrink fit on the flywheel, and renewal entails drilling the old ring then splitting it with a chisel. The new ring must then be heated so that it expands slightly, and allowed to cool when in position on the flywheel. As it cools, it contracts to a smaller diameter than the flywheel so as to provide a tight interference fit. The temperatures involved in this operation are critical to avoid damaging the ring gear, and the work should be carried out by a Rover dealer or motor engineering works.

The clutch friction surface on the flywheel should be checked for grooving or cracks, the latter being caused by overheating. If these conditions are evident, renewal of the flywheel is necessary.

On manual and automatic models, check the condition of the reluctor ring teeth. If any are bent, broken. or in any way damaged, renew the ring, which is bolted to the flywheel or driveplate.

---

24 Lubrication system – description

The pressed-steel sump is attached to the underside of the crankcase, and acts as a reservoir for the engine oil. The oil pump draws oil through a strainer attached to the pick-up pipe and submerged in the oil. The pump passes the oil along a short passage and into the full-flow filter, which is screwed onto the pump housing. The freshly filtered oil flows from the filter and enters the main cylinder block oil gallery, which feeds the crankshaft main bearings. Oil passes from the main bearings, through drillings in the crankshaft to the big-end bearings.

As the crankshaft rotates, oil is squirted from the hole in each connecting rod, and splashes the thrust side of the pistons and cylinder bores.

A drilling from the main oil gallery feeds the cylinder head gallery, via a restrictor located just below the top face of the cylinder block. The cylinder head contains an oil gallery on each side, with drillings to lubricate each camshaft journal and hydraulic tappet bore. The oil then drains back into the sump via large drillings in the cylinder head and cylinder block.

A pressure relief valve is incorporated in the oil pump housing, to maintain the oil pressure within specified limits.

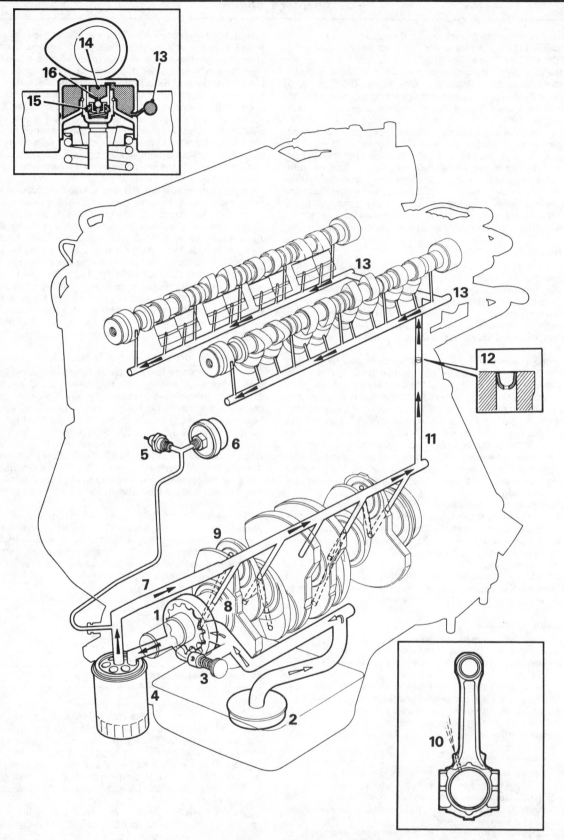

Fig. 1.13 Diagrammatic layout of the lubrication system (Sec 24)

1	Oil pump	6	Oil pressure transducer
2	Pick-up pipe strainer	7	Main oil gallery
3	Pressure relief valve	8	Crankshaft main bearings
4	Filter cartridge	9	Big-end bearing journals
5	Oil pressure switch		

10	Connecting rod oil squirt holes	14	Hydraulic tappet low pressure chamber
11	Feed to cylinder head	15	Tappet high pressure chamber
12	Restrictor	16	Ball valve
13	Cylinder head oil gallery		

25 Engine mountings – removal and refitting

Front mounting

1 Remove the battery as described in Chapter 12, then undo the retaining bolts and remove the battery tray.
2 Remove the air intake trunking as described in Chapter 3.
3 Undo the nut securing the mounting to the engine mounting bracket, and the two bolts securing the mounting to the front chassis member.
4 Using a jack and interposed block of wood, raise the engine slightly until the mounting stud can be withdrawn from the bracket, then remove the mounting from the car.
5 Renew the mounting if it shows any sign of damage, contamination or separation of the rubber-to-metal bond.
6 Refitting is the reverse sequence to removal, but ensure that the small peg on the mounting top face engages with the hole in the bracket, and tighten the bolts and nut to the specified torque.

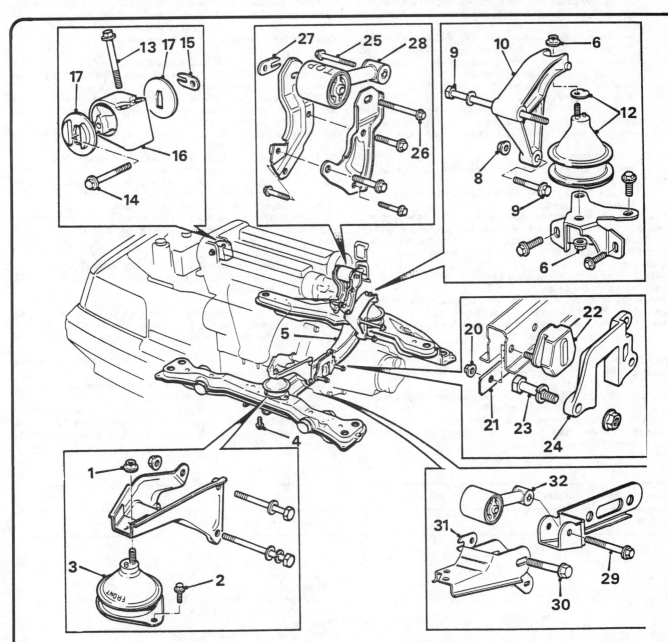

Fig. 1.14 Engine mounting components and attachments (Sec 25)

1	Front mounting-to-engine bracket retaining nut	6	Rear mounting-to-mounting bracket nuts	15	Forked nut	26	Rear tie-bar-to-engine bracket through-bolt

1   Front mounting-to-engine bracket retaining nut
2   Front mounting-to-chassis member bolts
3   Front mounting
4   Longitudinal support member retaining bolt
5   Longitudinal support member
6   Rear mounting-to-mounting bracket nuts
8   Engine bracket retaining nut
9   Engine bracket retaining bolt
10 Engine bracket
12 Rear mounting and spacer
13 Right-hand mounting-to-engine bracket bolt
14 Mounting through-bolt
15 Forked nut
16 Right-hand mounting
17 Snubber plates
20 Snubber retaining nut
21 Backing plate
22 Snubber
23 Snubber bracket bolt
24 Snubber bracket
25 Rear tie-bar-to-body bracket through-bolt
26 Rear tie-bar-to-engine bracket through-bolt
27 Forked nut
28 Rear tie-bar
29 Lower tie-bar-to-engine bracket through-bolt
30 Lower tie-bar-to-chassis bracket through-bolt
31 Forked nut
32 Lower tie-bar

Rear mounting

7 Disconnect the battery negative terminal. (Refer to Chapter 12, Section 1, before doing this).

8 Remove the air intake trunking as described in Chapter 3.

9 Jack up the front of the car and support it on axle stands.

10 Undo the bolts and remove the longitudinal support member from beneath the engine.

11 Support the engine and gearbox/transmission assembly on a jack with interposed block of wood.

12 Undo and remove all the nuts and bolts securing the mounting to its mounting bracket and chassis member, and the mounting bracket to the engine.

13 Withdraw the mounting bracket from below, followed by the mounting. If there is a spacer located between the mounting and mounting bracket, retain this for refitting with the existing mounting, but discard it if the mounting is being renewed.

14 Renew the mounting if it shows any sign of damage, contamination or separation of the rubber-to-metal bond.

15 Refitting is the reverse sequence to removal, but ensure that the small peg on the mounting top face engages with the hole in the bracket, and tighten the bolts and nut to the specified torque.

Right-hand mounting

16 Disconnect the battery negative terminal. (Refer to Chapter 12, Section 1, before doing this).

17 Position a jack and interposed block of wood under the sump, and just take the weight of the engine.

18 Undo the bolts securing the power steering pipe support brackets, and move the pipes slightly to gain access to the right-hand mounting.

19 Undo the mounting through-bolt, and recover the special nut. Note that the forked end of the nut plate locates over a stud on the body bracket.

20 Undo the two bolts and remove the mounting and snubber plates from the bracket on the engine.

21 Renew the mounting if it shows any sign of damage, contamination or separation of the rubber-to-metal bond.

22 Refitting is the reverse sequence to removal, but tighten the bolts to the specified torque.

Rear tie-bar

23 Disconnect the battery negative terminal. (Refer to Chapter 12, Section 1, before doing this).

24 On cars equipped with single-point fuel injection, remove the air cleaner assembly as described in Chapter 3.

25 Drain the cooling system as described in Chapter 2, then disconnect the heater hoses and coolant hoses in the vicinity of the tie-bar as necessary to provide access.

26 Undo the two through-bolts securing the tie-bar to its mounting brackets. Note that at the larger end of the tie-bar, the through-bolt is retained by a forked nut which engages over a peg on the engine bracket.

27 Using a screwdriver if necessary, prise the tie-bar from its brackets and remove it from the car.

28 Renew the tie-bar if it shows any sign of damage, contamination or separation from the rubber-to-metal bond.

29 Refitting is the reverse sequence to removal, but ensure that the tie-bar is positioned with the word TOP, on the larger end of the bar, uppermost. Tighten the through-bolts to the specified torque, then refit the air cleaner as described in Chapter 3, and refill the cooling system as described in Chapter 2 on completion.

Snubber (manual gearbox models only)

30 Disconnect the battery negative terminal. (Refer to Chapter 12, Section 1, before doing this).

31 Jack up the front of the car and support it on axle stands.

32 Undo the retaining bolts and remove the longitudinal support member from under the engine.

33 Undo the nuts and remove the backing plate and snubber from the longitudinal support member.

34 If required, undo the nuts and bolts and remove the snubber bracket from the gearbox adaptor plate.

35 Renew the snubber if it shows any sign of damage, contamination or separation of the rubber-to-metal bond. Check also for signs of wear on the snubber bracket, and renew if necessary.

36 Refitting is the reverse sequence to removal. Centralise the snubber in its bracket before tightening the bolts and nuts to the specified torque.

Lower tie-bar (automatic transmission models only)

37 Disconnect the battery negative terminal. (Refer to Chapter 12, Section 1, before doing this).

38 Jack up the front of the car and support it on axle stands.

39 Undo the two through-bolts securing the tie-bar to its mounting brackets. Note that at the larger end of the tie-bar, the through-bolt is retained by a forked nut which engages over a peg on the mounting bracket.

40 Using a screwdriver if necessary, prise the tie-bar from its brackets and remove it from the car.

41 Renew the tie-bar if it shows any signs of damage, contamination or separation of the rubber-to-metal bond.

42 Refitting is the reverse sequence to removal, but ensure that the tie-bar is positioned with the letters BTM, on the larger end of the bar, facing downwards, and tighten the through-bolts to the specified torque.

26 Fault diagnosis – engine

Symptom	Reason(s)
Engine fails to start	Discharged battery
	Loose battery connections
	Moisture on spark plugs, distributor cap or HT leads
	Incorrect spark plug gaps
	Cracked distributor cap or rotor arm
	Other ignition system fault (see Chapter 4)
	Empty fuel tank
	Other fuel system fault (see Chapter 3)
	Faulty starter motor
	Low cylinder compressions
Engine idles erratically	Idling adjustment incorrect
	Inlet manifold air leak
	Disconnected or damaged crankcase ventilation hoses
	Leaking cylinder head gasket
	Incorrect valve timing
	Worn camshaft lobes
	Faulty hydraulic tappet(s)
	Uneven cylinder compressions
	Other fuel system fault (see Chapter 3)
	Other ignition system fault (see Chapter 4)

Symptom	Reason(s)
Engine misfires	Spark plugs worn, or incorrectly gapped
	Burnt out valve
	Leaking cylinder head gasket
	Distributor cap cracked
	Incorrect valve timing
	Worn camshaft lobes
	Faulty hydraulic tappet(s)
	Disconnected or damaged crankcase ventilation hoses
	Uneven cylinder compressions
	Other fuel system fault (see Chapter 3)
	Other ignition system fault (see Chapter 4)
Engine stalls	Idling adjustments incorrect
	Disconnected or damaged crankcase ventilation hoses
	Inlet manifold air leak
	Other fuel system fault (see Chapter 3)
	Other ignition system fault (see Chapter 4)
Excessive oil consumption	Worn pistons, piston rings or cylinder bores
	Valve guides, valve stems or valve stem oil seals worn
	Oil seal or gasket leakage
Engine lacks power	Low cylinder compressions
	Excessive carbon build-up in engine
	Air cleaner choked
	Other fuel system fault (see Chapter 3)
	Other ignition system fault (see Chapter 4)

Chapter 2 Cooling system

Contents

Specifications

System type .... Pressurized, water pump-assisted thermo-syphon, with front-mounted radiator and electric cooling fan

Thermostat
Type .... Wax
Starts-to-open temperature .... 76° to 80°C (169° to 176°F)
Fully-open temperature .... 88°C (190°F)
Lift height .... 8.1 mm (0.32 in)

Expansion tank cap pressure .... 1.0 bar (14.5 lbf/in²)

Cooling fan operating temperature .... 90°C (194°F)

System capacity .... 10.0 litres (17.6 Imp pts)

Antifreeze
Type .... Ethylene glycol based antifreeze (Duckhams Universal Antifreeze and Summer Coolant)

33% antifreeze (by volume):
  Commences freezing .... −19°C (−2°F)
  Frozen solid .... −36°C (−33°F)

Antifreeze	**Water**
3.3 litres	6.7 litres
(5.8 Imp pts)	(11.8 Imp pts)

  Quantities (system refill) ....

50% antifreeze (by volume):
  Commences freezing .... −36°C (−33°F)
  Frozen solid .... −48°C (−54°F)

Antifreeze	**Water**
5.0 litres	5.0 litres
(8.8 Imp pts)	(8.8 Imp pts)

  Quantities (system refill) ....

Torque wrench settings

	Nm	lbf ft
Water outlet elbow to thermostat housing	25	18
Thermostat housing to cylinder head	25	18
Water pump bolts	6	4
Water pump housing bolts	6	4
Water pump support strut bolt	6	4
Engine mounting bracket bolts	25	18
Timing belt tensioner plate	See text – Section 12	
Lower backplate bolts	6	4
Coolant temperature thermistor	7	5
Radiator centre platform bolts	8	6
Cooling fan to radiator	6	4
Bonnet safety catch to centre platform	6	4

1 General description

The cooling system is of the pressurized, pump-assisted thermo-syphon type. The system consists of the radiator, water pump thermostat, electric cooling fan, expansion tank and associated hoses. The impeller type water pump is mounted on the right-hand end of the engine, and is driven by the timing belt.

The system functions as follows. Cold coolant in the bottom of the radiator left-hand tank passes, via hoses and pipes, to the water pump, where it is pumped around the cylinder block and head passages. After cooling the cylinder bores, combustion surfaces and valve seats, the coolant reaches the underside of the thermostat, which is initially closed, and is diverted through a bypass hose to the heater matrix. After passing through the heater, the coolant travels through the water jacket of the inlet manifold or throttle housing as applicable, before returning to the water pump inlet hose. When the engine is cold, the thermostat remains closed, and the coolant only circulates as described. When the coolant reaches a predetermined temperature,

however, the thermostat opens, and the coolant passes through the top hose to the radiator right-hand tank. As the coolant circulates around the radiator, it is cooled by the inrush of air when the car is in forward motion. Airflow is supplemented by the action of the electric cooling fan when necessary. Upon reaching the left-hand side of the radiator, the coolant is now cooled and the cycle is repeated.

When the engine is at normal operating temperature, the coolant expands, and some of it is displaced into the expansion tank. This coolant collects in the tank, and is returned to the radiator when the system cools.

The electric cooling fan mounted on the radiator is controlled by a thermostatic switch, located in the radiator right-hand side tank. At a predetermined coolant temperature, the switch contacts close, thus actuating the fan.

On models equipped with automatic transmission, a fluid cooler is mounted to the transmission casing by a hollow centre bolt. The fluid cooler is connected to the main cooling system, engine coolant being the transmission fluid cooling medium.

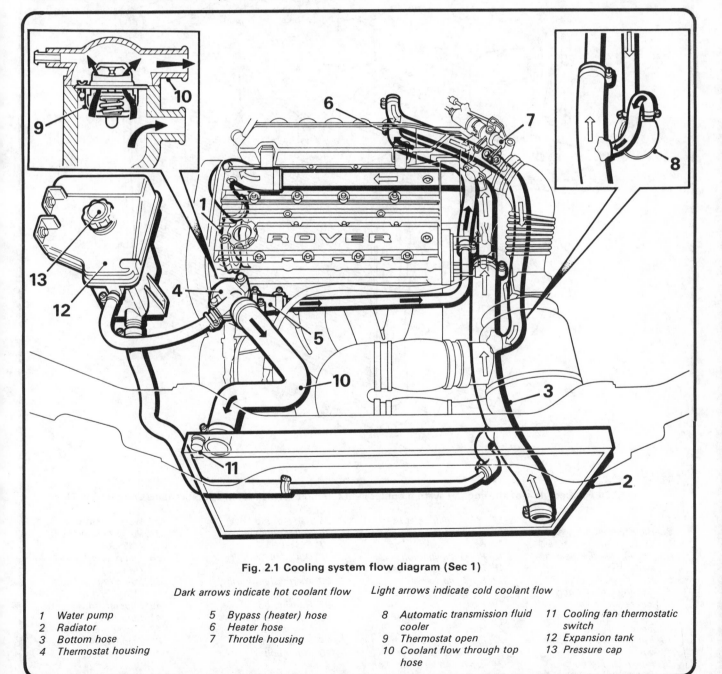

Fig. 2.1 Cooling system flow diagram (Sec 1)

Dark arrows indicate hot coolant flow   *Light arrows indicate cold coolant flow*

1 Water pump	5 Bypass (heater) hose	8 Automatic transmission fluid cooler	11 Cooling fan thermostatic switch
2 Radiator	6 Heater hose	9 Thermostat open	12 Expansion tank
3 Bottom hose	7 Throttle housing	10 Coolant flow through top hose	13 Pressure cap
4 Thermostat housing			

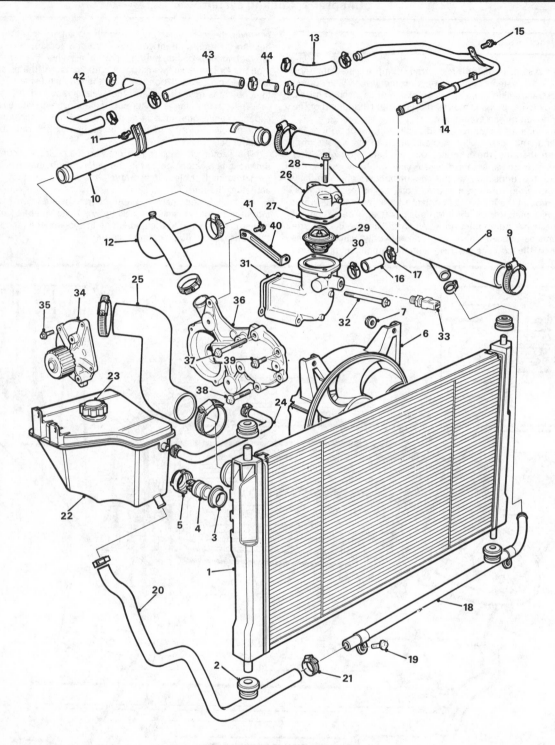

Fig. 2.2 Exploded view of the cooling system components – single-point fuel injection models shown (Sec 1)

1	Radiator	12	Water pump inlet hose
2	Radiator mounting grommet	13	Heater inlet hose
3	Thermostatic switch seal	14	Bypass (heater) pipe
4	Cooling fan thermostatic switch	15	Pipe retaining bolt
5	Retaining ring	16	Bypass (heater) hose
6	Cooling fan assembly	17	Hose clip
7	Fan retaining nut	18	Expansion tank pipe
8	Radiator bottom hose	19	Pipe bolt
9	Hose clips	20	Expansion tank hose
10	Bottom hose connecting pipe	21	Hose clip
11	Pipe retaining bolts	22	Expansion tank
		23	Pressure cap
		24	Expansion tank vent hose

25	Radiator top hose	36	Water pump housing
26	Water outlet elbow	37	Pump housing bolt (M8x60)
27	Gasket	38	Pump housing bolt (M8x70)
28	Outlet elbow bolt	39	Pump housing bolt (M8x25)
29	Thermostat	40	Support strut
30	Thermostat housing	41	Strut bolt
31	Gasket	42	Heater outlet hose
32	Housing bolt	43	Manifold outlet hose
33	Coolant temperature thermistor	44	Adaptor pipe
34	Water pump		
35	Pump bolt		

2 Maintenance and inspection

1   Check the coolant level in the system weekly and, if necessary, top up when the engine is cold, using a water-and-antifreeze mixture (photo), until the level just covers the pipe outlet on the seam of the tank. With a sealed type cooling system, topping-up should only be necessary at very infrequent intervals. If this is not the case, and frequent topping-up is required, it is likely that there is a leak in the system, or that the engine is overheating. Check all hoses and joint faces for any staining or actual wetness, and rectify as necessary. If no leaks can be found, it is advisable to have the system pressure-tested, as the leak could possibly be internal. It is a good idea to keep a careful check on the engine oil level in these circumstances, as a serious internal coolant leak can often cause the level in the sump to rise, thus confirming suspicions.
2   At the service intervals given in *Routine maintenance* at the beginning of this manual, carefully inspect all the hoses, hose clips and visible joint gaskets for cracks, corrosion, deterioration or leakage. Renew any hoses and clips that are suspect, and also renew any gaskets or reseal any joint faces, if necessary.
3   At the less-frequent service intervals indicated drain, flush and refill the cooling system using fresh antifreeze, as described in Sections 3, 4, and 5 respectively.

2.1 Top up through the expansion tank with a water-and-antifreeze mixture

3 Cooling system – draining

1   It is preferable to drain the cooling system when the engine is cold. *If the engine is hot, the pressure in the cooling system must be released before attempting to drain the system.* Place a cloth over the pressure cap of the expansion tank to avoid scalding and turn the cap one complete turn anti-clockwise. Wait until all the pressure is released, then remove the cap slowly from the tank.
2   Undo the retaining bolts and remove the undertray from beneath the radiator (photo).
3   Place a suitable container beneath the left-hand side of the radiator. Slacken the hose clip and carefully ease the bottom hose off the radiator outlet (photo). Allow the coolant to drain into the container.
4   If the cooling system is to be flushed after draining, see the next Section, otherwise refit the bottom hose and undertray, then refill the system as described in Section 5.

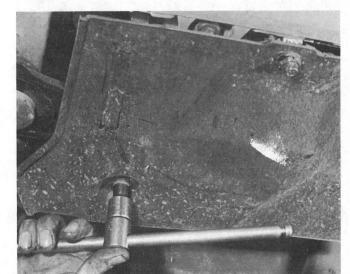

3.2 Undo the five bolts and remove the undertray

4 Cooling system – flushing

1   With time, the cooling system may gradually lose its efficiency, as the radiator core becomes choked with rust, scale deposits from the water, and other sediment.
2   To flush the system, first drain the coolant as described in the previous Section.
3   Disconnect the top hose at the thermostat housing water outlet elbow, and leave the bottom hose disconnected at the radiator outlet.
4   Insert a garden hose into the top hose, and allow water to circulate through the radiator until it runs clear from the bottom outlet.
5   Disconnect the small hose that connects the heater pipe to the thermostat housing (photo). Connect the garden hose, and allow water to circulate through the heater and manifold and out through the bottom hose until clear. Refit the heater hose on completion.
6   To flush the engine, remove the thermostat as described in Section 10, and insert the garden hose into the thermostat housing. Allow water to flow through the engine until it runs clear from the bottom hose. Refit the thermostat on completion.
7   In severe cases of contamination, reverse-flushing of the radiator may be necessary. To do this, remove the radiator as described in Section 7, invert it and insert the garden hose into the bottom outlet. Continue flushing until clear water runs from the top hose outlet.
8   The use of chemical cleaners should only be necessary as a last resort. The regular renewal of antifreeze should prevent excessive contamination of the system.

3.3 Slacken the hoseclip (arrowed) and remove the bottom hose

4.5 Disconnect the hose connecting the heater pipe to the thermostat housing

5.3 Tighten the bleed screw (arrowed) when coolant flows free from air bubbles

5 Cooling system – filling

1   If the system has been flushed, refit any hoses or components that were removed for this purpose.
2   Slacken the bleed screw, which is located on the hose connecting the main coolant pipe to the water pump at the rear of the engine.
3   Fill the system slowly through the expansion tank with the appropriate mixture of water and antifreeze (see Section 6), until the level is just below the filler neck. Tighten the bleed screw as soon as coolant flows out free of air bubbles (photo).
4   Recheck the coolant level in the expansion tank, then refit the pressure cap.
5   Start the engine, run it for approximately two minutes, then switch off.
6   Slowly unscrew the pressure cap one complete turn, wait until all the pressure escapes, then remove the cap. Check that the coolant just covers the pipe outlet on the seam of the tank, top up if necessary, then refit the cap.

6 Antifreeze mixture

1   The antifreeze should be renewed at regular intervals (see *Routine maintenance*). This is necessary not only to maintain the antifreeze properties, but also to prevent corrosion which would otherwise occur as the corrosion inhibitors become progressively less effective.
2   Always use an ethylene glycol based antifreeze with non-phosphate corrosion inhibitors, containing no methanol, and which is suitable for use in mixed metal cooling systems.
3   Before adding antifreeze, the cooling system should be completely drained and flushed, and all hoses checked for condition and security.
4   The ratio of antifreeze to water should be maintained at least 33% all year round. The quantity of antifreeze and levels of protection are indicated in the Specifications.
5   After filling with antifreeze, a label should be attached to the radiator, stating the type and concentration of antifreeze used, and the date installed. Any subsequent topping-up should be made with the same type and concentration of antifreeze.
6   Do not use engine antifreeze in the screen washer system, as it will cause damage to the vehicle paintwork. Screen washer antifreeze is available from most motor accessory shops.

7 Radiator – removal, inspection, cleaning and refitting

1   Drain the cooling system as described in Section 3. Leave the bottom radiator hose disconnected.

2   Slacken the retaining clip and disconnect the radiator top hose (photo).
3   Disconnect the radiator cooling fan multi-plug at the wiring connector.
4   Disconnect the two wires at the thermostatic switch just below the top hose outlet.
5   Undo the radiator grille retaining screws, release the lower catches, and remove the grille from the front of the car.
6   Undo the two bolts each side securing the centre platform to the body side members (photo).
7   Undo the nut and retaining bolt securing the bonnet safety catch to the centre platform (photo).
8   Lift the centre platform upwards, turn it over, and cut off the cable ties securing the bonnet release cable to the platform underside (photo). Remove the platform from the car.
9   Lift the radiator upwards, and carefully remove it from the car.
10 Radiator repair is best left to a specialist, but minor leaks may be sealed using a proprietary coolant additive. Clear the radiator matrix of flies and small leaves with a soft brush, or by hosing.
11 Reverse-flush the radiator, as described in Section 4. Renew the top and bottom hoses and clips if they are damaged or have deteriorated.

7.2 Radiator top hose connection (arrowed)

12 Refitting the radiator is the reverse sequence to removal, but ensure that the lower mounting lugs engage in the rubber grommets (photo), and the centre platform grommets locate over the radiator upper lugs (photo). Re-secure the bonnet release cable to the centre platform, using new cable ties. On completion, fill the cooling system as described in Section 5.

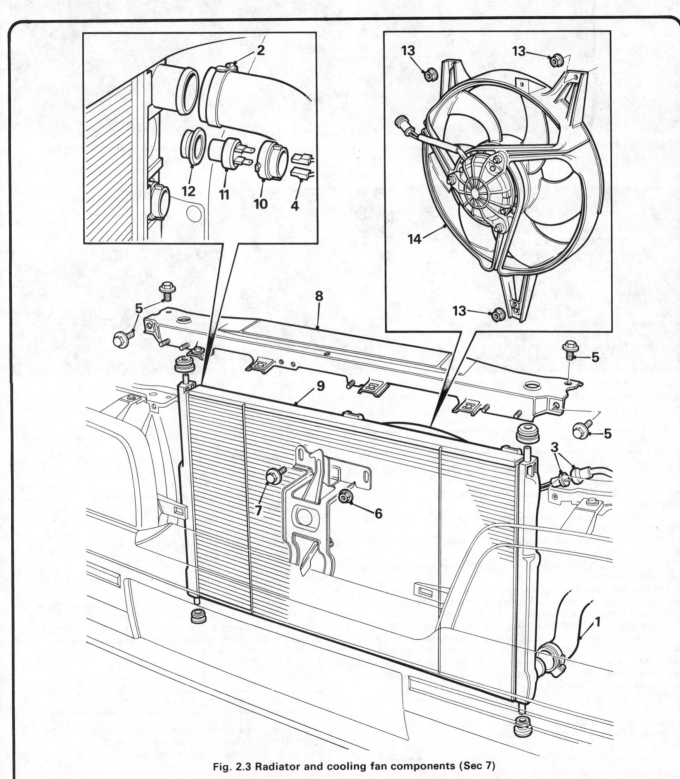

Fig. 2.3 Radiator and cooling fan components (Sec 7)

1 Bottom hose
2 Top hose
3 Cooling fan multi-plug
4 Thermostatic switch wires
5 Centre platform retaining bolts

6 Bonnet safety catch retaining nut
7 Bonnet safety catch retaining bolt

8 Centre platform
9 Radiator
10 Thermostatic switch retaining ring

11 Thermostatic switch
12 Seal
13 Fan shroud retaining nuts
14 Fan and shroud assembly

7.6 Centre platform retaining bolts – right-hand side (arrowed)

7.7 Remove the bonnet safety catch from the centre platform

7.8 Cut off the cable ties securing the bonnet release cable

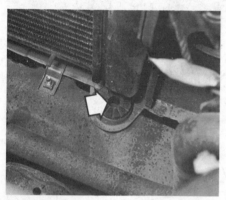

7.12A Ensure that the radiator lower lugs (arrowed) engage with the rubber grommets ...

7.12B ... and the centre platform grommets (arrowed) locate over the radiator upper lugs

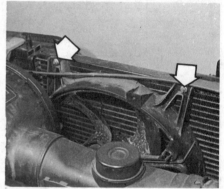

8.6 Cooling fan upper retaining nuts (arrowed)

8 Cooling fan assembly – removal and refitting

Note: *On cars equipped with air conditioning, a second cooling fan for the condenser is mounted alongside the main cooling fan for the radiator. The following procedures are applicable to both types of installation.*

1 Undo the radiator grille retaining screws, release the lower catches, and remove the grille from the front of the car.
2 Undo the two bolts each side securing the centre platform to the body side members.
3 Undo the nut and retaining bolt securing the bonnet safety catch to the centre platform.
4 Lift the centre platform upwards, turn it over, and cut off the cable ties securing the bonnet release cable to the platform underside. Remove the platform from the car.
5 Disconnect the cooling fan multi-plug at the wiring connector.
6 Undo the two upper retaining nuts (photo) and the single lower nut, then carefully lift out the cooling fan assembly. Note that the cooling fan, motor and cowl are a balanced assembly, and should not be dismantled. Should renewal be necessary, all three components are supplied as an assembled unit.
7 Refitting is the reverse sequence to removal.

9 Cooling fan thermostatic switch – testing, removal and refitting

Note: *On cars equipped with air conditioning, a second thermostatic switch for the condensor fan is mounted below the main thermostatic switch for the radiator cooling fan. The following procedures are applicable to both types of installation*

1 The radiator cooling fan (and condenser fan on cars equipped with air conditioning) are each operated by thermostatic switches, located on the right-hand side of the radiator. When the coolant exceeds a predetermined temperature, the switch contacts close and the fan(s) are activated.
2 If the operation of the fan or switch is suspect, run the engine until normal operating temperature is reached, and then allow it to idle. If the fan does not cut in within a few minutes, switch off the engine and disconnect the two wires from the thermostatic switch. Bridge the two wires with a length of wire, and switch on the ignition. If the fan now operates, the thermostatic switch is faulty, and must be renewed. If the fan still fails to operate, check that battery voltage is present at the two wires. If not, check for a blown fuse or wiring fault. If voltage is present, the fan motor is faulty.
3 To remove switch, partially drain the cooling system (approximately 2.5 litres/ 4.5 pints), using the procedure described in Section 3.
4 Disconnect the two wires, remove the switch retaining ring, which is a bayonet fitting, and withdraw the switch and seal from the radiator.
5 Refitting is the reverse sequence to removal, but renew the switch seal if the old one has deteriorated. On completion, fill the cooling system as described in Section 5.

10 Thermostat – removal, testing and refitting

1 Partially drain the cooling system (approximately 2.5 litres/ 4.5 pints), using the procedure described in Section 3.
2 Slacken the clips and detach the radiator top hose and expansion tank hose from the water outlet elbow on the thermostat housing (photo).
3 Undo the two bolts and remove the water outlet elbow (photos). Remove the gasket.
4 Withdraw the thermostat from its seat in the housing (photo).
5 To test the thermostat, suspend it on a string in a saucepan of cold water, together with a thermometer. Do not allow the thermostat or thermometer to touch the bottom of the pan. Heat the water, and note

10.2 Detach the radiator top hose and expansion tank hose at the water outlet elbow

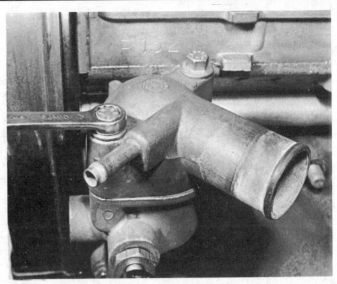
10.3A Undo the two retaining bolts ...

10.3B ... and remove the water outlet elbow

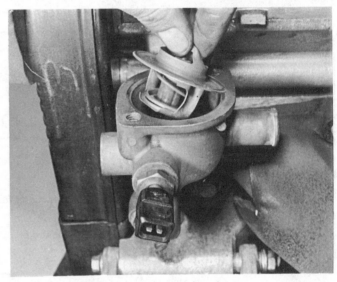
10.4 Withdraw the thermostat from the housing

the temperature at which the thermostat begins to open. Continue heating the water until the thermostat is fully open, note the temperature, then remove the unit from the water.

6 The temperatures at which the thermostat should start to open, and be fully open, are given in the Specifications. The fully-open temperature is also stamped on the wax capsule at the base of the thermostat. If the unit does not start to open, or is not fully open, at the specified temperatures, or if it does not close when removed from the water, then it must be discarded, and a new unit fitted. Under no circumstances should the car be used without a thermostat, as uneven cooling of the cylinder walls and head passages will occur, causing distortion and possible seizure of the engine internal components.

7 Refitting the thermostat is the reverse sequence to removal, bearing in mind the following points:

(a) Position the unit with its support legs across the heater outlet pipe, as shown in Fig. 2.4
(b) Clean away all traces of old gasket from the mating faces, and use a new gasket, lightly smeared with jointing compound

(c) Tighten the water outlet elbow retaining bolts to the specified torque
(d) Top up the cooling system with reference to Section 5

11 Thermostat housing – removal and refitting

1 Remove the thermostat as described in the previous Section.
2 Disconnect the coolant temperature thermistor wiring multi-plug.
3 Slacken the retaining clips, and disconnect the heater pipe connecting hose from the side of the housing.
4 Undo the two bolts, and remove the thermostat housing and gasket from the cylinder head (photos).
5 Refitting is the reverse sequence to removal, bearing in mind the following points:

(a) Clean away all traces of old gasket from the mating faces, and use a new gasket, lightly smeared with jointing compound
(b) Tighten the retaining bolts to the specified torque

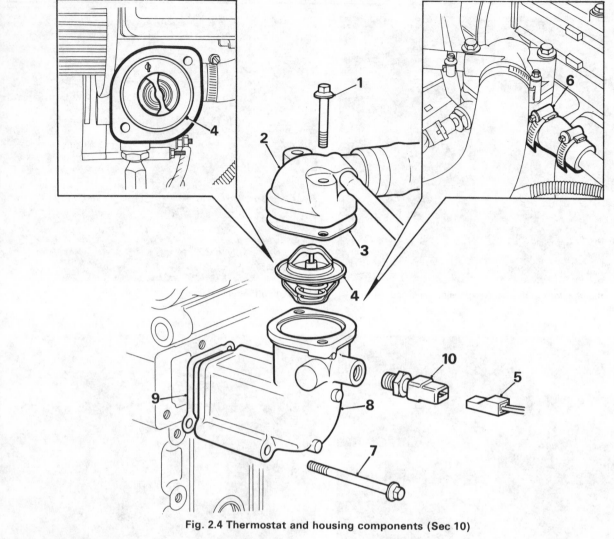

Fig. 2.4 Thermostat and housing components (Sec 10)

1	Outlet elbow bolt	4	Thermostat (inset shows	6	Connecting hose clip	9	Gasket
2	Water outlet elbow		correct fitted position)	7	Housing bolt	10	Coolant temperature
3	Gasket	5	Wiring plug	8	Thermostat housing		thermistor

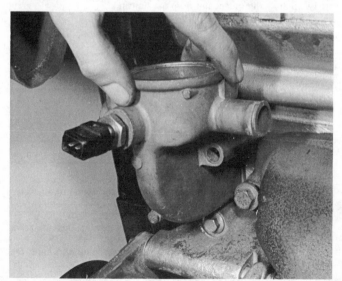

11.4A Remove the thermostat housing ...

11.4B ... followed by the gasket

12 Water pump – removal and refitting

Note: *Water pump failure is indicated by water leaking from the gland at the front of the pump, or by rough and noisy operation, usually accompanied by excessive play of the pump spindle. Repair or overhaul of a faulty pump is not possible, as internal parts are not available separately. In the event of failure, a replacement pump must be obtained.*

1 Drain the cooling system as described in Section 3.
2 Remove the alternator drivebelt as described in Chapter 12.
3 Refer to Chapter 1 and remove the timing belt.
4 Undo the three remaining bolts securing the lower backplate to the engine, noting that one bolt also retains a breather hose clip, and one retains an oil pipe clip. Remove the lower backplate (photo).
5 Undo the three bolts or Torx type / socket-headed screws, as applicable, and remove the timing belt tensioner mounting plate (photo).
6 Undo the five bolts securing the water pump to its housing (photo).
7 Have a container handy to catch any remaining coolant, then withdraw the pump from the housing. If necessary, carefully tap the pump body with a soft-faced mallet to free it.
8 With the pump removed, scrape away all traces of RTV sealant from the pump and housing mating faces, ensuring that both are competely clean and dry.
9 Before refitting the pump, it will be necessary to obtain three new bolts or socket-headed screws, as applicable, that retain the timing belt tensioner mounting plate. These are all of the micro-encapsulated type that incorporate a locking compound in their threads, and consequently, they can only be used once. Note also that considerable modification has taken place in this area during the course of production, and there are currently three versions of mounting plate and fastenings available. These are shown in Figs. 2.5 to 2.7. To identify the type fitted to the engine being worked on, compare the part number stamped on the mounting plate face with those shown in the illustrations, and obtain new screws or bolts from a Rover dealer accordingly.
10 Apply a thin, continuous bead of RTV sealant to the pump mating face, and place the pump in position on the housing.
11 Refit the pump retaining bolts and tighten them progressively, and in a diagonal sequence, to the specified torque.
12 Locate the timing belt tensioner mounting plate in position, and fit the three bolts or screws finger-tight. These must now be tightened in the correct sequence, according to type as follows:

First version (Fig. 2.5)
Tighten screws 'A' progressively to 9 to 12 Nm (6.6 to 8.8 lbf ft) then tighten bolt 'B' to 7 to 10 Nm (5.1 to 7.3 lbf ft)

Second version (Fig. 2.6)
Tighten in numerical order shown, to 11 to 14 Nm (8.1 to 10.3 lbf ft) for screws 1 and 2, and 7 to 10 Nm (5.1 to 7.3 lbf ft) for bolt 3

Third version (Fig. 2.7)
Tighten all, in the numerical order shown, to 11 to 14 Nm (8.1 to 10.3 lbf ft)

Do not attempt to retighten any of the screws or bolts after the locking compound has set (approximately two minutes), otherwise the locking properties will be destroyed, and the screws may loosen in service.
13 Refit the lower backplate to the engine, and secure with the three bolts.
14 Refer to Chapter 1 and refit the timing belt.
15 Refit the alternator drivebelt as described in Chapter 12, then refill the cooling system as described in Section 5.

12.4 Remove the lower backplate from the engine

12.5 Timing belt tensioner mounting plate bolts/screws (arrowed)

12.6 Undo the five bolts (arrowed) and remove the water pump

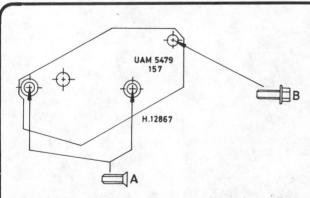

Fig. 2.5 Timing belt tensioner mounting plate – first version (Sec 12)

A   Hexagon drive countersunk screws
B   Flange head bolt

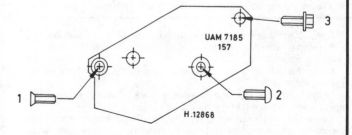

Fig. 2.6 Timing belt tensioner mounting plate – second version (Sec 12)

1   Torx type countersunk screw   3   Flange head bolt
2   Torx type pan head screw

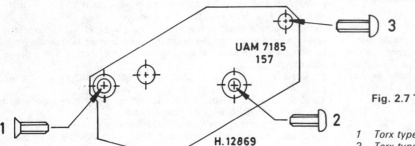

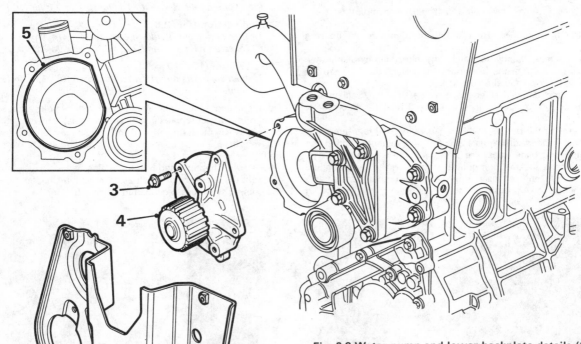

Fig. 2.7 Timing belt tensioner mounting plate – third
version (Sec 12)

1   Torx type countersunk screw   3   Torx type pan head screw
2   Torx type pan head screw

Fig. 2.8 Water pump and lower backplate details (Sec 12)

1   Lower backplate bolts   4   Water pump assembly
2   Lower backplate   5   Bead of RTV sealant applied
3   Water pump bolts   to pump housing face

13 Water pump housing – removal and refitting

1   Remove the water pump as described in the previous Section.
2   Slacken the clip and detach the water inlet hose from the rear of the
pump housing (photo).
3   Undo the bolt securing the support strut to the rear of the pump
housing (photo).
4   Using a suitable jack and interposed block of wood, support the
engine under the sump at the timing belt end.
5   Undo the four bolts securing the right-hand engine mounting
bracket to the water pump housing (photo), and the two bolts
securing the bracket to the engine mounting, then remove the bracket.
6   Undo the remaining two retaining bolts (photo), and remove the
water pump housing from the cylinder block.
7   Clean away all traces of RTV sealant from the housing and cylinder
block mating faces, ensuring that both surfaces are clean and dry.
8   Apply a thin, continuous bead of RTV sealant to the cylinder block
mating face (photo), and locate the housing in position.

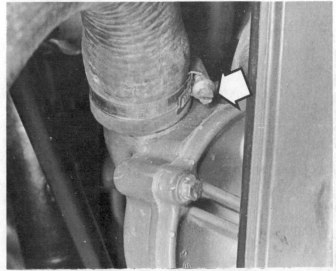

13.2 Water inlet hose connection (arrowed) at rear of water pump
housing

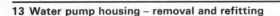

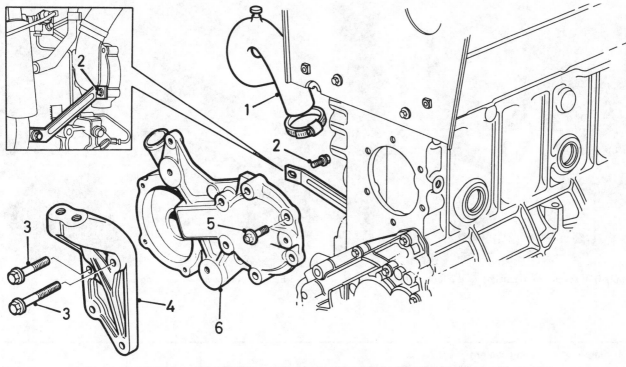

Fig. 2.9 Water pump housing details (Sec 13)

1 Water inlet hose
2 Support strut bolt
3 Engine mounting bracket
   bolts
4 Engine mounting bracket
5 Pump housing bolts
6 Water pump housing

9 Apply thread sealer to the two housing retaining bolts, and fit them finger-tight at this stage.
10 Apply thread sealer to the four engine mounting bracket-to-pump housing bolts, fit the bracket and tighten the bolts to the specified torque. Now tighten the two pump bolts fitted previously.
11 Secure the engine mounting bracket to the mounting, and remove the support jack.
12 Refit the bolt securing the support strut to the rear of the pump housing.
13 Reconnect the inlet water hose to the housing.
14 Refit the water pump as described in the previous Section.

14 Expansion tank – removal and refitting

1 Drain the cooling system as described in Section 3.
2 Slacken the clips and detach the two hoses on the side of the tank.

3 Undo the two upper (photo) and one lower retaining screw(s), and remove the tank.
4 Refitting is the reverse sequence to removal.

15 Coolant temperature thermistor – removal and refitting

1 The thermistor contains an element, the resistance of which alters according to coolant temperature. The unit controls the operation of the temperature gauge, and is also used by the fuel and ignition system control units to determine engine temperature.
2 Partially drain the cooling system (approximately 2.5 litres/ 4.5 pints), using the procedure described in Section 3.
3 Disconnect the wiring multi-plug, then unscrew the thermistor from its location in the thermostat housing.
4 Refitting is the reverse sequence to removal, but refill the cooling system with reference to Section 5.

13.3 Undo the bolt (arrowed) securing the support strut to the housing

13.5 Engine mounting bracket bolt locations (arrowed)

13.6 Water pump housing retaining bolts (arrowed)

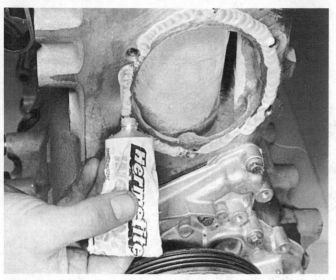

13.8 Apply RTV sealant to the mating face prior to refitting

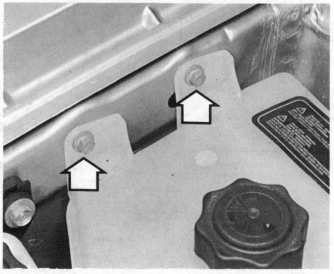

14.3 Expansion tank upper retaining bolts (arrowed)

16 Fault diagnosis – cooling system

Symptom	Reason(s)
Overheating	Low coolant level (this may be the result of overheating for other reasons) Radiator blockage (internal or external), or grille restricted Thermostat defective Ignition system fault Faulty cooling fan thermostatic switch Faulty cooling fan Blown cylinder head gasket Water pump defective Expansion tank pressure cap faulty Brakes binding
Overcooling	Thermostat missing, defective or wrong heat range Incorrect reading on gauge (faulty gauge or temperature thermistor)
Water loss – external	Loose hose clips Perished or cracked hoses Radiator core leaking Heater matrix leaking Expansion tank pressure cap leaking Boiling due to overheating Water pump or thermostat housing leaking Core plug leaking Other joint face leak
Water loss – internal	Cylinder head gasket blown Cylinder head cracked or warped Cylinder head cracked
Corrosion	Infrequent draining and flushing Incorrect antifreeze mixture, or inappropriate type Combustion gases contaminating coolant

Chapter 3 Fuel and exhaust systems

Contents

Specifications

Part A : Single-point fuel injection system
System type .... Indirect single-point injection, with microprocessor control

Fuel pump
Type .... Electric, self-priming centrifugal
Make .... Nippon Denso FP3
Output pressure .... 4.1 bar (59.4 lbf/in²)
Regulated pressure .... 1.0 bar (14.5 lbf/in²)
Delivery rate (at 1.0 bar/14.5 lbf/in², and 12 volts) .... 85 litres/hr (150 pints/hr)
Voltage at pump .... 9.0 to 10.0 volts

General
ECU-controlled idle speed:
    Manual gearbox models .... 700 to 800 rpm
    Manual transmission models .... 650 to 750 rpm
Base idle speed:
    Manual gearbox models .... 625 to 675 rpm
    Automatic transmission models .... 575 to 625 rpm
Idle mixture CO content .... 2.0 to 3.0%
Throttle potentiometer voltage .... 315 to 335 mV
Throttle lever lost motion gap .... 0.5 to 0.9 mm (0.020 to 0.035 in)
Fuel octane rating .... 4 star (97 RON – leaded) or Premium (95 RON – unleaded)

Torque wrench settings

	Nm	lbf ft
Inlet air temperature sensor	7	5
Fuel filter banjo union bolts	50	37
Throttle body-to-manifold nuts	25	18
Fuel pump banjo union bolt	22	16
Fuel pump retaining nuts	6	4
Fuel tank drain plug	50	37
Fuel tank strap locknuts	18	13
Inlet manifold support stay bolts	25	18
Inlet manifold to cylinder head	25	18
Inlet manifold heater bolts	10	7
Exhaust manifold to cylinder head	45	33
Exhaust front pipe to manifold	30	22
Exhaust section flange nuts	30	22
Exhaust heat shield retaining bolts	25	18

Part B : Multi-point fuel injection system

System type

Indirect multi-point injection, with microprocessor control

Fuel pump

Type	Electric, self-priming centrifugal
Make	Nippon Denso FP3
Output pressure	4.1 bar (59.4 lbf/in²)
Regulated pressure range	3.0 to 2.3 bar (43.5 to 33.4 lbf/in²)
Delivery rate (at 3.0 bar/43.5 lbf/in², and 12 volts)	70 litres/hr (123.2 pints/hr)

General

ECU-controlled idle speed:	
Manual gearbox models	850 to 950 rpm
Automatic transmission models	800 to 900 rpm
Base idle speed:	
Manual gearbox models	725 to 775 rpm
Automatic transmission models	675 to 725 rpm
Idle mixture CO content	0.5 to 1.5%
Throttle potentiometer voltage	315 to 335 mV
Fuel octane rating	4 star (97 RON – leaded) or Premium (95 RON – unleaded)

Torque wrench settings

	Nm	lbf ft
Airflow meter retaining bolts	6	4
Throttle housing retaining nuts	8	6
Fuel filter banjo union bolts	50	37
Fuel pressure regulator retaining bolts	6	4
Brake servo hose banjo union bolt	50	37
Plenum chamber to camshaft cover	6	4
Plenum chamber to inlet manifold	8	6
Fuel rail to inlet manifold	8	6
Fuel pump banjo union bolt	22	16
Fuel pump retaining nuts	6	4
Fuel tank drain plug	50	37
Fuel tank strap locknuts	18	13
Inlet manifold to cylinder head	25	18
Exhaust manifold to cylinder head	45	33
Exhaust front pipe to manifold	30	22
Exhaust section flange nuts	30	22
Exhaust heat shield retaining bolts	25	18

PART A : SINGLE-POINT FUEL INJECTION SYSTEM

1 General description

The fuel system used on Rover 820e and Se models consists of a centrally-mounted fuel tank, electric fuel pump and single-point fuel injection (SPi) system, together with its related electrical and mechanical components. A more detailed description of the SPi system is contained in Section 10.

The exhaust system consists of a front, intermediate and rear section, suspended from the underbody on rubber mountings, and bolted to a cast iron manifold at the front. A ball-and-socket universal joint is incorporated in the front section, to allow for engine and exhaust system movement.

Warning: *Many of the procedures in this Chapter entail the removal of fuel pipes and connections, which may result in some fuel spillage. Before carrying out any operations on the fuel system, refer to the precautions given in* Safety first! *at the beginning of this manual, and follow them implicitly. Petrol is a highly dangerous and volatile liquid, and the precautions necessary when handling it cannot be overstressed.*

2 Maintenance and inspection

1 At the intervals given in *Routine maintenance* at the beginning of this manual, carry out the following service operations on the fuel and exhaust system components.

2 With the car raised on a vehicle lift or securely supported on axle stands, carefully inspect the fuel pipes, hoses and unions for chafing, leaks, and corrosion. Renew any pipes that are severely pitted with corrosion, or in any way damaged. Renew any hoses that show signs of cracking or other deterioration.

3 Check the security of the fuel tank mountings, and check the tank

for signs of corrosion or damage. Refer to Section 7 if the tank condition is suspect.

4   Check condition of the exhaust system as described in Section 26.

5   From within the engine compartment, check the security of all fuel hose attachments, and inspect the fuel hoses and vacuum hoses for kinks, chafing or deterioration.

6   Renew the air cleaner element, and clean the air cleaner body and cover, as described in Section 3.

7   Check the operation of the accelerator linkage, and lubricate the linkage, cable and pedal pivot with a few drops of oil.

8   Renew the fuel filter as described in Section 4.

9   Check the fuel injection system base idle speed and mixture settings as described in Section 12.

3   Air cleaner and element – removal and refitting

1   To renew the air cleaner element, remove the cover from the air cleaner body by carefully prising it off using a screwdriver around the periphery (photo).

2   Withdraw the element from the body, and bend it upwards to clear the front body panel (photo).

3   Using a clean rag, wipe out the inside of the body and cover.

4   Carefully fit the new element, ensuring that its centre is located over the lip at the base of the air cleaner body.

5   Refit the cover, and push it firmly into place.

6   To remove the complete air cleaner assembly, slacken the hose clip securing the intake trunking to the air cleaner body, and release the HT cable from the support clip.

7   Undo the five upper bolts securing the air box to the injector housing and support bracket.

8   Lift up the air box, and disconnect the wiring multi-plug at the air temperature sensor, and the vacuum hose at the fuel trap (photos).

9   Disconnect the vacuum hose from the inlet manifold connection, and from the vacuum motor on the air cleaner (photos). Remove the air box and intake trunking assembly.

10 Undo the bolts securing the air cleaner body and the forward air trunking assembly to their support brackets (photos). Lift the body and trunking, disconnect the hot air intake tube, and release the trunking

3.1 Remove the air cleaner cover ...

3.2 ... and withdraw the element

3.8A Lift up the air box ...

3.8B ... and disconnect the air temperature sensor multi-plug

3.9A Disconnect the vacuum hose at the inlet manifold ...

3.9B ... and at the vacuum motor

3.10A Undo the air cleaner body left-hand retaining bolt (arrowed) ...

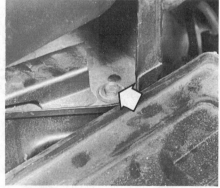
3.10B ... and right-hand retaining bolt (arrowed) ...

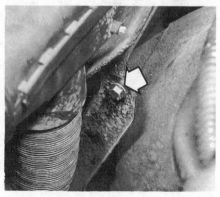
3.10C ... and the air cleaner trunking-to-support bracket bolt (arrowed)

from the connecting duct at the front of the car. Remove the air cleaner body and trunking.

11 If the cold air side intake is to be removed, refer to Chapter 12 and remove the battery.

12 Undo the bolt securing the side intake to the body, and remove the intake and duct (photo).

13 Refitting is the reverse sequence to removal, but ensure that all the ducts and trunking are fully engaged before tightening the various retaining bolts.

4 Fuel filter – removal and refitting

Note: Refer to the warning note in Section 1 before proceeding.

1 Disconnect the battery negative terminal. (Refer to Chapter 12, Section 1, before doing this.)

2 Place absorbent rags around the fuel filter outlet union banjo bolt (photo), then slowly unscrew the bolt to release the fuel system pressure.

3 Unscrew the filter inlet and outlet union banjo bolts, and recover the copper washers (photo).

4 Undo the filter bracket retaining nuts, and remove the filter.

5 Refitting is the reverse sequence to removal, but use new copper washers on the banjo unions.

5 Fuel pump – removal and refitting

Note: Refer to the warning note in Section 1 before proceeding.

1 Disconnect the battery negative terminal. (Refer to Chapter 12, Section 1, before doing this).

2 Release the fuel system pressure as described in Section 4,

paragraph 2. Tighten the fuel filter banjo bolt after the pressure has been released.

3 Remove the floor carpet from the luggage compartment.

4 Refer to Chapter 11 and remove the rear seats.

5 Release the eight studs and remove the seat squab backing from the body.

6 Release the two studs and remove the luggage compartment backboard from the body.

7 Remove the cover board over the spare wheel, and remove the tool kit.

8 Undo the four screws and lift off the pump access panel (photos). Move the panel to one side.

9 Disconnect the pump wiring multi-plug, then unscrew the fuel hose banjo union bolt and recover the copper washers (photo).

10 Slacken the clip and disconnect the fuel return hose.

11 Undo the pump retaining nuts, and withdraw the pump from the tank. Remove the seal from the pump flange.

12 Refitting is the reverse sequence to removal, but renew the flange seal if it shows any sign of deterioration.

6 Fuel gauge sender unit – removal and refitting

Note: Refer to the warning note in Section 1 before proceeding.

1 Follow the procedure given in Section 5, paragraphs 1 to 8 inclusive, with the exception of paragraph 2.

2 Disconnect the two leads at the sender unit.

3 Engage a screwdriver, flat bar or other suitable tool with the lugs of the locking ring, and turn the ring anti-clockwise to release it.

4 Withdraw the locking ring, seal and sender unit.

5 Refitting is the reverse sequence to removal, but renew the seal if it shows any sign of deterioration.

3.12 Side intake-to-body retaining bolt (arrowed)

4.2 Fuel filter outlet union banjo bolt (arrowed)

4.3 Undo the banjo unions and recover the copper washers

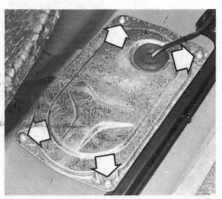

5.8A Undo the four retaining screws (arrowed) ...

5.8B ... and lift off the fuel pump access panel

5.9 Fuel pump wiring multi-plug connection (A) and fuel hose banjo union (B)

7 Fuel tank – removal and refitting

Note: *Refer to the warning note in Section 1 before proceeding.*
1 Follow the procedure given in Section 5, paragraphs 1 to 8 inclusive.
2 Disconnect the fuel pump wiring multi-plug, and the two leads at the fuel gauge sender unit.
3 Remove the fuel tank filler cap.
4 With suitable sealed containers handy, undo the drain plug at the base of the tank, and drain the fuel into the containers. Recover the drain plug sealing washer. When all the fuel has drained, refit the plug, using a new sealing washer if necessary.
5 Chock the front wheels, prise off the rear wheel trim and slacken the wheel nuts. Jack up the rear of the car and support it on axle stands. Remove the left-hand rear roadwheel.
6 Slacken the retaining clip and disconnect the filler hose from the filler neck. Move the hose aside.

7 Slacken the retaining clips and disconnect the five breather hoses from the breather pipes.
8 Refer to Section 26 and remove the exhaust system rear and intermediate sections, together with the rear heat shield.
9 Slacken the retaining clip and disconnect the fuel return hose from the pipe on the side of the tank. Plug the disconnected pipe and hose.
10 Undo the union connector and disconnect the fuel feed hose from the pipe. Plug the disconnected pipe and hose.
11 Support the tank on a jack with interposed block of wood.
12 Slacken the two tank retaining strap locknuts (photo), release the hook bolts from the body slots, and move the straps clear.
13 Lower the tank and remove it from under the car.
14 If the tank is contaminated with sediment or water, remove the sender unit as described in Section 6, and swill the tank out with clean fuel. If the tank is damaged, or leaks, it should be repaired by a specialist, or alternatively renewed. **Do not** *under any circumstances solder or weld the tank.*
15 Refitting is the reverse sequence to removal.

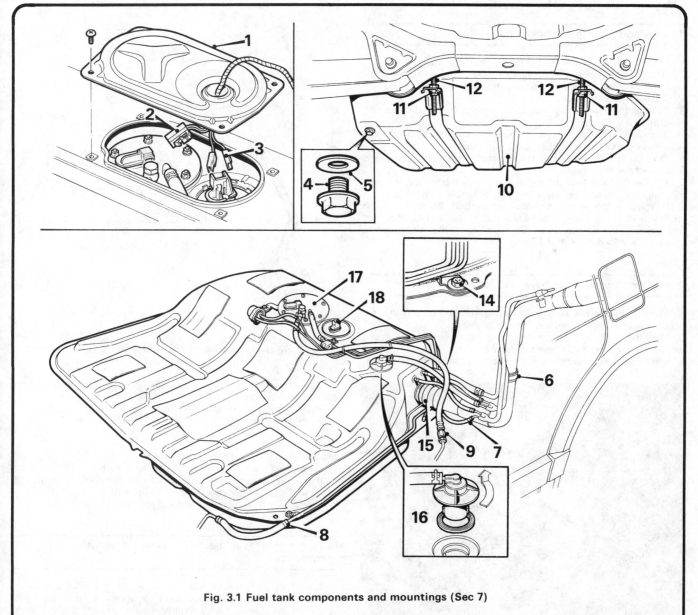

Fig. 3.1 Fuel tank components and mountings (Sec 7)

1 Fuel pump access panel	6 Filler hose-to-filler neck connection	10 Fuel tank	15 Filler hose-to-tank connection
2 Pump wiring multi-plug	7 Breather hose	11 Retaining strap locknuts	16 Cut-off valve
3 Sender unit wiring	8 Fuel return hose	12 Hook bolts	17 Fuel pump
4 Drain plug	9 Fuel feed hose union	14 Breather pipe support bracket	18 Fuel gauge sender unit
5 Sealing washer			

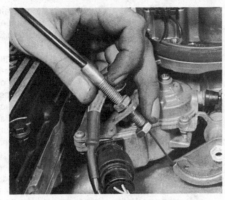

7.12 Fuel tank retaining strap and locknut   8.2 Undo the accelerator cable locknut ...   8.3 ... and release the cable end (arrowed) from the throttle cam

8 Accelerator cable – removal and refitting

1   Refer to Section 3 and remove the air cleaner air box.
2   Unscrew the accelerator outer cable locknut nearest to the cable end, pull the outer cable upwards, and slide the inner cable out of the slot in the support bracket (photo).
3   Release the inner cable end from the slot in the throttle cam (photo).
4   From inside the car, release the turnbuckles and lift out the trim panel over the clutch, brake and accelerator pedals.
5   Prise the retaining clip from the top of the accelerator pedal, and disconnect the inner cable.
6   Release the cable from the engine compartment bulkhead and from the support clips, and withdraw the complete cable from the car.
7   Refitting is the reverse sequence to removal. Adjust the cable initially by means of the outer cable locknuts, to give a small amount of free play with the throttle closed. On completion, check the base idle speed as described in Section 12.

9 Accelerator pedal – removal and refitting

1   From inside the car, release the turnbuckles and lift out the trim panel over the clutch, brake and accelerator pedals.
2   Prise the retaining clip from the top of the accelerator pedal, and disconnect the inner cable from the pedal arm.
3   Undo the bolts securing the pedal bracket to the bulkhead (photo),

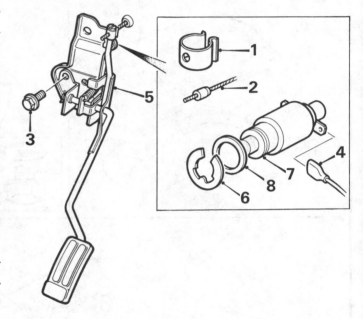

Fig. 3.2 Accelerator pedal and pedal switch components (Sec 9)

1   Cable retaining clip   5   Pedal and bracket assembly
2   Accelerator cable   6   C-clip
3   Pedal bracket retaining bolts   7   Pedal switch
4   Pedal switch wiring   8   Washer

and withdraw the bracket and pedal assembly.
4   Disconnect the switch wiring and remove the bracket and pedal.
5   If the accelerator pedal switch is to be removed, prise off the retaining C-clip and remove the switch and washer.
6   Refitting is the reverse sequence to removal.

10 Single-point fuel injection system – description and operation

The single-point fuel injection (SPi) system is a microprocessor-controlled fuel management system, designed to overcome the limitations associated with conventional carburettor induction. This is achieved by continuously monitoring the engine using various sensors, whose data is input to the fuel system electronic control unit (ECU). Based on this information, the ECU program and memory then determine the exact amount of fuel necessary, which is injected into the throttle body by a single injector, for all actual and anticipated driving conditions.

9.3 Accelerator pedal bracket retaining bolts (arrowed)

The main components of the system are shown in Figs. 3.3 and 3.4, and their individual operation is as follows.

Fuel ECU: The fuel ECU is a microprocessor which controls the injector opening time, and therefore the amount of fuel supplied. Contained in the ECU memory is a program from which a pulse is derived, the length of which determines the fuel injector opening duration. Information received from the various engine sensors will cause the ECU to alter the fuel requirements, by changing the pulse length. Airflow measurement is based on the speed/density method, in which the inlet air temperature and inlet manifold pressure are measured under the assumption that the engine is a calibrated vacuum pump, with its characteristics stored in the ECU memory. The air/fuel ratio requirements for all engine speeds and loads are also stored in the ECU. This information on the engine's basic fuel requirements is constantly amended, according to the information received from the various sensors. In addition to this, the engine idle speed is also controlled by the ECU, which uses a stepper motor to open or close the throttle as required. Two separate programs control the ECU functions.

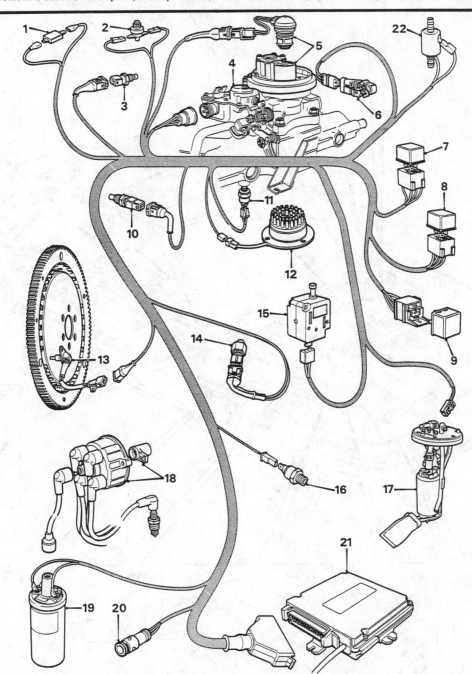

Fig. 3.3 Main components of the single-point fuel injection system (Sec 10)

1 Ambient air temperature sensor
2 Accelerator pedal switch
3 Inlet air temperature sensor
4 Throttle body and idle speed stepper motor
5 Fuel injector and fuel pressure regulator
6 Throttle potentiometer
7 Main fuel system relay
8 Fuel pump relay
9 Oil pressure relay
10 Coolant temperature thermistor
11 Manifold heater temperature sensor
12 Manifold heater
13 Crankshaft sensor
14 Knock sensor
15 Inertia switch
16 Oil pressure switch
17 Fuel pump
18 Distributor cap and rotor arm
19 Ignition coil
20 Diagnostic plug connector
21 Fuel/ignition ECU
22 Idle solenoid (models with air conditioning)

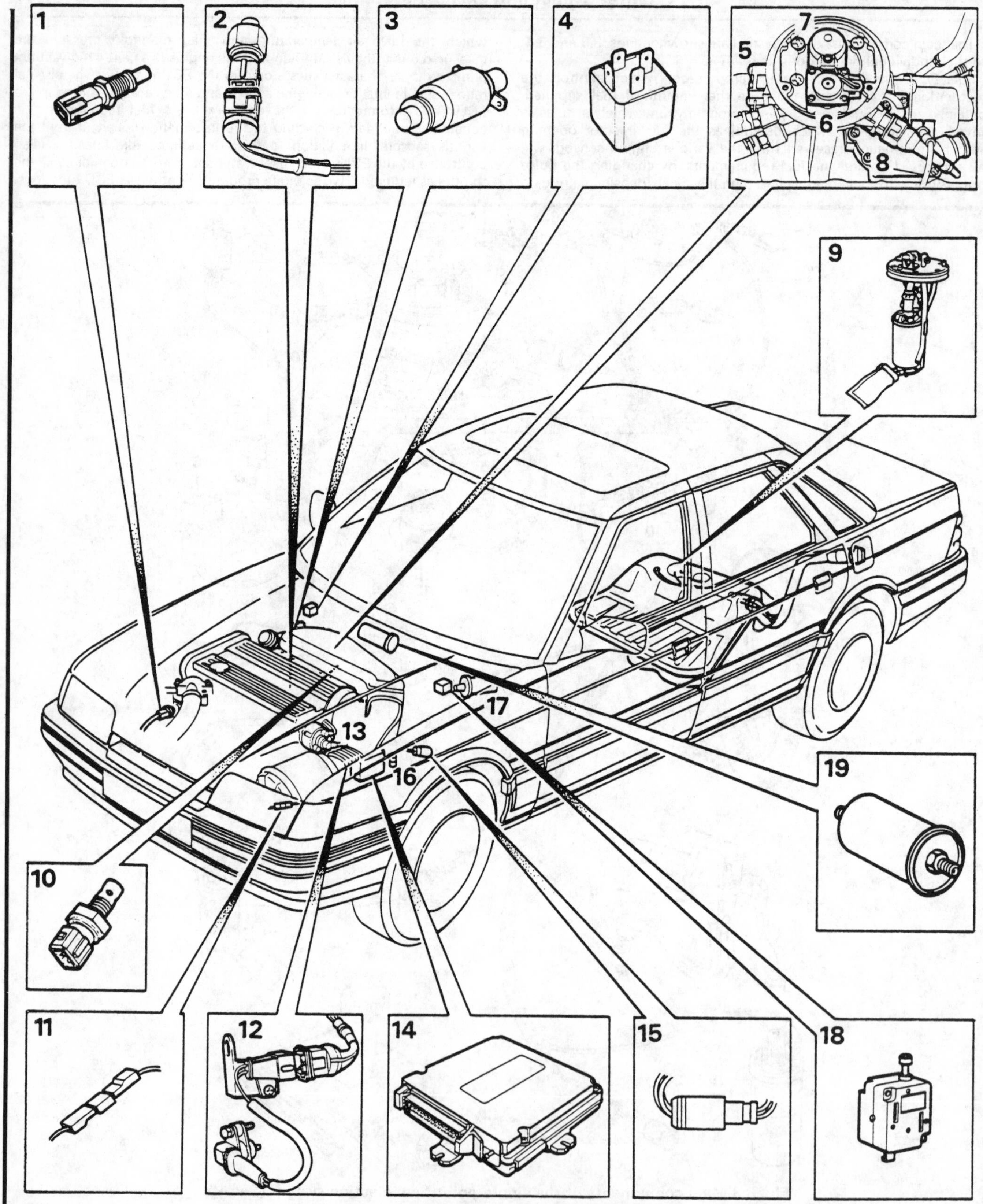

Fig. 3.4 Single-point injection system component location (Sec 10)

1 Coolant temperature thermistor
2 Knock sensor
3 Accelerator pedal switch
4 Fuel pump relay
5 Throttle potentiometer
6 Fuel pressure regulator
7 Fuel injector
8 Idle speed stepper motor
9 Fuel pump
10 Inlet air temperature sensor
11 Ambient air temperature sensor
12 Crankshaft sensor
13 Distributor cap and rotor arm
14 Fuel/ignition ECU
15 Diagnostic plug connector
16 Main fuel system relay
17 Ignition coil
18 Inertia switch
19 Fuel filter

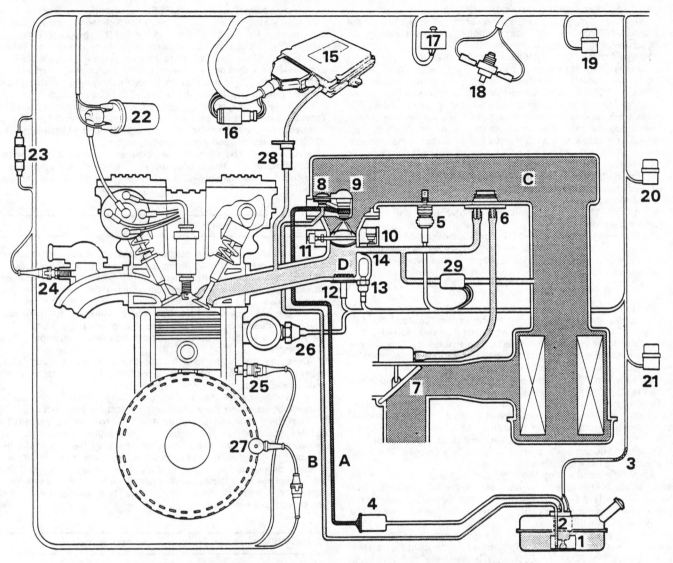

Fig. 3.5 Schematic layout of the single-point fuel injection system (Sec 10)

1 Fuel return swirl pot	11 Throttle potentiometer	19 Main fuel system relay
2 Fuel pump	12 Manifold heater	20 Oil pressure relay
3 Fuel pump resistive wire	13 Manifold heater temperature	21 Fuel pump relay
4 Fuel filter	sensor	22 Ignition coil
5 Inlet air temperature senose	14 Inlet manifold vacuum port	23 Ambient air temperature
6 Thermac switch	15 Fuel/ignition ECU	sensor
7 Vacuum motor and air flap	16 Diagnostic plug	24 Coolant temperature
8 Fuel pressure regulator	17 Inertia switch	thermistor
9 Fuel injector	18 Accelerator pedal switch	25 Knock sensor
10 Idle speed stepper motor		

26 Oil pressure switch
27 Crankshaft sensor
28 Fuel trap
29 Idle solenoid (models with
   air conditioning)
A Regulated fuel pressure
B Return fuel
C Inlet airflow
D Manifold vacuum

One program operates under cruise conditions, and the other at idle. The idle program can be altered completely using electronic test equipment, or partially by using the procedures described in Section 13. Any changes to this program do not affect the cruise program, which cannot be accessed. Whenever the battery is disconnected, the idle program is lost, and the ECU reverts back to a set of nominal parameters until the information is reintroduced into the memory. This can only be done using the manufacturer's test equipment, but the performance of the engine at idle is only marginally affected in this condition. As well as control of the fuel injection system, the ECU is also used to control the ignition timing.

Fuel injector: The single fuel injector is a solenoid-operated ball valve, containing a fine gauze filter and a nozzle wirh six spray holes for complete fuel atomization. When a pulse is received from the ECU, the injector sprays fuel into the air stream through the throttle body.

Throttle potentiometer: The potentiometer is a variable resistor, attached to the throttle shaft on the throttle body. The unit is supplied with a constant input voltage, and as the resistance of the potentiometer varies with throttle shaft movement, the output voltage is proportionally affected. This allows the ECU to determine throttle valve position, and rate of change.

Idle speed stepper motor: This is a small electric motor, having four control windings to enable it to rotate in either direction. Under a signal from the ECU, the stepper motor will rotate in whichever direction is necessary, to open or close the throttle by means of pushrod acting directly against the base idle speed adjusting screw.

Inlet air temperature sensor: Located in the airflow through the air cleaner air box, the sensor is a thermistor (resistive device whose resistance quickly decreases with temperature increase).

Coolant temperature thermistor: This resistive device is screwed into the thermostat housing, where its element is in direct contact with the engine coolant. Changes in coolant temperature are detected by the ECU as a change in the thermistor resistance.

Ambient air temperature sensor: The sensor is located behind the left-hand headlamp, and responds to changes in ambient temperature with a corresponding change in resistance.

Manifold heater: A manifold heater, to improve atomization of the fuel/air mixture during warm-up conditions, is fitted to the underside of the inlet manifold. The heater is of the positive temperature coefficient (PTC) type, in which the current consumption of the heating element is high while it heats up, but is greatly reduced at operating temperature. The unit is controlled by a temperature sensor, screwed into the coolant jacket of the inlet manifold. When coolant temperature reaches 50°C (122°F), the sensor switches the manifold heater off. To avoid a heavy drain on the battery, current for the heater is supplied via the oil pressure switch relay, and consequently only switches on after the engine has started.

Fuel pressure regulator: The fuel pressure regulator is attached to the throttle body, and maintains fuel pressure at a constant 1.0 bar (14.5 lbf/in²). When the pressure exceeds this value, the regulator returns excess fuel to the tank via the fuel return line.

Inertia switch: An inertia switch is fitted in the ignition switch feed to the fuel pump relay, and is situated inside the car behind the left-hand side of the radio cassette player. In the event of sudden impact, the switch trips out, thus switching off the fuel pump relay. The switch can be reset by pressing down the reset button on the switch body.

Relays: The main fuel system relay is energised when the ignition is switched on, and supplies current to the ignition coil and the fuel system ECU. The relay remains energised for approximately five seconds after the ignition is switched off, to enable the stepper motor to cycle to the correct position for engine starting. The fuel pump relay is energised when the oil pressure relay is de-energised by the low oil pressure switch. When the engine is cranking, the fuel pump is fed from the starter solenoid via the de-energised fuel pump relay.

Fuel pump: The fuel pump is a self-priming centrifugal unit, located in the fuel tank, and totally submerged in the fuel. Fuel is supplied under pressure from the pump, through a non-return valve and in-line filter, to the fuel pressure regulator, and then to the fuel injector. The high capacity output of the pump is reduced by a resistive wire in the harness which reduces the supply voltage.

Accelerator pedal switch: When the accelerator pedal is at rest, the pedal switch is closed, and a signal is sent to the ECU indicating that the engine is idling. On receipt of this information, the ECU selects the idle program from its memory, and automatic idle speed control via the stepper motor is implemented.

The fuel injection system works in the following way. When the ignition is switched on, voltage is supplied to the main fuel system relay and to the ECU. The ECU relay is energised and voltage is supplied to the fuel injector, the ignition coil and to the stepper motor. This causes the stepper motor to cycle to the fast idle position (providing that the engine has cooled since last being run), and the throttle is opened by the stepper motor pushrod.

When the starter is operated, voltage is supplied to the fuel pump via the starter solenoid, and the various sensors send data on engine cranking speed, coolant temperarure, inlet air temperature and manifold pressure. From this data, the ECU calculates the amount of fuel required and the injector opening time. To provide fuel enrichment for starting, the injector-open time is extended above the normal rate for idling, but the number of pulses in which the injector opens are limited, to prevent flooding.

Once the engine starts and the solenoid is released, the ECU senses from the crankshaft sensor that the engine speed is in excess of 400 rpm. As the oil pressure builds up, the oil pressure switch opens, and the fuel pump relay is activated. The pump is now supplied with a lower voltage through the resistive wire in the harness. The open oil pressure switch also activates the manifold heater, which will operate until the coolant temperature reaches 50°C (122°F). Until the ambient air temperature sensor senses that air temperature has reached 14°C (57°F) the ECU will continue to extend the injector-open time to improve cold drivability.

During the warm-up period, the engine fast idle speed is controlled by the stepper motor. As the ECU senses engine temperature rise via the coolant thermistor, the stepper motor is allowed to progressively return to the idle speed setting. Should engine speed drop by more than 15 rpm from the idle setting, due for example to an additional electrical load on the alternator, the stepper motor will be operated to maintain a stabilised setting.

During normal driving, the ECU constantly monitors engine condition via the various sensors, and when a change in one or more of the input parameters is detected, the ECU program enters a sub-routine to determine the injector-open duration required. When the engine is accelerating, extra injector pulses are generated to compensate for throttle movement. Should the engine speed exceed 6700 rpm, the ECU will cut off the injector pulses until the speed falls to 6400 rpm, at which time they will gradually be re-instated.

When the engine is being restarted in a hot condition, the ECU provides extra fuel for two seconds after starting, and fast idle is instated via the stepper motor. This will counteract the possible effects of fuel vaporisation, and prevent engine stalling.

Under conditions of abrupt deceleration or impact, the inertia switch trips out, and breaks the supply voltage to the fuel pump relay. This cuts off the fuel supply, stops the engine and reduces the fire hazard.

11 Engine tuning – procedure

1   Before making any changes to the settings of the fuel injection system, ensure that the spark plug gaps are correctly set, the air cleaner element is clean, there are no leaks in the exhaust system, and the ignition system is operating correctly. Ensure that all breather and vacuum hoses are connected, and that none are perished or kinked.
2   Temperature effects, and engine and transmission oil drag, can adversely influence the base idle speed setting, and it is important that the following warm-up procedure is adopted before attempting any adjustments.
3   Drive the car on the road for approximately two to four miles, dependent on summer or winter conditions, in a normal manner, without excessive load, engine speed or road speed.
4   Return the car to the working area, switch off and connect a tachometer, following the equipment manufacturer's instructions.
5   Start the engine again, and run it at 2000 rpm for ten seconds to stabilise the mixture. The adjustment procedure described in the following Section can now commence. If during the procedure the cooling fan operates, or if adjustment is not completed within two minutes, accelerate the engine to 2000 rpm again, by means of the throttle linkage (not the accelerator pedal) and hold this speed for a further ten seconds. Repeat this every two minutes until the adjustments are completed.

12 Base idle speed and mixture – adjustment

Note: *The function of the fuel injection system is such that the base idle speed and idle mixture settings are controlled by the electronic control unit, and of these two, only the base idle speed can be adjusted without the use of the manufacturer's test equipment. The idle mixture setting will not normally require attention unless the battery is disconnected, in which case the settings in the ECU memory will be lost. If the battery is disconnected for any reason, the ECU can be recalibrated using the procedure described in Section 13 as a temporary measure. Should poor idle quality be experienced, the base idle speed should be checked, and if necessary adjusted, using the following procedure. If the idle quality is still poor after adjustment, the idle mixture should be checked by a dealer.*

1   Refer to the information contained in Section 11 before starting.
2   Switch off the engine, and ensure also that all electrical circuits are switched off throughout the procedure.
3   Undo the five bolts and lift off the air cleaner air box. Place the air box alongside the engine, without disconnecting any of the hoses or ducts.
4   Operate the throttle by hand, and check that it opens fully and returns to rest against the stepper motor pushrod.
5   Start the engine and using the throttle linkage, not the accelerator pedal, increase the engine speed to 1200 rpm, and hold it at this speed. Check that the stepper motor pushrod has retracted fully, then disconnect the stepper motor multi-plug (the round plug on the side of the throttle body below the accelerator cable).
6   Release the throttle and allow the engine to stabilise at idle speed.
7   Check the engine base idle speed on the tachometer, and compare the reading with the figure given in the Specifications. If adjustment is required, slacken the adjusting screw locknut and turn the adjusting

screw as necessary to obtain the correct setting (photos). Tighten the locknut when the speed is correct.

8   Check the lost motion gap by inserting a feeler gauge of the specified size between the forked end of the throttle lever and the peg on the linkage (photo). If the gap requires adjustment, slacken the accelerator cable locknuts and reposition the outer cable until the correct setting is achieved (photo). Tighten the locknuts when the gap is correct.

9   Reconnect the stepper motor multi-plug.

10   Switch off the ignition, wait three seconds and switch the ignition on once more. After a further three seconds, switch off the ignition again. The stepper motor will now be in the correct position for the next engine start.

11   On cars equipped with automatic transmission, refer to Chapter 7 and check the kickdown cable adjustment.

12   Refit the air cleaner air box on completion.

13 Electronic control unit – calibration

Note: *Whenever the battery is disconnected, the idle mixture setting stored in the ECU memory will be lost. On reconnection of the battery,*

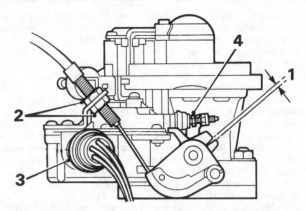

Fig. 3.6 Base idle speed adjustment (Sec 12)

1   *Lost motion gap*
2   *Accelerator cable locknuts for lost motion gap adjustment*
3   *Stepper motor multi-plug*
4   *Base idle speed adjusting screw*

12.7A Slacken the base idle speed adjusting screw locknut ...

12.7B ... and turn the adjusting screw (arrowed) to obtain the correct setting

12.8A Insert a feeler gauge between the throttle lever and peg ...

12.8B... then adjust the lost motion gap at the accelerator cable

the following procedure may be used to recalibrate the unit temporarily, until such time as the car can be taken to a dealer for accurate setting on Rover dedicated test equipment.
1   Run the engine with all electrical circuits switched off, until the engine cooling fan operates then stops.
2   Switch off the engine immediately the cooling fan stops.
3   Switch the ignition on to position two of the key.
4   Depress the accelerator pedal through at least half its travel, then release it, five times.
5   Wait until the high engine temperature warning light starts to flash.
6   As soon as the high engine temperature warning light stops flashing, start the engine **without depressing the accelerator pedal,** and allow it to idle. If the accelerator pedal is depressed, or if an electrical unit is switched on, the calibration will cease. (This also applies to the interior lights operated by the door pillar switches, so keep the doors closed.)
7   Wait for two to three minutes until the warning light flashes again, indicating that calibration is complete.

14 Thermac switch – removal and refitting

1   Refer to Section 3 and remove the air cleaner air box.
2   Disconnect the two vacuum hoses at the thermac switch on the base of the air box (photo).
3   Remove the air box intake trunking for access to the switch.
4   Carefully prise off the switch retaining clip, and remove the switch from inside the air box.
5   Refitting is the reverse sequence to removal, but position the unit so that the large diameter pipe is towards the air temperature sensor. Connect the vacuum hose from the manifold to the pipe with the small diameter hole, and the vacuum hose from the air cleaner vacuum motor to the pipe with the large diameter hole.

15 Inlet air temperature sensor – removal and refitting

1   Refer to Section 3 and remove the air cleaner air box.
2   Unscrew the sensor from the adaptor on the base of the air box. If

the adaptor unscrews with the sensor, unscrew the adaptor and refit it to the air box.
3   Refit the sensor to the adaptor, and refit the air box.

16 Throttle potentiometer – removal and refitting

1   Refer to Section 3 and remove the air cleaner air box.
2   Disconnect the multi-plug from the side of the potentiometer body.
3   Using a dab of paint, mark the position of the throttle potentiometer in relation to the mounting adaptor.
4   Undo the two screws, remove the potentiometer, and lift off the adaptor (photo).
5   Refitting is the reverse sequence to removal. Ensure that the potentiometer lever engages to the right of the throttle lever, and align the previously-made mark before tightening the retaining screws.
6   Have the potentiometer position adjusted accurately by a Rover dealer on completion.

17 Injector housing – removal and refitting

1   Refer to Section 4, paragraphs 1 to 3 inclusive, and carry out the operations described to release the fuel system pressure. Tighten the fuel filter banjo union bolt after the pressure has been released.
2   Refer to Section 3 and remove the air cleaner air box.
3   Using pliers, release the two fuel hose retaining clips at the injector housing, and disconnect the two hoses (photos). Plug the hoses after removal.
4   Disconnect the injector wiring multi-plug.
5   Undo the four screws securing the injector housing to the throttle body, and lift off the housing (photos). The housing may be initially tight, due to the two locating dowels. Recover the gasket from the throttle body.
6   This is the limit of dismantling that can be undertaken on the injector housing assembly. Should it be necessary to renew the fuel injector or fuel pressure regulator, a complete injector housing assembly must be obtained.
7   Clean the mating faces of the injector housing and throttle body,

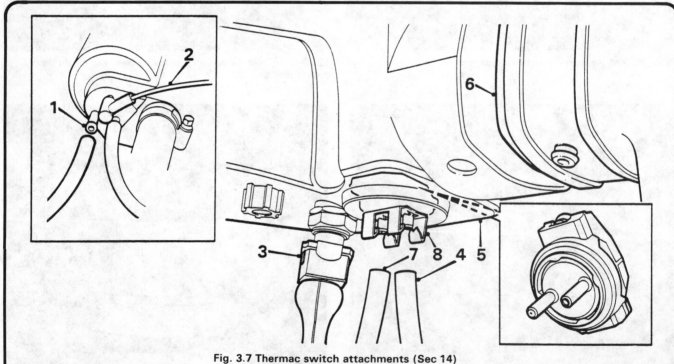

Fig. 3.7 Thermac switch attachments (Sec 14)

1 *Manifold vacuum connection to thermac switch*	2 *Manifold vacuum connection to fuel trap and ECU*	3 *Air temperature sensor multi-plug* 4 *Vacuum hose-to-air cleaner*	*vacuum motor* 5 *Air cleaner air box* 6 *Intake trunking*	7 *Vacuum hose to manifold* 8 *Switch retaining clip*

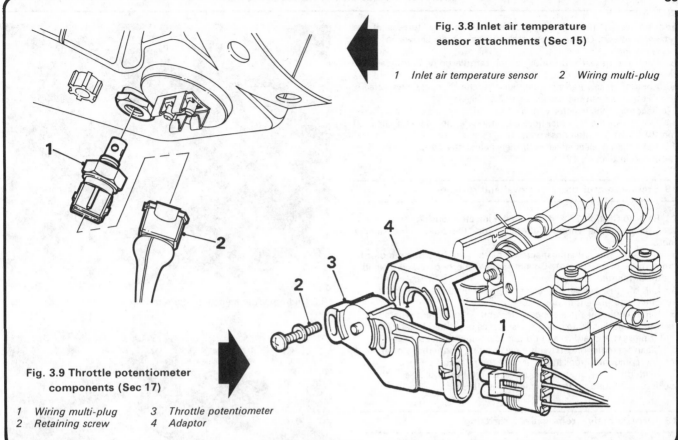

Fig. 3.8 Inlet air temperature sensor attachments (Sec 15)

1   Inlet air temperature sensor   2   Wiring multi-plug

Fig. 3.9 Throttle potentiometer components (Sec 17)

1   Wiring multi-plug   3   Throttle potentiometer
2   Retaining screw   4   Adaptor

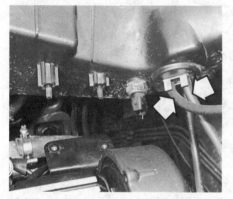

14.2 Thermac switch vacuum hoses (arrowed)

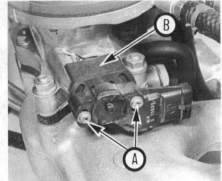

16.4 Throttle potentiometer retaining screws (A) and adaptor (B)

17.3A Release the fuel hose retaining clips (arrowed) ...

17.3B ... and disconnect the two hoses

17.5A Undo the four injector housing retaining screws (arrowed) ...

17.5B ... and lift off the housing

and remove all the old locking compound from the threads of the retaining screws. Obtain a new gasket if the original shows any signs of deterioration.

8   Place the gasket in position on the throttle body, and locate the injector housing over the gasket.

9   Apply a thread-locking compound to the four retaining screws, then fit and tighten the screws securely.

10   Reconnect the injector wiring multi-plug.

11   Reconnect the two fuel hoses, then locate the retaining clips 3.0 mm (0.12 in) from the hose ends.

12   Refit the air cleaner air box, then adjust the base idle speed as described in Section 12.

18 Stepper motor unit – removal and refitting

1   Refer to Section 17 and remove the injector housing.

2   Disconnect the wiring multi-plug from the side of the stepper motor.

3   Undo the four outermost screws that secure the stepper motor to the throttle body (photo). Do not remove the two screws near the centre of the unit.

4   Lift off the accelerator cable support bracket, with cable still attached, and place it to one side.

5   Carefully lift off the stepper motor unit (photo), and where fitted, recover the gasket. Note that the gasket was only fitted to early models, and if present, discard it, and do not fit another on reassembly.

6   Clean the components with a clean cloth, and remove all the old locking compound from the threads of the retaining screws.

7   Refitting is the reverse sequence to removal, but use a thread-locking compound on the retaining screw threads.

19 Throttle body – removal and refitting

1   Refer to Section 17 and remove the injector housing.

2   Disconnect the wiring multi-plugs to the stepper motor and throttle potentiometer.

3   Disconnect the two breather hoses on the side of the throttle body (photo).

4   Slacken the accelerator cable locknuts, open the throttle fully and slip the cable end out of the throttle cam. Unscrew the lower cable locknut fully, and remove the accelerator cable from the support bracket.

5   On automatic transmission models, disconnect the kickdown cable, using the same procedure as for the accelerator cable.

6   Undo the four nuts securing the throttle body to the manifold.

7   Lift off the throttle body, and recover the manifold spacer, with gaskets.

8   Clean the mating faces on the manifold and throttle body, and renew the gaskets on the spacer if they show any sign of deterioration. If the gaskets are being renewed, attach them to the spacer using non-drying jointing compound.

9   Place the spacer with gaskets over the manifold studs, then place the throttle body in position. Secure the throttle body with the four nuts tightened securely.

10   Reconnect the breather hoses and the wiring multi-plugs.

11   Refit the accelerator cable and adjust it, by means of the locknuts, to give a small amount of free play in the throttle-closed position.

12   On automatic transmission models, refit and adjust the kickdown cable as described in Chapter 7.

13   Refer to Section 17 and refit the injector housing.

20 Electronic control unit – removal and refitting

1   Disconnect the battery negative terminal. (Refer to Chapter 12, Section 1, before doing this).

2   Disconnect the wiring multi-plug from the ECU, which is located on the left-hand side of the engine compartment behind the battery. To do this, press the retaining tab upwards, release the bottom of the multi-plug, then disengage the top lug (photo).

3   Disconnect the vacuum supply hose.

4   Undo the two retaining screws, disengage the locating lug and remove the unit from its mounting bracket.

18.3 Undo the four stepper motor retaining screws (arrowed) ...

18.5 ... and lift off the stepper motor unit

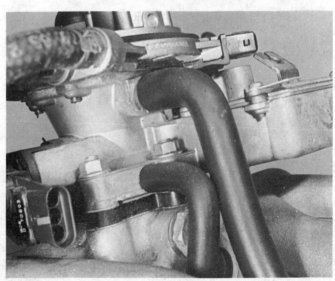

19.3 Breather hose attachments at the throttle body

5   Refitting is the reverse sequence to removal.

21 Resonator unit – removal and refitting

1   Apply the handbrake, jack up the front of the car and support it on axle stands.
2   Undo the two screws and one bolt securing the access panel to the underside of the front wheel arch on the left-hand side.
3   Disengage the access panel from the front spoiler, and remove it from under the car.
4   Undo the two bolts and withdraw the resonator from under the front wheel arch.
5   Remove the spacers and rubber mountings from the resonator.
6   Refitting is the reverse sequence to removal.

22 Inertia switch – removal and refitting

1   From inside the car, remove the stud from the centre console side cover on the left-hand side, and remove the cover.
2   Undo the two screws securing the inertia switch to the mounting plate, disconnect the wiring multi-plug and remove the switch.
3   Check the operation of the switch by striking the forward-facing side hard against the palm of your hand. The setting button should trip out when this is done. If not, renew the switch.
4   Refitting is the reverse sequence to removal. Press the button down to reset the switch after installation.

23 Manifold heater – removal and refitting

1   Disconnect the battery negative terminal. (Refer to Chapter 12, Section 1, before doing this).
2   Refer to Section 3 and remove the air cleaner air box.

20.2 Disconnect the ECU wiring multi-plug

3   Refer to Section 4, paragraphs 1 to 3 inclusive, and carry out the operations described to release the fuel system pressure. Tighten the fuel filter banjo union bolt after the pressure has been released.
4   Release the clips and disconnect the two fuel hoses at the injector housing.
5   Disconnect the manifold heater wiring connector.
6   Undo the two bolts securing the fuel pipe clips and the heater to the manifold, and move the pipes aside (photo).
7   Undo the remaining heater retaining bolt.
8   Open the throttle fully, and remove the heater by pushing down with a long screwdriver through the throttle aperture.

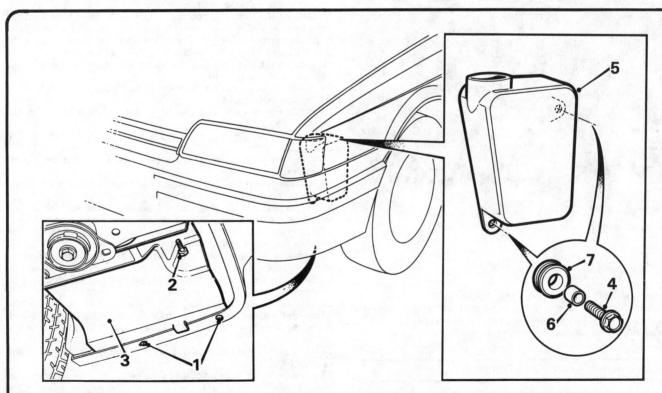

Fig. 3.10 Resonator unit location and mountings (Sec 21)

1 Access panel retaining screws	2 Access panel retaining bolt	4 Resonator unit retaining bolt	6 Spacer
	3 Access panel	5 Resonator unit	7 Rubber mounting

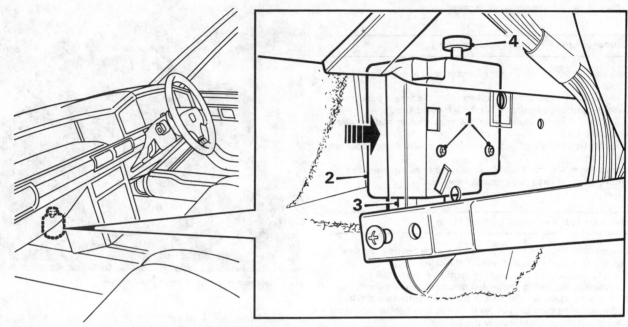

Fig. 3.11 Inertia switch location and mountings (Sec 22)

1   Switch retaining screws   2   Inertia switch   3   Wiring multi-plug   4   Setting button

23.6 Inlet manifold heater and fuel pipe clip retaining bolts

9   Remove the O-ring and gasket from the heater.
10   Clean the mating faces of the heater and manifold, and renew the gasket and O-ring if they show any sign of deterioration.
11   Refitting is the reverse sequence to removal.

24 Inlet manifold – removal and refitting

1   Disconnect the battery negative terminal. (Refer to Chapter 12, Section 1, before doing this).
2   Refer to Section 3 and remove the air cleaner air box.
3   Refer to Section 4, paragraphs 1 to 3 inclusive, and carry out the operations described to release the fuel system pressure. Tighten the filter banjo union bolt after the pressure has been released.

4   Release the hose clips and disconnect the two fuel hoses from the fuel pipes (photo).
5   Refer to Section 19 and remove the throttle body.
6   Refer to Chapter 2 and drain the cooling system.
7   Undo the brake servo banjo hose union at the manifold, and recover the two copper washers (photo).
8   Slacken the hose clip and disconnect the coolant hose from the right-hand end of the manifold (photo).
9   Disconnect the vacuum hoses from the left-hand end of the manifold, after noting their respective positions for reassembly.
10   Slacken the hose clip and disconnect the remaining coolant hose from the manifold (photo).
11   Undo the bolt securing the manifold to the support bracket under the coolant hose outlet.
12   Undo the bolt securing the upper end of the stay bar to the manifold.
13   Apply the handbrake, jack up the front of the car and support it on axle stands.
14   Undo the manifold stay bar lower retaining bolt and remove the stay (photo).
15   Release the clip and disconnect the breather hose from the oil separator (photo).
16   Disconnect the breather hose from the lower end of the oil separator at the cylinder block, and at the sump outlet (photos).
17   Disconnect the lead at the oil pressure switch and disconnect the pressure transducer lead at the wiring connector.
18   Unscrew the pipe union nut at the oil pressure switch adaptor.
19   Unscrew the bolt securing the oil pressure switch adaptor and oil separator to the cylinder block and remove the adaptor and oil separator.
20   Disconnect the wiring plug at the knock sensor on the cylinder block, and the two leads at the manifold heater temperature sensor under the manifold (photo). Move the wiring harness clear of the manifold.
21   Slacken the nine nuts and bolts securing the manifold to the cylinder head.
22   Remove all the bolts followed by the two nuts, then withdraw the manifold off the studs and remove it from the engine. Recover the manifold gasket.
23   Clean the manifold and cylinder head mating faces, and obtain a new gasket if the sealing lips of the original are in any way damaged.
24   Refitting is the reverse sequence to removal, but tighten the manifold retaining nuts and bolts in the sequence shown in Fig. 3.13, to the specified torque.

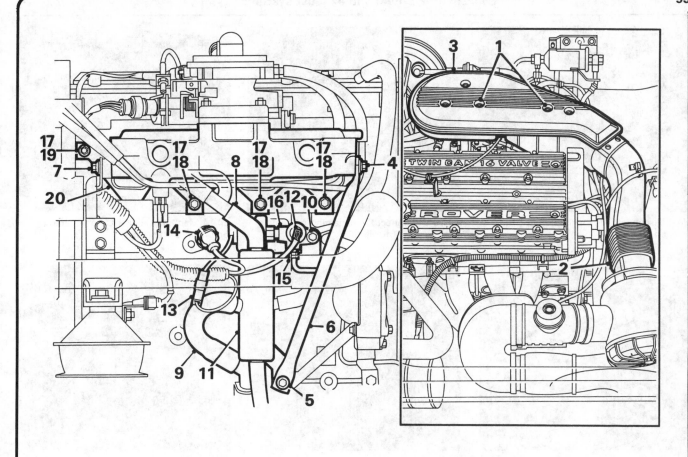

Fig. 3.12 Inlet manifold and related component attachments (Sec 24)

1 Air box retaining bolts
2 Intake trunking
3 Air box
4 Stay bar upper retaining bolt
5 Stay bar lower retaining bolt
6 Manifold stay bar
7 Manifold-to-support bracket bolt
8 Breather hose
9 Breather hose
10 Oil pressure switch adaptor, and oil separator retaining bolt
11 Oil separator
12 Oil pressure switch lead
13 Oil pressure transducer lead
14 Knock sensor wiring plug
15 Oil pipe union nut
16 Oil pressure switch adaptor
17 Manifold retaining nuts and bolts
18 Manifold bolt locations
19 Manifold nut locations
20 Manifold gasket

24.4 Release the clips and disconnect the fuel hoses

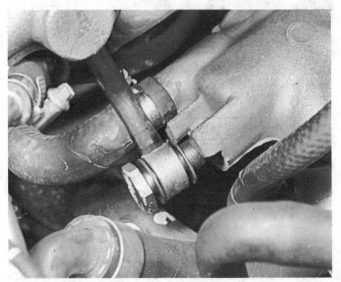

24.7 Undo the brake servo vacuum hose union

24.8 Disconnect the manifold right-hand coolant hose

24.10 Disconnect the remaining coolant hose from the manifold

24.14 Manifold stay bar lower retaining bolt location (arrowed)

24.15 Disconnect the breather hose (A) from the oil separator (B)

24.16A Disconnect the breather hose at the cylinder block ...

24.16B ... and at the sump

24.20 Disconnect the leads at the manifold heater temperature sensor

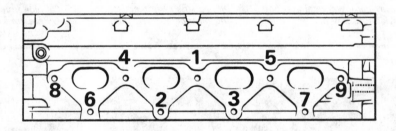

Fig. 3.13 Inlet manifold nut and bolt tightening sequence (Sec 24)

25 Exhaust manifold – removal and refitting

1   Disconnect the battery negative terminal. (Refer to Chapter 12, Section 1, before doing this).
2   Refer to Section 3 and remove the air cleaner components as necessary to provide total access to the front and side of the engine.
3   Drain the cooling system as described in Chapter 2.
4   Remove the dipstick from the dipstick tube.
5   Remove the distributor cap and place it to one side.
6   Apply the handbrake, jack up the front of the car and support it on axle stands.
7   Undo the four bolts securing the exhaust front pipe flange to the manifold (photo). Separate the flange and recover the gasket (photo).
8   Undo the bolts on both sides securing the two halves of the manifold stove together, and remove the outer half (photos).
9   Undo the bolt securing the heater bypass pipe to the cylinder head

and to the main coolant pipe support bracket (photos).
10   Slacken the clip securing the bypass pipe connecting hose to the thermostat housing.
11   Undo the five nuts and bolts securing the manifold to the cylinder head, noting that the upper nut also secures the bypass pipe bracket (photo).
12   Release the connecting hose from the thermostat housing, and withdraw the bypass pipe from the manifold stud.
13   Remove the manifold from the cylinder head, followed by the inner half of the stove and the manifold gasket (photos).
14   Clean the manifold and cylinder head mating faces, and obtain a new gasket if the original is in any way damaged.
15   Refitting is the reverse sequence to removal, but tighten the manifold retaining nuts and bolts in the sequence shown in Fig. 3.15, to the specified torque. Make sure that the inner half of the stove is in position before fitting the manifold.

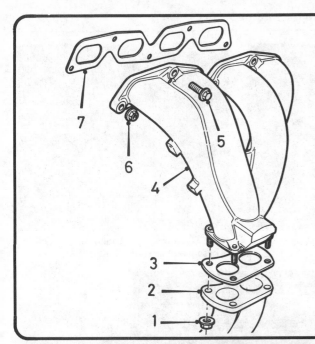

Fig. 3.14 Exhaust manifold attachments (Sec 25)

1 Front pipe flange retaining nuts
2 Front pipe
3 Flange gasket
4 Exhaust manifold
5 Retaining bolts
6 Retaining nuts
7 Manifold gasket

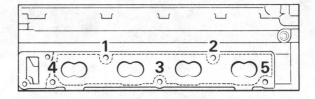

Fig. 3.15 Exhaust manifold nut and bolt tightening sequence (Sec 25)

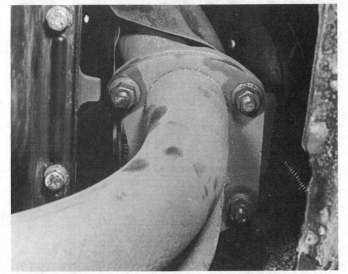

25.7A Undo the front pipe-to-manifold flange retaining bolts ...

25.7B ... and recover the gasket

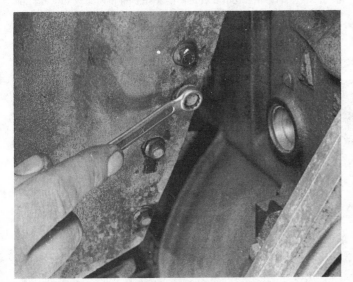

25.8A Undo the bolts on both sides of the manifold stove ...

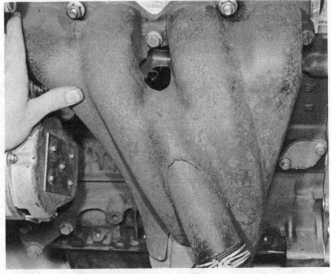

25.8B ... and remove the stove outer half

25.9A Undo the bolt securing the bypass pipe to the cylinder head (arrowed) ...

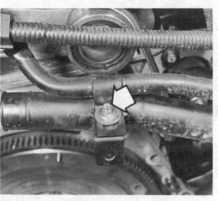

25.9B ... and to the main coolant pipe bracket (arrowed)

25.11 Undo the nut securing the front of the bypass pipe to the manifold

25.13A Remove the inner half of the manifold stove ...

25.13B ... and the exhaust manifold gasket

26 Exhaust system – checking, removal and refitting

1   The exhaust system should be examined for leaks, damage and security at regular intervals (see *Routine maintenance*). To do this, apply the handbrake, and allow the engine to idle in a well-ventilated area. Lie down on each side of the car in turn, and check the full length of the system for leaks, while an assistant temporarily places a wad of cloth over the end of the tailpipe. If a leak is evident, stop the engine and use a proprietary repair kit to seal it. If the leak is excessive, or damage is evident, renew the section. Check the rubber mountings for deterioration, and renew them if necessary.
2   To remove the system, raise the vehicle by means of axle stands or ramps to provide adequate working clearance underneath.
3   To remove the rear section, undo the three nuts securing the rear section to the intermediate section at the flange joint, and separate the joint (photo). Recover the flange gasket. Disengage the rubber mountings at the side and rear (photos), and remove the section from under the car.
4   To remove the intermediate section, undo the nuts securing the intermediate section to the front and rear sections at the flange joints (photo), and separate the joints. Recover the flange gaskets. Disengage the side rubber mountings and remove the section from under the car (photo).
5   To remove the front section, undo the nuts securing the front section to the manifold and intermediate section, separate the flange joints and remove the section from under the car. Recover the flange gaskets.
6   If necessary, the front and rear heat shields can be removed after removing the relevant exhaust section, then undoing the heat shield retaining bolts.
7   Refitting is the reverse sequence to removal, but use new gaskets if the originals show any sign of deterioration. Tighten the flange retaining nuts to the specified torque.

26.3A Exhaust rear section flange joint ...

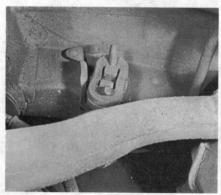

26.3B ... side rubber mounting ...

26.3C ... and rear rubber mounting

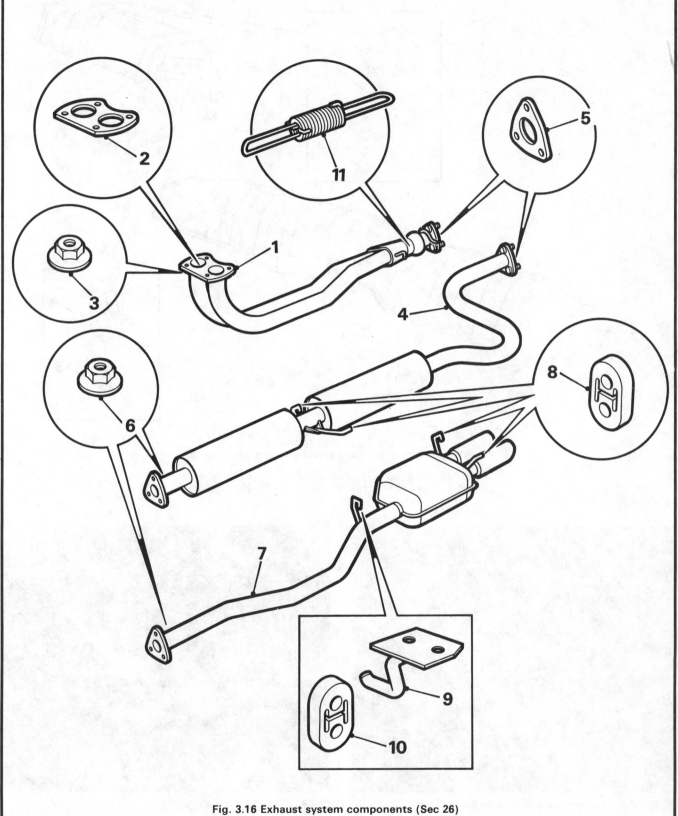

Fig. 3.16 Exhaust system components (Sec 26)

1	Front pipe	5	Flange gasket	9	Mounting bracket
2	Flange gasket	6	Locknut	10	Rubber mounting
3	Locknut	7	Rear section	11	Tensioning spring
4	Intermediate section	8	Rubber mountings		

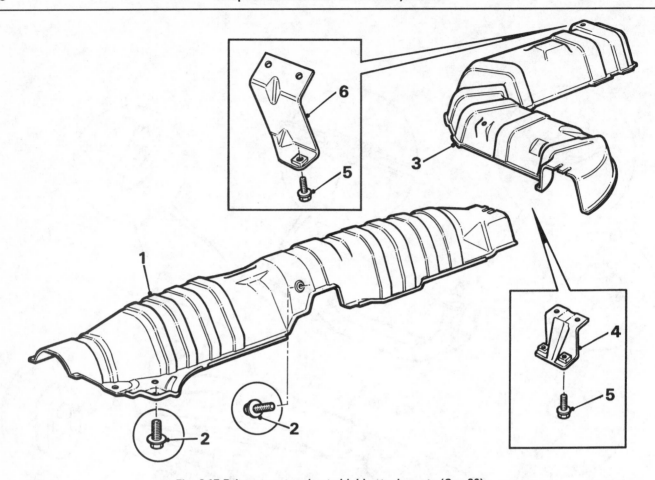

Fig. 3.17 Exhaust system heat shield attachments (Sec 26)

1	Front heat shield	3	Rear heat shield	5	Retaining bolts
2	Retaining bolts	4	Mounting bracket	6	Mounting bracket

26.4A Exhaust intermediate section flange joint ...

26.4B ... and rubber mountings

27 Fault diagnosis – fuel and exhaust systems (single-point fuel injection system)

Owing to the complexity of the electronic circuitry, and the nature of the computer-controlled operation, special test equipment has been developed for fault diagnosis on the fuel injection system. Therefore, any suspected faults on the system or its related components should be referred to a suitably-equipped Rover dealer.

PART B:
MULTI-POINT FUEL INJECTION SYSTEM

28 General description

The fuel system used on Rover 820i and Si models consists of a centrally-mounted fuel tank, electric fuel pump and indirect multi-point fuel injection (MPi) system, together with its related electrical and mechanical components. A more detailed description of the MPi system is contained in Section 37.

The exhaust system consists of a front, intermediate and rear section, suspended from the underbody on rubber mountings, and bolted to a cast iron manifold at the front. A ball-and-socket universal joint is incorporated in the front section, to allow for engine and exhaust system movement.

Warning: *Many of the procedures in this Chapter entail the removal of fuel pipes and connections, which may result in some fuel spillage. Before carrying out any operations on the fuel system, refer to the precautions given in* Safety first! *at the beginning of this manual and follow them implicitly. Petrol is a highly dangerous and volatile liquid, and the precautions necessary when handling it cannot be overstressed.*

29 Maintenance and inspection

1   At the intervals given in *Routine maintenance* at the beginning of this manual, carry out the following service operations on the fuel and exhaust system components.
2   With the car raised on a vehicle lift, or securely supported on axle stands, carefully inspect the fuel pipes, hoses and unions for chafing, leaks, and corrosion. Renew any pipes that are severely pitted with corrosion, or in any way damaged. Renew any hoses that show signs of cracking or other deterioration.
3   Check the security of the fuel tank mountings, and check the tank for signs of corrosion or damage. Refer to Section 34 if the tank condition is suspect.
4   Check the condition of exhaust system as described in Section 53.
5   From within the engine compartment, check the security of all fuel hose attachments, and inspect the fuel hoses and vacuum hoses for kinks, chafing or deterioration.
6   Renew the air cleaner element, and clean the air cleaner body and cover, as described in Section 30.
7   Check the operation of the accelerator linkage, and lubricate the linkage, cable and pedal pivot with a few drops of oil.
8   Renew the fuel filter as described in Section 31.
9   Check the fuel injection system base idle speed and mixture settings as described in Section 39.

30 Air cleaner and element – removal and refitting

1   To renew the air cleaner element, disconnect the vacuum hose from the air cleaner body cover (photo), release the retaining spring clips and lift off the cover.
2   Withdraw the element from the body, and bend it upwards to clear the front body panel.
3   Using a clean rag, wipe out the inside of the body and cover.
4   Carefully fit the new element, ensuring that its centre is located over the lip at the base of the air cleaner body.
5   Refit the cover and clip it into place.
6   To remove the complete air cleaner assembly, slacken the hose clip and disconnect the air trunking at the throttle housing (photo).
7   Disconnect the airflow meter wiring connector, and release the cable from the support clip.
8   Undo the two air cleaner body and airflow meter support bracket bolts, and the two bolts securing the forward air trunking to its support bracket (photo).
9   Withdraw the air cleaner body, complete with airflow meter and forward air trunking, release the trunking from the connecting duct at the front of the car, and remove the assembly from the engine compartment.
10   If the cold air side intake is to be removed, refer to Chapter 12 and remove the battery.
11   Undo the bolt securing the side intake to the body, and remove the intake and duct.
12   Refitting is the reverse sequence to removal, but ensure that all the ducts and trunking are fully engaged before tightening the various retaining bolts.

31 Fuel filter – removal and refitting

Note: *Refer to the warning note in Section 28 before proceeding.*
1   Disconnect the battery negative terminal.
2   Place absorbent rags around the fuel filter outlet union banjo bolt, then slowly unscrew the bleed screw in the centre of the bolt to release the fuel system pressure. Tighten the bleed screw when the pressure is released.
3   Unscrew the filter inlet and outlet union banjo bolts, and recover the copper washers.
4   Undo the filter bracket retaining nuts and remove the filter.
5   Refitting is the reverse sequence to removal, but use new copper washers on the banjo unions.

32 Fuel pump – removal and refitting

Note: *Refer to the warning note in Section 28 before proceeding.*
1   Disconnect the battery negative terminal.
2   Release the fuel system pressure as described in Section 31, paragraph 2.
3   Remove the floor carpet from the luggage compartment.
4   Refer to Chapter 11 and remove the rear seats.
5   Release the eight studs and remove the seat squab backing from the body.
6   Release the two studs and remove the luggage compartment backboard from the body.

30.1 Disconnect the vacuum hose at the air cleaner body cover

30.6 Disconnect the air trunking at the throttle housing

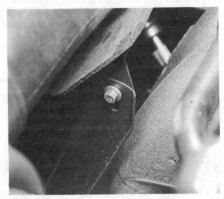
30.8 Forward air trunking-to-support bracket bolt

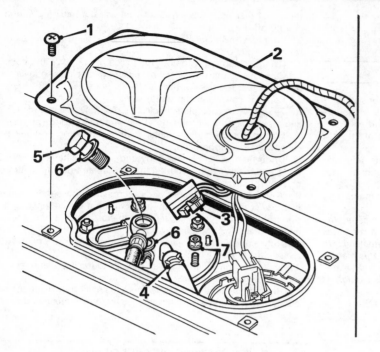

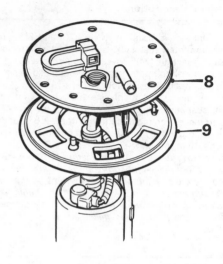

Fig. 3.18 Fuel pump and related component attachments (Sec 32)

1 *Access panel retaining* *screws*	4 *Fuel return hose*	7 *Pump retaining nuts*
2 *Access panel*	5 *Fuel feed hose banjo union* *bolt*	8 *Fuel pump*
3 *Pump wiring multi-plug*	6 *Copper washers*	9 *Pump seal*

7   Remove the cover board over the spare wheel, and remove the tool kit.

8   Undo the four screws and lift off the pump access panel. Move the panel to one side.

9   Disconnect the pump wiring multi-plug, then unscrew the fuel hose banjo union bolt and recover the copper washers.

10 Slacken the clip and disconnect the fuel return hose.

11 Undo the pump retaining nuts, and withdraw the pump from the tank. Remove the seal from the pump flange.

12 Refitting is the reverse sequence to removal, but renew the flange seal if it shows any sign of deterioration.

33 Fuel gauge sender unit – removal and refitting

Note: *Refer to the warning note in Section 28 before proceeding.*

1   Follow the procedure given in Section 32, paragraphs 1 to 8 inclusive, with the exception of paragraph 2.

2   Disconnect the two leads at the sender unit.

3   Engage a screwdriver, flat bar or other suitable tool with the lugs of the locking ring, and turn the ring anti-clockwise to release it.

4   Withdraw the locking ring, seal and sender unit.

5   Refitting is the reverse sequence to removal, but renew the seal if it shows any sign of deterioration.

34 Fuel tank – removal and refitting

Note: *Refer to the warning note in Section 28 before proceeding.*

1   Follow the procedure given in Section 32, paragraphs 1 to 8 inclusive.

2   Disconnect the fuel pump wiring multi-plug, and the two leads at the fuel gauge sender unit.

3   Remove the fuel tank filler cap.

4   With suitable sealed containers handy, undo the drain plug at the base of the tank, and drain the fuel into the containers. Recover the drain plug sealing washer. When all the fuel has drained, refit the plug, using a new sealing washer if necessary.

5   Chock the front wheel, prise off the rear wheel trim and slacken the

wheel nuts. Jack up the rear of the car and support it on axle stands. Remove the left-hand rear roadwheel.

6   Slacken the retaining clip and disconnect the filler hose from the filler neck. Move the hose aside.

7   Slacken the retaining clips and disconnect the five breather hoses from the breather pipes.

8   Refer to Section 53 and remove the exhaust system rear and intermediate sections, together with the rear heat shield.

9   Slacken the retaining clip and disconnect the fuel return hose from the pipe on the side of the tank. Plug the disconnected pipe and hose.

10 Undo the union connector and disconnect the fuel feed hose from the pipe. Plug the disconnected pipe and hose.

11 Support the tank on a jack with interposed block of wood.

12 Slacken the two tank retaining strap locknuts (photo), release the hook bolts from the body slots, and move the straps clear.

13 Lower the tank and remove it from under the car.

14 If the tank is contaminated with sediment or water, remove the sender unit as described in Section 34, and swill the tank out with clean fuel. If the tank is damaged, or leaks, it should be repaired by a specialist, or alternatively renewed. **Do not** *under any circumstances solder or weld the tank.*

15 Refitting is the reverse sequence to removal.

35 Accelerator cable – removal and refitting

1   Open the throttle fully by hand, and slip the inner cable end out of the slot on the throttle lever (photo).

2   Slacken the outer cable locknuts, and unscrew the outer locknut, nearest to the cable end, fully.

3   Remove the washer and rubber bush, then withdraw the cable from the support bracket.

4   From inside the car, release the turnbuckles and lift out the trim panel over the clutch, brake and accelerator pedals.

5   Prise the retaining clip from the top of the accelerator pedal, and disconnect the inner cable.

6   Release the cable from the engine compartment bulkhead, and from the support clips, and withdraw the complete cable from the car.

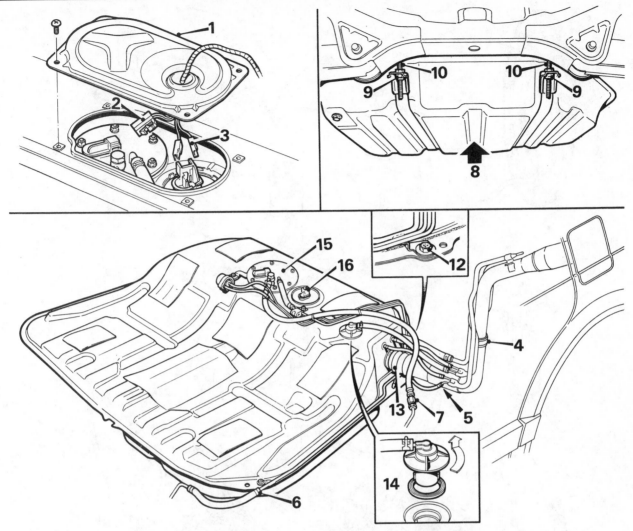

Fig. 3.19 Fuel tank components and mountings (Sec 34)

1	Fuel pump access panel	5	Breather hose	10	Hook bolts
2	Pump wiring multi-plug	6	Fuel return hose	12	Breather pipe support bracket
3	Sender unit wiring	7	Fuel feed hose union	13	Filler hose-to-tank connection
4	Filler hose-to-filler neck connection	8	Fuel tank	14	Cut-off valve
		9	Retaining strap locknuts	15	Fuel pump
				16	Fuel gauge sender unit

35.1 Accelerator cable end fitting attachment at the throttle lever (A) and outer cable locknuts (B)

7   Refitting is the reverse sequence to removal. Adjust the cable initially by means of the outer cable locknuts, to give a small amount of free play with the throttle closed. On completion, check the base idle speed as described in Section 39.

36 Accelerator pedal – removal and refitting

Refer to Part A, Section 9.

37 Multi-point fuel injection system – description and operation

The multi-point fuel injection (MPi) system is a microprocessor-controlled fuel management system, designed to overcome the limitations associated with conventional carburettor induction. This is achieved by continuously monitoring the engine using various sensors, whose data is input to the fuel system electronic control unit (ECU). Based on this information, the ECU program and memory then determine the exact amount of fuel necessary, which is then injected directly into the inlet manifold, for all actual and anticipated driving conditions.

The main components of the system are shown in Figs. 3.20 and 3.21, and their individual operation is as follows.

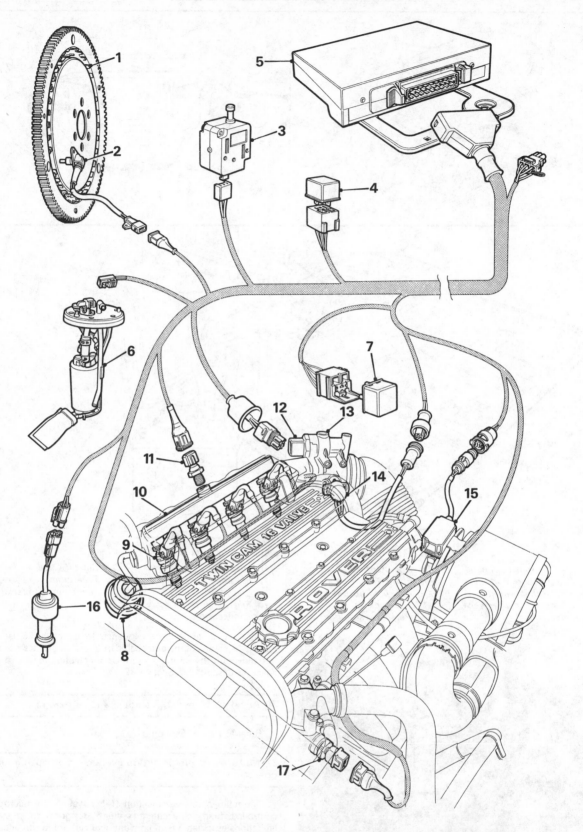

Fig. 3.20 Main components of the multi-point fuel injection system (Sec 37)

1 Flywheel reluctor ring
2 Crankshaft sensor
3 Inertia switch
4 Fuel pump relay
5 Fuel ECU

6 Fuel pump
7 Fuel system main relay
8 Fuel pressure regulator
9 Fuel injector
10 Fuel rail

11 Fuel temperature switch
12 Idle speed stepper motor
13 Throttle housing
14 Throttle potentiometer

15 Airflow meter
16 Speedometer transducer
17 Coolant temperature
    thermistor

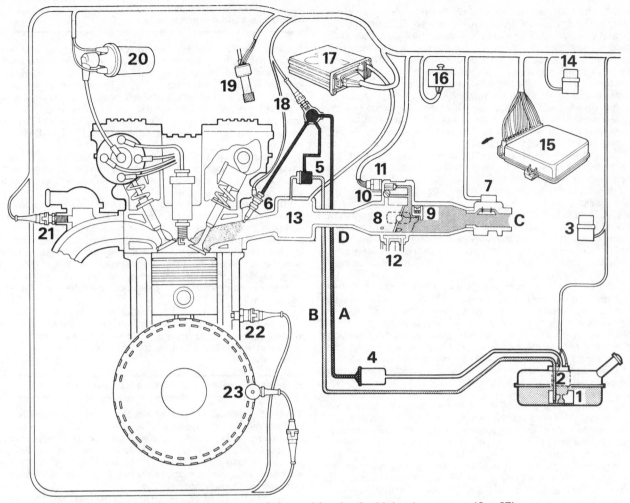

Fig. 3.21 Schematic layout of the multi-point fuel injection system (Sec 37)

1	Fuel return swirl pot	9	Base idle speed adjusting	14	Fuel system main relay
2	Fuel pump		screw	15	Fuel ECU
3	Fuel pump relay	10	Idle mixture adjustment	16	Inertia switch
4	Fuel filter		screw	17	Ignition ECU
5	Fuel pressure regulator	11	Idle speed stepper motor	18	Fuel temperature switch
6	Fuel injectors	12	Coolant and crankcase	19	Speedometer transducer
7	Airflow meter		breather ports	20	Ignition coil
8	Throttle potentiometer	13	Inlet manifold and plenum		
			chamber		

21	Coolant temperature thermistor
22	Knock sensor
23	Crankshaft sensor
A	Regulated fuel pressure
B	Return fuel
C	Inlet airflow
D	Manifold vacuum

Fuel ECU: The fuel ECU is a microprocessor, which controls the entire operation of the fuel system. Contained in the ECU memory is a program which controls the fuel supply to the injectors, and their opening duration. The program enters sub-routines to alter these parameters, according to inputs from the other components of the system. In addition to this, the engine idle speed is also controlled by the ECU, which uses a stepper motor to open or close an air valve as required.

Fuel injectors: Each fuel injector consists of a solenoid-operated needle valve, which opens under commands from the fuel ECU. Fuel from the fuel rail is then delivered through the injector nozzle into the inlet manifold.

Coolant temperature thermistor: This resistive device is screwed into the thermostat housing, where its element is in direct contact with the engine coolant. Changes in coolant temperature are detected by the ECU as a change in thermistor resistance.

Airflow meter: The airflow meter contains two resistive elements mounted in the intake air stream, one of which is heated by a current passing through it. Air passing over the heated wire alters its resistance by cooling it, while the temperature of the air is sensed by the other wire. An electronic module within the airflow meter monitors the reaction of the elements to the airflow, and provides a proportional signal to the fuel ECU.

Throttle potentiometer: The potentiometer is a variable resistor, attached to the throttle shaft in the throttle housing. The unit is supplied with a constant input voltage, and as the resistance of the potentiometer varies with throttle shaft movement, the output voltage is proportionally affected. This allows the fuel ECU to determine throttle valve position, and rate of change.

Idle speed stepper motor: This is a small electric motor, having two control windings to enable it to rotate in either direction. Under a signal from the fuel ECU, the stepper motor will rotate in whichever direction is necessary, to open or close the air valve in the throttle housing. This allows air to bypass the throttle valve and maintain a stabilised idling speed.

Fuel pump: The fuel pump is a self-priming centrifugal unit, located in the fuel tank, and totally submerged in the fuel. Fuel is supplied under pressure from the pump, through an in-line filter, to the fuel rail and fuel pressure regulator.

Fuel pressure regulator: The regulator is a vacuum-operated mechanical device, which ensures that the pressure differential between fuel in the fuel rail and fuel in the inlet manifold is maintained at a constant value. As manifold depression increases, the regulated fuel pressure is reduced in direct proportion. When fuel pressure in the fuel rail exceeds the regulator setting, the regulator opens to allow fuel to return via the return line to the tank.

Relays: The main relay is energised when the ignition is switched on, and provides the fuel ECU supply voltage. The fuel relay is energised by the fuel ECU for a short period after the ignition is initially switched on, and then continuously when the engine is running.

Fuel temperature switch: The fuel temperature switch contacts remain open during normal engine operation, and only close when the temperature of the fuel in the fuel rail exceeds a preset value. When the contacts close, a signal is sent to the fuel ECU, overriding the coolant thermistor signal. The ECU then alters the opening duration of the injectors accordingly, to minimise the effects of fuel vaporisation.

Inertia switch: The switch is a mechanically-controlled accelerator, connected in the electrical circuit between the ignition switch and the fuel ECU and fuel relay. Under violent deceleration or impact, the switch trips out, and cuts off the supply voltage. Depressing a button on the switch body resets the switch.

The fuel injection system works in the following way. When the ignition is switched on, a voltage is supplied via the inertia switch to the main relay and fuel ECU. The ECU energises the fuel pump relay, and voltage is supplied to the pump. The pump is allowed to run for a short period of time to pressurise the system. Excess fuel is returned to the tank by the action of the fuel pressure regulator. At the same time, the stepper motor cycles to close off the air valve, thus maintaining a richer mixture for starting.

When the starter is operated, voltage is supplied directly to the fuel pump, bypassing the fuel pump relay. Inputs to the fuel ECU from the road speed transducer, coolant temperature thermistor, throttle potentiometer, airflow meter and ignition ECU enables the fuel ECU to establish the amount of fuel required, and the injector opening duration, to allow the engine to start and run. During starting, the injectors operate simultaneously, and at each ignition pulse, so that fuel is sprayed into the inlet manifold at twice the normal rate, giving the necessary enrichment for starting.

When the engine fires and runs, the supply voltage for the fuel pump is diverted back through the fuel pump relay. During engine idling, the fuel ECU modifies the injector opening duration and fuel supply rate, according to data received from the various sensors. Additionally, the stepper motor cycles as necessary to open or close the air valve, to maintain a stablised idling speed.

During normal driving, any changes in the information from the sensors causes the fuel ECU program to enter a sub-routine, and determine the new fuel supply and injector opening durations accordingly.

During full throttle acceleration, the injectors are held open for a longer duration, thus providing the necessary enrichment to avoid hesitation. Under overrun conditions, the fuel supply is cut off by the fuel ECU, providing the engine has reached a predetermined temperature, and the accelerator pedal is released. When the engine speed decreases, or the accelerator pedal is depressed, the fuel supply is gradually re-instated to eliminate hesitation.

During hot start conditions, inputs to the fuel ECU from the coolant temperature thermistor and fuel temperature switch cause the fuel ECU to alter the injector opening duration accordingly, to counteract vaporisation.

Under conditions of abrupt deceleration or impact, the inertia switch opens, and breaks the system supply voltage. This shuts down the fuel system, stops the engine, and reduces the fire hazard.

38 Engine tuning – procedure

1   Before making any changes to the settings of the fuel injection system, ensure that the spark plug gaps are correctly set, the air cleaner element is clean, there are no leaks in the exhaust system, and the ignition system is operating correctly. Ensure that all breather and vacuum hoses are connected, and that none are perished or kinked.

2   Check that there is at least 5.0 mm (0.20 in) of free play in the accelerator cable, and that the throttle lever rests against its stop in the released condition. Adjust the cable as described in Section 35 if necessary.

3   Temperature effects, and engine and transmission oil drag, can adversely influence the idle speed and mixture settings, and it is important that the following warm-up procedure is adopted before attempting any adjustments.

4   Drive the car on the road for approximately two to four miles, dependent on summer or winter conditions, in a normal manner, without excessive load, engine speed or road speed.

5   Return the car to the working area, and without switching off the engine, connect an exhaust gas analyser (CO meter) in accordance with the equipment manufacturer's instructions. The analyser should be warmed up, correctly calibrated and ready for immediate use. Commence the adjustment procedure described in Section 39 immediately.

6   If, during the adjustment procedure, the cooling fan operates, or if adjustment is not completed within two minutes, accelerate the engine to 2000 rpm, and hold this speed for ten seconds. Repeat this every two minutes until the adjustments are completed.

39 Base idle speed and mixture – adjustment

Note: *The fuel injection system is such that the engine idle speed and mixture settings are controlled by the fuel ECU. Unless a new component has been fitted, the idle speed or mixture screws have been tampered with, or the idle quality is unsatisfactory, no adjustment should normally be necessary. If, however, the settings are to be altered, an accurate exhaust gas analyser (CO meter), tachometer, and voltmeter will be required.*

1   Refer to the information contained in Section 38 before starting.

2   Switch off all electrical accessories, and ensure that they remain switched off throughout the adjustment procedure.

3   With the engine idling and the exhaust gas analyser connected, take a reading of the exhaust gas CO content. If this is not as given in the Specifications, hook out the tamperproof plug over the idle mixture adjustment screw (photo), and turn the screw clockwise to enrich the mixture, or anti-clockwise to weaken it as necessary.

4   With the CO content correctly adjusted, switch off the engine and connect a tachometer according to the equipment manufacturer's instructions.

5   Before adjusting the base idle speed, the stepper motor must be cycled to its fully-extended position, using the following procedure.

   (a)   Switch on the ignition

39.3 Idle mixture adjustment screw tamperproof plug (arrowed)

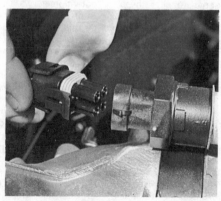

39.5 Disconnect the stepper motor wiring multi-plug

39.8 Base idle speed adjusting screw tamperproof plug (arrowed)

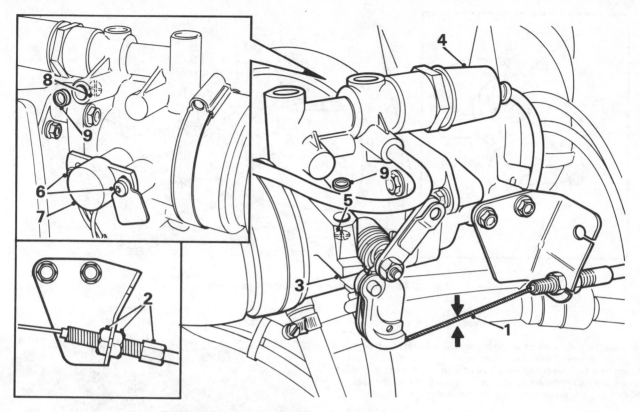

Fig. 3.22 Base idle speed and mixture adjustment (Sec 39)

1 Accelerator cable free play	4 Stepper motor multi-plug	6 Throttle potentiometer retaining screws
2 Cable locknuts for free play adjustment	5 Base idle speed adjusting screw	7 Throttle potentiometer
3 Throttle lever stop		

8 Idle mixture adjustment screw	9 Tamperproof plug

(b) Disconnect the stepper motor wiring multi-plug on the top of the throttle housing (photo)
(c) Switch off the ignition, wait five seconds, and reconnect the stepper motor multi-plug
(d) Switch on the ignition, wait five seconds, and disconnect the stepper motor multi-plug again
(e) Switch off the ignition, wait five seconds, and reconnect the stepper motor multi-plug
(f) Switch on the ignition, wait five seconds, and disconnect the stepper motor multi-plug once more. The stepper motor is now fully extended

6 Start the engine, and allow it to idle until normal operating temperature is again reached.
7 Check the reading on the tachometer, and compare this with the base idle speed figure given in the Specifications.
8 If adjustment is necessary, hook out the tamperproof plug over the idle speed adjusting screw (photo), and turn the adjusting screw as necessary to achieve the correct setting.
9 Increase the engine speed to 2000 rpm for ten seconds, then return it to idle.
10 Recheck the exhaust CO content, as described earlier in this Section.
11 Switch off the ignition, and pull back the dust cover over the throttle potentiometer wiring multi-plug.
12 Insert the probes from the voltmeter into the back of the multi-plug so that the voltmeter black lead is connected to the pink/black wire, and the red lead is connected to the light green/pink wire.
13 Select millivolts on the voltmeter, then switch on the ignition.
14 Check that the reading on the voltmeter scale is now equal to the throttle potentiometer voltage, as given in the Specifications. If this is not the case, slacken the two retaining screws (photo), and slowly move the potentiometer body until the correct reading is obtained. Tighten the screws securely.
15 Open and close the throttle several times, then with it closed, check the voltmeter reading once more. Repeat the adjustment if the reading

is now outside the specified tolerance.
16 With the adjustments complete, switch off the engine and disconnect the test instruments.

39.14 Throttle potentiometer retaining screws (arrowed)

40 Airflow meter – removal and refitting

1 Slacken the hose clip and detach the air trunking from the airflow meter.

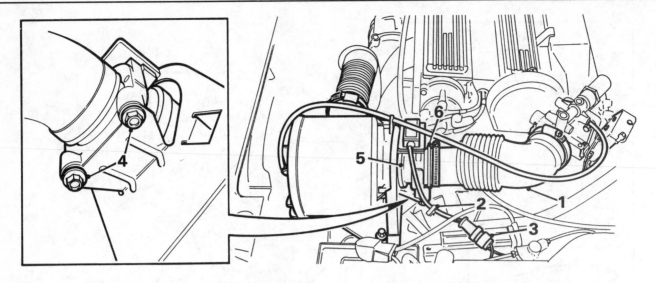

Fig. 3.23 Airflow meter attachments (Sec 40)

1	*Air trunking*	*3*	*Wiring multi-plug*	*5*	*Airflow meter*
2	*Wiring harness retaining clip*	*4*	*Retaining bolts*	*6*	*Seal location*

2   Release the airflow meter wiring harness from its retaining clip, and disconnect the wiring multi-plug (photo).
3   Undo the two bolts securing the unit to its mounting bracket, withdraw the unit from the air cleaner body, and recover the seal.
4   Refitting is the reverse sequence to removal.

41 Idle speed stepper motor – removal and refitting

1   Slide back the rubber dust cover (where fitted), and disconnect the stepper motor wiring multi-plug.
2   Using a 32 mm spanner, unscrew the stepper motor from the throttle housing.
3   Refitting is the reverse sequence to removal.

42 Throttle potentiometer – removal and refitting

1   Disconnect the throttle potentiometer wiring harness multi-plug.
2   Using a dab of paint, mark the position of the potentiometer in relation to the throttle housing, so that if the original unit is refitted, its position can be restored.
3   Undo the two screws, remove the unit from the throttle housing, and recover the gasket.
4   Refit the potentiometer and gasket, align the previously-made mark, then tighten the two retaining screws. If a new unit is being fitted, position it centrally within its adjustment range.
5   Adjust the base idle speed and mixture settings as described in Section 39.

43 Throttle housing – removal and refitting

1   Drain the cooling system as described in Chapter 2.
2   Slacken the hose clip and detach the air intake trunking from the throttle housing.
3   Disconnect the throttle potentiometer and stepper motor wiring multi-plugs.
4   Disconnect the air valve hose from the top of the housing (photo), and the breather hose from below.
5   Slacken the clips and disconnect the two coolant hoses from the housing.
6   Open the throttle fully by hand, and slip the accelerator inner cable end out of the slot on the throttle lever.
7   Slacken the outer cable locknuts, and unscrew the outer locknut, nearest to the cable end, fully.

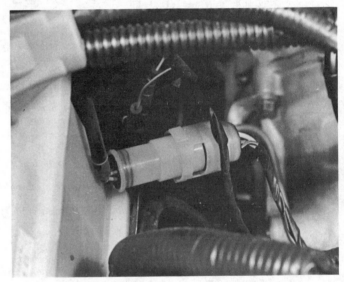

40.2 Airflow meter wiring multi-plug

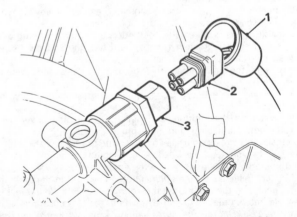

Fig. 3.24 Idle speed stepper motor details (Sec 41)

1	*Multi-plug dust cover*	*3 Stepper motor*
2	*Wiring multi-plug*	

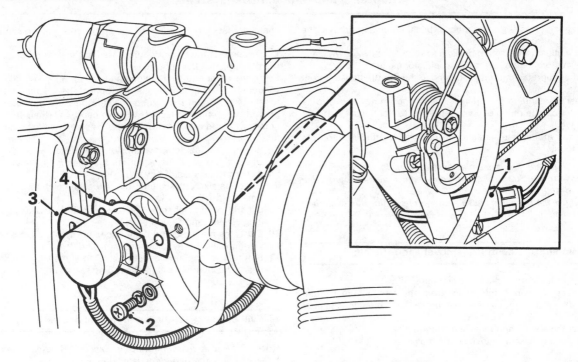

Fig. 3.25 Throttle potentiometer components (Sec 42)

1 *Wiring multi-plug*   2 *Retaining screws*   3 *Throttle potentiometer*   4 *Gasket*

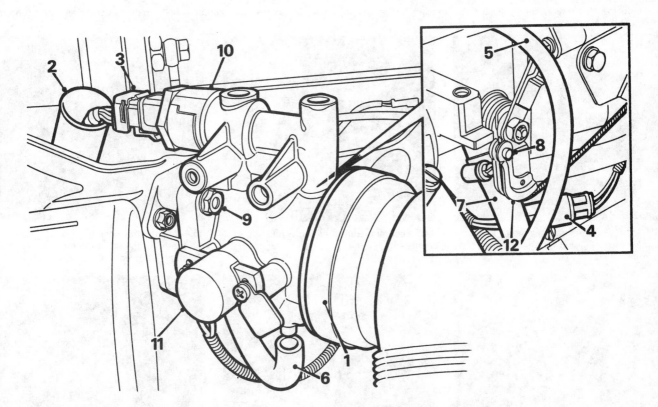

Fig. 3.26 Throttle housing components and attachments (Sec 43)

1 *Air intake trunking*	4 *Throttle potentiometer multi-plug*	7 *Coolant hoses*	10 *Stepper motor*
2 *Stepper motor multi-plug cover*	5 *Air valve hose*	8 *Accelerator cable end fitting*	11 *Throttle potentiometer*
3 *Stepper motor multi-plug*	6 *Breather hose*	9 *Throttle housing retaining nuts*	12 *Throttle lever*

8 Remove the washer and rubber bush, then withdraw the accelerator cable from the support bracket.

9 On automatic transmission models, disconnect the kickdown cable using the same procedure as for the accelerator cable.

10 Undo the four retaining nuts and remove the throttle housing from its mounting.

11 If further dismantling is required, the stepper motor and throttle potentiometer can be removed, with reference to Sections 41 and 42 respectively.

12 Refitting is the reverse sequence to removal, bearing in mind the following points:

   (a) Refill the cooling system as described in Chapter 2
   (b) On automatic transmission models, adjust the kickdown cable as described in Chapter 7
   (c) Adjust the base idle speed and mixture settings as described in Section 39

44 Fuel temperature switch – removal and refitting

1 Disconnect the battery negative terminal.

2 Disconnect the wiring multi-plug from the temperature switch, located in the centre of the fuel rail behind the plenum chamber (photo).

3 Unscrew the switch and remove it from the fuel rail.

4 Refitting is the reverse sequence to removal.

45 Plenum chamber – removal and refitting

1 Disconnect the battery negative terminal.

2 Slacken the hose clip and detach the air intake trunking from the throttle housing.

3 Undo the four nuts securing the throttle housing to the plenum chamber, ease the housing off the studs, and move it slightly to one side.

4 Disconnect the two vacuum hoses at the throttle housing end of the plenum chamber (photo).

5 At the other end of the plenum chamber, unscrew the brake servo vacuum hose banjo union bolt, disconnect the vacuum hose adjacent to the banjo union, and undo the fuel pressure regulator mounting bracket bolt (photo). Recover the two copper washers from the banjo union, and note that the hose locates between two locating pegs in its fitted position.

6 Remove the fuel temperature switch as described in Section 44.

7 Undo the two bolts securing the plenum chamber mounting brackets to the camshaft cover (photo).

8 Undo the six bolts securing the rear of the plenum chamber to the inlet manifold (photo).

9 Lift the plenum chamber off the manifold, and recover the four locating sleeves and O-ring seals.

10 Clean the manifold and plenum chamber mating faces, and renew the O-ring seals if they show any sign of deterioration.

11 Refitting is the reverse sequence to removal. Fit the locating sleeves to the manifold before the O-ring seals, and tighten all nuts and bolts to the specified torque.

46 Fuel pressure regulator – removal and refitting

Note: Refer to the warning note in Section 28 before proceeding.

1 Disconnect the battery negative terminal.

2 Place absorbent rags around the fuel filter outlet union banjo bolt, then slowly unscrew the bleed screw in the centre of the bolt to release the fuel system pressure. Tighten the bleed screw when the pressure is released.

3 Detach the breather hose from the camshaft cover, and move the hose aside (photo).

4 Disconnect the vacuum hose from the top of the regulator (photo).

43.4 Air intake trunking retaining clip (A), air valve hose (B), and throttle housing upper retaining nuts (C)

44.2 Fuel temperature switch wiring multi-plug

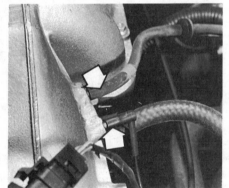

45.4 Vacuum hose connections at the throttle housing end of the plenum chamber (arrowed)

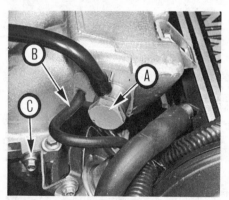

45.5 Brake servo vacuum hose banjo union (A), additional vacuum hose (B), and fuel pressure regulator mounting bracket bolt (C)

45.7 Plenum chamber mounting bracket-to-camshaft cover bolt (arrowed)

45.8 Plenum chamber-to-inlet manifold retaining bolts

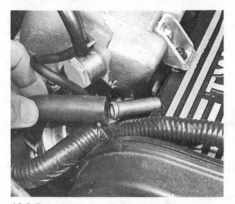

46.3 Detach the breather hose from the camshaft cover

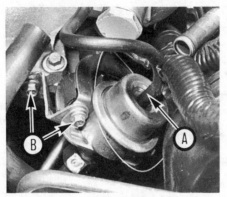

46.4 Fuel pressure regulator vacuum hose (A) and mounting bracket bolts (B)

48.3 Remove the ECU cover from under the driver's seat

5   Unscrew the fuel return hose union from the base of the regulator.
6   Undo the regulator bracket retaining bolts, and withdraw the regulator from the fuel rail.
7   Refitting is the reverse sequence to removal.

47 Fuel injectors – removal and refitting

Note: *Refer to the warning note in Section 28 before proceeding.*
1   Disconnect the battery negative terminal.
2   Place absorbent rags around the fuel filter outlet union banjo bolt, then slowly unscrew the bleed screw in the centre of the bolt to release the fuel system pressure. Tighten the bleed screw when the pressure is released.
3   Remove the plenum chamber as described in Section 45.
4   Remove the fuel temperature switch as described in Section 44.
5   Detach the breather hose from the camshaft cover, and move the hose aside.
6   Disconnect the fuel pressure regulator vacuum hose.
7   Undo the fuel pressure regulator mounting bracket bolts.
8   Undo the union nut, and disconnect the fuel supply hose from the fuel rail.
9   Undo the union nut, and disconnect the fuel return hose from the fuel pressure regulator.
10 Disconnect the multi-plugs from each of the four injectors.
11 Undo the two bolts securing the fuel rail to the inlet manifold.
12 Ease the four injectors out of their inlet manifold locations, and lift up the injector and fuel rail assembly. Recover the O-ring seal from each injector outlet.
13 Extract the retaining clips, and remove the injectors from the fuel rail. Recover the O-ring seal from each injector inlet.
14 Refitting is the reverse sequence to removal, but renew the injector inlet and outlet O-rings.

48 Electronic control unit – removal and refitting

1   Disconnect the battery negative terminal.
2   Slide the driver's seat fully forwards.
3   From under the driver's seat, undo the two screws and lift off the ECU cover (photo).
4   Undo the bolt securing the rear of the mounting bracket to the floor (photo).
5   Slide the driver's seat fully rearwards, and undo the two bolts securing the front of the mounting bracket to the floor.
6   Withdraw the ECU and mounting bracket assembly from under the seat.
7   Depress the multi-plug retaining tab, and pull the plug straight from the socket.
8   Remove the ECU from the car.
9   Refitting is the reverse sequence to removal.

49 Resonator unit – removal and refitting

Refer to Part A, Section 21.

48.4 ECU mounting bracket retaining bolt (arrowed)

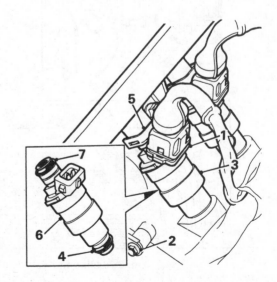

Fig. 3.27 Fuel injector and fuel rail details (Sec 47)

1 Injector multi-plug	5 Injector-to-fuel rail retaining
2 Fuel rail retaining bolt	clip
3 Fuel injector location on	6 Injector body
inlet manifold	7 Injector inlet O-ring seal
4 Injector outlet O-ring seal	

50 Inertia switch – removal and refitting

Refer to Part A, Section 22.

51 Inlet manifold – removal and refitting

1   Remove the fuel injectors, complete with fuel rail, as described in Section 47.
2   Release the clip and disconnect the breather hose from the oil separator.
3   Disconnect the breather hose from the lower end of the oil separator and the sump outlet.
4   Disconnect the wires at the oil pressure switch, oil pressure transducer and knock sensor.
5   Slacken the nine nuts and bolts securing the manifold to the cylinder head.
6   Remove all the bolts, followed by the two nuts, then withdraw the manifold off the studs and remove it from the engine. Recover the manifold gasket.
7   Clean the manifold and cylinder head mating faces, and obtain a new gasket if the sealing lips of the original are in any way damaged.
8   Refitting is the reverse sequence to removal, but tighten the manifold retaining nuts and bolts in the sequence shown in Fig. 3.13 and to the specified torque.

52 Exhaust manifold – removal and refitting

Refer to Part A, Section 25, but ignore the instructions to remove the manifold stove, which is not fitted to models with multi-point fuel injection.

53 Exhaust system – checking, removal and refitting

Refer to Part A, Section 26.

54 Fault diagnosis – fuel and exhaust systems (multi-point fuel injection system)

Refer to Part A, Section 27.

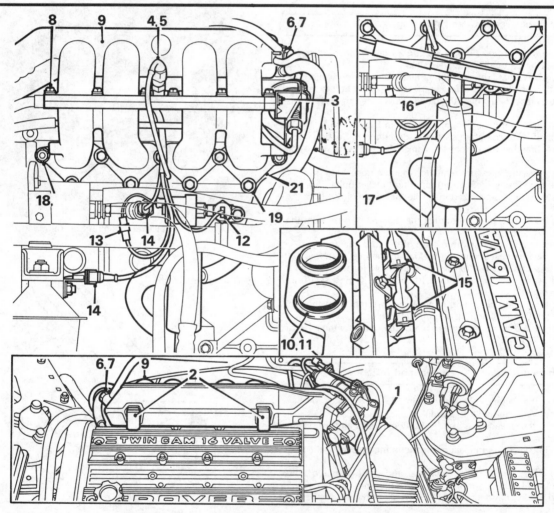

Fig. 3.28 Inlet manifold and related component attachments (Sec 15)

1 Air intake trunking	6 Brake servo vacuum hose banjo union bolt	11 O-ring seals	16 Oil separator upper breather hose
2 Plenum chamber mounting brackets	7 Banjo union copper washers	12 Oil pressure switch wire	17 Oil separator lower breather hose
3 Fuel pressure regulator mounting bracket bolt	8 Plenum chamber-to-inlet manifold retaining bolts	13 Oil pressure transducer wire	18 Manifold retaining nuts
4 Fuel temperature switch multi-plug	9 Plenum chamber	14 Knock sensor and crankshaft sensor wiring multi-plugs	19 Manifold retaining bolts
5 Fuel temperature switch	10 Locating sleeves	15 Fuel injector wiring multi-plugs	21 Inlet manifold

Chapter 4 Ignition system

Contents

Specifications

System type .... Programmed electronic ignition

Firing order .... 1-3-4-2 (No 1 at timing belt end)

Direction of rotor arm rotation .... Anti-clockwise

Ignition coil
Type .... Unipart GCL 141
Current consumption – engine idling .... 0.25 to 0.75 amps (average)
Primary resistance at 20°C (68°F) .... 0.71 to 0.81 ohms

Ignition timing*
Engines with single-point fuel injection:
  Vacuum connected .... 16° BTDC at ECU-controlled idle speed
Engines with multi-point fuel injection:
  Vacuum connected .... 22° to 28° BTDC at 1500 rpm
  Vacuum disconnected .... 12° BTDC at 1500 rpm
* Non-adjustable, for information only

Spark plugs
Type .... Unipart GSP 4662 or 3662, Champion RC9YC, or equivalent
Electrode gap .... 1.0 mm (0.040 in)

Torque wrench settings

	Nm	lbf ft
Spark plugs	18	13
Spark plug cover bolts	6	4
Crankshaft sensor bolts	6	4
Knock sensor	12	9
Ignition coil mounting bracket	24	18

1 General description

All models covered by this manual are equipped with a programmed electronic ignition system, which utilizes computer technology and electro-magnetic circuitry to simulate the main functions of a conventional ignition distributor.

A reluctor ring on the periphery of the engine flywheel, and a crankshaft sensor whose inductive head runs between the reluctor ring teeth, replace the operation of the contact breaker points in a conventional system. The reluctor ring utilizes 34 teeth spaced at 10° intervals, with two spaces, 180° apart, corresponding to TDC for Nos 1 and 4 pistons, and Nos 2 and 3 pistons respectively. As the crankshaft rotates, the reluctor ring teeth pass over the crankshaft sensor, which transmits a pulse to the ignition electronic control unit (ECU) every time a tooth passes over it. The ECU recognises the absence of a pulse every 180°, and consequently establishes the TDC position. Each subsequent pulse then represents 10° of crankshaft rotation. This, and the time interval between pulses, allows the ECU to determine accurately crankshaft position and speed.

A small bore pipe connecting the inlet manifold to a pressure transducer within the ECU supplies the unit with information on engine load. From this constantly-changing data, the ECU selects a particular advance from a range of ignition characteristics stored in its memory. The basic setting can be further advanced or retarded, according to information sent to the ECU from the coolant temperature thermistor and knock sensor.

With the firing point established, the ECU triggers the ignition coil, which delivers HT voltage to the spark plugs in the conventional manner. The cycle is then repeated many times a second for each cylinder in turn.

In addition to the above operations, many of the ignition system components have a second function in the control and operation of the fuel injection system. Further details will be found in Chapter 3.

Warning: *The voltages produced by the electronic ignition system are considerably higher than those produced by a conventional system. Extreme care must be used when working on the system with the ignition switched on, particularly by persons fitted with a cardiac pacemaker.*

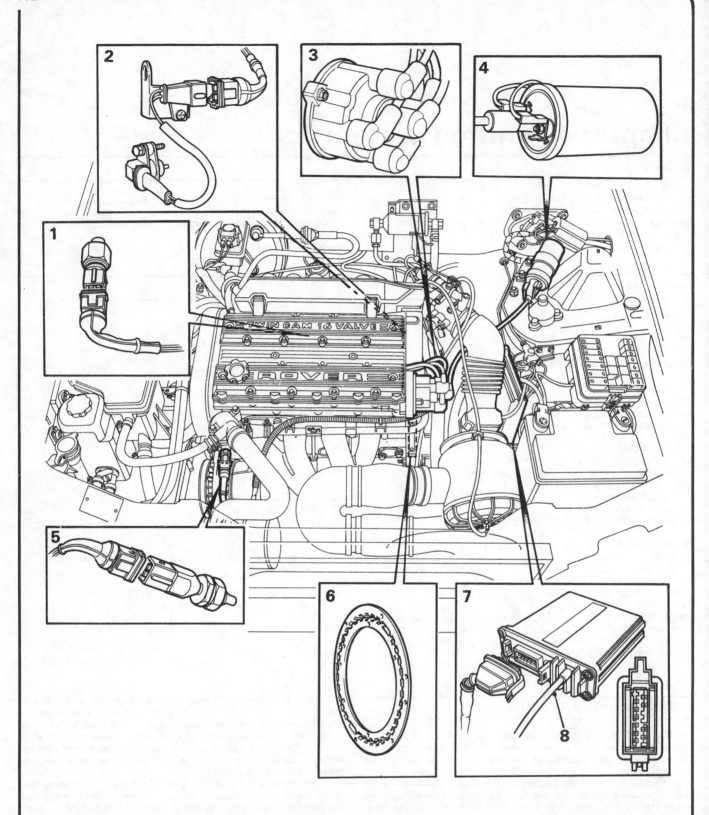

Fig. 4.1 Layout of the programmed electronic ignition system components (Sec 1)

1 Knock sensor
2 Crankshaft sensor
3 Distributor cap
4 Ignition coil
5 Coolant thermistor
6 Reluctor ring
7 Electronic control unit
8 Vacuum hose

2 Maintenance and inspection

1   At the intervals given in *Routine maintenance* at the beginning of this manual, remove the distributor cap and thoroughly clean it inside and out with a dry lint-free cloth. Examine the four HT lead segments inside the cap. If the segments appear badly burnt or pitted, renew the cap. Check the carbon brush in the centre of the cap, ensuring that it is free to move and that it stands proud of its holder.

2   Check all ignition wiring, cables and HT leads for security and cleanliness, and wipe them over with a clean rag if necessary. Pay particular attention to the wiring and HT lead connection at the coil tower. Dirt or moisture in this area can increase the likelihood of HT leakage due to arcing.

3   Remove, clean and reset, or renew, the spark plugs, using the procedure described in Section 9. It is recommended by the manufacturers that the spark plugs should be renewed every 24 000 miles (40 000 km) or two years, whichever occurs first. Practical experience has shown that this, in some circumstances, is considerably in excess of the practical working life of some makes of spark plug. In terms of performance and reliability, it may be considered beneficial to renew the plugs at the 12 000 mile (20 000 km), or 12 month, service interval.

4   This is the limit of routine maintenance necessary on the ignition system, as adjustment of the ignition timing, for example, is not necessary – nor is it possible.

3 Distributor cap and rotor arm – removal and refitting

1   Using an open-ended spanner, undo the two retaining screws and lift off the distributor cap from the cylinder head (photo). Clean and check the cap as described in Section 2.

2   If the cap is to be renewed, record the position of the HT leads in relation to the cap, then pull them off. Transfer the leads to a new cap, refitting them in the same position.

3   To renew the rotor arm, withdraw the plastic shield (photo), then undo the grub retaining screw using a suitable Allen key (photo). Withdraw the rotor arm from the end of the camshaft.

4   Refitting the rotor arm, shield and distributor cap is the reverse sequence to removal.

4 Crankshaft sensor – removal and refitting

1   Jack up the front of the car and support it on stands.

2   Disconnect the multi-plug from the crankshaft sensor wiring socket, attached to the gearbox/transmission adaptor plate on the rear-facing side of the engine.

3   Undo the retaining screw and remove the wiring socket from its mounting bracket.

4   Undo the two bolts securing the crankshaft sensor to the adaptor plate, and withdraw the sensor, complete with spacer and wiring socket.

5   Refitting is the reverse sequence to removal.

5 Knock sensor – removal and refitting

1   The knock sensor is located in the centre of the rear-facing side of the cylinder block, beneath the inlet manifold.

2   Jack up the front of the car and support it on stands.

3   Disconnect the wiring multi-plug, then unscrew the sensor from its location (photos).

4   Refitting is the reverse sequence to removal, but ensure that the sensor and cylinder block mating faces are clean.

6 Coolant thermistor – removal and refitting

Removal and refitting procedures for this component are contained in Chapter 2.

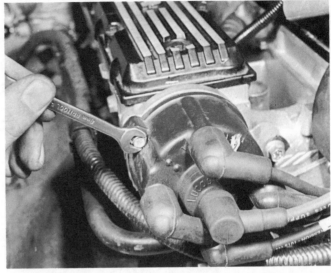
3.1 Undo the distributor cap screws using an open-ended spanner

3.3A Withdraw the plastic shield ...

3.3B ... then undo the rotor arm grub screw with an Allen key

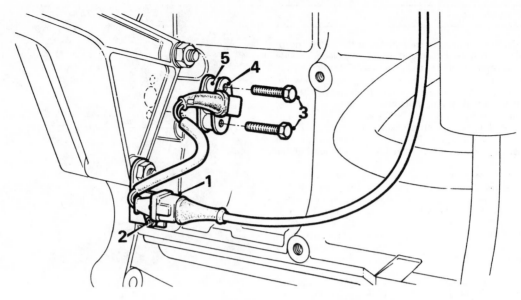

Fig. 4.2 Crankshaft sensor attachments (Sec 4)

1 Wiring multi-plug	*2 Wiring socket retaining screw*	*3 Sensor retaining bolts*
		4 Crankshaft sensor
		5 Spacer

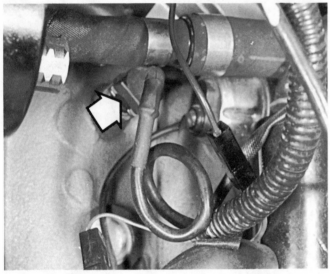

5.3A Disconnect the knock sensor wiring multi-plug (arrowed) ...

5.3B ... then unscrew the sensor

7   Electronic control unit – removal and refitting

Note: *The following procedure is applicable to engines with multi-point fuel injection. For engines equipped with single-point fuel injection, reference should be made to the procedures contained in Chapter 3.*

1   Disconnect the battery negative terminal.
2   Disconnect the wiring multi-plug from the electronic control unit (ECU), which is located on the left-hand side of the engine compartment, behind the battery. To do this, press the retaining tab upwards, release the bottom of the multi-plug, then disengage the top lug.
3   Disconnect the vacuum supply hose.
4   Undo the retaining screw, slide the unit out of its mounting bracket to disengage the retaining lug, and remove the ECU from the engine compartment.
5   Refitting is the reverse sequence to removal.

8   Ignition coil – general

1   The ignition coil is mounted on the left-hand side of the engine compartment, on the suspension strut tower.
2   To remove the coil, disconnect the LT leads at the coil positive and negative terminals, and the HT lead at the centre terminal.
3   Undo the mounting bracket retaining bolt and remove the coil.
4   Note the position of the positive and negative terminals in relation to the mounting bracket, then slacken the mounting bracket screw and slide out the coil.
5   Refitting is the reverse sequence to removal.
6   Accurate checking of the coil output requires the use of special test equipment, and should be left to a Rover dealer or suitably-equipped automotive electrician. It is however possible to check the primary winding resistance, using an ohmmeter as follows.
7   To check the primary winding resistance, disconnect the LT and HT wiring at the coil, and connect an ohmmeter across the positive and

negative LT terminals. The resistance should be as given in the Specifications at the beginning of this Chapter. If the resistance is not as specified, the coil should be renewed.

8 If the coil is to be renewed, ensure that the new coil is of the manufacturer's specified type for use in programmed electronic ignition systems. Failure to do so could cause irreparable damage to the electronic control unit.

9 Spark plugs and HT leads – general

1 The correct functioning of the spark plugs is vital for the proper running and efficiency of the engine. The spark plugs should be renewed at the intervals given in *Routine maintenance* at the beginning of this manual and section 2, paragraph 3 of this Chapter. If

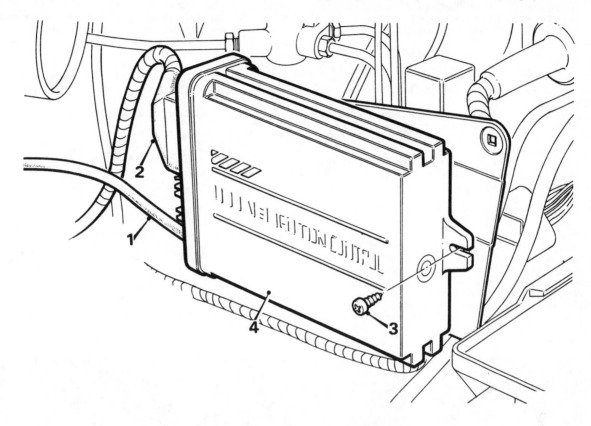

Fig. 4.3 Electronic control unit attachments (Sec 7)

1 *Vacuum hose*	2 *Wiring multi-plug*	3 *Retaining screw*	4 *Electronic control unit*

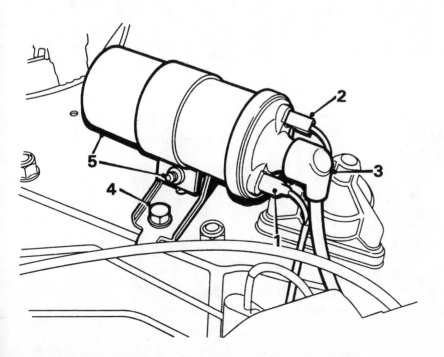

Fig. 4.4 Ignition coil details (Sec 8)

1 *LT negative lead*
2 *LT positive lead*
3 *HT lead*
4 *Mounting bracket retaining bolt*
5 *Coil-to-bracket retaining screw*

misfiring or bad starting is experienced within the service period, they must be removed, cleaned and regapped.

2   To remove the spark plugs, undo the two bolts securing the plastic spark plug cover to the centre of the cylinder head. Note the location of the accelerator cable support bracket on the right-hand bolt (photo).

3   Lift off the cover and release the HT cable support grommet from the distributor cap end (photo).

4   With the cover removed, withdraw the No 1 HT lead support clip from the lead and the retaining bolt stud (photo).

5   Mark the HT leads to ensure correct refitment, and carefully pull them off the plugs (photo).

6   Using a spark plug spanner or suitable deep socket and extension bar, unscrew each spark plug in turn and remove it from the engine (photo).

7   The condition of the spark plugs will also tell much about the condition of the engine.

8   If the insulator nose of the spark plug is clean and white, with no deposits, this is indicative of a weak mixture, or too hot a plug (a hot plug transfers heat away from the electrode slowly – a cold plug transfers it away quickly).

9   If the tip and insulator nose are covered with hard, black-looking deposits then this is indicative that the mixture is too rich. Should the plug be black and oily, then it is likely that the engine is fairly worn, as well as the mixture being too rich.

10 If the insulator nose is covered with light tan to greyish-brown deposits, then the mixture is correct, and it is likely that the engine is in good condition.

11 If there are any traces of long brown tapering stains on the outside of the white portion of the plug, then the plug will have to be renewed as this shows that there is a faulty joint between the plug body and the insulator, and compression is being lost.

12 Plugs should be cleaned by a sand blasting machine, which will free them from carbon more thoroughly than cleaning by hand. The machine will also test the condition of the plugs under compression. Any plug that fails to spark under test conditions should be renewed.

13 The spark plug gap is of considerable importance, as if it is too large or too small, the size of the spark and its efficiency will be seriously impaired. The spark plug gap should be set to the figure given in the Specifications at the beginning of this Chapter.

14 To set it, measure the gap with a feeler gauge, and then bend open, or close, the *outer* earth electrode until the correct gap is obtained. The centre electrode should *never* be bent, as this may crack the insulation and cause plug failure, if nothing worse.

15 To refit the plugs, first clean the seat area in the cylinder head, then screw the plugs in by hand initially, finally tightening to the specified torque. It a torque wrench is not available, tighten the plugs until initial resistance is felt as the sealing washer contacts its seat, and then tighten by a further quarter of a turn. Refit the HT leads in the correct order, ensuring that they are a tight fit over the plug ends. Refit the spark plug cover using the reverse of the removal sequence.

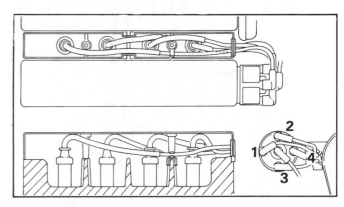

Fig. 4.5 Spark plug (HT) lead arrangement (Sec 9)

9.2 Accelerator cable support bracket location on spark plug cover

9.3 Release the HT cable grommet from the cover

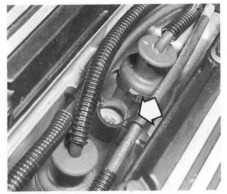

9.4 Withdraw the No 1 HT lead support clip (arrowed)

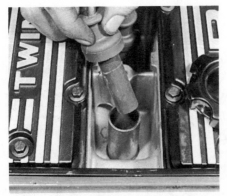

9.5 Carefully pull the HT leads off the spark plugs

9.6 Remove the spark plugs from the recesses in the cylinder head

Measuring plug gap. A feeler gauge of the correct size (see ignition system specifications) should have a slight 'drag' when slid between the electrodes. Adjust gap if necessary

Adjusting plug gap. The plug gap is adjusted by bending the earth electrode inwards, or outwards, as necessary until the correct clearance is obtained. Note the use of the correct tool

Normal. Grey-brown deposits, lightly coated core nose. Gap increasing by around 0.001 in (0.025 mm) per 1000 miles (1600 km). Plugs ideally suited to engine, and engine in good condition

Carbon fouling. Dry, black, sooty deposits. Will cause weak spark and eventually misfire. Fault: over-rich fuel mixture. Check: carburettor mixture settings, float level and jet sizes; choke operation and cleanliness of air filter. Plugs can be re-used after cleaning

Oil fouling. Wet, oily deposits. Will cause weak spark and eventually misfire. Fault: worn bores/piston rings or valve guides; sometimes occurs (temporarily) during running-in period. Plugs can be re-used after thorough cleaning

Overheating. Electrodes have glazed appearance, core nose very white — few deposits. Fault: plug overheating. Check: plug value, ignition timing, fuel octane rating (too low) and fuel mixture (too weak). Discard plugs and cure fault immediately

Electrode damage. Electrodes burned away; core nose has burned, glazed appearance. Fault: pre-ignition. Check: as for 'Overheating' but may be more severe. Discard plugs and remedy fault before piston or valve damage occurs

Split core nose (may appear initially as a crack). Damage is self-evident, but cracks will only show after cleaning. Fault: pre-ignition or wrong gap-setting technique. Check: ignition timing, cooling system, fuel octane rating (too low) and fuel mixture (too weak). Discard plugs, rectify fault immediately

10 Fault diagnosis – ignition system

Problems associated with the programmed electronic ignition system can usually be grouped into one of two areas, those caused by the more conventional HT side of the system such as spark plugs, HT leads, rotor arm and distributor cap, and those caused by the LT circuitry, including the electronic control unit and its related components.

The following checks are concerned with the HT side of the system, where the majority of ignition system problems occur. If, after carrying out these checks the fault still exists, then it will be necessary to seek the help of a Rover dealer, who will have the necessary dedicated test equipment to check accurately the remainder of the system.

Before carrying out any of the following tests, ensure that the battery terminals are clean and secure, and that the battery is fully charged and capable of cranking the engine on the starter motor. If this is not the case, refer to Chapter 12.

Engine fails to start

1   One of the most common reasons for bad starting is wet or damp spark plug leads and distributor cap. Remove the distributor cap. If condensation is visible internally, dry the cap with a rag and wipe over the leads. Refit the cap.

2   If the engine still fails to start, check that current is reaching the plugs, by disconnecting each plug lead in turn at the spark plug end, and holding the end of the lead about $3/16$ inch (5 mm) away from the cylinder block. Spin the engine on the starter motor.

3   Sparking between the end of the lead and the block should be fairly strong, with a regular blue spark. (Hold the lead with rubber to avoid electric shocks). If current is reaching the plugs, then remove them, and clean and regap them. The engine should now start.

4   If there is no spark at the plug leads, disconnect the HT lead from the centre of the distributor cap, and hold it to the block as before. Spin the engine on the starter once more. A rapid succession of blue sparks between the end of the lead and the block indicates that the coil is in good order, and that the distributor cap is cracked, the rotor arm faulty, or the carbon brush in the top of the distributor cap is not making good contact with the rotor arm.

5   If there are no sparks from the end of the coil lead, check the connections at the coil for security. If these are in order, check the coil primary resistance (see Section 8), which will give some idea of the condition of the coil, or preferably test by substitution of a new coil.

6   If all these checks have failed to highlight the problem, then the fault is likely to lie with the electronic control unit or its related components. It will therefore be necessary to refer the problem to a Rover dealer, as further checks can only be carried out using the manufacturer's test equipment and systematic checking procedure.

Engine misfires

7   If the misfire is regular and even, run the engine at a fast idle and pull off each of the plug HT leads in turn while listening to the note of the engine. Hold the lead with a dry cloth or rubber glove as additional protection against shock from the HT supply.

8   No difference in engine running will be noticed when the lead from the defective cylinder is removed. Removing the lead from one of the good cylinders will accentuate the misfire.

9   Stop the engine, remove the plug lead from the end of the defective plug and hold it about $3/16$ inch (5 mm) away from the block. Restart the engine. If the sparking is fairly strong and regular, the fault must lie in the spark plug.

10 The plug may be loose, the insulation may be cracked, or the electrodes may have burnt away, giving too wide a gap for the spark to jump. Either renew the plug, or clean it, reset the gap, and then test it.

11 If there is no spark at the end of the plug lead, or if it is weak and intermittent, check the HT lead from the distributor cap to the plug. If the insulation is cracked or perished, renew the lead. Even if the lead appears to be sound externally, there may be an internal break which will not be visually apparent. Substitute a known good lead for the suspect one, and repeat the checks.

12 If there is still no spark, examine the distributor cap carefully for tracking. This can be recognised by a very thin black line running between two or more electrodes, or between an electrode and some other part of the cap. These lines are paths which now conduct electricity across the cap, thus letting it run to earth. The only answer in this case is a new distributor cap.

13 Other causes of misfiring have already been described under the section dealing with failure of the engine to start. To recap, these are:

(a) The coil may be faulty giving an intermittent misfire
(b) There may be a damaged wire or loose connection in the low tension circuit
(c) There may be a fault in the electronic control unit

14 If all these areas appear satisfactory, then the fault may lie with the fuel system, or there may be an internal engine fault. Further information will be found in Chapters 3 and 1 respectively.

Chapter 5 Clutch

Contents

Specifications

Type	Single dry plate, diaphragm spring, hydraulically operated
Clutch disc diameter	215 mm (8.47 in)
Clutch fluid type	Hydraulic fluid to FMVSS 116 DOT 4 (Duckhams Universal Brake and Clutch Fluid)
Clutch pedal height	179.0 mm (7.0 in)

Torque wrench settings	Nm	lbf ft
Clutch cover to flywheel	26	19
Master cylinder retaining nuts	12	9
Fluid damper retaining nuts	12	9
Slave cylinder retaining bolts	22	16
Pedal bracket retaining nuts	12	9
Pedal bracket retaining bolt	25	18

1 General description

All manual transmission models are equipped with a single dry plate diaphragm spring clutch, operated hydraulically by a master and slave cylinder.

The clutch components comprise a steel cover assembly, clutch disc, release bearing and release mechanism. The cover assembly, which is bolted and dowelled to the rear face of the flywheel, contains the pressure plate and diaphragm spring.

The clutch disc is free to slide along the gearbox mainshaft splines, and is held in position between the flywheel and pressure plate by the pressure of the diaphragm spring.

Friction material is riveted to the clutch disc, which has a spring-cushioned hub to absorb transmission shocks, and to help ensure a smooth take-up of the drive.

The hydraulic components of the clutch mechanism consist of a master cylinder, mounted on the engine compartment side of the bulkhead in front of the driver, and a slave cylinder, mounted on the front of the gearbox. The two are connected by a hydraulic fluid pipe, incorporating a hydraulic damper for smooth operation. Hydraulic fluid is supplied by a combined brake and clutch fluid reservoir, mounted on the brake master cylinder. A short pushrod connects the clutch master cylinder to the pendant clutch pedal.

Depressing the clutch pedal moves the piston in the master cylinder forwards, so forcing hydraulic fluid through the hydraulic pipe to the slave cylinder, via the damper. The piston in the slave cylinder moves forward under the action of the fluid, and actuates the clutch release arm by means of a short pushrod. The opposite end of the release arm is forked, and is located behind the release bearing. As the release arm moves backwards, the release bearing moves forward to bear against the fingers of the diaphragm spring, so moving the centre of the diaphragm spring inwards. The spring is sandwiched between two annular rings, which act as fulcrum points. As the release bearing pushes the spring fingers in, the outer circumference pivots out, so moving the pressure plate away from the flywheel and releasing its grip on the clutch disc.

When the pedal is released, the diaphragm spring forces the pressure plate into contact with the friction linings of the clutch disc. The disc is now firmly sandwiched between the pressure plate and the flywheel, thus transmitting drive to the gearbox.

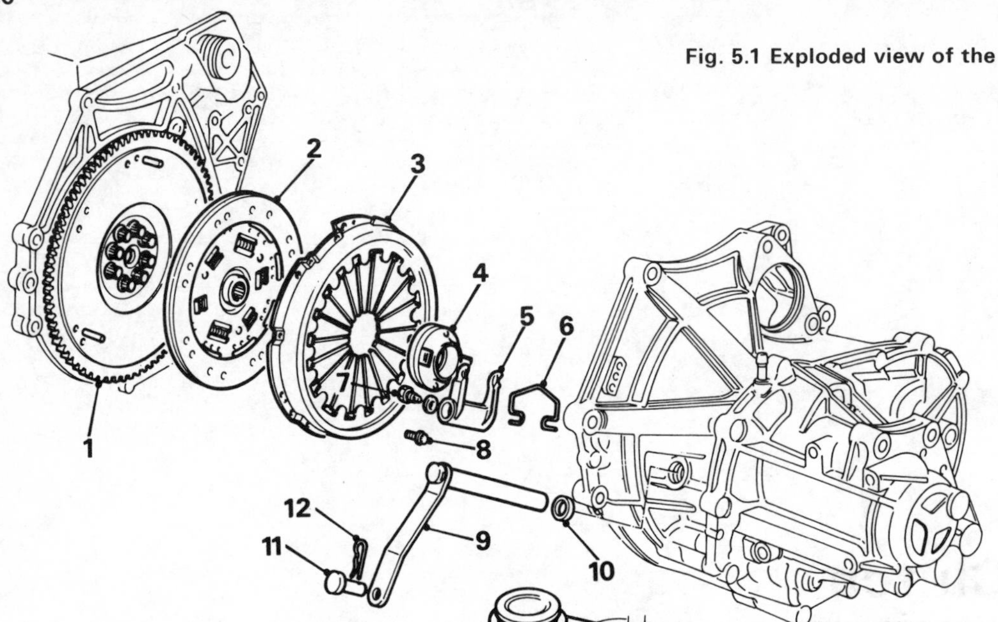

Fig. 5.1 Exploded view of the clutch components (Sec 1)

1 Flywheel
2 Clutch disc
3 Cover assembly
4 Release bearing
5 Release fork
6 Bearing spring clip
7 Release fork retaining bolt
8 Cover assembly retaining bolts
9 Release arm
10 Seal
11 Clevis pin
12 Spring clip

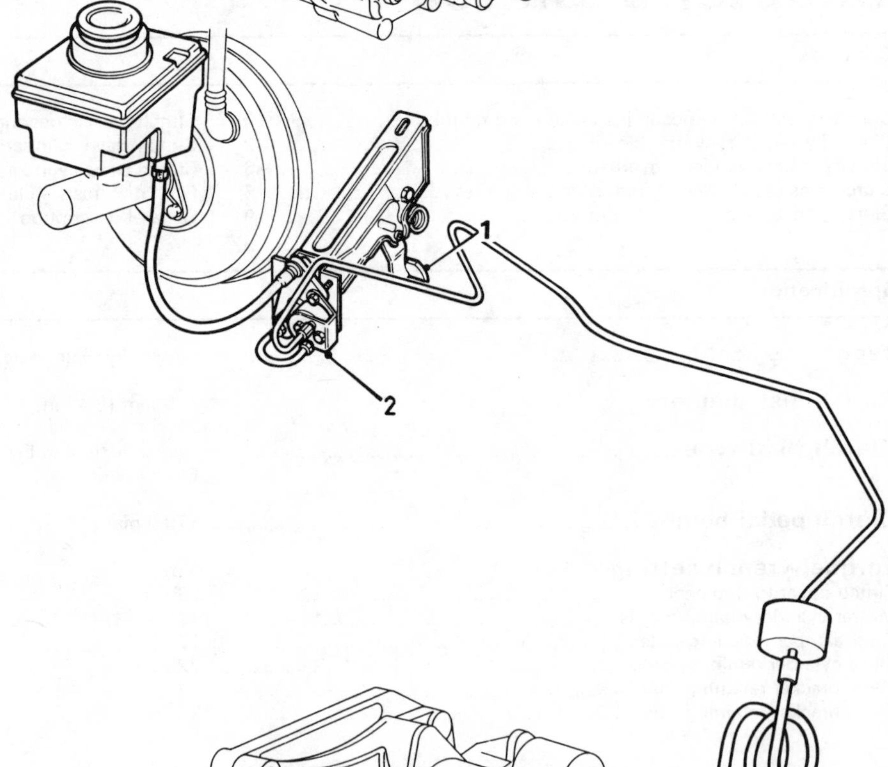

Fig. 5.2 Clutch component layout (Sec 1)

1 Clutch pedal
2 Master cylinder and damper
3 Slave cylinder
4 Release arm
5 Release bearing

2 Clutch hydraulic system – bleeding

1 Obtain a clean glass jar, a length of plastic or rubber tubing which will fit tightly over the bleed screw on the slave cylinder, a tin of the specified brake and clutch hydraulic fluid, and the help of an assistant. Alternatively, if a one-man brake bleeding kit is available, this can be used equally well for the clutch hydraulic system (see Chapter 9 for further information on these kits).

2 Check that the hydraulic fluid reservoir on top of the brake master cylinder is full, and top up if necessary. Also pour some fluid into the glass jar.

3 Remove the dust cap from the slave cylinder bleed screw, located on the lower front facing side of the gearbox (photo), and place one end of the rubber tube securely over the screw. Insert the other end of the tube into the glass jar, so that the end of the tube is below the level of the fluid.

4 Using a suitable spanner, slacken the bleed screw approximately one turn.

5 Have your assistant depress the clutch pedal, and hold it down at the end of its stroke. Close the bleed screw, then allow the pedal to return to its normal position.

6 Continue this series of operations (paragraphs 4 and 5) until clean fluid, without any trace of air bubbles, emerges from the end of the tubing. Make sure that the fluid reservoir is checked frequently to ensure that the level does not drop too far, thus letting further air into the system.

7 When no more air bubbles appear, tighten the bleed screw at the end of a downstroke and remove the tubing. Discard the expelled fluid, as it is unsuitable for further use in the hydraulic system.

8 Finally, check the level of fluid in the reservoir once more, top up if necessary, and refit the filler cap.

3 Clutch assembly – removal, inspection and refitting

1 Remove the gearbox as described in Chapter 6.

2 In a diagonal sequence, half a turn at a time, slacken the bolts securing the clutch cover assembly to the flywheel (photo).

3 When all the bolts are slack, remove them, and then ease the cover assembly off the locating dowels. Collect the clutch disc, which will drop out when the clutch cover is removed (photo).

4 With the clutch assembly removed, clean off all traces of asbestos dust using a dry cloth. This is best done outside or in a well-ventilated area; *asbestos dust is harmful and must not be inhaled.*

5 Examine the linings of the clutch disc for wear and loose rivets, and the disc for rim distortion, cracks, broken torsion springs, and worn splines. The surface of the friction linings may be highly glazed, but as long as the friction material pattern can be clearly seen, this is satisfactory. If there is any sign of oil contamination, indicated by a continuous, or patchy, shiny black discolouration, the disc must be renewed, and the source of the contamination traced and rectified. This will be either a leaking crankshaft oil seal or gearbox mainshaft oil seal – or both. Renewal procedures are given in Chapters 1 and 6 respectively. The disc must also be renewed if the lining thickness has worn down to, or just above, the level of the rivet heads.

6 Check the machined faces of the flywheel and pressure plate. If either is grooved, or heavily scored, renewal is necessary. The pressure plate must also be renewed if any cracks are apparent, or if the diaphragm spring is damaged, or its pressure suspect.

7 With the gearbox removed, it is advisable to check the condition of the release bearing, as described in the following Section.

8 To refit the clutch assembly, place the clutch disc in position with the raised portion of the spring housing facing away from the flywheel. The words FLYWHEEL SIDE will also usually be found on the other side of the disc that faces the flywheel (photo).

9 Hold the disc in place, and refit the cover assembly loosely on the dowels. Refit the retaining bolts, and tighten them finger-tight, so that the clutch disc is gripped, but can still be moved.

10 The disc must now be centralised, so that when the engine and gearbox are mated, the gearbox mainshaft splines will pass through the splines in the centre of the disc hub.

11 Centralisation can be carried out quite easily by inserting a round bar, or long screwdriver through the centre of the hub, so that the end of the bar rests in the hole in the centre of the crankshaft. Moving the

2.3 Clutch slave cylinder bleed screw and dust cap (arrowed)

3.2 Slacken the cover plate bolts in a diagonal sequence

3.3 Collect the clutch disc

3.8 Clutch disc marking

3.11 Using a clutch aligning tool to centralise the disc

bar sideways, or up-and-down, will move the disc in whichever direction is necessary to achieve centralisation. With the bar removed, view the clutch disc hub in relation to the hole in the centre of the crankshaft. When the hub appears exactly in the centre, all is correct. Alternatively, if a clutch aligning tool can be obtained, this will eliminate all the guesswork, obviating the need for visual alignment (photo).

12 Tighten the cover retaining bolts gradually, in a diagonal sequence, to the specified torque.

13 The gearbox can now be refitted, as described in Chapter 6.

4 Clutch release bearing – removal, inspection and refitting

1 Remove the gearbox as described in Chapter 6.

2 Disengage the ends of the retaining spring clip from the release fork, and slide the bearing off the gearbox mainshaft sleeve (photo).

3 Check the bearing for smoothness of operation, and renew it if there is any roughness or harshness as the bearing is spun.

4 If required, the release shaft and fork can be removed after undoing the bolt securing the fork to the shaft (photo). Slide the shaft out of the gearbox and recover the fork. Check the condition of the shaft and the oil seal, and renew any components as necessary.

5 Refitting is the reverse sequence to removal, but lubricate the shaft and mainshaft sleeve with molybdenum disulphide grease, and ensure that the retaining spring clip ends locate behind the release fork.

5 Clutch master cylinder – removal and refitting

1 From within the engine compartment, clamp the fluid supply hose from the fluid reservoir to the master cylinder, using a brake hose clamp, a G-clamp, or other similar tool. This will minimise fluid loss during subsequent operations.

2 Release the hose clip and disconnect the fluid supply hose at the master cylinder (photo).

3 Undo the union nut and disconnect the rigid fluid pipe at the upper connection on the damper. Release the retaining clip and carefully move the pipe aside for access.

4 From inside the car, release the turnbuckles and lift out the trim panel over the clutch, brake and accelerator pedals (photo).

5 Extract the retaining clip and withdraw the clevis pin securing the master cylinder pushrod to the clutch pedal (photo).

6 Undo the two nuts securing the master cylinder to the bulkhead, then remove the cylinder and damper assembly from the engine compartment. Recover the master cylinder-to-bulkhead gasket.

7 With the assembly on the bench, undo the two union nuts and remove the connecting fluid pipe between the cylinder and damper.

8 Undo the two nuts and separate the master cylinder from the damper.

9 Refit the master cylinder and damper using the reverse sequence to removal, then bleed the hydraulic system as described in Section 2.

10 After installation, it is advisable to check the clutch pedal height with reference to Fig. 5.4. To do this, measure the distance from the centre of the pedal pad to the floor (carpets removed), and if necessary alter the pedal position by slackening the locknut and turning the master cylinder pushrod. Tighten the locknut when the height is as specified.

6 Clutch master cylinder – overhaul

1 Remove the master cylinder as described in Section 5.

2 Ease back the rubber dust cover from the pushrod end, and then, using circlip pliers, release the circlip that retains the pushrod assembly. Lift out the pushrod complete with disc cover, circlip and washers.

3 Tap the end of the master cylinder on a block of wood to release the piston assembly complete with seals. Also withdraw the return spring

4.2 Removing the release bearing from the mainshaft sleeve

4.4 Clutch release fork-to-shaft retaining bolt (arrowed)

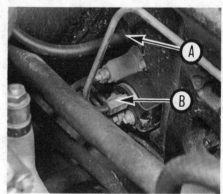

5.2 Fluid supply hose (A) and rigid fluid pipe connection (B) at the master cylinder

5.4 Interior trim panel retaining turnbuckles (arrowed)

5.5 Extract the clevis pin retaining spring clip (arrowed)

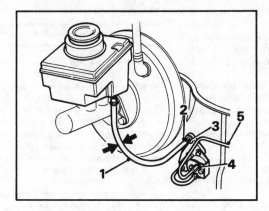

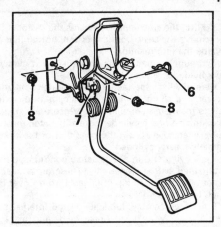

Fig. 5.3 Master cylinder attachment details (Sec 5)

1 *Fluid supply hose (arrows indicate clamping point)*
2 *Supply hose clip*
3 *Supply hose-to-master cylinder connection*
4 *Rigid pipe connection at fluid damper*
5 *Rigid pipe retaining clip*
6 *Clevis pin retaining clip*
7 *Clevis pin*
8 *Master cylinder retaining nuts*
9 *Master cylinder*
10 *Flange gasket*
11 *Connecting fluid pipe master cylinder union*
12 *Connecting fluid pipe damper union*
13 *Connecting fluid pipe*
14 *Damper retaining nut*
15 *Damper*

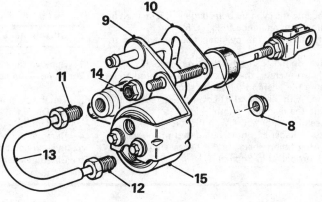

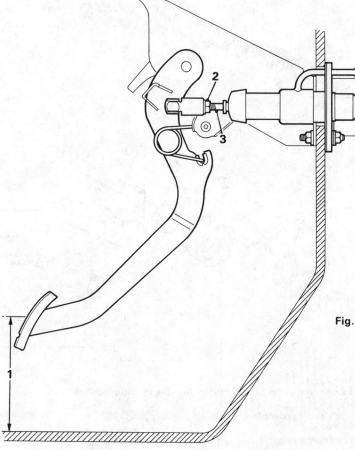

Fig. 5.4 Clutch pedal height adjustment details (Sec 5)

1 *Pedal height dimension = 179 mm (7.0 in)*
2 *Locknut*
3 *Pushrod*

noting that the small end is towards the piston.

4   Remove the seals from the piston, noting that their sealing lips are towards the return spring.

5   Thoroughly clean all the components in methylated spirit or clean brake fluid.

6   Carefully examine the internal cylinder bore and piston for scoring or wear, and all components for damage or distortion. In order for the seals to maintain hydraulic fluid pressure adequately without leakage, the condition of the cylinder bore and piston must be perfect. If in any doubt whatsoever about the condition of the components, renew the complete master cylinder.

7   If the cylinder is in a satisfactory condition, a new set of seals must be obtained before reassembly. These are available in the form of a master cylinder repair kit, obtainable from Rover dealers or brake and clutch factors.

8   Before reassembly, lubricate all the internal parts and the master cylinder bore with clean brake fluid, and make sure that they are assembled wet.

9   Insert the return spring into the cylinder bore, large end first, then fit the new seals to the piston with reference to Fig. 5.5.

10 Carefully insert the piston into the cylinder, taking care not to damage the seal edges.

11 If the rubber dust cover on the pushrod is to be renewed, it will be necessary to slacken, then unscrew, the locknut and pushrod fork. Before doing this, measure the pushrod length as shown in Fig. 5.5, and record this dimension. With the new dust cover fitted, reassemble the pushrod and reset it to the recorded length.

12 Refit the pushrod assembly, and secure with the circlip.

13 The assembled master cylinder can now be refitted to the car, as described in Section 5. After fitting check, and if necessary reset, the clutch pedal height (also described in Section 5).

7   Clutch slave cylinder – removal and refitting

1   Jack up the front of the car and support it on stands.

2   From within the engine compartment, clamp the fluid supply hose from the fluid reservoir to the clutch master cylinder, using a brake hose clamp, a G-clamp, or other similar tool. This will minimise fluid loss during subsequent operations.

3   From under the front of the car, unscrew the union nut and remove the fluid pipe at the slave cylinder (photo).

4   Extract the retaining spring clip, and withdraw the clevis pin securing the slave cylinder pushrod to the clutch release arm (photo).

5   Undo the two slave cylinder retaining bolts, and remove the cylinder from the car.

6   Refitting is the reverse sequence to removal, but on completion bleed the hydraulic system as described in Section 2.

8   Clutch slave cylinder – overhaul

1   Remove the slave cylinder from the car as described in Section 7.

2   Remove the pushrod from the cylinder, then release the rubber dust cover.

3   Tap the cylinder on a block of wood to release the piston and return spring. Do not attempt to remove the plastic filter from the base of the cylinder bore.

4   Remove the seal from the piston, then clean all the components in methylated spirit or clean brake fluid.

5   Carefully examine the internal cylinder bore and piston for signs of

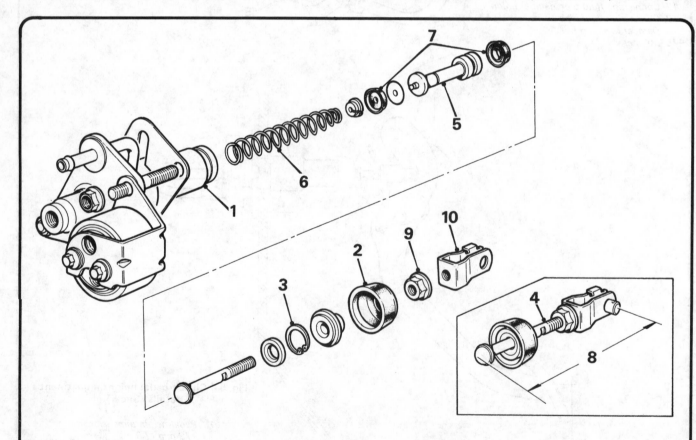

Fig. 5.5 Exploded view of the clutch master cylinder (Sec 6)

1 Master cylinder	4 Pushrod assembly	7 Piston seals	9 Locknut
2 Dust cover	5 Piston	8 Pushrod length (measured	10 Pushrod fork
3 Circlip	6 Piston spring	before dismantling)	

7.3 Fluid pipe union nut (A) and slave cylinder retaining bolts (B)

7.4 Removing the pushrod clevis pin retaining spring clip

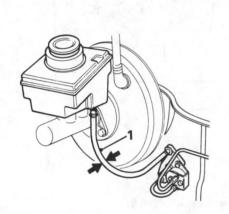

Fig. 5.6 Slave cylinder attachment details (Sec 7)

1 Fluid supply hose (arrows   2 Fluid pipe   4 Clevis pin   6 Slave cylinder
   indicate clamping point)   3 Clevis pin retaining clip 5 Slave cylinder retaining bolts

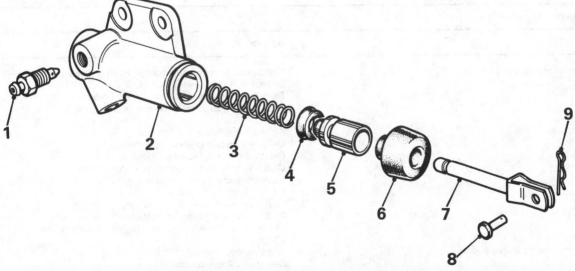

Fig. 5.7 Exploded view of the clutch slave cylinder (Sec 8)

1 Bleed screw   4 Piston seal   6 Dust cover   8 Clevis pin
2 Slave cylinder   5 Piston   7 Pushrod   9 Clevis pin retaining clip
3 Return spring

scoring or wear, and if evident, renew the complete slave cylinder. If the components are in a satisfactory condition, a new set of rubber seals must be obtained before reassembly. These are available in the form of a repair kit, obtainable from Rover dealers or brake and clutch factors.

6 Lubricate the piston, seal, and cylinder bore with clean brake fluid, and assemble the components wet.

7 Fit the new seal to the piston, with the sealing lip towards the return spring.

8 Fit the return spring to the cylinder bore, followed by the piston, dust cover and pushrod.

9 The assembled slave cylinder can now be fitted to the car as described in Section 7.

9 Clutch pedal – removal and refitting

1 From inside the car, release the turnbuckles and lift out the trim panel over the clutch, brake and accelerator pedals.

2 Depress the clutch pedal fully, release the pedal return spring from the pedal, then remove the spring from the pedal bracket.

3 Extract the retaining spring clip, and withdraw the clevis pin securing the master cylinder pushrod to the pedal.

4 Undo the two nuts and one bolt securing the pedal bracket to the bulkhead, and remove the bracket and pedal assembly from the car.

5 Undo the pedal pivot bolt and remove the pedal from the bracket.

6 Prise out the two pedal bushes and withdraw the centre spacer tube.

7 Check the condition of the components and renew as necessary.

8 Refitting is the reverse sequence to removal.

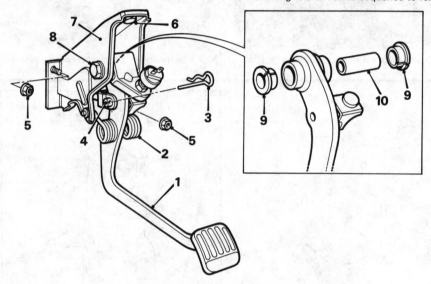

Fig. 5.8 Clutch pedal attachment details (Sec 9)

1 Clutch pedal	4 Clevis pin	7 Pedal bracket	9 Pedal bushes
2 Pedal return spring	5 Pedal bracket retaining nuts	8 Pedal pivot bolt	10 Centre spacer tube
3 Clevis pin retaining clip	6 Pedal bracket retaining bolt		

10 Fault diagnosis – clutch

Symptom	Reason(s)
Judder when taking up drive	Clutch disc linings contaminated with oil, or worn Defective clutch cover assembly Defective master cylinder or slave cylinder Clutch disc hub sticking on mainshaft splines
Clutch fails to disengage	Air in hydraulic system Defective master or slave cylinder Clutch disc linings contaminated with oil Clutch disc hub sticking on mainshaft splines Incorrect pedal height adjustment
Clutch slips	Faulty pressure plate or diaphragm spring Clutch disc linings contaminated with oil, or worn Clutch release mechanism sticking or partially seized
Noise when depressing clutch pedal	Worn release bearing Defective release mechanism Defective clutch cover assembly
Noise when releasing clutch pedal	Broken clutch disc torsion springs Defective clutch cover assembly Dry or worn pedal pivot bushes Gearbox internal wear

Chapter 6 Manual gearbox

Contents

Specifications

Type .... Five forward speeds (all synchromesh) and reverse. Final drive integral with main gearbox

Identification number .... G6 DT

Gear ratios

Up to approximately June 1988:

1st	3.25:1
2nd	1.89:1
3rd	1.31:1
4th	1.00:1
5th	0.85:1
Reverse	3.00:1
Final drive	3.94:1

From approximately June 1988 onwards:

1st	3.25:1
2nd	1.89:1
3rd	1.22:1
4th	0.93:1
5th	0.76:1
Reverse	3.00:1
Final drive	4.20:1

Lubrication

Lubricant type/specification*	Multigrade engine oil, viscosity SAE 10W/40, to API SF or SF/CD (Duckhams QXR, Hypergrade, or 10W/40 Motor Oil)
Lubricant capacity	2.3 litres (4.0 Imp pts)

* **Note:** *Austin Rover specify a 10W/40 oil to meet warranty requirements. Duckhams QXR and 10W/40 Motor Oil are available to meet these requirements.*

Gearbox overhaul data

Mainshaft endfloat	0.14 to 0.21 mm (0.005 to 0.008 in)
Endfloat adjustment	Selective circlips
Mainshaft bearing clearances:	
2nd to 3rd gear clearance:	
Standard	0.06 to 0.21 mm (0.002 to 0.008 in)
Wear limit	0.30 mm (0.012 in)
3rd gear thickness:	
Standard	35.42 to 35.47 mm (1.395 to 1.397 in)
Wear limit	35.30 mm (1.390 in)
4th gear to distance collar:	
Standard	0.06 to 0.21 mm (0.002 to 0.008 in)
Wear limit	0.30 mm (0.012 in)

Distance collar dimension 'A':
    Standard .... 26.03 to 26.08 mm (1.025 to 1.027 in)
    Wear limit .... 26.01 mm (1.024 in)
4th gear thickness:
    Standard .... 33.45 to 33.47 mm (1.317 to 1.318 in)
    Wear limit .... 33.33 mm (1.313 in)
5th gear to distance collar:
    Standard .... 0.06 to 0.21 mm (0.002 to 0.008 in)
    Wear limit .... 0.3 mm (0.012 in)
Distance collar dimension 'B':
    Standard .... 26.03 to 26.08 mm (1.025 to 1.027 in)
    Wear limit .... 26.01 mm (1.024 in)
5th gear thickness:
    Standard .... 31.92 to 31.97 mm (1.257 to 1.259 in)
    Wear limit .... 31.80 mm (1.252 in)
Countershaft endfloat:
    Standard .... 0.03 to 0.08 mm (0.0012 to 0.003 in)
    Wear limit .... 0.18 mm (0.007 in)
Endfloat adjustment .... Selective distance collars and thrustwashers
Synchro baulk ring to gear clearance:
    Standard .... 0.85 to 1.10 mm (0.033 to 0.043 in)
    Wear limit .... 0.40 mm (0.016 in)
Selector fork to synchro sleeve clearance:
    Standard .... 0.45 to 0.65 mm (0.017 to 0.025 in)
    Wear limit .... 1.00 mm (0.039 in)
Selector fork thicknesses:
    1st/2nd .... 8.90 to 9.00 mm (0.350 to 0.354 in)
    3rd/4th .... 8.40 to 8.50 mm (0.330 to 0.334 in)
    5th .... 5.40 to 5.50 mm (0.212 to 0.216 in)
Reverse gear fork to gear clearance:
    Standard .... 0.50 to 1.10 mm (0.019 to 0.043 in)
    Wear limit .... 1.80 mm (0.070 in)
Shift arm guide to 3rd/4th selector fork clearance:
    Standard .... 0.20 to 0.50 mm (0.007 to 0.019 in)
    Wear limit .... 0.80 mm (0.031 in)
Gearchange arm to shift arm clearance:
    Standard .... 0.05 to 0.35 mm (0.002 to 0.013 in)
    Wear limit .... 0.60 mm (0.023 in)
Gearchange arm to interlock clearance:
    Standard .... 0.05 to 0.25 mm (0.002 to 0.009 in)
    Wear limit .... 0.50 mm (0.020 in)
Shift arm to guide clearance:
    Standard .... 0.20 to 0.30 mm (0.007 to 0.012 in)
    Wear limit .... 0.55 mm (0.021 in)
Differential endfloat .... 0.15 mm (0.006 in)
Endfloat adjustment .... Selective circlips

Torque wrench settings

	Nm	lbf ft
Oil filler plug	45	33
Oil drain plug	40	30
Speedometer pinion retainer plate bolt	11	8
Gearbox steady rod bolt	25	18
Gear lever to gearchange rod	22	16
Remote control housing to underbody	22	16
Clutch slave cylinder bolts	22	16
Front engine mounting to gearbox bracket	80	59
Front engine mounting bracket to gearbox	40	30
Rear engine mounting bracket to gearbox	40	30
Engine rear tie-bar to mounting bracket	45	33
Longitudinal support member to underbody	45	33
Engine snubber bracket to gearbox	45	33
Reversing light switch	25	18
Gearcase to bellhousing bolts	45	33
Reverse idler shaft retaining bolt	55	41
Countershaft access plug	70	52
Reverse gear fork bracket bolts	15	11
Gearchange holder and interlock assembly:		
Long bolt	28	21
Intermediate bolt	15	11
Short bolt	12	9
Gearchange shaft detent plug	22	16
Gearchange arm to shaft bolt	30	22
Countershaft bearing retaining plate bolts	12	9
Countershaft nut	110	81
Roadwheel nuts	70	52

1 General description

The manual gearbox fitted to all 820 series models is of Honda design, incorporating five forward gears and one reverse. Synchromesh gear engagement is used on all forward gears.

The mainshaft and countershaft carry the constant mesh gear cluster assemblies, and are supported on ball and roller bearings. The short input end of the mainshaft eliminates the need for additional support from a crankshaft spigot bearing. The synchromesh gear engagement is by spring rings which act against baulk rings under the movement of the synchroniser sleeves. Gear selection is by means of a floor-mounted lever, connected by a remote control housing and gear change rod to the gearchange shaft in the gearbox. Gearchange shaft movement is transmitted to the selector forks via the gearchange holder and interlock assembly.

The final drive differential unit is integral with the main gearbox, and is located between the bellhousing and gearcase. The gearbox and final drive components both share the same lubricating oil.

2 Maintenance and inspection

1 At the intervals given in *Routine maintenance* at the beginning of this manual, carry out the following service operations on the gearbox.
2 Carefully inspect the gearbox joint faces and oil seals for signs of damage, deterioration or oil leakage.
3 At the same service intervals, check and if necessary top up the gearbox oil. The filler plug is located on the left-hand side of the gearcase, and can be reached from above the engine compartment. Wipe the area around the filler plug with a rag before unscrewing the plug. Top up if necessary, using the specified grade of oil, to bring the level up to the filler plug orifice (photo).
4 At the specified intervals, the gearbox oil should be renewed. To do this, jack up the front of the car and support it on axle stands. Place a suitable container beneath the drain plug, which is located below the driveshaft inner constant velocity joint on the same side as the filler plug (photo). Undo the plug using a square key, and allow the oil to drain. If a suitable key is not available, the 3/8 in square drive end of a socket bar will suffice. Refit the plug after draining, then refill with fresh oil through the filler orifice.
5 At less-frequent intervals, check for excess free play or wear in the gear linkage and gear lever joints and pivots.

3 Gearbox – removal and refitting

1 Disconnect the battery negative terminal. (Refer to Chapter 12, Section 1, before doing this).
2 Remove the air cleaner assembly as described in Chapter 3.
3 Remove the starter motor as described in Chapter 12.
4 Extract the retaining clips and release the support struts from the bonnet. Tie the bonnet back in the fully open position.
5 Apply the handbrake, prise off the front wheel trim and slacken the wheel nuts. Jack up the front of the car and support it on axle stands. Remove the front roadwheels.

6 Drain the gearbox oil as described in Section 2.
7 Remove the engine undershield and the access panel from the left-hand inner wing.
8 Remove the front suspension tie-rod on the left-hand side, as described in Chapter 10.
9 Undo the bolt and disconnect the earth lead from the gearbox (photo).
10 Slide up the rubber boot and disconnect the leads at the reversing light switch.
11 Disconnect the speedometer transducer wiring multi-plug.
12 Undo the bolts securing the longitudinal support member to the underbody, and remove the member.
13 Undo the three bolts and remove the engine snubber bracket from the gearbox (photo).
14 Extract the spring clip and withdraw the clevis pin securing the clutch slave cylinder pushrod to the release arm (photo).
15 Undo the two slave cylinder retaining bolts, and move the cylinder aside.
16 Undo the bolt in the centre of the gearbox steady rod. Remove the dished washer, slide off the steady rod and remove the inner flat washer (photos).
17 Remove the spring clip to expose the gearchange rod-to-gearchange shaft retaining roll pin (photo).
18 Using a parallel pin punch, tap out the roll pin, and slide the gearchange rod rearwards, off the shaft (photo).
19 Undo the nut securing the right-hand steering knuckle balljoint to the lower suspension arm, then release the balljoint from the arm using a universal balljoint separator tool or two-legged puller – refer to Chapter 10 if necessary.
20 Pull the steering knuckle outwards, then using a suitable flat bar or large screwdriver, lever between the driveshaft inner constant velocity joint and the differential housing to release the joint from the gearbox (photo).
21 Move the driveshaft clear of the gearbox, then repeat these procedures on the left-hand driveshaft.
22 Attach a suitable hoist to the engine using rope slings, or chains attached to brackets secured to the cylinder head. Raise the hoist to just take the weight of the engine.
23 Support the gearbox using a jack and interposed block of wood.
24 Undo the nut securing the front engine mounting to its gearbox bracket.
25 Undo the two bolts securing the front mounting bracket to the gearbox, and remove the bracket.
26 Undo the bolts securing the rear engine mounting bracket to the gearbox, noting the location of the crankshaft sensor bracket. Remove the bolts and move the sensor aside (photo).
27 Undo the bolt securing the larger end of the engine rear tie-bar to its mounting bracket. Remove the through-bolt, and recover the special nut.
28 Undo all the remaining bolts securing the gearbox to the engine.
29 Ease the gearbox away from the engine after releasing it from the locating dowels, then lower the jack and engine hoist until clearance exists to enable the gearbox to be withdrawn fully from the side of the engine. Withdraw the unit from under the car.
30 Refitting the gearbox is the reverse sequence to removal. Tighten all nuts and bolts to the specified torque, and fill the gearbox with oil as described in Section 2 on completion.

2.3 Topping-up the gearbox oil

2.4 Gearbox drain plug location (arrowed)

3.9 Gearbox earth lead retaining bolt (arrowed)

3.13 Undo the three bolts and remove the snubber bracket

3.14 Clutch slave cylinder pushrod clevis pin and spring clip

3.16A Undo the bolt in the centre of the steady rod (arrowed) ...

3.16B ... slide off the steady rod and remove the inner flat washer (arrowed)

3.17 Remove the gearchange rod spring clip ...

3.18 ... tap out the roll pin, and withdraw the gearchange rod off the shaft

3.20 Removing the driveshaft inner constant velocity joint

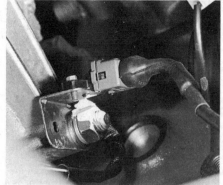

3.26 Crankshaft sensor bracket location

4 Gearbox overhaul – general

1 Dismantling, overhaul and reassembly of the gearbox is reasonably straightforward, and can be carried out without recourse to the manufacturer's special tools, although a reasonably comprehensive standard tool kit will be required. It should be noted, however, that any repair or overhaul work on the final drive differential must be limited to the renewal of the carrier support bearings. Owing to the complicated nature of this unit and the costs involved, the advice of a Rover dealer should be sought if further repair is necessary.

2 Read through all the applicable Sections of this Chapter, and familiarise yourself with the procedures involved before contemplating any repair or overhaul task. Make sure that you have all the necessary tools required (or have access to any you don't have), and enquire about the availability of any parts thay may be needed for repair.

3 Before starting any work on the gearbox, clean the exterior of the casings using paraffin or a suitable solvent. Dry the unit with a lint-free rag. Make sure that an uncluttered working area is available, with some small containers and trays handy to store the various parts. Label everything as it is removed.

4 Before starting reassembly, all the components must be spotlessly clean, and should be lubricated with the specified grade of oil during reassembly.

5 Gearbox – dismantling

1   Stand the gearbox on its bellhousing face on the bench, and begin dismantling by removing the reversing light switch.

2   Undo the bolt, remove the retaining plate, and lift out the speedometer transducer and pinion assembly.

3   Undo all the gearcase-to-bellhousing retaining bolts, noting the location of the breather hose and bracket, which are also retained by one of the case bolts. Remove the breather hose and bracket (photo).

4   Undo the reverse idler shaft retaining bolt, located on the side of the gearcase (photo).

5   Using a large Allen key, hexagonal bar, or suitable bolt with two nuts locked together, undo the countershaft access plug on the end of the gearcase (photo).

6   Using circlip pliers inserted through the access plug aperture, spread the countershaft retaining circlip, while at the same time lifting upwards on the gearcase. Tap the case with a soft mallet if necessary. When the circlip is clear of its groove, lift the case up and off the bellhousing and gear clusters (photos).

7   Undo the two retaining bolts and remove the reverse gear fork and bracket.

8   Lift out the reverse gear idler shaft, then remove the gear and thrustwasher from the shaft.

9   Undo the three bolts and remove the gearchange holder and interlock assembly. Note that the holder locates in a slot in the 1st/2nd selector shaft.

10 With the help of an assistant, lift the mainshaft and countershaft as an assembly upwards slightly, then withdraw the selector shafts and forks from the bellhousing and gear clusters (photo).

11 Lift the mainshaft and countershaft out of their respective bearings in the bellhousing (photo).

12 Finally, remove the differential from the bellhousing (photo).

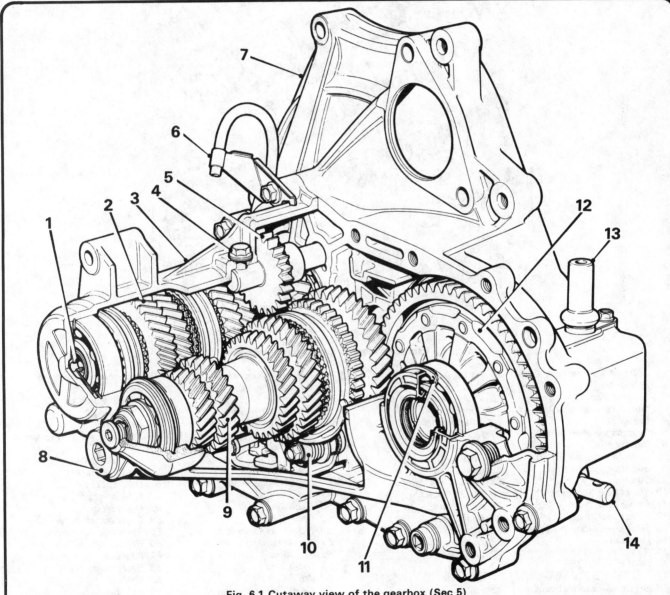

Fig. 6.1 Cutaway view of the gearbox (Sec 5)

1 Oil guide plate	5 Reverse idler gear	9 Countershaft assembly	12 Final drive differential
2 Mainshaft assembly	6 Gearbox breather and	10 Gearchange holder and	13 Speedometer pinion and
3 Gearcase	bracket	interlock assembly	transducer assembly
4 Reverse idler shaft retaining	7 Bellhousing	11 Differential endfloat circlip	14 Gearchange shaft
bolt	8 Countershaft access plug	shim	

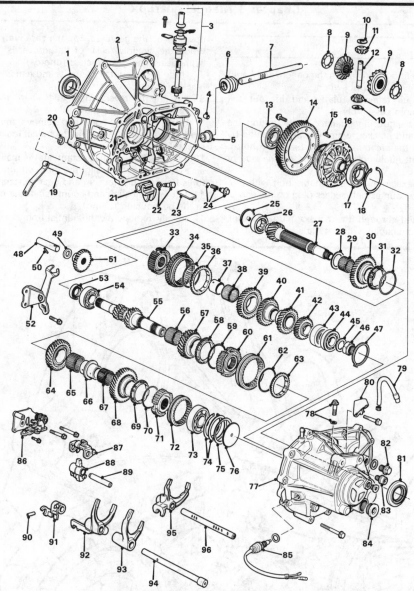

Fig. 6.2 Exploded view of the components (Sec 5)

1	Differential oil seal
2	Bellhousing
3	Speedometer pinion and transducer assembly
4	Dowel
5	Gearchange shaft oil seal
6	Rubber boot
7	Gearchange shaft
8	Sun gear thrustwasher
9	Sun gear
10	Planet gear thrustwasher
11	Planet gear
12	Planet gear shaft
13	Final drive support bearing
14	Final drive gear
15	Roll pin
16	Final drive casing
17	Final drive support bearing
18	Differential endfloat circlip shim
19	Clutch operating lever
20	Clutch operating lever oil seal
21	Gearchange arm
22	Dowel bolt and washer
23	Magnet
24	Detent ball, spring and plug
25	Oil guide plate
26	Countershaft roller bearing
27	Countershaft
28	Thrustwasher
29	Needle roller bearing
30	1st gear
31	Baulk ring
32	Spring ring
33	1st/2nd synchro hub
34	1st/2nd synchro sleeve
35	Spring ring
36	Baulk ring
37	Distance collar
38	Needle roller bearing
39	2nd gear
40	3rd gear
41	4th gear
42	5th gear
43	Countershaft roller bearing
44	Countershaft ball bearing
45	Washer
46	Retaining nut
47	Circlip
48	Reverse idler shaft
49	Reverse idler gear thrustwasher
50	Roll pin
51	Reverse idler gear
52	Reverse gear fork and bracket
53	Mainshaft oil seal
54	Mainshaft ball bearing
55	Mainshaft
56	Needle roller bearing
57	3rd gear
58	Baulk ring
59	Spring ring
60	3rd/4th synchro hub
61	3rd/4th synchro sleeve
62	Spring ring
63	Baulk ring
64	4th gear
65	Needle roller bearing
66	Distance collar
67	Needle roller bearing
68	5th gear
69	Baulk ring
70	Spring ring
71	5th gear synchro hub
72	5th gear synchro sleeve
73	Mainshaft ball bearing
74	Selective circlips
75	Belleville washer
76	Oil guide plate
77	Gearcase
78	Reverse idler shaft retaining bolt
79	Gearbox breather
80	Breather bracket
81	Differential oil seal
82	Filler/level plug
83	Drain plug
84	Countershaft access plug
85	Reversing light switch
86	Gearchange holder
87	Interlock
88	Gearchange arm
89	Shaft
90	Roll pin
91	5th/reverse gear selector
92	3rd/4th gear selector fork
93	5th gear selector fork
94	5th/reverse selector shaft
95	1st/2nd gear selector shaft
96	1st/2nd gear selector shaft

5.3 Gearbox breather bracket and case retaining bolt

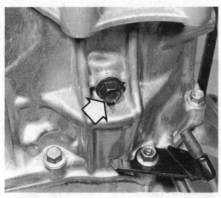

5.4 Reverse idler shaft retaining bolt (arrowed)

5.5 Countershaft access plug (arrowed)

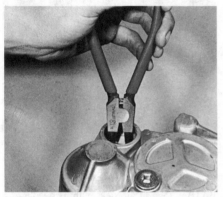

5.6A Release the countershaft bearing retaining circlip ...

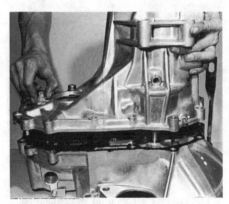

5.6B ... then withdraw the gearcase

5.10 Lift the mainshaft and countershaft, then remove the selector shafts and forks

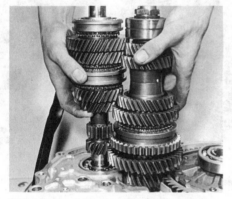

5.11 Remove the mainshaft and countershaft together from the bellhousing

5.12 Remove the differential from the bellhousing

6 Mainshaft – dismantling and reassembly

1 Remove the mainshaft bearing using a two- or three-legged puller if necessary, unless the bearing remained in the gearcase during removal.
2 Withdraw the 5th gear synchroniser hub and sleeve assembly from the mainshaft, using a puller if it is tight. Recover the 5th gear baulk ring from the cone face of 5th gear and place it, together with the spring ring, on the synchroniser unit.
3 Slide off 5th gear, followed by the 5th gear needle roller bearing.
4 Withdraw the distance collar, followed by 4th gear and the needle roller bearing.
5 Remove the 3rd/4th synchro hub and sleeve assembly, complete with baulk rings and spring rings.
6 Remove 3rd gear and its needle roller bearing.
7 Carry out a careful inspection of the mainshaft components as

described in Section 10, and obtain any new parts as necessary.
8 During reassembly, lightly lubricate all the parts with the specified grade of oil as the work proceeds.
9 Slide the 3rd gear needle roller bearing onto the mainshaft, followed by the 3rd gear, with its flat face towards the other gears on the shaft (photos).
10 Place the 3rd gear baulk ring and spring ring on the cone face of 3rd gear, then fit the 3rd/4th synchro hub and sleeve assembly. Ensure that the lugs on the baulk ring engage with the slots in the synchro hub (photos).
11 Locate the 4th gear spring ring and baulk ring in the synchro unit, then slide on 4th gear with its needle roller bearing (photos).
12 Fit the distance collar (photo).
13 Place the 5th gear needle roller bearing over the collar, then slide 5th gear onto the bearing (photos).
14 Locate the 5th gear baulk ring and spring ring in the 5th gear

6.9A Fit the 3rd gear needle roller bearing to the mainshaft ...

6.9B ... followed by 3rd gear

6.10A Place the baulk ring and spring ring on 3rd gear ...

6.10B ... then fit the 3rd/4th synchro hub and sleeve assembly

6.11A Locate the spring rig and baulk ring on the synchro unit ...

6.11B ... then fit 4th gear with its needle roller bearing

6.12 Fit the distance collar

6.13A Place the 5th gear needle roller bearing over the collar ...

6.13B ... then slide on 5th gear

synchro unit, then fit this assembly to the mainshaft (photo).
15 Fit the mainshaft bearing, and drive it fully home using a hammer and tube of suitable diameter in contact with the bearing inner race.
16 The mainshaft bearing clearances should now be checked, using feeler gauges as follows. If any of the clearances are found to be outside the tolerances given in the Specifications, it will be necessary to dismantle the mainshaft again so that the adjacent gear or distance collar can be measured, and then renewed if necessary. To avoid having to dismantle the mainshaft repeatedly, measure *all* the clearances first, then dismantle and renew the components as required.
17 Measure the clearance between 2nd gear and 3rd gear, and compare the figure obtained with that given in the Specifications. If the clearance is excessive, dismantle the mainshaft and measure the thickness of 3rd gear. If this is outside the specified tolerance, renew the gear. If the thickness is satisfactory, renew the 3rd/4th synchro hub.
18 Measure the clearance between 4th gear and the distance collar flange. If the clearance is excessive, dismantle the mainshaft and measure the distance from the 4th gear side of the distance collar

shoulder to the end of the collar (dimension 'A' in Fig. 6.3). If this dimension is outside the specified tolerance, renew the distance collar. If the measured distance is satisfactory, measure the 4th gear thickness. If this is outside the specified tolerance, renew the gear. If the thickness is satisfactory, renew the 3rd/4th synchro hub.
19 Measure the clearance between 5th gear and the distance collar flange. If the clearance is excessive, dismantle the mainshaft and measure the distance from the 5th gear side of the distance collar shoulder to the end of the collar (dimension 'B' in Fig. 6.3). If this dimension is outside the specified tolerance, renew the distance collar. If the measured distance is satisfactory, measure the 5th gear thickness. If this is outside the specified tolerance, renew the gear. If the thickness is satisfactory, renew the 5th gear synchro hub.
20 If the mainshaft, mainshaft components, the gearcase or bellhousing have been renewed, then the mainshaft endfloat must be checked and if necessary adjusted. To do this, it will be necessary to remove the mainshaft ball-bearing in the gearcase, remove the selective circlips, Belleville washer and oil guide, then refit the bearing.
21 Position the assembled mainshaft in the bellhousing, fit the

6.14 Fit the 5th gear synchro unit, complete with spring ring and baulk ring

gearcase, and temporarily secure it with several evenly-spaced bolts. Tighten the bolts securely.

22 Support the bellhousing face of the gearbox on blocks, so as to provide access to the protruding mainshaft.

23 Place a straight edge across the bellhousing face, in line with the mainshaft, then accurately measure and record the distance from straight edge to mainshaft (Fig. 6.4).

24 Turn the gearbox over so that the bellhousing is uppermost, and gently tap the mainshaft back into the gearcase using a soft-faced mallet. Take a second measurement of the mainshaft-to-straight edge distance.

25 Subtract the first measurement from the second measurement, and identify this as dimension A.

26 Measure the thickness of the Belleville washer, and add an allowance of 0.17 mm (0.006 in), which is the nominal mainshaft endfloat. Identify this as dimension B.

27 Subtract dimension B from dimension A, and the value obtained is the thickness of selective circlip(s) required to give the specified mainshaft endfloat.

28 Remove the gearcase and mainshaft. Remove the bearing from the gearcase, refit the oil guide, Belleville washer, and circlips of the required thickness, then refit the bearing.

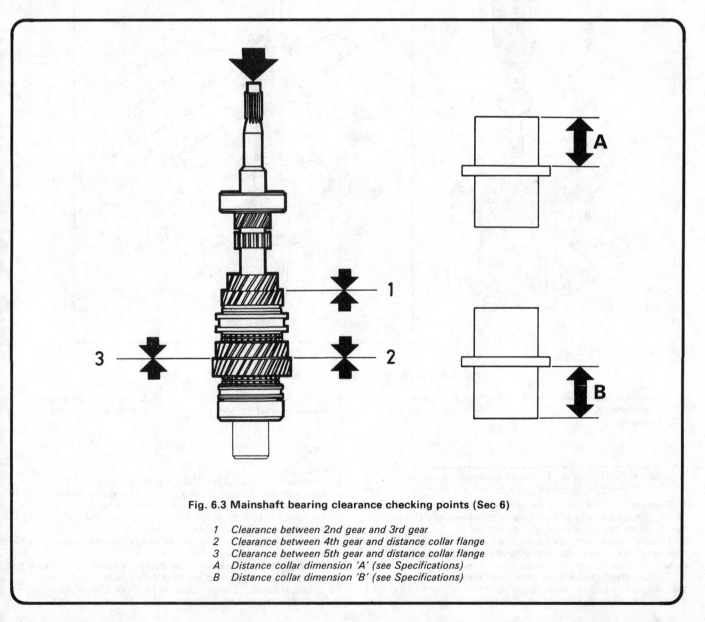

Fig. 6.3 Mainshaft bearing clearance checking points (Sec 6)

1 Clearance between 2nd gear and 3rd gear
2 Clearance between 4th gear and distance collar flange
3 Clearance between 5th gear and distance collar flange
A Distance collar dimension 'A' (see Specifications)
B Distance collar dimension 'B' (see Specifications)

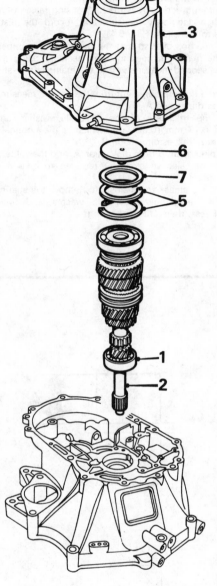

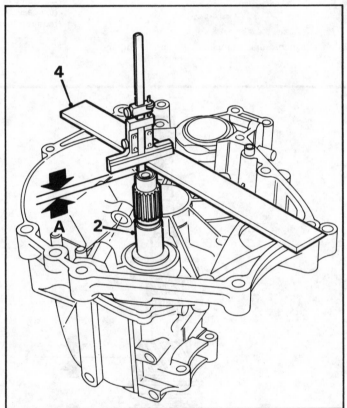

Fig. 6.4 Mainshaft endfloat adjustment (Sec 6)

1	*Mainshaft ball-bearing*	4	*Straight edge*
2	*Mainshaft*	5	*Selective circlips*
3	*Gearcase*		

6	*Oil guide plate*	A	*Measured clearance –*
7	*Belleville washer*		*straight edge-to-mainshaft*

7 Countershaft – dismantling and reassembly

1   Support the pinion gear on the countershaft between two blocks of wood. Tighten the vice just sufficiently to prevent the countershaft turning as the bearing retaining nut is undone.

2   Using a small punch, release the staking on the countershaft nut, then undo and remove the nut. Note that the nut has a left-hand thread, and must be turned clockwise to unscrew it.

3   Remove the dished washer, then draw off the two countershaft bearings using a two- or three-legged puller.

4   Slide 5th, 4th, 3rd, and 2nd gears off the countershaft, noting their fitted directions.

5   Remove the 2nd gear baulk ring and spring ring.

6   Slide off the 2nd gear needle roller bearing, followed by the distance collar. Use two screwdrivers to lever off the collar if it is tight.

7   Remove the 1st/2nd synchro hub and sleeve assembly, followed by the 1st gear baulk ring and spring ring.

8   Slide off first gear, followed by the needle roller bearing and thrust washer.

9   Carry out a careful inspection of the countershaft components as described in Section 10, and obtain any new parts as necessary.

10   During reassembly, lightly lubricate all the parts with the specified grade of oil as the work proceeds.

11 Fit the thrustwasher to the countershaft, followed by the needle roller bearing and 1st gear (photos).

12 Fit the baulk ring and spring ring to the cone face of 1st gear, then slide on the 1st/2nd synchro unit. The synchro unit must be fitted with the selector fork groove in the synchro sleeve away from 1st gear. As the unit is fitted, ensure that the lugs on the baulk ring engage with the slots in the synchro hub (photos).

13 Warm the distance collar in boiling water, then slide it onto the countershaft with the oil hole offset towards 1st gear (photo).

14 Fit the 2nd gear needle roller bearing to the distance collar (photo).

15 Locate the 2nd gear baulk ring and spring ring on the synchro unit, then slide 2nd gear into place over the needle roller bearing (photos).

16 Fit 3rd gear to the countershaft with its longer boss away from 2nd gear (photo).

17 Fit 4th gear with its boss towards the 3rd gear boss (photo).

18 Fit 5th gear with its flat face towards 4th gear (photo), then tap the countershaft bearings into position using a hammer and suitable tube.

19 Fit the dished washer with its dished side towards the bearings, followed by a new countershaft nut. Hold the pinion between blocks of wood in the vice as before, and tighten the nut to the specified torque.

20 Using feeler gauges, measure the clearance between the thrustwasher and 1st gear, and between the 2nd and 3rd gear faces (photos). Compare the measurements with the endfloat dimension given in the Specifications. If the recorded clearances are outside the tolerance range, dismantle the countershaft again, and fit an alternative thickness thrustwasher or distance collar from the range available.

21 With the countershaft assembled and the endfloat correctly set, recheck the torque of the countershaft nut, then peen its edge into the countershaft groove using a small punch.

7.11A Fit the thrustwasher to the countershaft ...

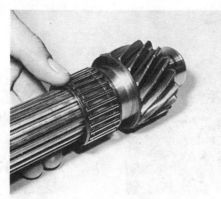

7.11B ... followed by the needle roller bearing ...

7.11C ... and 1st gear

7.12A Fit the baulk ring and spring ring to 1st gear ...

7.12B ... then slide on the 1st/2nd synchro unit

7.13 Fit the distance collar with its oil hole (arrowed) offset towards 1st gear

7.14 Locate the 2nd gear needle roller bearing over the collar

7.15A Fit the baulk ring and spring ring ...

7.15B ... followed by 2nd gear

7.16 Fit 3rd gear with its boss away from 2nd gear

7.17 Fit 4th gear with its boss towards 3rd gear

7.18 Fit 5th gear with its flat face towards 4th gear

7.20A Check the clearance between the thrustwasher and 1st gear ...

7.20B ... and between 2nd and 3rd gears

8 Gearcase – inspection and overhaul

1   Check the gearcase for cracks, or any damage to its bellhousing mating face. Renew the case if damaged.
2   Check the condition of the mainshaft bearing in the gearcase, and ensure that it spins smoothly, with no trace of roughness or harshness. The bearing must be removed if it is worn, if the gearcase is to be renewed, or if it is necessary to gain access to the mainshaft endfloat selective circlips located behind it.
3   Removal of the bearing entails the use of a slide hammer, with adaptor consisting of externally-expanding flange or legs, to locate behind the inner race. A Rover special tool is available for this purpose, but it should be possible to make up a suitable alternative with readily-available tools. Whichever option is chosen, it is quite likely that the oil guide plate will be damaged or broken in the process. If so a new one must be obtained.
4   If any of the mainshaft components are being renewed during the course of overhaul, do not refit the bearing, the circlips, the Belleville washer or the oil guide plate until after the mainshaft endfloat has been checked and adjusted.
5   When the bearing is fitted, this can be done by tapping it squarely into place, using a hammer and tube of suitable diameter in contact with the bearing outer race.
6   If there is any sign of leakage, the differential oil seal in the gearcase should be renewed. Drive or hook out the old seal, and install the new one with its open side facing inwards, ie towards the bearing. Tap the seal squarely into place, using a suitable tube or the old seal. Smear a little grease around the sealing to aid refitting of the driveshaft. **Note:** *If the differential or differential bearings have been renewed or disturbed from their original positions, do not fit the oil seal until the gearbox has been completely reassembled.* The differential bearing clearances are checked through the oil seal aperture, and cannot be done with the seal in place.

9 Bellhousing – inspection and overhaul

1   With the mainshaft and countershaft removed, lift out the magnet from its location in the bellhousing edge (photo).
2   Remove the clutch release bearing, release fork and arm as described in Chapter 5.
3   Undo the gearchange shaft detent plug bolt, and lift out the detent spring and ball (photos).
4   Undo the bolt securing the gearchange arm to the shaft, and slide the arm off the shaft (photo).
5   Withdraw the gearchange shaft from the bellhousing, and recover the rubber boot.
6   Check the condition of the ball and roller bearings in the bellhousing, ensuring that they spin smoothly, with no trace of roughness or harshness.
7   Removal of the bearing entails the use of a slide hammer, with adaptor consisting of externally-expanding flange or legs, to locate behind the inner race. A Rover special tool is available for this purpose, but it should be possible to make up a suitable alternative with readily-available tools. Another alternative would be to take the bellhousing along to your dealer, and have him renew the bearings for you. Whichever option is chosen, it is quite likely that the oil guide plate behind the countershaft roller bearing will be damaged or broken in the process (assuming this bearing is to be renewed), and if so a new one must be obtained (photo).
8   Refit the bearings by tapping them squarely into place, using a hammer and tube of suitable diameter. Ensure that the oil hole in the countershaft bearing faces the gearbox interior.
9   Carefully inspect all the oil seals in the bellhousing, and renew any that show signs of leakage or deterioration. The old seals can be driven out with a tube or punch, and the new seals tapped squarely into place using a block of wood or the old seal. Ensure that in all cases the open side of the seal faces inwards. In the case of the mainshaft oil seal, it

9.1 Remove the magnet from the bellhousing

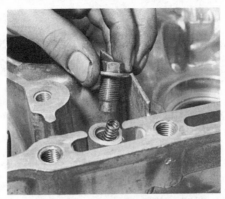

9.3A Undo the gearchange shaft detent plug bolt ...

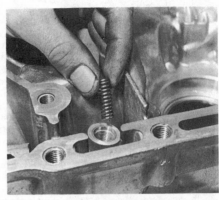

9.3B ... then lift out the spring ...

9.3C ... and detent ball

9.4 Gearchange arm retaining bolt (arrowed)

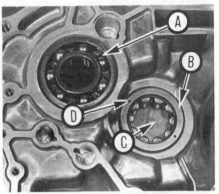

9.7 Mainshaft ballbearing (A) countershaft roller bearing(B), oil guide plate (C), and bearing oil holes (D)

will be necessary to remove the mainshaft bearing to enable a new seal to be fitted.

10 Inspect the gearchange shaft for distortion or wear across the detent grooves, and check the gearchange arm for wear of the forks. Renew these components if wear is evident.

11 With the new bearings and seals in position, and any other new parts obtained as necessary, refit the gearchange shaft and rubber boot with the detent grooves facing outwards, ie towards the gear clusters.

12 Slide on the gearchange arm so that its forked side is facing away from the bellhousing starter motor aperture. Refit the retaining bolt and washer, and tighten to the specified torque.

13 Refit the detent ball, followed by the spring and plug bolt. Tighten the bolt to the specified torque.

14 Refit the clutch release mechanism as described in Chapter 5.

15 Refit the magnet to its location in the bellhousing edge.

10 Mainshaft and countershaft components and synchro units – inspection and overhaul

1 With the mainshaft and countershaft dismantled, examine the shafts and gears for signs of pitting, scoring, wear ridges or chipped teeth. Check the fit of the gears on the mainshaft and countershaft splines, and ensure that there is no lateral free play.

2 Check the smoothness of the bearings, and check for any signs of scoring on the needle roller bearing tracks and distance collars.

3 Check the mainshaft and countershaft for straightness, check for damaged threads or splines, and ensure that the lubrication holes are clear (photos).

4 Mark one side of each synchro hub and sleeve before separating the two parts, so that they may be refitted in the same position.

5 Withdraw the hub from the sleeve, and examine the internal gear teeth for wear ridges. Ensure that the hub and sleeve are a snug sliding

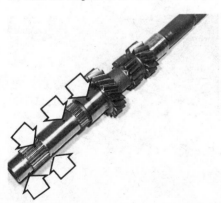

10.3A Gearbox mainshaft showing oil holes (arrowed) ...

10.3B ... and gearbox countershaft

10.8 Oversized teeth in synchro sleeve (arrowed) engaged with corresponding grooves in hub

fit, with the minimum of lateral movement.

6   Check the fit of the selector forks in their respective synchro sleeve grooves. If the clearance exceeds the figure given in the Specifications, measure the selector fork thicknesses, and renew any that are outside the specified tolerance range.

7   Place each baulk ring on the cone face of its respective gear, and measure the distance between the baulk ring and the gear face. If the clearance is less than specified, renew the baulk ring. Renew them also if there is excessive wear or rounding-off of the dog teeth around the periphery, if they are cracked, or if they are in any way damaged. If the gearbox is in reasonable condition and is to be rebuilt, it is advisable to renew all the baulk rings as a matter of course. The improvement in the synchromesh action when changing gear will justify the expense.

8   When reassembling the synchro units, make sure that the two oversize teeth in the synchro sleeve engage with the two oversize grooves in the hub (photo).

9   If any of the gears on the mainshaft are to be renewed, then the corresponding gear on the countershaft must also be renewed, and *vice-versa*. This applies to the countershaft and differential final drive gear as well.

11 Selector forks, shafts and gearchange mechanism – inspection and overhaul

1   Visually inspect the selector forks for obvious signs of wear ridges, cracks or deformation.

2   Slide the selector forks off the shafts, noting their fitted positions, and check the detent action as the fork is removed. Note that the detent balls and springs are located in the selector forks themselves, and cannot be removed. If the detent action is weak, or if there is evidence of a broken spring or damaged ball, the fork must be renewed.

3   Check the fit of the selector forks in their respective synchro sleeve grooves. If the clearance exceeds the figure given in the Specifications, measure the selector fork thicknesses, and renew any that are outside the specified tolerance range.

4   Examine the selector shafts for wear ridges around the detent grooves, and for any obvious signs of distortion. Renew any suspect shafts.

5   Examine the gearchange and interlock assembly for any visible signs of wear or damage, then measure the clearances as shown in the accompanying illustrations. It is advisable not to dismantle the mechanism unless it is obviously worn and in need of renewal. If this is the case, it can be separated into three main units, and the worn parts can be renewed.

6   Having obtained any new parts as required, reassemble the selector forks back onto the shafts, and reassemble the gearchange holder and interlock components if these were dismantled for renewal.

12 Final drive differential – inspection and renewal

1   As mentioned earlier, the only parts that can be renewed as a practical proposition are the two main support bearings on the final drive casing. The differential unit should be examined for any signs of wear or damage, but if any is found, it is recommended that you seek the advice of your dealer. Differential parts are supplied in sets, ie final drive gear and matching countershaft; sun gears and matching planet gears etc, and consequently are extremely expensive. The cost of individual parts may even equal, or exceed, the price of a complete exchange reconditioned gearbox.

2   Check that the bearings spin freely, with no sign of harshness or roughness. If renewal is necessary, remove the bearings by levering them off the differential using two screwdrivers or a small puller.

3   Fit the new bearings by tapping them into place, using a hammer and tube in contact with the bearing inner race.

13 Gearbox – reassembly

1   Position the differential in its location in the bellhousing, and tap it down gently, using a soft-faced mallet, to ensure that the bearing is fully seated.

2   Fit the gearcase to the bellhousing, and secure it temporarily with several bolts tightened to the specified torque.

3   Using feeler gauges inserted through the oil seal aperture in the

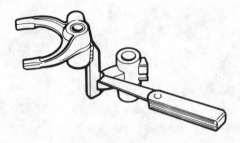

Fig. 6.5 Checking shift arm guide-to-3rd/4th selector fork clearance (Sec 11)

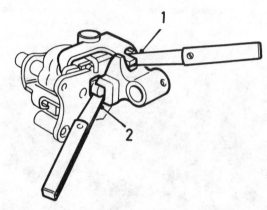

Fig. 6.6 Checking gearchange arm-to-shift arm clearance (1), and gearchange arm-to-interlock clearance (2) (Sec 11)

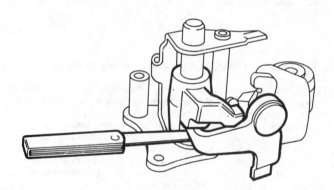

Fig. 6.7 Checking shift arm-to-guide clearance (Sec 11)

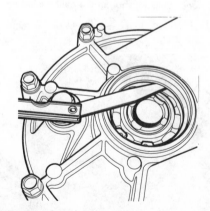

Fig. 6.8 Checking differential endfloat (Sec 13)

Feeler gauges inserted through oil seal aperture

gearcase, measure the clearance between the bearing and the circlip in the bearing recess. If the clearance is not equal to the differential endfloat dimension given in the Specifications, slacken the gearcase retaining bolts, extract the circlip through the oil seal aperture, and substitute a thicker or thinner circlip as required from the range available. Repeat this procedure until the correct endfloat is obtained, then remove the gearcase. Gearbox reassembly can now proceed as follows.

4   Insert the magnet into its location in the edge of the bellhousing.

5   Refit the gearchange shaft and arm as described in Section 9, if this has not already been done.

6   With the bearings in place in the bellhousing, hold the assembled mainshaft and countershaft together, and insert them into their locations.

7   With the help of an assistant, lift up the mainshaft and countershaft assemblies together, approximately 12.0 mm (0.5 in). Engage the selector forks with their respective synchro sleeves, and locate the selector shafts in the bellhousing (photo). Return the mainshaft and countershaft to their original positions, ensuring that the selector shafts engage fully with their holes in the bellhousing.

8   Refit the gearchange holder and interlock assembly, noting that the holder locates in a slot in the 1st/2nd selector shaft (photo).

9   Refit the three gearchange holder and interlock retaining bolts, and tighten them to the specified torque (photo).

10   Refit the reverse gear idler shaft, thrustwasher and reverse gear, and engage the roll pin on the shaft with the slot in the bellhousing (photo).

11   Engage the reverse gear fork over the reverse gear teeth, and over the peg on the 5th/reverse selector. Secure the reverse gear fork bracket with the two retaining bolts, tightened to the specified torque (photo).

12   Apply a thin, continuous bead of RTV sealant to the gearcase mating face. Lower the gearcase over the gear clusters, and engage the shafts and bearings in their locations. Using circlip pliers inserted through the countershaft access plug aperture, spread the circlip, and tap the gearcase fully into position using a soft-faced mallet. Release the circlip, ensuring that it enters the groove on the countershaft bearing.

13   Refit the gearcase retaining bolts and breather bracket, then tighten the bolts progressively and in a diagonal sequence to the specified torque.

14   Refit the reverse idler shaft retaining bolt, and tighten it to the specified torque.

15   Apply thread sealant to the countershaft access plug, refit the plug and tighten it to the specified torque.

16   Refit the speedometer transducer and pinion assembly, and the reversing light switch.

17   Refit the final drive differential oil seal to the gearcase, if not already done.

18   Check the operation of the gearchange mechanism, ensuring that all gears can be engaged, then refit the gearbox to the car as described in Section 3.

14 Gear lever and remote control housing – removal and refitting

Gear lever

1   Jack up the front of the car and support it on axle stands.

2   Undo the bolts securing the front heat shield to the underbody.

3   Release the exhaust system front rubber mounting, then remove the heat shield by twisting it around the exhaust front pipe.

4   Undo the nut and remove the bolt securing the gear lever to the gearchange remote control rod (photo).

5   Remove the centre console as described in Chapter 11.

6   Remove the rubber boot and dust cover over the gear lever (photos).

7   Extract the retaining circlip, and withdraw the gear lever from the remote control housing (photo).

8   Release the sealing washers, extract the bushes, and slide out the spacer, complete with O-ring seals, located at the base of the gear lever. Examine the components for wear.

9   Inspect the O-rings and gear lever seat in the remote control housing for signs of wear or damage.

10   Renew any worn or damaged parts, then reassemble and refit the gear lever, using the reverse sequence to removal.

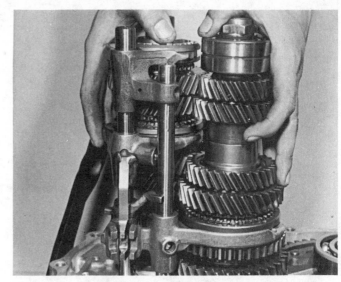

13.7 Lift up the mainshaft and countershaft to allow fitment of the selector forks and shafts

13.8 Fit the gearchange holder and interlock assembly ...

13.9 ... and secure with the three retaining bolts (arrowed)

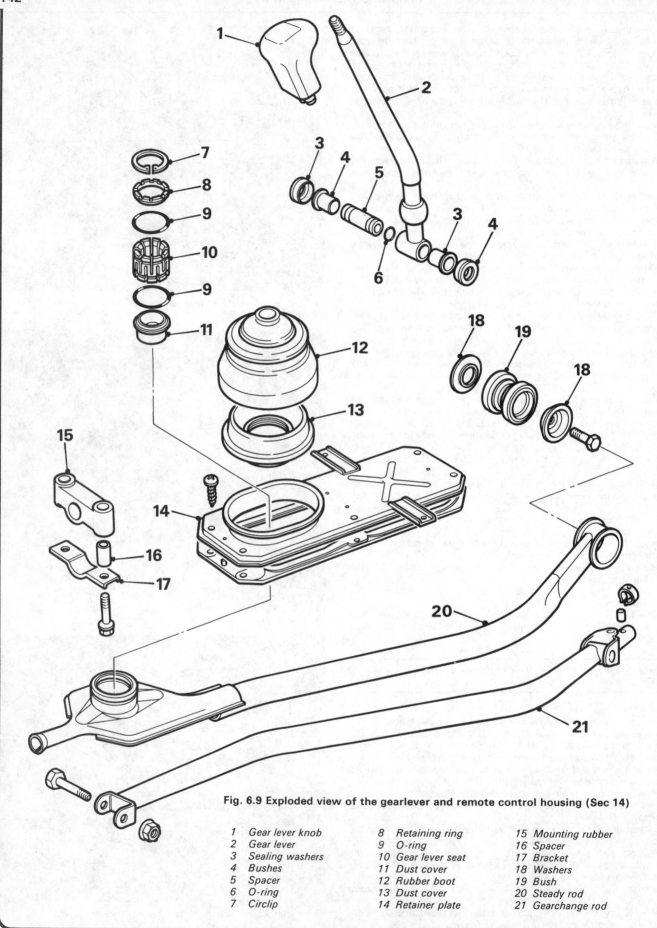

Fig. 6.9 Exploded view of the gearlever and remote control housing (Sec 14)

1 Gear lever knob	8 Retaining ring	15 Mounting rubber
2 Gear lever	9 O-ring	16 Spacer
3 Sealing washers	10 Gear lever seat	17 Bracket
4 Bushes	11 Dust cover	18 Washers
5 Spacer	12 Rubber boot	19 Bush
6 O-ring	13 Dust cover	20 Steady rod
7 Circlip	14 Retainer plate	21 Gearchange rod

13.10 Fit the reverse idler shaft, thrustwasher and gear

13.11 Engage the reverse gear fork with reverse gear, and with the 5th/reverse selector peg (arrowed)

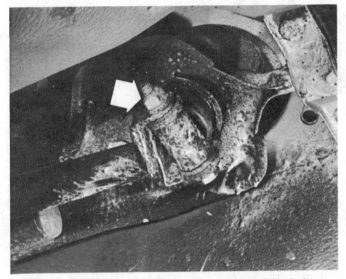

14.4 Gear lever-to-gearchange remote control rod retaining bolt (arrowed)

14.6A Remove the gear lever rubber boot ...

14.6B ... and dust cover

14.7 Gear lever retaining circlip location (arrowed)

Remote control housing

11 Carry out the operations described previously in paragraphs 1 to 5 inclusive.

12 Undo the bolt in the centre of the gearbox steady rod. Remove the dished washer, slide off the steady rod and remove the inner flat washer.

13 Remove the spring clip to expose the gearchange rod-to-gearchange shaft retaining roll pin.

14 Using a parallel pin punch, tap out the roll pin and slide the gearchange rod rearwards, off the shaft.

15 At the remote control housing end, undo the two bolts securing the mounting bracket to the underbody (photo), and withdraw the remote control assembly from under the car.

16 Refitting is the reverse sequence to removal.

14.14 Remote control housing mounting bracket retaining bolts (arrowed)

19 Fault diagnosis – manual gearbox

Symptom	Reason(s)
Gearbox noisy in neutral	Mainshaft bearings worn
Gearbox noisy only when moving (in all gears)	Countershaft bearings worn
	Differential bearings worn
	Differential final drive gear or countershaft pinion chipped or worn
Gearbox noisy in only one gear	Worn, damaged or chipped gear teeth
	Worn needle roller bearings
Gearbox jumps out of gear	Worn synchro hubs or synchro sleeves
	Weak or broken selector shaft detent spring
	Weak or broken gearchange shaft detent spring
	Worn shaft detent grooves
	Worn selector forks
	Excessive mainshaft or countershaft endfloat
Ineffective synchromesh	Worn baulk rings or synchro hubs
Difficulty in engaging gears	Clutch fault
	Ineffective synchromesh
	Worn gear lever bushes and/or linkage

Chapter 7 Automatic transmission

Contents

Specifications

General

Transmission type	ZF Type 4 HP 14
Transmission ratios:	
1st	2.412 : 1
2nd	1.369 : 1
3rd	1.000 : 1
4th	0.739 : 1
Reverse	2.828 : 1

Automatic transmission fluid

Fluid type	Dexron IID type ATF (Duckhams D-Matic)
Fluid capacity:	
From dry	6.0 litres (10.5 Imp pts)
At service fluid change	2.0 litres (3.5 Imp pts)

Torque wrench settings

	Nm	lbf ft
Drain plugs	15	11
Selector cable clamp nut	8	6
Selector cable-to-selector housing nut	15	11
Oil cooler retaining bolt	50	37
Starter inhibitor/reversing light switch	40	30
Sump pan screws	10	7
Dipstick/filler tube bracket bolt	9	6
Fluid filter housing screws	10	7
Front engine mounting bracket-to-transmission bolts	40	30
Longitudinal support member bolts	45	33
Engine tie-bars-to-mounting bracket through-bolts	45	33
Engine mountings-to-transmission bracket nuts	80	59
Roadwheel nuts	70	52

1 General description

The ZF four-speed automatic transmission fitted to Rover 820 series models comprises a hydrodynamic torque converter, a planetary gear set controlled by hydraulically operated clutches and brakes, and an integral final drive differential.

The torque converter operates on the split-torque principle, whereby engine torque is transmitted to the geartrain by hydraulic or mechanical means, in accordance with the gear selected. In first, second and reverse gears, the torque converter provides a totally hydraulic coupling between engine and geartrain. In third gear, approximately 40% of engine torque is transmitted hydraulically, the remaining 60% being transmitted mechanically by the torque converters integrated torsion damper. In fourth gear, 100% of engine torque is transmitted mechanically, thus eliminating the hydraulic slip within the torque converter at high engine speeds, and resulting in greater efficiency and improved fuel economy.

The planetary geartrain provides one of the four forward or single reverse gear ratios, according to which of its component parts are held

stationary or allowed to turn. In addition to two mechanical one-way clutches, the geartrain components are held or released by three clutches and three brake bands, which are activated by hydraulic valves. An oil pump within the transmission provides the necessary hydraulic pressure to operate the clutches and brakes.

Driver control of the transmission is by a seven-position selector lever, which provides fully-automatic operation with a hold facility on the first, second and third gear ratios. A kickdown (downshift) facility is provided for overtaking, actuated by flooring the accelerator pedal.

Fluid used in the transmission is common to the geartrain and final drive, but separate drain plugs are provided in the casing to ensure complete draining. An oil cooler is located on the side of the transmission, and uses engine coolant flow as the fluid cooling medium.

Due to the complexity of the automatic transmission, any repair or overhaul work must be entrusted to a Rover dealer or automatic transmission specialist with the necessary equipment for fault diagnosis and repair. The contents of this Chapter are therefore confined to supplying general information and any service information and instructions that can be used by the owner.

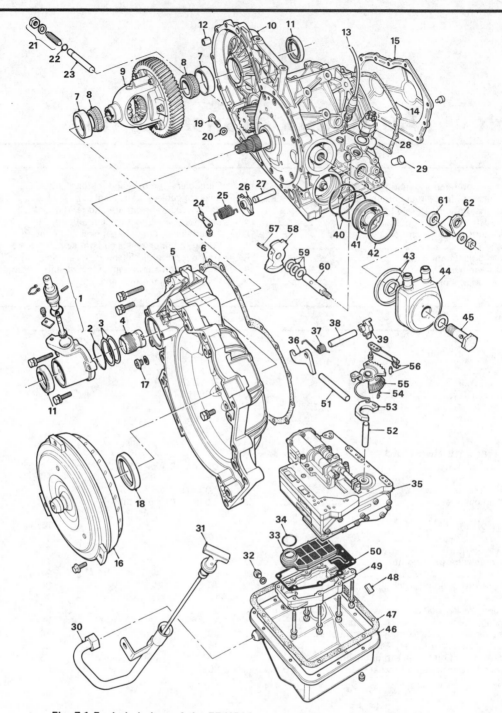

Fig. 7.1 Exploded view of the ZF HP14 automatic transmission (Sec 1)

1	Speedometer pinion assembly	16	Torque converter	31	Dipstick
2	O-ring	17	Drain plug	32	Drain plug
3	Selective shims	18	Oil seal	33	Fluid filter
4	Speedometer drivegear	19	Countershaft bearing locating bolt	34	O-ring
5	Torque converter housing	20	Washer	35	Valve block
6	Gasket	21	Brake band adjuster	36	Parking pawl
7	Bearing outer track	22	O-ring	37	Spring
8	Differential taper roller bearing	23	Adjuster plate	38	Parking pawl shaft
9	Final drive differential	24	Retaining plate	39	Oil diverter
10	Transmission casing	25	Spring	40	O-rings
11	Oil seal	26	Kickdown cam	41	Servo cover
12	Dowel	27	Kickdown cam shaft	42	Snap-ring
13	Kickdown cable	28	Starter/inhibitor switch	43	Oil cooler seals
14	Gasket	29	Transmission breather	44	Oil cooler
15	End cover	30	Dipstick/filler tube	45	Oil cooler retaining bolt
				46	Sump pan

47	Gasket
48	Magnet
49	Filter housing
50	Gasket
51	Parking pawl pushrod
52	Park lock cam shaft
53	Locking cam
54	Spring
55	Selector stop-plate
56	Detent spring and roller
57	Roll pin
58	Selector cam
59	Shims
60	Selector shaft
61	Oil seal
62	Selector lever

2 Maintenance and inspection

1   At the intervals given in *Routine maintenance* at the beginning of this manual, carefully inspect the transmission joint faces and oil seals for any signs of damage, deterioration or oil leakage.
2   Check the transmission fluid level as described in the following Section, and at the less-frequent intervals specified, renew the fluid as described in Section 4.
3   Carry out a thorough road test, ensuring that all gear changes occur smoothly without snatching and without an increase in engine speed between changes. Check that all gear positions can be engaged with the appropriate movement of the gear selector and, with the vehicle at rest, check the operation of the parking pawl when 'P' is selected.

3 Automatic transmission fluid – level checking

1   Check the fluid level at the intervals specified in *Routine maintenance*, with the car standing on a level surface. The check may be carried out with the engine/transmission hot or cold, but hot is preferable.

Engine/transmission cold

2   Apply the handbrake and select 'P'. Start the engine, and as soon as it idles evenly, withdraw the dipstick and wipe it clean on paper or a non-fluffy cloth.
3   Insert the dipstick fully, and immediately withdraw it. The fluid level should be between the MIN and MAX marks on the COLD side of the dipstick.
4   If more fluid is required, top up via the dipstick/filler tube, using the specified fluid, to the mid-point between the marks. Do not overfill. The difference between the MAX and MIN marks is 0.3 litres (0.5 Imp pts). Note that checking the fluid level cold is only approximate – ideally it should be checked hot.

Engine/transmission hot

5   The engine/transmission should be at normal operating temperature, preferably after a short journey.
6   Level checking and topping-up are as described in paragraphs 2 to 4, but check the level against the HOT side of the dipstick.

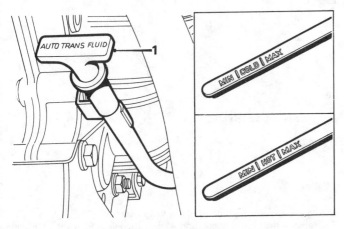

Fig. 7.2 Transmission fluid dipstick (1) and level markings (Sec 3)

4 Automatic transmission fluid – draining and refilling

1   Prior to draining, the engine/transmission should be at normal operating temperature, preferably after a short journey.
2   Apply the handbrake, select 'P', jack up the front of the car and support it on axle stands.
3   Position a large container beneath the transmission, and undo the two socket-headed drain plugs – one on the side of the sump pan, and one on the transmission casing (Fig. 7.3). Allow the fluid to drain into

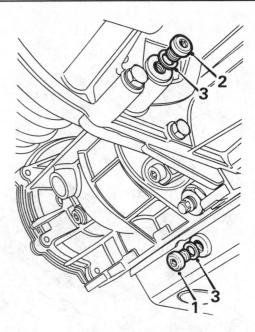

Fig. 7.3 Drain plug locations (Sec 4)

1   *Sump pan drain plug*   3   *Sealing washers*
2   *Transmission casing drain plug*

the container. **Warning:** *Take care to avoid scalding – the transmission fluid will be very hot.*
4   Clean and refit the drain plugs, using new sealing washers if the old ones are damaged.
5   Lower the car to the ground.
6   Refill through the dipstick/filler tube, using the specified fluid, until the fluid level is at MAX on the cold side of the dipstick.
7   Start the engine, and as soon as it idles evenly, move the selector lever slowly through all gear positions to circulate fluid through the transmission, then return it to 'P'.
8   Check the fluid level against the COLD side of the dipstick, as described in the previous Section, and top up if necessary.
9   Recheck the fluid level with the engine/transmission hot after taking the car for a short journey.

5 Transmission sump pan – removal and refitting

1   Remove the front suspension tie-rod on the left-hand side, as described in Chapter 10.
2   Drain the automatic transmission fluid as described in the previous Section.
3   Undo the bolt securing the dipstick/filler tube to the engine.
4   Undo the retaining screws and withdraw the sump pan and gasket.
5   Clean the interior of the sump pan, and remove and clean the swarf-collecting magnet.
6   Refit the sump pan using a new gasket, and tighten the retaining screws progressively and in a diagonal sequence to the specified torque.
7   Refit the dipstick/filler tube retaining bolt.
8   Refit the tie-rod as described in Chapter 10.
9   Lower the car to the ground, and refill the transmission with fresh fluid as described in Section 4.

6 Transmission fluid filter – removal, cleaning and refitting

1   This is not a routine maintenance operation, and will normally only be required after very high mileage, or if contaminants are evident in the fluid at the time of regular fluid renewal.
2   Remove the transmission sump pan as described in the previous Section.
3   Undo the nine screws securing the filter housing to the valve block,

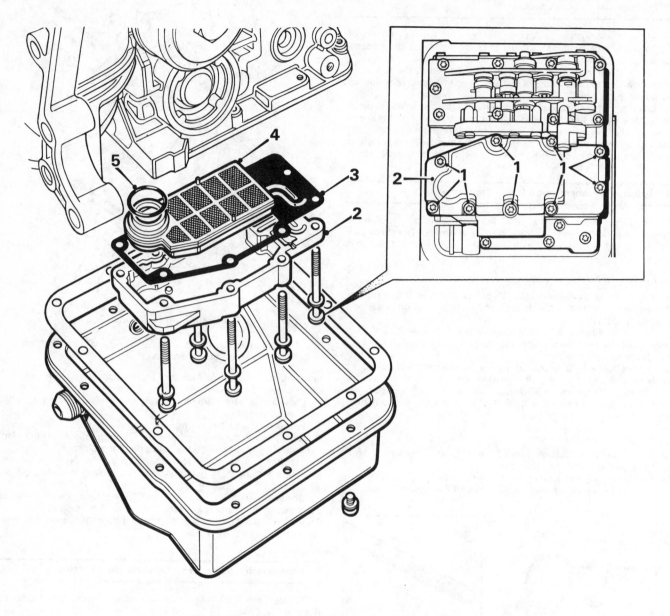

Fig. 7.4 Transmission fluid filter components (Sec 6)

1	Filter housing retaining screws	2	Filter housing	4	Fluid filter
		3	Gasket	5	O-ring seal

noting the locations of the different length screws.

4   Remove the filter housing and gasket, then withdraw the filter and O-ring seal.

5   Clean the filter and filter housing in clean transmission fluid. If the filter is badly contaminated, it should be renewed. Also renew the filter housing gasket and the O-ring seal as a matter of course.

6   Refit the components using the reverse sequence to removal, tightening the housing retaining screws to the specified torque. Refit the sump pan as described in the previous Section.

7   Valve block – removal and refitting

1   Remove the transmission sump pan as described in Section 5.

2   Undo the nine screws securing the filter housing to the valve block,

noting the locations of the different length screws.

3   Remove the filter housing and gasket, then withdraw the filter and O-ring seal.

4   Undo the remaining screws securing the valve block, and withdraw the valve block from the transmission.

5   Clean the valve block, filter and filter housing in clean transmission fluid. If the filter is badly contaminated, it should be renewed. Also renew the filter housing gasket and the O-ring seal as a matter of course.

6   Move the selector lever in the car to position '1'.

7   Fit the valve block to the transmission, ensuring that the manual shift valve engages with the kickdown cable cam.

8   With the O-ring in position, fit the filter to the valve block followed by the filter housing and gasket. Secure the housing and valve block with the retaining screws, tightened to the specified torque.

9   Refit the sump pan as described in Section 5.

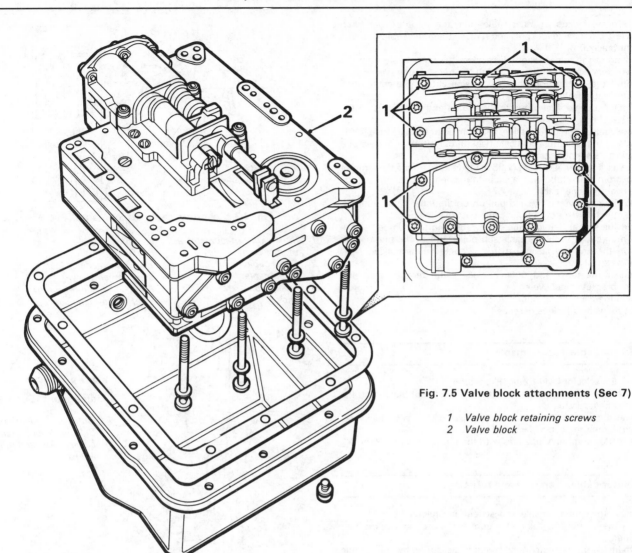

Fig. 7.5 Valve block attachments (Sec 7)

1   Valve block retaining screws
2   Valve block

8   Kickdown cable – adjustment

1   Refer to Chapter 3 and remove the air cleaner components as necessary to gain access to the kickdown cable and linkage.
2   Slacken the kickdown cable locknuts at the abutment bracket on the side of the throttle housing to release the tension in the cable.
3   Open the throttle and hold it in the fully-open position.
4   Pull the kickdown inner cable upwards until the detent is felt, then adjust the outer cable locknuts to eliminate the slack in the inner cable.
5   Release the throttle, and check that the gap between the crimped sleeve on the inner cable, and the end of the outer cable, is between 0.5 and 1.0 mm (0.02 and 0.04 in) (Fig. 7.6). Reposition the crimped sleeve if the gap is incorrect.
6   Tighten the cable locknuts securely, and refit the air cleaner components.

9   Kickdown cable – removal and refitting

1   Refer to Chapter 3 and remove the air cleaner components as necessary to gain access to the kickdown cable and linkage.
2   Remove the valve block as described in Section 7.
3   Record the routing of the cable so that the cable can be refitted in the same way.

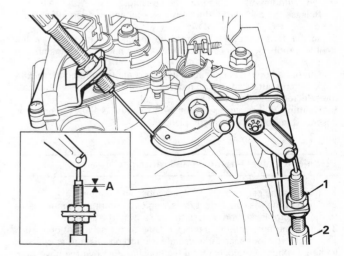

Fig. 7.6 Kickdown cable adjustment (Sec 8)

1   Kickdown cable locknuts
2   Outer cable
A   = 0.5 to 1.0 mm (0.02 to 0.04 in) – see text

4   Release the kickdown inner cable from the throttle lever, then unscrew the outer cable locknuts and remove the outer cable from the abutment bracket.

5   Working at the transmission, disconnect the inner cable from the kickdown cam, and the outer cable from the transmission casing.

6   Remove the O-ring from the transmission end of the cable, then remove the cable from the car.

7   To refit the cable, first lubricate the O-ring and position it on the outer cable.

8   Fit the cable to the transmission, and connect the inner cable to the kickdown cam after turning the cam back through three-quarters of a turn against its spring tension.

9   Make up a spacer, 41.5 mm (1.63 in) in length, from a thin strip of metal, or from metal tube with a slit along its length to allow it to be slipped over the inner cable (Fig. 7.7).

10 Hold the cable vertically, and pull up on the inner cable until the first detent is felt. Do not pull the cable past the detent.

11 Insert the spacer between the outer cable and the crimped sleeve on the inner cable. With the cable still pulled out to the first detent, reposition the crimped sleeve so that it contacts the spacer. Now remove the spacer.

12 Connect the inner and outer cables to the throttle lever and abutment bracket respectively.

13 Adjust the cable as described in Section 8.

14 Refit the valve block as described in Section 7.

10 Selector cable – adjustment

1   Move the selector lever to the 'P' position.

2   Slacken the outer cable clamp nut at the abutment bracket on the side of the transmission.

3   Rotate the selector lever at the transmission fully anti-clockwise, and then tighten the cable clamp nut.

4   Check the starter only operates with the transmission in 'P' or 'N'.

11 Selector cable – removal and refitting

1   Remove the centre console as described in Chapter 11.

2   Apply the handbrake, jack up the front of the car and support it on axle stands.

3   From inside the car, extract the spring clip securing the inner cable to the selector lever, and release the cable from the lever.

4   Undo the nut securing the outer cable to the selector housing. A $^{15}/_{16}$ inch crowfoot spanner is useful for undoing this nut, as space is limited. Withdraw the cable from the housing.

5   Release the cable from the body brackets and support clips under the car.

6   At the transmission end, extract the spring clip and withdraw the steel and rubber washers securing the inner cable to the transmission selector lever.

7   Undo the outer cable retaining nut at the abutment bracket, release the inner and outer cables, and recover the inner cable spacer. Remove the selector cable from the car.

8   Refitting is the reverse sequence to removal. Adjust the cable as described in Section 10 on completion.

12 Selector lever – removal and refitting

1   Remove the centre console as described in Chapter 11.

2   From inside the car, extract the spring clip securing the inner cable to the selector lever, and release the cable from the lever.

3   Undo the nut securing the outer cable to the selector housing. A $^{15}/_{16}$ inch crowfoot spanner is useful for undoing this nut, as space is limited. Withdraw the cable from the housing. Remove the olive from the cable.

4   Apply the handbrake, jack up the front of the car and support it on axle stands.

5   Undo the five bolts and remove the engine undertray.

6   Undo the nuts securing the exhaust front pipe to the manifold.

7   Release the exhaust system front rubber mounting, and lower the

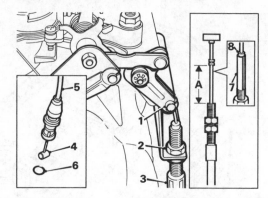

Fig. 7.7 Kickdown cable attachments (Sec 9)

1   Inner cable attachments at throttle cam
2   Outer cable locknuts
3   Outer cable
4   Inner cable – transmission end
5   Outer cable
6   O-ring
7   Home made spacer
8   Crimped sleeve
A   = 41.5 mm (1.63 in) – length of home-made spacer (see text)

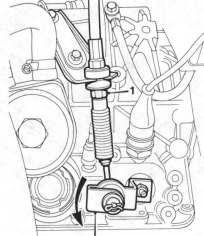

Fig. 7.8 Selector cable adjustment (Sec 10)

1   Outer cable clamp nut
2   Selector lever (rotate anti-clockwise during adjustment)

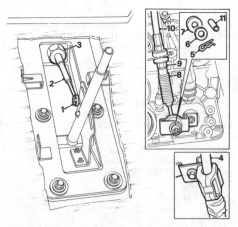

Fig. 7.9 Selector cable attachments (Sec 11)

1   Selector cable-to-lever spring clip
2   Inner cable
3   Outer cable-to-housing retaining nut
4   Underbody bracket
5   Spring clip
6   Steel washer
7   Rubber washer
8   Rubber gaiter
9   Outer cable-to-abutment bracket retaining nut
10 Outer cable
11 Inner cable spacer

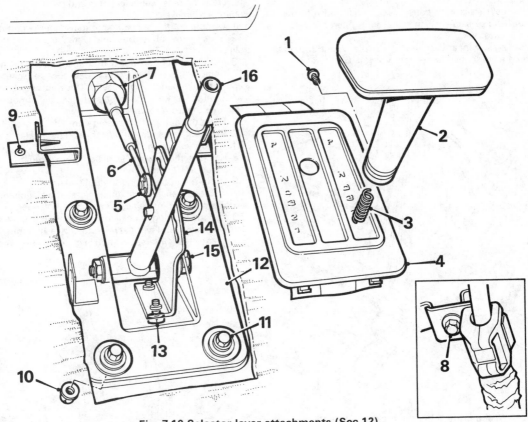

Fig. 7.10 Selector lever attachments (Sec 12)

1 Grub screw	5 Selector cable-to-lever	8 Underbody bracket
2 Selector lever knob	spring clip	9 Housing rivets
3 Spring	6 Inner cable	10 Housing retaining nut
4 Top panel	7 Outer cable-to-housing	11 Housing retaining bolt
	retaining nut	12 Selector housing

13   Detent bracket retaining
bolts
14   Detent bracket
15   Selector lever pivot bolt
16   Selector lever

exhaust slightly at the front. Recover the front pipe-to-manifold gasket.

8   Undo the retaining bolts and remove the exhaust front heat shield.

9   Undo the bolt and release the cable support bracket from the underbody.

10 Withdraw the selector cable from the selector housing.

11 From inside the car, move the carpets aside and drill out the four rivets on the sides of the housing.

12 Undo the nuts and bolts securing the housing and console mounting bracket, then remove the selector housing from the car.

13 With the assembly on the bench, undo the two bolts and remove the detent bracket from the housing.

14 Undo the nut, remove the selector lever pivot bolt and withdraw the lever from the housing.

15 Refitting is the reverse sequence to removal, but adjust the selector cable as described in Section 10 on completion.

13 Starter inhibitor/reversing light switch – removal and refitting

1   From within the engine compartment, release the ignition/fuel electronic control unit from its mounting bracket below the battery, and move the unit to one side.

2   Slide up the rubber grommet over the starter inhibitor/reversing light switch wiring terminals, and disconnect the four wires. Note that the two white/red wires are connected to the two larger terminals on the switch.

3   Unscrew the switch from the transmission and recover the sealing washer.

4   Refitting is the reverse sequence to removal, but use a new sealing

washer if necessary. On completion, check the operation of the reversing lights, and check that the starter only operates with the selector lever in 'P' or 'N'.

14 Brake band – adjustment

1   This is not a routine operation but is worth checking, along with the other adjustments contained in this Chapter, in the event of an elementary malfunction, or suspected fault in the transmission.

2   Apply the handbrake, jack up the front of the car and support it on axle stands.

3   Move the selector lever to 'N'.

4   Slacken the brake band adjuster locknut located above the sump pan drain plug.

5   Tighten the adjuster screw to 10 Nm (7.0 lbf ft), then unscrew the adjuster exactly two turns.

6   Hold the adjuster screw in this position, and tighten the locknut.

7   Lower the car to the ground.

15 Oil cooler – removal and refitting

1   Drain the cooling system as described in Chapter 2.

2   Undo the air cleaner bracket retaining bolts, and release the bracket for access.

3   Slacken the retaining clips and disconnect the two coolant hoses at the oil cooler.

4   Undo the centre retaining bolt and recover the seal.

5   Withdraw the oil cooler from the transmission, and recover the two seals.

6 Check the condition of the seals, and renew if necessary. Clean the oil cooler and the cooler-to-transmission mating faces.
7 Lubricate the new seals with transmission fluid, and refit the oil cooler using the reverse sequence to removal. Tighten the retaining bolt to the specified torque.
8 Refill the cooling system as described in Chapter 2, and top up the transmission fluid as described in Section 3 of this Chapter.

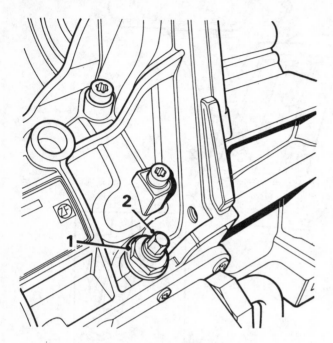

Fig. 7.11 Brake band adjuster locknut (1) and adjuster screw (2) (Sec 14)

16 Speedometer pinion – removal and refitting

1 Disconnect the speedometer transducer wiring multi-plug.
2 Slide up the rubber boot and extract the transducer retaining spring clip.
3 Withdraw the transducer from the pinion housing.
4 Undo the screw and remove the pinion housing retaining plate.
5 Withdraw the pinion housing from the transmission, and recover the O-ring seals.
6 Tap out the retaining pin in the housing and withdraw the pinion. Recover the small O-ring seal.
7 Check the condition of the components, and renew as necessary.
8 Lubricate the pinion shaft and O-rings with transmission fluid, then refit using the reverse sequence to removal.

17 Automatic transmission – removal and refitting

1 Disconnect the battery negative terminal. (Refer to Chapter 12, Section 1, before doing this).
2 Remove the air cleaner assembly as described in Chapter 3.
3 Drain the cooling system as described in Chapter 2.
4 Extract the retaining clips and release the support struts from the bonnet. Tie the bonnet back in the fully-open position.
5 Disconnect the earth lead at the transmission.
6 Slacken the clips and disconnect the two coolant hoses at the transmission oil cooler.
7 Slide up the rubber boot and disconnect the four wires at the reversing light/starter inhibitor switch. Note that the two white/red wires are connected to the two larger switch terminals.
8 Extract the spring clip and withdraw the steel and rubber washers securing the selector cable end to the transmission selector lever.
9 Undo the outer cable retaining nut at the abutment bracket, release the inner and outer cables, and recover the inner cable spacer.

10 Release the kickdown inner cable from the throttle lever, then unscrew the outer cable locknuts and remove the outer cable from the abutment bracket.
11 Disconnect the speedometer transducer wiring multi-plug.
12 Slide up the rubber boot and extract the transducer retaining spring clip.
13 Withdraw the transducer from the pinion housing.
14 Remove the starter motor as described in Chapter 12.
15 Apply the handbrake, prise off the front wheel trim and slacken the wheel nuts. Jack up the front of the car and support it on axle stands. Remove the front roadwheels.
16 Drain the automatic transmission fluid as described in Section 4.
17 Remove the engine undershield and the access panel from the left-hand inner wing.
18 Remove the front suspension tie-rod on the left-hand side, as described in Chapter 10.
19 Undo the nut securing the right-hand steering knuckle balljoint to the lower suspension arm, then release the balljoint from the arm using a universal balljoint separator tool or two-legged puller.
20 Pull the steering knuckle outwards, then using a suitable flat bar or large screwdriver, lever between the driveshaft inner constant velocity joint and the differential housing to release the joint from the transmission.

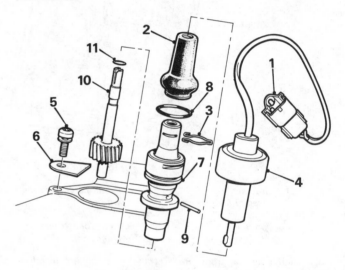

Fig. 7.12 Exploded view of the speedometer pinion components (Sec 16)

1 Transducer wiring multi-plug	6 Pinion housing retaining plate
2 Rubber boot	7 Pinion housing
3 Spring clip	8 O-ring
4 Transducer	9 Pinion retaining pin
5 Retaining screw	10 Speedometer pinion
	11 O-ring

21 Move the driveshaft clear of the transmission, then repeat these procedures on the left-hand driveshaft.
22 Attach a suitable hoist to the engine using rope slings, or chains attached to brackets secured to the cylinder head. Raise the hoist to just take the weight of the engine.
23 From under the front of the car, undo the bolt securing the larger end of the engine lower tie-bar to its mounting bracket. Remove the through-bolt and recover the special nut.
24 Undo the bolts securing the longitudinal support member to the underbody, and remove the member.
25 Undo the two bolts securing the bracket at the smaller end of the engine lower tie-bar to the transmission. Undo the mounting bracket bolts and remove the lower tie-bar assembly.
26 Turn the crankshaft as necessary, using a socket or spanner on the crankshaft pulley bolt, until one of the torque converter retaining bolts becomes accessible through the starter motor aperture. Undo the bolt, then turn the crankshaft and remove the remaining two bolts in the same way.
27 Support the transmission using a jack and interposed block of wood positioned under the sump pan.

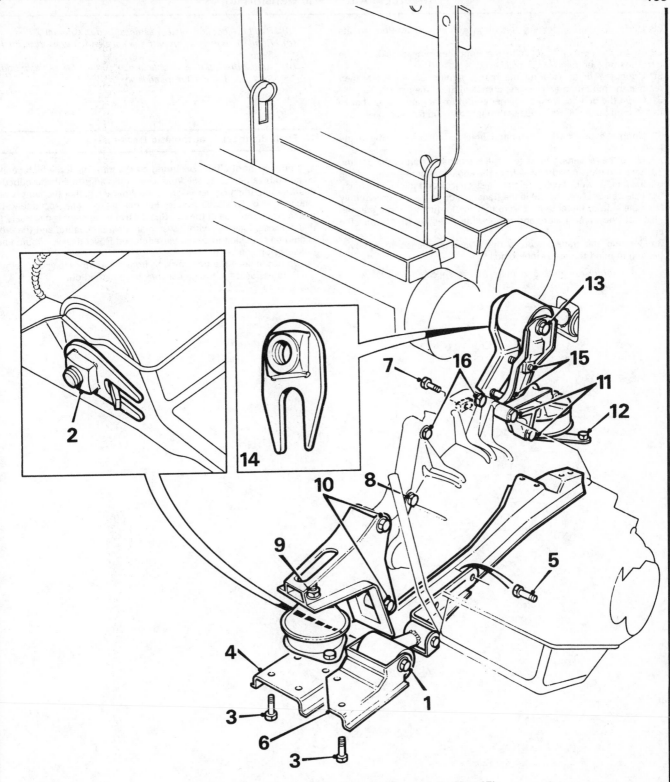

Fig. 7.13 Automatic transmission mounting details (Sec 17)

1 Engine lower tie-bar-to-mounting bracket bolt
2 Special nut
3 Longitudinal support member and tie-bar bracket bolts
4 Longitudinal support member
5 Engine lower tie-bar-to-transmission bracket bolts
6 Engine lower tie-bar assembly
7 Torque converter retaining bolts
8 Transmission-to-engine bolt
9 Front engine mounting-to-transmission bracket nut
10 Front engine mounting bracket retaining bolts
11 Rear engine mounting bracket retaining bolts
12 Rear engine mounting bolts
13 Engine rear tie-bar-to-mounting bracket bolt
14 Special nut
15 Rear tie-bar mounting bracket bolts
16 Transmission-to-engine bolts

28 Undo the nut securing the front engine mounting to its transmission bracket.
29 Undo the two bolts securing the front mounting bracket to the transmission, and remove the bracket.
30 Undo the bolts securing the rear mounting and bracket, then remove the mounting and bracket complete, from the car.
31 Undo the bolt securing the larger end of the engine rear tie-bar to its mounting bracket. Remove the through-bolt and recover the special nut.
32 Undo the rear tie-bar mounting bracket bolts, and remove the bracket.
33 Undo the remaining bolts securing the transmission to the engine.
34 Ease the transmission away from the engine, after releasing it from the locating dowels. Lower the transmission jack and the engine hoist, until clearance exists to enable the transmission to be withdrawn fully from the side of the engine. Ensure that the torque converter stays in place on the transmission, and remove the assembly from under the car.
35 Refitting the transmission is the reverse sequence to removal, bearing in mind the following points:

(a) *Tighten all nuts and bolts to the specified torque, where applicable*

(b) *Refill the cooling system as described in Chapter 2*
(c) *Refill the transmission with the specified fluid as described in Section 4*
(d) *Adjust the kickdown cable and selector cable as described in Sections 8 and 10 respectively*

18 Fault diagnosis – automatic transmission

In the event of a fault occurring on the transmission which cannot be cured by attention to the fluid level or the adjustments described in this Chapter, it is first necessary to determine whether the fault is of a mechanical or hydraulic nature. For this to be done accurately, the transmission must be in the car. Special test equipment is necessary for this purpose, together with a systematic test procedure, and the work should be entrusted to a suitably-equipped Rover dealer, or automatic transmission specialist.

Do not remove the transmission from the car for repair or overhaul until professional fault diagnosis has been carried out.

Chapter 8 Driveshafts

Contents

Specifications

Type .... Unequal-length solid steel, splined to inner and outer constant velocity joints

Lubrication
Overhaul only – see text
Lubricant type:
    Outer constant velocity joint .... Mobil 171A-M3 grease or equivalent
    Inner constant velocity joint .... Mobil 525 grease or equivalent
Quantity:
    Outer constant velocity joint .... 80 to 100 ml
    Inner constant velocity joint .... 175 to 185 ml

Torque wrench settings

	Nm	lbf ft
Driveshaft retaining nut	290	214
Strut forked member clamp bolt	50	37
Strut forked member to lower arm	90	66
Steering knuckle balljoint nut	100	74
Steering tie-rod balljoint nut	44	32
Roadwheel nuts	70	52

1 General description

Drive is transmitted from the differential to the front wheels by means of two unequal-length, solid steel driveshafts.

Both driveshafts are fitted with constant velocity joints at each end. The outer joints are of the ball-and-cage type, and are splined to accept the driveshaft and wheel hub drive flange. The inner joints are of the sliding tripod type, allowing lateral movement of the driveshaft to cater for suspension travel. The inner joints are splined to accept the driveshaft and differential sun gears.

To eliminate driveshaft-induced harmonic vibrations and resonance, a rubber-mounted steel damper is attached to the longer, right-hand, driveshaft.

Driveshaft repair procedures are limited, as only the inner and outer rubber boots, and outer constant velocity joints, are available separately. The driveshafts and inner joints are supplied as complete assemblies.

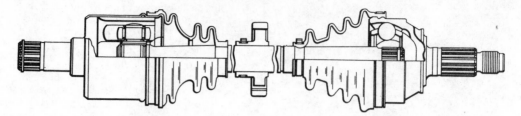

Fig. 8.1 Sectional view of the right-hand driveshaft assembly (Sec 1)

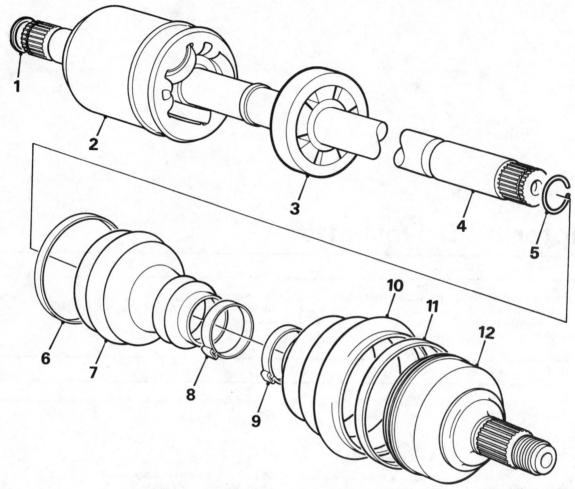

Fig. 8.2 Exploded view of the right-hand driveshaft components (Sec 1)

1 Circlip	4 Driveshaft	7 Inner joint rubber boot	10 Outer joint rubber boot
2 Inner constant velocity joint	5 Circlip	8 Rubber boot retaining clip	11 Rubber boot retaining clip
3 Damper	6 Rubber boot retaining clip	9 Rubber boot retaining clip	12 Outer constant velocity joint

2 Maintenance and inspection

1   At the intervals given in *Routine maintenance* at the beginning of this manual carry out a thorough inspection of the driveshafts and joints as follows.

2   Jack up the front of the car and securely support it on stands.

3   Slowly rotate the roadwheel, and inspect the condition of the outer joint rubber boots. Check for signs of cracking, splits or deterioration of the rubber, which may allow the grease to escape and lead to water and grit entry into the joint. Also check the condition and security of the retaining clips. Repeat these checks on the inner constant velocity joints. If any damage or deterioration is found, the boots should be renewed as described in Section 5.

4   Continue rotating the roadwheel, and check for any distortion or damage to the driveshaft itself. Check for any free play in the joints by first holding the driveshaft and attempting to rotate the wheel. Repeat this check by holding the inner joint and attempting to rotate the driveshaft. Any appreciable movement indicates wear in the joints, wear in the driveshaft splines, or a loose driveshaft retaining nut. Further investigation will be necessary if any wear is detected.

5   Road test the car and listen for a metallic clicking from the front as the car is driven slowly in a circle with the steering on full lock. If a clicking noise is heard, this indicates wear in the outer constant velocity joint(s), caused by excessive clearance between the balls in the joint and the tracks in which they run. Remove and inspect the joint as described in Section 4.

6   If vibration consistent with roadspeed is felt through the car when accelerating, there is a possibility of wear in the inner constant velocity joint(s). If so, renewal of the relevant driveshaft complete with inner joint will be necessary.

3 Driveshaft – removal and refitting

1   While the car is standing on its wheels, firmly apply the handbrake and put the transmission in gear (PARK on automatic transmission models).

2   Remove the wheel trim and, using a small punch, knock up the staking that secures the driveshaft retaining nut to the groove in the constant velocity joint stub shaft. Note that a new retaining nut will be needed for reassembly.

3   Using a socket, sturdy T-bar and long extension tube for leverage, slacken the retaining nut half a turn. Note that the retaining nut is tightened to a very high torque setting, and considerable effort will be required to slacken it.

4   Slacken the wheel nuts, jack up the front of the car and support it on stands. Remove the roadwheel and return the transmission to neutral.

5   Drain the gearbox oil as described in Chapter 6, or the automatic transmission fluid as described in Chapter 7.

6   Unscrew the nut and remove the clamp bolt securing the front suspension strut forked member to the strut – refer to Chapter 10 if necessary (photo).

7   Unscrew the nut and remove the bolt securing the forked member to the suspension lower arm (photo).

8   Remove the forked member from the strut and lower arm. If the member is tight on the strut, tap a screwdriver into the slot below the clamp bolt hole to spread the member slightly.

9   Undo the nut securing the steering knuckle balljoint to the lower arm, then release the balljoint from the arm using a universal balljoint separator tool or two-legged puller.

10 Extract the split pin and undo the nut securing the steering tie-rod balljoint to the steering knuckle arm. Release the balljoint using a universal balljoint separator tool or two-legged puller.

11 Remove the previously-slackened retaining nut.

12 Twist the steering knuckle onto full lock, then push the constant velocity joint out of the hub flange. It may be necessary to tap the end

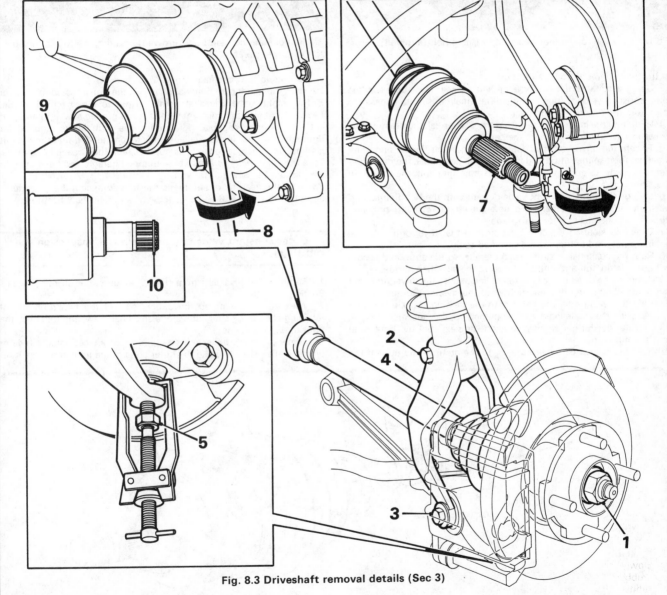

Fig. 8.3 Driveshaft removal details (Sec 3)

1 Driveshaft retaining nut	4 Forked member	7 Removal of constant velocity joint from steering knuckle hub flange	8 Removal of constant velocity joint from differential sun gear
2 Forked member clamp bolt	5 Steering knuckle ball joint nut and two-legged puller for joint separation		9 Driveshaft
3 Forked member-to-lower arm bolt			10 Inner joint retaining circlip

3.6 Unscrew the forked member-to-strut clamp bolt (arrowed)

3.7 Remove the nut and bolt (arrowed) securing the forked member to the suspension arm

of the joint to free it from its location.

13 Using a suitable flat bar or large screwdriver, lever between the inner constant velocity joint and the differential housing to release the joint from the differential sun gear.

14 Withdraw the inner joint fully from the differential, then remove the driveshaft assembly from under the car.

15 To refit the driveshaft, place it in position under the car and enter the inner joint splines into the differential sun gear. Push the driveshaft firmly inwards, to engage the retaining spring ring with the groove in the sun gear.

16 Engage the outer constant velocity joint with the hub flange, and push the joint fully home. Fit a new driveshaft retaining nut, and tighten it moderately tight at this stage.

17 Enter the steering knuckle balljoint into the lower arm, refit the retaining nut, and tighten to the specified torque.

18 Refit the suspension strut forked member to the strut, and secure with the clamp bolt and nut, tightened to the specified torque.

19 Connect the other end of the forked memebr to the lower arm, refit the bolt and retaining nut, and tighten to the specified torque.

20 Refit the steering tie-rod balljoint to the steering knuckle arm, and secure with the castellated nut, tightened to the specified torque. Tighten the nut further slightly, to align the next split pin hole, then lock the nut with a new split pin.

21 Refit the roadwheel, lower the car to the ground, and tighten the

wheel nuts to the specified torque.

22 With the handbrake firmly applied and the transmission in gear (or PARK), tighten the driveshaft retaining nut to the specified torque. Peen the nut into the constant velocity joint groove after tightening. If a torque wrench capable of recording the high figure required for tightening this nut is not available, it is recommended that the old nut is fitted, tightened as securely as possible, and then peened into place. Take the car directly to a suitably-equipped garage, and have them fit and tighten the new nut for you.

23 Refill the gearbox or automatic transmission using the procedures described in Chapter 6 or 7 respectively, and refit the wheel trim.

4 Outer constant velocity joint – removal, inspection and refitting

1 Remove the driveshaft from the car as described in the previous Section.

2 With the driveshaft on the bench, cut off the two rubber boot retaining clips using side cutters or a small hacksaw, and fold back the boot to expose the outer joint.

3 Firmly grasp the driveshaft or support it in a vice. Using a hide or plastic mallet, sharply strike the outer edge of the joint and drive it off

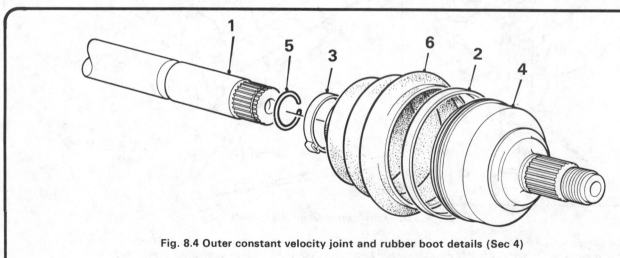

Fig. 8.4 Outer constant velocity joint and rubber boot details (Sec 4)

1 Driveshaft	3 Rubber boot retaining clip	5 Circlip
2 Rubber boot retaining clip (large)	(small)	6 Rubber boot
	4 Outer constant velocity joint	

the shaft. The outer joint is retained on the driveshaft by an internal circular section circlip, and striking the joint in the manner described forces the circlip to contract into a groove, so allowing the joint to slide off.

4   Remove the rubber boot from the driveshaft.

5   Thoroughly clean the constant velocity joint using paraffin or a suitable solvent, and dry it, preferably using compressed air. Ensure that the joint is completely dry inside, with all traces of paraffin or the solvent removed.

6   Move the inner splined driving member from side to side, to expose each ball in turn at the top of its track. Examine the balls for cracks, flat spots, surface pitting or severe scuff marks,

7   Inspect the ball tracks on the inner and outer members. If the tracks have worn, the balls will no longer be a tight fit. At the same time, check the ball cage windows for wear or for cracking between the balls.

8   If any of the above checks indicate wear in the joint, it will be necessary to renew it complete, as the internal parts are not available separately. If the joint is in a satisfactory condition, obtain a repair kit consisting of a new rubber boot and retaining clips. Also obtain a suitable quantity of the special lubricating grease (see Specifications).

9   Slide the small retaining clip and the new rubber boot over the end of the driveshaft, and locate the boot end in the driveshaft groove.

10 Place the retaining clip over the rubber boot, and fully tighten it by gently squeezing the raised portion with pliers.

11 The help of an assistant will be necessary while fitting the constant velocity joint to the driveshaft. Ensure that the circlip is undamaged and correctly located in its driveshaft groove.

12 Fold back the rubber boot and position the constant velocity joint over the splines on the driveshaft until it abuts the circlip.

13 Using two small screwdrivers placed either side of the circlip, compress the clip, and at the same time have your assistant firmly strike the end of the joint with a hide or plastic mallet.

14 The joint should slide over the compressed circlip and into position on the shaft. It will probably take several attempts until you achieve

success. If the joint does not spring into place the moment it is struck, remove it, reposition the circlip and try again. Do not force the joint, otherwise the circlip will be damaged.

15 With the joint tapped fully home, pack it thoroughly with the specified quantity of the special grease. Work the grease well into the ball tracks while twisting the joint, and fill the rubber boot with any excess.

16 Fold the rubber boot back over the joint, fit the large retaining clip, and secure the clip by squeezing the raised portion with pliers.

17 The driveshaft can now be refitted to the car as described in Section 3.

5   Constant velocity joint rubber boots – removal and refitting

1   Remove the driveshaft from the car as described in Section 3.

Outer joint rubber boot

2   Remove the outer constant velocity joint from the driveshaft as described in Section 4. Renewal of the rubber boot is also covered in Section 4, as it is an integral part of the outer joint removal and refitting procedure.

Inner joint rubber boot

3   Remove the outer constant velocity joint and rubber boot as described in Section 4.

4   If working on the right-hand driveshaft, cut off the damper retaining clips using side cutters or a small hacksaw, and slide the damper off the driveshaft.

5   Cut off the inner joint rubber boot retaining clips, and slide the boot off the driveshaft.

6   Clean out as much of the grease in the inner constant velocity joint as possible, using a wooden spatula and old rags. It is advisable not to

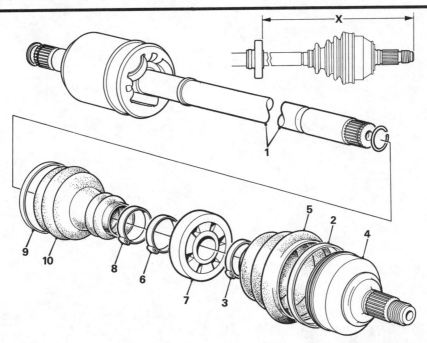

Fig. 8.5 Inner constant velocity joint, damper and rubber boot details (Sec 5)

1 Driveshaft	4 Outer constant velocity joint	8 Rubber boot retaining clip (small)
2 Rubber boot retaining clip (large)	5 Outer joint rubber boot	9 Rubber boot retaining clip (large)
3 Rubber boot retaining clip (small)	6 Damper retaining clip	10 Inner joint rubber boot
	7 Damper (right-hand driveshaft only)	

X = Damper setting dimension:
Manual gearbox models .... 538.25 to 546.25 mm (21.20 to 21.52 in)

Automatic transmission
models .... 522.25 to 527.25 mm (20.57 to 20.77 in)

clean this type of joint using paraffin or solvents, as it is impossible to remove all the solvent and dry the joint thoroughly after cleaning.

7 Examine the bearing tracks in the joint outer member for signs of scoring, wear ridges or evidence of lack of lubrication. Also examine the three bearing caps in the same way, and check for evidence of excessive play between the roller bearing caps and their tracks in the outer member.

8 If any of the above checks indicate wear in the joint, it will be necessary to renew the driveshaft and inner joint as an assembly; they are not available separately. If the joint is in a satisfactory condition, obtain a repair kit consisting of a new rubber boot and retaining clips. Also obtain a suitable quantity of the special lubricating grease (see Specifications).

9 Pack the constant velocity joint with the specified quantity of the special grease. Work the grease well into the joint while moving it from side to side. Fill the rubber boot with any excess.

10 Fit the new rubber boot and large retaining clip to the driveshaft, and locate the boot and clip over the joint. Secure the boot by squeezing the raised portion of the clip using side cutters.

11 Secure the other end of the boot in the same way with the small retaining clip.

12 Refit the damper and retaining clip to the driveshaft (where applicable), position the damper as shown in Fig. 8.5, and secure with the clip.

13 Refit the outer constant velocity joint and rubber boot as described in Section 4, then refit the driveshaft as described in Section 3.

6 Fault diagnosis – driveshafts

Symptom	Reason(s)
Vibration and/or noise on turns	Worn outer constant velocity joint(s)
Vibration when accelerating	Worn inner constant velocity joint(s) Bent or distorted driveshaft
Vibration or resonance at a particular roadspeed	Loose, incorrectly positioned or damaged vibration damper
Noise on taking up drive	Worn driveshaft or constant velocity joint splines Worn constant velocity joints Loose driveshaft retaining nut

See also Fault diagnosis – suspension and steering (Chapter 10)

Chapter 9 Braking system

Contents

Specifications

System type

.... Diagonally-split, dual-circuit hydraulic with pressure-reducing valve in rear hydraulic circuit, and cable-operated handbrake. Anti-lock braking system available on later models.

Front brakes

Type .... Ventilated disc with single-piston sliding calipers
Make .... Girling
Disc diameter .... 262.0 mm (10.32 in)
Disc thickness:
    New .... 21.0 mm (0.827 in)
    Minimum .... 19.0 mm (0.748 in)
Maximum thickness variation .... 0.015 mm (0.0006 in)
Maximum disc run-out .... 0.075 mm (0.003 in)
Caliper piston diameter .... 57.0 mm (2.24 in)
Brake pad thickness (including backing, but excluding shims):
    New .... 17.4 mm (0.68 in)
    Minimum .... 8.2 mm (0.32 in)

Rear brakes

Type .... Solid disc with single-piston sliding calipers
Make .... Girling
Disc diameter .... 260.0 mm (10.24 in)
Disc thickness:
    New .... 10.0 mm (0.394 in)
    Minimum .... 8.0 mm (0.315 in)
Maximum thickness variation .... 0.015 mm (0.0006 in)
Maximum disc run-out .... 0.075 mm (0.003 in)
Caliper piston diameter .... 38.0 mm (1.49 in)
Brake pad thickness (including backing):
    New .... 14.5 mm (0.57 in)
    Minimum .... 7.2 mm (0.28 in)

Handbrake
Handbrake linkage lever-to-stop pin clearance .... 0.5 to 2.0 mm (0.019 to 0.078 in)

General
Brake fluid type .... Hydraulic fluid to FMVSS 116 DOT 4 (Duckhams Universal Brake and Clutch Fluid)

Master cylinder bore diameter .... 23.81 mm (0.938 in)
Servo unit boost ratio 4.6:1
Wheel speed sensor-to-reluctor ring clearance (ABS):
    Front .... 0.30 to 1.02 mm (0.011 to 0.04 in)
    Rear .... 0.16 to 1.03 mm (0.006 to 0.04 in)

Torque wrench settings

	Nm	lbf ft
Caliper guide pin bolts	33	24
Front caliper carrier bracket to steering knuckle	75	55
Rear caliper carrier bracket to hub carrier	45	33
Caliper bleed screws	10	7
Brake hose banjo union bolts	35	26
Brake pipe union nuts:		
Without ABS	14	10
With ABS	22	16
Brake disc retaining screws	12	9
Handbrake linkage cover to rear caliper	10	7
Handbrake lever to floor	25	18
Handbrake front cable guide plate bolts	25	18
Handbrake rear cable support clip bolts	10	7
Master cylinder-to-servo unit nuts	25	18
Servo unit-to-bulkhead nuts	25	18
Brake pedal pivot bolt	25	18
Pressure reducing valve mounting bracket bolts	10	7
Hydraulic modulator mounting nuts (ABS)	10	7
Wheel speed sensor-to-sensor bracket bolt (ABS)	10	7
Wheel speed sensor bracket bolts (ABS)	25	18
Wheel speed sensor wiring clips and bracket bolts (ABS)	10	7
Roadwheel nuts	70	52

1 General description

The braking system is of the servo-assisted, dual-circuit hydraulic type, incorporating disc brakes at the front and rear. A diagonally-split dual circuit hydraulic system is employed, in which each circuit operates one front and one diagonally opposite rear brake from a tandem master cylinder. Under normal conditions, both circuits operate in unison; however, in the event of hydraulic failure in one circuit, full braking force will still be available at two wheels. A pressure-reducing valve is incorporated in the rear brake hydraulic circuit. This valve regulates the hydraulic pressure applied to each rear brake, and reduces the possibility of the rear wheels locking under heavy braking.

Self-adjusting single-piston sliding type calipers are used in conjunction with ventilated and solid discs at the front and rear respectively. A cable-operated handbrake provides an independent mechanical means of rear brake application.

An anti-lock braking system (ABS) is available as an optional extra on models produced from approximately June 1988 onwards. Further information on this system will be found in the relevant Sections of this Chapter.

2 Maintenance and inspection

1   At the intervals given in *Routine maintenance* at the beginning of this manual, the following service operations should be carried out on the braking system components.
2   Check the brake fluid level, and if necessary top up with the specified fluid to the MAX mark on the reservoir (photos). Any need for frequent topping-up indicates a fluid leak somewhere in the system, which must be investigated and rectified immediately.
3   Check the front and rear brake pads for wear, and inspect the condition of the discs using the procedures described in Sections 3 and 7 respectively.
4   Check the condition of the hydraulic pipes and hoses as described in Section 15. At the same time, check the condition of the handbrake cables, lubricate the exposed cables and linkages, and if necessary adjust the handbrake as described in Section 18.

2.2A Top up with the specified fluid ...

2.2B ... to the MAX mark on the reservoir (arrowed)

2.5 Brake pad wear warning light wiring plug (arrowed)

5   The operation of the three-function braking system warning light should be tested as follows. Apply the handbrake with the ignition switched on, and check that the light illuminates as the handbrake is applied. To test the low brake fluid warning function, place the car in gear (or in PARK on automatic transmission models), release the handbrake and switch on the ignition. The light should illuminate when the flexible contact cover in the centre of the brake fluid reservoir filler cap is depressed. To check the brake pad wear warning function, disconnect the warning lamp wiring plug attached to the left-hand front brake caliper (photo) and connect a bridging wire across the two terminals in the harness plug. With the ignition switched on, the warning light should illuminate when the bridging wire is earthed. Repeat this check at the left-hand rear caliper as a test for wiring continuity. If the warning light fails to illuminate under any of the test conditions, then either the bulb is blown, a fuse is at fault, or there is a wiring fault in the circuit concerned.

6   Renew the brake hydraulic fluid at the specified intervals by draining the system and refilling with fresh fluid, using the bleeding procedure described in Section 16.

7   The flexible brake hoses and rubber seals in the brake calipers and master cylinder should also be renewed at the intervals given. Details of these operations will be found in the relevant Sections of this Chapter.

3   Front brake pads – inspection and renewal

1   Apply the handbrake, prise off the front wheel trim and slacken the wheel nuts. Jack up the front of the car and support it on axle stands. Remove the front roadwheels.

2   The thickness of the brake pads can now be checked by viewing through the slot in the front of the caliper body. If any of the pads has worn down to, or below, the minimum specified thickness, all four pads must be renewed as a complete set. The pads must also be renewed if there is any sign of oil or fluid contamination caused by leaking seals. If so, the cause of the contamination must be traced and rectified before new pads are fitted.

3   Disconnect the pad wear warning light wiring plug (left-hand caliper only) and using a suitable spanner, unscrew the lower guide pin bolt (photo) while holding the guide pin with a second spanner.

4   Pivot the caliper body upwards (photo) and tie it up using a length of string to a suitable place under the wheelarch.

5   Lift out the two brake pads together with their shims (photo), then, where fitted, remove the upper and lower anti-rattle shims from the caliper carrier bracket (photos). If the pads are to be re-used, suitably identify them so that they can be refitted in their original positions.

6   Remove the heat shield from the caliper piston (photo).

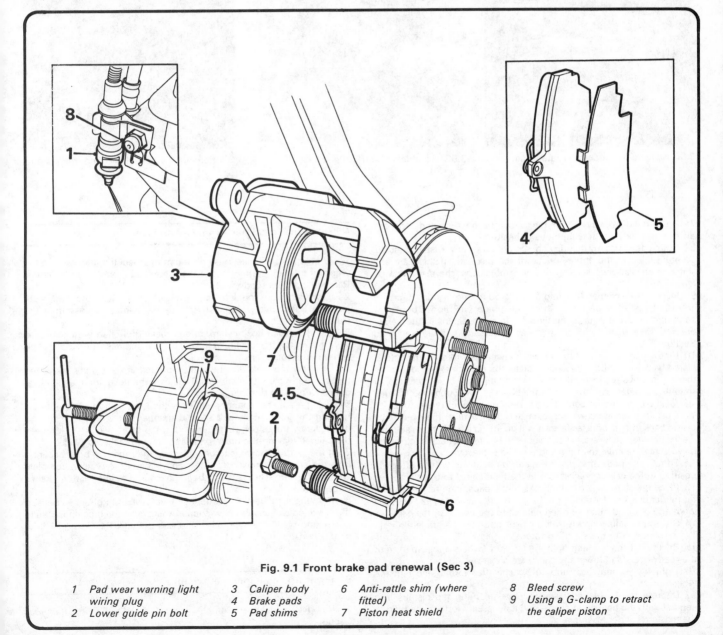

Fig. 9.1 Front brake pad renewal (Sec 3)

1 Pad wear warning light wiring plug	3 Caliper body	6 Anti-rattle shim (where fitted)	8 Bleed screw
2 Lower guide pin bolt	4 Brake pads 5 Pad shims	7 Piston heat shield	9 Using a G-clamp to retract the caliper piston

3.3 Unscrew the caliper lower guide pin bolt

3.4 Pivot the caliper body upwards

3.5A Lift out the brake pads together with their shims

3.5B Remove the upper anti-rattle shim ...

3.5C ... and lower anti-rattle shim

3.6 Remove the heat shield from the piston

7   Brush the dust and dirt from the caliper, piston, disc, and pads, but **do not inhale it,** as it is injurious to health.

8   Rotate the disc by hand, and scrape away any rust and scale. Carefully inspect the entire surface of the disc, and if there are any signs of cracks, deep scoring or severe abrasions, the disc must be renewed.

9   Inspect the caliper for fluid leaks around the piston, signs of corrosion, or other damage. Check the guide pin rubber boots for condition, and the pins themselves for free movement in the carrier bracket. Renew any suspect parts as necessary, with reference to Section 5.

10   If new pads are to be fitted, it will be necessary to push the caliper piston back into its bore to accommodate the new, thicker pads. To do this first remove the protective cap, then fit a plastic or rubber tube, of suitable diameter, over the end of the bleed screw. Submerge the free end of the tube in a jar containing a small quantity of brake fluid.

11   Open the bleed screw approximately half a turn, then push the piston back into its bore, as far as it will go, using a G-clamp or suitable pieces of wood as levers. When the piston has fully retracted, close the bleed screw, remove the tube and refit the protective cap.

12   To refit the pads, first place the anti-rattle shims (where fitted) in position in the carrier bracket and fit the heat shield to the piston.

13   Place the shims against the backs of the pads, then fit the pads to the carrier bracket. If working on the left-hand caliper, the pad with the warning light lead must be fitted nearest to the centre of the car.

14   Swing the caliper down over the pads and refit the guide pin bolt. Tighten the bolt to the specified torque.

15   Reconnect the warning light wiring plug (where applicable), refit the roadwheels and lower the car to the ground.

16   Tighten the roadwheel nuts to the specified torque and refit the wheel trims.

17   Depress the brake pedal several times to bring the pistons into contact with the pads then check, and if necessary top up, the fluid in the master cylinder reservoir.

4   Front brake caliper – removal and refitting

1   Apply the handbrake, prise off the front wheel trim and slacken the wheel nuts. Jack up the front of the car and support it on axle stands. Remove the front roadwheel.

2   If working on the left-hand caliper, disconnect the pad wear warning light wiring plug and release the wiring harness from the support clip.

3   Using a brake hose clamp, or self-locking wrench with protected jaws, clamp the flexible brake hose. This will minimise fluid loss during subsequent operations.

4   Unscrew the brake hose banjo union bolt at the caliper body, and recover the two copper washers. Tape over the hose union and caliper orifice to prevent dirt ingress.

5   Using a suitable spanner, unscrew the lower guide pin bolt while holding the guide pin with a second spanner.

6   Unscrew the upper guide pin bolt in the same way, then lift away the caliper, leaving the brake pads and carrier bracket in place.

7   If the carrier bracket is to be removed, undo the two bolts securing it to the steering knuckle (photo), and remove the bracket complete with brake pads. The pads can be removed, if required, with reference to Section 3.

8   Refitting is the reverse sequence to removal, but tighten all bolts to the specified torque. Use new copper washers on the brake hose banjo union, and bleed the hydraulic system as described in Section 16, on completion.

5   Front brake caliper – overhaul

1   Remove the caliper from the car as described in the previous Section.

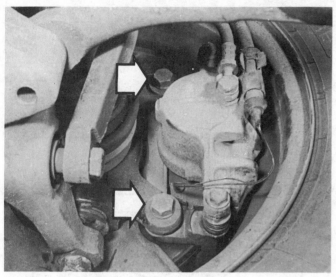

4.7 Carrier bracket-to-steering knuckle retaining bolts (arrowed)

7 Clean all the parts in methylated spirit, or clean brake fluid, and dry with a lint-free cloth. Inspect the piston and caliper bore for signs of damage, scuffing or corrosion, and if these conditions are evident, renew the caliper assembly complete. Also renew the guide pins in the carrier bracket if they are bent or damaged, or if their rubber boots are split or perished.

8 If the components are in a satisfactory condition, a repair kit consisting of new seals and dust cover should be obtained.

9 Thoroughly lubricate the caliper bore, piston, piston seal and dust cover with clean brake fluid, and carefully fit the seal to the caliper bore.

10 Position the dust cover over the innermost end of the piston, so that the caliper bore sealing lip protrudes beyond the base of the piston. Using a blunt instrument, if necessary, engage the sealing lip of the dust cover with the groove in the caliper. Now push the piston into the caliper bore until the other sealing lip of the dust cover can be engaged with the groove in the piston. Having done this, push the piston fully into its bore. Ease the piston out again slightly, and make sure that the dust cover lip is correctly seating in the piston groove.

11 Remove the guide pins from the carrier bracket, if not already done, and smear them with high-melting-point brake grease. Fit new rubber boots to the guide pins if necessary, and refit them to the carrier bracket.

12 The caliper can now be refitted as described in the previous Section.

2 With the caliper on the bench wipe away all traces of dust and dirt, but **avoid inhaling the dust,** as it is injurious to health.

3 Remove the shim from the caliper piston.

4 Using low air pressure, such as that generated by a tyre foot pump, eject the piston by holding the pump hose against the caliper fluid inlet port.

5 Remove the dust cover from the piston.

6 Using a blunt instrument such as a knitting needle, carefully extract the piston seal from the caliper bore.

6 Front brake disc – inspection, removal and refitting

1 Apply the handbrake, prise off the front wheel trim and slacken the wheel nuts. Jack up the front of the car and support it on axle stands. Remove the front roadwheel.

2 Undo the two bolts securing the brake caliper carrier bracket to the steering knuckle.

3 Withdraw the carrier bracket, complete with caliper and brake pads, from the disc and steering knuckle. Tie the caliper assembly from a

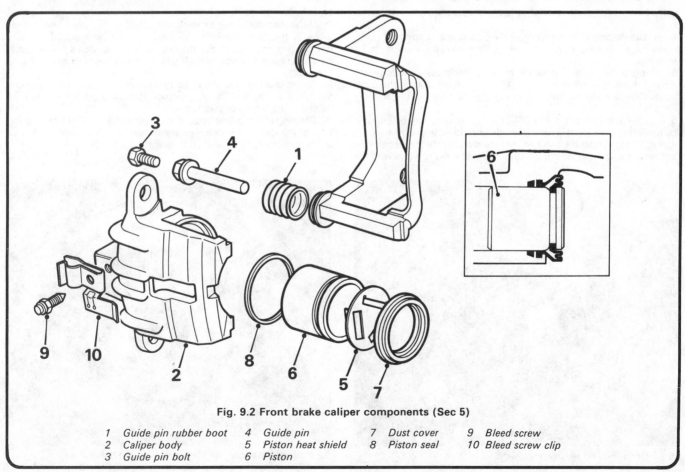

Fig. 9.2 Front brake caliper components (Sec 5)

1 Guide pin rubber boot	4 Guide pin	7 Dust cover	9 Bleed screw
2 Caliper body	5 Piston heat shield	8 Piston seal	10 Bleed screw clip
3 Guide pin bolt	6 Piston		

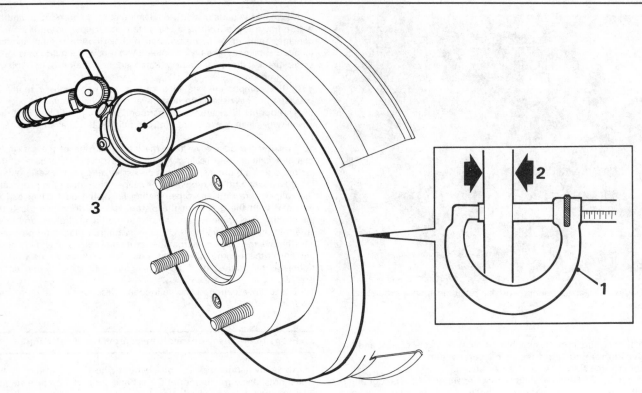

Fig. 9.3 Checking front brake disc thickness and run-out (Sec 6)

1   *Micrometer*   2   *Specified disc thickness*   3   *Dial test indicator*

convenient place under the wheel arch to avoid straining the brake hose.

4   Rotate the disc and examine it for deep scoring or grooving on both sides. Light scoring is normal, but if excessive the disc must be renewed.

5   Using a micrometer, measure the disc thickness at four places around the disc at approximately 10.0 mm (0.4 in) in from the outer edge. Compare the thickness with the figures given in the Specifications.

6   If a dial test indicator is available, the disc run-out can be checked by mounting the indicator with its probe positioned approximately 6.0 mm (0.25 in) in from the outer edge of the disc. Rotate the disc slowly, and note the reading on the indicator. Compare the run-out with the figures given in the Specifications.

7   If the disc thickness, or thickness variation, is outside the figures given in the Specifications, the disc must be renewed. If the disc run-out is excessive, remove the disc, turn it through 180°, refit it and check the run-out once more. If still excessive, renewal of the disc is necessary.

8   To remove the disc, undo the two retaining screws and withdraw the disc from the hub flange (photos). If it is tight, tap it lightly from behind using a hide or plastic mallet.

9   Refitting is the reverse sequence to removal. Ensure that the mating face of the disc and hub flange are thoroughly clean, and tighten all retaining bolts to the specified torque.

6.8A Undo the two retaining screws ...

6.8B ... and withdraw the front disc from the hub flange

7 Rear brake pads – inspection and renewal

1   Chock the front wheels, remove the rear wheel trim and slacken the rear wheel nuts. Jack up the rear of the car and support it on axle stands. Remove the rear roadwheels and ensure that the handbrake is released.

2   The thickness of the brake pads can now be checked by viewing through the slot in the front of the caliper. If any of the pads has worn down to, or below, the minimum specified thickness, all four pads must be renewed as a complete set. The pads must also be renewed if there is any sign of oil or fluid contamination caused by leaking seals. If so, the cause of the contamination must be traced and rectified before new pads are fitted.

3   Undo the three bolts securing the handbrake linkage cover (photo), and remove the cover from the side of the caliper.

4   Disconnect the pad wear warning light wiring plug (left-hand caliper only).

5   Using a suitable spanner, unscrew the upper and lower guide pin bolts (photo).

6   Withdraw the caliper and handbrake linkage assembly off the brake pads and carrier bracket.

7   Lift out the two brake pads, then, where fitted, remove the upper and lower anti-rattle shims from the caliper carrier bracket (photos). If the pads are to be re-used, suitably identify them so that they can be refitted in their original positions.

8   Brush the dust and dirt from the caliper, piston, disc, and pads, but **do not inhale it,** as it is injurious to health.

9   Rotate the disc by hand, and scrape away any rust and scale. Carefully inspect the entire surface of the disc, and if there are any signs of cracks, deep scoring or severe abrasions, the disc must be renewed.

10 Inspect the caliper for fluid leaks around the piston, signs of corrosion, or other damage. Check the guide pin rubber boots for condition, and the pins themselves for free movement in the carrier bracket. Renew any suspect parts as necessary, with reference to Section 9.

11 If new pads are to be fitted, it will be necessary to retract the caliper piston back into its bore to accommodate the new, thicker pads. To do this first remove the protective cap, then fit a plastic or rubber tube, of suitable diameter, over the end of the bleed screw. Submerge the free end of the tube in a jar containing a small quantity of brake fluid.

12 Open the bleed screw approximately half a turn, then screw the piston back fully into its bore by turning it clockwise with a pair of angled circlip pliers (photo) or other similar tool. With the piston fully retracted, close the bleed screw, remove the tube and refit the protective cap.

13 To refit the pads, first place the anti-rattle shims (where fitted) in position in the carrier bracket.

14 Fit the pads to the carrier bracket, noting that the pad with the warning light lead (left-hand caliper only) must be fitted nearest to the centre of the car.

15 Place the caliper over the pads, and secure with the guide pin bolts, tightened to the specified torque.

16 Refit the warning light wiring plug (where applicable) and the handbrake linkage cover.

17 Refit the roadwheels and lower the car to the ground. Tighten the roadwheel nuts to the specified torque and refit the wheel trim.

18 Depress the brake pedal several times to bring the pistons into contact with the pads then check, and if necessary top up, the fluid in the master cylinder reservoir. There may be excessive free travel of the handbrake initially after completing these operations, but this will self-adjust automatically after the car has been driven a few miles.

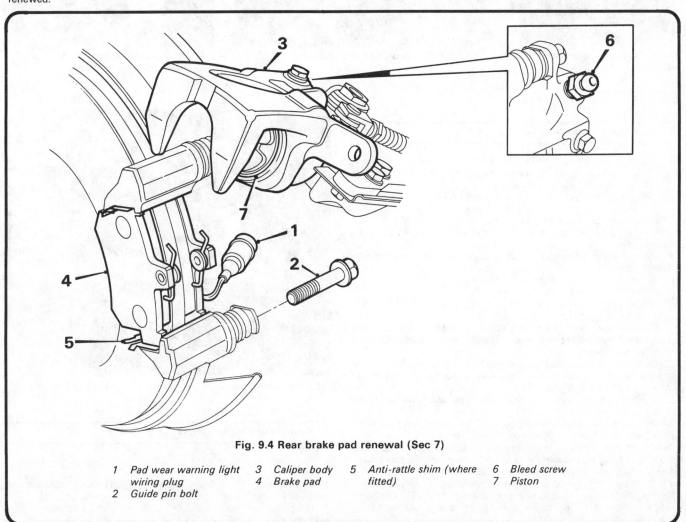

Fig. 9.4 Rear brake pad renewal (Sec 7)

1 Pad wear warning light wiring plug	3 Caliper body	5 Anti-rattle shim (where fitted)
2 Guide pin bolt	4 Brake pad	6 Bleed screw
		7 Piston

7.3 Undo the three handbrake linkage cover retaining bolts (arrowed)

7.5 Rear caliper upper and lower guide pin bolt locations (arrowed)

7.7A Lift out the two brake pads ...

7.7B ... followed by the upper anti-rattle shim ...

7.7C ... and lower anti-rattle shim

7.12 Using angled circlip pliers to screw the piston back into the caliper

8   Rear brake caliper – removal and refitting

1   Chock the front wheels, remove the rear wheel trim and slacken the rear wheel nuts. Jack up the rear of the car and support it on axle stands. Remove the rear roadwheel.

2   Undo the three bolts securing the handbrake linkage cover, and remove the cover from the side of the caliper.

3   If working on the left-hand caliper, disconnect the pad wear warning light wiring plug and release the wiring harness from the support clip.

4   Undo the two bolts and remove the front half of the handbrake linkage cover.

5   Extract the retaining clip and withdraw the clevis pin from the end of the handbrake cable (photo).

6   Prise off the handbrake cable retaining clip and withdraw the cable from the mounting bracket.

7   Using a brake hose clamp, or self-locking wrench with protected jaws, clamp the flexible brake hose. This will minimise fluid loss during subsequent operations.

8   Unscrew the brake hose banjo union bolt at the caliper body, and recover the two copper washers. Tape over the hose union and caliper orifice to prevent dirt ingress.

9   Using a suitable spanner, unscrew the upper and lower guide pin bolts.

10   Withdraw the caliper and handbrake linkage assembly off the brake pads and carrier bracket, and remove it from the car.

11   If the carrier bracket is to be removed, undo the two bolts securing it to the hub carrier, and remove the bracket complete with brake pads. The pads can be removed, if required, with reference to Section 7.

12   Refitting is the reverse sequence to removal, but tighten all bolts to the specified torque. Use new copper washers on the brake hose banjo union, and bleed the hydraulic system as described in Section 16, on completion.

8.5 Handbrake cable clevis pin (A) and cable retaining clip (B)

9   Rear brake caliper – overhaul

1   Remove the caliper from the car as described in the previous Section.

2   With the caliper on the bench, wipe away all traces of dust and dirt, but **avoid inhaling the dust,** as it is injurious to health.

3   Undo the two bolts and remove the handbrake linkage bracket assembly from the caliper.

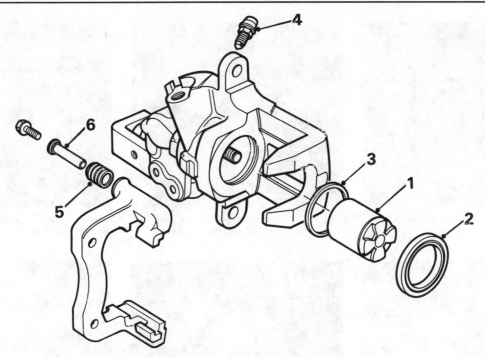

Fig. 9.5 Rear brake caliper components (Sec 9)

1 Piston	3 Piston seal	5 Guide pin rubber boot
2 Dust cover	4 Bleed screw	6 Guide pin

4   Using a pair of angled circlip pliers or other similar tool, turn the piston anti-clockwise to unscrew it from the caliper.

5   Remove the dust cover from the piston.

6   Using a blunt instrument such as a knitting needle, carefully extract the piston seal from the caliper bore.

7   Clean all the parts in methylated spirit, or clean brake fluid, and dry with a lint-free cloth. Inspect the piston and caliper bore for signs of damage, scuffing or corrosion, and if these conditions are evident, renew the caliper assembly complete. Also renew the guide pins in the carrier bracket if they are bent or damaged, or if their rubber boots are split or perished.

8   If the components are in a satisfactory condition, a repair kit consisting of new seals and dust cover should be obtained.

9   Thoroughly lubricate the caliper bore, piston, piston seal and dust cover with clean brake fluid, and carefully fit the seal to the caliper bore.

10 Position the dust cover over the innermost end of the piston, so that the caliper bore sealing lip protrudes beyond the base of the piston. Using a blunt instrument, if necessary, engage the sealing lip of the dust cover with the groove in the caliper. Screw the piston into the caliper bore until the other sealing lip of the dust cover can be engaged with the groove in the piston. With the piston screwed in all the way, make sure that the dust cover is correctly located in the piston and caliper grooves.

11 Remove the guide pins from the carrier bracket, if not already done, and smear them with high-melting-point brake grease. Fit new rubber boots to the guide pins if necessary, and refit them to the carrier bracket. Ensure that the guide pin with the rubber insert is fitted in the rearmost position.

12 Attach the handbrake linkage bracket assembly to the caliper and secure with the two bolts.

13 The caliper can now be refitted to the car as described in the previous Section.

10 Rear brake disc – inspection, removal and refitting

1   Chock the front wheels, remove the rear wheel trim and slacken the rear wheel nuts. Jack up the rear of the car and support it on axle stands. Remove the rear roadwheel.

2   Undo the two bolts securing the brake caliper carrier bracket to the rear hub carrier (photo).

3   Undo the retaining bolt and release the flexible brake hose support clip from the suspension strut (photo).

4   Withdraw the carrier bracket, complete with caliper and brake pads, from the disc and hub carrier. Tie the caliper assembly from a convenient place under the wheel arch to avoid straining the brake hose (photo).

5   The inspection procedures are the same as for the front brake disc, and reference should be made to Section 6, paragraphs 4 to 7 inclusive.

6   To remove the disc, undo the two retaining screws and withdraw the disc from the hub flange (photos). If it is tight, tap it lightly from behind using a hide or plastic mallet.

7   Refitting is the reverse sequence to removal. Ensure that the mating face of the disc and hub flange are thoroughly clean, and tighten all retaining bolts to the specified torque.

11 Master cylinder – removal and refitting

1   Working under the front of the car, remove the dust cover from the bleed screw on each front brake caliper. Obtain two plastic or rubber tubes of suitable diameter to fit snugly over the bleed screws, and place the other ends in suitable receptacles.

2   Open both bleed screws approximately half a turn, then operate the brake pedal until the master cylinder reservoir is empty. Tighten the bleed screws and remove the tubes. Discard the expelled brake fluid.

3   Disconnect the warning light wiring plug from the reservoir filler cap.

4   Place rags beneath the master cylinder to absorb any remaining brake fluid when the pipe unions are undone. If any brake fluid is spilled on the car paintwork, wash it off immediately with copious amounts of cold water.

5   On manual gearbox models, detach the clutch fluid supply hose from the side of the reservoir.

6   Unscrew the two brake pipe union nuts, and carefully withdraw the pipes from the master cylinder (photo). Tape over the pipe ends to prevent dirt ingress.

7   Undo the two nuts, remove the washers, and withdraw the master

10.2 Carrier bracket-to-rear hub carrier retaining bolts (arrowed)

10.3 Release the rear flexible brake hose support clip from the suspension strut

10.4 Tie up the caliper assembly to avoid straining the brake hose

10.6A Undo the two retaining screws ...

10.6B ... and withdraw the rear disc from the hub flange

11.6 Unscrew the two brake pipe unions (arrowed) at the master cylinder

cylinder from the servo unit. Recover the O-ring seal between master cylinder and servo.

8   Refitting is the reverse sequence to removal. Renew the master cylinder-to-servo O-ring seal, and tighten all retaining nuts to the specified torque. Bleed the hydraulic system as described in Section 16 on completion. On manual gearbox models, bleed the clutch hydraulic system as described in Chapter 5.

12 Master cylinder (non-ABS models) – overhaul

Note: *The following procedure is applicable to cars which are not fitted with an anti-lock braking system (ABS). For cars with ABS, refer to Section 13.*

1   Remove the master cylinder from the car as described in the previous Section. Drain any fluid remaining in the reservoir, and prepare a clean, uncluttered working surface ready for dismantling.
2   Hold the cylinder body firmly, and push the reservoir sideways to release it from its seals. Lift the reservoir off, and remove the two seals from the fluid inlet ports.
3   Push the primary piston down the cylinder bore slightly, and hold it there. Locate the stop-pin in the secondary inlet port, and withdraw the pin using pointed-nose pliers.
4   With the piston still held down, extract the circlip, using circlip pliers, from the end of the cylinder bore, and remove the washer behind the circlip.
5   Using a small blunt screwdriver, hook out the O-ring seal from the groove in the cylinder bore.
6   Remove the primary piston.
7   Lubricate the cylinder bore with clean brake fluid to aid removal of the secondary piston.
8   Tap the cylinder body on a block of wood to release the secondary piston, then withdraw the piston from the cylinder bore.
9   Refer to Fig. 9.6 and remove the secondary piston spring, seal retainer, rear seal, washer and front seal.

10   Remove the seal housing, seal and washer from the primary piston. Do not dismantle the primary piston further, as seals are not available separately. If the master cylinder is in a serviceable condition, and is to be re-used, a complete new primary piston assembly is included in the repair kit.
11   With the master cylinder dismantled, clean all the components in methylated spirit, or clean brake fluid, and dry with a lint-free cloth.
12   Carefully examine the cylinder bore and secondary piston for signs of wear, scoring or corrosion, and if evident, renew the complete master cylinder assembly.
13   If the components are in a satisfactory condition, obtain a repair kit consisting of new seals, springs and primary piston assembly.
14   Lubricate the cylinder bore, pistons and seals thoroughly in clean brake fluid, and assemble them wet.
15   Using your fingers only, fit the front seal to the secondary piston, followed by the washer, rear seal, seal retainer and spring.
16   Fit the washer, seal housing and seal to the primary piston.
17   Insert the secondary piston into the cylinder bore, using a circular rocking motion to avoid turning over the lips of the seals.
18   Fit the primary piston in the same way.
19   Fit a new O-ring seal to the groove in the cylinder bore, then refit the washer and circlip.
20   Push the primary piston down the bore, and refit the stop-pin to the secondary inlet port.
21   Fit two new seals to the reservoir fluid inlet ports, then push the reservoir firmly into place.
22   Fit a new seal to the reservoir filler cap, then refit the master cylinder to the car as described in Section 11.

13 Master cylinder (ABS models) – overhaul

Note: *The following procedure is applicable to cars which are fitted with an anti-lock braking system (ABS). For cars without ABS, refer to Section 12.*

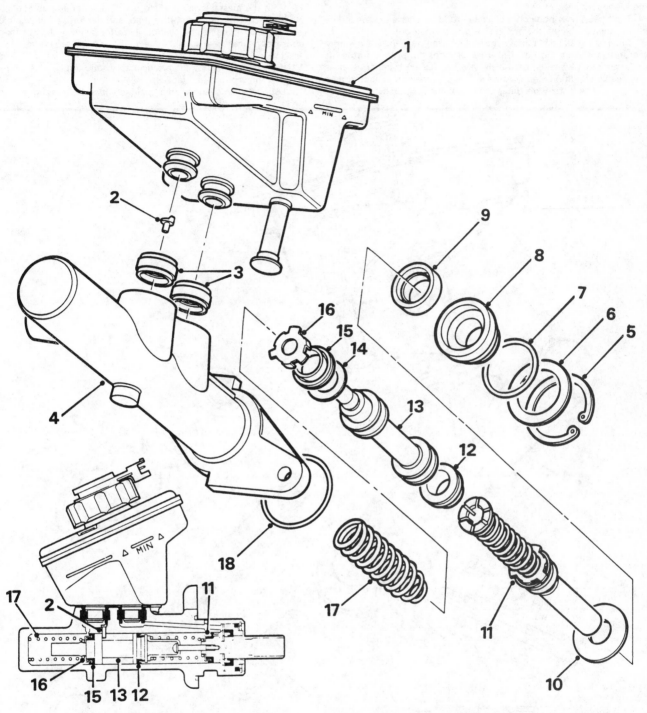

Fig. 9.6 Exploded view of the master cylinder – non-ABS models (Sec 12)

1 Reservoir	6 Washer	11 Primary piston assembly	15 Secondary piston rear seal
2 Stop-pin	7 O-ring seal	12 Secondary piston front seal	16 Secondary piston seal
3 Reservoir seals	8 Primary piston seal housing	13 Secondary piston	retainer
4 Cylinder body	9 Primary piston seal	14 Secondary piston washer	17 Secondary piston spring
5 Piston retaining circlip	10 Primary piston washer		18 O-ring

1   Remove the master cylinder from the car as described in Section 11. Drain any fluid remaining in the reservoir, and prepare a clean, uncluttered working surface ready for dismantling.

2   Hold the cylinder body firmly, and push the reservoir sideways to release it from its seals. Lift the reservoir off, and remove the two seals from the fluid inlet ports.

3   Push the primary piston down the cylinder bore slightly, and hold it there. Locate the stop-pin in the secondary inlet port, and withdraw the pin using pointed-nose pliers.

4   With the piston still held down, extract the circlip, using circlip pliers, from the end of the cylinder bore, and remove the washer behind the circlip.

5   Using a small blunt screwdriver, hook out the O-ring seal from the groove in the cylinder bore.

6   Remove the primary piston.

7   Lubricate the cylinder bore with clean brake fluid to aid removal of

the secondary piston.

8   Tap the cylinder body on a block of wood to release the secondary piston, then withdraw the piston from the cylinder bore.

9   Refer to Fig. 9.7 and remove the seal housing, seal and washer from the primary piston. Do not dismantle either of the pistons further as seals are not available separately. If the master cylinder is in a serviceable condition, and is to be re-used, a repair kit including new primary and secondary piston assemblies will be required.

10 With the master cylinder dismantled, clean all the components in methylated spirit, or clean brake fluid, and dry with a lint-free cloth.

11 Carefully examine the cylinder bore for signs of wear, scoring or corrosion, and if evident, renew the complete master cylinder assembly.

12 If the components are in a satisfactory condition, obtain a repair kit and two new piston assemblies.

13 Lubricate the cylinder bore, pistons and seals thoroughly in clean

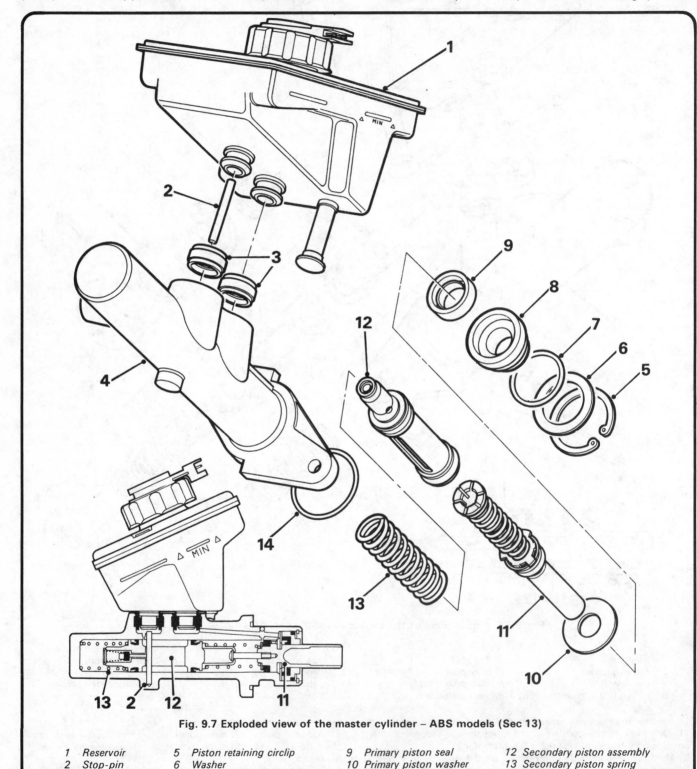

Fig. 9.7 Exploded view of the master cylinder – ABS models (Sec 13)

1 Reservoir	5 Piston retaining circlip	9 Primary piston seal	12 Secondary piston assembly
2 Stop-pin	6 Washer	10 Primary piston washer	13 Secondary piston spring
3 Reservoir seals	7 O-ring seal	11 Primary piston assembly	14 O-ring
4 Cylinder body	8 Primary piston seal housing		

brake fluid, and assemble them wet.

14 Fit the washer, seal housing and seal to the primary piston.

15 Insert the secondary piston into the cylinder bore, using a circular rocking motion to avoid turning over the lips of the seals. Align the slot in the piston with the stop-pin hole in the cylinder secondary inlet port.

16 Fit the primary piston in the same way.

17 Fit a new O-ring seal to the groove in the cylinder bore, then refit the washer and circlip.

18 Push the primary piston down the bore, and refit the stop-pin to the secondary inlet port.

19 Fit two new seals to the reservoir fluid inlet ports, then push the reservoir firmly into place.

20 Fit a new seal to the reservoir filler cap, then refit the master cylinder to the car as described in Section 11.

14 Pressure-reducing valve – description, removal and refitting

1 The pressure-reducing valve is mounted on the left-hand side of the engine compartment behind the battery.

2 The purposes of the valve is to distribute brake fluid to the front and rear brakes (rear brakes only on cars fitted with ABS), and to limit the fluid pressure supplied to the rear brakes under heavy braking.

3 The operation of the valve may be suspect if one or both rear wheels continually lock under heavy braking. It is essential, however, before condemning the valve to ensure that the brake assemblies themselves, or adverse road conditions, are not causing this condition. In the event of a valve internal failure, brake fluid will be seen seeping from the vent plug on the front of the valve which is covered by a plastic strap. Repair or overhaul of the valve is not possible, and the unit must be renewed as a complete assembly if faulty.

4 Remove the master cylinder reservoir filler cap, place a piece of polythene over the filler neck, and seal it tightly with an elastic band. This will minimise brake fluid loss during subsequent operations.

5 Place rags beneath the valve to collect any brake fluid that may escape when the pipe unions are undone. If any brake fluid is spilled on the car paintwork, wash it off immediately with copious amounts of cold water.

6 Identify the locations of each of the brake pipe unions, unscrew the union nuts and carefully withdraw the pipes clear of the valve (photo). Tape over the pipe ends and valve orifices to prevent dirt ingress.

7 Undo the two bolts securing the valve mounting bracket to the inner wing, and remove the valve assembly.

8 Refitting is the reverse sequence to removal. Bleed the hydraulic system as described in Section 16 on completion.

15 Hydraulic pipes and hoses – inspection, removal and refitting

1 At the intervals given in *Routine maintenance*, carefully examine all brake pipes, hoses, hose connections and pipe unions.

2 First check for signs of leakage at the pipe unions. Then examine the flexible hoses for signs of cracking, chafing or deterioration of the rubber.

3 The brake pipes must be examined carefully and methodically. They must be cleaned off and checked for signs of dents, corrosion or other damage. Corrosion should be scraped off and, if the depth of pitting is significant, the pipes renewed. The pipes are however protected by a plastic sleeve, and any corrosion that does occur is likely to be near the pipe unions where the sleeve protection ends.

4 If any section of pipe or hose is to be removed, first unscrew the master cylinder reservoir filler cap and place a piece of polythene over the filler neck. Secure the polythene with an elastic band, ensuring that an airtight seal is obtained. This will minimise brake fluid loss when the pipe or hose is removed.

5 As the front-to-rear brake pipes run inside the car, it will be necessary to determine the route of the pipe, then remove any interior trim panels as necessary for access (see Chapter 11). Once this is done, the union nuts at each end can be unscrewed, the pipe and union pulled out, and the pipe removed from the car or underbody clips as applicable. Where the union nuts are exposed, unprotected from the full force of the weather, they can sometimes be quite tight. As only an open-ended spanner can be used, burring of the flats on the nuts is not uncommon when attempting to undo them. For this reason, a self-locking wrench is often the only way to separate a stubborn union.

6 To remove a flexible hose, wipe the unions and brackets free of dirt and undo the union nut at the brake pipe end.

7 Next extract the hose retaining clip, and lift the end of the hose out of its bracket (photo).

8 If a front hose is being removed, undo the two bolts securing the hose support bracket to the steering knuckle (photo). At the rear, a single bolt secures the support bracket to the shock absorber strut.

9 Undo the banjo bolt securing the hose to the brake caliper (photo), recover the two copper washers, one on each side of the union, and remove the hose. Use new copper washers when refitting.

10 Brake pipes can be obtained individually, or in sets, from Rover dealers or larger accessory shops, cut to length and with the end flares and union nuts in place. The pipe is then bent to shape, using the old pipe as a guide, and is ready for fitting to the car.

11 Refitting the pipes and hoses is a reverse of the removal sequence. Make sure that the hoses are not kinked when in position, and will not chafe any suspension or steering component with suspension movement. Ensure also that the brake pipes are securely supported in their clips. After refitting, remove the polythene from the reservoir and bleed the hydraulic system as described in Section 16.

16 Hydraulic system – bleeding

1 The correct functioning of the brake hydraulic system is only possible after removing all air from the components and circuit; this is achieved by bleeding the system. Note that only clean, unused brake fluid of the specified type may be used.

2 If there is any possibility of incorrect fluid being used in the system, the brake lines and components must be completely flushed with uncontaminated fluid and new seals fitted to the components.

3 **Never** re-use brake fluid which has been bled from the system.

14.6 Pressure-reducing valve mountings and pipe attachments

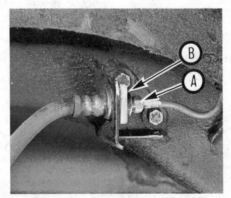

15.7 Flexible brake hose rigid pipe union nut (A) and hose retaining clip (B)

15.8 Front brake hose support bracket on the steering knuckle

15.9 Front brake hose-to-caliper banjo union bolt (arrowed)

4   During the procedure, do not allow the level of brake fluid to drop below the MIN mark on the reservoir.
5   Before starting work, check that all pipes and hoses are secure, unions tight, and bleed screws closed. Take great care not to allow brake fluid to come into contact with the car paintwork, otherwise the finish will be seriously damaged. Wash off any spilled fluid immediately with cold water.
6   If brake fluid has been lost from the master cylinder due to a leak in the system, ensure that the cause is traced and rectified before proceeding further.
7   There are a number of one-man, do-it-yourself, brake bleeding kits currently available from motor accessory shops. It is recommended that one of these kits is used wherever possible, as they greatly simplify the bleeding operation, and also reduce the risk of expelled air and fluid being drawn back into the system. If one of these kits is not available, it will be necessary to gather together a clean jar and a suitable length of plastic or rubber tubing, which is a tight fit over the bleed screw, and also to engage the help of an assistant.
8   If the hydraulic system has only been partially disconnected and suitable precautions were taken to minimise fluid loss, it should only be necessary to bleed that part of the system (ie primary or secondary circuit).
9   If the complete system is to be bled, then it should be done in the following sequence:

   Secondary circuit: Left-hand front, then right-hand rear
   Primary circuit: Right-hand front, then left-hand rear

Bleeding – two-man method

10   Check the fluid level in the master cylinder reservoir, and top up if necessary.
11   Clean the area around the bleed screw on the appropriate brake caliper, and remove the dust cap.
12   Push one end of the bleed tube onto the bleed screw and immerse the other end in the jar, which should contain enough fluid to cover the end of the tube.
13   Open the bleed screw approximately half a turn, and have your assistant depress the brake pedal with a smooth steady stroke, then release it. Tighten the bleed screw at the end of each pedal downstroke to obviate any chance of air or fluid being drawn back into the system.
14   Repeat this operation (paragraph 13) until clean brake fluid, free from air bubbles, can be seen flowing from the end of the tube.
15   Tighten the bleed screw at the end of a pedal downstroke, remove the bleed tube and refit the dust cap. Repeat these procedures on the remaining bleed screws as necessary.

Bleeding – using a one-way valve kit

16   Follow the instructions supplied with the kit, as the procedure may

vary slightly according to the type being used, but generally they are as follows.
17   Clean the area around the bleed screw on the appropriate brake caliper, and remove the dust cap.
18   Attach the tube to the bleed screw, and open the screw approximately half a turn.
19   Depress the brake pedal with a smooth steady stroke, then release it. The one-way valve in the kit will prevent expelled air and fluid from returning at the end of each pedal downstroke. Repeat this operation several times to be sure of ejecting all air from the system. Some kits incorporate a translucent container, which can be positioned so that the air bubbles can be seen flowing from the end of the tube.
20   Tighten the bleed screw, remove the tube and refit the dust cap. Repeat these procedures on the remaining bleed screws as necessary.

Bleeding – using a pressure-bleeding kit

21   These kits are also available from accessory shops, and are usually operated by air pressure from the spare tyre.
22   By connecting a pressurised, fluid-filled container to the master cylinder reservoir, bleeding is then carried out by simply opening each bleed screw in turn and allowing the fluid to run out, rather like turning on a tap, until no air is visible in the expelled fluid.
23   By using this method, the large reservoir of brake fluid provides a safeguard against air being drawn into the master cylinder during bleeding, which often occurs if the fluid level in the reservoir is not maintained.
24   Pressure bleeding is particularly effective when bleeding 'difficult' systems, or when bleeding the complete system at the time of routine fluid renewal. It is also advisable to use this method if the car is equipped with an anti-lock braking system.

All methods

25   When bleeding is completed, check and top up the fluid level in the master cylinder reservoir.
26   Check the feel of the brake pedal. If it feels at all spongy, air must still be present in the system, and further bleeding is indicated. Failure to bleed satisfactorily after a reasonable repetition of the bleeding operations may be due to worn master cylinder seals.
27   Discard brake fluid which has been bled from the system. It is almost certain to be contaminated with moisture and air, making it unsuitable for further use. Clean fluid should always be stored in an airtight container, as it is hygroscopic (absorbs moisture readily). This lowers its boiling point, and could affect braking performance under severe conditions.

17 Brake pedal – removal and refitting

1   From inside the car, release the turnbuckles and lift out the trim panel over the clutch, brake and accelerator pedals.
2   Disconnect the return spring from the brake pedal and pedal bracket.
3   Extract the retaining spring clip and withdraw the clevis pin securing the brake servo pushrod to the pedal.
4   Undo the nut, remove the washer and withdraw the brake pedal pivot bolt from the pedal bracket. Remove the pedal from the car.
5   Prise out the two pedal bushes and withdraw the spacer tube.
6   Check the condition of the components, and renew as necessary.
7   Refitting is the reverse sequence to removal.

18 Handbrake – adjustment

1   Due to the self-adjusting action of the rear brakes, adjustment of the handbrake should normally only be necessary after removal and refitting of any of the handbrake components.
2   To check the adjustment, chock the front wheels, remove the rear wheel trim and slacken the roadwheel nuts. Jack up the rear of the car and support it on axle stands. Remove both rear roadwheels and release the handbrake.
3   Undo the three bolts each side securing the handbrake linkage covers to the rear brake calipers, and remove the covers.
4   Check the clearance between the handbrake linkage lever and the stop-pin on both calipers (Fig. 9.9). If the clearance on either side is outside the tolerance given in the Specifications, adjust the handbrake

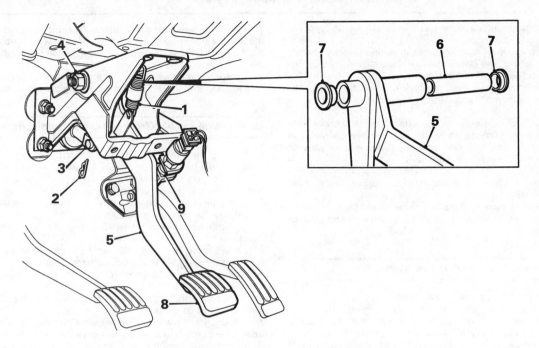

Fig. 9.8 Brake pedal mounting details (Sec 17)

1	Return spring	4	Pedal pivot bolt	6	Spacer tube	8	Pedal pad
2	Clevis pin spring clip	5	Brake pedal	7	Pedal bushes	9	Stop-light switch
3	Clevis pin						

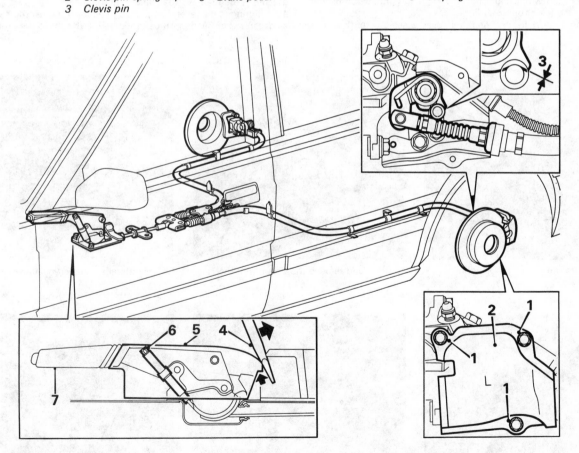

Fig. 9.9 Handbrake adjustment details (Sec 18)

1 Handbrake linkage cover retaining bolts
2 Handbrake linkage cover
3 Handbrake linkage lever-to-stop-pin clearance measuring point
4 Using a lever to prise up the handbrake lever trim cover
5 Handbrake lever trim cover
6 Handbrake adjuster
7 Handbrake lever

using the following procedure. If the clearance is satisfactory, proceed to paragraph 9.

5   From inside the car, carefully prise out the coin holders or switch panels on each side of the centre console, then raise the lid on the cassette holder at the rear of the console.

6   Using a screwdriver as a lever, carefully prise up the rear of the handbrake lever trim cover (photos), and remove the cover from the lever.

7   Turn the handbrake adjuster on the side of the handbrake lever (photo) to increase or decrease the previously-measured clearance, as necessary. Turning the adjuster clockwise will decrease the clearance, and turning it anti-clockwise will increase it.

8   Operate the handbrake two or three times, and recheck the clearance once more. Make a final adjustment if required, then refit the trim cover to the lever.

9   Refit the linkage covers to the brake calipers, refit the roadwheels and lower the car to the ground. Tighten the wheel nuts and refit the wheel trim.

19 Handbrake lever – removal and refitting

1   Refer to Chapter 11 and remove the centre console.

2   Chock the front wheels, remove the rear wheel trim and slacken the wheel nuts. Jack up the rear of the car and support it on axle stands. Remove the rear roadwheels and release the handbrake.

3   From inside the car, unscrew the handbrake adjuster on the side of the lever, and remove the adjuster and spacing washer from the front cable (photo).

4   Detach the front cable from the handbrake lever.

5   Disconnect the wiring plug from the warning light switch on the other side of the lever (photo).

6   Undo the four bolts securing the lever assembly to the floor (photo).

7   Lift up the lever assembly, release the cable and gaiter, and recover the lever to floor gasket. Remove the lever assembly from the car.

8   If required, the warning light switch can be removed after undoing the two screws.

9   Refitting is the reverse sequence to removal. Adjust the handbrake as described in Section 18 before lowering the car to the ground.

20 Handbrake cable (front) – removal and refitting

1   Refer to Chapter 11 and remove the centre console.

2   Chock the front wheels, remove the rear wheel trim and slacken the wheel nuts. Jack up the rear of the car and support it on axle stands. Remove the rear roadwheels and release the handbrake.

3   Undo the bolts securing the exhaust system front heat shield to the underbody. Release the exhaust system front rubber mountings, and remove the heat shield by twisting it around the exhaust system (photo).

4   Extract the spring clip and withdraw the clevis pin securing the front handbrake cable to the compensator (photo).

5   Undo the two bolts securing the front cable guide plate to the underbody (photo).

6   From inside the car, undo the four bolts securing the handbrake lever assembly to the floor.

7   Disconnect the wiring plug from the warning light switch on the side of the handbrake lever, then remove the lever assembly, complete with front cable, from the car. Recover the lever-to-floor gasket.

8   Unscrew the handbrake adjuster on the side of the lever, and remove the adjuster and spacing washer from the front cable.

9   Release the front cable and gaiter from the handbrake lever assembly, then remove the cable from the gaiter.

10 Refitting is the reverse sequence to removal. Adjust the handbrake as described in Section 18 before lowering the car to the ground.

18.6A Prise up the rear of the handbrake lever trim cover ...

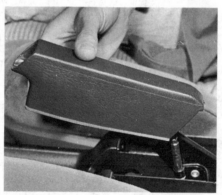

18.6B ... and remove the cover from the lever

18.7 Handbrake adjuster location (arrowed)

19.3 Undcrew the handbrake adjuster on the side of the lever

19.5 Disconnect the warning light switch wiring plug (arrowed)

19.6 Undo the four handbrake lever retaining bolts (arrowed)

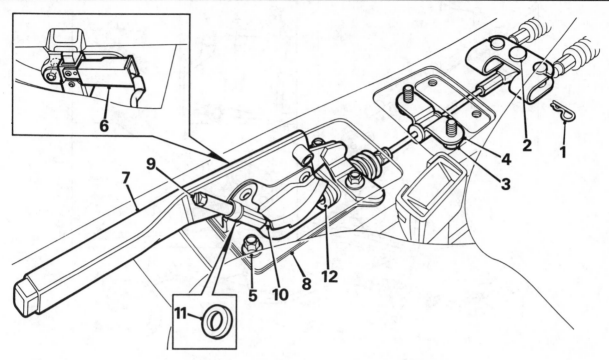

Fig. 9.10 Front handbrake cable attachments (Sec 20)

1   Clevis pin spring clip
2   Clevis pin
3   Cable guide plate retaining bolts
4   Cable guide plate
5   Handbrake lever retaining bolts
6   Warning light switch
    wiring plug
7   Handbrake lever
8   Lever-to-floor gasket
9   Handbrake adjuster
10 Front cable-to-lever attachment
11 Spacing washer
12 Gaiter

20.3 Removing the front heat shield from the exhaust system

20.4 Extract the cable retaining spring clip and clevis pin (arrowed)

20.5 Undo the front cable guide plate retaining bolts (arrowed)

21 Handbrake cable (rear) – removal and refitting

1   Chock the front wheels, remove the rear wheel trim and slacken the wheel nuts. Jack up the rear of the car and support it on axle stands. Remove the rear roadwheels and release the handbrake.
2   Release the exhaust system rubber mountings, lower the system at the rear, and support it on blocks to avoid straining the front flexible joint.
3   Undo the retaining bolts and remove the front and rear exhaust system heat shields (photo).
4   Undo the three bolts and remove the handbrake linkage cover from the brake caliper.
5   Extract the spring clip and withdraw the clevis pin securing the handbrake cable to the linkage lever on the caliper (see Section 8, photo 8.5).
6   Withdraw the spring clip securing the cable to the abutment bracket, and remove the cable from the caliper.

7   Undo the bolts and release the cable support clips on the suspension arm, chassis member and underbody (photos).
8   Disconnect the return spring, extract the spring clip and withdraw the clevis pin securing the front handbrake cable to the compensator (photo).
9   Turn the rear cable end through 90°, and release it from the slot in the compensator.
10 Withdraw the cable from the abutment bracket, and remove it from under the car. Remove the support clips from the cable.
11 Refitting is the reverse sequence to removal. Adjust the handbrake as described in Section 18 before lowering the car to the ground.

22 Stop-light switch – removal, refitting and adjustment

1   From inside the car, release the turnbuckles and lift out the trim panel over the clutch, brake and accelerator pedals.

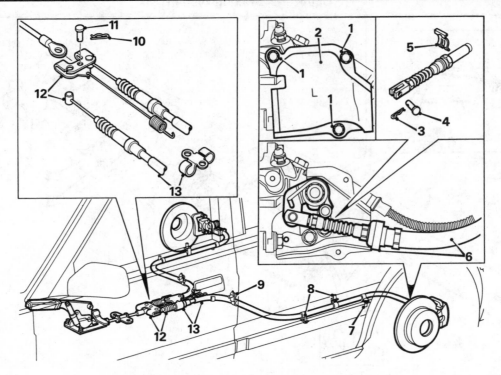

Fig. 9.11 Rear handbrake cable attachments (Sec 21)

1	Handbrake linkage cover retaining bolts	
2	Handbrake linkage cover	
3	Clevis pin spring clip	
4	Clevis pin	
5	Cable retaining spring clip	
6	Handbrake cable	
7	Suspension arm support clip	
8	Chassis member support clips	
9	Underbody support clip	
10	Clevis pin spring clip	
11	Clevis pin	
12	Cable attachment at compensator	
13	Abutment bracket	

21.3 Removing the rear heat shield from the exhaust system

21.7A Cable support on the chassis member ...

21.7B ... and rear underbody

21.7C Front cable support retaining bolts (arrowed)

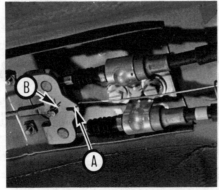

21.8 Handbrake cable return spring (A) and retaining clevis pin (B)

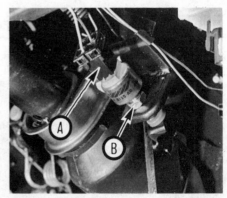

22.2 Stop-light switch wiring multi-plug (A) and locknut (B)

2 Disconnect the switch wiring multi-plug, then slacken the locknut and unscrew the switch from the brake pedal bracket (photo).
3 Refit the switch using the reverse of the removal procedure, and adjust its position so that the stop-lights illuminate after 6.0 mm (0.25 in) of brake pedal travel. When turning the switch during adjustment, disconnect the wiring multi-plug to avoid twisting the harness.
4 When adjustment is correct, tighten the locknut, then refit the trim panel.

23 Vacuum servo unit – description and testing

1 A vacuum servo unit is located between the brake pedal and master cylinder, to provide assistance to the driver when the brake pedal is depressed. This reduces the effort required by the driver to operate the brakes under all braking conditions.
2 The unit operates by vacuum obtained from the inlet manifold, and consists basically of a diaphragm, control valve and non-return valve.
3 With the brake pedal released, vacuum is channelled to both sides of the diaphragm, but when the pedal is depressed, one side is opened to atmosphere. The resultant unequal pressures are harnessed to assist in depressing the master cylinder pistons.
4 Normally, the servo unit is very reliable, but if the unit becomes faulty it must be renewed complete, as repair is not possible. In the event of failure, the hydraulic system is in no way affected, except that higher pedal pressures will be necessary.
5 To test the servo unit, depress the brake pedal several times with the engine switched off, to destroy the vacuum.
6 Apply moderate pressure to the brake pedal, then start the engine. The pedal should move down slightly as the vacuum is restored, if the servo is operating correctly.
7 Now switch off the engine and wait five minutes. Vacuum should still be available for at least one assisted operation of the pedal.

24 Vacuum servo unit – removal and refitting

1 Remove the master cylinder as described in Section 12 or 13 as applicable.
2 From inside the car, release the turnbuckles and lift out the trim panel over the clutch, brake and accelerator pedals.
3 Extract the retaining clip and withdraw the clevis pin securing the servo pushrod to the brake pedal.
4 From within the engine compartment, remove the vacuum hose elbow from the front face of the servo by prising it out of its grommet.
5 Unscrew the four retaining nuts inside the car, and withdraw the servo unit from the engine compartment bulkhead.
6 With the servo removed, the air filter can be renewed if necessary. Withdraw the dust cover over the air filter and pushrod. Hook out the washer and old filter, and cut the filter to allow removal over the pushrod fork. Similarly cut the new filter, place it in position in the housing, and refit the washer and dust cover.
7 Refitting is the reverse sequence to removal. Use a new gasket on the servo-to-bulkhead mating face, and tighten the retaining nuts to the specified torque. Refit the master cylinder as described in Sections 12 or 13 as applicable.

25 Anti-lock braking system – description and operation

Later Rover 820 models are available with an anti-lock braking system (ABS) as an optional extra. The system is used in conjunction with the normal braking system to provide greater stability, improved steering control and shorter stopping distances under all braking conditions. A brief description of the system operation is as follows. Each wheel is provided with a wheel speed sensor, which monitors the wheel rotational speed. The sensor consists of a magnetic core and coil, and is mounted at a predetermined distance from a toothed reluctor ring. The reluctor rings for the front wheels are pressed onto the driveshaft outer constant velocity joints, and those for the rear wheels are pressed onto the rear hubs. When each hub turns, the magnetic field of the sensor is altered as the reluctor ring teeth pass the sensor head, thus inducing an alternating voltage, the frequency of which varies according to wheel speed.

Signals from the wheel speed sensors are sent to an electronic control unit, which can accurately determine whether a wheel is accelerating or decelerating in relation to a reference speed. Information from the electronic control unit is sent to the hydraulic modulator, which contains four solenoids, each operating one inlet and one exhaust valve for one brake, and all working independently of each other in three distinct phases:
Pressure build-up phase: The solenoid inlet valves are open, and hydraulic pressure from the master cylinder is applied directly to the brake calipers.
Constant pressure phase: The solenoid inlet and exhaust valves are closed, and hydraulic pressure at the calipers is maintained at a constant level, even though master cylinder pressure may increase.
Pressure reduction phase: The solenoid inlet valve is closed to prevent further hydraulic pressure reaching the caliper and, in addition, the exhaust valve is open, to reduce existing pressure and release the brake. Fluid is returned to the master cylinder in this phase via the return pump in the hydraulic modulator.

The braking cycle for one wheel is therefore as follows, and will be the same for all four wheels, although independently.

Wheel rotational speed is measured by the wheel speed sensors, the information is processed by the electronic control unit. By comparing the signals received from each wheel, the control unit can determine a reference speed, and detect any variation from this speed, which would indicate a locking brake. Should a lock-up condition be detected, the control unit initiates the constant pressure phase, and no further increase in hydraulic pressure is applied to the affected brake. If the lock-up condition is still detected, the pressure reduction phase is initiated to allow the wheel to turn. The control unit returns to the constant pressure phase until the wheel rotational speed exceeds a predetermined value, then the cycle repeats with the control unit re-initiating the pressure build-up phase. This control cycle is continuously and rapidly repeated, until the brake pedal is released or the car comes to a stop.

Additional circuitry within the electronic control unit monitors the functioning of the system, and informs the driver of any fault condition by means of a warning light. Should a fault occur, the system switches off allowing normal braking, without ABS, to continue.

26 Anti-lock braking system components – removal and refitting

Hydraulic modulator

1 Refer to Chapter 12 and remove the battery.
2 To remove the modulator control relays, undo the screw and lift off the plastic cover. Remove the relays by pulling them out of their location. The large relay controls the return pump operation, and the small relay controls the solenoid valve operation. Refitting is the reversal of removal.
3 To remove the complete modulator unit, remove the relay cover, unscrew the cable clamp and disconnect the modulator wiring multi-plug. Undo the earth terminal nut and disconnect the earth lead from the modulator.
4 Remove the master cylinder reservoir filler cap, and place a piece of polythene over the filler neck. Seal the polythene with an elastic band, ensuring that an airtight seal is obtained. This will minimise brake fluid loss during subsequent operations. Place rags beneath the modulator as an added precaution against fluid spillage.
5 If no identification labels are present on the modulator brake pipe unions, identify each pipe and its location as an aid to refitting. The modulator ports should be stamped on the modulator body with a two-letter code as follows:

VR = Right-hand front
VL = Left-hand front
HR = Right-hand rear
HL = Left-hand rear

6 Unscrew each brake pipe union at the modulator, withdraw the pipe, and immediately plug the pipe end and orifice. Release the pipe support bracket from the side of the modulator, and carefully ease the pipes clear.
7 Slacken the modulator mounting nuts and remove the unit from its location. Do not attempt to dismantle the modulator, as it is a sealed

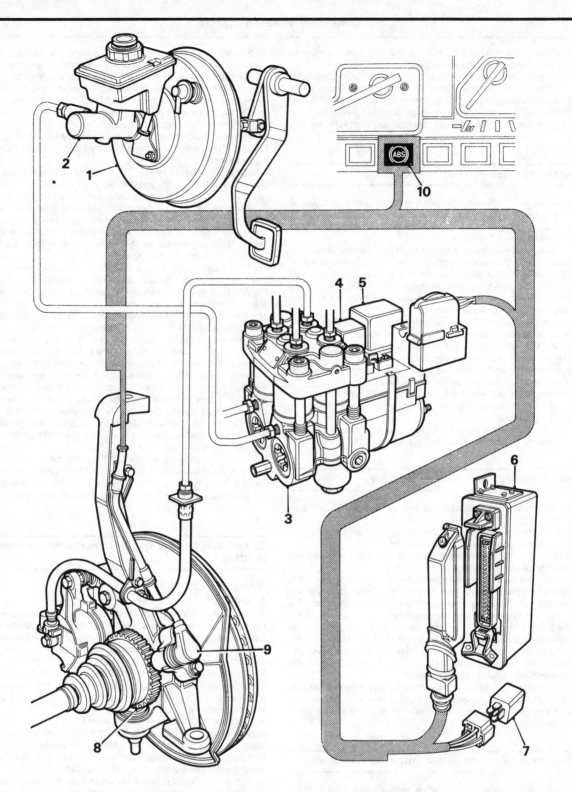

Fig. 9.12 Anti-lock braking system main components (Sec 25)

1 Vacuum servo unit
2 Master cylinder
3 Hydraulic modulator
4 Modulator control relay –
   solenoid valve operation
5 Modulator control relay –
   return pump operation
6 Electronic control unit
7 Over-voltage protection
   relay
8 Front wheel speed sensor
   reluctor ring
9 Front wheel speed sensor
10 ABS warning light

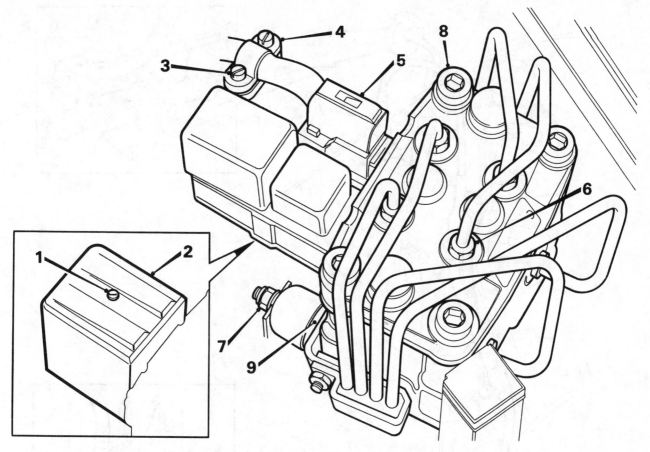

Fig. 9.13 Hydraulic modulator attachments (Sec 26)

1 Cover retaining screw	4 Cable clamp	6 Brake pipe unions	8 Modulator
2 Modulator relay cover	5 Multi-plug	7 Mounting nuts	9 Mounting rubbers
3 Cable clamp screws			

unit, and no repairs are possible.

8 Refitting is the reverse sequence to removal. Bleed the hydraulic system as described in Section 16 on completion.

Electronic control unit

9 Disconnect the battery negative terminal. (Refer to Chapter 12, Section 1, before doing this).

10 Working in the luggage compartment on the left-hand side, release the turnbuckle and lift off the control unit cover.

11 Disconnect the wiring multi-plug by depressing the spring tab at the cable end, lift the plug up at the cable end, then disengage the tab at the other end.

12 Undo the retaining bolts and remove the unit from its location.

13 Refitting is the reverse sequence to removal, but ensure that the wiring multi-plug engages securely with an audible click from the spring tab.

Over-voltage protection relay

14 Working in the luggage compartment, release the turnbuckle and lift off the cover over the electronic control unit.

15 Withdraw the relay from its socket located below the control unit.

16 Refitting is the reverse sequence to removal.

Front wheel speed sensor

17 Apply the handbrake, prise off the front wheel trim and slacken the wheel nuts. Jack up the front of the car and support it on axle stands. Remove the front roadwheel.

18 Undo the bolts securing the cable harness support brackets to the steering knuckle and inner wheel arch panel.

19 From within the engine compartment, release the wiring connector from its holder, and separate the connector. Release the wheel arch

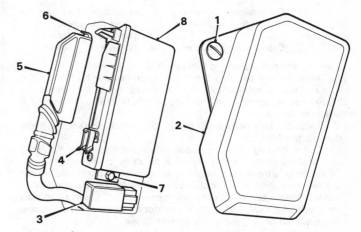

Fig. 9.14 Electronic control unit and over-voltage protection relay details (Sec 26)

1 Turnbuckle	5 Wiring multi-plug
2 Control unit cover	6 Multi-plug tab
3 Over-voltage protection relay	7 Retaining bolt
4 Spring tab	8 Electronic control unit

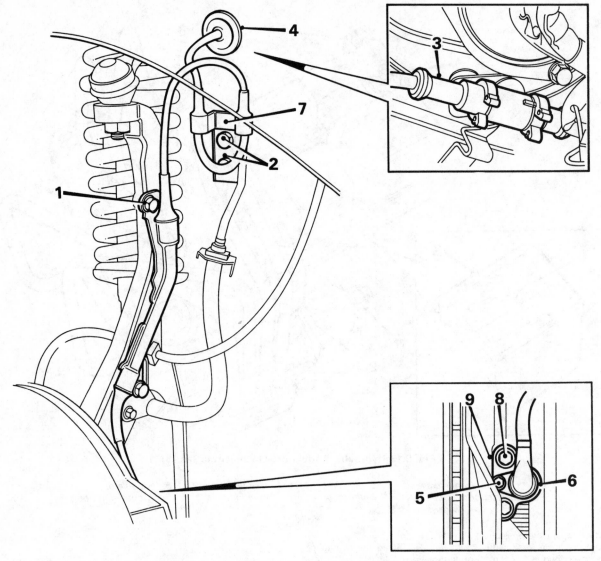

Fig. 9.15 Front wheel speed sensor attachments (Sec 26)

1	Cable harness support bracket bolt on steering knuckle	5	Sensor-to-sensor bracket retaining bolt
2	Cable harness support	6	Sensor

1   Cable harness support bracket bolt on steering knuckle
2   Cable harness support
    bracket and bolt on inner wheel arch panel
3   Wiring connector
4   Wheel arch grommet
5   Sensor-to-sensor bracket retaining bolt
6   Sensor
7   Harness support bracket
8   Sensor bracket-to-steering knuckle retaining bolt
9   Sensor bracket

grommet and pull the wiring through to the wheel arch.

20 Undo the bolt securing the sensor to the sensor bracket on the steering knuckle, and carefully prise the sensor out of the bracket.

21 Release the sensor wiring from the support bracket, and remove the unit from the car.

22 Undo the two bolts and remove the sensor bracket from the steering knuckle.

23 Prior to refitting, clean the sensor, sensor bracket and the mounting area on the steering knuckle, removing all traces of dirt and grit.

24 Refitting is the reverse sequence to removal. Lubricate the sensor and sensor bracket with Rocol J166 or Molykote FB180, and ensure that the bracket bosses face the hub when fitting. Tighten all bolts to the specified torque, and check the sensor-to-reluctor ring clearance, which should be as given in the Specifications.

Rear wheel speed sensor

25 Chock the front wheels, prise off the rear wheel trim and slacken the wheel nuts. Jack up the rear of the car and support it on axle stands. Remove the rear roadwheel.

26 Working in the luggage compartment on the left-hand side, release the turnbuckle and lift off the cover over the electronic control unit.

27 Remove the left-hand side trim panel for access to the wiring around the control unit.

28 Disconnect the wheel speed sensor wiring at the cable connector.

29 Undo the two screws and remove the plastic liner on the front face of the rear wheel arch.

30 Release the grommets in the luggage compartment floor and inner wheel arch, then pull the wiring through to the wheel arch.

31 Undo the two bolts and remove the cable cover and guide from the chassis member.

32 Release the cable ties and retaining clips securing the sensor wiring to the chassis member.

33 Undo the three bolts securing the cable harness support bracket to the rear suspension arm.

34 Undo the three bolts and remove the handbrake linkage cover from the brake caliper.

35 Undo the bolt securing the sensor to the sensor bracket on the hub carrier, and carefully prise the sensor out of the bracket.

36 Manipulate the sensor and wiring out from under the wheel arch, and remove it from car.

37 Prior to refitting, clean the sensor, sensor bracket and the mounting area on the hub carrier, removing all traces of dirt and grit.

38 Refitting is the reverse sequence to removal. Lubricate the sensor and sensor bracket with Rocol J166 or Molykote FB180, and tighten all bolts to the specified torque. Check the sensor-to-reluctor ring clearance, which should be as given in the Specifications.

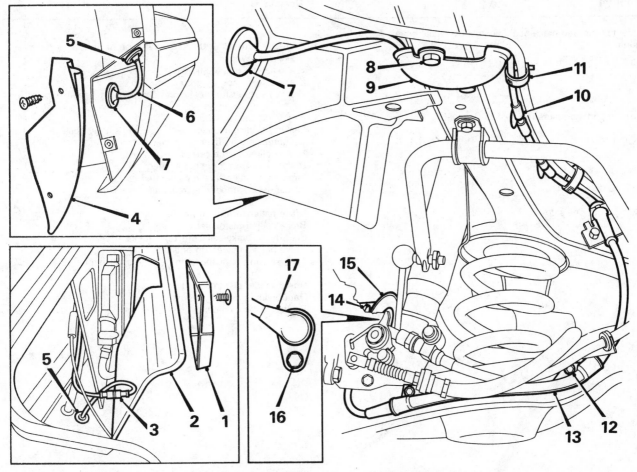

Fig. 9.16 Rear wheel speed sensor attachments (Sec 26)

1 Electronic control unit cover
2 Left-hand side trim panel
3 Cable connector
4 Rear wheel arch plastic liner
5 Luggage compartment floor grommet
6 Sensor wiring
7 Inner wheel arch grommet
8 Cover bolts
9 Cable cover and guide
10 Cable retaining clip
11 Cable tie
12 Support bracket bolt
13 Cable harness support bracket on suspension arm
14 Handbrake linkage cover bolts
15 Handbrake linkage cover
16 Sensor-to-sensor bracket retaining bolt
17 Wheel speed sensor

Wheel speed sensor reluctor rings

39 The reluctor rings for the front and rear wheel speed sensors are an integral part of the driveshaft outer constant velocity joints (front) and rear wheel hub flanges (rear), and cannot be renewed separately.

40 If a reluctor ring is damaged, or in any way unserviceable, a new driveshaft outer constant velocity joint or rear hub flange must be obtained as applicable. Removal and refitting procedures are covered in Chapters 8 and 10 respectively.

27 Fault diagnosis – braking system

Note: *Fault diagnosis on the anti-lock braking system (where fitted) should be entrusted to a suitably-equipped Rover dealer, due to the need for special gauges and test equipment.*

Symptom	Reason(s)
Excessive pedal travel	Rear brake self-adjust mechanism inoperative Air in hydraulic system Faulty master cylinder Worn or incorrectly adjusted hub bearings
Brake pedal feels spongy	Air in hydraulic system Faulty master cylinder

Symptom	Reason(s)
Judder felt through brake pedal or steering wheel when braking	Excessive run-out or thickness variation of discs Brake pads worn Brake caliper guide pins worn Brake caliper mounting bolts loose Wear in suspension or steering components – see Chapter 10
Excessive pedal pressure required to stop car	Faulty vacuum servo unit Leaking or disconnected servo vacuum supply hose Vacuum servo air filter choked Brake caliper piston seized Brake pads worn or contaminated Incorrect grade of brake pads fitted Primary or secondary hydraulic circuit failure
Brakes pull to one side	Brake pads worn or contaminated Brake caliper piston seized Seized rear brake self-adjust mechanism Brake pads renewed on one side only Tyre, steering or suspension defect – see Chapter 10
Brakes binding	Brake caliper piston seized Handbrake incorrectly adjusted Faulty master cylinder

Chapter 10 Suspension and steering

Contents

Specifications

Front suspension

Type .... Independent, by unequal length upper and lower suspension arms, with coil springs, telescopic shock absorbers and anti-roll bar

Trim height (measured from the centre of the front hub to the
edge of the wheel arch) .... 397 to 417 mm (15.6 to 16.4 in)
Hub bearing endfloat .... 0.05 mm (0.02 in)

Rear suspension

Type .... Independent, by transverse and trailing links, with coil springs, telescopic shock absorbers and anti-roll bar. Self-levelling suspension optional on certain models

Trim height (measured from the centre of the rear hub to the
edge of the wheel arch):
    Standard suspension .... 379 to 399 mm (14.9 to 15.7 in)
    Self-levelling suspension (after being driven for 0.6 mile/
    1.0 km) .... 348 to 368 mm (13.7 to 14.5 in)
Hub bearing endfloat .... 0.10 mm (0.004 in)

Steering

Type .... Power-assisted rack and pinion
Turns lock-to-lock 3.2
Fluid type .... Dexron 11D type ATF (Duckhams D-Matic)

Front wheel alignment

Toe setting	Parallel ± 0° 8'
Camber	0° 11' ± 0° 30' positive
Castor	1° 54' ± 0° 15' positive
Steering axis inclination	8°

Rear wheel alignment

Toe setting	0° 10' ± 0° 4' toe-in
Camber	0° ± 30'

Roadwheels

Wheel size:

Standard	6J x 14 or 6J x 15 pressed-steel
Optional	6J x 15 light alloy

Tyres

Tyre size	195/ 70 HR x 14 or 195/ 65 VR x 15 steel-braced radial ply	
Tyre pressures – cold, bar (lbf/ in²):	**Front**	**Rear**
195/ 70 HR x 14 and 195/ 65 VR x 15	1.9 (28)	1.9 (28)

For speeds in excess of 100 mph (160 kph), increase pressure by 0.4 bar (6.0 lbf/ in²) for 195/ 70 HR x 14 tyres, and by 0.7 bar (10.0 lbf/ in²) for 195/ 65 VR x 15 tyres

Torque wrench settings

	Nm	lbf ft
Front suspension		
Anti-roll bar connecting link bolts	50	37
Anti-roll mounting bracket bolts	22	16
Driveshaft retaining nut	290	214
Steering knuckle balljoint nut	100	74
Upper suspension arm balljoint nut	50	37
Strut forked member to lower arm	90	66
Strut forked member clamp bolt	50	37
Shock absorber top mounting nuts	25	18
Shock absorber spindle nut	50	37
Upper suspension arm mounting nuts	80	59
Upper suspension arm pivot bolt	90	66
Lower suspension arm inner mounting bolt	50	37
Tie-bar front mounting nut	90	66
Tie-bar-to-lower suspension arm bolts	170	125
Rear suspension		
Anti-roll bar connecting link nuts	45	33
Anti-roll bar mounting bracket bolts	22	16
Hub carrier-to-trailing link bolt	70	52
Hub carrier-to-transverse link bolt	70	52
Shock absorber-to-hub carrier clamp bolt	70	52
Shock absorber upper mounting nuts	25	18
Shock absorber spindle nut	52	38
Hub flange retaining nut	245	181
Transverse link inner mounting bolt	50	37
Trailing link front mounting nut	45	33
Trailing link adjustment plate retaining bolt	70	52
Trailing link adjustment plate eccentric bolt	70	52
Steering		
Steering wheel nut	50	37
Steering column upper mounting nuts	14	10
Steering column lower mounting bolts	22	16
Column universal joint clamp bolts	22	16
Steering tie-rod balljoint nut	44	32
Steering gear fluid pipe unions	18	13
Steering gear mounting bolts	45	33
Drivebelt tensioner wheel retaining nut (rear-mounted pump)	45	33
Drivebelt idler pulley retaining nut (front-mounted pump)	45	33
Camshaft pulley retaining bolts	10	7
Longitudinal support member bolts	45	33
Power steering pump retaining bolts:		
Rear-mounted pump	25	18
Front-mounted pump	10	7
Power steering pump pulley nut (rear-mounted pump)	82	61
Power steering pump pulley bolts (front-mounted pump)	25	18
Roadwheels		
Roadwheel nuts	70	52

1 General description

The independent front suspension is by unequal length upper and lower suspension arms, and utilizes coil springs and telescopic shock absorbers. Each spring and shock absorber assembly is attached to the body turret at its upper end by a rubber-cushioned mounting, and to the lower suspension arm by a forged, forked-shaped member. Fore and aft location of each suspension assembly is by a tie-bar, and an anti-roll bar is used to minimise body roll. The front steering knuckles, which carry the hub bearings, brake calipers and the hub/ disc assemblies, pivot on balljoints – one incorporated in the upper suspension arm, and one secured to the lower part of the steering knuckle itself.

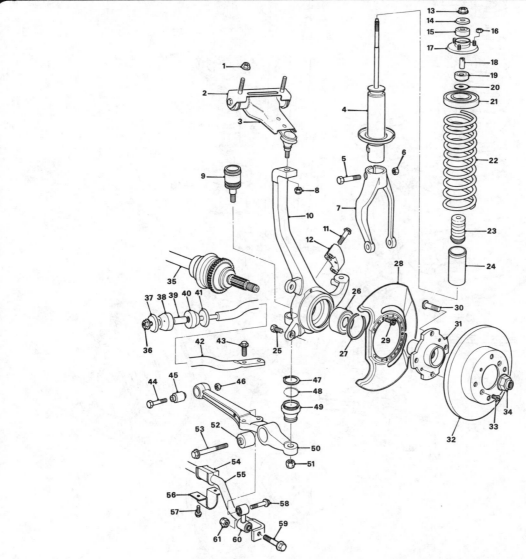

Fig. 10.1 Exploded view of the front suspension components (Sec 1)

1 Mounting bracket nut	16 Upper mounting nut	32 Brake disc	48 Dust cover locking ring
2 Upper suspension arm mounting bracket	17 Shock absorber upper mounting plate	33 Disc retaining screw	49 Balljoint dust cover
3 Upper suspension arm	18 Threaded collar	34 Driveshaft retaining nut	50 Lower suspension arm
4 Shock absorber	19 Lower bush (where fitted)	35 Driveshaft	51 Balljoint retaining nut
5 Forked member clamp bolt	20 Washer	36 Tie-bar front mounting nut	52 Forked member mounting bush
6 Clamp bolt nut	21 Spring seat	37 Washer	53 Forked member through bolt
7 Forked member	22 Coil spring	38 Outer mounting bush	54 Anti-roll bar mounting bush
8 Balljoint nut	23 Bump-stop	39 Spacer	55 Anti-roll bar
9 Steering knuckle balljoint	24 Dust cover	40 Inner mounting bush	56 Anti-roll bar mounting bracket
10 Steering knuckle	25 Brake caliper carrier bracket bolt	41 Washer	57 Mounting bracket bolt
11 Wheel speed sensor bolt (where applicable)	26 Hub bearing	42 Tie-bar	58 Connecting link bolt
12 Wheel speed sensor bracket (where applicable)	27 Bearing retaining circlip	43 Tie-bar-to-lower suspension arm bolt	59 Connecting link bolt
13 Shock absorber spindle nut	28 Disc shield	44 Lower suspension arm inner mounting bolt	60 Connecting link
14 Washer	29 Disc shield bolt	45 Inner mounting bush	61 Connecting link nut
15 Upper bush	30 Wheel stud	46 Mounting bolt nut	
	31 Hub flange	47 Balljoint retaining circlip	

The independent rear suspension is by transverse and trailing links with coil springs, telescopic shock absorbers, and an anti-roll bar. The shock absorbers are attached to the body at their upper ends by rubber-cushioned mountings, and clamped to the hub carriers at their lower ends. Lateral location of each suspension assembly is provided by the transverse link, which also provides the lower location of the coil spring. Fore and aft location of each suspension assembly is controlled by the trailing link, which is attached to the hub carrier by means of a bracket incorporating an eccentric mounting bolt for rear wheel toe adjustment.

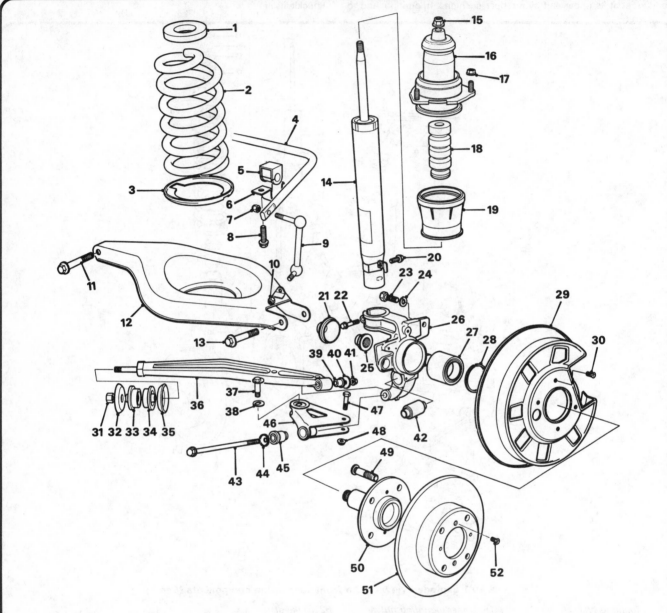

Fig. 10.2 Exploded view of the rear suspension components (Sec 1)

1 Upper spring seat	14 Shock absorber	27 Hub bearing	41 Through-bolt nut
2 Coil spring	15 Shock absorber spindle nut	28 Bearing retaining circlip	42 Transverse link-to-hub
3 Lower spring seat	16 Shock absorber upper	29 Disc shield	carrier mounting bush
4 Anti-roll bar	mounting	30 Disc shield screw	43 Trailing link-to-hub carrier
5 Anti-roll bar mounting bush	17 Upper mounting nut	31 Trailing link front mounting	through-bolt
6 Anti-roll bar mounting	18 Bump-stop	nut	44 Washer
bracket	19 Dust cover	32 Outer washer	45 Rear mounting bush
7 Connecting link nut	20 Brake hose bracket bolt	33 Outer bush	46 Adjustment plate
8 Mounting bracket bolt	21 Nut cover	34 Inner bush	47 Adjustment plate bolt
9 Connecting link	22 Shock absorber clamp bolt	35 Inner washer	48 Adjustment plate nut
10 Connecting link nut	23 Brake caliper carrier bracket	36 Trailing link	49 Wheel stud
11 Transverse link inner	bolt	37 Eccentric bolt	50 Hub flange
mounting bolt	24 Washer	38 Eccentric washer	51 Brake disc
12 Transverse link	25 Hub flange retaining nut	39 Rear mounting bush	52 Brake disc screw
13 Transverse link-to-hub	26 Hub carrier	40 Washer	
carrier bolt			

Self-levelling rear suspension, which reacts to vehicle loading and automatically maintains the normal trim heights, is available as an option on all later models. The self-levelling units are sealed dampers fitted in place of the normal rear shock absorbers. A pump in the damper operates under the action of the suspension to raise the rear of the car until normal trim height is regained. On an undulating road, this process will be carried out within one mile. When the additional load is removed, the suspension remains at the correct level.

Power-assisted rack and pinion steering gear is standard equipment on all models. Movement of the steering wheel is transmitted to the steering gear by a steering column shaft containing two universal joints. These allow for provision of a rake-adjustable column assembly, and also allow the necessary upward deflection of the column, for driver safety, in the event of front end impact. The front wheels are connected to the steering gear by tie-rods, each having an inner and outer balljoint. On early models, hydraulic fluid pressure for the power assistance is provided by a pump, mounted on the left-hand end of the engine and belt-driven from a pulley on the inlet camshaft. On later models, the pump is mounted on the forward-facing side of the engine, for improved access, and is belt-driven from the crankshaft pulley.

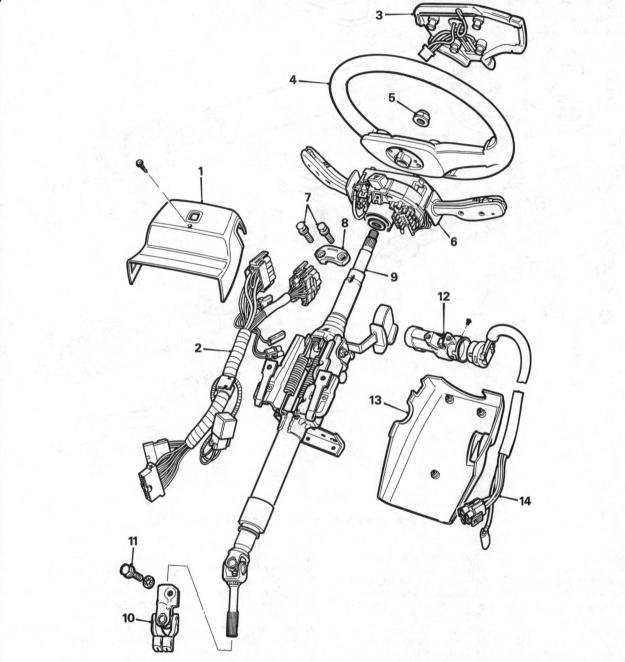

Fig. 10.3 Exploded view of the steering column components (Sec 1)

1	Steering column upper shroud	5	Steering wheel nut
2	Wiring harness	6	Steering column switches
3	Steering wheel pad	7	Steering lock shear-bolts
4	Steering wheel	8	Lock saddle
		9	Steering column shaft
10	Universal joint	13	Steering column lower shroud
11	Clamp bolt	14	Ignition switch wiring harness
12	Steering column lock/ignition switch		

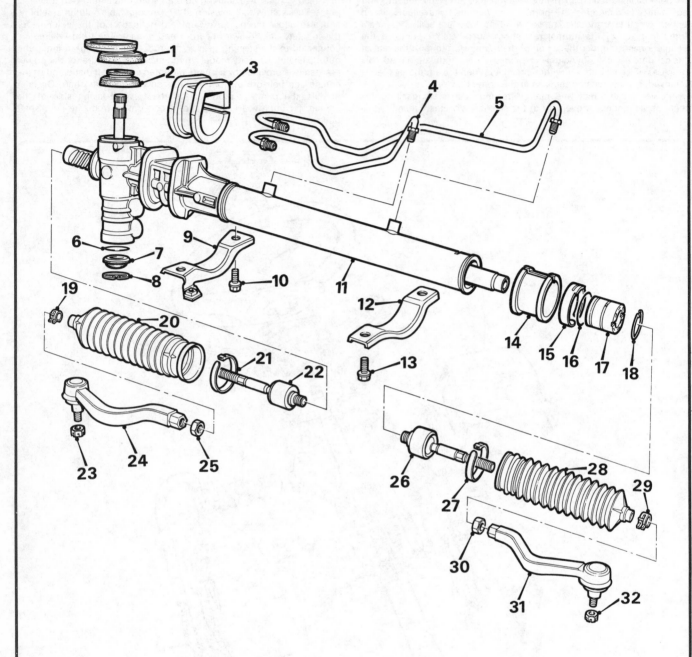

Fig. 10.4 Exploded view of the rack and pinion steering gear (Sec 1)

1	Pinion shield	10	Mounting bracket bolt
2	Pinon dust cover	11	Rack housing
3	Right-hand rubber mounting	12	Left-hand mounting bracket
4	Fluid pipe	13	Mounting bracket bolt
5	Fluid pipe	14	Left-hand rubber mounting
6	O-ring	15	Bush retainer
7	Pinion cover	16	O-ring
8	Circlip	17	Rack support bush
9	Right-hand mounting bracket	18	Locking wire

19	Gaiter clip	26	Left-hand inner tie-rod balljoint
20	Right-hand rubber gaiter	27	Gaiter clip
21	Gaiter clip	28	Left-hand rubber gaiter
22	Right-hand inner tie-rod balljoint	29	Gaiter clip
23	Balljoint	30	Tie-rod locknut
24	Right-hand steering tie-rod	31	Left-hand steering tie-rod
25	Tie-rod locknut	32	Balljoint nut

2 Maintenance and inspection

1 At the intervals given in *Routine maintenance* at the beginning of this manual, a thorough inspection of all suspension and steering components should be carried out, using the following procedures as a guide.

Front suspension and steering

2 With the engine switched off, check the fluid level in the power steering reservoir as follows.

3 Wipe the area around the black filler cap on the reservoir (photo), turn the cap anti-clockwise and remove it.

4 Wipe the dipstick on a clean cloth, refit the cap fully, then remove it once more. Check the fluid level, which must be between the MIN mark on one side of the dipstick, and the MAX mark on the other. If necessary, top up using the specified fluid to bring the level up to the MAX mark (photo). Refit the cap and tighten it securely.

5 Apply the handbrake, jack up the front of the car and support it securely on axle stands.

6 Visually inspect the upper and lower balljoint dust covers and the steering gear rubber gaiters for splits, chafing or deterioration. Renew any components showing signs of wear or damage as described in the appropriate Section of this Chapter.

7 Check the power steering fluid hoses for chafing or deterioration, and the pipe and hose unions for fluid leaks. Also check for any signs of fluid leakage from the rubber gaiters, which would indicate failed fluid seals within the steering gear itself. Rectify any faults found using the procedures described later in this Chapter.

8 Grasp the roadwheel at the 12 o'clock and 6 o'clock positions, and try to rock it. Very slight free play may be felt, but if the movement is appreciable, further investigation is necessary to determine the source. Continue rocking the wheel while an assistant depresses the footbrake. If the movement is now eliminated or significantly reduced, it is likely that the hub bearings are at fault. If the free play is still evident with the footbrake depressed, then there is wear in the suspension joints or mountings. Pay close attention to the upper and lower balljoints and the suspension arm mounting bushes. Renew any worn components as described in the appropriate Sections of this Chapter.

9 Now grasp the wheel at the 9 o'clock and 3 o'clock positions, and try to rock it as before. Any excessive movement felt now may again be caused by wear in the hub bearings or the steering tie-rod inner or outer balljoints. If the outer balljoint is worn, the visual movement will be obvious. If the inner joint is suspect, it can be felt by placing a hand over the rack and pinion rubber gaiter and grasping the tie-rod. If the wheel is now rocked, movement will be felt at the inner joint if wear has taken place. Repair procedures are described in Section 25.

10 Using a large screwdriver or flat bar, check for wear in the anti-roll bar mountings by carefully levering against these components. Some movement is to be expected as the mounting bushes are made of rubber, but excessive wear should be obvious. Renew any bushes that are worn.

11 With the car standing on its wheels, have an assistant turn the steering wheel back and forth about one-eighth of a turn each way. There should be minimal lost movement between the steering wheel and roadwheels (some free play within the rack and pinion steering gear itself is normal, due to design tolerances). If the free play is excessive, closely observe the joints and mountings previously described, but in addition check the steering column shaft and universal joints for wear, and also the rack and pinion steering gear itself. Any wear should be visually apparent and must be rectified, as described in the appropriate Sections of this Chapter.

12 Have the front wheel alignment checked, and if necessary adjusted, (see Section 30) if there is any sign of abnormal wear of the front tyres.

Rear suspension

13 Chock the front wheels, jack up the rear of the car and support it securely on axle stands.

14 Visually check the rear suspension components, attachments and linkages for any visible signs of wear or damage.

15 Grasp the roadwheel at the 12 o'clock and 6 o'clock positions, and try to rock it. Any excess movement here indicates wear in the hub bearings, which may also be accompanied by a rumbling sound when the wheel is spun, or wear in the hub carrier lower mounting bush. Repair procedures are described in later Sections of this Chapter.

2.3 Power steering reservoir and filler cap

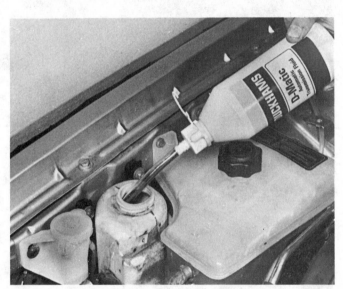

2.4 Top up the reservoir using the specified fluid

16 Have the rear wheel alignment checked, and if necessary adjusted, (see Section 30) if there is any sign of abnormal wear of the rear tyres.

Wheels and tyres

17 Carefully inspect each tyre, including the spare, for signs of uneven wear, lumps, bulges or damage to the sidewalls or tread face. Refer to Section 31 for further details.

18 Check the condition of the wheel rims for distortion, damage or excessive run-out. Also make sure that the balance weights are secure, with no obvious signs that any are missing. Check the torque of the roadwheel nuts, and check the tyre pressures.

Shock absorbers

19 Check for signs of fluid leakage around the shock absorber body, or from the rubber boot around the piston rod (where fitted). Should any fluid be noticed, the shock absorber is defective internally, and renewal is necessary.

20 The efficiency of the shock absorber may be checked by bouncing the car at each corner. Generally speaking, the body will return to its normal position and stop after being depressed. If it rises and returns on a rebound, the shock absorber is probably suspect. Examine also the shock absorber upper and lower mountings for any signs of wear. Renewal procedures are contained in Section 6, 7 and 14.

3 Front steering knuckle assembly – removal and refitting

1   While the car is standing on its wheels, firmly apply the handbrake and put the transmission in gear (PARK on automatic transmission models),
2   Remove the wheel trim, and using a small punch, knock up the staking that secures the driveshaft retaining nut to the groove in the constant velocity joint stub shaft (photo). Note that a new retaining nut will be needed for reassembly.
3   Using a socket, sturdy T-bar and long extension tube for leverage, slacken the retaining nut half a turn. Note that the retaining nut is tightened to a very high torque setting, and considerable effort will be required to slacken it.
4   Slacken the wheel nuts, jack up the front of the car and support it on stands. Remove the roadwheel and return the transmission to neutral.
5   Remove the driveshaft retaining nut.
6   Undo the two bolts securing the brake caliper carrier bracket to the steering knuckle (photo), and the two bolts securing the brake hose bracket to the knuckle.
7   Withdraw the caliper and carrier bracket assembly, complete with brake pads, off the disc, and tie it up using string or wire from a convenient place under the wheel arch. Take care to avoid straining the brake hose.
8   Undo the two retaining screws (photo) and remove the disc from the hub flange.
9   On cars equipped with ABS brakes, remove the front wheel speed sensor and wiring harness from the steering knuckle, as described in Chapter 9.
10 Extract the split pin and unscrew the nut securing the steering tie-rod balljoint to the steering knuckle arm (photo). Release the balljoint from the arm using a universal balljoint separator tool.
11 Undo the nut securing the steering knuckle balljoint to the lower suspension arm. Release the balljoint from the arm using a separator tool or two-legged puller (photo).
12 Undo the nut securing the upper suspension arm balljoint to the steering knuckle (photo), and release the balljoint using the same

3.2 Knock up the staking (arrowed) securing the driveshaft retaining nut

3.6 Brake caliper carrier bracket retaining bolts (arrowed)

3.8 Brake disc retaining screws (arrowed)

3.10 Extract the tie-rod balljoint nut split pin (arrowed)

3.11 Using a two-legged puller to release the steering knuckle balljoint

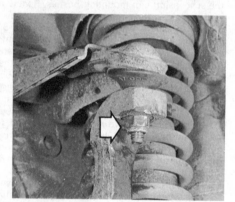

3.12 Undo the upper suspension arm balljoint nut (arrowed)

3.13 Removing the steering knuckle from the driveshaft

3.14 Tighten the new driveshaft retaining nut fully **only** when the weight of the car is on the roadwheels

procedure as for the lower balljoint.

13 Disengage the balljoint shanks, then withdraw the steering knuckle from the driveshaft (photo). If necessary, tap the end of the driveshaft with a copper or plastic mallet to release it from the hub splines. Remove the steering knuckle assembly from the car.

14 Refitting the steering knuckle is the reverse sequence to removal, bearing in mind the following points:

(a) Tighten all retaining nuts and bolts to the specified torque and use a new split pin to secure the steering tie-rod balljoint nut

(b) Use a new driveshaft retaining nut but **do not attempt to tighten this nut fully until the weight of the car is on the roadwheels** (photo). Peen the nut into the driveshaft groove using a small punch after tightening. If a torque wrench capable of recording the high figure required for tightening is not available, it is recommended that the old nut is fitted, tightened as securely as possible, then peened into place. Take the car directly to a suitably-equipped garage, and have them fit and tighten the new nut for you.

(c) On cars equipped with ABS brakes, refit the wheel speed sensor as described in Chapter 9

---

4 Front hub bearing – renewal

---

1 Remove the steering knuckle from the car as described in the previous Section.

2 Support the steering knuckle on blocks with the hub flange facing downwards. Using a hammer and socket or tube of suitable diameter in contact with the inner edge of the hub flange (photo), drive the flange

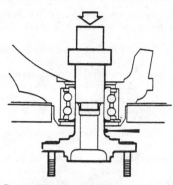

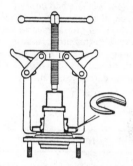

Fig. 10.5 Removing the hub flange from the steering knuckle and bearing (Sec 4)

Fig. 10.6 Using a puller and horseshoe-shaped strip of metal to draw off the bearing inner race from the hub flange (Sec 4)

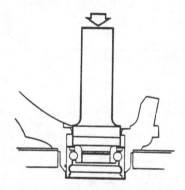

Fig. 10.7 Removing the hub bearing from the steering knuckle (Sec 4)

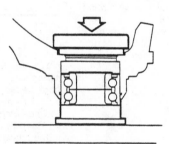

Fig. 10.8 Fitting the new hub bearing to the steering knuckle (Sec 4)

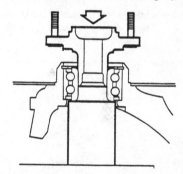

Fig. 10.9 Fitting the hub flange to the new bearing (Sec 4)

4.2A Remove the hub flange using a socket or tube in contact with its outer edge (arrowed) ...

4.2B ... or preferably, use a hydraulic press

out of the hub bearing. Alternatively, if a press is available, support the steering knuckle on the press bed and press the hub flange out (photo).

3 As the hub flange is withdrawn, one of the bearing inner races will come away with it, and must now be removed. To do this, engage the legs of a two-legged puller under the inner race and draw it off. It may be easier to do this if a horseshoe-shaped strip of metal is placed under the inner race, to give the puller legs greater purchase (Fig. 10.6).

4 With the hub flange removed, undo the four screws and remove the disc shield.

5 Using circlip pliers, extract the bearing retaining circlip from the steering knuckle.

6 Support the steering knuckle face-down on blocks, or on the press bed as before, and with the tube or mandrel in contact with the edge of the outer bearing, drive or press the bearing out.

7 Fit the new bearing in the same way, ensuring that it is pressed fully home to the shoulder in the steering knuckle. Keep the bearing square as it is fitted, otherwise it will jam and continued pressure could cause the outer race to crack. If the bearing does jam, tap or press it out, remove any burrs in the bore of the steering knuckle and try again.

8 Secure the bearing with the circlip, then refit the disc shield.

9 Support the bearing inner race on a socket or tube of suitable diameter, and drive or press the hub flange into place.

10 The steering knuckle can now be refitted to the car as described in the previous Section.

5 Steering knuckle balljoint – removal and refitting

1 Remove the steering knuckle from the car as described in Section 3.

2 Extract the balljoint retaining circlip (photo) and remove the dust cover.

3 Support the steering knuckle in a wide-opening vice or on a press bed, and using suitable tubes as mandrels and distance pieces, press the balljoint out of the knuckle. Fig. 10.10 shows the manufacturer's special tools being used for this purpose, to give an idea of the arrangement, but lengths of tubular steel work equally well.

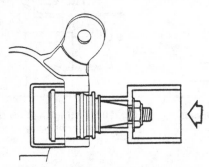

Fig. 10.10 Rover special tool for steering knuckle balljoint removal (Sec 5)

4 Using the same basic procedure, fit the new balljoint until its shoulder contacts the steering knuckle flange.

5 Fit the new dust cover and secure the assembly with the circlip.

6 Refit the steering knuckle to the car as described in Section 3.

6 Front shock absorber and coil spring assembly – removal and refitting

1 Apply the handbrake, prise off the front wheel trim and slacken the wheel nuts. Jack up the front of the car and support it on axle stands. Remove the front roadwheel.

2 Place a jack beneath the lower suspension arm and raise the arm slightly.

3 Undo the nut and remove the through-bolt securing the forked member to the lower suspension arm.

4 Undo the nut and remove the clamp bolt securing the forked member to the shock absorber.

5 Slowly lower the jack, and remove the forked member from the shock absorber and lower suspension arm (photo). It may be necessary to tap the member down using a copper or plastic mallet to release it from the shock absorber.

6 Have an assistant hold the assembly, from below, then undo the three nuts securing the shock absorber top mounting to the body turret in the engine compartment (photo).

7 Remove the shock absorber and spring assembly from under the wheel arch.

8 Refitting is the reverse sequence to removal. Tighten all nuts and bolts to the specified torque, but do not fully tighten the forked member-to-lower arm bolt and nut until the weight of the car is on the roadwheels.

7 Front shock absorber and coil spring assembly – dismantling and reassembly

Note: *Before attempting to dismantle the shock absorber and coil spring assembly, a suitable tool to hold the spring in compression must be obtained. Adjustable coil spring compressors are readily available, and are recommended for this operation. Any attempt at dismantling without such a tool is likely to result in damage or personal injury.*

1 Remove the shock absorber and coil spring assembly as described in the previous Section.

2 Position the spring compressors on either side of the spring, and compress the spring evenly until there is no tension on the spring seat or upper mounting.

5.2 Balljoint retaining circlip (arrowed)

6.5 Removing the front suspension forked member

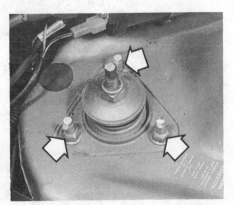

6.6 Shock absorber top mounting retaining nuts (arrowed)

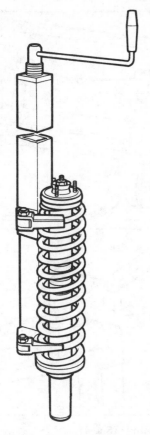

Fig. 10.11 Coil spring and shock absorber assembly, showing spring compressor tool in position (Sec 7)

3   Hold the unthreaded end of the shock absorber spindle with a self-locking wrench or similar tool, and unscrew the upper mounting retaining nut (photo).
4   Withdraw the washer under the nut, followed by the upper bush, the upper mounting plate and the spring seat.
5   To remove the threaded collar on the shock absorber spindle, it will be necessary to make up a suitable tool which will engage in the slots on the collar, enabling it to be unscrewed. A tool can be made out of a

7.3 Remove the retaining nut (arrowed) from the shock absorber spindle

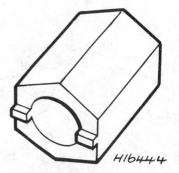

Fig. 10.12 Shock absorber threaded collar home-made removal tool (Sec 7)

large nut, with one end suitably shaped by cutting or filing so that two projections are left, which will engage with the collar slots (Fig. 10.12).
6   Engage the home-made tool with the threaded collar slots, then screw two 10 mm nuts onto the threaded end of the spindle, and lock them together. Hold these locknuts to prevent the spindle turning, and unscrew the threaded collar.
7   Remove the locknuts, home-made tool and collar, then withdraw the lower bush and washer.
8   Lift off the spring, then remove the bump-stop and shock absorber dust cover.
9   Examine the shock absorber for signs of fluid leakage. Check the spindle for signs of wear or pitting along its entire length, and check the shock absorber body for signs of damage or corrosion. Test the operation of the shock absorber, while holding it in an upright position, by moving the spindle through a full stroke, and then through short strokes of 50 to 100 mm (2 to 4 in). In both cases, the resistance felt should be smooth and continuous. If the resistance is jerky or uneven, or if there is any visible sign of wear, damage or fluid leakage, renewal is necessary.
10   If any doubt exists about the condition of the coil spring, remove the spring compressors and check the spring for distortion or damage. The spring free length can only be assessed by comparing it with a new item, and this should be done if the spring is suspect or if the vehicle ride height has been measured and found to be less than the specified figure. Renew the spring if necessary, ideally in pairs (both sides).
11   Check the condition of the spring seat and upper mounting components, and renew any parts which are suspect.
12   Begin reassembly by refitting the shock absorber dust cover and bump-stop.
13   Refit the spring compressors, if previously removed, and place the spring in position on the shock absorber.
14   Refit the washer, lower bush and threaded collar. Tighten the collar using the same procedure as for removal.
15   Refit the spring seat, upper mounting plate, upper bush and washer. Secure the upper mounting assembly with the retaining nut, tightened to the specified torque.
16   Remove the spring compressors, and refit the spring and shock absorber to the car as described in Section 6.

8   Front upper suspension arm – removal and refitting

Note: *The upper suspension arm incorporates the steering knuckle upper support balljoint as a riveted integral assembly. If wear of the balljoint necessitates renewal, a complete upper suspension arm must be obtained*

1   Apply the handbrake, prise off the front wheel trim and slacken the wheel nuts. Jack up the front of the car and support it on axle stands. Remove the front roadwheel.
2   Undo the nut securing the upper suspension arm balljoint to the steering knuckle (photo). Release the balljoint using a separator tool or two-legged puller.
3   From within the engine compartment, undo the two nuts securing the suspension arm mounting bracket to the inner wing valance. For access to the rearmost nut, it may be necessary to move the wiring harness connectors aside, or if working on the left-hand suspension

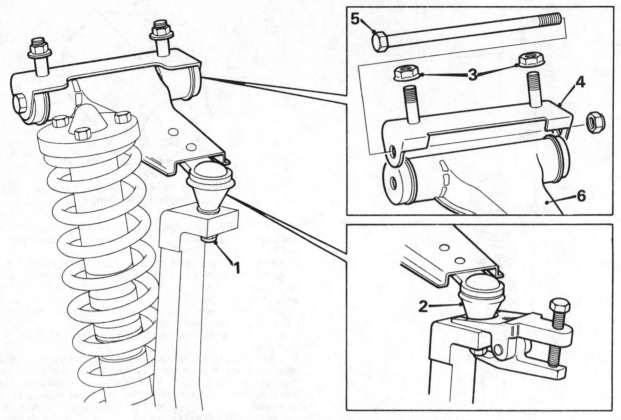

Fig. 10.13 Upper suspension arm attachment details (Sec 8)

1	Balljoint-to-steering knuckle retaining nut	2	Releasing the balljoint with a separator tool	3	Mounting bracket retaining nuts	4	Mounting bracket

1   Balljoint-to-steering knuckle
    retaining nut
2   Releasing the balljoint with
    a separator tool
3   Mounting bracket retaining
    nuts
4   Mounting bracket
5   Pivot bolt
6   Upper suspension arm

arm, to undo the bolts and move the wiper motor bracket slightly.
4   Withdraw the upper suspension arm assembly from under the wheel arch.
5   With the arm on the bench, undo the nut and withdraw the pivot bolt then remove the arm from its mounting bracket.
6   Check the condition of the balljoint dust cover, and check the joint itself for excess free play. Also check the condition of the pivot bushes and the arm itself. The bushes can be renewed by drifting them out then pressing in new ones. If the balljoint, balljoint dust cover or the suspension arm show signs of damage or wear, a complete new assembly must be obtained. Examine the pivot bolt for signs of wear ridges, and check the mounting bracket for elongation of the pivot bolt holes. Renew any components as necessary.
7   Refitting is the reverse sequence to removal, but tighten all nuts and bolts to the specified torque.

9   Front lower suspension arm – removal and refitting

1   Apply the handbrake, prise of the front wheel trim and slacken the wheel nuts. Jack up the front of the car and support it on axle stands. Remove the front roadwheel.
2   Undo the nut securing the steering knuckle balljoint to the lower suspension arm (photo). Release the balljoint using a separator tool or two-legged puller.
3   Undo the nut and remove the through-bolt securing the shock absorber forked member to the arm.
4   Undo the bolt securing the anti-roll bar connecting link to the arm.
5   Undo the two bolts securing the tie-bar to the arm.
6   Undo the nut and remove the suspension arm inner mounting bolt (photo).

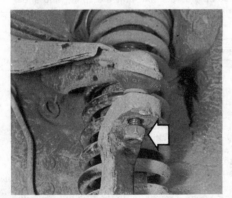

8.2 Undo the nut securing the balljoint to the steering knuckle (arrowed)

9.2 Undo the nut securing the steering knuckle balljoint to the lower suspension arm

9.6 Lower suspension arm inner mounting bolt (arrowed)

7 Withdraw the suspension arm from its inner mounting location, and remove it from under the wheel arch.

8 Check the condition of the two suspension arm bushes, and renew these if worn or damaged. To do this, a press will be required, together with suitable mandrels and distance tubes. If this equipment is not available, have this work done by a Rover dealer or suitably-equipped garage.

9 Refitting is the reverse sequence to removal, but tighten all nuts and bolts to the specified torque. Do not fully tighten the inner mounting bolt or the forked member retaining bolt until the weight of the car is on its roadwheels.

10 Front anti-roll bar – removal and refitting

1 Apply the handbrake, prise off the front wheel trim and slacken the wheel nuts. Jack up the front of the car and support it on axle stands. Remove the front roadwheels.

2 Undo the single bolt each side securing the anti-roll bar connecting links to the lower suspension arms (photo).

3 Undo the two bolts each side securing the anti-roll bar mounting brackets to the chassis members (photo), and remove the bar from under the car.

4 If required, the connecting links can be removed after undoing the retaining nut and bolt on each side.

5 Check the condition of the connecting link bushes and the anti-roll bar mounting bushes, and renew any that show signs of deterioration. The connecting link bushes come complete with new connecting links, and the mounting bushes are slit along their length to allow removal and refitting over the bar.

6 Refitting is the reverse sequence to removal. Tighten the mounting and connecting link bushes to the specified torque only with the weight of the car on its roadwheels.

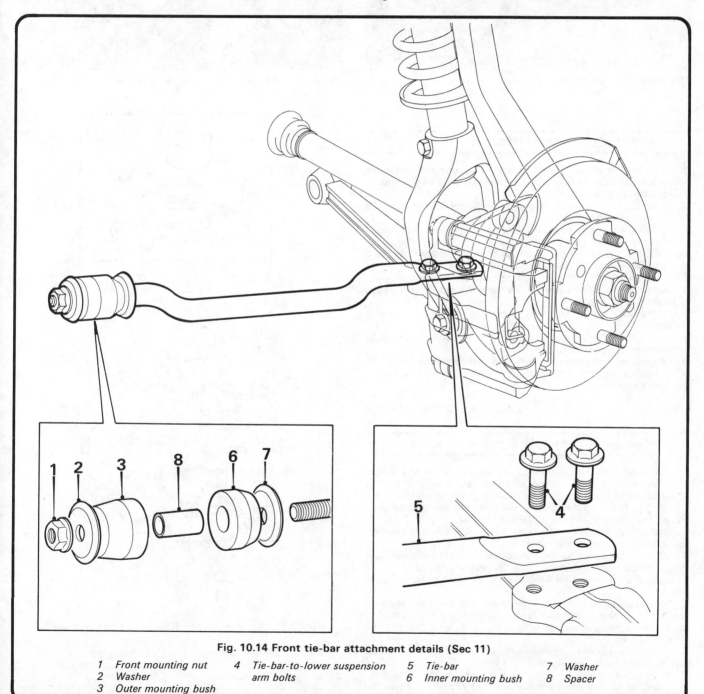

Fig. 10.14 Front tie-bar attachment details (Sec 11)

1	Front mounting nut	4	Tie-bar-to-lower suspension	5	Tie-bar	7	Washer
2	Washer		arm bolts	6	Inner mounting bush	8	Spacer
3	Outer mounting bush						

10.2 Anti-roll bar connecting link bolt (arrowed)

10.3 Anti-roll bar mounting bracket bolts (arrowed)

11 Front tie-bar – removal and refitting

1   Apply the handbrake, prise off the front wheel trim and slacken the wheel nuts. Jack up the front of the car and support it on axle stands. Remove the front roadwheel.
2   Undo the five bolts and remove the undertray for access to the tie-bar front mounting.
3   Undo the front mounting nut and remove the tie-bar washer and outer mounting bush.
4   Undo the two bolts securing the tie-bar to the lower suspension arm, and remove the bar from under the car.
5   Withdraw the spacer, inner mounting bush and washer.
6   Renew the mounting bushes if they show any sign of deformation or swelling of the rubber.
7   Fit the washer, inner bush and spacer, then locate the tie-bar in position.
8   Secure the tie-bar to the lower suspension arm, with the two bolts tightened to the specified torque.
9   Fit the outer bush and washer, followed by the retaining nut, but do not tighten the nut fully until the weight of the car is on its roadwheels.
10 Refit the undertray.

12 Rear hub carrier – removal and refitting

1   Chock the front wheels, prise off the rear wheel trim and slacken the wheel nuts. Jack up the rear of the car and support it on axle stands. Remove the rear roadwheel and release the handbrake.
2   Refer to Chapter 9 if necessary, and undo the two bolts securing the brake caliper carrier bracket to the hub carrier.
3   Undo the retaining bolt and release the flexible brake hose support bracket from the shock absorber strut.
4   Withdraw the carrier bracket, complete with caliper and brake pads, from the disc and hub carrier. Tie the caliper assembly from a convenient place under the wheel arch to avoid straining the brake hose.
5   On cars equipped with ABS, withdraw the rear wheel speed sensor and wiring harness from the hub carrier, as described in Chapter 9.
6   Undo the two screws and remove the brake disc from the hub flange (photos).
7   Undo the nut and release the anti-roll bar connecting link from the suspension lower transverse link.
8   Place a jack beneath the transverse link, and raise the link slightly.
9   Undo the nut and remove the through-bolt and washers securing the hub carrier to the trailing link.

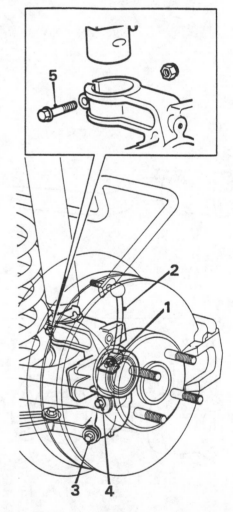

Fig. 10.15 Rear hub carrier attachment details (Sec 12)

1   Anti-roll bar connecting link nut
2   Anti-roll bar connecting link
3   Hub carrier-to-trailing link
    through-bolt
4   Hub carrier-to-transverse link retaining bolt
5   Shock absorber clamp bolt

12.6A Undo the two screws (arrowed) ...

12.6B ... and remove the brake disc

10 Undo the nut and remove the bolt securing the hub carrier to the transverse link.
11 Undo the nut and clamp bolt securing the shock absorber strut to the hub carrier.
12 Lower the jack slightly, and release the hub carrier from the shock absorber strut. If the strut is tight, spread the slot in the hub carrier with a screwdriver, and tap the carrier down with a copper or plastic mallet.
13 Withdraw the hub carrier from the transverse and trailing links, and remove it from the car.
14 Refitting is the reverse sequence to removal. Tighten all nuts and bolts to the specified torque, but do not fully tighten the transverse and trailing link retaining nuts until the weight of the car is on the roadwheels.

13 Rear hub bearing – renewal

1 Remove the rear hub from the car as described in the previous Section.
2 Prise off the cover over the hub flange retaining nut at the rear of the hub carrier, then secure the hub flange in a vice.

3 Using a small punch or screwdriver, tap up the staking, then unscrew the hub flange retaining nut. Note that a new nut will be required for reassembly.
4 Support the hub carrier in a vice, and tap the hub flange out of the bearing.
5 Undo the four screws and remove the disc shield.
6 Extract the bearing retaining circlip, then support the hub carrier face-down on blocks or on a press bed. Using a tube or mandrel in contact with the edge of the outer bearing, drive or press the bearing out.
7 Fit the new bearing in the same way, ensuring that it is pressed fully home to the shoulder in the hub carrier. Keep the bearing square as it is fitted, otherwise it will jam, and continued pressure could cause the outer race to crack. If the bearing does jam, tap or press it out, remove any burrs in the bore of the carrier and try again.
8 Secure the bearing with the circlip, then refit the disc shield.
9 Tap the hub flange into the bearing and fit a new retaining nut. Tighten the nut to the specified torque, and secure by staking the nut flange into the groove in the hub. Tap on the nut cover.
10 Refit the hub carrier to the car as described in the previous Section.

Fig. 10.16 Cover (1) and hub flange retaining nut (2) at the rear of the hub carrier (Sec 13)

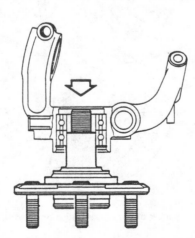

Fig. 10.17 Removing the hub flange from the bearing (Sec 13)

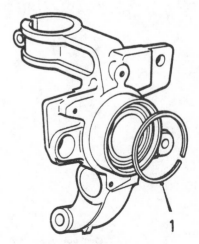

Fig. 10.18 Rear hub bearing retaining circlip (1) (Sec 13)

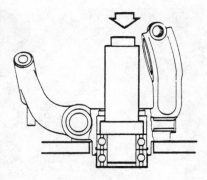

Fig. 10.19 Using a suitable mandrel for removal of the hub bearing (Sec 13)

14 Rear shock absorber – removal and refitting

Note: *The following procedures are applicable equally to cars with standard suspension or self-levelling damper units*

1   Chock the front wheels, prise of the rear wheel trim and slacken the wheel nuts. Jack up the rear of the car and support it on axle stands. Remove the rear roadwheel.
2   Undo the retaining bolt and release the flexible brake hose support bracket from the shock absorber strut.
3   Undo the nut and release the anti-roll bar connecting link from the suspension lower transverse link.
4   Place a jack below the transverse link, and raise the link slightly.
5   Undo the nut and remove the through-bolt and washers securing the hub carrier to the trailing link.
6   Undo the nut and remove the bolt securing the hub carrier to the transverse link.
7   Undo the nut and clamp bolt securing the shock absorber strut to the hub carrier.
8   Lower the jack slightly, and release the hub carrier from the shock

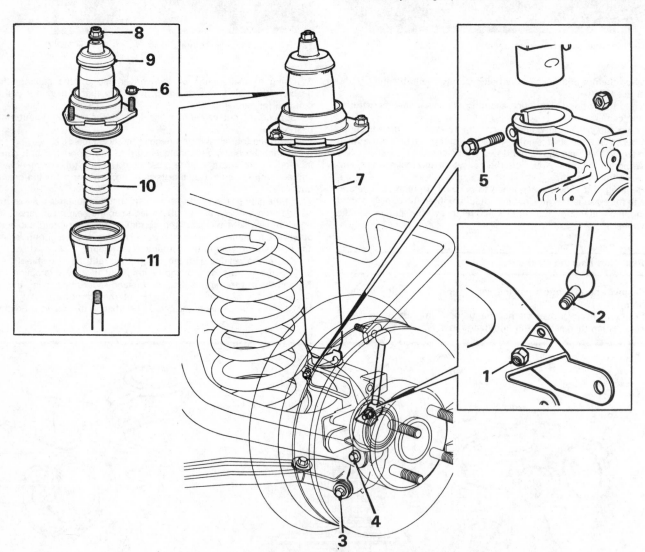

Fig. 10.20 Rear shock absorber attachment details (Sec 14)

1 Connecting link retaining nut	4 Transverse link retaining bolt	8 Shock absorber spindle nut
2 Anti-roll bar connecting link	5 Shock absorber clamp bolt	9 Upper mounting
3 Trailing link retaining through-bolt	6 Upper mounting retaining nut	10 Bump-stop
	7 Shock absorber	11 Dust cover

absorber strut. If the strut is tight, spread the slot in the hub carrier with a screwdriver, and tap the carrier down with a copper or plastic mallet.
9 From inside the luggage compartment, remove the trim as necessary to gain access to the shock absorber upper mounting.
10 Undo the three nuts securing the upper mounting to the body, and remove the shock absorber from under the wheel arch.
11 If the upper mounting is to be removed, undo the shock absorber spindle nut and withdraw the upper mounting, followed by the bump-stop and dust cover.
12 Examine the shock absorber for signs of fluid leakage. Check the spindle for signs of wear or pitting along its entire length, and check the shock absorber body for signs of damage or corrosion. Test the operation of the shock absorber, while holding it in an upright position, by moving the spindle through a full stroke, and then through short strokes of 50 to 100 mm (2 to 4 in). In both cases, the resistance felt should be smooth and continuous. If the resistance is jerky or uneven, or if there is any visible sign of wear, damage or fluid leakage, renewal is necessary. Also check the condition of the upper mounting, bump-stop and dust cover, and renew any components as necessary.
13 Refitting is the reverse sequence to removal. Tighten all nuts and bolts to the specified torque, but do not fully tighten the transverse and trailing link retaining nuts until the weight of the car is on the roadwheels.

15 Rear coil spring – removal and refitting

1 Refer to Section 14 and carry out the operations described in paragraphs 1 to 6 inclusive, with the exception of paragraph 2.
2 Ease the hub carrier away from the trailing link, and move the trailing link end clear as much as possible.
3 Lower the jack slowly and carefully to release the tension on the coil spring.
4 When all the tension is released, withdraw the spring from its location, and recover the upper and lower spring seats. Note the fitted position of the lower seat in the transverse link as it is removed.
5 Examine the spring carefully for signs of distortion or damage. The spring free length can only be assessed by comparing it with a new item, and this should be done if the spring is suspect or if the vehicle ride height has been measured and found to be less than the specified figure. Renew the spring if necessary, ideally in pairs (both sides). Also check the condition of the upper and lower spring seats, and renew any components as necessary.
6 Refitting is the reverse sequence to removal, but ensure that the tang on the lower spring seat engages with the slot in the transverse link. Tighten all nuts and bolts to the specified torque, but do not fully tighten the transverse and trailing link retaining nuts until the weight of the car is on the roadwheels.

16 Transverse link – removal and refitting

1 Remove the rear coil spring as described in the previous Section.
2 Undo the nut and remove the transverse link inner mounting bolt (photo).
3 Ease the link away from its inner location, and remove it from under the car.
4 If the transverse link inner mounting bush requires renewal, a hydraulic press and suitable mandrels will be needed to press out the old bush and press in a new one. If this equipment is not available, have the work carried out by a Rover dealer or suitably-equipped garage. A similar procedure must be used for renewal of the outer bush, which is located in the hub carrier, after removal of this component from the car (see Section 12).
5 Refitting is the reverse sequence to removal, but do not fully tighten the inner mounting nut until the weight of the car is on the roadwheels.

17 Trailing link – removal and refitting

1 Chock the front wheels, prise off the rear wheel trim and slacken the wheel nuts. Jack up the rear of the car and support it on axle stands. Remove the rear roadwheel.

16.2 Transverse link inner mounting bolt (arrowed)

17.2 Trailing link front mounting

17.3 Trailing link-to-hub carrier through-bolt (arrowed)

2   Undo the trailing link front mounting nut (photo) and remove the outer washer and bush.

3   Undo the nut and remove the through-bolt and washers securing the trailing link to the hub carrier (photo).

4   Ease the link away from the hub carrier, withdraw the front mounting from its location and remove the link from under the car.

5   Withdraw the front mounting inner bush and washer, and the two rear mounting bushes.

6   If the adjustment plate is to be removed, first mark the position of the forward eccentric bolt in relation to the plate, so that an approximate rear wheel toe setting can be obtained on reassembly. Undo the nuts, remove the retaining bolt and eccentric bolt, then withdraw the adjustment plate from the trailing link.

7   Examine all the mounting bushes for damage, deformation or swelling of the rubber, and check the remaining components for damage or distortion. Renew any parts as necessary.

8   Refit the adjustment plate to the link, and secure with the retaining

and adjustment bolts and nuts. Before fully tightening the nuts, set the eccentric adjustment bolt in the position marked before removal.

9   The remainder of the refitting procedure is the reverse sequence to removal. Do not fully tighten the trailing link-to-hub carrier through-bolt until the weight of the car is on the roadwheels.

10   On completion, have the rear wheel alignment checked and if necessary adjusted (see Section 30).

18 Rear anti-roll bar – removal and refitting

1   Apply the handbrake, prise off the rear wheel trim and slacken the wheel nuts. Jack up the rear of the car and support it on axle stands. Remove the rear roadwheels.

2   Undo the single nut each side securing the anti-roll bar connecting links to the rear suspension transverse links.

3   Undo the two bolts each side securing the anti-roll bar mounting

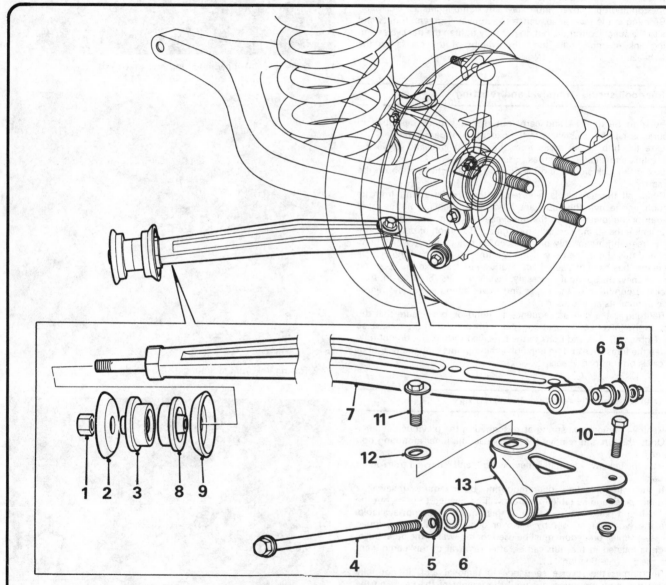

Fig. 10.21 Exploded view of the trailing link components and attachments (Sec 17)

1 Front mounting nut	5 Washer	9 Inner washer	11 Eccentric bolt
2 Outer washer	6 Bush	10 Adjustment plate retaining	12 Eccentric washer
3 Outer bush	7 Trailing link	bolt	13 Adjustment plate
4 Trailing link through-bolt	8 Inner bush		

brackets to the chassis members (photo), and remove the bar from under the car.

4 If required, the connecting links can be removed after undoing the retaining nut on each side.

5 Check the condition of the connecting link bushes and the anti-roll bar mounting bushes, and renew any that show signs of deterioration. The mounting bushes are slit along their length to allow removal and refitting over the bar.

6 Refitting is the reverse sequence to removal. Tighten the mounting and connecting link bushes to the specified torque only with the weight of the car on its roadwheels.

19 Steering wheel – removal and refitting

1 Disconnect the battery negative terminal. (Refer to Chapter 12, Section 1, before doing this).

2 Set the front wheels in the straight-ahead position.

3 Carefully prise off the steering wheel pad, disconnect the two horn switch leads and remove the pad (photos).

4 With an assistant holding the wheel, undo and remove the centre retaining nut using a socket and bar (photo).

5 Mark the steering wheel and column shaft in relation to each other, and withdraw the wheel from the shaft splines.

6 Before refitting, check that the wheels are still in the straight-ahead position, and turn the direction indicator cancelling bush so that the slot is pointing upwards (photo).

7 Engage the steering wheel over the shaft splines, ensuring that the previously-made marks are aligned, and make sure that the lug on the wheel boss engages with the slot in the direction indicator cancelling bush (photo).

8 Refit the retaining nut and tighten it to the specified torque while your assistant holds the wheel.

9 Reconnect the horn switch wires and refit the steering wheel pad.

10 Reconnect the battery.

18.3 Anti-roll bar right-hand side mounting bracket

19.3A Prise off the steering wheel pad ...

19.3B ... and disconnect the two horn switch leads

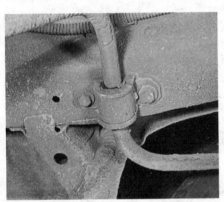

19.4 Undo the steering wheel retaining nut

19.6 Position the direction indicator cancelling bush with the slot pointing upwards

19.7 Ensure that the lug on the steering wheel boss (A) engages the cancelling bush slot (B)

20 Steering column lock – removal and refitting

1 Disconnect the battery negative terminal. (Refer to Chapter 12, Section 1, before doing this).

2 From inside the car, release the turnbuckles and lift out the trim panels over the clutch, brake and accelerator pedals.

3 Release the rake lock on the side of the steering column, and move the column to its lowest position.

4 Undo the single upper screw and the three lower screws, and remove the upper and lower steering column shrouds.

5 Undo the two nuts and remove the washers from the steering column upper mounting.

6 Undo the two bolts and remove the mounting strap from the column lower mounting. Lower the column slightly, and support it in this position.

7 Disconnect the ignition switch wiring multi-plug and the additional switch lead.

8 Centre-punch the steering column lock shear-bolts, then drill off the bolt heads.

9 Remove the lock saddle, then withdraw the lock from the column.

10 With the lock removed, unscrew the shear-bolt studs with a self-locking wrench or a pair of grips on the protruding bolt ends.

11 Refitting is the reverse sequence to removal, but tighten all the mounting bolts and nuts to the specified torque. Use new shear-bolts to secure the lock, and tighten them until the heads shear off, but check the operation of the lock before doing this.

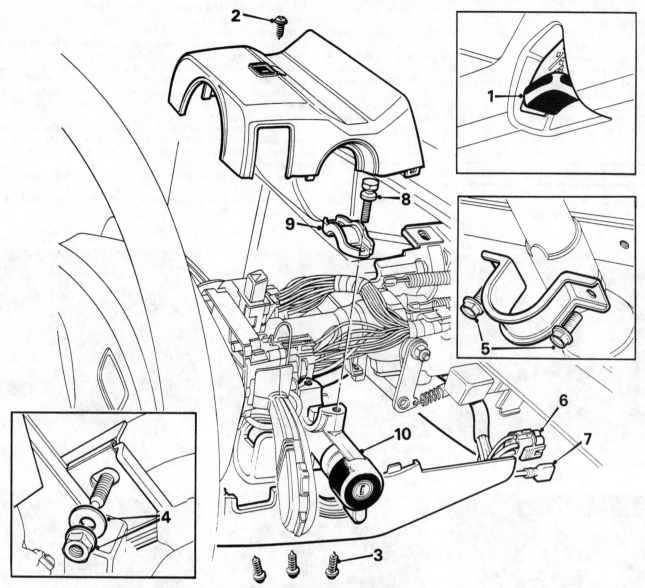

Fig. 10.22 Steering column lock attachments (Sec 20)

1	Steering column rake lock
2	Upper shroud retaining screw
3	Lower shroud retaining screws
4	Column upper mounting nut and washer
5	Column lower mounting bolts
6	Ignition switch wiring multi-plug
7	Additional switch lead
8	Shear-bolt
9	Lock saddle
10	Steering column lock

21 Steering column – removal and refitting

1   Disconnect the battery negative terminal. (Refer to Chapter 12, Section 1, before doing this).

2   Remove the steering wheel as described in Section 19.

3   From inside the car, release the turnbuckles and lift out the trim panels over the clutch, brake and accelerator pedals (photos).

4   Release the rake lock on the side of the steering column, and move the column to its lowest position.

5   Undo the single upper screw and the three lower screws, and remove the upper and lower steering column shrouds.

6   At the base of the steering column, release the two retaining clips and slide up the cover over the column shaft universal joint.

7   Move the carpets aside to gain access to the floor-mounted cover plate.

8   Prise out the retaining studs to release the cover plate and gasket from the floor.

9   Undo the clamp bolt securing the universal joint to the steering gear pinion.

10 Undo the two nuts and remove the washers from the steering column upper mounting (photo).

11 Undo the two bolts and remove the mounting strap from the column lower mounting (photo). Lower the column slightly, and support it in this position.

12 Release the flasher unit from its bracket above the fusebox.

13 Disconnect the two main wiring harness multi-plugs adjacent to the fusebox.

14 Lift the steering column assembly upwards to disengage the universal joint from the steering gear pinion, then remove the column from the car.

15 If the universal joint is to be removed, first mark the joint in relation to the column shaft. Undo the clamp bolt and slide the joint off the shaft.

16 Before refitting the column, set the roadwheels to the straight-ahead position.

17 Refit the universal joint to the column shaft (if previously removed), ensuring that the marks made during removal are aligned.

18 Engage the universal joint with the steering gear pinion, and push it fully home.

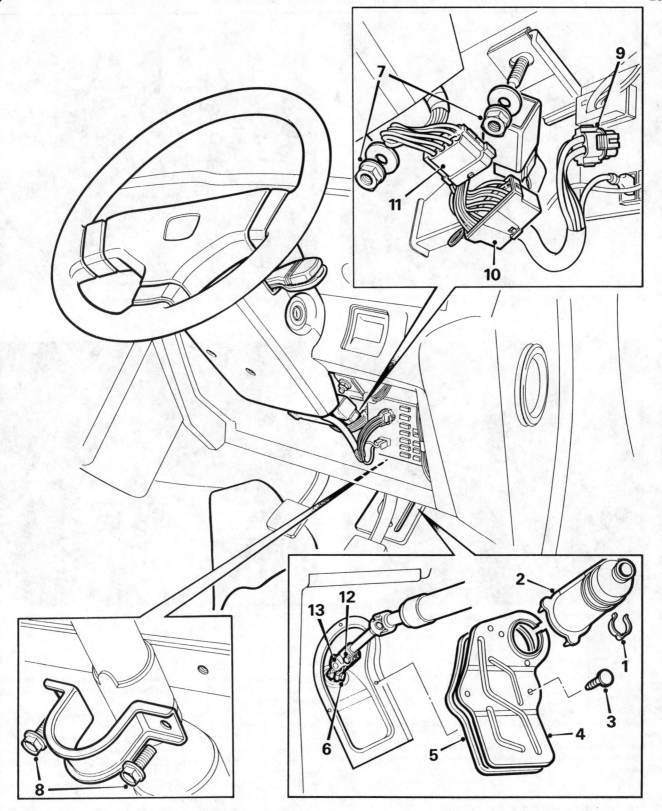

Fig. 10.23 Steering column attachments and components (Sec 21)

1 Universal joint cover
   retaining clip
2 Universal joint cover
3 Cover plate retaining studs
4 Cover plate

5 Gasket
6 Universal joint clamp bolt
7 Column upper mounting
   nuts

8 Column lower mounting
   bolts
9 Flasher unit
10 Main wiring multi-plug

11 Main relay harness
    multi-plug
12 Universal joint clamp bolt
13 Universal joint

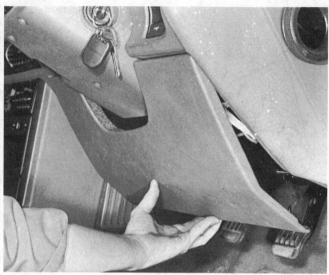

21.3A Remove the upper trim panel ...

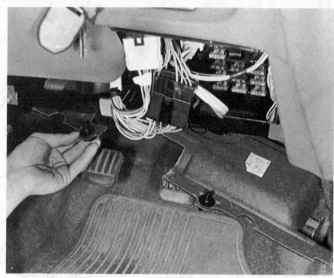

21.3B ... and lower trim panel over the pedals

21.10 Steering column upper mounting nut (arrowed)

21.11 Steering column lower mounting bolt (arrowed)

19 Reconnect the wiring multi-plugs and refit the flasher unit.
20 Refit the column mountings, and tighten the nuts and bolts to the specified torque.
21 Tighten the universal joint clamp bolt.
22 Refit the cover plate and gasket, followed by the universal joint cover.
23 Refit the steering column shrouds and the trim panels.
24 Refit the steering wheel as described in Section 19, then reconnect the battery.

22 Steering tie-rod – removal and refitting

1   Apply the handbrake, prise off the front wheel trim and slacken the wheel nuts. Jack up the front of the car and support it on axle stands. Remove the front roadwheel.
2   Slacken the tie-rod retaining locknut by a quarter of a turn (photo).
3   Extract the split pin, then unscrew the nut securing the tie-rod balljoint to the steering knuckle arm (photo).
4   Using a universal balljoint separator tool, release the tapered ball-pin from the arm (photo).

5   Engage a spanner over the flats on the inner tie-rod that protrudes from the rubber gaiter, then unscrew the steering tie-rod and outer balljoint assembly.
6   Fit the new tie-rod by screwing it on to the inner tie-rod until it contacts the locknut.
7   Insert the balljoint into the steering knuckle arm and refit the retaining nut. Tighten the nut to the specified torque, then tighten it further, slightly, to align the next split pin hole. Secure the nut with a new split pin.
8   Tighten the tie-rod retaining locknut securely, refit the roadwheel and lower the car to the ground.
9   Check the front wheel alignment as described in Section 30.

23 Steering gear rubber gaiter – renewal

1   Remove the steering tie-rod as described in the previous Section.
2   Count and record the number of exposed threads from the end of the inner tie-rod to the locknut, then unscrew and remove the locknut.
3   Release the rubber gaiter retaining clips, and withdraw the gaiter from the steering gear and inner tie-rod.

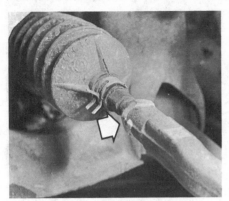

22.2 Tie-rod retaining locknut (arrowed)

22.3 Extract the split pin and remove the tie-rod retaining nut (arrowed)

22.4 Using a universal balljoint separator tool to release the tie-rod balljoint

4   Slide the new gaiter into position and secure it with new retaining clips.
5   Refit the locknut to the inner tie-rod, and position it so that the same number of threads are exposed as counted on removal.
6   Refit the steering tie-rod as described in the previous Section.

24 Steering gear – removal and refitting

1   From inside the car, release the two retaining clips and slide up the cover over the universal joint at the base of the steering column.
2   Move the carpets aside to gain access to the floor-mounted cover plate.
3   Prise out the retaining studs to release the cover plate and gasket from the floor.
4   Undo the clamp bolt securing the universal joint to the steering gear pinion.
5   Apply the handbrake, prise off the front wheel trim and slacken the wheel nuts. Jack up the front of the car and support it on axle stands. Remove the front roadwheels.
6   Remove the exhaust front pipes as described in Chapter 3.
7   Extract the split pins, then unscrew the nuts securing each tie-rod balljont to the steering knuckle arm.
8   Using a universal balljoint separator tool, release the balljoint tapered ball-pins from the arms.
9   Position a suitable container beneath the pinion end of the steering gear.
10 Wipe clean the area around the fluid pipe unions, then unscrew the two rearward-facing union nuts on the pinion housing (photo). Allow the power steering fluid to drain into the container.
11 Remove the two O-ring seals from the disconnected pipes, then plug or tape over the pipe ends and orifices.
12 Undo the two bolts each side securing the steering gear to the chassis members, and remove the mounting brackets (photos).

13 Lower the steering gear to release the pinion from the column universal joint, then manipulate the assembly sideways and out through the wheel arch.
14 Check the condition of the rubber mountings, and renew them if there is any sign of deterioration or swelling of the rubber.
15 Refitting the steering gear is the reverse sequence to removal, bearing in mind the following points:

   (a) Tighten all nuts, bolts and unions to the specified torque
   (b) Use new O-ring seals on the pipe unions, and new split pins on the balljoint retaining nuts
   (c) Fill the system with fresh fluid, and bleed the steering gear as described in Section 26
   (d) If necessary, reposition the steering wheel so that the spokes are horizontal when the steering gear is in the straight-ahead position (see Section 19)

25 Steering gear – overhaul

1   Remove the steering gear from the car as described in the previous Section.
2   Clean the assembly externally with a rag, paying particular attention to the area around the pipe unions.
3   Remove both steering tie-rods and rubber gaiters, with reference to the procedures contained in Sections 22 and 23 respectively.
4   To remove the inner tie-rods and balljoints, ideally Rover tool 18G 1440 should be used. This tool consists of two clamps, one for the balljoint housing and one for the rack itself. The clamps are tightened securely, allowing the balljoint housing complete with inner tie-rod to be unscrewed using one clamp, while the rack is held with the other clamp. Fig. 10.25 shows the arrangement. In practice however, it is possible to do this using self-locking wrenches, pipe-grips, or similar tools, provided that the jaws are protected and care is taken not to

24.10 Unscrew the two fluid pipe union nuts (arrowed)

24.12A Steering gear right-hand mounting bracket bolts (arrowed) ...

24.12B ... and left-hand mounting bracket bolts (arrowed)

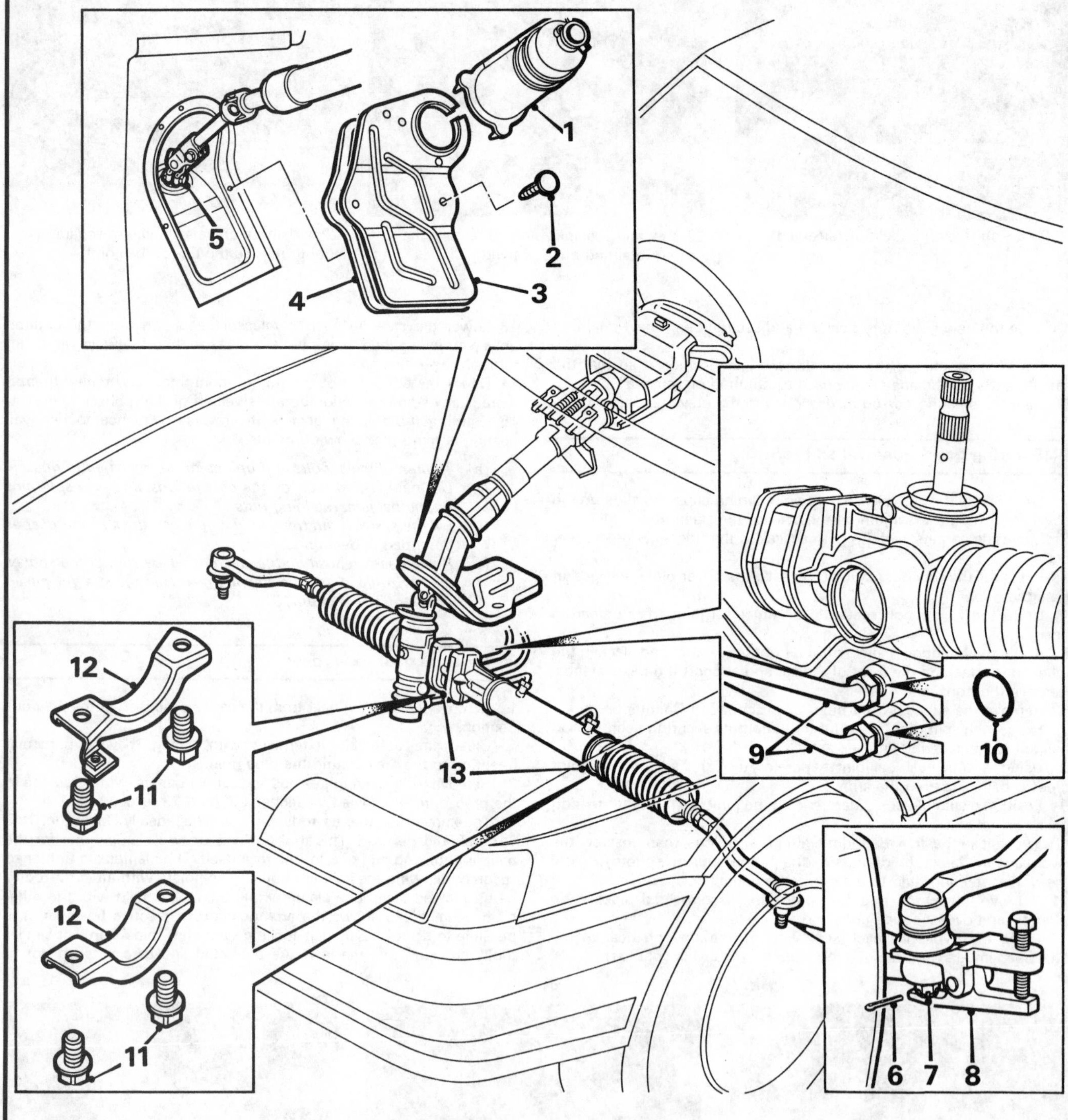

Fig. 10.24 Steering gear removal details (Sec 24)

1 Universal joint cover	5 Universal joint clamp bolt	8 Balljoint separator tool	11 Mounting bracket bolts
2 Cover plate retaining studs	6 Split pin	9 Fluid pipe unions	12 Mounting brackets
3 Cover plate	7 Tie-rod balljoint retaining	10 O-ring	13 Mounting points
4 Gasket	nut		

score the parts being gripped, particularly the rack. Note that the balljoint housing is peened into place on the rack, so it will be tight to unscrew initially.

5 With the inner tie-rod and balljoint assemblies removed, prise out the rack support bush retainer, followed by the O-ring seal, support bush and bush locking wire.

6 Unscrew the remaining four pipe unions, and remove the two fluid pipes.

7 Extract the circlip at the base of the pinion housing, remove the pinion cover and withdraw the O-ring seal.

8 This is the limit of dismantling that can be undertaken on the steering gear, as no other parts are available separately.

9 Examine all the dismantled components, and renew any that are worn. The O-ring seals and rubber gaiters should be renewed as a matter of course.

10 Reassembly of the steering gear is the reverse sequence to removal, bearing in mind the following points:

(a) *Clean all the old sealant from the bush retainer sealant hole in the rack housing, and apply fresh RTV sealant on reassembly*

(b) *Lubricate all the seals with the specified power steering fluid*

(c) *Tighten the inner tie-rod balljoint housing using the same procedure as used for removal, then peen the rack, using a small punch, to secure the assembly*

(d) *Refit the steering tie-rods and rubber gaiters, with reference to Sections 22 and 23*

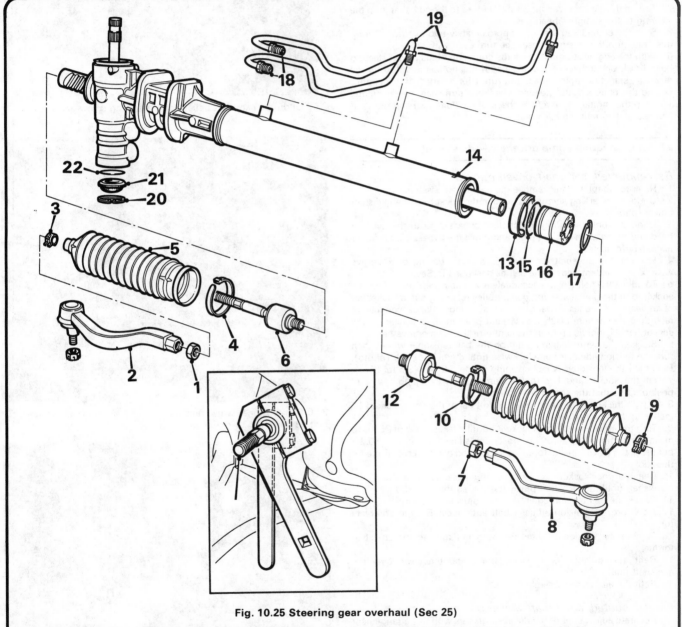

Fig. 10.25 Steering gear overhaul (Sec 25)

1	Right-hand steering tie-rod locknut	7	Left-hand steering tie-rod locknut	12	Left-hand inner tie-rod balljoint
2	Right-hand steering tie-rod	8	Left-hand steering tie-rod	13	Bush retainer
3	Gaiter clip	9	Gaiter clip	14	Bush retainer sealant hole
4	Gaiter clip	10	Gaiter clip	15	O-ring
5	Right-hand rubber gaiter	11	Left-hand rubber gaiter	16	Rack support bush
6	Right-hand inner tie-rod balljoint				

17	Locking wire
18	Fluid pipe unions
19	Fluid pipes
20	Circlip
21	Pinion cover
22	O-ring

Inset shows Rover special tool for removal of the inner tie-rod balljoints

26 Power steering gear – bleeding

1   Remove the filler cap on the power steering fluid reservoir, and fill the reservoir with the specified fluid until the level is up to the MAX mark on the cap dipstick.
2   Disconnect the HT lead from the centre of the ignition coil.
3   Crank the engine on the starter motor for five seconds to prime the power steering pump.
4   Top up the reservoir, then crank the engine again for a further five seconds.
5   Turn the steering onto full right-hand lock, and crank the engine for five seconds.
6   Turn the steering onto full left-hand lock, and crank the engine for five seconds.
7   Top up the reservoir, reconnect the HT lead to the coil, then turn the steering to the straight-ahead position.
8   Start the engine and run it for approximately two minutes. During this time, turn the steering wheel one turn each way.
9   With the engine stopped, check the condition of the power steering fluid. If it is aerated, leave it until clear. If it is not aerated, top up the reservoir, start the engine again and run it for a further two minutes. During this time, turn the steering wheel one turn each way as before.
10 Stop the engine, make a final check of the fluid level and top up if necessary, then refit the filler cap.

27 Power steering pump drivebelt – adjustment

Rear-mounted, camshaft-driven pump

1   Refer to Chapter 3 and remove the air cleaner assembly.
2   Undo the retaining screw and remove the cover over the camshaft pulley (photo).
3   Undo the bolts securing the coolant bypass pipe to the cylinder head and to the main coolant pipe, and move the bypass pipe aside as necessary for access.
4   Examine the drivebelt for signs of cracking, fraying or excessive wear, and if evident, renew the belt as described in Section 28.
5   To adjust the belt tension accurately it will be necessary to obtain a socket to fit the power steering pump pulley retaining nut, a socket bar of at least 12 inches in length, and a spring balance capable of recording a minimum of 25 lbs. Make a paint mark or similar on the socket bar, 12 inches up from the centre of the square drive end.
6   Slacken the centre retaining nut on the belt tensioner wheel, then turn the tension adjuster bolt clockwise until the belt is slack (photo). Retighten the tensioner wheel retaining nut to 5.0 Nm (3.6 lbf ft).
7   Fit the socket and bar to the pump pulley retaining nut, and position it so that the socket bar is vertical.
8   Attach the spring balance to the socket bar at the point marked 12 inches up from the square drive end.
9   Turn the adjuster bolt anti-clockwise until it takes a pull of 25 lbs to make the pump pulley slip. This procedure is illustrated in Fig. 10.26, but using the Rover special tool. The socket and bar are a substitute for this tool.
10 Remove the socket, bar and spring balance, then turn the crankshaft until the camshaft pulley has turned through 180°.
11 Check the belt tension again, and re-adjust if necessary.
12 Now turn the tension adjuster bolt anti-clockwise two complete turns.
13 Tighten the tensioner wheel retaining nut fully to the specified torque.
14 Refit the coolant pipe retaining bolts, and the cover over the camshaft pulley.
15 Refit the air cleaner assembly.

Front-mounted, crankshaft-driven pump

16 Accurate adjustment of the drivebelt on cars with this arrangement can only be achieved with the Rover belt tensioning tool, and ideally this operation should be carried out by a Rover dealer. However, if a new belt has been fitted, or if the existing tension is extremely slack, a rough approximation as a temporary measure can be achieved using the following procedure.
17 Jack up the front of the car and securely support it on axle stands.
18 From under the front of the car, examine the drivebelt for signs of cracking, fraying or excessive wear, and if evident, renew the belt as described in Section 28.

27.2 Undo the camshaft pulley cover retaining screw

27.6 Belt tensioner wheel retaining nut (A) and tension adjuster bolt (B) on the rear-mounted pump

27.19 Idler pulley retaining nut (A) and adjuster bolt (B) on the front-mounted pump

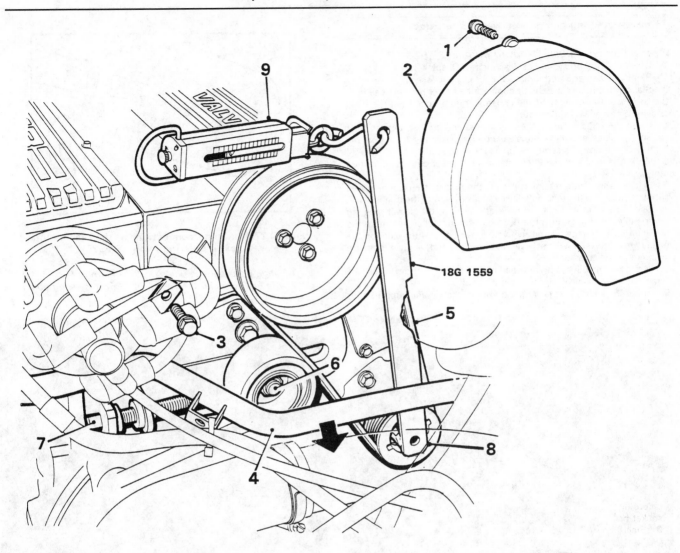

Fig. 10.26 Power steering pump drivebelt adjustment – rear-mounted pump (Sec 27)

1 Camshaft pulley cover retaining screw	retaining bolt	6 Belt tensioner wheel centre retaining nut	8 Rover special tool for checking tension
2 Camshaft pulley cover	4 Coolant bypass pipe	7 Tension adjuster bolt	9 Spring balance
3 Coolant pulley pipe	5 Drivebelt		

19 To adjust the belt tension, refer to Fig. 12.1 (Chapter 12) and slacken the idler pulley retaining nut (photo), then turn the adjuster bolt clockwise to increase the tension or anti-clockwise to decrease it, until it is just possible to twist the belt by hand through 90° at a point midway between the crankshaft and power steering pump pulleys.
20 When the tension is correct, tighten the idler pulley retaining nut to the specified torque and lower the car to the ground.
21 Refit the air cleaner assembly.

28 Power steering pump drivebelt – removal and refitting

Rear-mounted, camshaft-driven pump

1 Refer to Chapter 3 and remove the air cleaner assembly.
2 Undo the retaining screw and remove the cover over the camshaft pulley.
3 Undo the bolts securing the coolant bypass pipe to the cylinder head and to the main coolant pipe, and move the bypass pipe aside as necessary for access.
4 Slacken the centre retaining nut on the belt tensioner wheel, then

turn the tensioner adjuster bolt clockwise until the belt is slack.
5 Undo the three camshaft pulley retaining bolts, withdraw the pulley and recover the spacer behind the pulley.
6 Remove the belt from the camshaft and power steering pump pulleys.
7 Place the new belt in position, then fit the spacer and camshaft pulley. Tighten the pulley retaining bolts to the specified torque.
8 Tension the belt using the procedure described in Section 27, but on completion, do not refit the camshaft cover or coolant pipe retaining bolts.
9 Start the engine, and run it for approximately 10 minutes at 1500 rpm to settle the new belt.
10 Switch off the engine, then refer to Section 27 again, and carry out the complete adjustment procedure once more.

Front-mounted, crankshaft-driven pump

11 Jack up the front of the car and securely support it on axle stands.
12 Slacken the idler pulley retaining nut, then turn the adjuster bolt anti-clockwise until all the tension is removed from the drivebelt.
13 Slip the drivebelt off the pulleys, then place a new belt in position.
14 Adjust the belt tension using procedure contained in Section 27.

29 Power steering pump – removal and refitting

Rear-mounted, camshaft-driven pump

1   Drain the cooling system as described in Chapter 2.
2   Refer to Chapter 3 and remove the air cleaner assembly.
3   Slacken the hose clips and disconnect the heater bypass hose from the thermostat housing, and the radiator bottom hose from the main coolant pipe below the distributor.
4   Undo the bolts securing the heater pipe and coolant pipe to their support brackets, and move the pipe and hose assembly away from the vicinity of the power steering pump as far as possible.
5   Undo the retaining screw and remove the cover over the camshaft pulley.
6   Slacken the centre retaining nut on the drivebelt tensioner wheel (photo), then turn the tension adjuster clockwise until the bolt is slack.
7   Using a socket and bar, unscrew and remove the power steering pump pulley retaining nut (photo). To prevent the pulley turning as the nut is undone, engage a large screwdriver with one of the slots on the pulley, rest the screwdriver over the socket, and apply clockwise leverage to the screwdriver.
8   Withdraw the pulley and drivebelt from the pump (photo). Use two screwdrivers to lever off the pulley if it is tight.
9   Apply the handbrake, jack up the front of the car and support it on

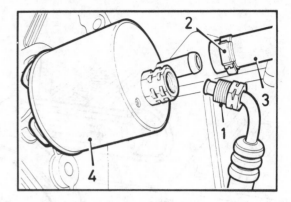

Fig. 10.27 Fluid pipe connections at the rear-mounted power steering pump (Sec 29)

1   High pressure pipe union   3   Return hose
2   Return hose clip   4   Power steering pump

29.6 Slacken the tensioner wheel retaining nut

29.7 Unscrew the pump pulley retaining nut

29.8 Remove the pulley and drivebelt

29.14 Undo the four pump retaining bolts

axle stands.

10 Undo the bolts securing the longitudinal support member to the underbody beneath the engine and remove the member.

11 Position a suitable container beneath the engine, below the power steering pump.

12 Wipe clean the area around the pipe and hose unions at the rear of the pump.

13 Unscrew the union nut and slacken the hose clip, then disconnect the high pressure pipe and return hose from the pump. Allow the power steering fluid to drain into the container. Plug or tape over the disconnected unions when the fluid has drained.

14 Undo the four power steering pump retaining bolts (photo), and remove the pump from under the car.

15 Refitting is the reverse sequence to removal, bearing in mind the following points:

(a) Tighten all nuts, bolts and unions to the specified torque
(b) Adjust the drivebelt tension as described in Section 27
(c) Bleed the power steering gear as described in Section 26
(d) Refill the cooling system and refit the air cleaner as described in Chapters 2 and 3 respectively

Front-mounted, crankshaft-driven pump

16 Position a suitable container beneath the engine, below the power steering pump.

17 Wipe clean the area around the pipe and hose unions at the rear of the pump.

18 Unscrew the union nut and slacken the hose clip, then disconnect the high pressure pipe and return hose from the pump. Allow the power steering fluid to drain into the container. Plug or tape over the disconnected unions when the fluid has drained.

19 Jack up the front of the car and securely support it on axle stands.

20 Slacken the idler pulley retaining nut, then turn the adjuster bolt anti-clockwise until all the tension is removed from the drivebelt.

21 Remove the belt from the pulleys.

22 Undo the three bolts and remove the power steering pump pulley.

23 Undo the four bolts securing the pump to its mounting bracket. Slide the pump out of the bracket, and remove it from under the car.

24 Refitting is the reverse sequence to removal, bearing in mind the following points:

(a) Tighten all nuts, bolts and unions to the specified torque
(b) Adjust the drivebelt tension as described in Section 27
(c) Bleed the power steering gear as described in Section 26

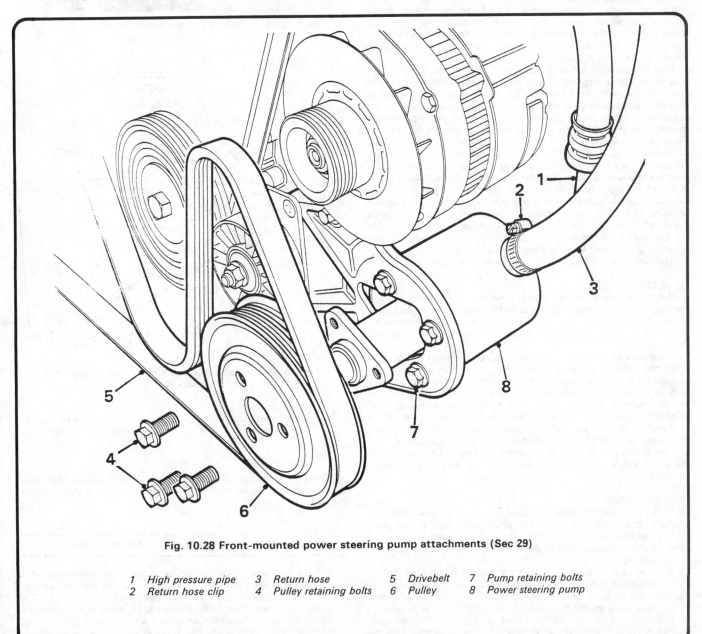

Fig. 10.28 Front-mounted power steering pump attachments (Sec 29)

1	High pressure pipe	3	Return hose	5	Drivebelt	7	Pump retaining bolts
2	Return hose clip	4	Pulley retaining bolts	6	Pulley	8	Power steering pump

30 Wheel alignment and steering angles

1   Accurate wheel alignment is essential to provide positive steering and handling characteristics, and to prevent excessive tyre wear. Before considering the steering/ suspension geometry, check that the tyres are correctly inflated, the front wheels are not buckled, and the steering linkage and suspension joints are in good order, without slackness or wear.

2   Wheel alignment consists of four factors:

Camber is the angle at which the roadwheels are set from the vertical when viewed from the front or rear of the vehicle. Positive camber is the angle (in degrees) that the wheels are tilted outwards at the top from the vertical.

Castor is the angle between the steering axis and a vertical line when viewed from each side of the vehicle. Positive castor is indicated when the steering axis is inclined towards the rear of the vehicle at its upper end.

Steering axis inclination, also known as kingpin inclination or KPI, is the angle, when viewed from the front or rear of the vehicle, between the vertical and an imaginary line drawn between the steering knuckle upper and lower balljoints.

Toe is the amount by which the distance between the front inside edges of the roadwheel rims differs from that between the rear inside edges. If the distance at the front is less than at the rear, the wheels are said to 'toe-in'. If the distance at the front inside edges is greater than at the rear, the wheels 'toe-out'.

3   Due to the need for special gauges to check the steering and suspension angles accurately, it is preferable to leave this work to your Rover dealer. Apart from the front and rear toe settings, all other steering and suspension angles are set in production, and are not adjustable. If these angles are ever checked and found to be outside specification, then either the suspension components are damaged or distorted, or wear has occurred in the bushes at the attachment points.

4   The front and rear toe settings are adjustable, and two methods are available to the home mechanic for doing this. One method is to use a gauge to measure the distance between the front and rear inside edges of the roadwheels. The other method is to use a scuff plate, in which the roadwheel is rolled across a movable plate which records any deviation, or scuff, of the tyre relative to the straight-ahead position, as it moves across the plate. Relatively inexpensive equipment of both types is available from accessory outlets to enable these checks, and subsequent adjustments, to be carried out at home.

5   The checking and adjustment procedures are as follows.

Front toe setting

6   With the car on level ground and the steering in the straight-ahead position, bounce the front and rear to settle the suspension, then push the car backwards then forwards. Follow the equipment manufacturer's instructions according to the equipment being used, and check the toe setting.

7   If adjustment is required, slacken the steering tie-rod locknuts on both sides (photo), and release the rubber gaiter retaining clips.

8   Using a spanner engaged with the flat on the inner tie-rod, turn both tie-rods, by equal amounts clockwise to increase the toe-in, or anti-clockwise to increase the toe-out. Push the car forwards, then recheck the setting. If a gauge is being used, take three readings, at 120° intervals around the wheel, pushing the car forward a little each time. Use the mean average of the three readings as the setting.

9   Repeat this procedure until the setting is as specified, then tighten the tie-rod locknuts and refit the gaiter clips. Ensure that the gaiters are not twisted.

Rear toe setting

10   With the car on level ground and the steering in the straight-ahead position, bounce the front and rear to settle the suspension, then push the car backwards then forwards. Follow the equipment manufacturer's instructions according to the equipment being used, and check the toe setting.

11   If adjustment is required, slacken the adjustment plate-to-trailing link retaining bolt locknut, and the eccentric bolt locknut on each side.

12   Turn both eccentric bolts, by equal amounts in whichever direction is necessary, then tighten the locknuts and recheck the toe setting.

13   If a gauge is being used, take three readings, at 120° intervals around the wheel, pushing the car forward a little each time. Use the mean average of the three readings as the setting.

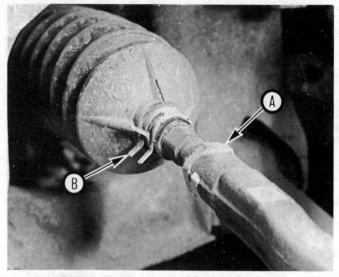

30.7 Steering tie-rod locknut (A) and gaiter clip (B)

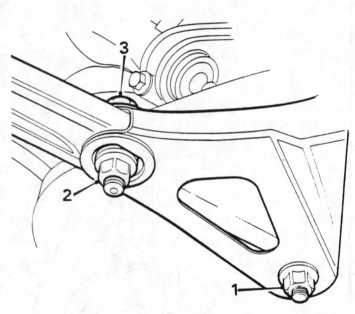

Fig. 10.29 Rear wheel toe setting adjustment points (Sec 30)

1 Adjustment plate retaining bolt locknut	2 Eccentric bolt locknut
	3 Eccentric bolt

14   Repeat this procedure until the setting is as specified, then fully tighten the retaining bolt and eccentric bolt locknuts to the specified torque.

31 Wheels and tyres – general care and maintenance

Wheels and tyres should give no real problems in use provided that a close eye is kept on them with regard to excessive wear or damage. To this end, the following points should be noted.

Ensure that tyre pressures are checked regularly and maintained correctly. Checking should be carried out with the tyres cold and not immediately after the vehicle has been in use. If the pressures are checked with the tyres hot, an apparently high reading will be obtained owing to heat expansion. Under no circumstances should an attempt be made to reduce the pressures to the quoted cold reading in this instance, or effective underinflation will result.

Underinflation will cause overheating of the tyre owing to excessive flexing of the casing, and the tread will not sit correctly on the road surface. This will cause a consequent loss of adhesion and excessive wear, not to mention the danger of sudden tyre failure due to heat build-up.

Overinflation will cause rapid wear of the centre part of the tyre tread coupled with reduced adhesion, harsher ride, and the danger of shock damage occurring in the tyre casing.

Regularly check the tyres for damage in the form of cuts or bulges, especially in the sidewalls. Remove any nails or stones embedded in the tread before they penetrate the tyre to cause deflation. If removal of a nail *does* reveal that the tyre has been punctured, refit the nail so that its point of penetration is marked. Then immediately change the wheel and have the tyre repaired by a tyre dealer. Do *not* drive on a tyre in such a condition. In many cases a puncture can be simply repaired by the use of an inner tube of the correct size and type. If in any doubt as to the possible consequences of any damage found, consult your local tyre dealer for advice.

Periodically remove the wheels and clean any dirt or mud from the inside and outside surfaces. Examine the wheel rims for signs of rusting, corrosion or other damage. Light alloy wheels are easily damaged by 'kerbing' whilst parking, and similarly steel wheels may become dented or buckled. Renewal of the wheel is very often the only course of remedial action possible.

The balance of each wheel and tyre assembly should be maintained to avoid excessive wear, not only to the tyres but also to the steering and suspension components. Wheel imbalance is normally signified by vibration through the vehicle's bodyshell, although in many cases it is particularly noticeable through the steering wheel. Conversely, it should be noted that wear or damage in suspension or steering components may cause excessive tyre wear. Out-of-round or out-of-true tyres, damaged wheels and wheel bearing wear/maladjustment also fall into this category. Balancing will not usually cure vibration caused by such wear.

Wheel balancing may be carried out with the wheel either on or off the vehicle. If balanced on the vehicle, ensure that the wheel-to-hub relationship is marked in some way prior to subsequent wheel removal so that it may be refitted in its original position.

General tyre wear is influenced to a large degree by driving style – harsh braking and acceleration or fast cornering will all produce more rapid tyre wear. Interchanging of tyres may result in more even wear, but this should only be carried out where there is no mix of tyre types on the vehicle. However, it is worth bearing in mind that if this is completely effective, the added expense of replacing a complete set of tyres simultaneously is incurred, which may prove financially restrictive for many owners.

Front tyres may wear unevenly as a result of wheel misalignment. The front wheels should always be correctly aligned according to the settings specified by the vehicle manufacturer.

Legal restrictions apply to the mixing of tyre types on a vehicle. Basically this means that a vehicle must not have tyres of differing construction on the same axle. Although it is not recommended to mix tyre types between front axle and rear axle, the only legally permissible combination is crossply at the front and radial at the rear. When mixing radial ply tyres, textile braced radials must always go on the front axle, with steel braced radials at the rear. An obvious disadvantage of such mixing is the necessity to carry two spare tyres to avoid contravening the law in the event of a puncture.

In the UK, the Motor Vehicles Construction and Use Regulations apply to many aspects of tyre fitting and usage. It is suggested that a copy of these regulations is obtained from your local police if in doubt as to the current legal requirements with regard to tyre condition, minimum tread depth, etc.

32 Fault diagnosis – suspension and steering

Note: *Before diagnosing suspension or steering faults, be sure that the trouble is not due to incorrect tyre pressures, mixture of tyre types, or binding brakes. More detailed fault diagnosis on the power-assisted steering gear entails the use of special test equipment. Apart from the general references listed below, faults on this system should be referred to a dealer*

Symptom	Reason(s)
Vehicle wanders or pulls to one side	Incorrect wheel alignment Wear in front suspension or steering components Wear in rear suspension components Weak shock absorbers Faulty tyre
Steering stiff and heavy	Power steering pump drivebelt slipping or broken Power steering system fault Seized steering or suspension balljoint Incorrect wheel alignment Steering rack or column bent or damaged
Excessive play in steering	Worn steering or suspension joints Worn steering column universal joint Worn rack and pinion steering gear
Wheel wobble and vibration	Roadwheels out-of-balance Roadwheels buckled or distorted Faulty or damaged tyre Worn steering or suspension joints Weak shock absorbers Worn hub bearings
Excessive tyre wear	Wheel alignment incorrect Worn steering or suspension components Roadwheels out-of-balance Accident damage

Chapter 11 Bodywork

Contents

Specifications

Torque wrench settings	Nm	lbf ft
Bonnet hinge bolts	10	7
Boot lid hinge bolts	10	7
Door hinge-to-body bolts	30	22
Door hinge-to-pillar bolts	22	16
Front seat retaining bolts	32	23
Seat belt retaining bolts	32	23
Bumper retaining bolts	22	16

1 General description

The bodyshell and underframe is of all-steel welded construction, and is of computer-originated design. The assembly and welding of the main body unit is completed entirely by computer-controlled robots, and the finished unit is checked for dimensional accuracy using modern computer and laser technology. In accordance with current practice, the bodyshell incorporates computer-calculated impact crumple zones at the front and rear, with a centre safety cell passenger compartment. During manufacture the body is dip-primed, fully sealed and undercoated, then painted with multi-layered base and top coats.

2 Maintenance – bodywork and underframe

The general condition of a vehicle's bodywork is the one thing that significantly affects its value. Maintenance is easy but needs to be regular. Neglect, particularly after minor damage, can lead quickly to further deterioration and costly repair bills. It is important also to keep watch on those parts of the vehicle not immediately visible, for instance the underside, inside all the wheel arches and the lower part of the engine compartment.

The basic maintenance routine for the bodywork is washing – preferably with a lot of water, from a hose. This will remove all the loose solids which may have stuck to the vehicle. It is important to flush these off in such a way as to prevent grit from scratching the finish. The wheel arches and underframe need washing in the same way to remove any accumulated mud which will retain moisture and tend to encourage rust. Paradoxically enough, the best time to clean the underframe and wheel arches is in wet weather when the mud is thoroughly wet and soft. In very wet weather the underframe is usually cleaned of large accumulations automatically and this is a good time for inspection.

Periodically, except on vehicles with a wax-based underbody protective coating, it is a good idea to have the whole of the underframe of the vehicle steam cleaned, engine compartment included, so that a thorough inspection can be carried out to see what minor repairs and renovations are necessary. Steam cleaning is available at many garages and is necessary for removal of the accumulation of oily grime which sometimes is allowed to become thick in certain areas. If steam cleaning facilities are not available, there are one or two excellent grease solvents available which can be brush applied. The dirt can then be simply hosed off. Note that these methods should not be used on vehicles with wax-based underbody protective coating or the coating will be removed. Such vehicles should be inspected annually, preferably just prior to winter, when the underbody should be washed down and any damage to the wax coating repaired. Ideally, a completely fresh coat should be applied. It would also be worth considering the use of such wax-based protection for injection into door panels, sills, box sections, etc, as an additional safeguard against rust damage where such protection is not provided by the vehicle manufacturer.

After washing paintwork, wipe off with a chamois leather to give an unspotted clear finish. A coat of clear protective wax polish will give added protection against chemical pollutants in the air. If the paintwork sheen has dulled or oxidised, use a cleaner/polisher combination to restore the brilliance of the shine. This requires a little effort, but such dulling is usually caused because regular washing has been neglected. Care needs to be taken with metallic paintwork, as special non-abrasive cleaner/polisher is required to avoid damage to the finish. Always check that the door and ventilator opening drain holes and pipes are completely clear so that water can be drained out. Bright work should be treated in the same way as paint work. Windscreens and windows can be kept clear of the smeary film which often appears by the use of a proprietary glass cleaner. Never use any form of wax or other body or chromium polish on glass.

3 Maintenance – upholstery and carpets

Mats and carpets should be brushed or vacuum cleaned regularly to keep them free of grit. If they are badly stained remove them from the vehicle for scrubbing or sponging and make quite sure they are dry before refitting. Seats and interior trim panels can be kept clean by wiping with a damp cloth. If they do become stained (which can be more apparent on light coloured upholstery) use a little liquid detergent and a soft nail brush to scour the grime out of the grain of the material. Do not forget to keep the headlining clean in the same way as the upholstery. When using liquid cleaners inside the vehicle do not over-wet the surfaces being cleaned. Excessive damp could get into the seams and padded interior causing stains, offensive odours or even rot. If the inside of the vehicle gets wet accidentally it is worthwhile taking some trouble to dry it out properly, particularly where carpets are involved. *Do not leave oil or electric heaters inside the vehicle for this purpose.*

4 Minor body damage – repair

The photographic sequences on pages 218 and 219 illustrate the operations detailed in the following sub-sections.
Note: *For more detailed information about bodywork repair, the Haynes Publishing Group publish a book by Lindsay Porter called The Car Bodywork Repair Manual. This incorporates information on such aspects as rust treatment, painting and glass fibre repairs, as well as details on more ambitious repairs involving welding and panel beating.*

Repair of minor scratches in bodywork

If the scratch is very superficial, and does not penetrate to the metal of the bodywork, repair is very simple. Lightly rub the area of the scratch with a paintwork renovator, or a very fine cutting paste, to remove loose paint from the scratch and to clear the surrounding bodywork of wax polish. Rinse the area with clean water.

Apply touch-up paint to the scratch using a fine paint brush; continue to apply fine layers of paint until the surface of the paint in the scratch is level with the surrounding paintwork. Allow the new paint at least two weeks to harden: then blend it into the surrounding paintwork by rubbing the scratch area with a paintwork renovator or a very fine cutting paste. Finally, apply wax polish.

Where the scratch has penetrated right through to the metal of the bodywork, causing the metal to rust, a different repair technique is required. Remove any loose rust from the bottom of the scratch with a penknife, then apply rust inhibiting paint to prevent the formation of rust in the future. Using a rubber or nylon applicator fill the scratch with bodystopper paste. If required, this paste can be mixed with cellulose thinners to provide a very thin paste which is ideal for filling narrow scratches. Before the stopper-paste in the scratch hardens, wrap a piece of smooth cotton rag around the top of a finger. Dip the finger in cellulose thinners and then quickly sweep it across the surface of the stopper-paste in the scratch; this will ensure that the surface of the stopper-paste is slightly hollowed. The scratch can now be painted over as described earlier in this Section.

Repair of dents in bodywork

When deep denting of the vehicle's bodywork has taken place, the first task is to pull the dent out, until the affected bodywork almost attains its original shape. There is little point in trying to restore the original shape completely, as the metal in the damaged area will have stretched on impact and cannot be reshaped fully to its original contour. It is better to bring the level of the dent up to a point which is about ⅛ in (3 mm) below the level of the surrounding bodywork. In cases where the dent is very shallow anyway, it is not worth trying to pull it out at all. If the underside of the dent is accessible, it can be hammered out gently from behind, using a mallet with a wooden or plastic head. Whilst doing this, hold a suitable block of wood firmly against the outside of the panel to absorb the impact from the hammer blows and thus prevent a large area of the bodywork from being 'belled-out'.

Should the dent be in a section of the bodywork which has a double skin or some other factor making it inaccessible from behind, a different technique is called for. Drill several small holes through the metal inside the area – particularly in the deeper section. Then screw long self-tapping screws into the holes just sufficiently for them to gain a good purchase in the metal. Now the dent can be pulled out by pulling on the protruding heads of the screws with a pair of pliers.

The next stage of the repair is the removal of the paint from the damaged area, and from an inch or so of the surrounding 'sound' bodywork. This is accomplished most easily by using a wire brush or abrasive pad on a power drill, although it can be done just as

This sequence of photographs deals with the repair of the dent and paintwork damage shown in this photo. The procedure will be similar for the repair of a hole. It should be noted that the procedures given here are simplified — more explicit instructions will be found in the text

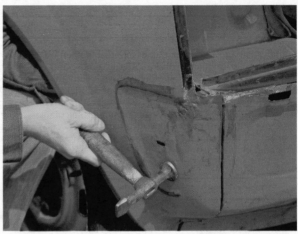

In the case of a dent the first job — after removing surrounding trim — is to hammer out the dent where access is possible. This will minimise filling. Here, the large dent having been hammered out, the damaged area is being made slightly concave

Now all paint must be removed from the damaged area, by rubbing with coarse abrasive paper. Alternatively, a wire brush or abrasive pad can be used in a power drill. Where the repair area meets good paintwork, the edge of the paintwork should be 'feathered', using a finer grade of abrasive paper

In the case of a hole caused by rusting, all damaged sheet-metal should be cut away before proceeding to this stage. Here, the damaged area is being treated with rust remover and inhibitor before being filled

Mix the body filler according to its manufacturer's instructions. In the case of corrosion damage, it will be necessary to block off any large holes before filling — this can be done with aluminium or plastic mesh, or aluminium tape. Make sure the area is absolutely clean before ...

... applying the filler. Filler should be applied with a flexible applicator, as shown, for best results; the wooden spatula being used for confined areas. Apply thin layers of filler at 20-minute intervals, until the surface of the filler is slightly proud of the surrounding bodywork

Initial shaping can be done with a Surform plane or Dreadnought file. Then, using progressively finer grades of wet-and-dry paper, wrapped around a sanding block, and copious amounts of clean water, rub down the filler until really smooth and flat. Again, feather the edges of adjoining paintwork

The whole repair area can now be sprayed or brush-painted with primer. If spraying, ensure adjoining areas are protected from over-spray. Note that at least one inch of the surrounding sound paintwork should be coated with primer. Primer has a 'thick' consistency, so will find small imperfections

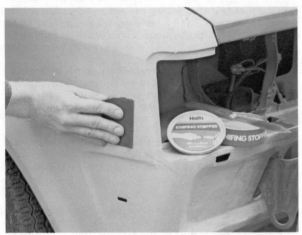

Again, using plenty of water, rub down the primer with a fine grade wet-and-dry paper (400 grade is probably best) until it is really smooth and well blended into the surrounding paintwork. Any remaining imperfections can now be filled by carefully applied knifing stopper paste

When the stopper has hardened, rub down the repair area again before applying the final coat of primer. Before rubbing down this last coat of primer, ensure the repair area is blemish-free — use more stopper if necessary. To ensure that the surface of the primer is really smooth use some finishing compound

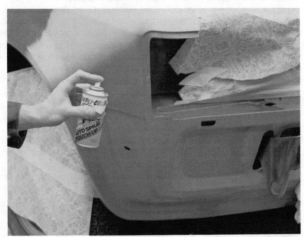

The top coat can now be applied. When working out of doors, pick a dry, warm and wind-free day. Ensure surrounding areas are protected from over-spray. Agitate the aerosol thoroughly, then spray the centre of the repair area, working outwards with a circular motion. Apply the paint as several thin coats

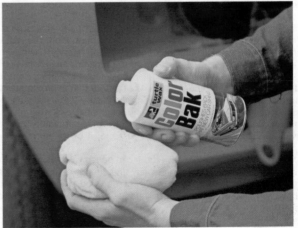

After a period of about two weeks, which the paint needs to harden fully, the surface of the repaired area can be 'cut' with a mild cutting compound prior to wax polishing. When carrying out bodywork repairs, remember that the quality of the finished job is proportional to the time and effort expended

effectively by hand using sheets of abrasive paper. To complete the preparation for filling, score the surface of the bare metal with a screwdriver or the tang of a file, or alternatively, drill small holes in the affected area. This will provide a really good 'key' for the filler paste.

To complete the repair see the Section on filling and re-spraying.

Repair of rust holes or gashes in bodywork

Remove all paint from the affected area and from an inch or so of the surrounding 'sound' bodywork, using an abrasive pad or a wire brush on a power drill. If these are not available a few sheets of abrasive paper will do the job just as effectively. With the paint removed you will be able to gauge the severity of the corrosion and therefore decide whether to renew the whole panel (if this is possible) or to repair the affected area. New body panels are not as expensive as most people think and it is often quicker and more satisfactory to fit a new panel than to attempt to repair large areas of corrosion.

Remove all fittings from the affected area except those which will act as a guide to the original shape of the damaged bodywork (eg headlamp shells etc). Then, using tin snips or a hacksaw blade, remove all loose metal and any other metal badly affected by corrosion. Hammer the edges of the hole inwards in order to create a slight depression for the filler paste.

Wire brush the affected area to remove the powdery rust from the surface of the remaining metal. Paint the affected area with rust inhibiting paint; if the back of the rusted area is accessible treat this also.

Before filling can take place it will be necessary to block the hole in some way. This can be achieved by the use of aluminium or plastic mesh, or aluminium tape.

Aluminium or plastic mesh is probably the best material to use for a large hole. Cut a piece to the approximate size and shape of the hole to be filled, then position it in the hole so that its edges are below the level of the surrounding bodywork. It can be retained in position by several blobs of filler paste around its periphery.

Aluminium tape should be used for small or very narrow holes. Pull a piece off the roll and trim it to the approximate size and shape required, then pull off the backing paper (if used) and stick the tape over the hole; it can be overlapped if the thickness of one piece is insufficient. Burnish down the edges of the tape with the handle of a screwdriver or similar, to ensure that the tape is securely attached to the metal underneath.

Bodywork repairs – filling and re-spraying

Before using this Section, see the Sections on dent, deep scratch, rust holes and gash repairs.

Many types of bodyfiller are available, but generally speaking those proprietary kits which contain a tin of filler paste and a tube of resin hardener are best for this type of repair. A wide, flexible plastic or nylon applicator will be found invaluable for imparting a smooth and well contoured finish to the surface of the filler.

Mix up a little filler on a clean piece of card or board – measure the hardener carefully (follow the maker's instructions on the pack) otherwise the filler will set too rapidly or too slowly. Using the applicator apply the filler paste to the prepared area; draw the applicator across the surface of the filler to achieve the correct contour and to level the filler surface. As soon as a contour that approximates to the correct one is achieved, stop working the paste – if you carry on too long the paste will become sticky and begin to 'pick up' on the applicator. Continue to add thin layers of filler paste at twenty-minute intervals until the level of the filler is just proud of the surrounding bodywork.

Once the filler has hardened, excess can be removed using a metal plane or file. From then on, progressively finer grades of abrasive paper should be used, starting with a 40 grade production paper and finishing with 400 grade wet-and-dry paper. Always wrap the abrasive paper around a flat rubber, cork, or wooden block – otherwise the surface of the filler will not be completely flat. During the smoothing of the filler surface the wet-and-dry paper should be periodically rinsed in water. This will ensure that a very smooth finish is imparted to the filler at the final stage.

At this stage the 'dent' should be surrounded by a ring of bare metal, which in turn should be encircled by the finely 'feathered' edge of the good paintwork. Rinse the repair area with clean water, until all of the dust produced by the rubbing-down operation has gone.

Spray the whole repair area with a light coat of primer – this will show up any imperfections in the surface of the filler. Repair these imperfections with fresh filler paste or bodystopper, and once more smooth the surface with abrasive paper. If bodystopper is used, it can be mixed with cellulose thinners to form a really thin paste which is ideal for filling small holes. Repeat this spray and repair procedure until you are satisfied that the surface of the filler, and the feathered edge of the paintwork are perfect. Clean the repair area with clean water and allow to dry fully.

The repair area is now ready for final spraying. Paint spraying must be carried out in a warm, dry, windless and dust free atmosphere. This condition can be created artificially if you have access to a large indoor working area, but if you are forced to work in the open, you will have to pick your day very carefully. If you are working indoors, dousing the floor in the work area with water will help to settle the dust which would otherwise be in the atmosphere. If the repair area is confined to one body panel, mask off the surrounding panels; this will help to minimise the effects of a slight mis-match in paint colours. Bodywork fittings (eg chrome strips, door handles etc) will also need to be masked off. Use genuine masking tape and several thicknesses of newspaper for the masking operations.

Before commencing to spray, agitate the aerosol can thoroughly, then spray a test area (an old tin, or similar) until the technique is mastered. Cover the repair area with a thick coat of primer; the thickness should be built up using several thin layers of paint rather than one thick one. Using 400 grade wet-and-dry paper, rub down the surface of the primer until it is really smooth. While doing this, the work area should be thoroughly doused with water, and the wet-and-dry paper periodically rinsed in water. Allow to dry before spraying on more paint.

Spray on the top coat, again building up the thickness by using several thin layers of paint. Start spraying in the centre of the repair area and then, using a circular motion, work outwards until the whole repair area and about 2 inches of the surrounding original paintwork is covered. Remove all masking material 10 to 15 minutes after spraying on the final coat of paint.

Allow the new paint at least two weeks to harden, then, using a paintwork renovator or a very fine cutting paste, blend the edges of the paint into the existing paintwork. Finally, apply wax polish.

Plastic components

With the use of more and more plastic body components by the vehicle manufacturers (eg bumpers, spoilers, and in some cases major body panels), rectification of more serious damage to such items has become a matter of either entrusting repair work to a specialist in this field, or renewing complete components. Repair of such damage by the DIY owner is not really feasible owing to the cost of the equipment and materials required for effecting such repairs. The basic technique involves making a groove along the line of the crack in the plastic using a rotary burr in a power drill. The damaged part is then welded back together by using a hot air gun to heat up and fuse a plastic filler rod into the groove. Any excess plastic is then removed and the area rubbed down to a smooth finish. It is important that a filler rod of the correct plastic is used, as body components can be made of a variety of different types (eg polycarbonate, ABS, polypropylene).

Damage of a less serious nature (abrasions, minor cracks etc) can be repaired by the DIY owner using a two-part epoxy filler repair material. Once mixed in equal proportions, this is used in similar fashion to the bodywork filler used on metal panels. The filler is usually cured in twenty to thirty minutes, ready for sanding and painting.

If the owner is renewing a complete component himself, or if he has repaired it with epoxy filler, he will be left with the problem of finding a suitable paint for finishing which is compatible with the type of plastic used. At one time the use of a universal paint was not possible owing to the complex range of plastics encountered in body component applications. Standard paints, generally speaking, will not bond to plastic or rubber satisfactorily. However, it is now possible to obtain a plastic body parts finishing kit which consists of a pre-primer treatment, a primer and coloured top coat. Full instructions are normally supplied with a kit, but basically the method of use is to first apply the pre-primer to the component concerned and allow it to dry for up to 30 minutes. Then the primer is applied and left to dry for about an hour before finally applying the special coloured top coat. The result is a correctly coloured component where the paint will flex with the plastic or rubber, a property that standard paint does not normally possess.

5 Major body damage – repair

Where serious damage has occurred, or large areas need renewal due to neglect, it means that complete new sections or panels will need welding in, and this is best left to professionals. If the damage is due to impact, it will also be necessary to check completely the alignment of the bodyshell, and this can only be carried out successfully using special jigs. If the body is left misaligned, it is primarily dangerous as the car will not handle properly, and secondly, uneven stresses will be imposed on the steering, suspension, and possibly transmission, causing abnormal wear, or complete failure, particularly to such items as the tyres.

6 Maintenance – hinges and locks

1 Oil the hinges of the bonnet, boot lid or tailgate, and doors with a few drops of light oil at regular intervals (photo).
2 At the same time lightly lubricate the bonnet release mechanism and the door locks (photo).
3 **Do not** attempt to lubricate the steering lock.

7 Bonnet – removal, refitting and adjustment

1 Open the bonnet and remove the sound-deadening material on the left-hand side by releasing the clip retainers (photo).
2 Undo the two screws securing the illumination lamp to the bonnet (photo), feed the lamp and wiring down behind the sound-deadening material and retrieve it from the bottom of the bonnet. Place the lamp and wiring to one side.

3 Disconnect the windscreen washer fluid feed hose at the two-way connector (photo).
4 Place some rags beneath the bonnet corners, by the hinges.
5 Mark the position of the hinges by drawing around them with a soft pencil, then loosen the retaining bolts (photo).
6 Engage the help of an assistant to support the bonnet.
7 Using a small screwdriver, prise out the clips securing the support struts to the pegs on the bonnet (photo). Release both struts from their pegs.
8 Undo the retaining bolts and carefully lift away the bonnet.
9 Refitting is the reverse sequence to removal, but adjust the bonnet position on the hinges to its original position initially, then check the alignment as follows.
10 Close the bonnet and check the alignment with the adjacent body panels. The bonnet can be moved forward and backward by adjusting its position at each hinge. If the bonnet is too low with respect to the adjacent wing, fit small shims between the hinge and bonnet.
11 Check the bonnet closure and ease of opening. If the striker pins do not engage smoothly with the lock plates, slacken the striker plate retaining bolts and reposition the plates. If necessary, slacken the locknut and adjust the striker pin height by turning the slotted end with a screwdriver.

8 Bonnet support strut – removal and refitting

1 Open the bonnet, and support it in the open position with the aid of an assistant or with a suitable prop.
2 Using a small screwdriver, prise out the retaining clips securing the strut ends to the mounting pegs.
3 Release the strut from the pegs and remove it from the bonnet.
4 Refitting is the reverse sequence to removal.

6.1 Lubricate the hinges with a few drops of light oil

6.2 Lubricate the bonnet release mechanism and the door locks

7.1 Release the sound-deadening material retaining clips

7.2 Remove the bonnet illumination lamp

7.3 Disconnect the windscreen washer fluid feed hose (arrowed)

7.5 Loosen the bonnet hinge retaining bolts (arrowed)

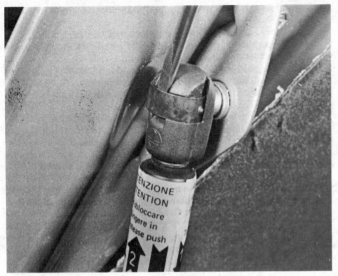

7.7 Prise out the support strut retaining clips

10.6 Release the cable from the retaining clip (arrowed)

9 Bonnet lock and release cable – removal and refitting

1   From inside the car, undo the bolts and withdraw the release lever from the right-hand side of the footwell.
2   Disengage the cables from the lever.
3   Working in the engine compartment, undo the bolts securing the relevant bonnet lock to the front body panel.
4   Withdraw the lock from under the body panel and disengage the release cable.
5   Release the cable from the retaining clips and ties in the engine compartment, and from the bulkhead grommet.
6   Feed the cable through into the engine compartment and remove it from the car.
7   Refitting is the reverse sequence to removal. Adjust the bonnet lock as described in Section 7, if necessary.

10 Boot lid (Saloon models) – removal, refitting and adjustment

1   Open the boot lid and remove the plastic cover over the lock.
2   Release the retaining clip and disconnect the link rod from the lock lever.
3   Disconnect the wiring at the connector adjacent to the lock.
4   Undo the two bolts and withdraw the lock from the boot lid.
5   Withdraw the lock release cable outer sheath from the lock bracket, and disconnect the inner cable from the lock lever.
6   Withdraw the grommet from the cable entry point above the boot lid hinge, and release the cable from the hinge cable clips and ties (photo). Withdraw the release cable and wiring from the bonnet.
7   With an assistant supporting the boot lid, undo the four hinge bolts and lift the boot lid away.
8   Refitting is the reverse sequence to removal. Engage the centre groove of the lock release cable sheath into the lock bracket slot initially, but use an alternative groove if the release lever action is unsatisfactory.
9   With the boot lid closed, check the relationship of the lid with the adjacent panels. If necessary, the boot can be repositioned by altering the position of the hinges at their body attachment. To do this, remove the rear seats as described in Section 42, and remove the parcel shelf. Slacken the hinge nuts and reposition the hinges as required. Tighten the nuts, then close the boot lid and check the operation of the lock. If necessary, slacken the striker plate bolts, reposition the striker plate and tighten the bolts (photo).
10 Refit the parcel shelf and rear seats on completion.

10.10 Boot lid striker plate retaining bolts (arrowed)

11 Boot lock (Saloon models) – removal and refitting

1   Open the boot lid and remove the plastic cover over the lock.
2   Release the retaining clip and disconnect the link rod from the lock lever.
3   Disconnect the wiring at the connector adjacent to the lock.
4   Undo the two bolts and withdraw the lock from the boot lid.
5   Withdraw the lock release cable outer sheath from the lock bracket, disconnect the inner cable from the lock lever, and remove the lock.
6   Refitting is the reverse sequence to removal. Engage the centre groove of the lock release cable sheath into the lock bracket slot initially, but use an alternative groove if the release lever action is unsatisfactory.

12 Boot lid private lock (Saloon models) – removal and refitting

1   Remove the number plate from the boot lid.
2   From inside the boot lid, undo the screws and remove the centre lens and reflector assembly (photo).
3   Extract the retaining circlip from the private lock lever, and withdraw the link rod.

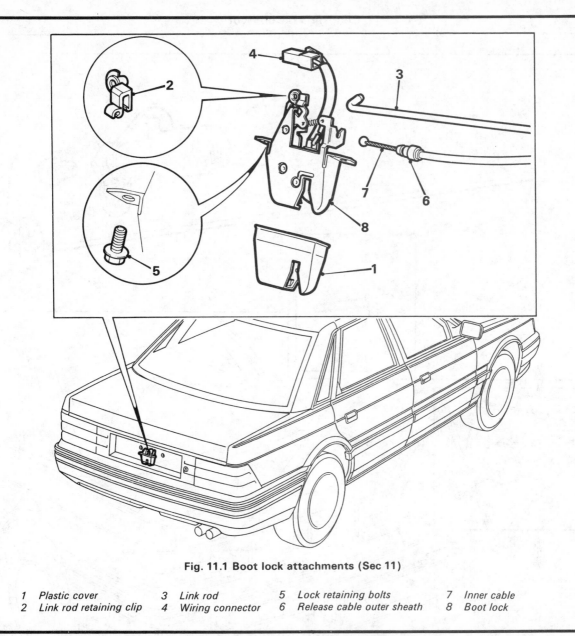

Fig. 11.1 Boot lock attachments (Sec 11)

1	Plastic cover	3	Link rod	5	Lock retaining bolts	7	Inner cable
2	Link rod retaining clip	4	Wiring connector	6	Release cable outer sheath	8	Boot lock

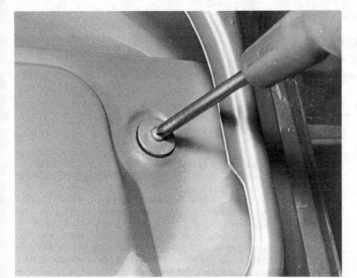

12.2 Undo the centre lens and reflector retaining screw

12.4 Boot lid private lock retaining rivets

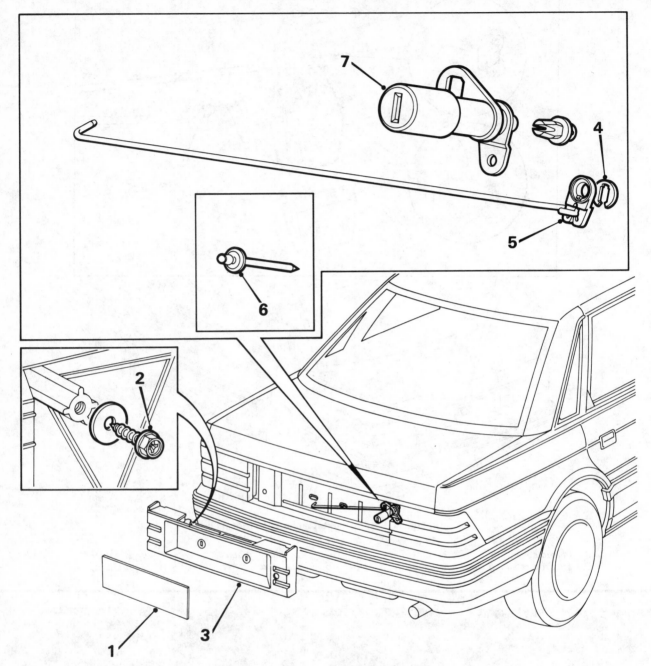

Fig. 11.2 Boot private lock attachments (Sec 12)

1 Number plate	3 Centre lens and reflector	4 Lever retaining circlip	6 Retaining rivets
2 Centre lens and reflector	assembly	5 Lever	7 Private lock
assembly screws		

4 Drill out the three retaining rivets (photo), and remove the private lock from the boot lid.
5 Refitting is the reverse sequence to removal.

13 Boot lid/tailgate and fuel filler flap release control – removal and refitting

1 Withdraw the knobs from the release levers inside the car (photo).
2 Undo the two screws securing the release control cover – one on the side face (photo), and one under a flap at the rear.
3 Withdraw the cover retaining stud on the inner face, then lift the

cover off the release control (photo).
4 Undo the screws securing the front sill tread plate, lift off the tread plate, and pull back the carpet around the release control.
5 Undo the three screws and withdraw the release control (photo).
6 Disconnect the inner cable ends and outer cable sheaths, and remove the control from the car.
7 Refitting is the reverse sequence to removal. Note that the boot/tailgate release cable with the single groove in the outer cable sheath is fitted to the upper location, and the fuel filler flap release with the three grooves in the outer cable sheath is fitted to the lower location. Engage the centre groove with the bracket when fitting the filler flap cable, and check the release operation. If unsatisfactory, use an alternate groove.

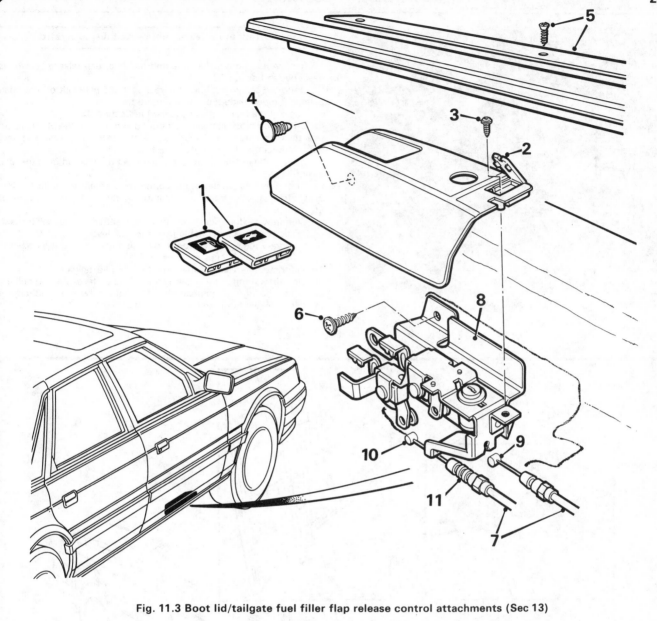

Fig. 11.3 Boot lid/tailgate fuel filler flap release control attachments (Sec 13)

1	Release lever knobs	5	Front sill tread plate screws
2	Access flap	6	Release control retaining
3	Cover retaining screws		screws
4	Cover retaining stud	7	Control cables

8	Release control
9	Boot release inner cable
10	Fuel filler flap release inner cable

11	Three grooves on fuel filler flap release outer cable sheath

13.1 Withdraw the boot lid/tailgate and fuel filler flap release lever knobs

13.2 Undo the release lever control cover retaining screws

13.3 Withdraw the cover ...

13.5 ... over the release lever assembly

14 Boot lid/tailgate release cable – removal and refitting

1   Remove the boot lid/tailgate and fuel filler flap release control as described in Section 13.

2   Undo the screws securing the rear sill tread plate, lift off the tread plate and move aside the carpet around the sill.

3   Remove the rear seat as described in Section 42.

4   On Saloon models, open the boot lid and remove the plastic cover over the lock. On Fastback models, open the tailgate, release the screw studs and remove the tailgate inner trim panel.

5   Release the retaining clip and disconnect the link rod from the lock lever.

6   Disconnect the wiring at the connector adjacent to the lock.

7   Undo the two bolts and withdraw the lock from the boot lid/tailgate.

8   Withdraw the lock release cable outer sheath from the lock bracket, and disconnect the inner cable from the lock lever.

9   Withdraw the grommet from the cable entry point and release the cable from the cable clips and ties.

10 Withdraw the release cable from the boot lid/tailgate.

11 Tie a drawstring to the release control end of the cable, and pull the cable into the luggage compartment. Untie the drawstring and remove the release cable from the car.

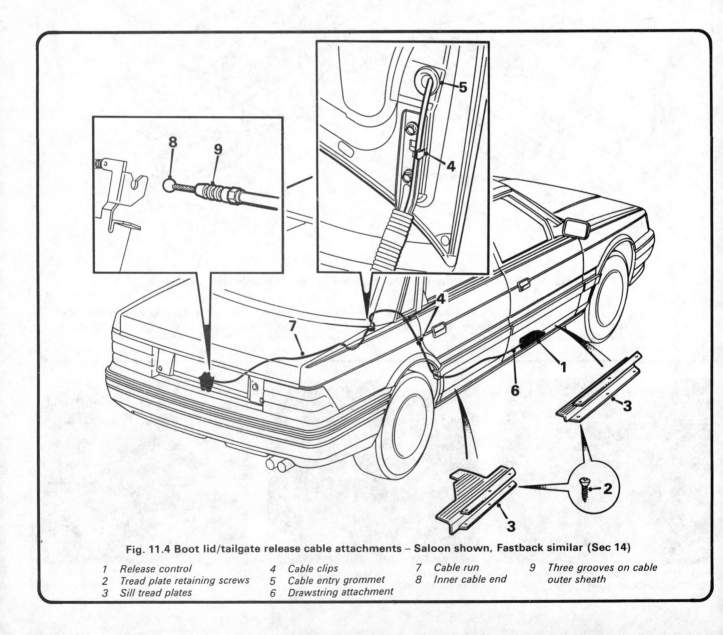

Fig. 11.4 Boot lid/tailgate release cable attachments – Saloon shown, Fastback similar (Sec 14)

1 Release control	4 Cable clips	7 Cable run	9 Three grooves on cable
2 Tread plate retaining screws	5 Cable entry grommet	8 Inner cable end	outer sheath
3 Sill tread plates	6 Drawstring attachment		

12 Tie the drawstring to the new cable, and pull it through into the car interior.

13 Refit the cable to the release lever and lock, then reassemble the components using the reverse sequence to removal. When refitting the cable to the lock, engage the centre groove of the cable sheath into the lock bracket slot initially, but use an alternative groove if the release lever action is unsatisfactory.

15 Fuel filler flap release cable – removal and refitting

1 Open the fuel filler flap, then remove the boot lid/tailgate and fuel filler flap release control, as described in Section 13.

2 Undo the screws securing the rear sill tread plate, lift off the tread plate and move aside the carpet around the sill.

3 Remove the rear seat as described in Section 42.

4 Extract the retaining clip securing the cable end at the filler flap end, and push the cable through into the luggage compartment (photo).

5 Release the cable from the retaining clips, and pull it into the car interior.

6 Where fitted, undo the screws and remove the cover strip over the cable beneath the rear seat location.

7 Release the cable from any further clips and ties, and remove it from the car.

8 Refitting is the reverse sequence to removal, with reference to Section 13 when refitting the cable to the release control.

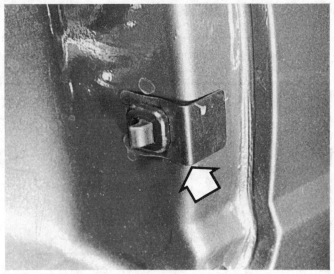

15.4 Fuel filler flap cable end retaining clip (arrowed)

16 Tailgate (Fastback models) – removal and refitting

1 Open the tailgate and release the parcel shelf support strings.

2 From inside the car, remove the headliner rear finisher for access to the tailgate hinge retaining nuts.

3 Disconnect the screen washer hose, and the tailgate wiring harness connectors.

4 Support the tailgate with the help of an assistant, or using a prop.

5 Extract the wire spring retainer securing each support strut to its tailgate ball-stud, and release the struts.

6 Undo the tailgate hinge retaining nuts and remove the tailgate from the car.

7 Refitting is the reverse sequence to removal, in conjunction with the following adjustment procedure.

8 With the tailgate closed, check the relationship of the tailgate with the adjacent panels. If necessary, it can be repositioned by altering the position of the hinges at their body attachment. Slacken the hinge nuts, and reposition the hinges are required. Tighten the nuts, then close the tailgate and check the operation of the lock. If necessary, slacken the striker plate bolts, reposition the striker plate and tighten the bolts.

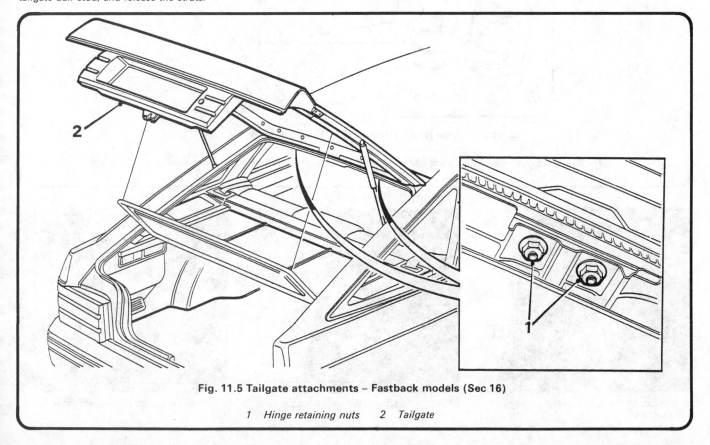

Fig. 11.5 Tailgate attachments – Fastback models (Sec 16)

1 Hinge retaining nuts   2 Tailgate

17 Tailgate support strut (Fastback models) – removal and refitting

1 Open the tailgate and support it with the help of an assistant, or using a prop.

2 Extract the wire spring retainer securing the upper end of the support strut to its tailgate ball-stud, and release the strut (photos).

3 Release the strut lower end clip, ease the strut from its stud (photo) and remove it from the car.

4 Refitting is the reverse sequence to removal.

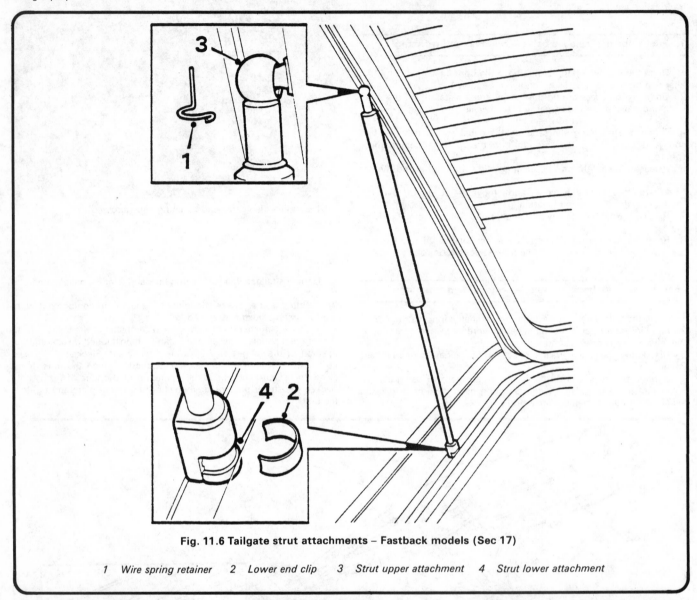

Fig. 11.6 Tailgate strut attachments – Fastback models (Sec 17)

1   Wire spring retainer   2   Lower end clip   3   Strut upper attachment   4   Strut lower attachment

17.2A Extract the support strut wire spring retainer ...

17.2B ... and release the strut from the stud

17.3 Release the strut lower end from its stud

18 Tailgate lock (Fastback models) – removal and refitting

1   Open the tailgate, release the screw studs (photo) and remove the tailgate inner trim panel.
2   Remove the plastic cover from the lock (photo).

3   Release the retaining clip from the link rod, and remove the link rod from the lock lever.
4   Disconnect the wiring multi-plugs, undo the two lock retaining bolts (photo) and remove the lock from the door.
5   Refitting is the reverse sequence to removal.

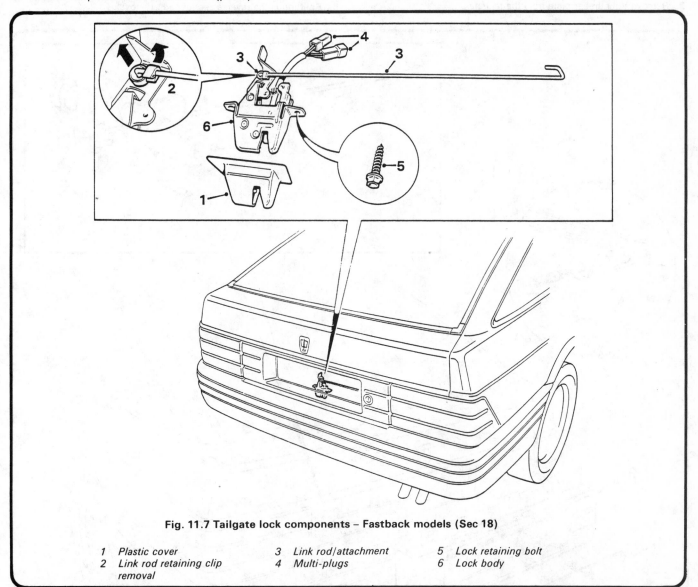

Fig. 11.7 Tailgate lock components – Fastback models (Sec 18)

1	Plastic cover	3 Link rod/attachment	5 Lock retaining bolt
2	Link rod retaining clip removal	4 Multi-plugs	6 Lock body

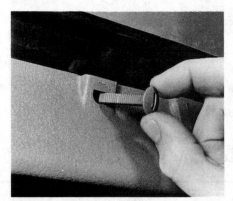

18.1 Release the screw studs and remove the tailgate inner trim panel

18.2 Remove the plastic cover from the lock

18.4 Undo the two lock retaining bolts (arrowed)

19 Tailgate private lock (Fastback models) – removal and refitting

1 Open the tailgate, release the screw studs and remove the tailgate inner trim panel.
2 Remove the number plate from the tailgate.

3 From inside the tailgate, undo the screws and remove the centre lens and reflector assembly.
4 Extract the retaining circlip from the private lock lever, and withdraw the lever from the lock (photo).
5 Drill out the three retaining rivets and remove the private lock from the tailgate.
6 Refitting is the reverse sequence to removal.

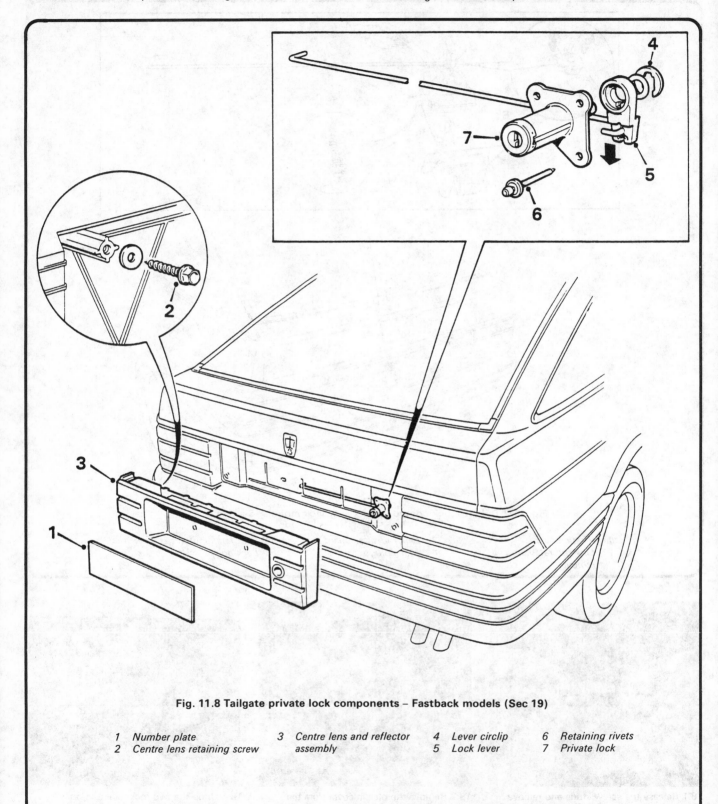

Fig. 11.8 Tailgate private lock components – Fastback models (Sec 19)

1 Number plate	3 Centre lens and reflector assembly	4 Lever circlip	6 Retaining rivets
2 Centre lens retaining screw		5 Lock lever	7 Private lock

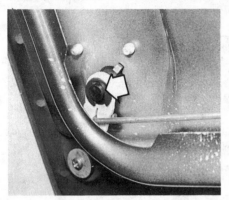

19.4 Private lock lever retaining circlip (arrowed)

21.1 Radiator grille upper retaining screws (arrowed)

21.2 Radiator grille lower retaining clip

20 Tailgate lock solenoid (Fastback models) – removal and refitting

1   Open the tailgate, release the screw studs and remove the tailgate inner trim panel.
2   Remove the number plate from the tailgate.
3   From inside the tailgate, undo the screws and remove the centre lens and reflector assembly.
4   Disconnect the solenoid wiring multi-plug.
5   Undo the two screws and remove the solenoid from the tailgate.
6   Refitting is the reverse sequence to removal.

21 Radiator grille – removal and refitting

1   Undo the four grille upper retaining screws (photo).
2   Release the two lower retaining clips (photo) and withdraw the grille from the car.
3   Refitting is the reverse sequence to removal.

22 Windscreen, rear window and tailgate window glass – removal and refitting

The primary window glass on Rover 820 models is flush-glazed, and secured to the body shell by direct bonding. Due to this method of retention, special tools and equipment are required for removal and refitting, and this task is definitely beyond the scope of the home mechanic. If it is necessary to have windscreen, rear window or tailgate window glass removed, this job should be left to a suitably-equipped specialist.

23 Front door inner trim panel – removal and refitting

Saloon models
1   Insert a small screwdriver into the slot at the rear of the interior locking button, and prise apart the outer moulded half of the locking button. Lift off the outer half, then remove the inner half from the locking rod (photos).
2   Carefully prise out the finisher trim from the inner handle, disconnect the tweeter speaker leads and remove the finisher (photos).

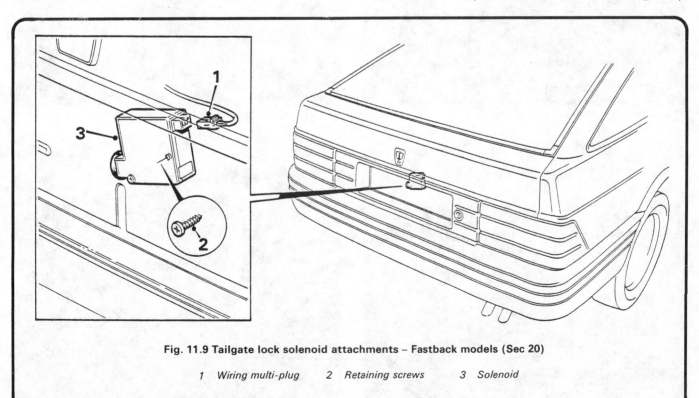

Fig. 11.9 Tailgate lock solenoid attachments – Fastback models (Sec 20)

1   Wiring multi-plug   2   Retaining screws   3   Solenoid

3   Carefully prise out the blanking plate from the bottom of the panel (photo).
4   Ease back the padded trim at the bottom of the panel to expose the retaining screw, then undo the screw (photo).
5   Pull out the blanking plug on the rear side of the panel, and undo the recessed screw behind (photos).
6   Undo the screw at the upper front corner of the panel (photo).
7   Undo the screw at each end of the storage bin (photos).
8   Working through the blanking plate aperture, undo the screw in the recess (photo).
9   Undo the screw at the top of the door pull below the interior handle (photo).
10 Using a suitable flat tool or your fingers, release the eight studs securing the panel to the door by prising the panel out, or sharply pulling it out, in the vicinity of each stud. Lift the panel upwards and withdraw it from the door (photo).
11 Disconnect the switch panel wiring multi-plug from the rear of the panel and remove the panel (photo).
12 Refitting is the reverse sequence to removal.

Fastback models
13 Insert a small screwdriver into the slot at the rear of the interior locking button, and prise apart the outer moulded half of the locking button. Lift off the outer half, then remove the inner half from the locking rod (photo).
14 Prise out the door inner handle centre finisher trim, and undo the two screws securing the trim surround to the door (photos).

15 Pull the door handle outwards, and manipulate the trim surround off the handle and door panel (photo).
16 Disconnect the tweeter speaker leads from the rear of the trim surround, and remove the surround (photo).
17 Where fitted, undo the screw from the bottom of the door pull finger grip, and remove the finger grip from the panel.
18 If the panel incorporates a moulded door pull, prise out the blanking plug and undo the recessed screw behind (photos).
19 Lift up the cap over the screw at the bottom rear corner of the panel, and undo the screw (photo).
20 Pull out the blanking plug on the rear side of the panel, and undo the recessed screw behind (photos).
21 Undo the screw at the upper front corner of the panel (photo).
22 Undo the screw at each end of the storage bin (photos).
23 Undo the screw at the top of the door pull below the interior handle (photo).
24 Release the rubber boot over the door mirror adjustment stalk, release the stalk retaining clips and push the stalk through to the inside of the panel (photos).
25 Using a suitable flat tool or your fingers, release the eight studs securing the panel to the door by prising the panel out, or sharply pulling it out, in the vicinity of each stud. Lift the panel upwards and withdraw it from the door.
26 Refitting is the reverse sequence to removal but push the door mirror stalk into position from the rear before refitting the panel (photo).

23.1A Prise apart the interior lock button ...

23.1B ... and lift out the outer half ...

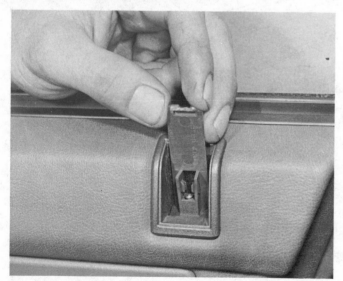

23.1C ... followed by the inner half

23.2A Prise out the inner handle finisher trim ...

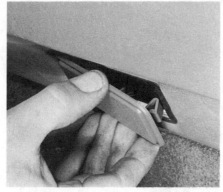

23.2B ... and disconnect the tweeter speaker leads

23.3 Prise out the blanking plate

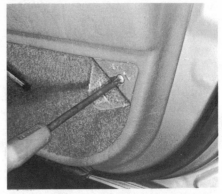

23.4 Undo the screw behind the padded trim

25.5A Pull out the blanking plug ...

23.5B ... and undo the recessed screw behind

23.6 Undo the screw at the upper front corner

23.7A Undo the screw at the front ...

23.7B ... and rear of the storage bin

23.8 Undo the screw in the blanking plate recess

23.9 Undo the screw at the top of the door pull

23.10 Withdraw the panel from the door

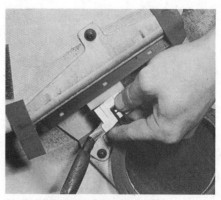

23.11 Disconnect the switch panel wiring multi-plug

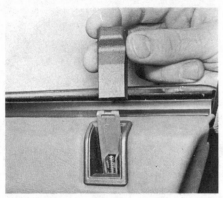
23.13 Remove the two halves of the locking button

23.14A Prise out the inner handle centre finisher trim ...

23.14B ... and undo the two trim surround screws

23.15 Manipulate the surround off the handle

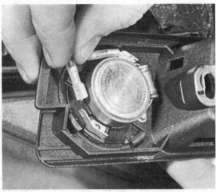
23.16 Disconnect the tweeter speaker leads

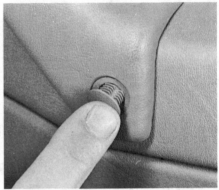
23.18A Prise out the blanking plug ...

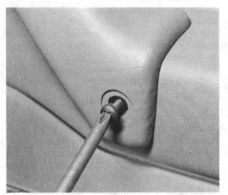
23.18B ... and undo the screw behind

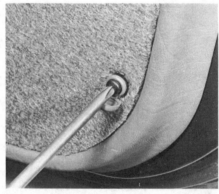
23.19 Lift off the cap and undo the panel bottom rear corner screw

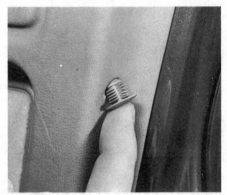
23.20A Pull out the blanking plug ...

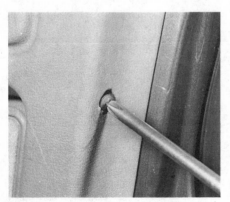
23.20B ... and undo the recessed rear side screw

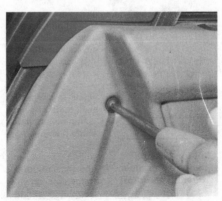
23.21 Undo the screw at the upper front corner

23.22A Undo the screw at the front ...

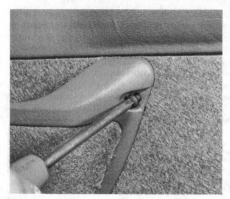

23.22B ... and rear of the storage bin

23.23 Undo the screw at the top of the door pull

23.24A Withdraw the rubber boot ...

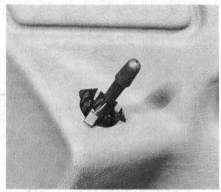

23.24B ... and release the mirror adjustment stalk

23.26 Refit the mirror adjustment stalk before fitting the panel

24 Front door – removal, refitting and adjustment

1   Remove the front door inner trim panel as described in Section 23.
2   Release the masking tape and carefully peel back the polythene condensation barrier as necessary for access to the internal wiring multi-plugs.
3   Identify the multi-plugs for refitting, then disconnect them from the door components. Withdraw the wiring harness from the door.
4   Using a suitable drift, tap out the door check strap retaining roll pin (photo).

5   With the help of an assistant, support the door on a padded jack, undo the four hinge retaining bolts and withdraw the door from the car.
6   Refitting is the reverse sequence to removal.
7   Check the fit of the door against the surrounding panels, and if necessary slacken the hinge bolts and reposition the door.
8   When the door fit is correct, check the operation of the lock, and if necessary slacken the striker plate screws and reposition the striker plate (photo). Tighten all the bolts and screws securely on completion.

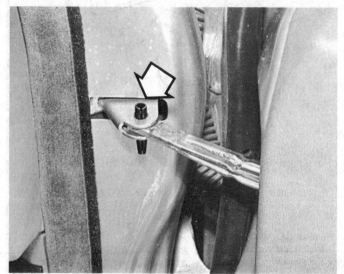

24.4 Remove the door check strap roll pin (arrowed)

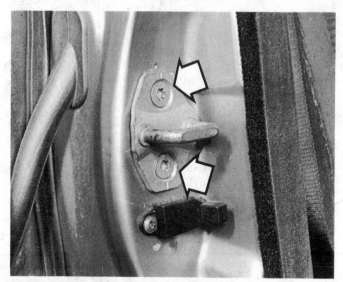

24.8 Door striker plate retaining screws (arrowed)

25 Front door lock – removal and refitting

1   Remove the front door inner trim panel as described in Section 23.
2   Release the masking tape and carefully peel back the polythene condensation barrier as necessary for access to the door lock area.
3   Carefully prise out the door lock link rod and control rod from their attachments at the private lock lever and exterior handle lever

respectively.
4   Undo the three screws securing the lock assembly to the door (photo).
5   Lower the lock assembly, and release the interior handle control rod and locking button rod from the lock levers.
6   Disconnect the central locking motor wiring multi-plug, and manipulate the lock assembly from the door.
7   Refitting is the reverse sequence to removal.

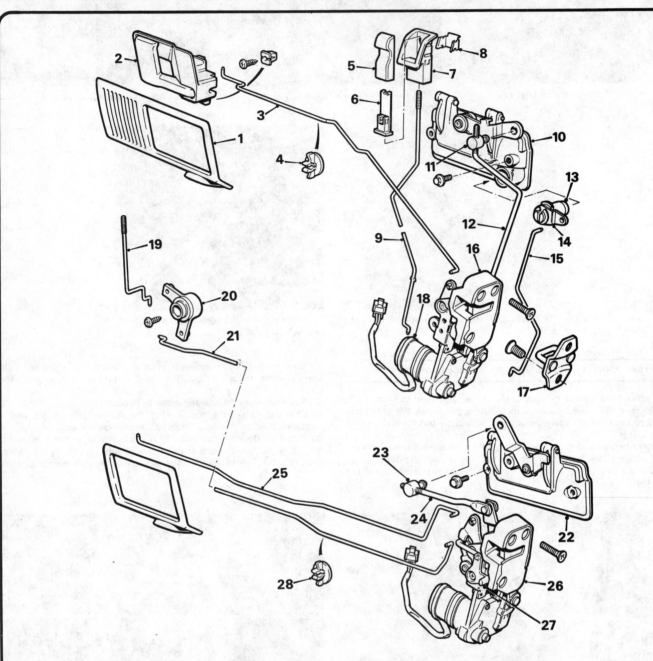

Fig. 11.10 Exploded view of the front and rear door locks and related components (Sec 25)

Front door
1   Finisher trim
2   Inner handle
3   Control rod
4   Rod guide
5   Locking button outer half
6   Locking button inner half
7   Sleeve

8   Clip
9   Link rod
10 Exterior handle
11 Trunnion
12 Control rod
13 Private lock
14 Private lock lever
15 Link rod

16 Door lock
17 Striker plate
18 Central locking motor

Rear door
19 Link rod
20 Bellcrank
21 Control rod

22 Exterior handle
23 Trunnion
24 Link rod
25 Link rod
26 Door lock
27 Childproof lock lever
28 Rod guide

25.4 Door lock retaining screws

26 Front door private lock – removal and refitting

1 Remove the front door inner trim panel as described in Section 23.
2 Release the masking tape and carefully peel back the polythene condensation barrier as necessary for access to the door lock area.
3 Extract the circlip from the end of the lock barrel, and remove the washer, plate and operating lever (photo).
4 Extract the private lock retaining wire clip, and withdraw the lock from the outside of the door.
5 Refitting is the reverse sequence to removal.

27 Front door exterior handle – removal and refitting

1 Remove the front door private lock as described in Section 26.
2 Carefully prise out the door lock control rod from the exterior handle lever.
3 Undo the two retaining bolts and remove the handle from the outside of the door (photo).

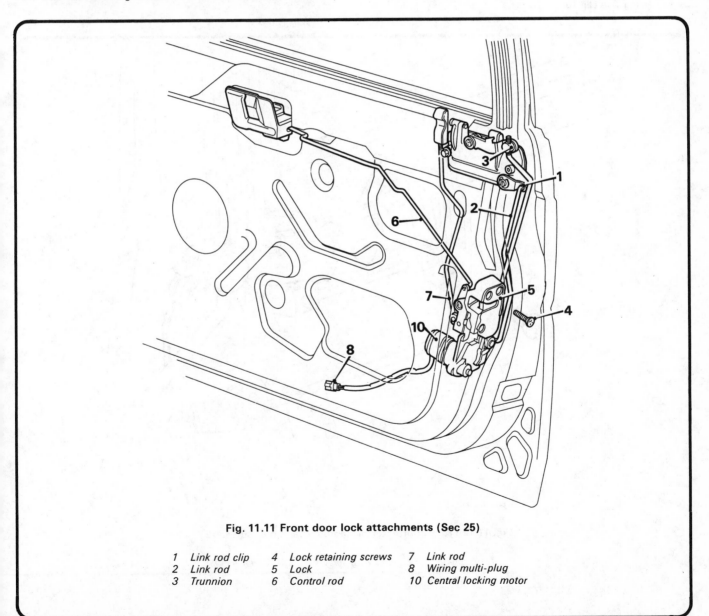

Fig. 11.11 Front door lock attachments (Sec 25)

1	Link rod clip	4	Lock retaining screws	7	Link rod
2	Link rod	5	Lock	8	Wiring multi-plug
3	Trunnion	6	Control rod	10	Central locking motor

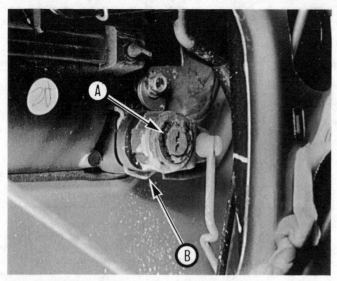

26.3 Lock barrel operating lever retaining circlip (A) and private lock retaining wire clip (B)

27.3 Front door exterior handle retaining bolts (arrowed)

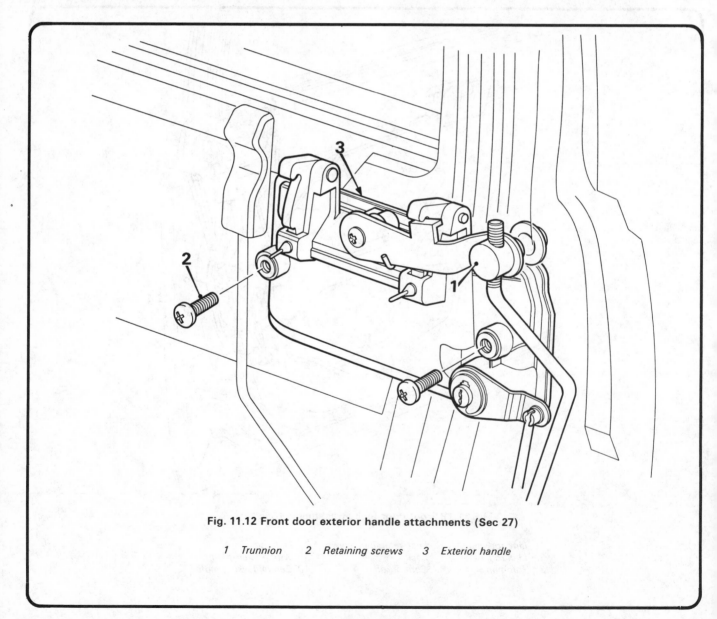

Fig. 11.12 Front door exterior handle attachments (Sec 27)

1   Trunnion   2   Retaining screws   3   Exterior handle

28 Front door interior handle – removal and refitting

1   Remove the front door inner trim panel as described in Section 23.
2   Remove the foam pad from the handle (photo).
3   Where applicable, undo the screws securing the handle to the door

panel.
4   Lift the locking tab at the front of the handle body, slide the handle rearwards and withdraw it from the door (photo).
5   Disconnect the operating rod and remove the handle.
6   Refitting is the reverse sequence to removal.

28.2 Remove the foam pad

28.4 Withdraw the handle from the door

29 Front door window glass – removal and refitting

1   Remove the front door inner trim panel as described in Section 23.
2   Using a screwdriver and protective rag, carefully prise up the waist seal from the upper edge of the door panel to release the retaining clips (photos).
3   Remove the front door main speaker, referring to Chapter 12 if necessary.
4   Where fitted, undo the three screws and remove the trim panel support bracket (photo).
5   Release the masking tape securing the wiring loom and loom connectors to the door panel (photo).
6   Release the wiring loom retaining clips and ease the loom away from the door (photos).
7   Undo the three screws securing the relay mounting plate, then move the plate and relays aside (photos).
8   Carefully peel back the condensation barrier, and pull it downwards to provide access inside the door (photo).
9   Lower the window until the two glass-to-lifting member retaining bolts are accessible through one of the door apertures.
10 Undo the two bolts securing the door glass to the lifting member, and lift the glass up and out of the door (photo).
11 Refitting is the reverse sequence to removal. Ensure that the condensation barrier is refitted securely over the entire door panel face, and position the waist seal retaining clips in the waist seal before refitting the seal to the door (photo).

30 Front door window lift motor – removal and refitting

1   Remove the front door window glass as described in Section 29.
2   Disconnect the motor wiring multi-plug (photo).
3   Undo the two lower bolts and one upper bolt securing the lifting channel to the door.
4   Undo the three nuts securing the motor to the door, then manipulate the motor and lifting channel out through the lower door aperture (photos).
5   Refitting is the reverse sequence to removal.

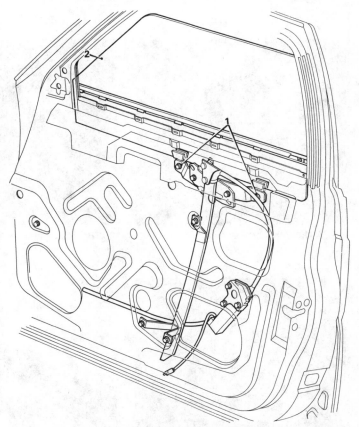

Fig. 11.13 Front door window glass attachments (Sec 29)

1   Glass-to-lifting member
    retaining bolts
2   Window glass

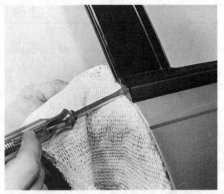
29.2A Prise up the waist seal ...

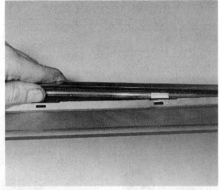
29.2B ... and release the retaining clips

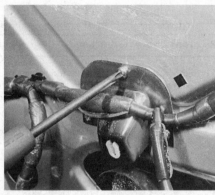
29.4 Remove the trim panel support bracket

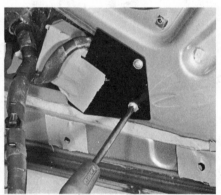
29.5 Release the masking tape

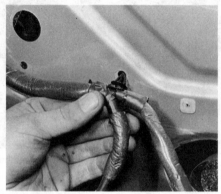
29.6A Release the retaining clips ...

29.6B ... and ease the wiring loom from the door

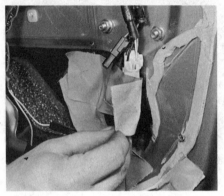
29.7A Undo the three screws ...

29.7B ... and withdraw the relay mounting plate

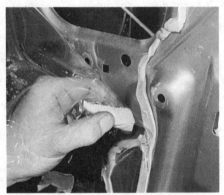
29.8 Peel back the condensation barrier

29.10 Lift the glass up and out of the door

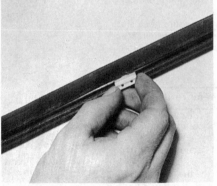
29.11 Fit the clips to the waist seal before refitting the seal

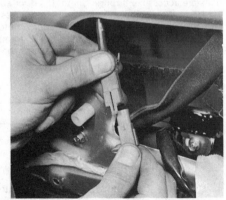
30.2 Disconnect the motor wiring multi-plug

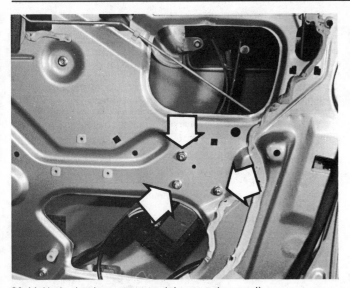

30.4A Undo the three motor retaining nuts (arrowed) ...

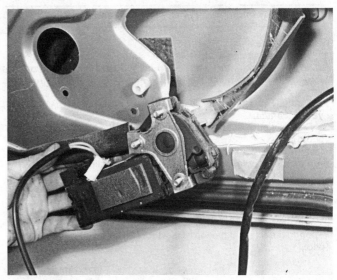

30.4B ... and remove the motor from the door

31 Front door mirror – removal and refitting

Manually controlled mirror

1   Remove the front door inner trim panel as described in Section 23.
2   Carefully prise off the triangular trim panel from the upper corner of the door (photo).
3   Undo the three mirror retaining screws (photo), release the cables from their retaining strap inside the door, and remove the mirror and cables from the door (photo).
4   Refitting is the reverse sequence to removal.

Electrically controlled mirror

5   Remove the front door inner trim panel as described in Section 23.
6   Carefully prise off the triangular trim panel from the upper corner of the door.
7   Peel back the condensation barrier as necessary to gain access to the mirror wiring multi-plugs, then disconnect them.
8   Undo the three mirror retaining screws and withdraw the mirror from the door.
9   Refitting is the reverse sequence to removal.

Fig. 11.14 Front door mirror details (Sec 31)

1   Trim panel   3   Mirror
2   Retaining screws   4   Wiring multi-plugs

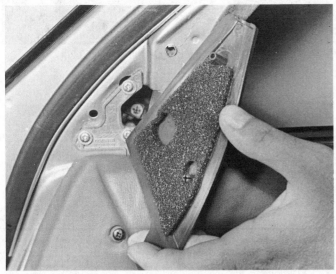

31.2 Prise out the trim panel

31.3 Undo the mirror retaining screws

32 Rear door inner trim panel – removal and refitting

Saloon models

1 Insert a small screwdriver into the slot at the rear of the interior locking button, and prise apart the outer moulded half of the locking button. Lift off the outer half, then remove the inner half from the locking rod (photos).

2 Carefully prise out the finisher trim from the inner handle, and remove the trim.

3 Carefully prise out the blanking plate from the bottom of the panel (photo).

4 If the window is manually operated, push in the escutcheon behind the regulator handle, extract the handle retaining clip and withdraw the handle from the regulator spindle.

5 Ease back the padded trim at the bottom of the panel to expose the retaining screw then undo the screw.

6 Working through the blanking plate aperture, undo the screw in the recess (photo).

7 Undo the screw at the top of the door pull below the interior handle (photo).

8 Pull out the blanking plug near the bottom of the panel, and undo the recessed screw behind (photos).

9 Using a suitable flat tool or your fingers, release the eight studs securing the panel to the door by prising the panel out, or sharply pulling it out, in the vicinity of each stud. Lift the panel upwards and withdraw it from the door.

10 Disconnect the wiring multi-plug at the rear of the window lift switches (where fitted) and remove the panel (photo).

11 Refitting is the reverse sequence to removal. Where fitted, locate the window regulator handle retaining clip in the handle groove before fitting the handle to the door.

Fastback models

12 Insert a small screwdriver into the slot at the rear of the interior locking button, and prise apart the outer moulded half of the locking button. Lift off the outer half, then remove the inner half from the locking rod.

13 Prise out the door inner handle centre finisher trim, and undo the two screws securing the trim surround to the door.

14 Pull the door handle outwards, and manipulate the trim surround off the handle and door panel.

32.1A Prise apart the locking button ...

32.1B ... and remove the inner and outer half

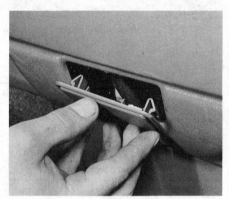
32.3 Prise out the blanking plate

32.6 Undo the screw in the blanking plate aperture

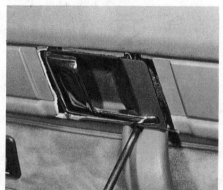
32.7 Undo the screw at the top of the door pull

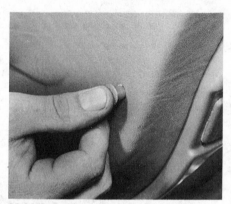
32.8A Pull out the blanking plug ...

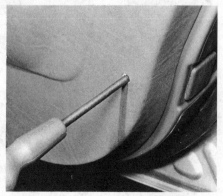
32.8B ... and remove the screw behind

32.10 Disconnect the wiring multi-plug

15 Undo the screw from the bottom of the door pull finger grip, and remove the finger grip from the panel.

16 Using a suitable flat tool or your fingers, release the eight studs securing the panel to the door by prising the panel out, or sharply pulling it out, in the vicinity of each stud. Lift the panel upwards and withdraw it from the door.

17 Refitting is the reverse sequence to removal. Where fitted, locate the window regulator handle retaining clip in the handle groove before fitting the handle to the door.

33 Rear door – removal, refitting and adjustment

The procedure for the rear door is virtually identical to that for the front door, and reference should be made to Section 24.

34 Rear door exterior handle – removal and refitting

1 Remove the rear door inner trim panel as described in Section 32.
2 Release the masking tape and carefully peel back the polythene condensation barrier as necessary for access to the door lock area.
3 Remove the access plug from the rear of the door.
4 Undo the screw securing the interior lock button control rod bellcrank.
5 Withdraw the bellcrank from the door, and disconnect the door lock control rod.
6 Undo the bolt securing the rear glass channel to the door, and remove the glass channel.
7 Undo the three screws securing the door lock to the rear face of the door.
8 Release the door lock control rod from the plastic guide on the inner face of the door.
9 Move the door lock aside, and undo the bolts securing the exterior handle to the door.
10 Withdraw the exterior handle, release the collar and remove the control rod from the exterior handle lever.
11 Remove the exterior handle from the door.
12 Refitting is the reverse sequence to removal.

35 Rear door lock – removal and refitting

1 Remove the rear door exterior handle as described in Section 34.
2 Release the door inner handle control rod from its plastic guide on the outer face of the door.
3 Carefully prise out the two control rods from their respective levers on the door lock.
4 Disconnect the central locking motor wiring multi-plug, and manipulate the lock assembly from the door.
5 Refitting is the reverse sequence to removal.

36 Rear door interior handle – removal and refitting

The procedure for the rear door is virtually identical to that for the front door, and reference should be made to Section 28.

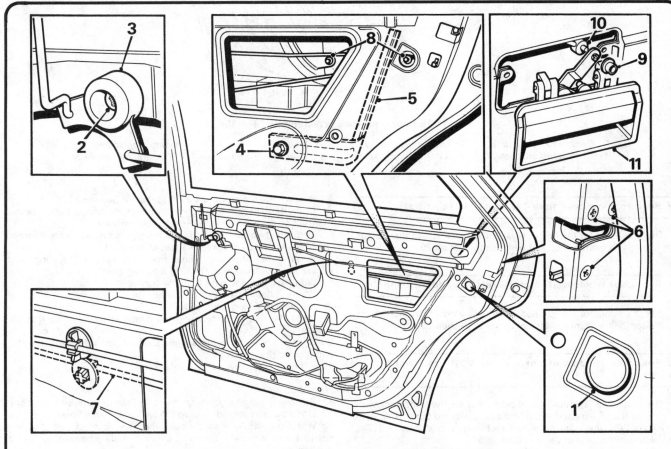

Fig. 11.15 Rear door exterior handle attachments (Sec 34)

1 Access plug	4 Rear glass channel retaining bolt	7 Control rod and guide	9 Collar
2 Bellcrank retaining screw	5 Rear glass channel	8 Exterior handle retaining bolts	10 Trunnion
3 Bellcrank	6 Lock retaining screws		11 Exterior handle

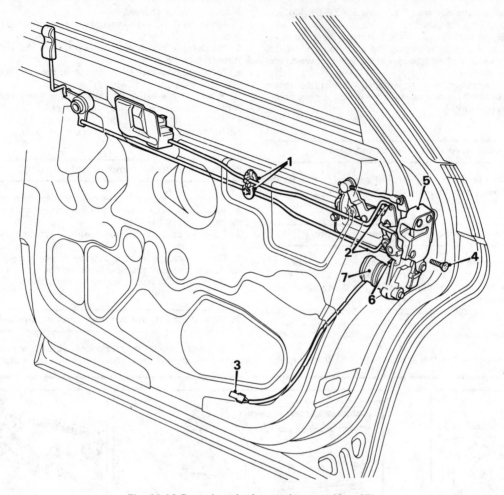

Fig. 11.16 Rear door lock attachments (Sec 35)

1	*Control rod and guide*	3	*Wiring multi-plug*	5	*Door lock*		*retaining screws*
2	*Control rod attachments*	4	*Lock retaining screws*	6	*Central locking motor*	7	*Central locking motor*

37 Rear door window glass – removal and refitting

The procedure for the rear door is virtually identical to that for the front door, and reference should be made to Section 29.

38 Rear door window lift motor – removal and refitting

The procedure for the rear door is virtually identical to that for the front door, and reference should be made to Section 30.

39 Rear door window lift manual regulator – removal and refitting

The procedure is virtually identical to that for the front door with electric lift motor, except that the regulator is secured to the door with two bolts, and there are no wiring multi-plugs to disconnect. The complete procedure is covered in Section 30.

40 Bumpers – removal and refitting

Front bumper
1 Refer to Chapter 12 and remove the headlamp lens units, and where fitted, the headlamp washer jets.

2 Remove the radiator grille as described in Section 21.
3 Undo the bolt and two screws securing the access panels below the front of each wheel arch. Remove both panels.
4 Undo the two nuts securing the bumper moulding to the frame at the front. Withdraw the washers and clamp plates.
5 Release the wheel arch liner from the bumper moulding, and release the moulding from the side retaining clips.
6 Withdraw the moulding from the bumper.
7 Where fitted, release the washer pipe clips and studs, and disconnect the wiring multi-plug.
8 Undo the two bolts securing the centre support member to the bumper.
9 Undo the two end bolts securing the bumper to the frame (photo) and remove the bumper.
10 Refitting is the reverse sequence to removal.

Rear bumper
11 Remove the plastic trim from the rear of the luggage compartment.
12 Undo the screws and remove the two wheel arch liners.
13 Withdraw the grommets from the rear face of the luggage compartment, and undo the two bumper moulding retaining nuts and washers.
14 Release the moulding from the side retaining clips, and withdraw the moulding from the bumper.
15 Remove the plastic cover over the rear towing eye.
16 Withdraw the grommets, and undo the two bolts each side securing the bumper to the frame (photo).
17 Remove the bumper from the car.
18 Refitting is the reverse sequence to removal.

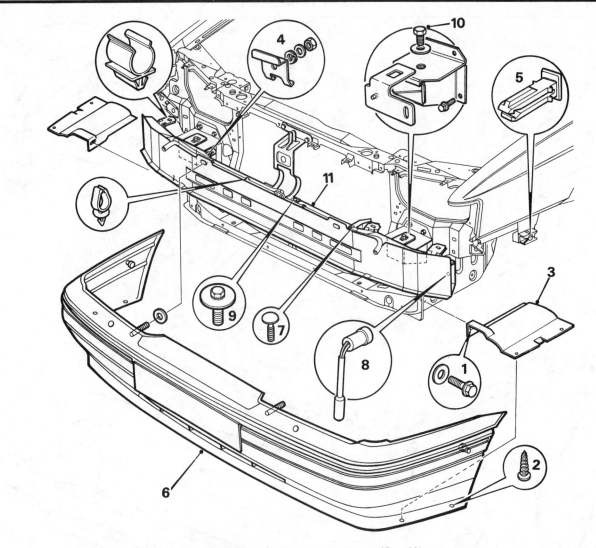

Fig. 11.17 Front bumper components (Sec 40)

1	Access panel retaining bolt	4 Bumper moulding clamp	7 Stud	10 Bumper retaining bolts
2	Access panel retaining screws	5 Bumper moulding side clips	8 Wiring multi-plug	11 Bumper mounting
3	Access panel	6 Bumper moulding	9 Centre support member bolts	

40.9 Front bumper retaining bolt

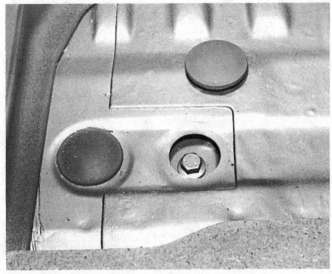

40.16 Rear bumper retaining bolt and cover grommet

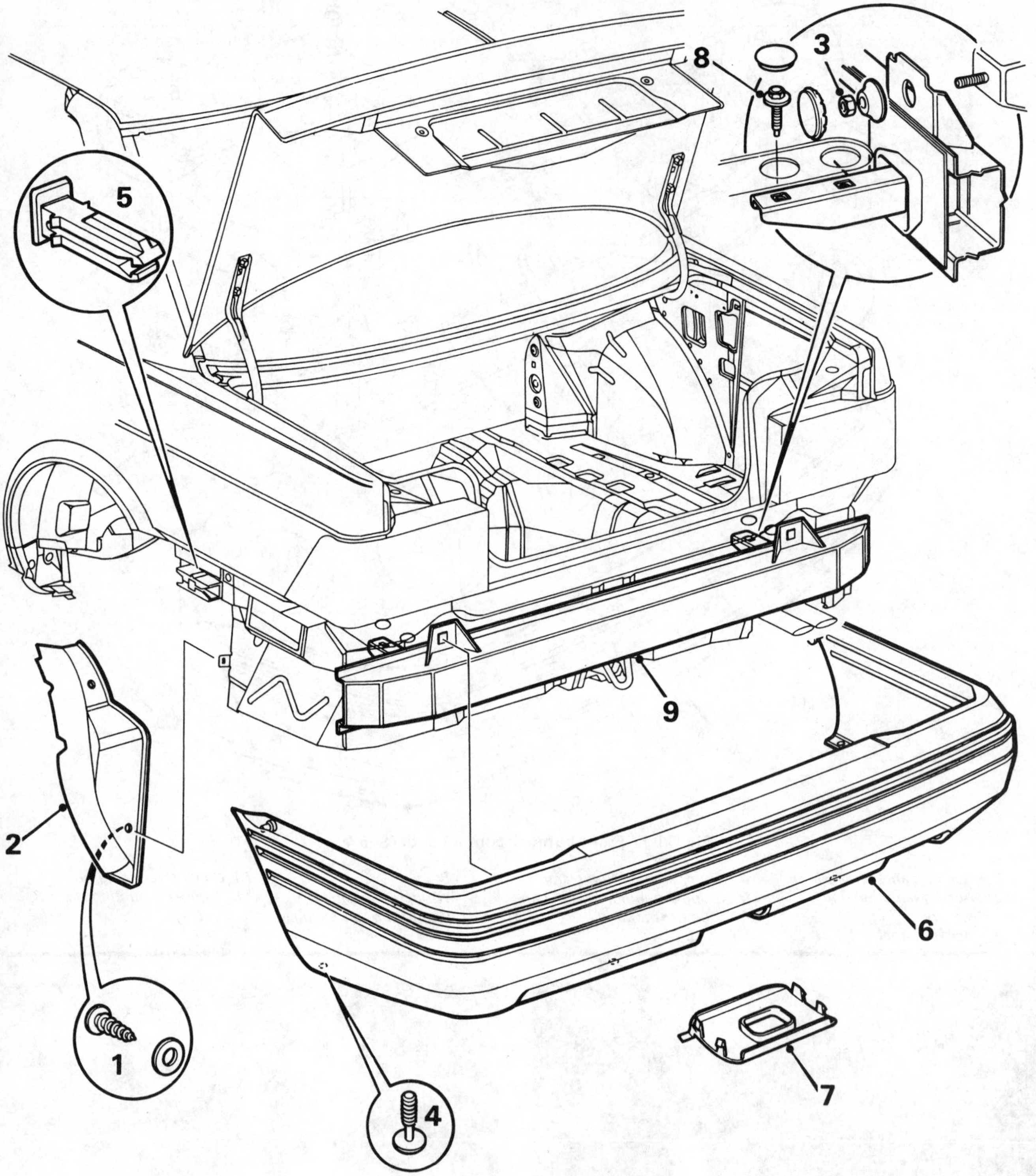

Fig. 11.18 Rear bumper components (Sec 40)

1   Wheel arch liner screws
2   Wheel arch liner
3   Bumper moulding nuts and
    grommets

4   Bumper moulding retaining
    bolts
5   Bumper moulding retaining
    clips

6   Bumper moulding
7   Towing eye cover

8   Bumper mounting bolts and
    grommets
9   Bumper mounting

41 Front seats – removal and refitting

1 Carefully prise off the trim caps, and undo the two screws securing the trim panel below the seat base. Remove the trim panel.
2 Undo the bolt securing the seat belt at the base of the seat.
3 Undo the four bolts securing the seat runners.
4 Undo the bolt securing the seat belt stalk, and remove the stalk.
5 Withdraw the seat from the car.
6 Refitting is the reverse sequence to removal.

42 Rear seats – removal and refitting

Saloon models
1 Push the seat base rearwards, and at the same time lift it up at the front to release the two retainers. Remove the seat base from the car.
2 Undo the four bolts at the base of the seat squab.
3 Release the two seat belts from the retainers.
4 Slide the squab downwards and forwards to release the rear locating pegs, then remove the squab from the car.
5 Refitting is the reverse sequence to removal.

Fastback models
6 Push the seat base rearwards, and at the same time lift it up at the front to release the two retainers. Remove the seat base from the car.
7 Undo the bolt at the base of each side cushion extension, lift the cushion extensions upwards to release the rear wire retainers, and remove the side cushions (photo).
8 Operate the release levers and tip the two seat squabs forward.
9 Undo the two bolts securing the hinge brackets at the ends of each squab (photo).
10 Release the seat belt stalks and remove the squabs from the car.
11 Refitting is the reverse sequence to removal.

43 Rear seat squab release lever and cable (Fastback models) – removal and refitting

1 Remove the luggage compartment lamp from the release lever surround.
2 Undo the screw in the lamp aperture, move the release lever surround forwards and outwards, then disengage the two rear locating lugs (photos).
3 Extract the outer cable retaining clip at the rear of the lever surround (photo).
4 Disengage the inner cable from the release lever, and remove the lever and surround assembly.
5 Extract the outer cable retaining clip at the squab locking mechanism (photo).
6 Disengage the inner cable from the lever, and remove the cable from the car.
7 Refitting is the reverse sequence to removal.

44 Seat belts – removal and refitting

Front seat belts
1 Move the front seat rearwards as far as it will go.
2 Carefully prise off the lower trim from the centre door pillar.
3 Undo the bolt at the seat belt anchorage.
4 Remove the trim cap over the top anchorage, undo the retaining bolt and recover the spacer and fibre washer.
5 Undo the retaining screw and remove the belt guide.
6 Undo the bolt at the base of the inertia reel, and remove the seat belt components.
7 Undo the bolt securing the seat belt stalk to the seat, and remove the stalk.
8 Refitting is the reverse sequence to removal.

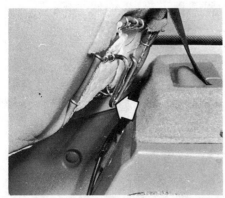

42.7 Release the side cushion wire retainer (arrowed)

42.9 Undo the hinge bracket bolts

43.2A Undo the release lever surround retaining screw ...

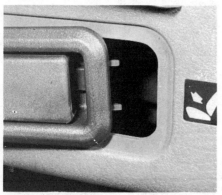

43.2B ... and disengage the locating lugs

43.3 Extract the outer cable retaining clip (arrowed) at the lever surround ...

43.5 ... and the clip at the locking mechanism (arrowed)

Rear seat belts

9   Remove the rear seat base and squab as described in Section 42.
10 Undo the bolt at the seat belt anchorage.
11 Remove the belt guide from the rear parcel shelf.
12 Remove the trim cap over the top anchorage, undo the retaining bolt and recover the spacer and fibre washer.
13 From within the luggage compartment, undo the bolt at the base of the inertia reel, and remove the seat belt assembly from the luggage compartment.
14 Undo the retaining bolts and remove the individual static belts as required.
15 Refitting is the reverse sequence to removal.

45 Sunroof – general

A mechanically operated steel sunroof is available as standard or optional equipment according to model.

The sunroof is maintenance-free, but any adjustment or removal and refitting of the component parts should be entrusted to a dealer, due to the complexity of the unit and the need to remove much of the interior trim and headlining to gain access. The latter operation is involved, and requires care and specialist knowledge to avoid damage.

46 Centre console – removal and refitting

1   On manual gearbox models, unscrew the gear lever knob and remove the gear lever boot (photo).
2   On automatic transmission models, undo the retaining screw and lift off the selector lever. Carefully prise up the selector lever quadrant, disconnect the wiring multi-plugs and remove the quadrant.
3   Prise up the coin trays (photo) or switch panels on each side of the handbrake lever. Remove the coin trays, or disconnect the multi-plugs and remove the switch panels.
4   Insert a screwdriver under the rear end of the cover trim over the handbrake lever. Prise up the cover rear end, then withdraw the cover

from the handbrake lever (photo).
5   Lift back the edges of the carpet under the coin holder or switch panel locations, and undo the two console retaining bolts under the carpet (photo).
6   Remove the rear ashtray, followed by the ashtray insert, then undo the two screws securing the rear of the console (photos).
7   Open the cassette holder lid, and undo the two screws at the base of the cassette racks (photo).
8   Apply the handbrake as hard as possible, then lift the rear of the console over the handbrake lever (photos). Slide the forward end of the console out from under the facia and remove the console from the car. There is barely sufficient clearance to allow the console to clear the handbrake under normal conditions, and if it proves impossible to do this, refer to Chapter 9 and slacken the handbrake adjuster to allow the lever to be pulled up further.
9   Refitting is the reverse sequence to removal. Adjust the handbrake as described in Chapter 9 if the adjuster position was disturbed.

47 Facia – removal and refitting

1   Remove the instrument panel and the radio cassette player as described in Chapter 12.
2   Release the turnbuckles and remove the trim panel under the facia on the driver's side. Remove the additional panel over the clutch, brake and accelerator pedals (photo).
3   Release the heater outer cable retaining clips on the lower right-hand side of the heater, and slip the inner cable ends off the lever studs (photo).
4   Pull off the control knobs on the heater control switches (photo).
5   Undo the two nuts and two bolts securing the steering column clamp and mounting bracket under the facia. Remove the clamp and lower the column.
6   Release the retaining button and withdraw the triangular-shaped trim panels at the base of the lower facia (photo).
7   Undo the retaining screw on each side now exposed, securing the lower facia side braces to the support bracket (photo).
8   Using a screwdriver, release the radio mounting plate side retainers

46.1 Unscrew the gear lever knob

46.3 Prise up the coin trays

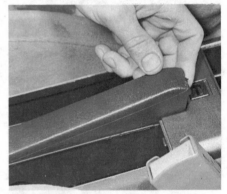
46.4 Lift up the handbrake lever cover trim at the rear

46.5 Console left-hand retaining bolt (arrowed)

46.6A Remove the rear ashtray ...

46.6B ... and undo the two rear screws

and remove the mounting plate (photos).

9 Undo the two screws at the base of the oddments tray below the digital clock (photo).

10 Withdraw the clock and oddments tray housing from the lower facia, and disconnect the clock wiring multi-plug (photo).

11 Undo the two upper screws securing the lower facia, and withdraw the lower facia from its location (photos).

12 Disconnect the wiring multi-plug at the rear (photo), and remove the lower facia from the car.

13 Undo the screw at each end of the cross-brace under the facia on the driver's side (photo).

14 Undo the bolt at each lower end of the facia (photo).

15 Undo the two bolts on the front support plate at the base of the console (photo).

16 Lift up the cover plate on the console top, at the centre below the windscreen (photo), and undo the bolt below the plate (photo).

17 Prise out the trim caps at each side of the console, adjacent to the door apertures, and undo the bolt behind (photos).

18 With the help of an assistant, lift the console from its location and withdraw it into the passenger compartment.

19 Disconnect the wiring multi-plug at the inertia switch, and at the fusebox, and disconnect the two main loom multi-plugs (photos).

20 With all the wiring disconnected, remove the facia from the car (photo).

21 Refitting is the reverse sequence to removal. When connecting the heater cables, adjust the position of the outer cables in their retaining clips so as to give full travel of the heater levers, consistent with full travel of the control levers.

46.7 Undo the two screws at the base of the cassette rack

46.8A Apply the handbrake fully

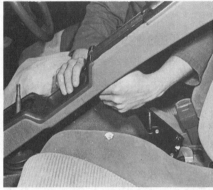

46.8B ... and lift the console over the handbrake

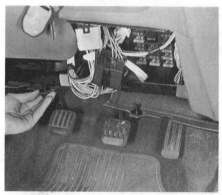

47.2 Remove the trim panel under the facia

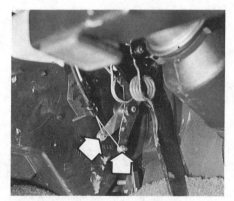

47.3 Release the heater cables at the heater (arrowed)

47.4 Pull off the heater knobs

47.6 Withdraw the trim panel at the base of the lower facia

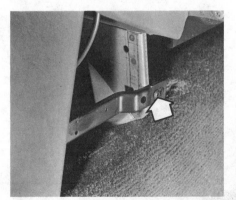

47.7 Undo the side brace retaining screws (arrowed)

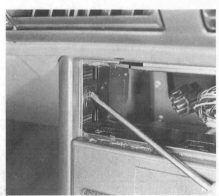

47.8A Release the radio mounting plate retainers ...

47.8B ... and remove the mounting plate

47.9 Undo the screws in the oddments tray

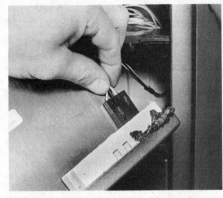
47.10 Disconnect the clock wiring multi-plug

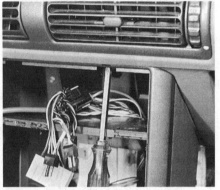
47.11A Undo the lower facia upper screws ...

47.11B ... and remove the lower facia

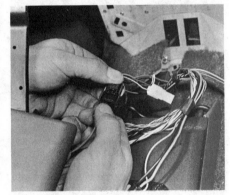
47.12 Disconnect the lower facia multi-plug

47.13 Undo the cross-brace screws

47.14 Undo the bolt at the facia lower end

47.15 Undo the front support plate bolts (arrowed)

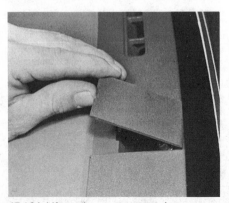
47.16A Lift up the centre cover plate ...

47.16B ... and undo the retaining bolt

47.17A Prise out the trim caps ...

47.17B ... and undo the bolts in the door apertures

47.19A Disconnect the inertia switch wiring ...

47.17B ... the fusebox multi-plug ...

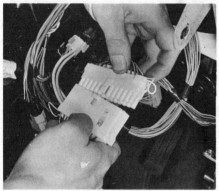

47.19C ... the large main wiring multi-plug

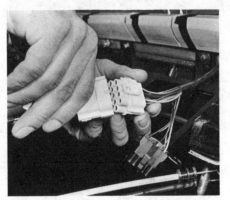

47.19D ... and the smaller main wiring multi-plug

47.20 Withdraw the facia with the help of an assistant

48 Heater blower motor and housing assembly – removal and refitting

1 Disconnect the battery negative terminal. (Refer to Chapter 12, Section 1, before doing this).
2 Remove the trim panel under the facia on the passenger's side.
3 Open the glovebox, undo the two screws securing the glovebox bar, and remove the glovebox.
4 Disconnect the air duct from the side of the unit, and recover the seals.
5 Release the screw cap and undo the facia retaining bolt at the extreme end, adjacent to the door aperture.
6 Disconnect the blower motor wiring multi-plug (photo).
7 Disconnect the vacuum hose at the solenoid (photo).
8 Undo the two upper bolts and one lower nut securing the heater housing assembly in position, and remove the unit from under the facia (photos).

9 Refitting is the reverse sequence to removal.

49 Heater blower motor – removal and refitting

1 Remove the assembly from the car as described in Section 48.
2 Extract the clips securing the two halves of the housing assembly, and lift off the upper half.
3 Remove the separator plate.
4 Undo the nut and remove the fan from the motor.
5 Disconnect the cooling hose and wiring multi-plug from the side of the motor.
6 Undo the motor retaining nuts, withdraw the motor and collect the gasket.
7 Refitting is the reverse sequence to removal.

48.6 Blower motor wiring multi-plug

48.7 Solenoid vacuum hose (arrowed)

48.8A Undo the two upper bolts (arrowed) ...

48.8B ... and lower nut (arrowed)

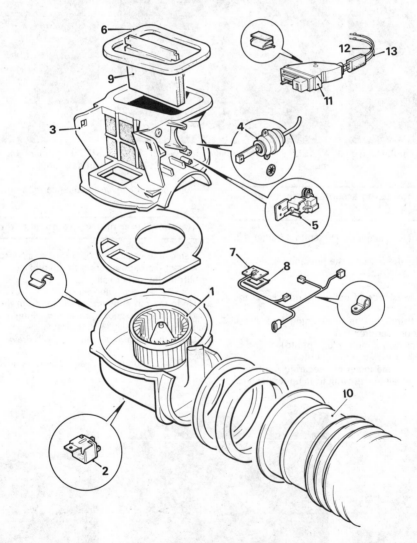

Fig. 11.19 Exploded view of the heater blower motor housing assembly (Sec 48)

1	Fan	5	Vacuum solenoid	8	Gasket	11 Control assembly
2	Relay	6	Seal	9	Air flap	12 Distribution cable
3	Air box	7	Harness	10	Air duct	13 Temperature cable
4	Vacuum actuator					

50 Heater vacuum servo unit – removal and refitting

1 Disconnect the battery negative terminal. (Refer to Chapter 12, Section 1, before doing this).
2 Remove the trim panel under the facia on the passenger's side.
3 Open the glovebox, undo the two screws securing the glovebox bar, and remove the glovebox.
4 Disconnect the air duct from the side of the heater blower assembly, and recover the two seals.
5 Disconnect the vacuum hose at the servo unit.
6 Extract the retaining spire clip, and release the servo arm from the heater lever.
7 Undo the two screws and remove the servo from the heater assembly.
8 Refitting is the reverse sequence to removal.

51 Heater solenoid valve – removal and refitting

1 Disconnect the battery negative terminal. (Refer to Chapter 12, Section 1, before doing this).
2 Remove the trim panel under the facia on the passenger's side.
3 Open the glovebox, undo the two screws securing the glovebox bar, and remove the glovebox.
4 Disconnect the air duct from the side of the heater blower assembly, and recover the two seals.
5 Disconnect the vacuum hose at the solenoid valve.
6 Disconnect the solenoid wiring multi-plug.
7 Undo the retaining screw and remove the solenoid from the car.
8 Refitting is the reverse sequence to removal.

52 Heater control unit and cables – removal and refitting

1 Remove the instrument cowl as described in Chapter 12.
2 Remove the trim panel under the facia on the driver's side.
3 Extract the outer cable retaining clips, and slip the cable ends off the heater levers.
4 Withdraw the control unit and cables from the facia.
5 Release the two inner and outer cables from the control unit.
6 Refitting is the reverse sequence to removal. When connecting the heater cables, adjust the position of the outer cables in their retaining clips so as to give full travel of the heater levers, consistent with full travel of the control levers.

53 Heater matrix – removal and refitting

1 Remove the facia as described in Section 47.
2 Drain the cooling system as described in Chapter 2.
3 From within the engine compartment, disconnect the heater hoses at the matrix pipe stubs.

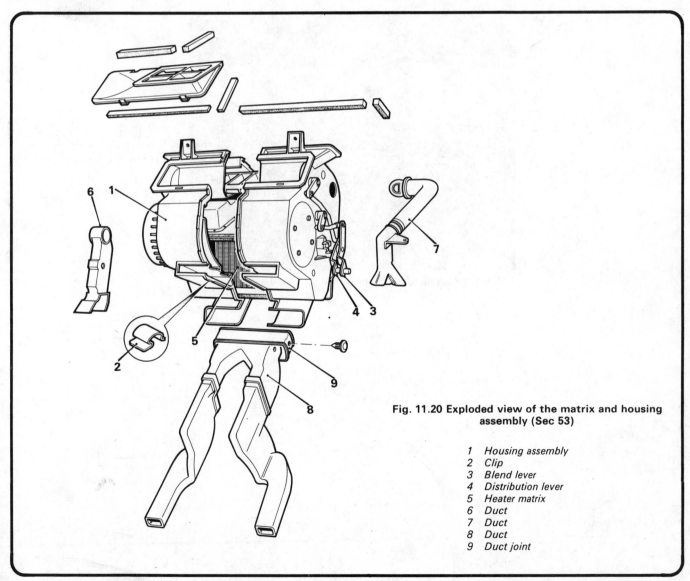

Fig. 11.20 Exploded view of the matrix and housing assembly (Sec 53)

1 Housing assembly
2 Clip
3 Blend lever
4 Distribution lever
5 Heater matrix
6 Duct
7 Duct
8 Duct
9 Duct joint

4   Remove the duct between the heater blower motor assembly and the matrix housing. Collect the two seals.

5   Extract the retaining stud from the driver's side footwell duct and remove the duct.

6   Extract the two studs securing the rear compartment duct to the matrix casing, and slide the duct rearwards.

7   Remove the two retaining clips at the base of the matrix housing.

8   Undo the two upper retaining bolts (photo) and remove the matrix housing from the car.

9   Remove the seal from the top of the housing.

10   Undo the screw and remove the left-hand duct.

11   Release the clips around the upper face aperture, and remove the face panel.

12   Release the clips securing the two halves of the matrix housing, and separate the housing.

13   Remove the matrix

14   Refitting is the reverse sequence to removal.

54 Air conditioning system – precautions and maintenance

1   Air conditioning is available as optional equipment on certain models covered by this manual. Due to the complexity of the system, the need for special equipment to carry out virtually all operations, and the dangers involved in any service or repair procedure, work on the air conditioning system components is considered beyond the scope of this manual. If, however, it is necessary to remove or disconnect a component as part of some other maintenance or repair procedure, observe the following.

2   Never disconnect any part of the air conditioner refrigerant circuit unless the system has been discharged by a dealer or qualified refrigerant engineer.

3   Where the compressor or condenser obstructs other mechanical operations, such as engine removal, it is permissible to unbolt their mountings and move them to the limit of their flexible hose deflection, but **not** to disconnect the hoses. If there is still insufficient room to carry out the required work, then the system must be discharged before disconnecting and removing the assemblies.

4   The system will, of course, have to be recharged on completion.

5   Regularly check the condenser for clogging with flies or dirt. Hose clean with water or compressed air.

6   Check the drivebelt condition, and if necessary adjust, or have it adjusted by a Rover dealer. The belt adjustment procedure requires a special tool to check the deflection, but the procedure is similar to that described in Chapter 12 for the alternator drivebelt.

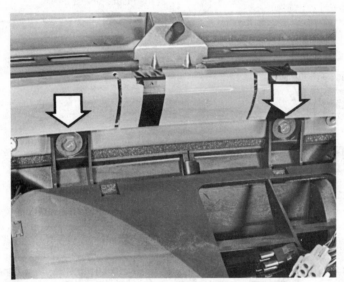

53.8 Matrix housing upper retaining bolts (arrowed)

Chapter 12 Electrical system

Contents

Specifications

System type	12 volt, negative earth
Battery	
Type	Unipart 'sealed for life'
Capacity	54 amp-hour
Performance – cold start current (amps)/reserve capacity (minutes)	480/90
Alternator	
Type	Lucas A127/65
Maximum output	65 amps
Brush length:	
New	20.0 mm (0.8 in)
Minimum	10.0 mm (0.4 in)
Starter motor	
Type	Lucas M78R
Power	1.0 or 1.4 kW

Bulbs

	Wattage
Headlamp dipped beam	60/55
Headlamp main beam	55
Sidelamps	5
Direction indicators	21
Side repeater lamps	5
Stop/tail lamps	21/5
Reversing lamps	21
Rear foglamp	21
Number plate lamps	5
Engine compartment lamp	5
Interior courtesy lamps	10
Map reading and courtesy lamps	4
Footwell and glovebox illumination lamps	5
Luggage compartment lamp	10
Instrument panel illumination and warning lamps	1.2
Ignition warning lamp	2
Switch illumination bulbs	0.36
Heater control illumination bulbs	0.36 and 1.2

Torque wrench settings

	Nm	lbf ft
Alternator pivot bolt	25	18
Alternator adjustment bracket bolts	12	9
Alternator drivebelt idler pulley nut	45	33
Alternator pulley nut	47	35
Starter motor retaining bolts:		
Manual gearbox	85	63
Automatic transmission	45	33

General description

The electrical system is of the 12 volt negative earth type, and consists of a 12 volt battery, alternator, starter motor and related electrical accessories, components and wiring. The battery is of the maintenance-free 'sealed for life' type, and is charged by an alternator which is belt-driven from the crankshaft pulley. The starter motor is of the pre-engaged type, incorporating an integral solenoid. On starting, the solenoid moves the drive pinion into engagement with the flywheel or driveplate ring gear before the starter motor is energised. Once the engine has started, a one-way clutch prevents the motor armature being driven by the engine until the pinion disengages from the ring gear.

Note: *On cars equipped with single-point fuel injection, the idle mixture settings stored in the memory of the fuel system electronic control unit will be lost whenever the battery is disconnected. When the battery is reconnected, the control unit will adopt a set of nominal parameters which will allow the engine to run, but the mixture setting will be outside the manufacturer's specification. Should the engine performance be unsatisfactory, the control unit can be calibrated as a temporary measure using the procedure described in Chapter 3, Section 13, until such time as the setting can be accurately adjusted by a dealer.*

2　Electrical system – precautions

1　It is necessary to take extra care when working on the electrical system to avoid damage to semi-conductor devices (diodes and transistors), and to avoid the risk of personal injury. In addition to the precautions given in *Safety first!* at the beginning of this manual, observe the following when working on the system.

2　*Always remove rings, watches, etc before working on the electrical system.* Even with the battery disconnected, capacitive discharge could occur if a component live terminal is earthed through a metal object. This could cause a shock or nasty burn.

3　*Do not reverse the battery connections.* Components such as the alternator, fuel and ignition control units, or any other having semi-conductor circuitry could be irreparably damaged.

4　If the engine is being started using jump leads and a slave battery, connect the batteries *positive to positive* and *negative to negative*. This also applies when connecting a battery charger.

5　Never disconnect the battery terminals, any electrical wiring or any test instruments, when the engine is running.

6　Never use an ohmmeter of the type incorporating a hand-cranked generator for circuit or continuity testing.

3　Maintenance and inspection

1　At regular intervals, (see *Routine maintenance*) carry out the following maintenance and inspection operations on the electrical system components.

2　Check the operation of all the electrical equipment, ie wipers, washers, lights, direction indicators, horn etc. Refer to the appropriate Sections of this Chapter if any of the components are found to be inoperative.

3　Visually check all accessible wiring connectors, harnesses and retaining clips for security, or signs of chafing or damage. Rectify any problems encountered.

4　Check the alternator drivebelt for cracks, fraying or damage. Renew the belt if worn, or if satisfactory, check and adjust the belt tension as described in Section 6.

5　Check the condition of the wiper blades, and if they show signs of deterioration or fail to clean the screen effectively, renew them as described in Section 37.

6　Check the operation of the windscreen, tailgate and headlamp washers, as applicable and adjust the windscreen or tailgate washers using a pin if necessary. Top up the screen washer reservoir (photo) and check the condition and security of the pump wires and water pipes.

7　Check the battery terminals and if there is any sign of corrosion, disconnect and clean them thoroughly. Smear the terminals and battery posts with petroleum jelly before refitting the plastic covers. If there is any corrosion on the battery tray, remove the battery, clean the deposits away and treat the affected metal with an anti-rust preparation. Repaint the tray in the original colour after treatment.

8　It is advisable to have the headlamp aim adjusted using optical beam setting equipment.

9　When carrying out a road test, check the operation of all the instruments and warning lights, and the various electrical accessories as applicable.

4　Battery – removal and refitting

Note: *Refer to Section 1 before proceeding.*

1　The 'sealed for life' battery is located on the left-hand side of the engine compartment.

3.6 Topping-up the washer reservoir

4.3 Lift off the plastic cover and disconnect the battery positive terminal

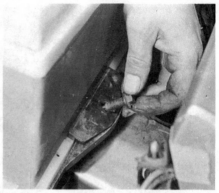

4.4 Removing the battery clamp retaining bolt

2 Slacken the negative (–) terminal clamp bolt and lift the terminal off the battery post.
3 Lift the plastic cover from the positive (+) terminal, slacken the clamp bolt and lift the terminal off the battery post (photo).
4 Undo the retaining bolt and remove the battery clamp plate (photo).
5 Lift the battery out of its tray and remove it from the car.
6 If required, the battery tray can be removed after undoing the three retaining bolts.
7 Refitting is the reverse sequence to removal, but make sure that the positive lead is connected first and the negative lead last. Do not overtighten the clamp bolts.

5 Battery charging

1 In winter, when a heavy demand is placed on the battery, such as when starting from cold and using more electrical equipment, it may be necessary to have the battery fully charged from an external source.
2 Charging should be done overnight, with the battery removed from the car, and at a 'trickle' rate of 1 to 1.5 amps. Owing to the design of certain maintenance-free batteries, rapid or boost charging is not recommended. If in any doubt about the suitability of certain types of charging equipment, consult a dealer or automotive electrical specialist.
3 The terminals of the battery and the leads of the charger must be connected positive to positive and negative to negative.
4 Battery charging must be carried out in a well-ventilated area. Explosive gases are given off as the battery is charged, and every precaution must be taken to avoid naked flames and sparks.

6 Alternator drivebelt – removal, refitting and adjustment

Note: *Accurate adjustment of the drivebelt can only be achieved with a Rover belt tensioning tool, and ideally this operation should be carried out by a dealer. However, if a new belt is to be fitted, or if the existing tension is extremely slack, a rough approximation as a temporary measure can be achieved using the following procedure.*

Cars with a rear-mounted power steering pump

1 Disconnect the battery negative terminal. (Refer to Section 1 before doing this).
2 Slacken the two alternator adjustment bracket bolts and the alternator pivot bolt and nut (photos).
3 Undo the timing belt lower cover retaining bolt below the drivebelt run.
4 Push the alternator in towards the engine and slip the drivebelt off the alternator pulley (photo).
5 Lift the lower edge of the timing belt cover and remove the belt from the crankshaft pulley.
6 Check the drivebelt for signs of fraying, splitting of the internal ribs, a build-up of rubber within the rib grooves, oil contamination, or general deterioration. Renew the belt if any of these conditions are evident.
7 Fit the new drivebelt over the pulleys, then lever the alternator away from the engine until the drivebelt is moderately tight. The alternator must only be levered with care at the drive end bracket. Hold the alternator in this position and tighten the adjustment bracket bolts.
8 Refit the timing belt lower cover bolt.
9 Check that it is just possible to twist the belt by hand through 90° at a point midway between the two pulleys. If necessary, slacken the adjustment bracket bolts and re-adjust the belt tension. When the tension is correct, tighten the pivot bolt and nut.
10 Reconnect the battery, then run the engine at a fast idle for five minutes. Switch off, recheck the tension and re-adjust if necessary.

Cars with a front-mounted power steering pump

11 Disconnect the battery negative terminal. (Refer to Section 1 before doing this).
12 Jack up the front of the car and support it on axle stands.
13 Slacken the nut in the centre of the idler pulley, then turn the adjuster bolt anti-clockwise until all tension is removed from the belt (photo).
14 Slip the belt off the crankshaft, alternator, power steering pump and idler pulleys, and remove it from under the car.
15 Check the drivebelt for signs of fraying, splitting of the internal ribs, a build-up of rubber within the rib grooves, oil contamination, or

6.2A Alternator adjustment bracket bolts (arrowed) ...

6.2B ... and pivot bolt retaining nut (arrowed)

6.4 Slip the drivebelt off the alternator pulley

6.13 Drivebelt adjuster bolt (arrowed) on cars with a front-mounted power steering pump

general deterioration. Renew the belt if any of these conditions are evident.

16 Fit a new drivebelt over the pulleys, then turn the adjuster bolt clockwise until it is just possible to twist the belt by hand through 90° at a point midway between the crankshaft and power steering pump pulleys.

17 Tighten the idler pulley retaining nut and lower the car to the ground.

18 Reconnect the battery, then run the engine for five minutes at a fast idle. Switch off, recheck the tension and repeat the adjustment procedure if necessary.

7 Alternator – removal and refitting

1 Remove the drivebelt as described in Section 6.

2 Undo the two nuts and remove the alternator rear cover.

3 Disconnect the electrical leads at the rear of the alternator (photo).

4 On cars with a rear-mounted power steering pump, remove the previously-slackened pivot bolt and adjustment arm bolt, then withdraw the alternator from the engine.

5 On cars with a front-mounted power steering pump, undo the alternator upper and lower mounting bolts, and remove the unit from the engine.

6 Refitting is the reverse sequence to removal, but adjust the drivebelt, as described in Section 6, before tightening the adjustment and mounting bolts.

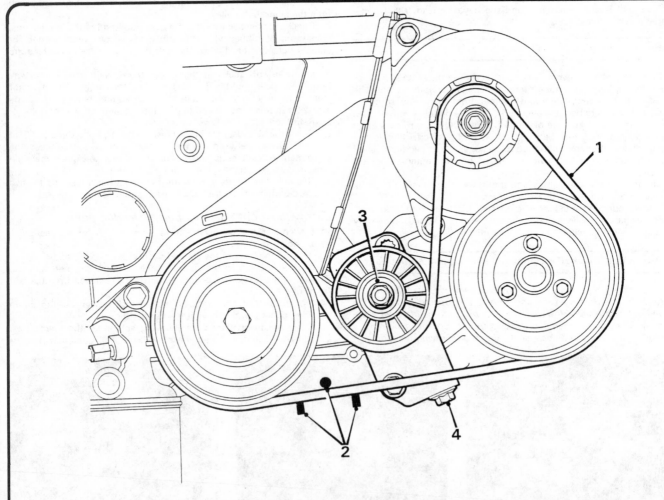

Fig. 12.1 Alternator drivebelt adjustment on cars with a front-mounted power steering pump (Sec 6)

1   Drivebelt   2   Checking gauge – Rover   3   Idler pulley retaining nut   4   Adjuster bolt
                        special tool

7.3 Disconnect the alternator electrical leads (arrowed)

8 Alternator – fault tracing and rectification

Due to the specialist knowledge and equipment required to test or repair an alternator, it is recommended that, if the performance is suspect, the car be taken to an automobile electrician who will have the facilities for such work. Because of this recommendation, information is limited to the inspection and renewal of the brushes and renewal of the voltage regulator. Should the alternator not charge, or the system be suspect, the following points should be checked before seeking further assistance:

(a) Check the drivebelt condition and tension
(b) Ensure that the battery is fully charged
(c) Check the ignition warning light bulb, and renew it if blown

9 Alternator brushes and regulator – removal, inspection and refitting

1 Remove the alternator as described in Section 9.
2 Undo the three small screws securing the regulator and brushbox assembly to the rear of the alternator (photo).
3 Tip the assembly upwards at the edge, and withdraw it from its location. Disconnect the wiring terminal and remove the regulator and brushbox from the alternator (photos).
4 Measure the brush length (photo) and renew the brushbox and

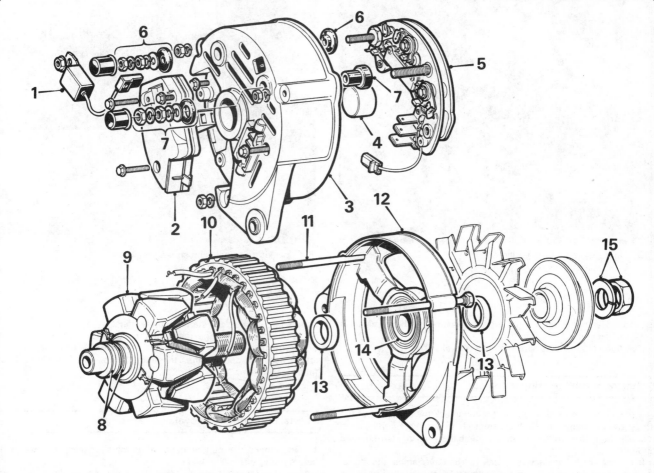

Fig. 12.2 Exploded view of the Lucas A127/65 alternator (Sec 9)

1 Suppression capacitor	6 Phase terminal attachments and insulating washers	9 Rotor assembly	13 Spacers
2 Regulator and brushbox		10 Stator	14 Drive end bearing
3 Slip ring end bracket	7 Main terminal attachments and insulating washers	11 Through-bolts	15 Pulley retaining nut and washer
4 Slip ring end bearing		12 Drive end bracket	
5 Rectifier pack	8 Slip rings		

9.2 Undo the regulator and brushbox retaining screws

9.3A Withdraw the regulator and brushbox ...

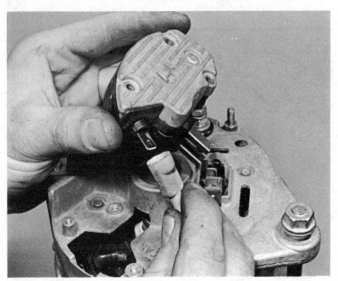

9.3B ... and disconnect the wiring

9.4 Checking alternator brush length

regulator assembly if the brushes are worn below the figure given in the Specifications.

5   Refitting is the reverse sequence to removal.

10 Starter motor – testing in the car

1   If the starter motor fails to operate, first check the condition of the battery by switching on the headlamps. If they glow brightly, then gradually dim after a few seconds, the battery is in a discharged condition.

2   If the battery is satisfactory, check the battery clamps, the starter motor main terminal and the engine earth cable for security. Check the terminal connections on the starter solenoid, located on top of the starter motor, for tightness.

3   If the starter still fails to turn, use a voltmeter, or 12 volt test lamp and leads, to ensure that there is battery voltage at the solenoid main terminal (containing the cable from the battery positive terminal).

4   With the ignition switched on and the ignition key in position III, check that voltage is reaching the solenoid terminal with the Lucar

connector, and also the starter main terminal.

5   If there is no voltage reaching the Lucar connector, there is a wiring, relay or ignition switch fault. If voltage is available, but the starter does not operate, then the starter or solenoid is likely to be at fault.

11 Starter motor – removal and refitting

1   Disconnect the battery negative terminal. (Refer to Section 1 before doing this).

2   Refer to Chapter 3 and remove the air cleaner air intake trunking as necessary to provide access to the starter motor.

3   Disconnect the main feed cable and the Lucar spade connector at the solenoid.

4   Undo the starter retaining bolts, then remove the unit from the transmission (photo).

5   Refitting is the reverse sequence to removal, but tighten the retaining bolts to the specified torque.

11.4 Removing the starter motor

12 Starter motor – overhaul

1   Remove the starter motor from the car as described in Section 11.
2   Undo the two nuts and withdraw the commutator end bracket (photo).
3   At the rear of the solenoid, unscrew the nut and lift away the lead from the solenoid 'STA' terminal.
4   Release the rubber grommet from the side of the yoke (photo) and withdraw the brush holder assembly complete with brushes.
5   Withdraw the yoke from the drive end bracket and armature (photo).
6   Undo the two screws and remove the solenoid body from the drive end bracket (photo).
7   Disengage the solenoid plunger from the engaging lever and remove the plunger (photo).
8   Lift the armature out of the reduction gearbox, and remove it from the drive end bracket (photo). Recover the armature drivegear from the gearbox (photo).
9   Release the engaging lever pivot and grommet from the drive end bracket, then withdraw the reduction gearbox, engaging lever and drive assembly from the drive end bracket.
10 Using a suitable tubular drift, tap the thrust collar on the end of the pinion shaft towards the pinion, to expose the jump ring. Prise the

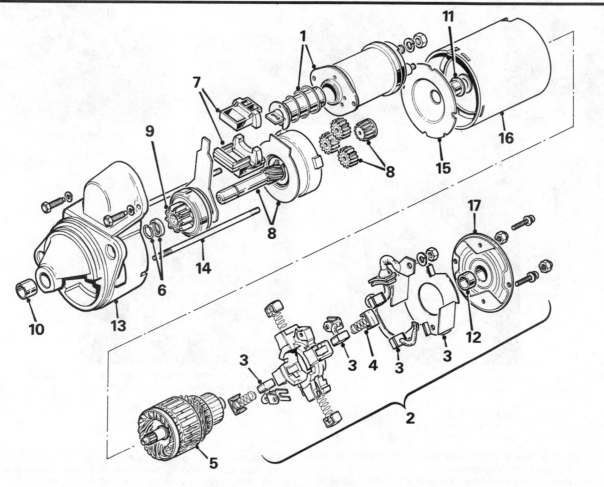

Fig. 12.3 Exploded view of the Lucas M78R starter motor (Sec 12)

1 Solenoid and plunger	6 Jump ring and thrust collar	9 Drive pinion assembly	13 Drive end bracket
2 Commutator end bracket and brush holder assembly	7 Engaging lever pivot and grommet	10 Drive end bracket bush	14 Through-bolts
3 Brushes	8 Pinion shaft and reduction gears	11 Intermediate bracket bush	15 Intermediate bracket
4 Brush springs		12 Commutator end bracket bush	16 Field coil yoke
5 Armature			17 Commutator end bracket

12.2 Withdraw the commutator end bracket

12.4 Release the rubber grommet (arrowed) and remove the brush holder

12.5 Withdraw the yoke

12.6 Remove the solenoid body

12.7 Disengage the solenoid plunger from the engaging lever

12.8A Remove the armature ...

12.8B ... and recover the drivegear

12.15 Using pointed-nose pliers to compress the brushes

jump ring out of its groove and slide it off the shaft. Withdraw the thrust collar and drive pinion assembly.

11 With the starter motor completely dismantled, check the condition of the brushes and the tension of the brush springs. If any appear excessively worn, or if the tension of any of the springs is suspect, renew the brush holder assembly.

12 Check the armature shaft for distortion, and examine the commutator for excessive wear or burns. If necessary, the commutator may be skimmed in a lathe and then polished with fine glass paper.

13 Check the drive pinion assembly, drive end housing, reduction gears, engaging lever and solenoid for wear or damage. Make sure that the drive pinion one-way clutch permits movement of the pinion in one direction only and renew the complete assembly, if necessary.

14 Accurate checking of the armature, commutator and field coil windings and insulation requires the use of special equipment. If the starter motor was inoperative when removed from the car and the previous checks have not highlighted the problem, then it can be assumed that there is a continuity or insulation fault, and the unit should be renewed.

15 If the starter is in a satisfactory condition, or if a fault has been traced and rectified, the unit can be reassembled using the reverse of the dismantling sequence. When refitting the brush holder assembly, carefully compress the brushes one at a time using pointed-nose pliers, tip the holder slightly and ease the brushes over the commutator (photo).

13 Fuses and relays – general

1   Two fuseboxes are used on Rover 820 models. One is located inside the car under the facia on the driver's side, and the other is located on the left-hand side of the engine compartment. The main vehicle system relays are located on a relay panel behind the interior fusebox, and also in the engine compartment fuse and relay box.

Interior fusebox

2   To gain access to the fuses, release the two turnbuckles at the base of the trim panel beneath the steering column, and lift away the panel (photo). The fuse locations, current rating and circuits protected are shown on a label attached to the inside of the panel (photo). Each fuse is also colour-coded, and has its rating stamped on it.

3   To remove a fuse from its location, withdraw the removal tool from the centre of the fusebox, push the tool over the fuse to be removed and pull out the fuse (photos). Refit the fuse by pressing it firmly into position. Spare fuses are located in a vertical row on the right-hand side of the fusebox.

4   Always renew the fuse with one of an identical rating. Never renew a fuse more than once without finding the source of the trouble.

5   To gain access to the relays behind the fusebox, undo the two fusebox retaining bolts, one at each end, and ease the unit away from its location. For greater access, mark the various wiring multi-plugs to avoid confusion when refitting, then disconnect them and remove the fusebox completely.

6   The fuse and relay locations, and circuits protected are shown in Figs. 12.4 and 12.5.

7   The relays can be removed by simply pulling them from their respective locations. If a system controlled by a relay becomes inoperative, and the relay is suspect, operate the system and if the relay is functioning it should be possible to hear it click as it is energised. If this is the case, the fault lies with the components of the system. If the relay is not being energised, then the relay is either not receiving a main supply voltage, a switching voltage, or the relay itself is faulty.

Engine compartment fuse and relay box

8   The engine compartment fuse and relay box contains additional fuses, some of the vehicle system relays, and the main wiring loom fusible links.

9   To gain access, press the upper edge of the retaining catch on the fuse and relay box cover, lift the cover at the front and disengage the rear tags (photo). A symbol identifying the function of each fuse is marked on the cover.

10   The fuses and relays can be renewed in the same way as for the interior fusebox described previously. The fuse removal tool, together with the spare fuses, is located at the front of the box. On certain models, additional fuses and relays are located on the outside edge of the box, with the fuses under a protective cover. Lift off the cover to renew each individual fuse (photo).

11   To gain access to the wiring loom fusible links, lift off the protective cover on the right-hand side of the fuse and relay box (photo). A blown fusible link indicates a serious wiring or system fault, which must be diagnosed before renewing the link.

12   The fuse, relay, and fusible link locations and circuits protected are shown in Figs. 12.6 and 12.7.

14 Direction indicator and hazard flasher system – general

1   The combined direction indicator and hazard flasher unit is located adjacent to the interior fusebox. To remove the unit, release the turnbuckles and lift away the trim panel below the steering column. Pull the flasher unit from its mounting bracket and disconnect the wiring plug. Fit the new unit, then replace the trim cover.

2   Should the flashers become faulty in operation, check the bulbs for security, and make sure that the contact surfaces are not corroded. If one bulb blows, or is making a poor connection due to corrosion, the system will not flash on that side of the car.

3   If the flasher unit operates in one direction and not the other, the fault is likely to be in the bulbs or wiring to the bulbs. If the system will

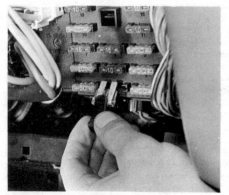
13.2A Lift away the trim panel for access to the fusebox ...

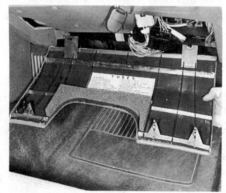
13.2B ... noting the fuse identification on the rear of the panel

13.3A Fuse removal tool location (arrowed)

13.3B Using the tool to remove a fuse

13.9 Removing the engine compartment fuse and relay box cover

13.10 Additional fuse located under a cover on the outside of the fuse and relay box

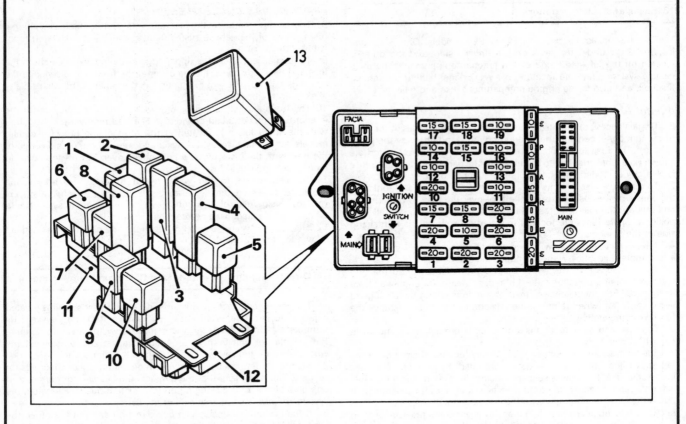

Fig. 12.4 Interior fusebox fuse and relay locations and circuits – pre-1988 models (Sec 13)

Note: *Some fuse and relay locations and circuits may vary from the following, according to model and equipment fitted*

Fuses

Fuse No	Circuit protected
1	Sun roof relays
2	Driver's front window relay
3	Passenger's front window relay
4	Cigar lighter, footwell lamp
5	Interior lamps, radio cassette player, headlamp delay unit, clock
6	Central door locking ECU
7	RH side/tail and number plate lamps, foglamp relay
8	LH side/tail and number plate lamps, panel illumination lamps
9	LH rear window relay
10	RH rear window relay
11	ABS voltage protection relay
12	Fuel ECU (multi-point injection models)
13	Inertia switch, fuel pump, oil pressure relay (single-point injection models)
14	Reversing lamps, direction indicators, instruments, digital clock, interior lamp delay unit
15	Ignition ECU (multi-point injection models), fuel/ignition ECU (single-point injection models)
16	Lighting, cooling fan, headlamp changeover, window lift and air conditioning compressor clutch relays
17	Washer pump, wiper relay
18	Heater relays, air conditioning relays, door mirrors
19	Radio memory, mirror memory

Relays

Relay No	Circuit
1	Wiper motor
2	Rear screen demister timer
3	Headlamp changeover unit
4	Headlamp delay timer
5	Rear window motors
6	Sidelamps
7	Rear foglamps
8	Interior lamps
9	Fuel pump
10	Front window motors
11	Wiper motor delay
12	Central door locking ECU
13	Flasher unit

Additional relays
Window lift control – located in driver's door
Sunroof – located in sunroof frame
ABS over-voltage protection – located in luggage compartment

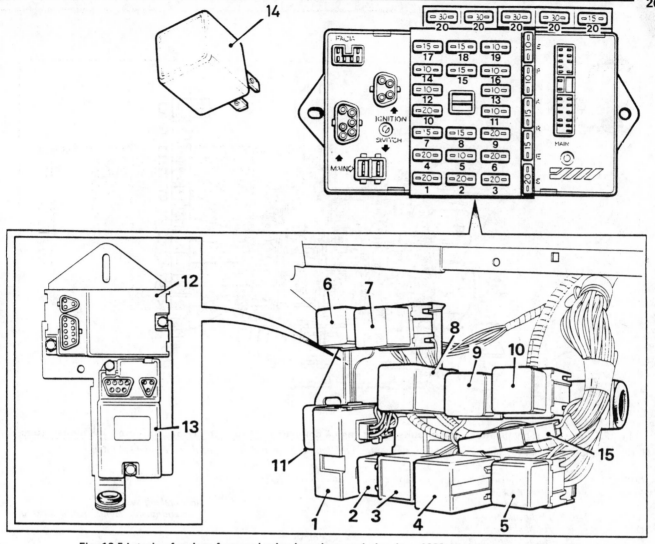

Fig. 12.5 Interior fusebox fuse and relay locations and circuits – 1988 models onwards (Sec 13)

Note: *Some fuse and relay locations and circuits may vary from the following according to model and equipment fitted*

Fuses

Fuse No	Circuit protected
1	Sunroof relays
2	Driver's front window relay
3	Passenger's front window relay
4	Cigar lighter, footwell lamp
5	Interior lamps, radio cassette player, headlamp delay unit, clock
6	Central door locking ECU
7	RH side/tail and number plate lamps, foglamp relay
8	LH side/tail and number plate lamps, panel illumination lamps
9	LH rear window relay
10	RH rear window relay
11	ABS voltage protection relay
12	Fuel ECU (multi-plug injection models)
13	Inertia switch, fuel pump, oil pressure relay (single-point injection models)
14	Reversing lamps, direction indicators, instruments, digital clock, interior lamp delay unit
15	Ignition ECU (multi-point injection models), fuel/ignition ECU (single-point injection models)
16	Lighting, cooling fan, headlamp changeover, window lift and air conditioning compressor clutch relays
17	Washer pump, wiper relay
18	Heater relays, air conditioning relays, door mirrors
19	Radio memory, mirror memory
20	Speaker power amplifier circuit

Relays

Relay No	Circuit
1	Rear wiper/washer timer (Fastback models)
2	Rear window motors
3	Headlamp changeover unit
4	Rear screen demister timer
5	Wiper motor
6	Front window motors
7	Cigar lighter
8	Interior lamp delay
9	Rear foglamps
10	Sidelamps
11	Front window motors
12	Windscreen wiper motor delay unit
13	Central door locking ECU
14	Flasher unit
15	Anti-run-on valve diode

Additional relays

Window lift control – located in driver's door
Sunroof – located in sunroof frame
ABS over-voltage protection – located in luggage compartment

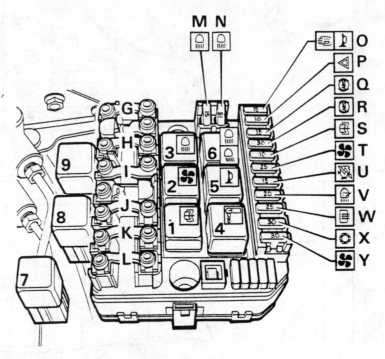

Fig. 12.6 Fuse and relay locations and circuits in the engine compartment fuse and relay box – pre-1988 models (Sec 13)

Note: *Some fuse and relay locations and circuits may vary from the following according to model and equipment fitted*

Fuses

Fuse	Circuit protected
M	RH headlamp
N	LH headlamp
O	Horn, stop-lamp relay
P	Hazard warning lamps
Q	ABS relay
R	ABS modulator
S	Fuel ECU (multi-point injection models)
T	Heater fan motor
U	Fuel/ignition ECU (single-point injection models)
V	Headlamp washer
W	Rear screen demister
X	Air conditioning fan/compressor clutch
Y	Radiator cooling fan

Fusible links	Circuit protected
G	Radio power amplifier
H	Ignition switch circuit
I	Alternator output
J	Window lift circuit
K	ABS braking system
L	Side and interior lamps, central locking

Relays

Relay No	Circuit
1	Cooling fan changeover, or inlet manifold heater (single-point injection models)
2	Radiator cooling fan
3	Lighting circuits
4	Starter solenoid
5	Horns
6	Headlamp main/dipped beams
7	Air conditioning changeover
8	Ignition/fuel ECU
9	Oil pressure transducer (single-point injection models)

Additional relays

Headlamp power wash timer – behind RH headlamp
Air conditioning compressor clutch – behind RH headlamp
ABS return pump – on top of ABS hydraulic modulator
ABS solenoid valve – on top of ABS hydraulic modulator

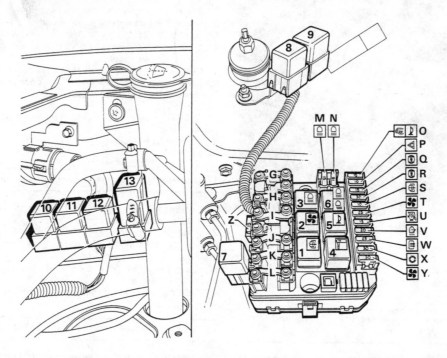

Fig. 12.7 Fuse and relay locations and circuits in the engine compartment fuse and relay box – 1988 models onwards (Sec 13)

Note: *Some fuse and relay locations and circuits may vary from the following according to model and equipment fitted*

Fuses

Fuse	Circuit protected
M	RH headlamp
N	LH headlamp
O	Horn, stop-lamp relay
P	Hazard warning lamps
Q	ABS relay
R	ABS modulator
S	Fuel ECU (multi-point injection models)
T	Heater fan motor
U	Fuel/ignition ECU (single-point injection models)
V	Headlamp washer
W	Rear screen demister
X	Air conditioning fan/compressor clutch
Y	Radiator cooling fan
Z	Headlamp dim/dip relay

Fusible links	Circuit protected
G	Radio power amplifier
H	Ignition switch circuit
I	Alternator output
J	Window lift circuit
K	ABS braking system
L	Side and interior lamps, central locking

Relays

Relay No	Circuit
1	Cooling fan changeover, or inlet manifold heater
2	Radiator cooling fan
3	Lighting circuits
4	Starter solenoid
5	Horns
6	Headlamp main/dipped beams
7	Air conditioning changeover
8	Inlet manifold heater (single-point injection models)
9	Ignition/fuel ECU

Additional relays

10 Fuel pump and oil pressure switch – RH headlamp
11 Not used on 820 models
12 Headlamp dim/dip – behind RH headlamp
13 Not used on 820 models

13.11 Lift off the protective cover for access to the fusible links

not flash in either direction, operate the hazard flashers. If these function, check for a blown fuse in position 14. If the fuse is satisfactory, renew the flasher unit.

15 Ignition switch/steering column lock – removal and refitting

The ignition switch is an integral part of the steering column lock, and removal and refitting procedures are given in Chapter 10.

16 Steering column switches – removal and refitting

1   Disconnect the battery negative terminal. (Refer to Section 1 before doing this).
2   Remove the steering wheel as described in Chapter 10.
3   Undo the three lower screws and the single upper screw, and remove the upper and lower steering column shrouds (photos).
4   Release the fibre optic lead from the bulbholder by carefully prising up the plastic tag (photo).
5   Depress the retainers at the top and bottom of the switch, then pull the switch out of the steering column boss (photos).
6   Disconnect the wiring multi-plug and remove the switch from the car.
7   The switch on the other side of the column is removed in the same way.
8   Refitting is the reverse sequence to removal.

17 Centre console switches – removal and refitting

1   Carefully prise up the coin holder or switch panel as applicable from the side of the centre console.
2   If individual switches are fitted, disconnect the wiring multi-plug, depress the lugs on the side of the switch and withdraw the switch from the coin holder panel (photo).
3   If a multi-switch pack is fitted, disconnect the wiring multi-plug and remove the switch panel complete.
4   Refitting is the reverse sequence to removal.

18 Door switches – removal and refitting

1   Remove the front or rear door inner trim panel as described in Chapter 11.

16.3A Undo the three lower screws ...

16.3B ... and single upper screw ...

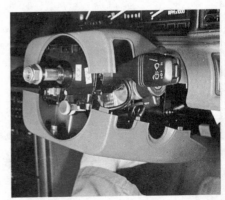

16.3C ... then lift off the steering column shrouds

16.4 Release the fibre optic lead from the bulbholder

16.5A Depress the top and bottom switch retainers ...

16.5B ... and remove the switch

2 Release the switch pack assemblies from the rear of the trim panel and carefully withdraw them. Note that the individual switches in the switch packs cannot be removed separately. If any are faulty, or if renewal of a switch is necessary for any reason, the complete switch pack must be obtained.

3 Refitting is the reverse sequence to removal.

19 Courtesy lamp door pillar switches – removal and refitting

1 Disconnect the battery negative terminal. (Refer to Section 1 before doing this).

2 Undo the retaining screw and withdraw the switch from the door pillar (photo).

3 Disconnect the wiring and remove the switch. Tie the wiring to the door striker plate while the switch is removed to prevent the wires dropping into the pillar.

4 Refitting is the reverse sequence to removal.

20 Instrument cowl and switch units – removal and refitting

1 Disconnect the battery negative terminal. (Refer to Section 1 before doing this).

2 Carefully prise out the cover plate at the extreme left-hand side of the cowl and undo the screw now exposed (photos).

3 Pull off the knobs on the heater and air conditioning controls as applicable (photo).

4 Undo the three screws securing the cowl to the facia above the instrument panel (photo).

5 Undo the two screws below the vent panel on the driver's side (photo) and the two screws below the heater control panel (photo).

6 Ease the cowl away from the facia slightly, and disconnect the switch panel and heater control wiring multi-plugs (photo).

7 Remove the cowl from the car.

8 If further dismantling is required, undo the four screws and remove the driver's vent panel.

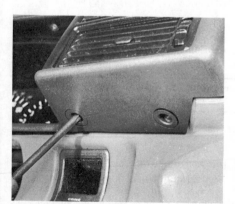
17.2 Centre console switch removal

19.2 Courtesy lamp door pillar switch location

20.2A Prise out the instrument cowl cover plate ...

20.2B ... and undo the screw behind

20.3 Pull off the heater control knobs

20.4 Undo the three screws above the instrument panel (arrowed)

20.5A Undo the two screws below the driver's vent panel ...

20.5B ... and the two screws below the heater controls

20.6 Withdraw the cowl and disconnect the multi-plugs

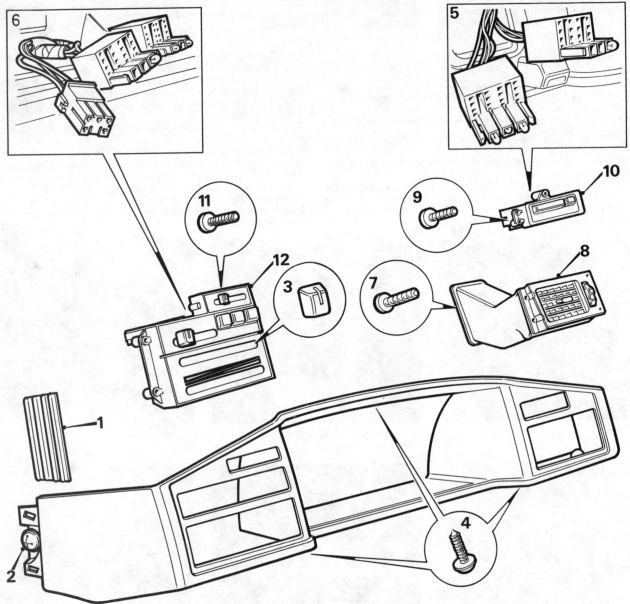

Fig. 12.8 Exploded view of the instrument cowl components (Sec 20)

1   Cover plate
2   Retaining screw
3   Air conditioning and heater
    control knobs
4   Retaining screw locations

5   Switch panel multi-plugs
    and bulbholders
6   Heater and air conditioning
    control multi-plugs and bulb
    holders

7   Vent panel retaining screws
8   Vent panel
9   Switch unit retaining screws
10 Switch unit

11 Heater and air conditioning
    control unit retaining screws
12 Heater and air conditioning
    control unit

9   Undo the three screws and remove the switch unit.
10 Undo the four screws and remove the heater and air conditioning control unit.
11 Refitting is the reverse sequence to removal.

21 Instrument panel – removal and refitting

1   Remove the upper and lower steering column shrouds as described in Section 16.
2   Remove the instrument cowl as described in Section 20.
3   Lower the steering column as far as it will go by means of the rake adjuster.
4   Undo the two screws at each end of the instrument panel (photo).
5   Ease the panel away from the facia, then disconnect the wiring multi-plugs and the earth lead Lucar connector (photos).

6   Remove the instrument panel from the car.
7   Refitting is the reverse sequence to removal.

22 Instrument panel and instruments – dismantling and reassembly

1   Remove the instrument panel from the car as described in Section 21.

Panel illumination and warning lamp bulbs

2   The bulbholders are secured to the rear of the instrument panel by a bayonet fitting, and are removed by turning the holders anti-clockwise (photo). Note that the illumination and warning lamp bulbs are renewed complete with their holders.
3   If a faulty bulb is not accessible, undo the five screws securing the

21.4 Instrument panel right-hand side retaining screws (arrowed)

21.5A Withdraw the instrument panel ...

21.5B ... and disconnect the multi-plugs

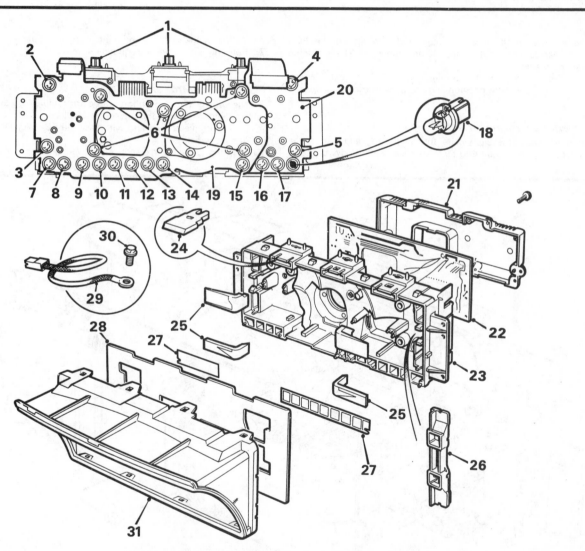

Fig. 12.9 Exploded view of the instrument panel (Sec 22)

1	Panel front illumination bulbs	7	RH direction indicator warning lamp bulb
2	Low oil pressure warning lamp bulb	8	Spare bulb
3	Ignition warning lamp bulb	9	Brake warning lamp bulb
4	High engine temperature warning lamp bulb	10	Spare bulb
5	Low fuel warning lamp bulb	11	ABS warning lamp bulb (where applicable)
6	Panel rear illumination bulb	12	Spare bulb
		13	Spare bulb
		14	Spare bulb

15	Sidelamp warning lamp bulb
16	Main beam warning lamp bulb
17	Trailer direction indicators warning lamp bulb
18	LH direction indicator warning lamp bulb
19	Secondary printed circuit
20	Main printed circuit
21	ECU cover

22	ECU
23	Instrument panel body
24	Front illumination prism
25	Gauge illumination prisms
26	Side housing
27	Warning lamp colour strips
28	Faceplate
29	Earth strap
30	Screw
31	Cowl and faceplate

22.2 Instrument panel warning lamp bulb renewal

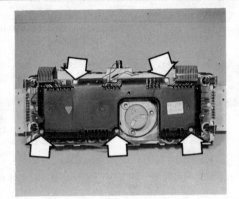

22.3 Instrument panel ECU retaining screws (arrowed)

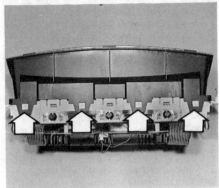

22.5 Instrument panel window upper retaining clips (arrowed)

ECU to the rear of the panel (photo), and carefully lift the ECU upwards. Take care not to strain the ribbon connectors. The remaining bulbs are now accessible.

4 Refit the bulbholders by turning clockwise to lock. Where applicable, lay the ECU in position and secure with the five screws.

Instrument panel window and faceplate

5 Carefully release the eight clips, four at the top and four at the bottom, securing the window to the instrument panel body (photo).

6 Withdraw the window and remove the faceplate.
7 Refitting is the reverse sequence to removal.

Electronic control unit (ECU)

8 Disconnect the two ribbon connector multi-plugs and the centre wiring multi-plug from the top of the ECU.
9 Undo the five screws and withdraw the ECU from the rear of the instrument panel.
10 Refitting is the reverse sequence to removal.

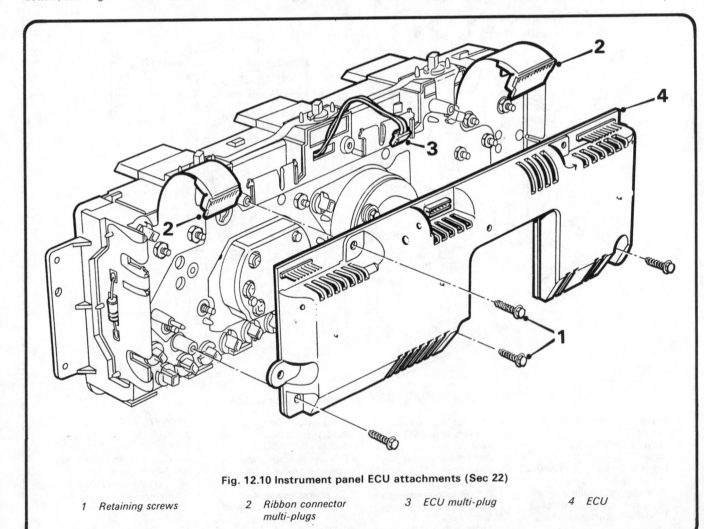

Fig. 12.10 Instrument panel ECU attachments (Sec 22)

| 1 Retaining screws | 2 Ribbon connector multi-plugs | 3 ECU multi-plug | 4 ECU |

Secondary printed circuit

11 Remove the ECU as described previously.
12 Undo the two voltmeter retaining nuts.
13 Remove the bulbholders as applicable.
14 Undo the five printed circuit retaining screws.
15 Release the five retaining studs.
16 Ease the printed circuit off the two locating pins, and remove it from the rear of the panel.
17 Refitting is the reverse sequence to removal.

Main printed circuit

18 Remove the instrument panel window and faceplate, the ECU and the secondary printed circuit as described previously.
19 Withdraw the warning lamp colour strips from the front of the panel.
20 Pull off the trip reset button.
21 Disconnect the ribbon connector from the tachometer by carefully levering off the metal retainer with a small screwdriver. Remove the metal retainer from the ribbon.
22 Remove the bulbholders.
23 Undo the nuts from the gauge studs.
24 Release the two printed circuit retaining studs.
25 Ease the printed circuit off the locating pins, and remove it from the rear of the panel.
26 Refitting is the reverse sequence to removal.

Speedometer

27 Remove the instrument panel window and faceplate, and the ECU as described previously.
28 Undo the three speedometer retaining screws, release the wiring harness and remove the speedometer from the instrument panel.
29 Refitting is the reverse sequence to removal.

Tachometer

30 Remove the instrument panel window and faceplate, and the ECU as described previously.
31 Undo the two tachometer retaining screws.
32 Disconnect the ribbon connector from the tachometer by carefully levering off the metal retainer with a small screwdriver. Remove the metal retainer from the ribbon.
33 Remove the tachometer from the instrument panel.
34 Refitting is the reverse sequence to removal.

Voltmeter, oil pressure, coolant temperature and fuel gauges

35 Remove the instrument panel window and faceplate, and the ECU as described previously.
36 Undo the two retaining nuts and remove the relevant gauge as applicable.
37 Refitting is the reverse sequence to removal.

23 Clock – removal and refitting

1 Disconnect the battery negative terminal. (Refer to Section 1 before doing this).
2 Undo the two screws at the base of the oddment tray opening.
3 Withdraw the oddment tray and disconnect the clock wiring multi-plug.
4 Remove the oddment tray. Undo the two clock retaining screws and remove the clock.
5 Refitting is the reverse sequence to removal.

24 Headlamp and sidelamp bulbs – renewal

Headlamp dipped beam bulb

1 From within the engine compartment, disconnect the wiring multi-plug at the rear of the headlamp bulb (photo), then pull off the rubber cover.

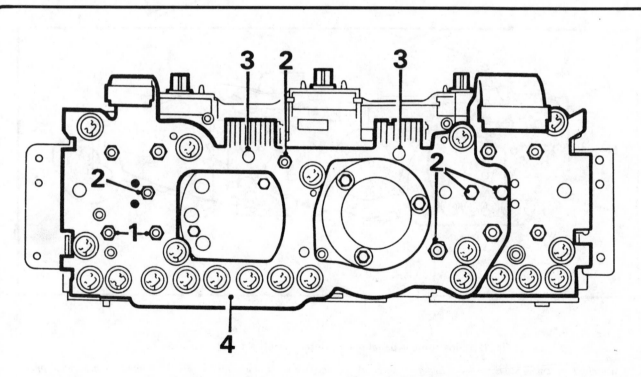

Fig. 12.11 Instrument panel secondary printed circuit attachments (Sec 22)

| 1 Voltmeter retaining nuts | 2 Printed circuit retaining screws | 3 Printed circuit studs | 4 Printed circuit locating pins |

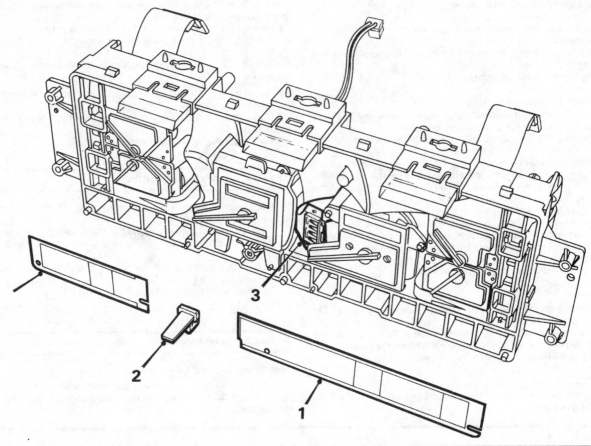

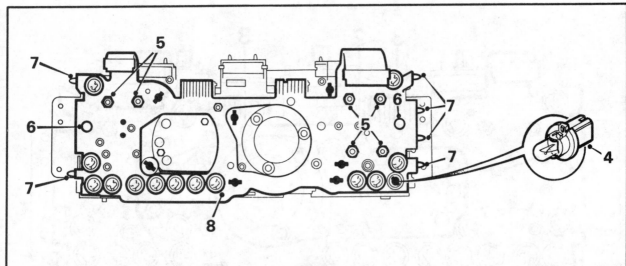

Fig. 12.12 Instrument panel main printed circuit attachments (Sec 22)

1	Warning lamp colour strips	3	Tachometer ribbon	5	Gauge retaining nuts	7	Printed circuit locating pins
2	Trip reset button		connector	6	Printed circuit studs	8	Printed circuit
		4	Bulbholders				

2 Release the wiring retaining clip and withdraw the bulb from its location in the headlamp (photo). Take care not to touch the bulb glass with your fingers; if touched, clean the bulb with methylated spirit.
3 Fit the bulb, ensuring that the lugs in the bulb engage with the slots in the headlamp.
4 Refit the retaining clip, rubber cover and wiring plug. Ensure that the tab marked TOP on the cover is uppermost.

Sidelamp bulb

5 From within the engine compartment, disconnect the wiring multi-plug at the rear of the headlamp bulb, then pull off the rubber cover.
6 Withdraw the sidelamp bulbholder from the headlamp unit (photo) and remove the bulb from the holder.
7 Fit a new bulb to the holder and fit the holder to the headlamp.
8 Refit the rubber cover and headlamp wiring plug. Ensure that the tab marked TOP on the cover is uppermost.

Headlamp main beam bulb

9 Withdraw the plastic cover, release the wire clip and withdraw the bulb from the headlamp (photo). Take care not to touch the bulb glass with your fingers; if touched, clean the bulb with methylated spirit.
10 Disconnect the wiring connectors and remove the bulb.
11 Connect the wiring to the new bulb and place the bulb in the headlamp, ensuring that the flange cut-out locates in the housing ridge.
12 Refit the wire clip and the plastic cover.

25 Front direction indicator bulb – renewal

1 From within the engine compartment, unhook the retaining spring (photo) and withdraw the lens unit and seal from the front wing.
2 Press and turn the bulbholder anti-clockwise to remove it from the

lens unit, then remove the bulb from the holder in the same way (photo).
3 Refit the bulb and holder, locate the lens unit in position and secure with the retaining spring.

26 Direction indicator side repeater bulb – renewal

1 Press the lamp unit to the right, free the left-hand retainer and withdraw the unit from the front wing.
2 Turn the bulbholder anti-clockwise to remove it from the lamp unit, then remove the push-fit bulb from the holder.
3 Fit a new bulb. Refit the bulbholder, and push the lamp unit into position in the wing.

27 Rear lamp cluster bulbs – renewal

1 From within the luggage compartment, press the retainer on the access panel and remove the panel (photo).
2 Lift the top retainer on the bulb panel, press the two bottom retainers and withdraw the panel (photo).
3 Remove the bulbs as required by depressing and turning anti-clockwise (photo).
4 Fit the new bulb(s), push the bulb panel into position and refit the access panel.

28 Number plate lamp bulb – renewal

Saloon models

1 Open the boot lid, turn the bulbholder anti-clockwise and withdraw the bulb and holder (photo).
2 Remove the push-fit bulb from the holder.
3 Refit the bulb and bulbholder.

24.1 Disconnect the headlamp bulb multi-plug

24.2 Headlamp bulb withdrawn

24.6 Sidelamp bulbholder withdrawn

24.9 Headlamp main beam bulb withdrawn

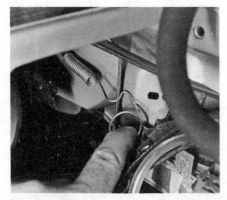

25.1 Unhook the direction indicator lens retaining spring

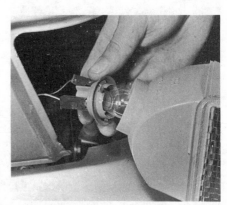

25.2 Withdraw the lens assembly and remove the bulbholder

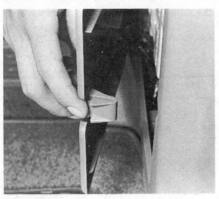

27.1 Press the retainer and remove the access panel

27.2 Remove the rear lamp cluster bulb panel

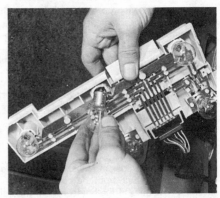

27.3 Rear lamp cluster bulb renewal

Fastback models

4   Open the tailgate, release the plastic retaining screws and remove the inner trim (photo).
5   Turn the bulbholder anti-clockwise (photo) and withdraw.
6   Remove the push-fit bulb from the holder.
7   Refit the bulb, bulbholder and trim.

29 Engine compartment lamp bulb – renewal

1   Open the bonnet, undo the two retaining screws and remove the lamp lens (photo).
2   Push and turn the bulb anti-clockwise to remove it from the holder.
3   Refit the bulb, lens and retaining screws.

30 Interior lamp bulbs – renewal

Interior courtesy lamp

1   Carefully prise the lens from the lamp body using a thin blade (photo).
2   Remove the festoon-type bulb from the contacts (photo).
3   Fit the new bulb and push the lens into place.

Map reading and courtesy lamp

4   Using a small screwdriver, carefully prise the map reading lamp from its housing, then turn the bulb anti-clockwise to remove.
5   Fit the new bulb and push the lens into place.
6   Renewal of the courtesy lamp bulb is the same as described in paragraphs 1 to 3.

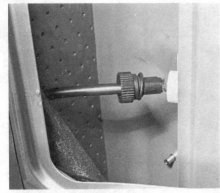

28.1 Number plate lamp bulbholder on Saloon models

28.4 Release the screws and remove the trim panel

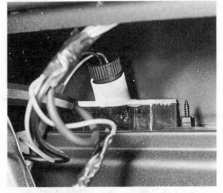

28.5 Number plate lamp bulbholder on Fastback models

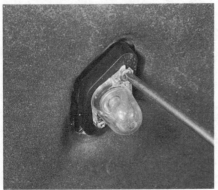

29.1 Remove the lens for access to the engine compartment lamp bulb

30.1 Prise off the courtesy lamp lens

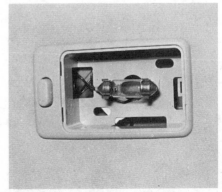

30.2 Remove the festoon bulb from the contacts

Footwell and glovebox lamps

7 From within the glovebox or under the footwell as applicable, carefully prise the lamp from its location using a small screwdriver.
8 Release the festoon-type bulb from its contacts (photo).
9 Fit the new bulb and push the lamp back into position.

Luggage compartment lamp

10 Using a small screwdriver, carefully prise the right-hand end of the lamp from its location under the rear parcel shelf on Saloon models, or on the rear side panels on Fastback models (photos).
11 Withdraw the lamp, turn the bulb anti-clockwise and remove it from the lamp (photo).
12 Fit the new bulb and push the lamp back into position.

---

31 Instrument panel illumination and warning lamp bulbs – renewal

Refer to Section 31.

---

32 Switch illumination bulbs – renewal

Facia switches and heater/air conditioner control switches

1 Remove the instrument cowl as described in Section 20.
2 With the wiring multi-plugs disconnected, remove the relevant bulb, which is a push-fit in the multi-plug holder.
3 Fit a new bulb, then refit the instrument cowl as described in Section 20.

Hazard warning switch

4 Lift off the switch lens on the steering column upper shroud, and remove the push-fit bulb.
5 Fit a new bulb, and press the lens into place.

Steering column switches

6 Undo the three lower screws and the single upper screw, and remove the upper and lower steering column shrouds.
7 Withdraw the bulbholder from the rear of the fibre optic diffuser unit (photo) then remove the bulb from the holder.
8 Fit a new bulb, push the bulbholder into place and refit the steering column shrouds.

---

33 Headlamp lens unit – removal and refitting

1 Remove the radiator grille as described in Chapter 11.
2 Remove the front direction indicator lamp assembly as described in Section 25.
3 Disconnect the wiring multi-plug at the rear of the headlamp dipped beam bulb, and separate the main beam wiring at the connector (photo).
4 Undo the two bolts securing the headlamp lens unit to the front body panel.
5 Release the unit from the two lower lugs (photo) and remove it from the car.
6 Refitting is the reverse sequence to removal.

---

34 Rear lamp cluster assembly – removal and refitting

1 From within the luggage compartment, press the retainer on the access panel and remove the panel.
2 Lift the top retainer on the bulb panel, press the two bottom retainers and withdraw the panel.
3 Undo the four nuts securing the lamp cluster to the rear wing, and withdraw the unit from the car (photos).
4 Refitting is the reverse sequence to removal.

30.8 Withdraw the glovebox lamp, and remove the bulb from the contacts

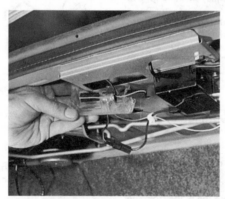

30.10A Renewing the luggage compartment lamp bulb on Saloon models

30.10B Withdraw the luggage compartment lamp lens from the rear side panel on Fastback models ...

30.11 ... for access to the bulb

32.7 Withdraw the bulbholder from the steering column switch fibre optic diffuser

33.3 Disconnect the headlamp lens unit wiring multi-plug

33.5 Release the lens unit from the lower lugs

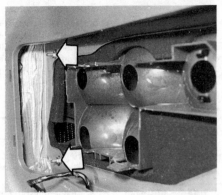

34.3A Rear lamp cluster side retaining nuts (arrowed)

34.3B Removing the rear lamp cluster assembly

35 Number plate lamp unit – removal and refitting

1   On Fastback models, remove the trim panel on the inside of the tailgate.
2   Undo the six retaining screws and remove the rear lens reflector and number plate assembly (photo).
3   Undo the two screws securing each number plate lamp unit and withdraw the unit(s) (photo).
4   Turn the bulbholder anti-clockwise to remove the bulb, then remove the lamp unit from the car.,
5   Refitting is the reverse sequence to removal.

36 Headlamp aim – adjustment

1   At regular intervals (see *Routine maintenance*) headlamp aim should be checked, and if necessary adjusted.
2   Due to the light pattern of the homofocal headlamp lenses fitted to Rover 820 models, optical beam setting equipment must be used to achieve satisfactory aim of the headlamps. It is recommended therefore that this work is entrusted to a dealer. If, however, you have access to beam setting equipment, the horizontal and vertical adjustment screws for each headlamp unit are shown in Fig. 12.13.

37 Wiper blades and arms – removal and refitting

Wiper blades

1   The blades should be renewed when they no longer clean the screen effectively.
2   Lift the wiper arm away from the screen.
3   Depress the spring retaining catch and separate the blade from the wiper arm (photos).
4   Insert the new blade into the arm, ensuring that the spring retaining catch engages fully. Note that the blade with the deflector is fitted to the driver's side.

Windscreen wiper arms

5   Open the bonnet, lift the wiper arm slightly and retain it in the raised position by inserting a pop-rivet, small drill bit or similar item through the hole in the side of the arm (photo).
6   Unscrew the arm-to-spindle retaining nut (photo) and withdraw the arm from the spindle.
7   If required, remove the blade from the arm as previously described, and pull out the rivet or drill bit. Relieve the spring tension of the arm as the rivet or bit is withdrawn.
8   Refitting is the reverse sequence to removal, but adjust the wiper arm park setting as described in Section 38 during the refitting sequence.

Tailgate wiper arm (Fastback models)

9   Lift off the cover over the wiper arm spindle.
10 Unscrew the wiper arm-to-spindle retaining nut and withdraw the arm from the blade.

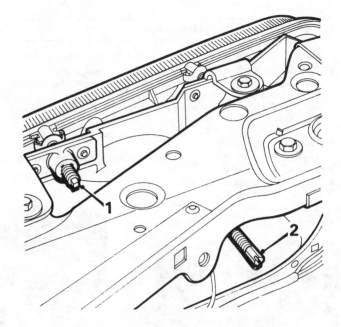

Fig. 12.13 Headlamp beam horizontal adjustment screw (1) and vertical adjustment screw (2) (Sec 36)

11 Refitting is the reverse sequence to removal, but position the arm along the bottom of the screen with the motor in the park position.

38 Windscreen wiper arm park setting – adjustment

1   Remove the wiper blades and wiper arms as described in Section 37.
2   Switch on the ignition and turn the wiper switch on and off, so that the motor operates then stops in the park position. Switch off the ignition.
3   Position the wiper arms so that they are resting on the top of the stop-pegs on the windscreen finisher. Engage the end of the arms with their respective spindles, and refit the retaining nut.
4   Refit the wiper blades, remove the rivet or drill bit, and position the arms in the normal park position against the side of the stop-pegs.
5   Operate the washers to wet the screen, then operate the wipers.
6   Switch the wipers off, and check that they park with the arms against the stop-pegs and the blades on the windscreen finisher.

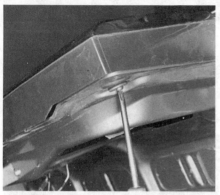

35.2 Remove the rear lens reflector and number plate assembly

35.3 Removing the number plate lamp unit

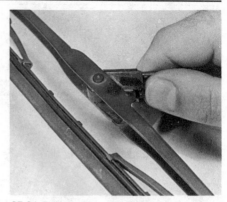

37.3A Depress the wiper blade spring retaining catch ...

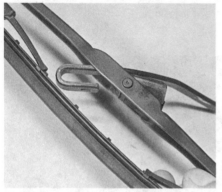

37.3B ... and release the blade from the arm

37.5 Insert a pop-rivet through the hole in the wiper arm

37.6 Wiper arm retaining nut

39 Windscreen wiper motor – removal and refitting

1   Disconnect the battery negative terminal. (Refer to Section 1 before doing this).
2   Remove the wiper arms as described in Section 37.
3   Carefully prise up the screw caps over the windscreen finisher retaining screws at the base of the windscreen (photo).
4   Undo the screws on the finisher front face and on the extreme edges, then remove the finisher from the car (photos).
5   Using pointed-nose pliers, release the rubber sealing strip retaining clips (photos). Be prepared for some of these clips to break during removal.

6   Lift off the centre grille and the left-hand plenum moulding (photos).
7   Working through the left-hand plenum chamber aperture, undo the retaining nut and remove the wiper linkage rotary link from the motor spindle (photo).
8   Disconnect the wiper motor wiring multi-plug (photo).
9   Undo the three bolts and remove the wiper motor and mounting bracket from the car (photo).
10 Withdraw the seal from the motor spindle, then remove the seal from the mounting plate.
11 Undo the three bolts and remove the motor from the mounting plate.
12 Refitting is the reverse sequence to removal.

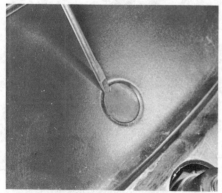

39.3 Prise up the windscreen finisher screw caps

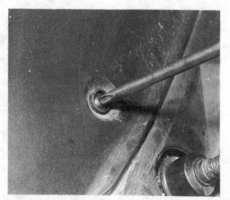

39.4A Undo the screws on the finisher front face ...

39.4B ... and at the extreme edges (arrowed)

39.5A Release the rubber sealing strip retaining clips ...

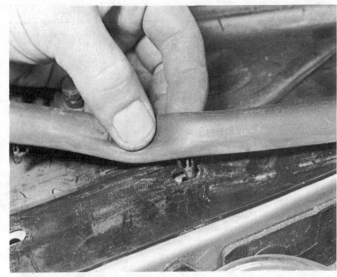

39.5B ... and withdraw the sealing strip

39.6A Lift off the centre grille ...

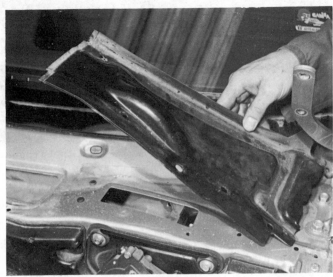

39.6B ... and the left-hand side plenum moulding

39.7 Undo the nut securing the linkage rotary link to the motor spindle

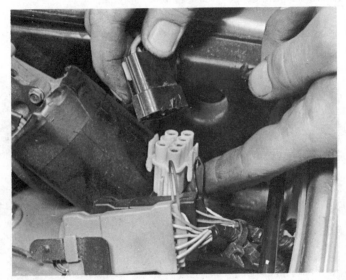

39.8 Disconnect the wiring multi-plug

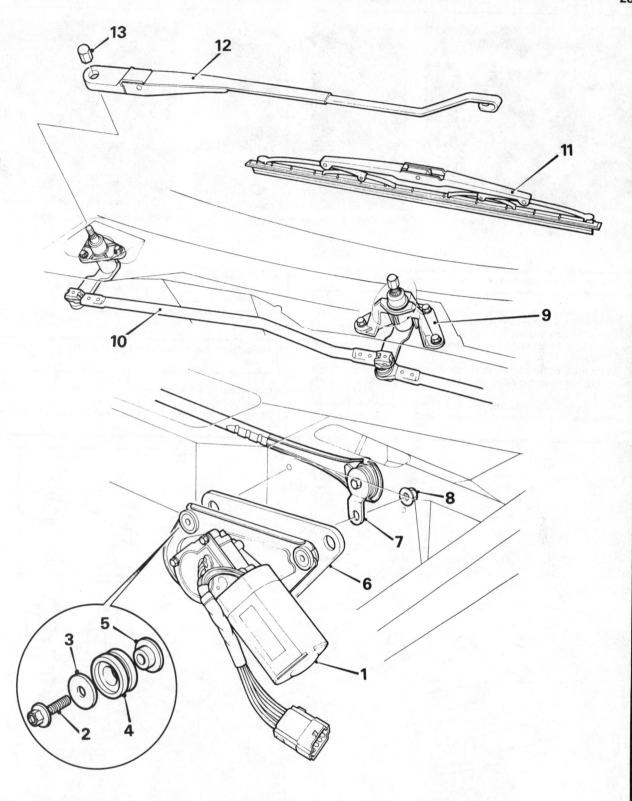

Fig. 12.14 Windscreen wiper motor and linkage components (Sec 39)

1	Wiper motor	4 Mounting bush	8 Rotary link retaining nut	11 Wiper blade
2	Mounting bracket retaining bolt	5 Sleeve	9 Linkage centre spindle	12 Wiper arm
3	Washer	6 Mounting bracket seal	10 Connecting link	13 Wiper arm retaining nut
		7 Rotary link		

39.9 Undo the motor mounting bracket retaining bolts (arrowed)

40.4A Wiper linkage centre spindle assembly ...

40.4B ... and right-hand spindle assembly

40 Windscreen wiper linkage – removal and refitting

1   Remove the windscreen wiper arms as described in Section 37.
2   Remove the wiper motor as described in Section 39.
3   Disconnect the primary link arm from the centre spindle assembly by pushing down to release the ball-and-socket joint. Remove the primary link.
4   Undo the four bolts securing the centre spindle assembly, and the three bolts securing the right-hand spindle assembly, to the scuttle (photos).
5   Feed the right-hand spindle assembly through the scuttle aperture, and draw out the linkage from the centre spindle opening. Remove the complete linkage assembly from the car.
6   Further dismantling is not possible, and if any of the parts are worn, a complete linkage assembly must be obtained.
7   Refitting is the reverse sequence to removal.

41 Tailgate wiper motor (Fastback models) – removal and refitting

1   Disconnect the battery negative terminal. (Refer to Section 1 before doing this).
2   Remove the wiper arm as described in Section 37.

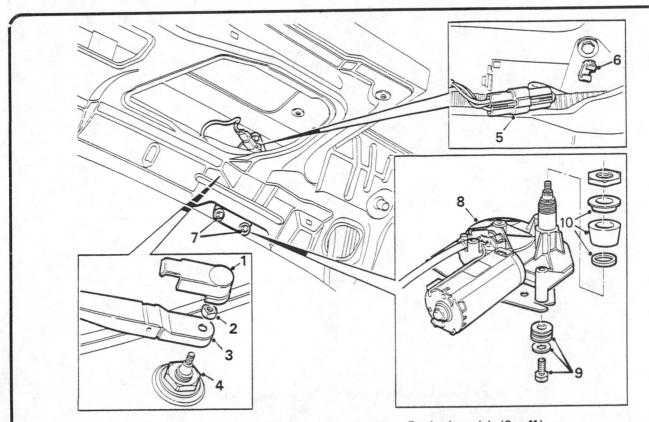

Fig. 12.15 Tailgate wiper motor attachments – Fastback models (Sec 41)

1 Wiper arm cover	retaining nut	bolts	washer
2 Wiper arm retaining nut	5 Wiring multi-plug	8 Motor assembly	10 Spindle seal, spacer and
3 Wiper arm	6 Wiring harness cable clip	9 Wiper motor-to-mounting	washer
4 Wiper motor spindle	7 Mounting plate retaining	plate bolt, spacer and	

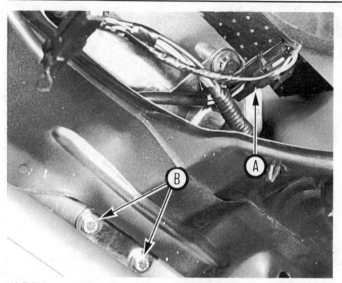

41.5 Tailgate wiper motor multi-plug (A) and mounting plate retaining bolts (B)

3 Release the plastic clip screws and remove the trim panel from inside the tailgate.
4 Undo the large retaining nut from the wiper motor spindle.
5 Disconnect the wiper motor multi-plug, and release the wiring from its cable clip (photo).
6 Undo the two bolts securing the motor mounting plate to the tailgate, then withdraw the motor and mounting plate.
7 Undo the three bolts and remove the motor from the mounting plate.
8 Withdraw the seal, spacer and washer components from the motor spindle.
9 Refitting is the reverse sequence to removal.

42 Washer reservoir and pumps – removal and refitting

1 Disconnect the battery negative terminal. (Refer to Section 1 before doing this).
2 Undo the screw securing the washer reservoir filler neck to the inner wing valance (photo).
3 Withdraw the filler neck from the reservoir, and disconnect the breather hose.
4 From under the wheel arch, undo the two screws and one bolt securing the access panel, and remove the panel.

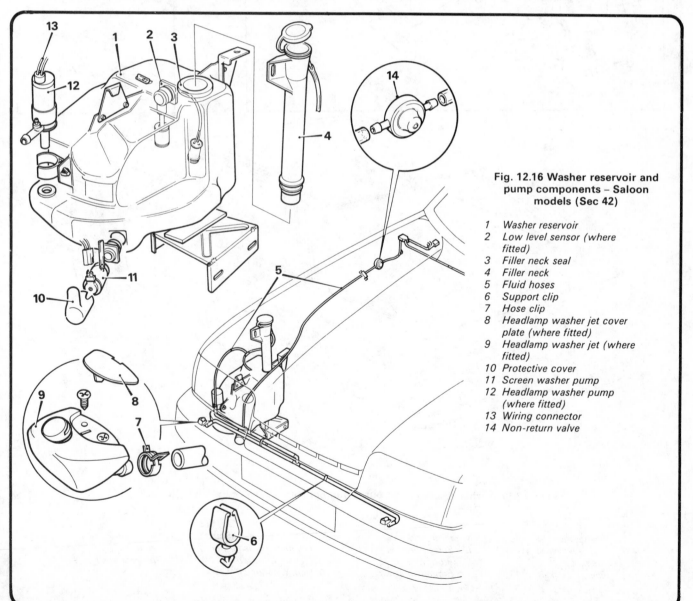

Fig. 12.16 Washer reservoir and pump components – Saloon models (Sec 42)

1 Washer reservoir
2 Low level sensor (where fitted)
3 Filler neck seal
4 Filler neck
5 Fluid hoses
6 Support clip
7 Hose clip
8 Headlamp washer jet cover plate (where fitted)
9 Headlamp washer jet (where fitted)
10 Protective cover
11 Screen washer pump
12 Headlamp washer pump (where fitted)
13 Wiring connector
14 Non-return valve

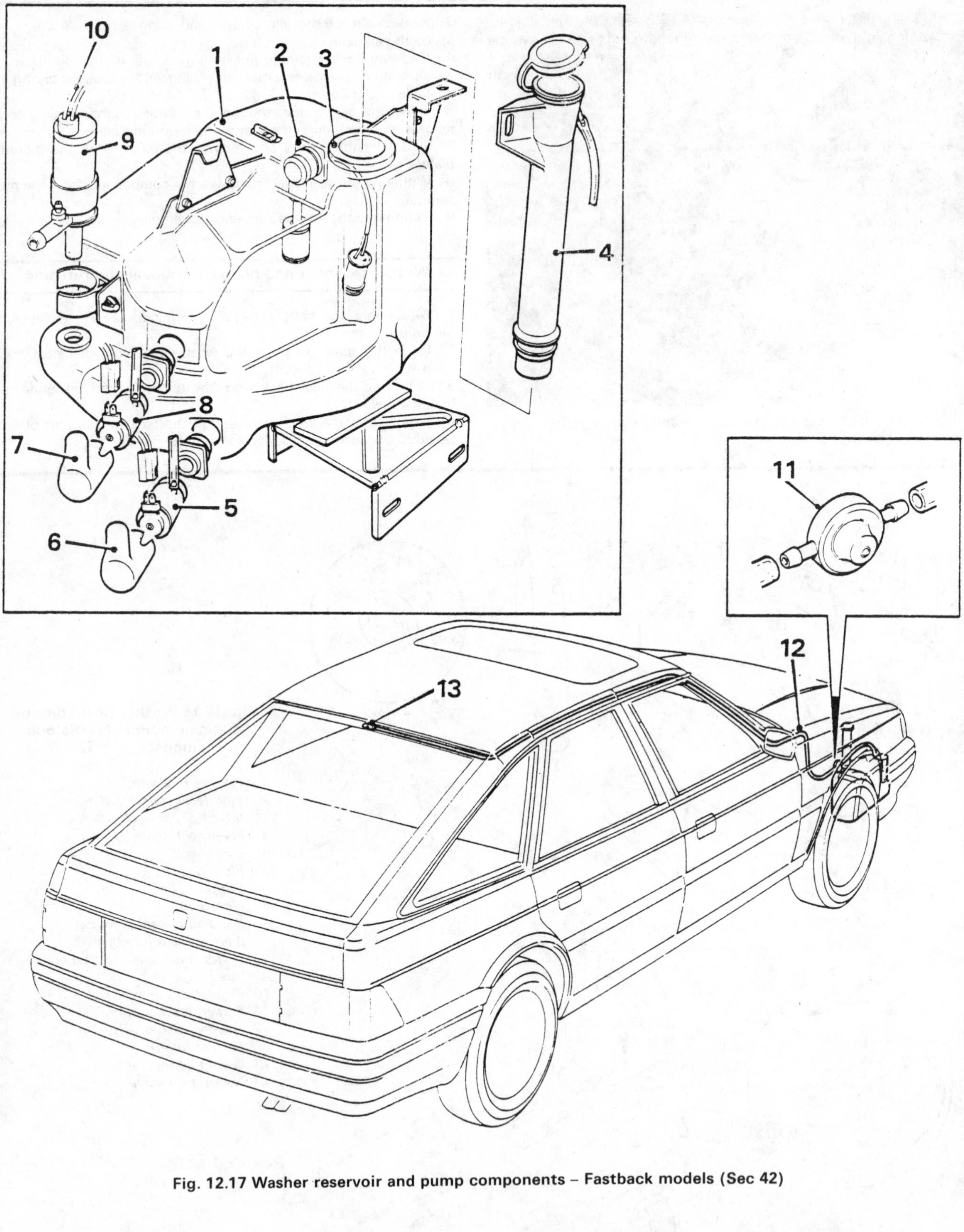

Fig. 12.17 Washer reservoir and pump components – Fastback models (Sec 42)

1 Washer reservoir	4 Filler neck	8 Tailgate washer pump	11 Non-return valve
2 Low level sensor (where fitted)	5 Screen washer pump	9 Headlamp washer pump (where fitted)	12 Fluid hose
3 Filler neck seal	6 Protective cover	10 Wiring connector	13 Tailgate washer jet
	7 Protective cover		

5 Undo the three reservoir retaining bolts and lower the unit slightly.
6 Disconnect the fluid hoses and wiring multi-plugs and remove the reservoir, complete with pumps, from under the wheel arch.
7 Remove the pumps as required from the reservoir by pulling them out of their locations.
8 Refitting is the reverse sequence to removal.

43 Headlamp washer jet – removal and refitting

1 Prise off the cover plate on the washer jet to expose the two retaining screws.
2 Undo the two screws and withdraw the jet from the front bumper.
3 Release the water hose clip, disconnect the hose and remove the jet.
4 Refitting is the reverse sequence to removal.

44 Horns – removal and refitting

1 Disconnect the battery negative terminal. (Refer to Section 1 before doing this).
2 From under the left-hand wheel arch, undo the two screws and one bolt securing the access panel and remove the panel.
3 Disconnect the electrical leads, undo the retaining nut and remove the horn(s) from the mounting bracket.
4 Refitting is the reverse sequence to removal.

45 Radio cassette player – removal and refitting

1 Disconnect the battery negative terminal. (Refer to Section 1 before doing this).
2 Insert a DIN standard radio removal tool into each pair of holes at the edge of the unit, and push the tools fully home to engage the radio retaining clips (photo). These tools are available from audio accessory shops or from Rover dealers.
3 Move the tools outward to depress the retaining clips, and withdraw the radio from the centre console sufficiently to gain access to the wiring at the rear (photo).
4 Note the location of the speaker wiring by recording the cable colours and their positions, then disconnect the speaker leads, aerial lead and wiring multi-plug (photo). Remove the unit from the car.
5 Disengage the removal tools from the retaining clips on the side of the radio, and remove the tools (photo).
6 Refitting is the reverse sequence to removal.

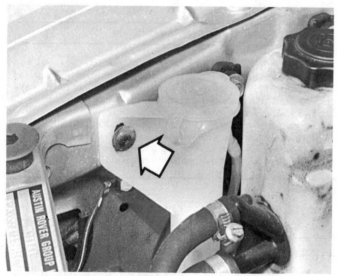

42.2 Washer reservoir filler neck retaining screw (arrowed)

45.2 Insert the radio removal tools into the holes on the edge of the unit

45.3 Withdraw the radio, using the tools to release the retaining clips.

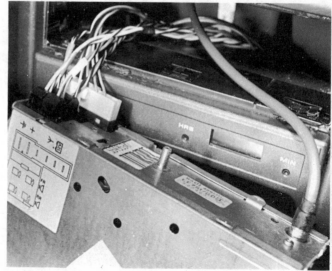

45.4 Disconnect the wiring at the rear of the radio

45.5 Release the removal tools from the retaining clips (arrowed)

46 Cassette unit tape head – cleaning

1   Remove the radio cassette player as described in Section 45.
2   Insert a screwdriver into the slot at the rear left-hand edge of the unit cover and lift the cover carefully upwards. Now insert the screwdriver into the slot on the other side, and lift carefully upwards until the retaining clips on the cover rear edge are released.
3   Pivot the cover upwards to disengage the retainer on the front edge and remove the cover.
4   Refer to Fig. 12.18 and press the arm on top of the unit rearwards to gain access to the playing mechanism.

5   Using a cotton wool pad moistened in a proprietary tape head cleaning fluid, clean the pinch wheel, capstan and tape head.
6   Return the arm to its original position and refit the unit cover.
7   Refit the radio cassette player as described in Section 45.

47 Rear speaker – removal and refitting

Saloon models

1   From inside the luggage compartment, disconnect the two leads and undo the four retaining nuts (photo).
2   Withdraw the speaker upwards into the car, and remove it from the rear parcel shelf (photo).
3   Refitting is the reverse sequence to removal.

Fastback models

4   Undo the three screws securing the trim panel to the parcel tray support (photo) and remove the trim panel.
5   Remove the speaker grille.
6   Undo the six speaker retaining screws (photo), lift the speaker from its location and disconnect the wiring connectors.
7   Remove the speaker from the car.
8   Refitting is the reverse sequence to removal.

48 Front speakers – removal and refitting

Main speaker and filter

1   Remove the front door inner trim panel as described in Chapter 11.
2   Undo the four screws securing the speaker to the door (photo).
3   Withdraw the speaker, disconnect the leads and remove the speaker from the door (photo).
4   To remove the filter, cut off the tape securing it to the wiring harness adjacent to the main speaker location.
5   Disconnect the leads at each end and remove the filter.
6   Refitting is the reverse sequence to removal.

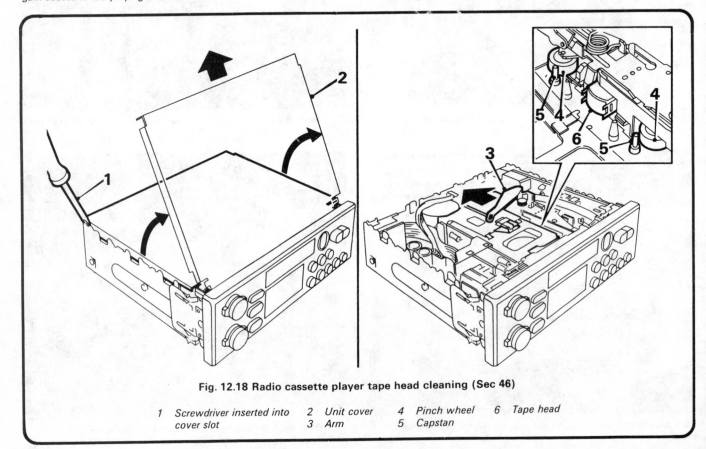

Fig. 12.18 Radio cassette player tape head cleaning (Sec 46)

1	Screwdriver inserted into cover slot	2	Unit cover	4	Pinch wheel	6	Tape head
		3	Arm	5	Capstan		

47.1 Rear speaker retaining nuts (arrowed) on Saloon models

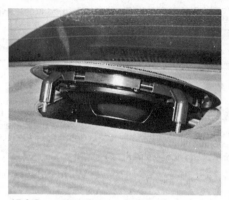

47.2 Removing the rear speaker from the parcel shelf

47.4 Remove the trim panel over the rear speaker on Fastback models

47.6 Undo the six screws and remove the speaker assembly

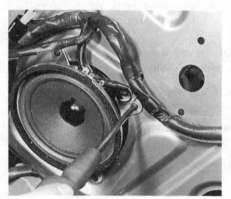

48.2 Undo the main door speaker retaining screws

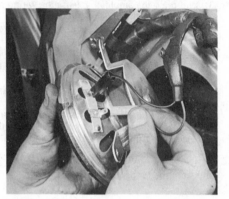

48.3 Withdraw the speaker and disconnect the wiring

Tweeter

7   Refer to 'Front door inner trim panel – removal and refitting' in Chapter 11 and remove the escutcheon around the door inner release handle.
8   Rotate the tweeter clockwise to release it from the escutcheon, then disconnect the leads and remove the tweeter (photo).
9   Refitting is the reverse sequence to removal.

---

49 Aerial amplifier – removal and refitting

Saloon models

1   Disconnect the battery negative terminal. (Refer to Section 1 before doing this).
2   From inside the luggage compartment, disconnect the two leads at the amplifier unit located under the rear parcel shelf (photo).
3   Disconnect the two amplifer leads at the connections to the rear screen demisting element.

4   Disconnect the aerial co-axial lead at the amplifier.
5   Undo the two screws and remove the amplifier from under the parcel shelf.
6   Refitting is the reverse sequence to removal.

Fastback models

7   Disconnect the battery negative terminal. (Refer to Section 1 before doing this).
8   Remove the trim panel from inside the tailgate.
9   Disconnect the leads at the amplifier unit located behind the stiffener panel in the tailgate.
10 Disconnect the leads at the connector to the rear screen demisting element.
11 Disconnect the aerial co-axial lead at the amplifier.
12 Undo the two screws and remove the amplifier from the tailgate (photo). Note that one of the screws also secures the wiring earth cable.
13 Refitting is the reverse sequence to removal.

48.8 Disconnect the wiring and remove the tweeter

49.2 Aerial amplifier unit located under the rear parcel shelf on Saloon models

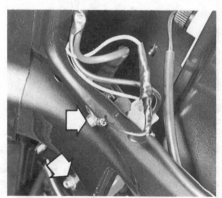

49.12 Aerial amplifier unit retaining bolts (arrowed) on Fastback models

50 Power amplifier – removal and refitting

Facia-mounted amplifier – early models

1   Disconnect the battery negative terminal. (Refer to Section 1 before doing this).
2   Release the turnbuckles and remove the trim panel over the fusebox, beneath the steering column.
3   Remove the radio cassette player as described in Section 45.
4   Disconnect the four multi-plugs connecting the speaker leads from the power amplifier to the wiring harness. Record the colour codes of each lead to ensure correct connection on reassembly.
5   Release the retaining stud and remove the small centre console trim panel from the footwell on the driver's side.
6   Working through the trim panel aperture, disconnect the power amplifier wiring multi-plug.
7   Undo the nut and two screws securing the power amplifier mounting bracket under the facia.
8   Withdraw the amplifier, release the wiring harness, and remove the unit from under the facia.
9   Refitting is the reverse sequence to removal.

Luggage compartment-mounted amplifier – later models

10 Disconnect the battery negative terminal. (Refer to Section 1 before doing this).
11 Remove the trim panel from the right-hand side of the luggage compartment.
12 Disconnect the rear speaker leads at the speakers or at the wiring connectors, and pass the disconnected leads through to the amplifier.
13 Disconnect the two multi-plugs and the DIN socket connector at the amplifier.
14 Undo the two amplifier mounting bracket screws, and remove the unit from the luggage compartment.

15 Refitting is the reverse sequence to removal.

51 Power amplifier filter – removal and refitting

1   Release the retaining stud and remove the small centre console trim panel from the footwell on the driver's side.
2   Working through the trim panel aperture, disconnect the multi-plugs at each end of the filter.
3   Release the cable tie and remove the filter from its location.
4   Refitting is the reverse sequence to removal.

52 Wiring diagrams – explanatory notes

1   The wiring diagrams included at the end of this Chapter are shown in continuous rail format. All the circuits which comprise the main wiring diagram for a particular model are positioned side by side in three rows, one above the other. The circuits are connected to each other by a common earth line, representing the vehicle chassis.
2   Grid references showing the location of the components on the diagram are included in the key. The component location on the diagram bears no relation, however, to the actual component location on the car.
3   Numbers shown within a triangle on the diagram represent interconnections from one circuit to another. An output is indicated by the lead being connected to the base of the triangle, and an input is indicated by the lead being connected to the triangle apex. A list of the connection point grid references is included in the key.
4   The numbers shown in boxes relate to the earth point locations, as shown on a supplementary diagram. A component without a number is earthed through its mountings, or through a cable earthed adjacent to the component.

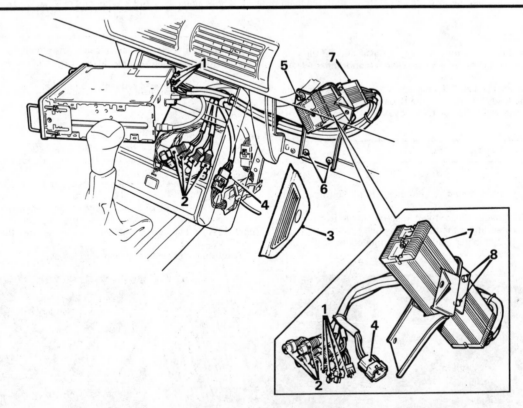

Fig. 12.19 Facia-mounted power amplifier attachments (Sec 50)

1	Speaker lead connections at radio	3	Console trim panel
2	Speaker lead connections at amplifier	4	Amplifier wiring multi-plug
		5	Mounting bracket retaining nut

6   Mounting bracket retaining screws
7   Amplifier unit

8   Amplifier-to-mounting bracket retaining screws

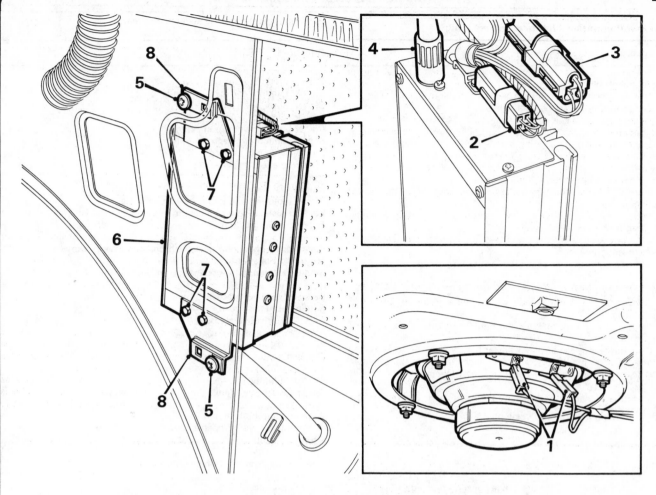

Fig. 12.20 Luggage compartment-mounted power amplifier attachments (Sec 50)

1 Left-hand speaker leads
2 Wiring multi-plug
3 Wiring multi-plug
4 DIN socket connector
5 Mounting bracket retaining screws
6 Luggage compartment stiffener panel
7 Amplifier-to-mounting bracket retaining screws
8 Amplifier mounting bracket

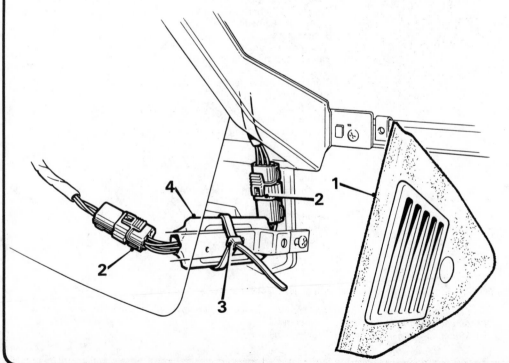

Fig. 12.21 Power amplifier filter attachments (Sec 51)

1 Console trim panel
2 Multi-plugs
3 Cable tie
4 Filter

53 Fault diagnosis – electrical system

Symptom	Reason(s)
Starter fails to turn engine	Battery discharged or defective
	Battery terminal and/or earth leads loose
	Starter motor connections loose
	Starter solenoid faulty
	Starter brushes worn or sticking
	Starter commutator worn or dirty
	Starter field coils earthed
	Starter solenoid relay faulty
Starter turns engine very slowly	Battery discharged
	Starter motor or solenoid connections loose
	Starter brushes worn or sticking
	Poor earth connection
Starter noisy	Pinion or flywheel ring gear teeth broken or badly worn
	Mounting bolts loose
	Starter motor armature bushes worn
Battery will not retain charge	Battery defective internally
	Battery terminals loose
	Alternator drivebelt slipping
	Alternator regulator faulty
	Wiring fault
	Electrical system not switching off
Ignition warning lamp stays on	Alternator faulty
	Alternator drivebelt faulty
Ignition warning lamp fails to come on	Warning lamp bulb blown
	Warning lamp wiring open-circuit
	Alternator faulty
Instrument readings erratic	Faulty instrument electronic control unit
Fuel, temperature or oil pressure gauges give no reading	Wiring open-circuit
	Sender, thermistor or transducer faulty
	Faulty instrument electronic control unit
Lamps inoperative	Bulb blown
	Fuse blown
	Relay faulty
	Fusible link blown
	Battery discharged
	Switch faulty
	Wiring open-circuit
	Bad connections due to corrosion
Failure of component motor	Component motor faulty
	Fuse blown
	Relay faulty
	Fusible link blown
	Poor or broken wiring connections
Failure of an individual component	Fuse blown
	Relay faulty
	Fusible link blown
	Poor or broken wiring connections
	Switch faulty
	Component faulty

Wiring diagram symbols and colour code

Colour code

B	Black	P	Purple
G	Green	R	Red
K	Pink	S	Slate
LG	Light green	U	Blue
N	Brown	W	White
O	Orange	Y	Yellow

Symbols

1 Fusible links
2 Fuse
3 Sealed joint
4 Connection point input
5 Connection point output

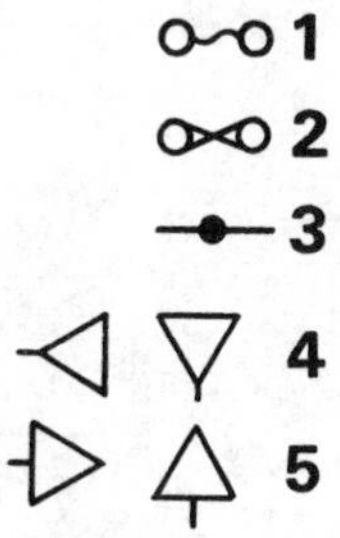

o⌒o **1**

o⌒⌒o **2**

•— **3**

◁ ▽ **4**

▷ △ **5**

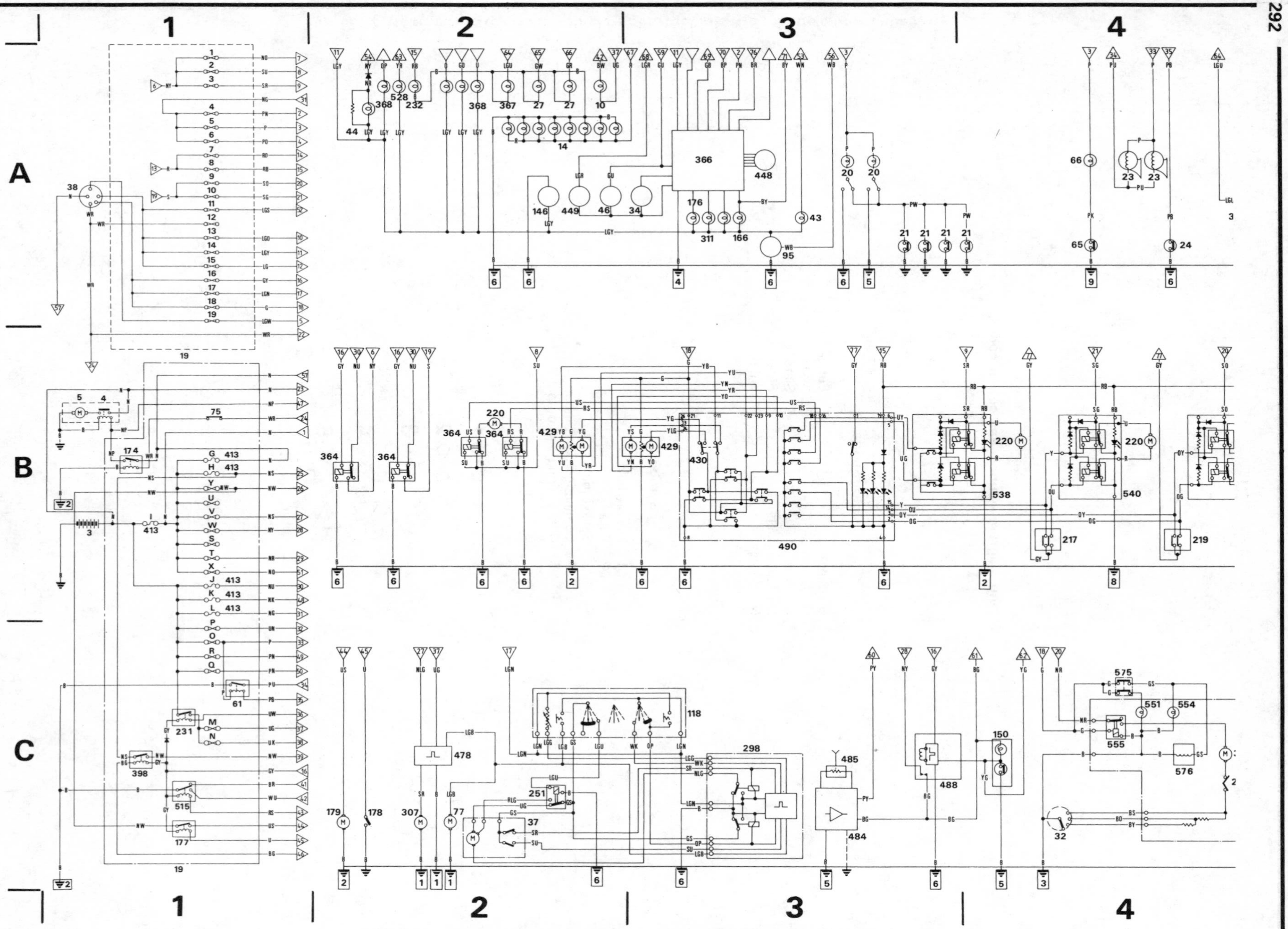

Fig. 12.22 Main wiring diagram – single-point fuel injection models

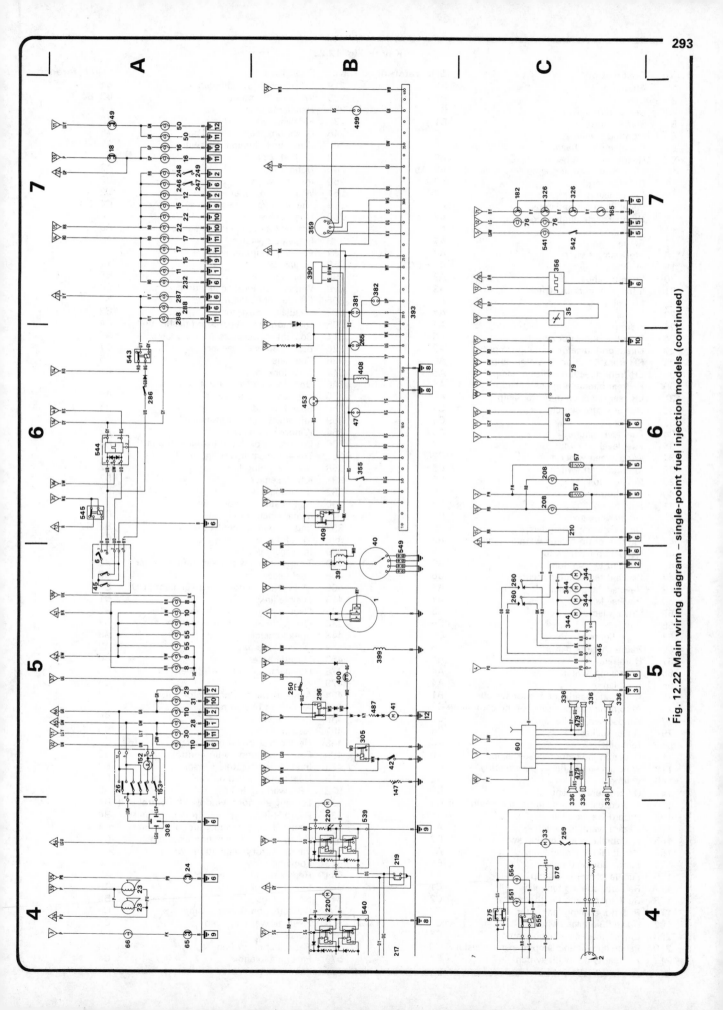

Fig. 12.22 Main wiring diagram – single-point fuel injection models (continued)

Key to Fig. 12.22

No	Description	Grid reference	No	Description	Grid reference
1	Alternator	B5	219	LH rear window lift switch	B4
3	Battery	B1	220	Window lift motor	B2, B4
4	Starter motor switch	B1	231	Headlamp relay	C1
5	Starter motor	B1	232	Sidelamp warning lamp	A2
6	Lighting switch	A5	246	Glove box illumination lamp	A6
8	Headlamp dip beam	A5	247	Glove box illumination switch	A7
9	Headlamp main beam	A5	248	Bonnet lamp	A7
10	Main beam warning lamp	A2, A5	249	Bonnet lamp switch	A2
11	RH sidelamp	A7	250	Inertia switch	B5
12	LH sidelamp	A7	251	Windscreen wiper relay	C2
14	Panel illumination lamps	A2	259	Thermal circuit breaker	C4
15	Number plate illumination lamps	A7	260	Door lock switch	C6
16	Stop-lamps	A7	265	Ambient air temperature sensor	B6
17	RH tail lamp	A7	286	Foglamp switch	A6
18	Stop-lamp switch	A7	287	Foglamp warning lamp	A7
19	Fusebox	A1,B1,C1	288	Foglamps	A7
20	Interior lamps	A3	296	Fuel pump relay	B5
21	Interior lamp door switch	A3	298	Windscreen wiper delay unit	C3
22	LH tail lamp	A7	305	Oil pressure switch relay	B5
23	Horns	A4	307	Headlamp wash motor	C2
24	Horn push	A4	308	Direction indicator/hazard flasher unit	A4
26	Direction indicator switch	A5	311	Coolant temperature warning lamp	A3
27	Direction indicator warning lamps	A2	326	Brake pad wear sensor	C7
28	RH front direction indicator lamp	A5	336	Speakers	C5
29	LH front direction indicator lamp	A5	344	Door lock motor	C5
30	RH rear direction indicator lamp	A5	345	Door lock motor control unit	C5
31	LH rear direction indicator lamp	A5	355	Accelerator pedal switch	B6
32	Heater motor switch	C4	356	Speed transducer	B6
33	Heater motor	C4	359	Idle speed stepper motor	B7
34	Fuel level gauge	A3	364	Window lift relay	B2
35	Fuel level tank unit	C7	366	Instrument pack multi-function unit	A3
37	Windscreen wiper motor	C2	367	Trailer indicator warning light	A2
38	Ignition/start switch	B5	368	Spare warning light	A2
39	Ignition coil	B5	381	Knock sensor	B7
40	Distributotr	B5	382	Crankshaft sensor	B7
41	Fuel pump	B5	390	Diagnostic junction – Engine management ECU	B7
42	Oil pressure switch	B5	393	Engine management ECU	B6, B7
43	Oil pressure warning lamp	A3	398	Manifold heater relay	C1
44	Ignition or no charge warning lamp	A2	399	Inlet manifold heater	B5
45	Headlamp flash switch	A5	400	Temperature switch – manifold heater	B5
46	Coolant temperature gauge	A2	408	Fuel injector	B6
47	Coolant temperature thermistor	B6	409	Main relay – Engine management ECU	B6
49	Reverse lamp switch	A7	413	Fusible link	B1
50	Reverse lamps	A7	429	Electric mirror motor/heater	B2
55	Driving lamps	A5	430	Electric mirror switch	B3
56	Clock	C6	448	Speedometer	A3
57	Cigar lighter	C6	449	Oil pressure gauge	A2
60	Radio cassette player	C5	453	Throttle potentiometer	B6
61	Horn relay	C1	478	Headlamp power wash timer unit	C2
65	Boot lamp switch	A4	479	Filter	C5
66	Boot lamp	A4	484	Aerial amplifier and isolator unit	C3
75	Automatic gearbox inhibitor switch	B1	485	Aerial and heated rear screen	C3
76	Automatic gearbox selector indicator lamp	C7	486	Resistor wire – harness	B5
77	Windscreen washer motor	C2	487	Resistive wire	B5
79	Trailer socket	C6	488	Heated rearscreen timer relay	C3
95	Tachometer	A3	490	Four door window lift control unit	B3
110	Direction indicator repeater lamps	A5	499	Inlet air temperature sensor	B7
118	Windscreen washer/wiper switch	C3	515	Headlamp main/dip relay	C1
146	Voltmeter	A2	528	ABS warning light	A2
147	Oil pressure transducer	B5	538	Passenger's door window lift control unit	B4
150	Heated rear screen switch and warning lamp	C4	539	Rear LH door window lift control unit	B4
152	Hazard warning lamp	A5	540	Rear RH door window lift control unit	B4
153	Hazard warning switch	A5	541	Vanity mirror illumination lamp	C7
165	Handbrake warning lamp switch	C7	542	Vanity mirror illumination switch	C7
166	Handbrake warning lamp	A3	543	Foglamp relay	A6
174	Starter solenoid relay	B1	544	Headlamp cut-off unit	A6
176	Fuel level warning lamp	A3	545	Sidelamp relay	A6
177	Radiator cooling fan relay	C1	549	Spark plugs	B5
178	Radiator cooling fan thermostat	C2	551	Recirculation warning lamp	C4
179	Radiator cooling fan motor	C2	554	Fresh air warning lamp	C4
182	Brake fluid level switch	C7	555	Heater relay	C4
208	Cigar lighter illumination lamp	C6	575	Recirculation switch	C4
210	Panel illumination lamp rheostat resistor	C6	576	Fresh air solenoid	C4
217	RH rear window lift switch	B4			

Key to Fig. 12.22 (continued)

Connection chart

No	Grid references	Supplementary circuit connections	No	Grid references	Supplementary circuit connections
1	B1, B5		37	A2, A5, C1	
2	A1, A3, C6	Courtesy lamp delay	38	A5, C1	
3	A1, A3, A4, C5, C6	Radio cassette player with power amplifier. Courtesy lamp delay	39	B5	
			40	A4, C1	
4	A1, C5	Central locking with remote control	41	A5, C1	
			42	A2, A5, C1	
5	A1, C5, C7	Radio cassette player with power amplifier	43	A5, C1	
			44	C1, C2	
6	A1, B2		45	C1, C2	
7	A1		46	A5, B5	
8	A1, B2		47	A5, B1, B5	
9	A1, B4	ABS brake system	48	B1, C1	ABS brake system
10	A1, B5		49	C1	ABS brake system
11	A1, A2, A3, A5, A7, C6	ABS brake system. Courtesy lamp delay	50	C1	ABS brake system
			51	B1	Cooling fans – models with air conditioning
12	A1, B6, C7				
13	A1, A6	ABS brake system	52	A2, B2	ABS brake system
14	A1, A6, A7, C6		53	A3, B5	
15	A1, A2, A7, B3, C6		54	A2, B5	ABS brake system
16	A1, A6, B2, C1, C3	Cooling fans – models with air conditioning	55	B5, B7	
			56	A3, B7	
17	A1, C2		57	A1, B1	
18	A1, B3, B6, C1, C4	Air conditioning	58	B6	Cooling fans – models with air conditioning
19	A1, B2				
20	A1, B4, C4		59	A3, B7	
21	A1, B4		60	C3, C5	Radio cassette player with power amplifier
22	A1, B7				
23	B1, B6		61	C4	Air conditioning
24	B1		62	C4	Air conditioning
25	B1	Radio cassette player with power amplifier	63	A2	ABS braking system
			64	A4, B2	
26	B1	Cooling fan – models with air conditioning	65	A5, B2, C6	
			66	A5, B2, C6	
27	B1, C2		67	A3, C6	Air conditioning
28	B1, C3		68	A3, B4	
29	B1, B6	Air conditioning	69	A3, C7	
30	B1, B2		70	A3, C7	
31	A1, A6, B1		71	A3, C7	
32	A5, C1		72	A7, C6	ABS brake system
33	A7, B1		73	A7, C6	
34	A4, B1, C1		74		Air conditioning
35	A4, B1, C1		76	A3, C7	
36	A6, B1, C1		77	B3, B4	

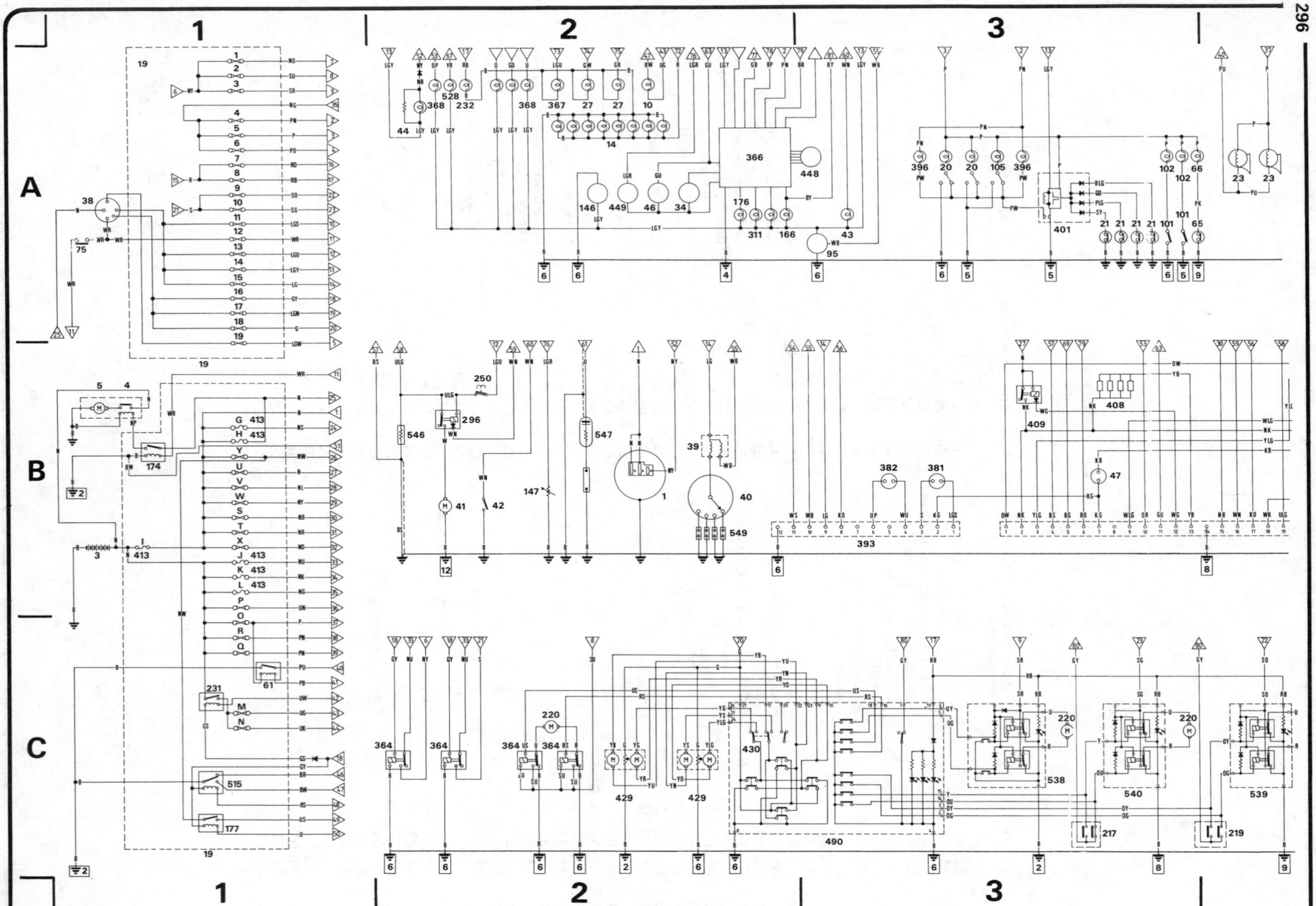

Fig. 12.23 Main wiring diagram – multi-point fuel injection models

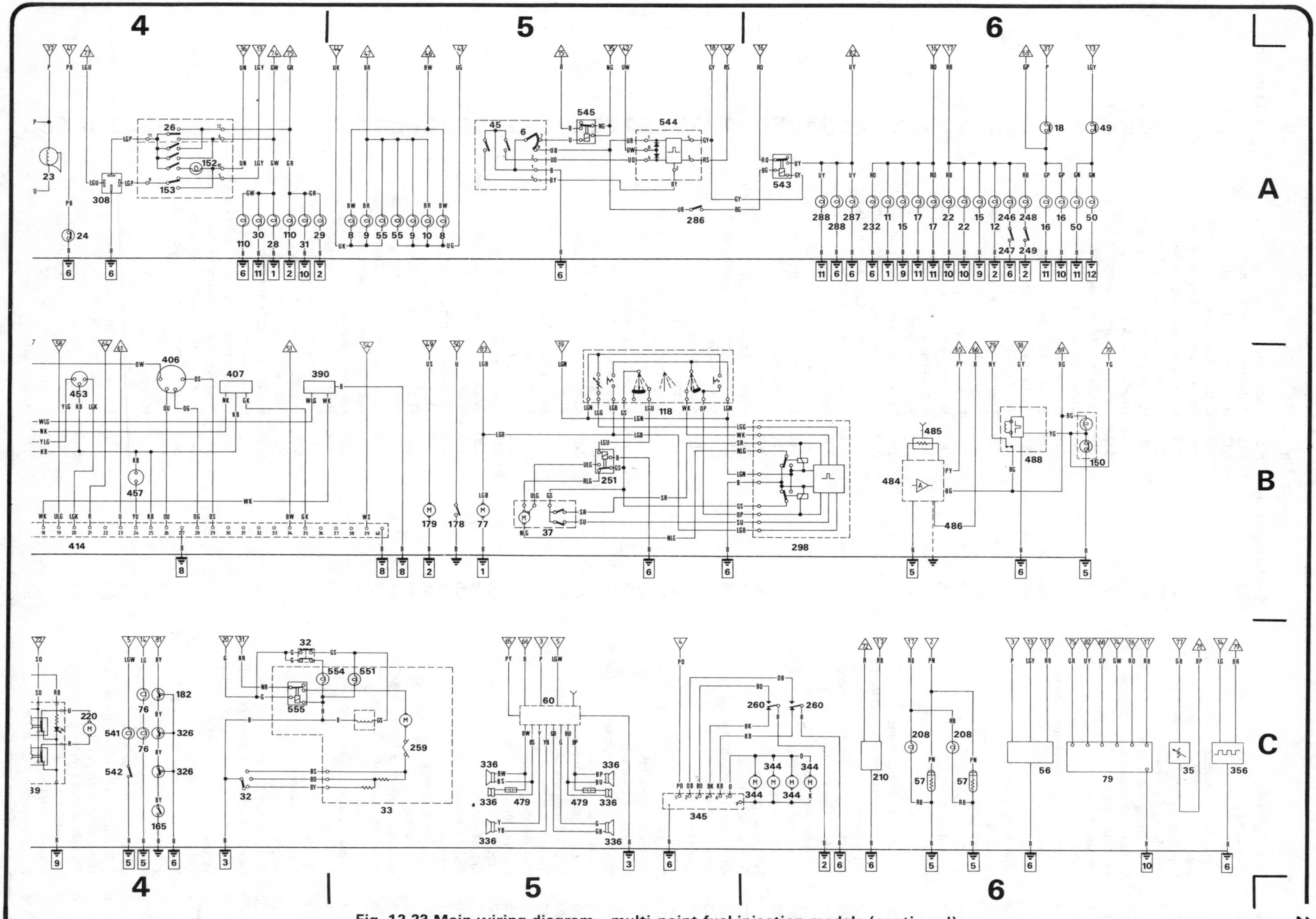

Fig. 12.23 Main wiring diagram – multi-point fuel injection models (continued)

Key to Fig. 12.23

No	Description	Grid reference	No	Description	Grid reference
1	Alternator	B2	179	Radiator cooling fan motor	B5
3	Battery	B1	182	Brake fluid level switch	C4
4	Starter motor switch	B1	208	Cigar lighter illumination lamp	C6
5	Starter motor	B1	210	Panel illumination lamp rheostat resistor	C6
6	Lighting switch	A5	217	RH rear window lift switch	C3
8	Headlamp dip beam	A5	219	LH rear window lift switch	C4
9	Headlamp main beam	A5	220	Window lift motor	C2, C3, C4
10	Main beam warning lamp	A2,A5	231	Headlamp relay	C1
11	RH sidelamp	A6	232	Sidelamp warning lamp	A2, A6
12	LH sidelamp	A6	246	Glove box illumination lamp	A6
14	Panel illumination lamps	A2	247	Glove box illumination switch	A6
15	Number plate illumination lamps	A6	248	Bonnet lamp	A6
16	Stop-lamps	A6	249	Bonnet lamp switch	A6
17	RH tail lamp	A6	250	Inertia switch	B2
18	Stop-lamp switch	A6	251	Windscreen wiper relay	B5
19	Fusebox	A1,B1,C1	259	Thermal circuit breaker	C5
20	Interior lamps	A3	260	Door lock switch	C6
21	Interior lamp door switch	A3	286	Foglamp switch	A5
22	LH tail lamp	A6	287	Foglamp warning lamp	A6
23	Horns	A4	288	Foglamps	A6
24	Horn push	A4	296	Fuel pump relay	B2
26	Direction indicator switch	A4	298	Windscreen wiper delay unit	B6
27	Direction indicator warning lamps	A2	308	Direction indicator/hazard flasher unit	A4
28	RH front direction indicator lamp	A4	311	Coolant temperature warning lamp	A2
29	LH front direction indicator lamp	A4	326	Brake pad wear sensor	C4
30	RH rear direction indicator lamp	A4	336	Speakers	C5
31	LH rear direction indicator lamp	A4	344	Door lock motor	C6
32	Heater motor switch	C4	345	Door lock motor control unit	C5
33	Heater motor	C5	356	Speed transducer	C6
34	Fuel level gauge	A2	364	Window lift relay	C2
35	Fuel level tank unit	C6	366	Instrument pack multi-function unit	A2
37	Windscreen wiper motor	B5	367	Trailer towing warning light	A2
38	Ignition/start switch	A1	368	Spare warning light	A2
39	Ignition coil	B2	381	Knock sensor	B3
40	Distributor	B2	382	Crankshaft sensor	B3
41	Fuel pump	B2	390	Diagnostic junction – Fuel ECU	B4
42	Oil pressure switch	B2	393	Programmed ignition ECU	B3
43	Oil pressure warning lamp	A3	396	Footwell illumination	A3
44	Ignition or no charge warning lamp	A2	401	Interior lamp delay unit	A3
45	Headlamp flash switch	A5	406	Air valve stepper motor	B4
46	Coolant temperature gauge	A2	407	Airflow meter electronic unit	B4
47	Coolant temperature thermistor	B3	408	Fuel injectors	B3
49	Reverse lamp switch	A6	409	Main relay – Fuel ECU	B3
50	Reverse lamps	A6	413	Fusible link	B1
55	Driving lamps	A5	414	Fuel ECU	B4
56	Clock	C6	429	Electric mirror motor/heater	C2
57	Cigar lighter	C6	430	Electric mirror switch	C2
60	Radio cassette player	C5	448	Speedometer	A3
61	Horn relay	C1	449	Oil pressure gauge	A2
65	Boot lamp switch	A3	453	Throttle potentiometer	B4
66	Boot lamp	A3	457	Fuel temperature sensor	B4
75	Automatic gearbox inhibitor switch	A1	479	Filter	C5
76	Automatic gearbox selector indicator lamp	C4	484	Aerial amplifier and isolator unit	B6
77	Windscreen washer motor	B5	485	Aerial and heated rear screen	B6
79	Trailer socket	C6	486	Aerial co-axial cable	B6
95	Tachometer	A3	488	Heated rearscreen timer relay	B6
101	Map light switch	A3	490	Four door window lift control unit	C3
102	Map light	A3	515	Headlamp main/dip relay	C1
105	Rear interior lamp	A3	528	ABS warning light	A2
110	Direction indicator repeater lamp	A4	538	Passenger's door window lift control unit	C3
118	Windscreen washer/wiper switch	B5	539	Rear LH door window lift control unit	C4
146	Voltmeter	A2	540	Rear RH door window lift control unit	C3
147	Oil pressure transducer	B2	541	Vanity mirror illumination lamp	C4
150	Heated rear screen switch and warning lamp	B6	542	Vanity mirror illumination switch	C4
152	Hazard warning lamp	A4	543	Foglamp relay	A6
153	Hazard warning switch	A4	544	Headlamp cut-off unit	A5
165	Handbrake warning lamp switch	C4	545	Sidelamp relay	A5
166	Handbrake warning lamp	A2	546	Lambda heater	B2
174	Starter solenoid relay	B1	547	Lambda sensor	B2
176	Fuel level warning lamp	A2	549	Spark plugs	B2
177	Radiator cooling fan relay	C1	551	Recirculation warning lamp	C5
178	Radiator cooling fan thermostat	B5	554	Fresh air warning lamp	C5
			555	Heater relay	C4

Key to Fig. 12.23 (continued)

Connection chart

No	Grid references	Supplementary circuit connections	No	Grid references	Supplementary circuit connections
1	B1, B2		39	C1	ABS brake system
2	A1, A2, A3, C6		40	A4, C1	
3	A1, A3, C3, C6	Radio cassette player with power amplifier	41	C1, A4	
4	A1, C5	Central locking with remote control	42	C1, A5	
5	B1, C4, C5	Radio cassette player with power amplifier	43	C1, A2, A5	
6	A1, C2		44	C1, A5	
7	A1		46	A5, C1	
8	A1, C2		47	A5, C1, A2	
9	A1, C3	ABS brake system	48	C1, A5	
10	A1		49	C1, B5	
11	A1, B1		50	C1, B5	
12	A1, B2		51	B4, B1	
13	A1, A2, A3, A4, A6, C6	ABS brake system	52	A2, B2	ABS brake system
14	A1, B2, B3, C4, C6		53	A2, B3	
15	A1, A5		54	B2, B5	
16	A1, A6, C6		55	B2, A3, B3	
17	A1, A2, A6, C3, C6	Air conditioning	56	B3, B4	
18	A1, A5, B6, C1, C2	Cooling fans – models with air conditioning	57	B2, B3	
19	A1, B5		58	B2, B4	
20	A1, C2, C4		59	B2, B4	
21	A1, C2		60	A3, B2	
22	A1, C4		61	B4, B2	
23	A1, C3		63	B3, A2	
24	B1	Radio cassette player with power amplifier	64	B4	Cooling fans – models with air conditioning
25	A1, B1		65	C5, B6	Radio cassette player with power amplifier
26	B1	Cooling fan – models with air conditioning	66	C5, B6	Radio cassette player with power amplifier
27	B1, B3		67	A2	ABS brake system
28	B1	Headlamp power wash	68	A6, C6	ABS brake system
29	B1, B6		69	B6, B3	Air conditioning
30	B1, B4		70	B6	Air conditioning
31	B1, C4	Air conditioning	72	C6, A2	Air conditioning
32	B1	Cooling fan – models with air conditioning	73	A4, A2	
33	B1, C2		74	A4, A2, C6	
34	B1	ABS brake system	75	A4, A2, C6	
35	B1, A1, A5		76	A2, B2	
36	B1, A4		77	A2, C6	
37	C1, A4, A6		78	C6, A2	
38	C1	ABS brake system	79	C6, A3, B3	
			80	C3	
			81	A3, C4	
			82	A6, C6	
			83	B5	Headlamp wash

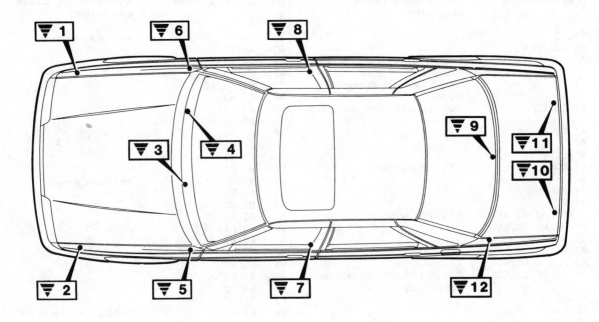

Fig. 12.24 Supplementary wiring diagram – earth point locations

1 Behind RH headlamp
2 Behind LH headlamp
3 Behind facia
4 Steering column bracket
5 Base of LH 'A' pillar
6 Base of RH 'A' pillar
7 Base of LH 'B' pillar

8 Base of RH 'B' pillar
9 Beneath rear parcel shelf
10 Beneath LH rear lamp
11 Beneath RH rear lamp
12 LH side panel in luggage
   compartment beneath carpet

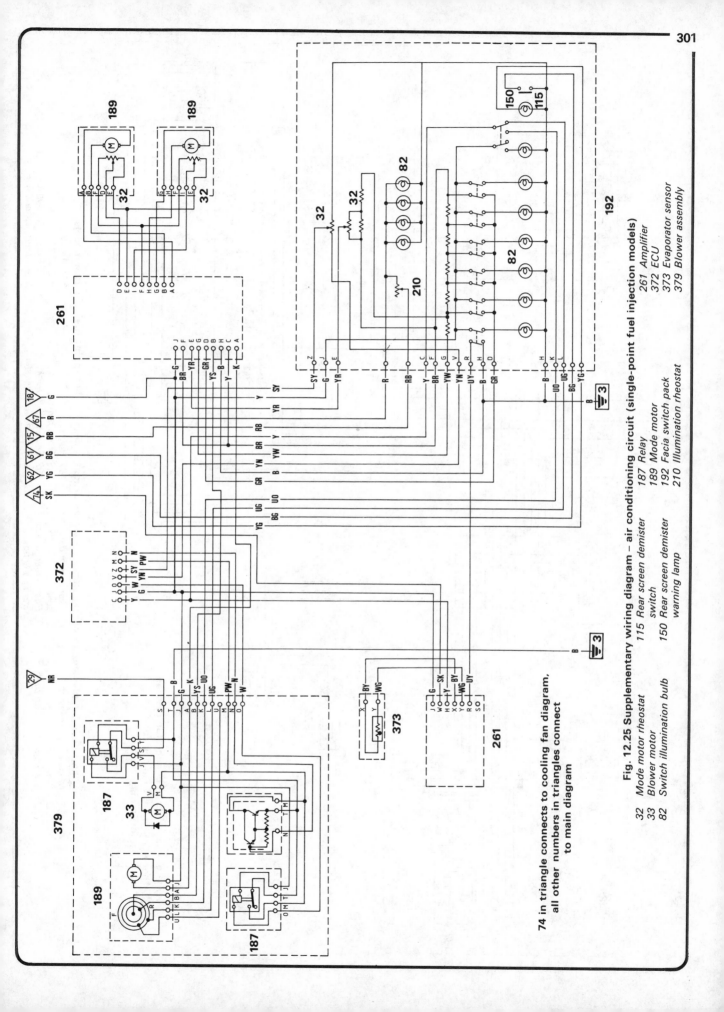

Fig. 12.25 Supplementary wiring diagram – air conditioning circuit (single-point fuel injection models)

32 Mode motor rheostat
33 Blower motor
82 Switch illumination bulb

115 Rear screen demister switch
150 Rear screen demister warning lamp

187 Relay
189 Mode motor
192 Facia switch pack
210 Illumination rheostat

261 Amplifier
372 ECU
373 Evaporator sensor
379 Blower assembly

74 in triangle connects to cooling fan diagram,
all other numbers in triangles connect
to main diagram

302

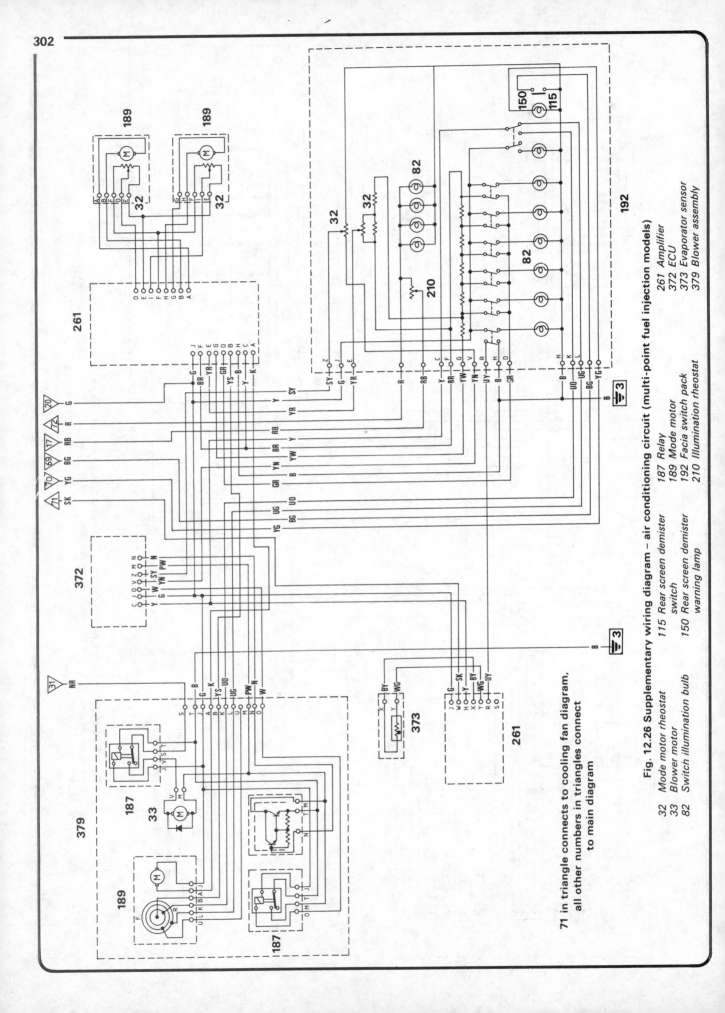

Fig. 12.26 Supplementary wiring diagram – air conditioning circuit (multi-point fuel injection models)

32	Mode motor rheostat	115	Rear screen demister	261	Amplifier
33	Blower motor		switch	372	ECU
82	Switch illumination bulb	150	Rear screen demister	373	Evaporator sensor
			warning lamp	379	Blower assembly
		187	Relay
		189	Mode motor
		192	Facia switch pack
		210	Illumination rheostat

71 in triangle connects to cooling fan diagram,
all other numbers in triangles connect
to main diagram

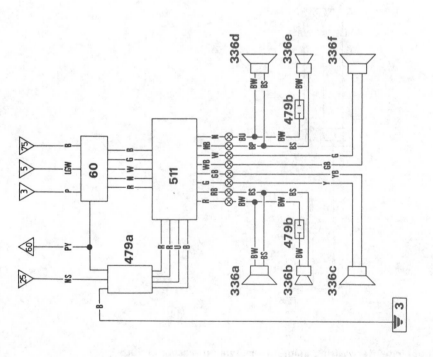

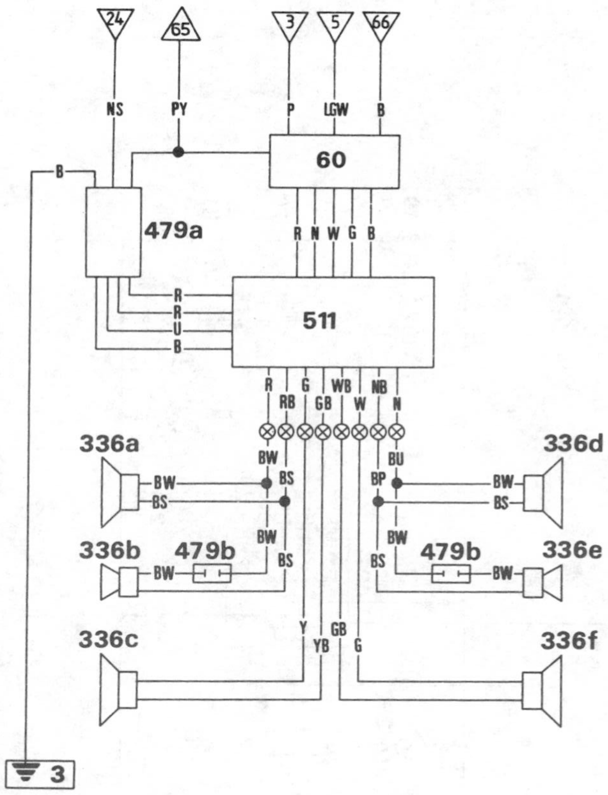

Fig. 12.28 Supplementary wiring diagram – radio cassette
player with power amplifier circuit (multi-point fuel
injection models)

60	Radio cassette player	336e	RH front tweeter
336a	LH front speaker	336f	RH rear speaker
336b	LH front tweeter	479a	Filter – power amplifier
336c	LH rear speaker	479b	Filter – speakers
336d	RH front speaker.	511	Power amplifier

Fig. 12.27 Supplementary wiring diagram – radio cassette
player with power amplifier circuit (single-point fuel
injection models)

60	Radio cassette player	336e	RH front tweeter
336a	LH front speaker	336f	RH rear speaker
336b	LH front tweeter	479a	Filter – power amplifier
336c	LH rear speaker	479b	Filter – speakers
336d	RH front speaker	511	Power amplifier

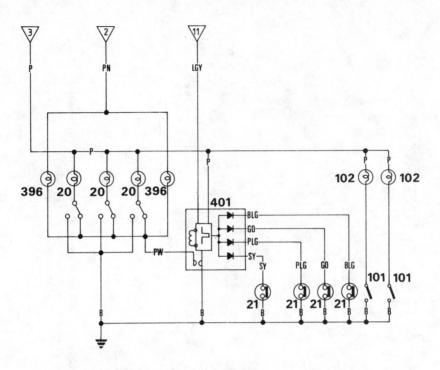

Fig. 12.29 Supplementary wiring diagram – courtesy lamp delay circuit

20 Interior lamps	21 Interior lamp door pillar switch	101 Map lamp switch	396 Footwell lamps
		102 Map reading lamps	401 Interior lamp delay unit

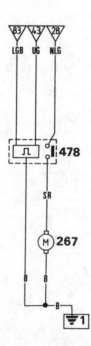

Fig. 12.30 Supplementary wiring diagram – headlamp washer circuit

267 Washer pump   478 Timer delay relay

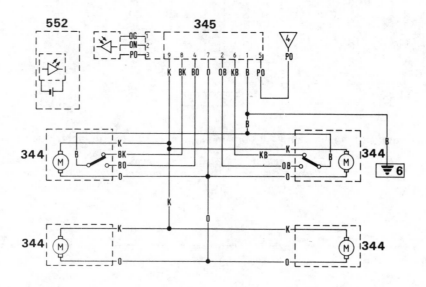

Fig. 12.31 Supplementary wiring diagram – central locking with remote control circuit

344 Door lock motor *345 ECU* *552 Remote control*

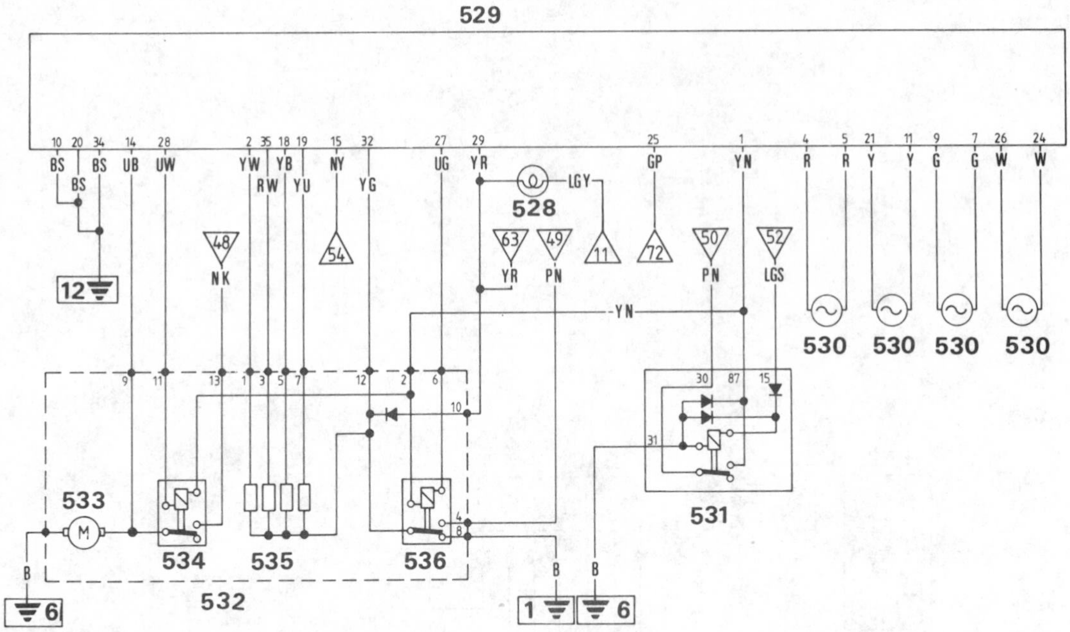

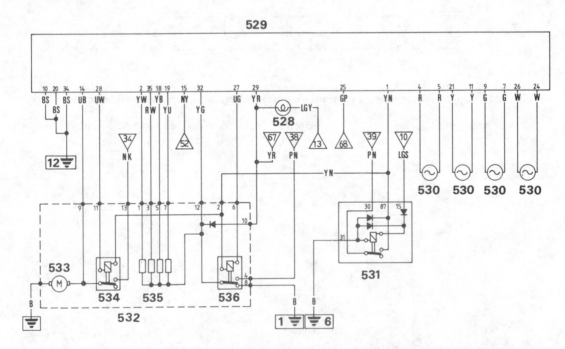

Fig. 12.32 Supplementary wiring diagram – ABS braking system circuit (single-point fuel injection models)

528 ABS warning lamp
529 ECU
530 Wheel speed sensor

531 ABS over-voltage
   protection relay
532 Hydraulic modulator

533 Return pump
534 Return pump relay

535 Solenoid valve
536 Solenoid valve relay

Fig. 12.33 Supplementary wiring diagram – ABS braking system circuit (multi-point fuel injection models)

528 ABS warning lamp
529 ECU
530 Wheel speed sensor

531 ABS over-voltage
   protection relay
532 Hydraulic modulator

533 Return pump
534 Return pump relay

535 Solenoid valve
536 Solenoid valve relay

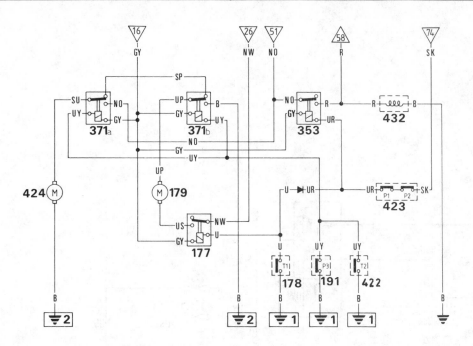

Fig. 12.34 Supplementary wiring diagram – cooling fan circuit (single-point fuel injection models with air conditioning)

177	Radiator cooling fan relay	191	Condenser cooling fan	371b	Condenser fan	423	Dual pressure switch
178	Radiator cooling fan		switch		changeover relay 2	424	Condenser cooling fan
	switch	371a	Condenser fan	353	Magnetic clutch relay		motor
179	Radiator cooling fan		changeover relay 1	422	Air conditioning	423	Compressor switch
	motor				thermostat switch		

74 in triangle connects to air conditioning diagram, all other numbers in triangles connect to main diagram

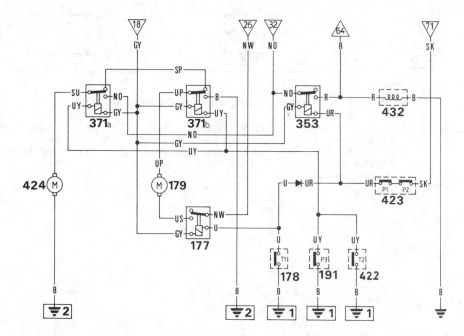

Fig. 12.35 Supplementary wiring diagram – cooling fan circuit (multi-point fuel injection models with air conditioning)

177	Radiator cooling fan relay	191	Condenser cooling fan	371b	Condenser fan	423	Dual pressure switch
178	Radiator cooling fan		switch		changeover ralay 2	424	Condenser cooling fan
	switch	371a	Condenser fan	353	Magnetic clutch relay		motor
179	Radiator cooling fan		changeover relay 1	422	Air conditioning	432	Compressor switch
	motor				thermostat switch		

71 in triangle connects to air conditioning diagram, all other numbers in triangles connect to main diagram

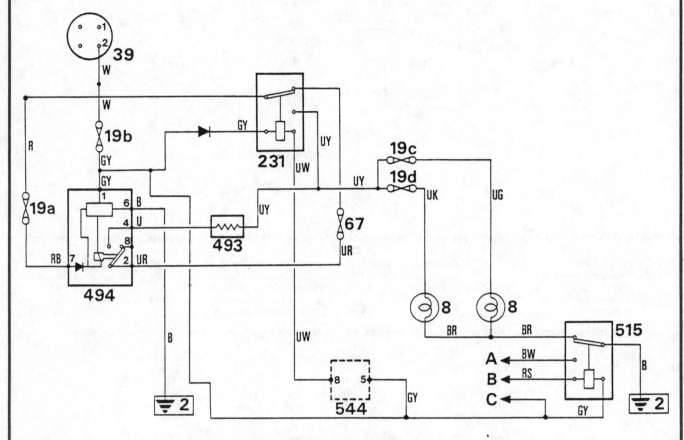

Fig. 12.36 Supplementary wiring diagram – dim-dip lighting circuit

8	Headlamp dipped beam	39	Ignition switch	515	Headlamp main/dipped
19a	Fuse 7	67	Line fuse		beam relay
19b	Fuse 16	231	Headlamp relay	544	Headlamp changeover relay
19c	Fuse M	493	Dim-dip resistor	A	From headlamp main
19d	Fuse N	494	Dim-dip relay		beams

B From headlamp changeover relay

C To radiator cooling fan relay

Index

Contents

Section I   Functions   1

1   Research: What, Why, and How   3

Research Methods for Criminology and Criminal Justice: A Primer

Second Edition

M.L. Dantzker, PhD
Professor
Criminal Justice Department
University of Texas-Pan American
Edinburg, Texas

Ronald D. Hunter, PhD
Professor and Department Head
Department of Applied Criminology
Western Carolina University
Cullowhee, North Carolina

JONES AND BARTLETT PUBLISHERS
Sudbury, Massachusetts
BOSTON   TORONTO   LONDON   SINGAPORE

World Headquarters
Jones and Bartlett Publishers
40 Tall Pine Drive
Sudbury, MA 01776
978-443-5000
info@jbpub.com
www.jbpub.com

Jones and Bartlett Publishers Canada
6339 Ormindale Way
Mississauga, Ontario L5V 1J2
Canada

Jones and Bartlett Publishers International
Barb House, Barb Mews
London W6 7PA
United Kingdom

Jones and Bartlett's books and products are available through most bookstores and online booksellers. To contact Jones and Bartlett Publishers directly, call 800-832-0034, fax 978-443-8000, or visit our website www.jbpub.com.

Substantial discounts on bulk quantities of Jones and Bartlett's publications are available to corporations, professional associations, and other qualified organizations. For details and specific discount information, contact the special sales department at Jones and Bartlett via the above contact information or send an email to specialsales@jbpub.com.

Production Credits
Chief Executive Officer: Clayton E. Jones
Chief Operating Officer: Donald W. Jones, Jr.
President, Higher Education and Professional Publishing: Robert W. Holland, Jr.
V.P., Sales and Marketing: William J. Kane
V.P., Production and Design: Anne Spencer
V.P., Manufacturing and Inventory Control: Therese Connell
Publisher, Public Safety Group: Kimberly Brophy
Acquisitions Editor: Stefanie Boucher
Editor: Christine Emerton
Production Editor: Jenny L. McIsaac
Director of Marketing: Alisha Weisman
Interior Design: Anne Spencer
Cover Design: Anne Spencer
Composition: Auburn Associates, Inc.
Cover Images: Cover art by Anne Spencer; photographic image © David Buffington/Photodisc/Getty Images;
  column © Ron Chapple/Thinkstock/Alamy Images
Chapter Opener Image: © Masterfile
Text Printing and Binding: Malloy
Cover Printing: Malloy

Library of Congress Cataloging-in-Publication Data

Dantzker, Mark L., 1958-
  Research methods for criminology and criminal justice / Mark L.
Dantzker and Ronald D. Hunter. — 2nd ed.
    p. cm.
  Includes bibliographical references and index.
  ISBN 0-7637-3615-5 (hardcover)
  1. Criminology—Research—Methodology. 2. Criminal justice,
Administration of—Research—Methodology.   I. Hunter, Ronald D.
II. Title.
  HV6024.5.D36 2006
  364.072—dc22
                                                                    2005024821

Printed in the United States of America
09 08 07 06 05   10 9 8 7 6 5 4 3 2 1

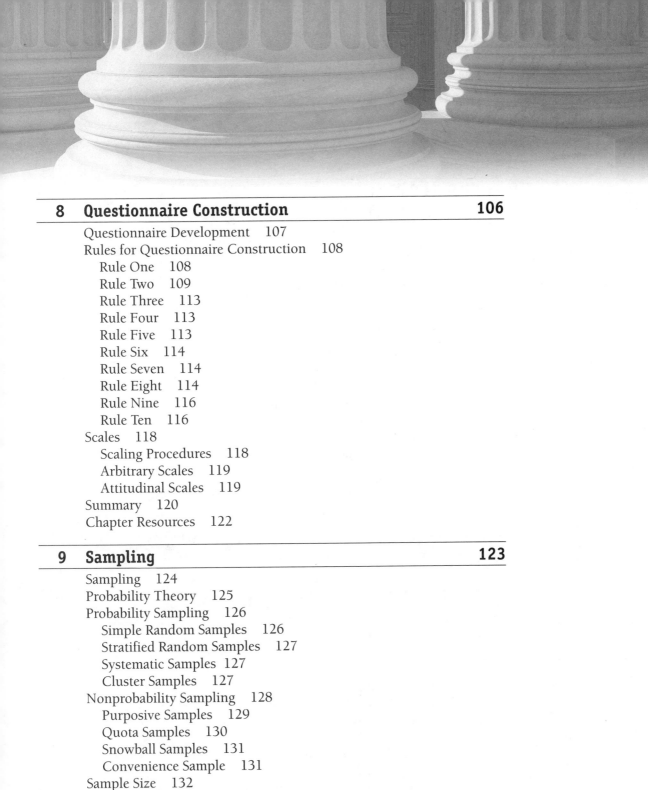

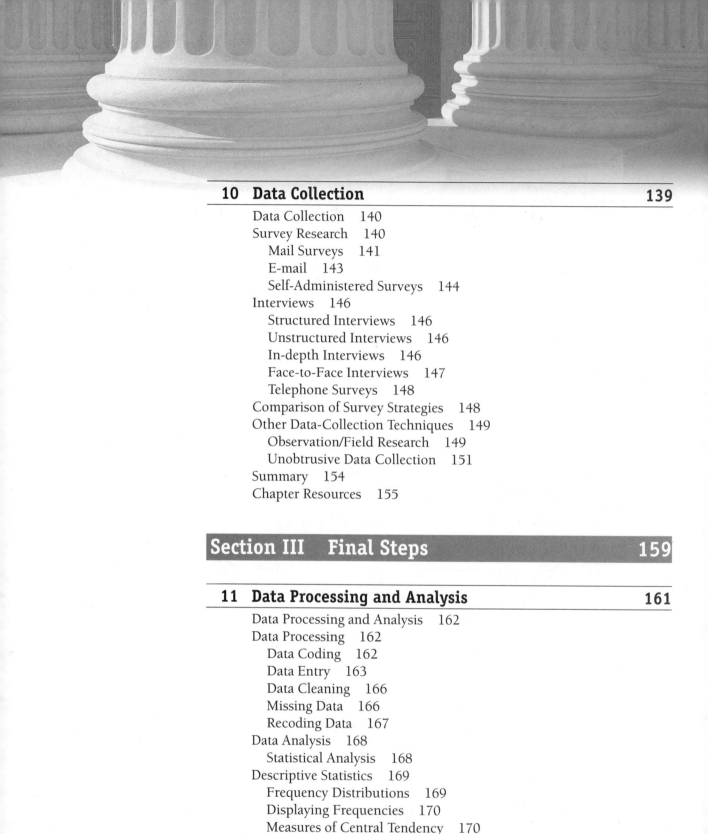

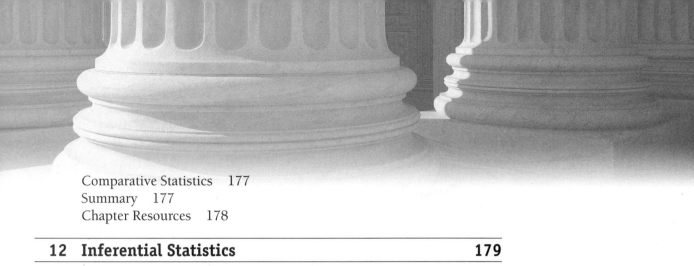

Whether research is done by a college student completing a project for his or her degree, (or just trying to understand an assigned reading) or by a professor meeting requirements or expectations associated with his or her position, it should be enjoyable and not a chore. The first step is to learn the basics for conducting research. A number of textbooks exist that can assist in this task, but many make learning about research—let alone conducting it—appear daunting. The authors have made every attempt to ease the task of learning how to conduct research less daunting and perhaps even to put the prospect of conducting research in a favorable light, thus it is called a primer. To accomplish this task, several pedagogical tools are used.

Each chapter begins with a Vignette that describes a situation students might find themselves in, which relates to the particular chapter's topic. By the end of the chapter, students should be able to identify how to address the confusion or problem presented in the vignette. Within the text, realistic examples are given to enhance the way the specific aspect of research is applicable to criminal justice and criminology. Another enhancement tool is the Methodological Link; these are excerpts from actual criminal justice and criminological research, which reinforce the concept under discussion. Finally, each chapter ends with Methodological Queries—questions and exercises requiring students to apply what has been learned from the chapter.

The text begins by discussing what research is, as well as why and how it is conducted. It addresses such questions as, What are criminal justice and criminological research? Why conduct this research? And, How can this research be completed? In general, it lays the foundation for conducting research.

In Chapter 2, *The Language of Research*, students are introduced to the researchese or terminology associated with conducting research, such as theory, hypothesis, population, sample, and variables. Furthermore, it briefly explores the processes required for conducting research through a researchese perspective.

Deciding what to conduct research on can often be frustrating. However, there are numerous sources available to assist in making a decision on what to research. Chapter 3, *Getting Started*, explores what sources to use and the issue of developing the research question, which often is the driving force behind social science research.

Because criminal justice research often deals with human behavior, the ethics associated with such research is important. Chapter 4, *Research Ethics*, discusses the ethics relevant to conducting research.

Because of its long-standing image of being an applied social science, and because of its lack of statistical sophistication, some of the research conducted and published has had its detractors. As a result, a debate continues as to what is more "academic," qualitative or quantitative research. Chapter 5, *Qualitative*

Preface

Research, does not enter the debate but simply explains how this type of research fits into both criminology and into criminal justice.

To help balance the debate over qualitative versus quantitative research, Chapter 6, *Quantitative Research,* takes over where Chapter 5 ends by exploring the other important type of research conducted in both criminology and criminal justice.

To successfully complete any type of research, it is important to establish a feasible plan or blueprint, known as the research design. Chapter 7, *Research Designs,* discusses the various research designs available for criminal justice and criminological research. They include historical, descriptive, inferential, developmental, case and field, correlational, and causal-comparative. A brief mention is made of true and quasi-experimental, and action designs.

One of the most popular means of collecting data is the questionnaire. Although a rule of thumb is to use an established questionnaire, many individuals choose to design their own. Chapter 8, *Questionnaire Construction,* discusses the intricacies of designing a questionnaire, including issues of measurement, reliability, and validity.

It would be great if information could be gathered from a complete population, but this is almost impossible for criminal justice and criminological research. Therefore, sampling is an important aspect of research. In Chapter 9, *Sampling,* this concept and its related issues are examined.

In establishing the research design, a key component is how the data is to be collected. The four primary means for collecting data—survey, observation, archival, and unobtrusive means—are identified and explored within Chapter 10, *Data Collection.*

Once the data is collected, the question is, what to do with it? There are a number of statistical techniques from which to choose. This is not a statistics book. However, to assist the student in better understanding the role of statistics in the research process, we offer Chapters 11, *Data Processing and Analysis,* and Chapter 12, *Inferential Statistics.*

Now that the data is collected and analyzed, all there is left to do is write up the findings. For many, this is a daunting task. To help ease the fear and frustration, Chapter 13, *Writing the Research,* takes the student through a step-by-step introduction to writing the research.

Finally, to bring all the information offered throughout this text into a handy reference guide, we offer Chapter 14, *Summing Up,* an extensive, yet simple review of all the main concepts.

A final note concerns what this text is not. *Research Methods for Criminology and Criminal Justice: A Primer, Second Edition,* is not a statistics book. However, it could be used in conjunction with a criminal justice statistics text. The fact is, separate books are often required to provide students the fullest extent of the knowledge required to conduct research and to analyze the data. This text allows students to learn how to conduct the research, leaving the statistics for another course and text.

We hope you will find the text as useful as it is intended to be. If nothing else, we hope it will help you at least feel more comfortable about reading or conducting criminal justice and criminological research.

—M.L. Dantzker and Ronald D. Hunter

Acknowledgments

As with each book, there are several people who deserve recognition and our gratitude. It all begins with the person who takes the chance of signing authors to write a book. In this case it was Chambers Moore, Acquisitions Editor; our thanks for her support and confidence.

We would also like to thank Christine Emerton, Jenny McIsaac, and Stefanie Boucher.

Finally, we'd like to thank our wives, Dr. Gail Dantzker and Mrs. Vi Hunter, for the constant love and support, especially during "crunch time." Thank you one and all.

Functions

I

Research: What, Why, and How

1

Vignette 1-1 The Research Paper

Research Methods: It is a required course, so you had no choice but to take it. But, you wondered, how hard could it be? The big project is just preparing to write a research paper. No big deal! You have written several "research papers" in college, so how hard could it be to simply go through the stages to prepare to write such a paper? The first class session is about to begin; you settle into your desk and wait to hear what, exactly, is expected in this course.

As the professor begins the introduction to the class, you recall that other students have said this professor is fair but extremely tough. She has very high expectations of students and does not give too many breaks. Again, no problem—you are not afraid of a little work or a challenge. Besides, you feel that you can write pretty well and have had fairly good grades on previous criminal-justice and criminology papers, so you should do all right. Suddenly your attention is caught when the professor advises the class that anyone who thinks they have written a research paper in their other major courses actually has not—but instead, has written what she calls a "literature review" paper. She explains that what is most often required in most college courses are papers where students choose a topic, find a certain amount of resources or "references," and then write a descriptive or explanatory paper. Yes, it might have had an introduction, thesis statement, evidence, and a conclusion, but it was not a research paper—at least not in the same sense as what you will be doing in this class.

The instructor continues by noting that in answering the following questions, you will soon see that there is a difference between what you had believed to be a research paper and what a research paper really is. The questions include: What is criminal-justice research? Why conduct the research? How is this research done? The professor finishes by advising the class that by the end of the first week, you will have been introduced to the foundations for conducting research on criminological and criminal-justice-related topics. So, let the learning begin!

Chapter Objectives

After studying this chapter, the student should be able to:

- Discuss tradition and authority as sources of human learning. Contrast their strengths and weaknesses.
- Present and discuss the errors that plague casual observation.
- Define what is meant by the scientific method. Explain how it seeks to remedy the errors of casual observation.
- Compare and contrast the relationship between theory and research within the inductive- and deductive-logic processes.
- Define research and explain its purpose.
- Compare and contrast basic, applied, and multipurpose research.
- Present and discuss the various types of research.
- Present and discuss the reasons for research in criminal justice and criminology.
- Present and discuss the various factors that influence research decisions.
- Describe the primary steps in conducting research.

The purpose of this text is to assist criminal-justice and criminology students in developing an understanding (and hopefully an appreciation) of the basic principles of social research. We do not seek to turn you into a research scientist in one short course of study. However, we do hope to give you a rudimentary foundation that can be built upon, should you be interested in doing criminological or criminal-justice research in the future. This primer will enable you to grasp the importance of scientific research, to read and comprehend all but the most complex research methodologies of others, and to provide you with the basic tools to conduct your own social research.

■ The Nature of Scientific Inquiry

It was not that long ago, at least in our minds, that we were criminal-justice students taking a first course in research methods. Our thoughts ran something like this: *We want to be police officers—why do we need to take this course? This is even worse than criminal theory, another useless course. What does it have to do with the real world that we want to work in?* Later, police experience in the "real world" taught us the value of both theory and research in the field of criminal justice. When we subsequently returned to school for graduate studies, the importance of theory and research was more readily apparent to us. We had learned that scientific investigation is very similar to criminal investigation: the use of a logical order and established procedures to solve real-world problems.

■ Social-Science Research and the "Real World"

As police officers, we (the authors) sought to determine whether a crime had been committed (what occurred and when it occurred), who had done it, how they had done it, and why they had done it. We then sought to use that investigatory knowledge to develop a successful prosecution of the offender. Our endeavors in the field taught us that the theory course that we had grudgingly endured had provided the rationale for human behavior upon which the strategies of policing, courts, and corrections were based. We also discovered that those theories were not developed in some esoteric vacuum. They were, in fact, the products of trial-and-error experiments conducted in policing, the courts, and corrections—experiments that had been refined and reapplied to their appropriate subject area. Today's police-deployment strategies, legal processes, and correctional techniques are all solidly based on prior theory and research.

The above statements can also be applied to social-science research in general. Typical "real-world" conclusions are often flawed due to a number of issues that cause our observations as well as our reasoning to be inaccurate. The scientific method seeks to provide a means of investigation to correct (or at least limit) the inaccuracies of ordinary human inquiry. Earl Babbie (2004) argues that we learn from direct observation and from what we are taught by others. How we interpret our own observations as well as what we learn from others is based on tradition and authority. Tradition is the cultural teaching about the real world: "Poisonous snakes are dangerous. Beware of them!" You don't have to be bitten by a rattlesnake to appreciate its hazard. You have been taught by other members of your culture to respect the threat to you. This is an example of positive learning from tradition. It is based on the experiences of others in your society who passed their knowledge on to you. Unfortunately, knowledge based on tradition is often erroneous. "Women are not suited to be police officers. They are too weak and too emotional." A multitude of highly competent and professional police officers have proved this sexist stereotype to be a fallacy.

The other source of secondhand knowledge cited by Babbie (2004) is authority. Authority refers to new knowledge that is provided from the observations of others whom we respect. The cool aunt or uncle (or older cousin) who explained the "facts of life" to you was an authority figure. How accurate their explanations were, we leave to you to decide. As you got older, you learned that much free advice was worth what you paid for it, and that a great deal of "bought advice" had little value as well. The importance of knowledge gained from authority figures depends on their qualifications relative to the subject being discussed. Therefore, you go to a physician for help with your health problems and you hire a plumber to fix a broken water pipe. These individuals are expected to have the expertise to provide solutions that laypeople do not have. Like tradition, the knowledge gained from dealings with authority figures can be extremely accurate or highly erroneous.

■ Science Versus Casual Inquiry

Casual inquiry is influenced by the sources of knowledge discussed in the previous section. In addition, there are other pitfalls that create errors in our own observations. It has been noted that casual inquiry may be flawed due to inaccurate observation, overgeneralization, selective observation, or illogical reasoning (Babbie, 2004; Glicken, 2003; Leedy & Ormond, 2005).

Inaccurate observation occurs when we make conclusions based on hasty or incomplete observations. As an example, a young police officer once walked by a break room where a young records clerk was in tears. Sitting on each side of her were the captain in charge of Internal Affairs and an IA investigator. In a harsh tone of voice, the captain was telling her to stop crying. The officer walking by immediately thought, "Those jerks. They could have at least taken her into their office before interrogating her." Several years later, the officer, then a sergeant for whom the woman in question now worked, learned that she had been extremely distraught over the breakup of her marriage, and that the captain was a father figure to her who had actually been consoling her.

Overgeneralization occurs when we make conclusions about individuals or groups based on our knowledge of similar individuals or groups. "All lawyers are liars!" would be an example. Despite the preponderance of lawyer jokes and any bad experiences that you or a friend may have had with an attorney, you cannot accurately make that conclusion about all lawyers. There are simply too many attorneys (men and women of honesty and integrity as well as those of questionable ethics) to make such a conclusion without an individual knowledge of the person.

Selective observation is when you see only those things that you want to see. Racial and ethnic stereotyping would be an example of negative selective observation. The attitude that "All whites are racists who seek to oppress minorities" may cause the observer to see what he or she believes in the behaviors of all European Americans with whom they come into contact. Selective observation may also be positively biased: "My darling wonderful child has never done anything like that." Such selective observation can lead to major disappointment, such as when "He's a wonderful man who caters to my every whim" becomes "He's a selfish jerk who doesn't ever consider my feelings."

Finally, illogical reasoning happens when we decide that despite our past observations, the future will be different. For example, the individual who plays the lottery, loyally believing that eventually he has to win because someone always does, is an example of illogical reasoning. If the odds of success are unlikely, it is illogical to assume that by sheer willpower you can make it occur.

By imposing order and rigor on our observations, science seeks to reduce the possibility of these common errors occurring. The means of doing so is the application of the scientific method.

The Scientific Method

The scientific method seeks to prevent the errors of casual inquiry by utilizing procedures that specify objectivity, logic, theoretical understanding, and knowledge of prior research in the development and use of a precise-measurement instrument designed to accurately record observations. The result is a systematic search for the most accurate and complete description or explanation of the events or behaviors that are being studied. Just as a criminal investigation is a search for "the facts," and a criminal trial is a search for "the truth," the scientific method is a search for knowledge. The criminological researcher seeks to use the principles of empiricism, skepticism, relativism, objectivity, ethical neutrality, parsimony, accuracy, and precision to assess a particular theoretical explanation.

In the above formula, empiricism is defined as seeking answers to questions through direct observation. Skepticism is the search for disconfirming evidence and the process of continuing to question the conclusions and the evidence that are found. Relativism refers to theories whose conceptions are not absolute but rather relative to the individual who proposes that theory. Objectivity mandates that conclusions be based on careful observation that sees the world as it really is, free from personal feelings or prejudices. Criminological researchers often acknowledge that total objectivity is unattainable, but every reasonable effort is made to overcome any subjective interests that might influence the research outcomes. This is known as intersubjectivity. Ethical neutrality builds on objectivity by stressing that the researcher's beliefs or preferences will not be allowed to influence the research process or its outcomes. Parsimony is the attempt to reduce to the smallest possible number the sum of possible explanations for an event or phenomenon. Accuracy requires that observations be recorded in a correct manner exactly as they occurred. Precision is specifying the number of available subcategories of a concept. (Definitions adapted from Adler & Clark, 2003; Fitzgerald & Cox, 2001; and Senese, 1997.)

The Relationship Between Theory and Research

As was discussed in a prior section, the practice of criminal justice is based on theories about the causes of crime and how to respond to them. Criminology is an academic discipline that studies the nature of crime, its causes, its consequences, and society's response to it. Criminal justice as an academic discipline tends to focus more on the creation, application, and enforcement of criminal laws to maintain social order. (For a detailed analysis of the complex interrelationships between criminology and criminal justice, *Criminology and Criminal Justice: Comparing, Contrasting, and Intertwining Disciplines* [Dantzker, 1998] is recommended reading.) There is so much of an overlap between the two disciplines that within this text we deal with the two as one discipline (as, indeed, many criminologists and criminal-justice experts consider them to be). Regardless of the reader's orientation, theory is integral to the development of research. Likewise, theory that has been validated by research is the basis for practice in the criminal-justice system.

■ Theory

Theory is that which explains how things are in reality, as opposed to what we might want them to be. Personal ideologies are of no value in criminological theory unless they can be evaluated scientifically. We define theory as "an attempt to explain why a particular social activity or event occurs." A theory is a generalization about the phenomenon that is being studied. From this broad theory, more-precise statements (concepts) are developed. Specific measurable statements are hypotheses. It is through observation and measurement that the validity (correctness or ability to actually predict what it seeks to examine) of a hypothesis is examined. If the hypothesis cannot be rejected, then support for the theory is shown. The method by which the hypothesis is observed and measured is research. The relationship between theory and research may be either inductive or deductive in nature.

Inductive Logic

In the stories by Sir Arthur Conan Doyle, his detective hero Sherlock Holmes continuously assails Dr. Watson, a man of science, about the merits of "deductive logic." It is through deductive logic that Holmes is said to solve his cases. In actuality, the process that Holmes describes is inductive logic. In this process, the researcher observes an event, makes empirical generalizations about the activity, and constructs a theory based on them. Only rarely does Holmes engage in the deduction of which he speaks so highly. Another example of inductive logic would be Sir Isaac Newton's alleged formulation of the theory of gravity after observing an apple fall from a tree.

Deductive Logic

Deductive logic begins with a theoretical orientation. The researcher then develops research hypotheses that are tested by observations. These observations lead to empirical generalizations that either support or challenge the theory in question. Had our hero Holmes followed up his theory construction with such observation, he then would have been engaged in deduction. The scientific method is based on deductive-theory construction and testing. In criminological research, the distinctions between inductive and deductive logic are often obscured because the two processes are actually complementary. Although it has been described as a circular model (Babbie, 2004; Wallace, 1971), the elements of both inductive and deductive logic may also be viewed as part of a never-ending continuum that begins with theory, which encourages creation of hypotheses, which in turn calls for observations. The result of observations is generalizations, and the conclusions of the generalizations assist in modification of the theory.

The Purpose of Research

The average college student truly believes he or she knows what it means to conduct research. Many have written a "research paper" either in high school or for a college course. Realistically, though, few have ever had the opportunity to truly write a research paper because even fewer have ever conducted scientific research.

■ What Research Is

Research is the conscientious study of an issue, problem, or subject. It is a useful form of inquiry designed to assist in discovering answers. It can also lead to the creation of new questions. For example, a judge wants to know how much effect her sentencing has had on individuals convicted of drug possession, particularly as it compares to another judge's sentencing patterns. She asks that research be conducted that focuses on recidivism of these individuals. The results indicate that 30 percent of drug offenders sentenced in her court are rearrested, compared with only 20 percent from the other judge's court. In comparing the two courts, the inquiring judge has discovered that her sentencing does not appear to be as effective. This answered the primary question of the research, but it has also created new questions, such as, Why are her methods not working as well as those of the other judge?

Research creates questions, but ultimately, regardless of the subject or topic under study, it is the goal of research to provide answers. One of the more common uses of the term *research* is a description of what a student might be asked to accomplish for a college class. Many times you hear instructors and students refer to the choosing of a topic, using several sources, and writing a descriptive paper on the topic as research. If done thoroughly and objectively, this may actually constitute qualitative research (discussed in detail in Chapter 5). Unfortunately, these "research papers" are too often essays based more on the individual's ideologies than on scientific discovery. For the purpose of this text, the emphasis shall be on *empirical research* that yields scholarly results.

There are many formal definitions for the term research. We use the following: *Research is the scientific investigation into or of a specifically identified phenomenon* (Dantzker, 1998, p. 128), and is applicable to recognizable and undiscovered phenomena. Therefore, in terms of criminal justice and criminology, related research can be viewed as *the investigation into or of any phenomenon linked to any or all aspects of the criminal-justice system*. Using this definition, criminal justice and criminological research are not limited to any one area.

Along with the plethora of research topics, there are several methods for conducting the research. They include surveys, observation, conducting case studies, and reviewing official records. These methods will be discussed in further detail, but before we do so, it is important to understand all the underlying characteristics of research. To begin with, criminal justice and criminological research are often divided into two forms: applied and basic.

Applied Research

Perhaps the most immediately useful type of research in criminal justice is applied research, which is primarily an inquiry of a scientific nature designed and conducted with practical application as its goal. In other words, applied research is the collection of data and the analysis of the collected data with respect to a specific issue or problem so that the applications of the results can influence change (see **Box 1-1**).

A major form of applied research is evaluative research, which focuses on answering questions (Eck & La Vigne, 1994, p. 6) such as:

1. *Is the program, policy, or procedure doing what it was meant to do?*

2. *If not, how is the program, policy, or procedure deficient?*

3. *How can it be improved?*

4. *Should it be continued as is, changed, or discontinued?*

In essence, applied research provides answers that can be used to improve, change, or help decide to eliminate the focus of study. It can be quite useful to criminal-justice practitioners. Despite its usefulness, applied research is not conducted as frequently in criminology or criminal-justice research as is basic research.

Basic Research

Basic research, sometimes referred to as "pure" research, is the conducting of scientific inquiries that may offer little "promise or expectation of immediate, direct relevance" (Talarico, 1980, p. 3). Instead, it is concerned with the acquisition of new information for the purpose of helping develop the scholarly discipline or field of study in which the research is being conducted. This type of research is more often consistent with criminological inquiries. The more common nature of this research is descriptive, and tries to respond to such questions as:

1. *How big is the issue or problem?*

2. *Whom or what does the issue or problem affect?*

3. *What causes the issue or problem? (Eck & La Vigne, 1994, p. 5)*

Box 1-1

Applied-Research Topics: Some Examples

Policing:
    Stress, patrol effectiveness, use of force, job satisfaction, response times
Courts:
    Types of sentencing, plea bargaining, race and sentencing, jury versus judge verdicts, death penalty
Corrections:
    Rehabilitation versus punishment, effectiveness of programs, boot camps, prisonization
Others:
    Criminal behavior, victimization, drugs, gangs, juvenile criminality

METHODOLOGICAL
LINKS

To evaluate the effectiveness of Florida's mandatory human-diversity course for police and correctional officers, Ford and Williams (1999) conducted a survey among justice personnel who had completed the course. Their findings indicated that the course was seen as important, but did little to change on-the-job conduct.

Metraux and Culhane (2004) examined the incidence of and interrelationships between shelter use and reincarceration among a cohort of 48,424 people. Their findings suggested that more use of shelters limited reincarceration rates.

The findings from basic research often have little if any applicable usage in the field of criminal justice. However, such research may become the foundation upon which subsequent applied research and criminal-justice policy are based. It is such research that leads to the development of the criminological theories that guide the actions of lawmakers, police, courts, and corrections.

Multipurpose Research

Both basic and applied research are vital to the study of crime and justice. However, a good portion of the research conducted by criminal-justice and criminological academicians tends to come under a third area of research

METHODOLOGICAL
LINKS

Mueller, Giacomazzi, and Wada (2004) surveyed panel chairs from the 2003 Academy of Criminal Justice Sciences meeting. Although this research does not appear to have any direct value to criminal-justice policy or processes, its outcomes could help steer the direction of future conferences.

Gaarder, Rodrigues, and Zatz (2004) examined whether and how gender, race/ethnicity, and class influence perceptions held by juvenile-court personnel, and how such perceptions may contribute to the already-limited treatment options for girls. Initially, the results of this research may not seem as if they would have any application. However, findings could assist in developing better training for court personnel on how to not let their perceptions cloud their judgment.

most accurately called *multipurpose research*. Multipurpose research is the scientific inquiry into an issue or problem that can be both descriptive and evaluative—that is, it is between the basic and applied realms. This type of research generally begins as exploratory, but is of such a nature that its results could ultimately be applicable. For example, a police chief is interested in the level of job satisfaction among his sworn employees. A job-satisfaction survey is conducted that offers a variety of findings related to officers' satisfaction. From a basic perspective, the data may simply describe how officers perceive their jobs, thus becoming descriptive in nature. However, these same findings could be used to evaluate the police agency by examining those areas where satisfaction is the lowest, and leading to efforts to determine how to improve them. This is the applied nature of the research. The result is research that is multipurpose.

Whether applied, basic, or multipurpose, research can provide interesting findings about a plethora of problems, events, issues, or activities. Regardless of the strategies utilized, criminological and criminal-justice research are necessary for understanding both crime and criminality as well as for developing suitable responses.

■ Types of Research

Prior to conducting research, one must understand something about research; that is, one must first study how research is correctly conducted. At some point in one's college career or during one's employment, a person may be asked to "look into something" or "research this topic." Often the individual has no clue where to look, how to begin, or what to look for. Then, once the information is obtained, the person may not understand how the information was found and what it actually means.

The primary reason for studying research is to be able to attain a better understanding of why it was done and how it may be used. Ultimately, if we do not understand what research is and how it works, we cannot understand the products of research. Therefore, the answer to why we study research is the same as the reason why we conduct research: to gain knowledge. This knowledge may occur in one of four formats or types: descriptive, explanatory, predictive, or intervening knowledge.

Descriptive Research

Knowledge that is descriptive allows us to understand what something is. Research of this nature helps us to gain a better grasp about an issue or problem we know little about. In other words, it tends to define or describe what we are trying to understand. This type of research is also very popular regarding opinions and perceptions.

Descriptive knowledge is a very common result of criminal-justice and criminological research. Although the results may be very informative, what can be done with this knowledge is often limited.

METHODOLOGICAL

Women have taken part in many forms of crime in the United States. One area we know little about is women in organized crime. To provide some insight into this arena of thought, Liddick (1999) examined the role of women in the numbers-gambling industry in New York City. The study's findings about women in this extremely lucrative form of criminality provided knowledge that had previously been unknown.

Ventura, Lambertt, Bryant, and Pasupuleti (2004) examined the differences in attitudes toward gays and lesbians among criminal-justice and non-criminal-justice majors. This research, although limited to one university, offered insight into attitudinal differences among students at this university, especially those majoring in criminal justice. Another example of descriptive research is Vaughn, Del Carmen, Perfecto, and Charand (2004), who offered a strictly descriptive study of the journals in criminal justice and criminology.

Explanatory Research

Explanatory research tries to tell us *why* something occurs, or the causes behind it. This research can be very important when trying to understand why certain types of individuals become serial murderers, or what factors contribute to criminality. Knowing the causes behind something can assist in finding ways to counteract the behavior or the problem.

Predictive Research

Knowledge that is predictive in nature helps to establish future actions. This type of research can be useful to all criminal-justice practitioners. For example, if research indicates that a large percentage of juveniles placed in boot-camp environments are less likely to become adult offenders, these results could be used in the future sentencing of juvenile offenders. Conversely, if boot camps are shown

METHODOLOGICAL

Why do people fear crime? What perpetuates this fear? Weitzer and Kubrin (2004) examined the role of the media in shaping crime fears. Kingsnorth and Macintosh (2004) examined more than 5,000 cases of domestic violence in an attempt to discover predictors of victim support for official action.

METHODOLOGICAL LINKS

Metraux and Culhane (2004) examined the incidence of and interrelationships between shelter use and reincarceration among a cohort of 48,424 people. Their findings suggested that more use of shelters limited reincarceration rates. The predictive value of these finding could assist in postsentencing decisions.

to have little or no effect, other alternatives may then be explored. Predictive knowledge gives some foresight into what may happen if something is implemented or tried. Because one of the concerns of criminal justice is to lower criminality, predictive knowledge could be quite useful in attaining this end.

Intervening Research

Finally, intervening knowledge allows one to intercede before a problem or issue gets too difficult to address. This type of research can be quite significant when a problem arises that currently available means are not addressing properly. Research on the effectiveness of certain community-policing programs is a good example of intervening research. It can demonstrate whether a specific type of action taken before a given point will provide the desired results. For example, current research has shown that community-policing initiatives from "foot patrol to limiting pay phones to outgoing calls," has helped meet desired outcomes of lowering drug-related crimes. (See Brodeur, 1998; Rosenbaum, 1994.)

Whether the research is descriptive, explanatory, predictive, or intervening, it is important to understand what research is and how it is valuable. If one fails to study research in and of itself, then all research is of little value. This becomes especially true for the criminal-justice and criminological academic or practitioner who wants to make use of previously conducted research or to conduct his or her own. It is important to have a grasp of what research is and why it is conducted, before one can actually conduct research.

■ Why Research Is Necessary

There are a number of specific reasons for conducting criminal-justice or criminological research. Three primary reasons include curiosity, addressing social problems, and the development and testing of theories.

Curiosity

Wanting to know about an existing problem, issue, policy, or outcome is being curious. For example, in an earlier Methodological Links, Mueller, Giacomazzi, and Wada (2004) were interested in the perceptions of panel chairs from a national conference. One might say that the study by Vaughn, Del Carmen, Perfecto, and Charand (2004) was also a study of curiosity.

Social Problems

The most salient social problem related to criminal justice is crime. Who commits it? Why do they act as they do? How do they do it? These are questions of interest for many criminal-justice and criminological practitioners and academics. Concern over the effects of crime on society only adds further reason to conduct related research. This research can help identify who is more likely to commit certain crimes and why, how to better deal with the offenders and the victims, and what specific parts of the system can do to help limit or alleviate crime. As a major social problem, crime provides many reasons for research as well as avenues for exploration.

Theory Testing

Linked more closely with pure criminological research, theories provide good cause to conduct research. The relationship between theory and research was discussed earlier in this chapter. Theory construction will be discussed in detail in the next chapter.

■ Factors That Influence Research Decisions

Regardless of why the research is conducted, one must be cognizant of factors that can influence why the research is conducted and how it is conducted. Of the many influential factors, the three that appear to be the most important are social and political, practicality, and ethical considerations (Kaplan, 1963; Kimmel, 1988, 1996; Leedy & Ormond, 2005)

The social and political influences are often specific to the given research. Criminology and criminal justice as social sciences are greatly influenced by social and political events that are taking place in society. For example, race and ethnicity, economics, and gender might be influential on research about prison environments. Research on whether a particular law is working might have political ramifications. The inability of the criminal-justice system to address problems identified by research may be due not to the lack of system resources, but to the lack of social desire or political will for the system to do so.

When it comes to conducting research, practicality can play an extremely important role. Economics and logistics are two elements of practicality. How much will the research cost? Can it be conducted in an efficient and effective manner? Would the benefits that are anticipated justify the social, political, and economic costs? Would limited resources be taken from other areas? These are just some of the questions of practicality that could influence the conducting of research and the subsequent uses of that research.

Because ethics plays an important role in conducting research, a more in-depth discussion is offered in Chapter 4. It is briefly noted here that there are three ethical considerations of importance: invasion of privacy, deception, and potential harm. Within a free society, citizens jealously protect their rights to privacy. These rights are not just expected by citizens but are protected by law. Deception can have adverse effects not only on the research findings but also on the individuals who were deceived by the researcher. Harm to others, especially to those who did not willingly accept such risks, must be avoided. Each of these concepts will be explored in greater detail later.

Whatever the reason, researchers must be aware of the influences that have led to the research and those that might affect the research outcomes. Each could be detrimental to the outcome of the research.

■ How Research Is Done

Whether the research is applied or basic, qualitative or quantitative (to be discussed in later chapters), certain basic steps are applicable to each. There are five primary steps in conducting research:

1. Identifying the research problem

2. Research design

3. Data collection

4. Data analysis

5. Reporting of results

Each of these will be given greater attention later in the text, but a brief introduction here is appropriate.

Identifying the Problem

Prior to starting a research project, one of the most important steps is recognizing and defining what is going to be studied. Identifying or determining the problem, issue, or policy to be studied sets the groundwork for the rest of the research. For example, embarking on the study of crime can be too great an undertaking without focusing on a specific aspect of crime, such as types, causes, or punishments. Therefore, it is important to specify the target of the research first. Doing this makes completing the remaining stages easier.

Research Design

The research design is the "blueprint," which outlines how the research is to be conducted. Although the design will depend on the nature of the research, there are several common designs used in criminal justice and criminology. Various designs will be presented in this section. They will be discussed in detail in later chapters.

Survey Research

Conducting surveys is one of the most often employed methods of research. This approach obtains data directly from the targeted source(s) and is often conducted through self-administered or interview questionnaires.

Field Research

Field research is when researchers gather data through firsthand observations of their targets. For example, if a researcher wanted to learn more about gang membership and activities, he or she might try "running" with a gang as a participant-observer.

Experimental Research

Experimental research is also observational research. Unlike field research, however, observational studies involve the administration of research stimuli to participants in a controlled environment. Due to ethical and economic concerns, this kind of experimental research is conducted less frequently in criminal justice than are other research strategies.

Life Histories or Case Studies

Probably one of the simplest methods of research in criminology and criminal justice is through the use of life histories or case studies. Often these studies require the review and analysis of documents such as police reports, court records, medical histories, and so forth. This type of research might focus on violent behavior where the researcher investigates the lives of serial murderers to try and comprehend why the perpetrators acted as they did.

Record Studies

When researchers evaluate and analyze official records for relevant data, they employ the *records study* research design. For example, to determine patterns and influences of robbery, the research design might utilize data from Uniform Crime Reports.

Content Analysis

In this research design, documents, publications, or presentations are reviewed and analyzed. A researcher might review old documents to determine how crime events were publicized in a prior century, or may monitor current television broadcasts to assess how the entertainment media influence public perceptions of crime.

Despite the options these designs offer, other design methods are possible, but will be discussed later in the text. Ultimately, the design used will depend on the nature of the study.

Data Collection

Regardless of the research design, data collection is a key component. A variety of methods (which will receive greater attention later in the text) exist. They include surveys, interviews, observations, and previously existing data.

Data Analysis

How to analyze and interpret the data is more appropriately discussed in another course, perhaps one focusing on statistics. Still, it is an important part of the design and cannot be ignored. The most common means for data analysis today is through the use of a computer and specifically oriented software.

Reporting

The last phase of any research project is the reporting of the findings. This can be done through various means: reports, journals, books, or computer presentations. How the findings are reported will depend on the target audience. Regardless of the audience or the medium used, the findings must be coherent and understandable or they are of no use to anyone.

Before leaving this section, there is one last area worthy of a brief discussion. Information has been offered on why and how to conduct research, but when is it inappropriate to conduct that research?

Often it appears that research is conducted with little concern as to its appropriateness. Failing to consider this might render the findings useless. Therefore, it is necessary that the prospective researcher be able to answer all the following questions with a negative response (Eck & La Vigne, 1994, p. 39):

1. *Does the research problem involve question(s) of value rather than fact?*
2. *Is the solution to the research question already predetermined, effectively annulling the findings?*
3. *Is it impossible to conduct the research effectively and efficiently?*
4. *Are the research issues vague and ill-defined?*

If the answer to any of these questions is yes, the research in question should be avoided.

■ Summary

Conducting criminological research goes beyond looking up material on a subject and writing a descriptive paper. Prior to conducting research, one must understand what it is, why it is, and how it might be conducted.

For the purposes of this text, criminal-justice and criminological research are defined together as *the investigation into or of any phenomenon linked to any or all aspects of the criminal justice system.* The type of research conducted can be applied, basic, or multipurpose. A primary reason for conducting research is to gain knowledge, which can be descriptive, explanatory, predictive, or intervening in nature. Studying research is required to better understand the results offered.

All research tends to follow five basic steps: recognizing and defining a problem, issue, or policy for study; designing the research; collecting data through survey, interviews, observation, or examining previously collected data; analyzing the data; and reporting the findings. Finally, it is important to determine whether it is prudent to conduct the research in question.

Research plays a very important role in criminal justice and criminology. It brings questions and answers, debates, and issues. Knowing what the research is, why it is done, and how it can be accomplished is necessary if one is to study crime and criminal behavior.

METHODOLOGICAL QUERIES

1. Your roommate has just returned from the first day of classes and says that he has to write two research papers. What questions will you ask in reference to these papers?

2. What is the first thing you need to do to prepare to start your first criminal-justice research paper? What will affect or influence this decision?

3. You have chosen a topic that fits the "multipurpose" research mode. What is that topic? Explain how it fits the applied and basic categories.

4. Identify and discuss what items might make researching your topic inappropriate.

REFERENCES

Adler, E. S., & Clark, R. (2003). *How it's done: An invitation to social research* (2nd ed.). Belmont, CA: Wadsworth.

Babbie, E. (2004). *The practice of social research* (10th ed.). Belmont, CA: Thomson/Wadsworth.

Brodeur, J. (Ed.). (1998). *How to recognize good policing: Problems and issues.* Thousand Oaks, CA: Sage.

Dantzker, M. L. (1998). *Criminology and criminal justice: Comparing, contrasting, and intertwining disciplines.* Woburn, MA: Butterworth-Heinemann.

Eck, J. E., & La Vigne, N. G. (1994). *Using research: A primer for law enforcement managers.* Washington, DC: Police Executive Research Forum.

Fitzgerald, J. D., & Cox, S.M. (2001). *Research methods and statistics in criminal justice: An introduction* (3rd ed.). Chicago: Nelson-Hall.

Ford, M. C., & Williams, L. (1999). Human/Cultural diversity training for justice personnel. In M. L. Dantzker (Ed.), *Readings for research methods in criminology and criminal justice* (pp. 37–60). Woburn, MA: Butterworth-Heinemann.

Gaarder, E., Rodrigues, N. & Zatz, M. S. (2004). Criers, liars, and manipulators: Probation officers' views of girls. *Justice Quarterly, 21*(3), 547–578.

Glicken, M. D. 2003. *Social research: A simple guide.* Boston: Allyn and Bacon.

Kaplan, A. (1963). *The conduct of inquiry: Methodology for behavioral science.* San Francisco: Chandler.

Kimmel, A. J. (1988). *Ethics and values in applied social research.* Thousand Oaks, CA: Sage.

Kimmel, A. J. (1996). *Ethical issues in behavioral research: A survey.* Cambridge, MA: Blackwell.

Kingsnorth, R. F., & Macintosh, R. C. (2004). Domestic violence: Predictors of victim support for official action. *Justice Quarterly, 21*(2), 301–328.

Leedy, P. D. & Ormond, J. E. (2005). *The practice of research* (7th ed.). Upper Saddle River, NJ: Prentice Hall.

Liddick, Jr., D. R. (1999). Women as organized criminals: An examination of the numbers gambling industry in New York City. In M. L. Dantzker (Ed.), *Readings for research methods in criminology and criminal justice* (pp. 123-138). Woburn, MA: Butterworth-Heinemann.

Metraux, S., & Culhane, D. P. (2004). Homeless shelter use and reincarceration following prison release. *Criminology and Public Policy, 3*(2), 139–160.

Mueller, D., Giacomazzi, A., & Wada, J. (2004). So how was your conference? Panel chairs' perceptions of the 2003 ACJS meeting in Boston. *Journal of Criminal Justice Education, 15*(2), 201–218.

Rosenbaum, D. P. (Ed.). (1994). *The challenge of community policing: Testing the promises.* Thousand Oaks, CA: Sage.

Senese, J. D. (1997). *Applied research methods in criminal justice.* Chicago: Nelson-Hall.

Talarico, S. M. (1980). *Criminal justice research: Approaches, problems, and policy.* Cincinnati, OH: Anderson Publishing.

Vaughn, M. S., Del Carmen, R. V., Perfecto, M., & Charand, K. X. (2004). Journals in criminal justice and criminology: An updated and expanded guide for authors. *Journal of Criminal Justice Education, 15*(1), 61–192.

Ventura, L. A., Lambertt, E. G. Bryant, M., & Pasupuleti, S. (2004). Differences in attitudes toward gays and lesbians among criminal justice and non-criminal justice majors. *American Journal of Criminal Justice, 28*(2), 165-179.

Wallace, W. (1971). *The logic of science in sociology.* New York: Aldine deGrutyer.

Weitzer, R., & Kubrin, C. E. (2004). Breaking news: How local TV news and real-world conditions affect fear of crime. *Justice Quarterly, 21*(3), 497–520.

Chapter Resources

The Language
of Research

2

Vignette 2-1   Researchese?

Still pondering the instructor's comments about research papers, you remain puzzled. In many previous classes, you have been asked to write research papers, and now you are being told you have never written one. You raise your hand. When called upon, you ask, "What do you mean that we have never written a research paper? I know I have written several." The instructor acknowledges expecting this query. Yet the response is not what you had expected. Your instructor asks, "Have you ever studied a foreign language?" You reply that you took a few years of Spanish in high school. The instructor then asks whether you recall a word or words that have a specific meaning yet are often broadly used. When you reply positively, the instructor says that this is precisely what is happening here with the word *research*. It is quite common for students and teachers alike to use the term research to describe a paper assignment that is actually a literature review. The instructor goes on to explain that it is necessary to understand the specific language of research before one can proceed with conducting research. Laypeople often refer to the use of legal terminology by lawyers as "legalese." In that same vein, one might refer to the language of research by criminal justice scholars as "researchese."

Chapter Objectives

After studying this chapter, the student should be able to:

- Define theory and explain how it relates to research.
- Describe the conceptualization process.
- Describe what takes place during operationalization.
- Define variable. Discuss how dependent and independent variables differ from one another.
- Describe a hypothesis and how it differs from an assumption. Present and discuss the types of hypotheses.
- Identify a population and discuss how it is related to a sample. Provide examples of some different types of samples.
- Define validity and describe the various types of validity.
- Define reliability. Explain how it relates to validity.
- Describe data and the four levels of data.
- Discuss the steps in the research process.

■ The Language of Research

It is quite common for students and teachers alike to use the term research to describe a paper assignment that is actually a literature review. As previously noted, with respect to criminal justice and criminology, there is more to research than reviewing literature. This synonymous use of the term *research* is just one example of the need to understand language associated with this field. In Chapter 1, the term research was defined. In this chapter, various associated terms—such as *theory*, *hypothesis*, and *variable*—will be defined or further expanded upon.

Theory

There is an interesting debate one could have regarding the term *theory*, which is reminiscent of the age-old argument: Which came first, the chicken or the egg? With respect to theory, one side of the debate argues that theories drive the research (theory-then-research) or deductive logic. The other side would argue that research creates the theory (research-then-theory) (Berg, 2004) or inductive logic (see **Box 2-1**).

In reality, the two types of logic are actually extensions of one another. Observation may lead to theory construction, which then leads to more observation in order to test the theory. Therefore, even research that is initially inductive in nature ultimately becomes deductive in that the theory that is generated is tested by observation. In short, all criminal-justice practice is grounded in criminological theory. Theory is defined here as *an explanation that offers to classify, organize, explain, predict, and/or understand the occurrence of specific phenomena.*

Box 2-1
Theory Debate Models

Theory-then-research
Theory =
Construction +
Selection +
Design +
Reject/Accept

Research-then-theory
Investigation +
Measurement +
Analysis +
Acceptance =
Theory

Based on the definition, a theory is a statement that attempts to make sense of reality. Reality consists of those phenomena that we can identify, recognize, and observe. For example, in criminology, criminal behavior is observed. Therefore, people breaking the law are a reality. A question that arises from this reality is, What causes people to break the law? It is here that theory comes into the picture. Criminology is replete with criminal-behavior theories that focus on causes that include biological, psychological, and sociological factors (see **Box 2-2**).

Research is conducted to determine if theories have any merit or are truly applicable. Proving that a theory is valid is a common goal of criminological and criminal-justice researchers. However, in order to research a theory, the first step is to focus on a concept.

Box 2-2
Examples of Theories in Criminology

Biological
1. A person's physique is correlated to the type of crime one commits.
2. Criminality is genetic.
3. A chemical imbalance in one's brain can lead to criminal behavior.

Psychological
1. Criminal behavior is the result of an inadequately developed ego.
2. Inadequate moral development during childhood leads to criminal behavior.
3. Criminals learn their behavior by modeling it after other criminals.

Sociological
1. Socializing with criminals produces criminal behavior.
2. Society's labeling of an individual as deviant or criminal breeds criminality.
3. Failure to reach societal goals through acceptable means leads to criminality.

Conceptualization

A concept is best defined as an *abstract label that represents an aspect of reality (usually in the form of an object, policy, issue, problem, or phenomenon)*. Every discipline has its own concepts. For example, common concepts in criminal justice and criminology include criminality, law, rehabilitation, and punishment.

Concepts are viewed as the beginning point for all research endeavors, and are often very broad in nature. They are the bases of theories, and serve as a means to communicate, introduce, classify, and build thoughts and ideas. To conduct research, the concept must first be taken from its conceptual or theoretical level to an observational level. In other words, one must go from the abstract to the concrete before research can occur. This process is often referred to as conceptualization. As with the definition of theory, there is more than one way to approach conceptualization. This text promotes the two-phase (theory and research levels), five-stage (conceptual level, conceptual components, conceptual definitions, operational definitions, and observational level) approach (Nachmias & Nachmias, 2000) (see **Box 2-3**). All too often, research fails to explain the conceptualization process. Therefore, it is important that the researcher provide a clear picture of how he or she took the concept from the abstract to the concrete.

To achieve the second part of the conceptualization model—the research phase— the concepts must now be measured. Although concepts can be qualitative, they are most often converted into variables through a process called *operationalization*.

Operationalization

The act of operationalizing is the describing of how a concept is measured. This process is best defined as *the conversion of the abstract idea or notion into a measurable item*. In other words, it involves taking something that is conceptual and making it observable, or going from abstract to concrete.

Box 2-3

Conceptualization-Process Model

Theoretical Phase
 Conceptual Level
  The main concept or theory
 Conceptual Components
  Concepts that are part of the main concept
 Conceptual Definitions
  Terms that describe and differentiate the concept

Research Phase
 Operational Definitions
  Procedures that describe activities to be undertaken
 Observational Level
  Responses to the operational definitions

METHODOLOGICAL LINKS

Researchers often do not report how they conceptualized their concept. When they do, it provides a better understanding of the research. From the following excerpt, can you fit the pieces into the first phase—the theoretical phase—of the conceptualization model?

Community empowerment is a concept used to describe individuals living in close proximity who as a group unite to combat a common problem. The focus of the group is the common problem. If a community is to be empowered, the residents must first be aware that a problem exists (community awareness) to such an extent that it is disturbing or troubling (community concern), resulting in organization of the community (community mobilization) to fight against it (community action) (Moriarty, 1999, p. 17).

Operationalization is one of the more important tasks prior to conducting any research. However, there is no one right way to go about operationalizing; how this is accomplished is up to the researcher. Unfortunately, it is common for researchers to publish their results without ever explaining how their concepts were operationalized. As a result, many students have difficulty fully comprehending the notions of conceptualizing and operationalizing variables. It is up to the researcher to clearly explain the process.

Variables

The primary focus of the operationalization process is the creation of variables and the subsequent development of a measurement instrument to assess those variables. Variables are concepts that may be divided into two or more categories or groupings known as attributes. The ability to divide the variables into categories enables us to study their relationships with other variables. Attributes are the grouping into which variables may be divided. As an example, "male" is an attribute of the variable "gender." There are two types of variables: dependent and independent.

Dependent Variables

A dependent variable is a factor that requires other factors to cause or influence change. Dependent variables are factors over which the researcher has no control. Basically, the dependent variable is the outcome factor or that which is being predicted. In criminal justice and criminology, criminal behavior is a dependent variable because it requires other factors in order for it to exist or change. These other factors are the independent variables.

Independent Variables

The independent variable is the influential or the predictor factor. These are the variables believed to cause the change or outcome of the dependent variable, and are something the researcher can control. Some better-known independent

METHODOLOGICAL

The following excerpt shows how a concept is operationalized. *Community awareness* was conceptualized as the level of knowledge about the use of alcohol and other drugs in the community. Four variables reflected community awareness: drug usage in the neighborhood, drug dealing in the neighborhood, alcohol-/drug-prevention messages; and availability of certain drugs (eight different drugs in all). The following are the actual questions used to establish each variable:

- Drug usage in the neighborhood: Respondents were asked, "How many people in this neighborhood use drugs?" Responses included "many, some, not many or no residents use drugs."
- Drug dealing in the neighborhood: Respondents were asked, "How often do you see drug dealing in this neighborhood?" The responses included "very often, sometimes, rarely, never."
- Alcohol/drug prevention message: Respondents were asked if they had heard or seen any drug or alcohol prevention messages in the past six months.
- Availability of certain drugs: Respondents were asked about the difficulty or ease of obtaining specific drugs in the county. The list of drugs included marijuana, crack cocaine, other forms of cocaine, heroin, other narcotics (methadone, opium, codeine, paregoric), tranquilizers, barbiturates, amphetamines, and LSD. Each drug available represents one variable. (Moriarty, 1999, p. 18)

variables used in criminal-justice and criminological research are gender, race, marital status, and education.

Identifying and recognizing the difference between the variables is important in research, but sometimes may get lost. Therefore, it is important for research to specifically call attention to the variables.

The key to any research is to be able to operationalize the concepts into understandable and measurable variables. Failing to complete this task will make the creation and testing of the hypothesis more difficult.

Hypotheses

Once the concept has been operationalized into variables that fit the theory in question, most research focuses on testing the validity of a statement called a hypothesis. The hypothesis is a *specific statement describing the expected relationship between the independent and dependent variables*. There are three common types of hypotheses: research, null, and rival.

Research Hypothesis

The foundation of a research project is the research hypothesis. This is a statement of the expected relationship between the dependent and independent vari-

METHODOLOGICAL LINKS

Researching attitudes among different criminal-justice practitioners is popular. Gordon (1999) looked at the attitudes of correctional officers toward delinquents and delinquency, and whether the type of institution they work in made a difference. In describing the research, she is clear as to the variables used and how they are measured. This makes the finding much easier to understand.

Variable	Measurement
Dependent Variables	
PUNITIVENESS	Examines attitudes toward punitiveness. Higher scores indicate disagreement with punitiveness as a means to reduce crime. Range 3–12, Mean 6.38.
DELINQUENCY	Examines attitudes toward delinquency. Higher scores indicate disagreement that crime is a result of environmental and opportunity factors. Range 3–12, Mean 7.49.
TREATMENT	Examines attitudes toward treatment of youth. Higher scores indicate disagreement with the ability of "treatment" programs to change offenders' behaviors. Range 4–16, Mean 10.34.
Independent Variables	
FACILITY	0 = Open-Security, 1 = Closed-Security
AGE	In years
GENDER	0 = Female, 1 = Male
RACE	0 = White, 1 = Nonwhite
EDUCATION	0 = Less than High School, 1 = High School, 2 = Some College, 3 = Bachelor Degree, 4 = Graduate Degree
LENGTH AT CURRENT POSITION	In months

ables. The statement may be specified as either a positive (as one increases, the other increases) or a negative (as one increases, the other decreases) relationship. The hypothesis is not always clearly delineated, but it is preferable for it to be.

Null Hypothesis

Some would argue that the results of the research should support the research hypothesis. Others will claim that the goal is to disprove the null hypothesis, which is a statement indicating that no relationship exists between the dependent and independent variables. For example, in Colomb and Damphouse (2004),

METHODOLOGICAL LINKS

Holcomb, Williams, and Demuth (2004), in their research of white females and death-penalty disparity, clearly stated their hypothesis: Defendants convicted of killing white females are significantly more likely to receive death sentences than are killers of victims with other race-gender characteristics (p. 877).

Cooper, McLearen, and Zapf (2004), in their study of police officers' dispositional decisions involving the mentally ill, used this hypothesis: Arrest dispositions would be chosen more often than involuntary-hospitalization dispositions, and experience will be correlated with lack of formal action (p. 295).

Finally, Wilson and Jasinski (2004), in looking at the public satisfaction with the police in domestic-violence cases, hypothesized that: Domestic-violence victims whose expectations are fulfilled by the police will be more satisfied than those victims whose expectations are not fulfilled (p. 235).

although their research hypothesis is not made clear to the reader, the null hypothesis is: A moral panic did not occur in the late 1990s regarding hate crimes because of the disproportionate amount of media attention given to the issue (p. 149).

By rejecting the null hypothesis, the research goal has been fulfilled. However, rejecting the null hypothesis does not necessarily mean that the results have established the validity of the research hypothesis.

Rival Hypothesis

Prior to starting the research, it is customary to establish the research hypothesis, which is generally what the researcher hopes to validate or demonstrate. However, sometimes the results may reject both the null hypothesis and the research hypothesis. This allows for the creation of what is called a rival hypothesis. The rival hypothesis is a statement offering an alternate prediction for the research findings.

For example, the research hypothesis of Holcomb, Williams, and Demuth (2004) that "defendants convicted of killing white females are significantly more likely to receive death sentences than are killers of victims with other race-gender characteristics" might call for a rival hypothesis, perhaps along the lines of "Nonwhite defendants convicted of killing white females are significantly more likely to receive death sentences than are white killers of white females."

It is usually the goal of the research to be able to reject the null hypothesis. Testing the research hypothesis becomes central to the research, making identifying the hypothesis an important aspect of the research. However, although hypotheses often take center stage in research, there is another type of statement that can find its way into the research: *assumptions*. However, these types of statements should be avoided whenever possible.

Assumptions

Hypotheses are educated guesses about the relationship between variables. These educated guesses must be proved by the research. An *assumption* is *a statement accepted as true with little supporting evidence*. From a research perspective, assumptions are problematic. It is expected that statements of inquiry or fact be backed up by research to substantiate them. Fortunately, assumptions can often lead to research. For example, a researcher might assume, based on the perceived natural caring instincts of women, that women would make better police officers than would males. Since there is little evidence to validate this assumption, and it would not be a readily accepted statement, at least among males, there would be a need to research this assumption. In this situation, the researcher could move beyond the untestable assumption that women would be better officers because they are more caring by converting it into hypotheses that can be tested. Variables could be created to measure what is meant by "caring" and what is meant by "officer performance."

Theory, concept, operationalize, variable, hypothesis, and *assumption* are all key words in the language of research. Still, they are just the building blocks and causes for other terms with which the student should be familiar.

■ Other Key Terms

There are many other terms a student should be familiar with before undertaking a research effort. Because these remaining terms are covered in greater detail in later chapters, only a brief definition will be offered, but in the same context as previous definitions.

Once the researcher has managed to conceptualize and operationalize his or her research, it is then time to choose who will be targeted to respond to the dependent variables. A unit of analysis is the level at which the researcher will focus his or her attention. It could be individuals, groups, communities, or even entire societies, depending on the nature of the research. The researcher then selects samples from the population that is being studied.

Population

A population is *the complete group or class from which information is to be gathered*. For example, police officers, probation officers, and correctional officers are each a population. For every member of a population to provide the information sought would in most cases be logistically impractical, not to mention inefficient and wasteful of the researcher's time and resources. Therefore, most researchers choose to obtain a sample from the targeted population.

Sample

A sample is *a group chosen from within a target population to provide information sought*. Choosing this group is referred to as sampling, and may take one of several forms. Sampling is important enough to warrant an entire chapter of its own later in the text. Some examples of samples follow.

> *Random: A random sample is one in which all members of a given population have the same chances of being selected. Furthermore, the selection of each member must be independent from the selection of any other members.*

> *Stratified Random: This is a sample that has been chosen from a population that has been divided into subgroups called strata. The sample is composed equally of members representing each stratum.*

> *Cluster: The sample comprises randomly selected groups rather than individuals.*

> *Snowball: This sample begins with an individual or individuals who provide names of other people for the sample.*

> *Purposive: Individuals are chosen to provide information based on the researcher's belief that they will provide the necessary information. This type of sample is also known as a judgmental or convenience sample.*

Once the sample has been identified, the information is collected. The various collection techniques will be covered in detail in a later chapter. In collecting this information, two concerns for the researcher are the validity and the reliability of the data-collection device.

Validity

Validity is a term describing whether the measure used accurately represents the concept it is meant to measure. There are four types of validity: face, content, construct, and criterion. Validity can also be categorized as either internal (truthfulness of the findings with respect to the individuals in the sample) or external (truthfulness of the findings with respect to individuals not in the sample).

> *Face Validity: This is the simplest form of validity, and basically refers to whether the measuring device appears, on its face, to measure what the researcher wants to measure. This is primarily a judgmental decision.*

> *Content Validity: Each item of the measuring device is examined to determine whether the element measures the concept in question.*

> *Construct Validity: This validity inquires as to whether the measuring device does indeed measure what it has been designed to measure. It refers to the fit between theoretical and operational definitions of the concept.*

> *Criterion (or Pragmatic) Validity: This type of validity represents the degree to which the measure relates to external criteria. It can be either concurrent (Does the measure enhance the ability to assess the current characteristics of the concept under study?) or predictive (the ability to accurately foretell future events or conditions).*

Reliability

Reliability refers to how consistent the measuring device would be over time. In other words, if the study is replicated, will the measuring device provide consistent results? The two key components of reliability are stability and consistency. Stability means the ability to retain accuracy and resist change. Consistency is the ability to yield similar results when replicated.

Having established the validity and reliability of the measuring device, the sample can now be approached for information. The information gathered is known as data.

Data

Data are simply pieces of information gathered from the sample. The pieces may describe events, beliefs, characteristics, people, or other phenomena. These data may exist at one of four levels:

1. Nominal Data: These data are categorical, based on some defined characteristic. The categories are exclusive and have no logical order. For example, gender is a nominal-level data form.

2. Ordinal Data: Ordinal data are also categorical, but their characteristics may be rank-ordered. These data categories are also exclusive, but are scaled in a manner representative of the amount of characteristics in question, along some dimension. For example, types of prisons may be broken down into the categories of minimum, medium, and maximum.

3. Interval Data: Categorical data for which there is a distinctive, yet equal, difference among the characteristics measured are interval data. The categories have order and represent equal units on a scale with no set zero starting point (for example, the IQ of prisoners).

4. Ratio Data: This type of data is ordered, has equal units of distance, and a true zero starting point (for example, age, weight, income).

As the text continues, other terms will be introduced and defined. Because a sufficient number of terms have been introduced, it is now possible to review the research process in a researchese manner.

■ The Research Process

Now that you have been introduced to research and its language, the last item you will need to understand is a model of the research process through terminology. This model begins with a theory usually identifying some concept. The concept is then conceptualized and operationalized to create dependent variables. Completing the identification of both the independent and dependent variables leads then to developing the hypothesis or hypotheses. Finally, a sample is chosen, measurement or information is gathered from the sample, the information is converted into the proper data for analysis, and the results are reported (see **Box 2-4**). This process will become functionally clearer as the text progresses.

Box 2-4
The Research Process in Brief

Conceptualization

Identify a relevant social issue or phenomenon worthy of study
Review prior research regarding the identified social issue
Decide what the focus of your research into the social issue is to be
Determine the theoretical orientation/explanation upon which the research is based
Determine the various concepts used within the primary theoretical explanation
Identify the concepts employed within the theoretical explanation
Define these concepts so that others can understand their meanings
Think about how these concepts may relate to one another

Operationalization

Create variables that may be used to measure concepts
Identify whether the variables are dependent or independent
Develop hypotheses that will enable you to evaluate the relationships among variables
Determine how you will collect data regarding your variables
Determine how you will analyze the data that are collected
Determine the population to be studied
Determine how the population is to be sampled
Determine what will be done with the results of the research

■ Summary

To become proficient in research, one needs to know the language. Several terms have been introduced that are important to mastering research as a language. The main terms include theory, concept, operationalize, variables, hypothesis, and sample. There are two types of variables: independent and dependent. A sample may be random, stratified, clustered, snowball, or purposive. Other terms are validity (face, content, construct, and criterion), reliability, and data (nominal, ordinal, interval, and ratio). With knowledge of these terms, the research process can be taken to the next level.

METHODOLOGICAL QUERIES

1. Taking both sides of the debate about theory, apply the definition of theory to this statement: Crime is a direct result of poverty.

2. How would you convert or operationalize the following concepts: professionalism, stress, and ethnicity?

3. What are the null hypotheses for the three research hypotheses offered in the Methodological Link?

4. Convert this assumption into a hypothesis: Due to the natural caring instincts of women, they will make better police officers.

5. How would you demonstrate the research process using the turnover rate of federal probation officers as the concept under study?

REFERENCES

Berg, B. L. (2004). *Qualitative research methods for the social sciences* (5th ed.). Boston: Allyn and Bacon.

Colomb, W., & Damphouse, K. (2004). Examination of newspaper coverage of hate crimes: A moral panic perspective. *American Journal of Criminal Justice, 28*(2), 149–163.

Cooper, V. G., McLearen, A. M., & Zapf, P. A. (2004). Dispositional decisions with the mentally ill: Police perceptions and characteristics. *Police Quarterly, 7*(3), 295–310.

Gordon, J. (1999). Correctional officers' attitudes toward delinquents and delinquency: Does the type of institution make a difference? In M. L. Dantzker (Ed.), *Readings for research methods in criminology and criminal justice* (pp. 85–98). Woburn, MA: Butterworth-Heinemann.

Holcomb, J. E., Williams, M. R., & Demuth, S. (2004). White female victims and death penalty disparity research. *Justice Quarterly, 21*(4), 877–902.

Moriarty, L. J. (1999). The conceptualization and operationalization of the intervening dimensions of social disorganization. In M. L. Dantzker (Ed.), *Readings for research methods in criminology and criminal justice* (pp. 15–26). Woburn, MA: Butterworth-Heinemann.

Nachmias, D., & Nachmias, C. (2000). *Research methods in the social sciences* (6th ed.) New York: Worth.

Wilson, S., & Jasinski, J. L. (2004). Public satisfaction with the police in domestic violence cases: The importance of arrest, expectations, and involuntary consent. *American Journal of Criminal Justice, 28*(2), 235–254.

3 Getting Started

Vignette 3-1   Picking a Topic

It is only about a third of the way through the fall semester, and you are already thinking about graduating in the spring. Next semester, you must take the senior seminar—a capstone course—in which you will have to write a research paper based on your own original research. That is why you waited until this semester to take the methods course. Older students have suggested that you start thinking about your topic before getting into that class because it will make things so much easier. The problem is, you have no idea what you would want to research. There are lots of areas that interest you, but which one intrigues you enough to research it in depth is another question. Where do you start? You are aware of several possible sources of information. Yet you are still a little confused and apprehensive.

Furthermore, you understand that the heart of your research revolves around something referred to as the research question, a statement explaining what it is you want to accomplish. Forming the research question then leads to the formation of hypotheses and the identification of variables. Obviously, there are several things yet to learn.

Chapter Objectives

After studying this chapter, the student should be able to:

- Discuss the issues that should be considered in selecting a research topic.
- Present and describe the three purposes of research.
- Describe what a literature review is and the sources that are available for such a review.

- Compare and contrast the various writing styles utilized by criminal-justice researchers.
- Define what an article critique is and discuss its details.
- Define what is meant by the research question. Give an example of a research question.
- Define hypothesis and describe the types of hypotheses.
- Define variable and describe the types of variables.

To this point, we have discussed why research is necessary and its related terminology. Although these are important topics that warrant serious consideration, if you are charged with writing an empirical research paper, you may find that there is still a great deal you need to know in order to satisfactorily complete such a project. In this chapter, we present and discuss a number of issues that must be considered when starting a research project, such as the selection of what to research, often referred to as the *research problem* (Babbie, 2004; Neuman, 2002; Schutt, 2001).

■ Picking a Topic

Prior to beginning the research project, one must first answer this: What should I study? Within the fields of criminology and criminal justice, there are numerous research topics available. All you have to do is choose one. However, that is not as easy as it appears.

Obviously, the beginning of any research project must focus on what is to be studied. Defining the problem is the most important stage of the research (Eck & La Vigne, 1994; Neuman, 2002; Schutt, 2001). To start, it should be something of personal interest. *If you are not interested in the topic before you begin, you will be sick of it before you are done.* It must also comply with any topic restrictions imposed by the individuals and/or organization for whom you are conducting the research. For example, in order to avoid emotional diatribes on controversial issues that are better left to experienced researchers, the authors frequently restrict the topics that their students may research. In addition, before the topic is chosen, one should consider:

1. *What currently exists in the literature*
2. *Any gaps in theory or the current state of art*
3. *The feasibility of conducting the research*
4. *Whether there are any policy implications*
5. *Possible funding availability (Berg, 2004; Eck & La Vigne, 1994; Fitzgerald & Cox, 1998; Hagan, 2000; Senese, 1997)*

A number of studies have been conducted on community policing. Many of them suggest and support how effective community policing can be. What appear to be lacking are studies that explain why it may be successful in some places and a failure in other places. Thus, a gap in theory exists that needs to be filled. Finding such gaps in the literature can assist in choosing a topic.

Once an interesting and intriguing topic is found, you must consider the feasibility of conducting the research. Feasibility is linked primarily to logistics (for example: Is a sample accessible? Does a data-collection instrument exist or must one be designed?). Sometimes the topic is a very good choice for researching, but attempting it is not feasible. Prior to finalizing the research topic, the prospective researcher needs to be sure that the study can actually be accomplished.

Because of the popularity of some topics—such as job stress, capital punishment, sentencing disparity, and community policing—there is usually a wealth of information available to help build a research base. However, there may be times when the topic is legitimate, but there may be little information in the literature to support your research question. This should not prevent the researcher from moving forward with the research. If the findings can be validated (shown to meet scientific rigor and supported by ensuing research), they may become a new and significant contribution to the literature, the discipline, and subsequently, the practice of criminal justice. Choosing a research topic that could have policy implications can be very useful because it can help to change or implement new policy.

Finally, although funding may not be applicable to many students' research efforts, it should be taken into consideration. One of the most popular means of funding research is through internal and external grants. Many universities offer both students and faculty opportunities to apply for internal grants that will at least allow the researcher to start the research project, and may also help offset personal costs. Ultimately, many researchers seek external grants. However, these are usually not sought by undergraduate students. Regardless of where the funding may come from, it is important to establish whether any moneys will be needed and from where they may be sought.

METHODOLOGICAL
LINKS

Willis, Mastrofski, and Weisburd (2004) conducted a case study of one department's experiences with COMPSTAT. Findings could be used to improve how the process is used. In Chapter 1, we discussed the Gaarder, Rodrigues, and Zatz (2004) study of probation officers' views of girls. Results from this study could be used to improve training and placement policies. Engel and Calnon (2004) examined the influence of drivers' characteristics during traffic stops. What effect could findings from this study have on policy? Metraux and Culhane (2004) examined the incidence of and interrelationships between shelter use and reincarceration among a cohort of 48,424 people. Their findings suggested that more use of shelters limited reincarceration rates.

■ The Purpose of the Research

Once consideration is given to these issues, the research can begin. However, in order to address these issues, one must have an idea of what the research will cover. Perhaps the best place to start is to decide what the research should accomplish. There are three possible expectations, or accomplishments: (1) exploring, (2) describing, and (3) explaining (Singleton & Straits, 1999).

Exploring

The majority of us are explorers. Our curiosity about things begins at a very early age and should last until we die. What we explore and how we explore change with age and time. Our exploration occurs either accidentally or intentionally. Intentional exploration may well be considered a form of research. Thus, when one wants to know more about something, the tendency is to explore the topic.

For example, before buying a new sport-utility vehicle (SUV), you might read what various magazines say about SUVs, then you will likely check out prices through various dealers, and you might even talk with current owners of such vehicles. When you are finished, you should have enough information to make an informed decision. You have conducted research. With respect to criminal justice and criminology, exploration of what interests us is usually formal and intentional, and is accomplished through some form of research.

Exploratory research provides information not previously known, or about which little is known. In other words, it seeks out information about something that is known to exist, but as to why or how, that remains to be discovered. Therefore, exploratory research offers additional insights about something for which there is awareness but limited knowledge.

Describing

What is the phenomenon? How does it work? What does it do? These are just three of the types of questions answered when conducting research for the purpose

METHODOLOGICAL **LINKS**

It can be argued that much of the published research in the criminal-justice field is exploratory. Here are a few possibilities: Ventura, Lambertt, Bryant, and Pasupuleti's (2004) study of attitudinal differences among criminal-justice and non-criminal-justice majors toward gays and lesbians; Batton's (2004) examination of the historical trends in the relationship between homicide and suicide rates, considering the extent to which gender differences exist; and Engel and Calnon's (2004) study of drivers' characteristics and how they might influence police behavior during traffic stops.

of describing. The basic purpose *is to be able to describe specific aspects or elements of the topic*. Generally, this type of research is informative in nature and is based on something we are already aware of, but know little about. For example, most people know what a prison is. Yet how many really know the details about a specific prison? A descriptive study could offer information about the inmates, correctional staff, programs, violent acts, and so forth, which would further enhance what is known about that prison. Descriptive studies are among the easier types of studies to conduct because the researcher simply needs to explain what he or she sees, hears, or reads with respect to the various elements of the topic.

From a purely academic perspective, some literature reviews might serve as a descriptive study. An example of a purely descriptive study would be Vaughn, Del Carmen, Perfecto, and Charand's (2004) examination of the criminal-justice and criminological journals, in which the authors offer descriptions of the various publications' editorial processes and other relevant information pertaining to publishing these journals.

Explaining

Undoubtedly the most in-depth and difficult purpose for conducting research is to provide an explanation. *Explanatory research attempts to analyze and fully understand the concept "why" as it applies to policies, procedures, objects, attitudes, opinions, and so forth.* Examples of such studies include the previously noted Ventura, Lambertt, Bryant, and Pasupuleti (2004) study of student attitudes toward gays and lesbians; the Gaarder, Rodrigues, and Zatz (2004) study of probation officers' perceptions of girls; and Wilson and Jasinski's (2004) examination of public satisfaction with the police in domestic-violence cases.

Although all three reasons for conducting research are valid, it is most often the explanatory reason that many criminologists and criminal-justice researchers pursue. This type of study relies on strong, clear research questions, hypotheses, and variables. Each of these will be discussed in greater length shortly. However, there is still the question of choosing a topic.

To demonstrate the myriad of possible topics for study, **Box 3-1** offers a short list of potential research topics. Still, the question lingers regarding how to go about choosing a topic. This can be aided through personal observations; suggestions from academics, scholars, and other students; and the existing literature in criminal justice and criminology. It is through this last means that a large number of research topics are chosen.

■ Reviewing the Literature

For many researchers, while the choice of an idea or concept to study may at times be frustrating, what becomes more frustrating is choosing a topic, and then finding either too little or too much information available in the current literature. Neither of these situations should prevent the individual from conducting the research, however. In criminal justice and criminology, there is usually a substantial amount of literature to support most topics one might wish to re-

Box 3-1

Possible Research Topics

1. Examine the role of criminal-justice programs in a given state
2. Survey education and job satisfaction among police, parole, or correctional officers
3. Compare and contrast criminal-justice educators: practitioner-academic vs. pure academic and their work products
4. Evaluate the relationships between job stress and race/ethnicity
5. Explore the causes and extent of criminality among high-school students
6. Conduct a cost-benefit analysis of private versus state prisons
7. Research drug usage among adolescents
8. Evaluate the success of electronic monitoring
9. Evaluate the effectiveness of community policing
10. Survey public attitudes toward corporal punishment

search. With the extensive number of journals currently available, data from government agencies, and Internet access to information, one can usually collect enough data to support a research effort.

Ultimately, the best way to begin a research effort is to focus on a particular issue, phenomenon, or problem that most interests the individual. In doing so, one must be sure to (1) determine what the problem, issue, or phenomenon is; and (2) organize what is known about it. This is where a literature search and review is valuable, and the best place to begin the search is the library.

Become Familiar with the Library

A first step in conducting a search of the literature is to familiarize oneself with the nearest library. As a criminal-justice/criminology student, you should have access to a good library. If not, find out how far it is to a better library and make arrangements to go there. Too frequently, students try to use the excuse that "it was not in our library"—after only a brief perusal of the available texts and journals. That is not an acceptable excuse. As an individual who is capable of thinking critically, you are expected to solve problems regarding the availability of resources, not to just bemoan them. Familiarize yourself with the layout of your particular library, the search vehicles that are available, and get to know the librarians. You may find that there are many more resources available to you than you had imagined.

Text/Journal Abstracts

Literature or topical searches can start with the use of a source called an abstract. Two popular ones are *Sociological Abstracts* and *Criminal Justice Abstracts*. With these sources, the researcher can look for a particular term (a key word or words, such as "job satisfaction"), concept, or topic to see what has already been published about this subject.

Scholarly Journals

From the abstracts, one can go directly to the proper journals. Scholarly journals are refereed (meaning that before being published, the article appearing in the journal had to pass review by other scholars, who were asked by the journal to critique the article's contents). How critiques are conducted will be discussed in a following section. The findings from a perusal of journal articles may not only help you determine a topic, but also guide you in your research.

Textbooks

For research purposes, introductory-level texts are generally not of sufficient depth to use as sources in your research. It is better to build from them by going to the sources that they cite within a subject area, or to rely on texts devoted to the subject in question. However, introductory-level texts are often excellent starting sources for selecting a research topic. If you are assigned a research project for a certain class, review the contents of the text that is being used in that class to determine if a topic of personal interest suggests itself.

Social-Science Indexes

Annual indexes for journals are another source of information. Today, journals are available on microfiche, as hard copy, or online. Government documents and the Internet are additional sources for helping choose a topic or for gathering information to support the research topic.

Internet Searches

A word of caution is appropriate regarding the use of the Internet. Although it is useful for gaining preliminary information about a topic, the Internet does not replace conducting a solid literature review of the subject area. For all its convenience, the Internet has a great deal of information that is unsubstantiated, if not outright false. *If the source is not clearly scholarly (such as a reputable online journal), be cautious about using it as a research reference.* The Internet augments the library and social-science indexes and/or abstracts as search vehicles; it does not replace them. Nor does it replace journals and textbooks. Although the Internet may provide legitimate sources, a reference page filled with numerous Web sites instead of text and journal citations is indicative of lazy scholarship on the part of the researcher.

Overall, there are a number of sources from which one can choose a topic or find support for a given topic. (**Box 3-2** provides a sampling of refereed journals that publish articles in criminology and/or criminal justice. This is not an exhaustive listing.) Once a literature search is completed, the research question(s) can be formulated.

■ Critiquing the Literature

In order to conduct a sound literature review (whether as a topical search or in developing the scholarly basis for the research that you are conducting), you must be able to properly interpret the research that you are reading. In this section, we

Box 3-2

Literature Review: Examples of Sources

Journals

American Journal of Criminal Justice
American Journal of Sociology
British Journal of Criminology
Canadian Journal of Criminology
Crime and Delinquency
Criminal Justice Policy Review
Criminology
Journal of Contemporary Criminal Justice
Journal of Criminal Justice
Justice Quarterly
Police Quarterly
Prison Journal

Compendiums

Criminal Justice Abstracts
Psychological Abstracts
Social Sciences Index
Sociological Abstracts

Government Agencies

Bureau of Justice Statistics (BJS) (www.ojp.usdoj.gov/bjs/)
National Criminal Justice Reference Service (NCJRS) (www.ncjrs.org)
National Institute of Justice (NIJ) (www.ojp.usdoj.gov/nij)

give you some guidance as to what to look for in evaluating other studies. These guidelines will also be helpful in preparing your own work for others to review. In a later chapter, we provide more detail on preparing your work for submission.

Understanding Writing Styles

Scholarly journals and textbooks conform to specific writing styles. The various styles are precisely detailed in publication manuals. In criminal justice and criminology, you will find that several styles are utilized. At some point in your research, you may view Turabian (which uses numbers to indicate citations, and footnotes at the bottom of each page); *Chicago* style (also uses numbers after citations, with endnotes instead of footnotes); American Psychological Association—APA (the most commonly used style in criminal justice/criminology; lists the author and year of publication within the text); and American Sociological Association—ASA (similar to APA, but may use endnotes for specific details, and varies in the format of the references). Occasionally, you may also see MLA—Modern Language Association—style, as well as other styles that are unique to specific law or criminal-justice journals (these are often variations of the above styles). When critiquing an article or text, it is important to know what style is utilized—and even more important to know what style is required when submitting a paper, article, or text for review. For example, the authors require their students to submit all papers in APA format. The best way to become familiar with this format is through the APA stylebook.

Knowing What to Look For

In critiquing another's work, there are a number of points that should be covered (Babbie, 2004; Brown & Curtis, 1987; Creswell, 2002; Neuman, 2002; Schutt, 2001; Singleton & Straits, 1999).

1. Synopsis of Article

This is nothing more than a brief overview of the article. What is the social issue that was studied? How was it investigated—exploration, description, explanation, or a combination of strategies? Who conducted the research? Who financed it (and is there a conflict of interest)? Was it well written and well organized, and did it have clarity of purpose? Were the findings reasonable based upon the research design? What were the conclusions and recommendations?

2. Clarity of Problem Statement

What was the problem being investigated? Did the literature review support the need for this research? What was the theoretical orientation? What was the research hypothesis? (Or, if more than one, what were the research hypotheses?) Were concepts properly defined? Were the dependent and independent variables identified?

3. The Literature Review

Did the literature review provide a thorough coverage of the prior research? Were previous studies adequately evaluated and discussed? Was the coverage complete (classic studies relevant to the research problem included as well as recent research)? Did the literature cited provide a justification for the current investigation?

4. Methodology Used

What was the research design? Was it clearly developed from the theoretical frame of reference alluded to in the problem statement? Who were the subjects, and how were they included in the study? Did the study conform to ethical standards? What was the sampling method, and was it adequate for this research? Was the measurement instrument/strategy satisfactory? How were the data analyzed? Were there any adverse effects or limitations due to the research design and the means of analysis being incompatible? Were measures of association and tests of significance clearly indicated and appropriately discussed? Were the measurement techniques valid and reliable?

5. Findings

Were the findings displayed in a concise and readily understandable manner? How were the data summarized? Were the tables logical and clear? Were the statistical techniques appropriate? Would other statistical techniques have been more appropriate? Did the findings relate to the problem, the method, and/or the theoretical framework? How did the findings relate to those of the prior research?

6. Discussion and Conclusions

Are the conclusions that were reached consistent with the findings that were presented? Are the conclusions compatible with the theoretical orientation presented in the problem statement? Based on the problem statement, the prior research, the

METHODOLOGICAL
LINKS

In Engel and Calnon (2004), rather than offer an actual hypothesis, the authors include a section called research issues that they are trying to address through their research. Ventura, Lambertt, Bryant, and Pasupuleti (2004) note that they are looking to answer a research question rather than a hypothesis. Bjerregaard and Lord (2004) offer four research questions regarding their study of ethical and value orientation of criminal-justice students.

methodology, and the findings, do the conclusions and/or recommendations make sense? Based on the problem statement and the literature, are the conclusions and/or recommendations of this study a significant contribution to the field of study?

■ The Research Question

Once a topic has been chosen, the next step is to create the research question(s). The research question is a statement answered through the research process. Its focus, which must be clearly stated, should inform readers of the actual purpose of the research.

The research question may be synonymous with the research problem. Essentially, what the researcher must do is decide what it is he or she is to study and why. It is the "why" that helps form the research question. Furthermore, it is common for researchers to forgo hypotheses for research questions.

The research question(s) should allow others to gain a clear understanding of why the research was conducted. A well-worded research question should give some indication of the outcomes one might expect at the conclusion of the research.

After establishing the research question(s), the researcher must next explain what specifically is going to be studied and the expected results. This is usually accomplished through statements or propositions referred to as hypotheses.

■ Hypotheses

As previously discussed, a hypothesis is *a specific statement describing the expected result or relationship between the independent and dependent variables*. Again, the three most common types are:

1. The *research hypothesis*, which is a statement of the expected relationship between variables offered in a positive manner
2. The *null hypothesis*, which is a statement that the relationship or difference being tested does not exist
3. The *rival hypothesis*, which is a statement offering an alternate explanation for the research findings

The research hypothesis, which is the most common of the hypothesis types, is generally a statement that fits the equation "If X, then Y." An example is: "If there is an increase in the number of patrol units in a given area, the amount of reported crime increases." Note that the statement suggests a relationship between two variables—patrol units and reported crime— in a manner indicating the belief that more patrol cars will cause there to be more crime reported. Therefore, the research would focus on examining this relationship in an effort to disprove the null hypothesis.

The null hypothesis fits the equation "X has no relationship with Y." For the previous research hypothesis, the null hypothesis would read: "The increase in patrol units will not increase the amount of reported crime (no relationship exists)." A successful research effort will disprove this, which in essence supports the research effort.

What if the increase in patrol units decreases the amount of reported crime? This would lead to the rival hypothesis that fits an equation, in the above circumstance, "The more of X, the less of Y." Again, although the general research goal is to support the research hypothesis by disproving the null hypothesis, one should not consider the inability to disprove the null hypothesis as a failure. On the contrary, the failure to support the null hypothesis may actually lead to new information or additional research not previously known or conducted.

Overall, whether establishing research questions, hypotheses, or both, their link to the topic is crucial. However, if you cannot decide on your topic, it will be all but impossible to establish either.

■ Summary

Prior to starting any research effort, a topic must be chosen, keeping in mind that the research effort can explore, describe, or explain. This topic should be relevant and of interest, and should have support in the literature through journals, government documents, or the Internet.

After choosing the topic, the research question is created, which advises others what is to be studied. From the research question comes the hypothesis (or perhaps hypotheses), a statement that indicates the nature of the relationship to be studied. The three main types of hypotheses are research, null, and rival. The goal is to disprove the null hypothesis.

METHODOLOGICAL QUERIES

From the following brief literature review,[1]

1. What are three possible research topics?

2. What is the hypothesis (or hypotheses) for each?

3. What might be the null and rival hypotheses for each?

4. What are the possible variables?

Conducting surveys to determine a community's satisfaction or perception of its police services is becoming a rapidly recognized means of ascertaining information, especially for police agencies practicing community policing. Depending on how one defines community, we may be looking at a specific segment of a city, a given population within a designated jurisdiction, or a city's complete population. Using this broad approach, one could consider a university's population as a community, or, as previously noted, as a community within a community (Fisher, Sloan, & Wilkins, 1995). Accepting this position, it would be feasible to consider a university police department's desires to learn how its community perceives how the department is doing. Conducting a survey would seem appropriate (Johnson & Bromley, 1999).

"One of the most often employed methods of research is the use of surveys" (Dantzker & Hunter, 2000, p. 17). For many years, the three primary methods of conducting survey research included personal interview, mail questionnaire, and telephone survey. With the proliferation of technology, a more recent means of conducting survey research has been with a computer and the use of electronic mail (e-mail). Although the use of e-mail for conducting survey research has not become a staple in criminal-justice research, it does appear to be very popular in other arenas, especially education research (Heflich & Rice, 1999; Schaefer & Dillman, 1998; Sheehan, 1999; Zhang, 2000).

A review of currently available literature reveals a growing interest in the use of e-mail to conduct surveys. Although a majority of the literature appears to support and promote the use of e-mail, there do seem to be some cautionary trends with respect to using e-mail versus regular mail. Furlong (1997) noted that e-mail surveys may not end up as representative as regular mail, although e-mail does save money and time. Meehan and Burns (1997) discussed problems with posting surveys and how respondents may need more notice on survey availability and response requests. Mavis and Brocato (1998) found that postal surveys were far superior to e-mail surveys with respect to return and response rates. They recommended that a decision to use e-mail surveys should be dependent upon issues such as cost, convenience, and timeliness.

Matz (1999) reported how response rates to Web surveys were not as high as with traditional methods, but that responses to Web surveys were gathered more quickly, supporting the cost and speed aspects. Handwerk, Carson, and Blackwell (2000), comparing response rates between e-mail respondents and

---

[1]This literature review was written by one of the authors a few years ago for a paper presented at a conference. The sources cited are real; however, for purposes of efficiency, the full citations are not provided here.

regular-mail respondents, had a higher response rate from the paper-and-pencil group than from the online sample. They report that students found the online survey advantageous, assuming that they could readily gain access to a computer. Underwood, Kim, and Matier (2000) also found that response rates were better for mail surveys than for the electronic surveys. An interesting aspect of their study was that women responded at greater rates then did men, regardless of the survey method. Finally, Paola, Bonaminio, Gibson, Partridge, and Kallail (2000) add further support to the position that mailed surveys yield a higher return rate.

Overall, it appears that while there is growing support for the use of e-mail to conduct surveys, the return rate is questionable. This paper contributes to the discussion of return rates, but adds a slightly different dimension. In this study, respondents received the survey only via e-mail, but could return it either via regular mail (actually through the university mail system) or by e-mail. Additionally, the paper offers the perceptions of those who returned survey instruments as to the effectiveness of the university's police department.

REFERENCES

Babbie, E. (2004). *The practice of social research* (10th ed.). Belmont, CA: Thomson/Wadsworth.

Batton, C. (2004). Gender differences in lethal violence: Historical trends in the relationship between homicide and suicide rates, 1960–2000. *Justice Quarterly, 21*(3), 423–461.

Berg, B. L. (2004). *Qualitative research methods for the social sciences* (5th ed.). Boston: Allyn and Bacon.

Bjerregaard, B., & Lord, V. B. (2004). An examination of the ethical and value orientation of criminal justice students. *Police Quarterly, 7*(2), 262–284.

Brown, S. E., & Curtis, J. H. (1987). *Fundamentals of criminal justice research.* Cincinnati, OH: Pilgrimage.

Creswell, J. W. (2002). *Research design: Qualitative, quantitative, and mixed methods approaches* (2nd ed.). Thousand Oaks, CA: Sage.

Eck, J. E., & La Vigne, N. G. (1994). *Using research: A primer for law enforcement managers* (2nd ed.). Washington, DC: Police Executive Research Forum.

Engel, R. S., & Calnon, J. M. (2004). Examining the influence of drivers' characteristics during traffic stops with police: Results from a national survey. *Justice Quarterly, 21*(1), 49–90.

Fitzgerald, J. D., & Cox, S. M. (1998). *Research methods in criminal justice: An introduction* (2nd ed.). Chicago: Nelson-Hall.

Gaarder, E., Rodrigues, N., & Zatz, M. S. (2004). Criers, liars, and manipulators: Probation officers' views of girls. *Justice Quarterly, 21*(3), 547–578.

Hagan, F. (2000). *Research methods in criminal justice and criminology* (5th ed.). Boston: Allyn and Bacon.

Neuman, W. L. (2002). *Social research methods* (5th ed.). Boston: Allyn and Bacon.

Schutt, R. K. (2001). *Investigating the social world: The process and practice of research* (3rd ed.). Thousand Oaks, CA: Pine Forge Press.

Senese, J. D. (1997). *Applied research methods in criminal justice*. Chicago: Nelson-Hall.

Singleton, R., Jr., & Straits, B. C. (1999). *Approaches to social research* (3rd ed.). New York: Oxford University Press.

Vaughn, M. S., Del Carmen, R. V., Perfecto, M., & Charand, K. X. (2004). Journals in criminal justice and criminology: An updated and expanded guide for authors. *Journal of Criminal Justice Education, 15*(1), 61–192.

Ventura, L. A., Lambertt, E. G., Bryant, M., & Pasupuleti. S. (2004). Differences in attitudes toward gays and lesbians among criminal justice and non-criminal justice majors. *American Journal of Criminal Justice, 28*(2), 165–179.

Willis, J. J., Mastrofski, S. D., & Weisburd, D. (2004). COMPSTAT and bureaucracy: A case study of challenges and opportunities for change. *Justice Quarterly, 21*(3), 463–496.

Wilson, S., & Jasinski, J. L. (2004). Public satisfaction with the police in domestic violence cases: The importance of arrest, expectations, and involuntary consent. *American Journal of Criminal Justice, 28*(2), 235–254.

4 Research Ethics

Vignette 4-1   A Question of Ethics?

While doing a literature search, you come across a study that is very similar to what you are considering for your senior project. Although the study is about 25 years old, much of what was written could be applicable today. The best thing about this study is that all the questions used to gather the data are listed. Knowing you are being encouraged to create your own survey questionnaire, you start to ponder using these questions. It is an old study, in a somewhat obscure journal. Who would know if you borrowed the questions and offered them as your own? Of course, that would be not only plagiarism, but also extremely unethical. Then again, is ethics that big a concern for you? Getting caught cheating might not go over well, but you think you would be able to get around that by pleading ignorance. The ethical dilemma is another story.

Later that evening, you meet with some friends at the local hangout to celebrate one of your friend's successful defense of her master's thesis. At one point during the evening, the topic of ethics in research arises. Informed consent—or, more appropriately, the lack of that consent—was an issue during your friend's defense. Apparently, your friend did a survey among individuals booked into the county jail during a six-month period, but never told the inmates what the survey was for or that they did not have to complete it. They were simply advised to fill it out during the booking process. There was a good deal of debate as to whether this method was right or wrong. Was it ethical? Obviously, the decision was in your friend's favor, but in the past 12 hours, you have been confronted with two ethical questions regarding research. How many others can there be?

```
Chapter Objectives
```

After studying this chapter, the student should be able to:

- Define what is meant by ethics and explain its importance to criminal-justice-related research.
- Present and discuss the various characteristics of ethical problems in criminal-justice-related research.
- Explain how the researcher's role influences, and is influenced by, ethical concerns.
- Discuss the various ethical considerations that were presented.
- Describe the relationship that exists between ethics and professionalism. Include "code of ethics" within this discussion.
- List and describe the four ethical criteria.
- Present and discuss the five reasons why confidentiality and privacy are important research concerns.
- Describe the impacts of institutional review boards (IRBs) and research guidelines (such as those mandated by the National Institute of Justice) upon criminal-justice-related research.

Learning how to conduct research is important. The previous chapters set the foundation for understanding what it means to conduct research in criminology and criminal justice. However, before we open the discussion of how to conduct research, we feel it is important to consider the ethical aspects of research methods.

Criminology and criminal justice are virtual playgrounds of ethical confrontations. There is no aspect of them—including research—in which ethical questions or dilemmas do not exist. This is particularly true when the research is of an applied nature.

The ethical issues encountered in applied social research are subtle and complex, raising difficult moral dilemmas that, at least on a superficial level, create ambivalence or irresoluteness on the part of the researcher. These dilemmas often require the researcher to strike a delicate balance between the scientific requirements of methodology and the human rights and values potentially threatened by the research (Kimmel, 1988, 1996).

As discussed in this chapter, ethics refers to doing what is morally and legally right in the conducting of research. This requires the researcher to be knowledgeable about what is being done; to use reasoning when making decisions; to be both intellectual and truthful in approach and reporting; and to consider the consequences—in particular, to be sure that the outcome of the research outweighs any negatives that might occur. Using this approach, ethical decisions will be much easier.

Criminal-justice and criminological research almost always involves dealings with humans and human behavior. It is prudent to be aware of the characteristics associated with ethical problems in social research. Although there does not appear to be a consensus as to what these characteristics are, nor is there a comprehensive list, the following have been identified as recognizable characteristics of ethical problems:

1. *A single research problem can generate numerous questions regarding appropriate behavior on the part of the researcher.*

2. *Ethical sensitivity is a necessity, but is not necessarily sufficient to solve problems that might arise.*

3. *Ethical dilemmas result from conflicting values as to what should receive priority on the part of the researcher.*

4. *Ethical concerns can relate to both the research topic and to how the research is conducted.*

5. *Ethical concerns involve both personal and professional elements in the research (Berg, 2004; Golden, 1976; Kimmel, 1988, 1996; Schutt, 2001).*

When dealing with humans, ethics plays an important role. It all begins with the researcher's role.

■ The Researcher's Role

Contrary to popular belief, the criminal-justice professional or criminologist who conducts research is considered a scientist. Ignoring the distinctions made between a natural scientist and a social scientist, both are scientists who are governed by the laws of inquiry (Kaplan, 1963). Both require an ethically neutral, objective approach to research. Ethical neutrality requires that the researcher's moral or ethical beliefs are not allowed to influence the gathering of data or the conclusions that are made from analyzing the data. Objectivity is striving to prevent personal ideology or prejudices from influencing the process. As you can see, the two have a similar concern: maintaining the integrity of the research. In addition to these concerns, the researcher, whether a nuclear physicist or a criminologist, must also ensure that the research concerns do not negatively impact upon the safety of others.

The researcher's role will often coexist—and, at times, even conflict—with other important roles, such as practitioner, teacher, academic, scholar, and citizen. This meshing of roles can often cause the researcher to lose objectivity in his or her approach to the collection, analysis, and reporting of the data. In particular, there are the concerns over the individual's morals, values, attitude, and beliefs interfering with completing an objective study.

We are each raised with certain ideals, identified as morals and values. What those are will commonly be reflected in our attitudes and behaviors. Weak or strong morals and values can affect how we conduct research. For example, individuals raised to believe that success is very important, regardless of the costs, might regard the "borrowing" of someone else's research efforts and passing them off as their own as acceptable; or they might accept the manipulation of data to gain more-desirable results. An even more repugnant scenario would be one in which the researcher continues with his or her research despite knowing that to do so will cause physical harm or emotional anguish for others. In each of these cases, the decisions are ethically wrong.

Because the researcher's role is intertwined with other roles, ethics becomes even more difficult to manage. Ultimately, it is up to the individual to decide the importance of personal ethics. However, this is just one aspect of ethics in research.

■ Ethical Considerations

Sometimes conducting research, in and of itself, can be problematic. Accessibility, funding, timing, and other factors may all impose limitations. As noted by Golden (1976, p. 28): "Ethical concerns can enter at every stage of the research process, from the selection of a research problem to the use of research results." With this in mind, the considerations about to be discussed should not be viewed as more important at any one particular time in the process, but rather, should apply throughout the research.

Ethical Ramifications

It is important for researchers to consider whether the topic to be studied has innate ethical ramifications. Some topics are controversial by their very nature. For instance, the individual interested in gangs might decide that the best way to gain data is to become a participant-observer. As such, chances are that the researcher may have to witness, or even be asked to participate in, illegal activity. Ethically as well as legally, this information should be given to the police, but doing so might jeopardize the research. Although it is apparent what decision should be made (in order to avoid such a dilemma, the research should be adjusted, or possibly even abandoned altogether), the research may be so important to the individual that he or she does not always make the right decision. Therefore, *before embarking on a research topic, the ethical implications of the research itself must be addressed.*

Harm to Others

Another consideration is what effects the research might have on the research targets. When the research involves direct human contact, ethics plays an important role. Whether the targets are victims, accused offenders, convicted offenders, practitioners, or the general public, a major consideration is whether the research might cause them any harm. Harm can be physical, psychological, or social.

Physical harm most often can occur during experimental or applied types of research, such as testing new drugs or weapons. Psychological harm might result through the type of information being gathered. For example, in a study of victims of sexual assault, the research might delve into the events prior to, during, and after the assault. This line of questioning may inflict more psychological harm in addition to that which already exists as a result of the assault. Finally, social harm may be inflicted if certain information is released that should not have been. Consider a survey of sexual orientation among correctional officers where it becomes public knowledge who is gay or lesbian. This information may cause those individuals to be treated differently, perhaps discriminated against, thus causing sociological harm. Obviously, it is important that, prior to starting the research, the researcher consider what type of harm may befall respondents or participants (Babbie, 2004).

Privacy Concerns

The right to privacy is another ethical consideration. Individuals in America have a basic right to privacy. In many cases, research efforts may violate that right. How far should individuals be allowed to pry into the private or public lives of others in the name of research? Ethically speaking, if a person does not want his or her life examined, then that right should be respected. We all have a right to anonymity (Fitzgerald & Cox, 2001; Kimmel, 1996; Berg, 2004). However, there are a variety of documents accessible to the public in which information can be gathered that individuals would prefer to be unavailable, such as arrest records, court dockets, and tax and property files. The ethical question that arises here is whether a person should have the right to consent to access to certain types of information in the name of research. Giving consent in general is a major ethical consideration (Berg, 2004; Fitzgerald & Cox, 2001; Kimmel, 1996; Schutt, 2001; Senese, 1997).

METHODOLOGICAL

LINKS

As part of the university's requirements for conducting research, Dantzker and Waters (1999) had to establish "informed consent." To meet this requirement, the following statement was read to all students prior to the distribution of the survey.

You are being asked to participate in a "Students' Perceptions of Policing" study being directed by Dr. M. L. Dantzker, Department of Political Science, Justice Studies Programs, Georgia Southern University. There are two major purposes to this research: to examine college students' perceptions of policing, both Criminal Justice majors and non-majors, and to measure changes in perceptions of same students, particularly those who may be taking a police course or attending a police academy. Participation is VOLUNTARY and CONFIDENTIAL. The only personal identifier you are being asked to provide is the last four digits of your social security number, or a four-digit identifier you can make up and recall for later use. (Note to reader: If not absolutely necessary, do not require an identifier. This will make your subjects feel more secure in their anonymity.) Participation or lack thereof will be used neither for nor against you. The data being collected will be used SOLELY FOR RESEARCH PURPOSES with the possibility of publishing of the results. Should you choose to participate, please follow the questionnaire's instructions for completion. Thank you for your assistance.

Informed Consent

Particularly in survey research, it is common for the researcher to either ask for specific consent from the respondents or at least to acknowledge that by completing the survey, the respondent has conferred consent. Normally, this requires only that the individual sign an "informed consent" form or that the instructions indicate that the survey is completely anonymous, voluntary, and that the information is being used only for the purpose of research.

Voluntary Participation

As you probably noted in the Methodological Links, not only did the researchers seek to obtain consent, they also informed students that their participation was voluntary. Too frequently, criminological researchers require their subjects to sign consent forms, but (particularly within institutional settings such as military organizations, schools, and prisons) neglect to inform the subjects that their participation is voluntary. In fact, in these environments, participation is often coerced. We are not stating that all research must use voluntary participation, but we do wish to stress that there must be valid reasons that can be given showing that the knowledge could not otherwise be reasonably obtained and that no harm will come to the participants from their compulsory involvement.

Regardless of the fact that the research was not intrusive and could cause no harm to the respondents, informed consent was required. The rule of thumb in these situations is: *If you have any doubt as to whether your research could be in any way construed to be intrusive, get consent from your subjects.* It is also best to assure them that their participation is voluntary and that they may choose not to take part in the study.

Within the academic setting, informed consent and voluntary participation do not appear to be an unusual requirement. To ensure that informed consent is provided, and to judge the value and ethical nature of the research, many universities have an institutional review board (IRB). The IRBs exist as a result of the Code of Federal Regulations (CFR), in particular Title 28 (Judicial Administration), Part 46, which specifies all aspects of the IRB, including membership, functions and operations, reviewing the research, and criteria for IRB approval (www.access.gpo.gov/nara/cfr/cfr-table-search.html).

Established primarily for the review of research, usually experimental or applied, dealing directly with human subjects, university IRBs often extend their review over any type of research involving human respondents (survey or otherwise). While having to attain IRB approval can be somewhat frustrating, it is a useful process because it helps to reaffirm the researcher's perceptions and beliefs about the research and can help identify prospective ethical problems. Also, reviewers may see problems overlooked by the researcher. It is better to err on the side of caution.

The process generally is not that difficult. It usually requires the researcher to submit basic information about the proposed research, often in a format designed by the university. At the end of this chapter is an example of a request submitted to an IRB for approval. While not all IRBs make use of the same format, the information required will be similar across institutions.

Informed consent is valuable because it is important that research targets be allowed the right to refuse to be part of the research. While consent may not be a major problem in survey research (because permission can be written into the documents), it does raise an interesting dilemma for observational research (when the researcher may not want the subjects to know they are being observed). The ethical consideration here is that as long as the subjects are doing what they normally would be doing and the observations will not in any way directly influence their behavior or harm them, it is ethically acceptable.

Deception

Some types of research (particularly field research that requires the researcher to in essence "go undercover") cannot be conducted if the subjects are aware that they are being studied. Such research is controversial and must be carefully thought out before it is undertaken (Babbie, 2004; Kimmel, 1996). All too often, the deception is based more on the researcher's laziness or bias rather than on a real need for secrecy. For example, a researcher is interested in studying juvenile behavior within the confines of a juvenile facility. Rather than explain to administrators and the subjects what he or she is doing, the researcher conducts his or her research under the guise of an internship or volunteer work.

Depending on the type of research, there is always some type of ethical consideration. What is interesting is that the science of research itself is viewed as ethically neutral or amoral. The ethical dilemmas rise from the fact that researchers themselves are not neutral. This fosters the need for regulation in the conducting of research so that it does meet ethical standards (Adler & Clark, 2003; Berg, 2004; Fitzgerald & Cox, 2001; Kimmel, 1996).

■ The Professionalism of Research

According to the *American Heritage Dictionary,* 4th ed. (2001, p. 671), professionalism is defined as "Professional status, methods, character, or standards." Research in itself is a profession. When research is conducted within other professions, there is an even greater need to conduct business in a professional manner. It has been offered that "professional ethics activities reflect the willingness of a profession to self-regulate the behavior of its members on behalf of the public and the profession" (Kimmel, 1988, p. 56). This typically means that the profession has established a code of ethics.

Although other professions tend to support written codes of ethics for research applicable to all members in the discipline (for example, the American Psychological Association), criminal justice and criminology are still attempting to establish such a code. Furthermore, there appears to be no universal code of ethics with respect to research. This may be a result of the wide variety of research conducted, as well as of calls for individually applied standards.

Grant-funded research is more likely to have ethical constraints imposed. For example, a popular source of funding for criminal-justice and criminological research is the National Institute of Justice (NIJ). The NIJ has developed its own code of ethics to which all grant recipients must agree. The NIJ is very specific in its guidelines, especially with respect to data confidentiality and the protection of human subjects (www.ojp.usdoj.gov/nij/humansubjects/index.html).

■ Ethical Research Criteria

Even though there is no universally recognized research code of ethics, there are some specifically identified criteria that, when applied or followed, will assist in producing ethical research:

1. Avoid harmful research.
2. Be objective in designing, conducting, and evaluating your research.
3. Use integrity in the performance and reporting of the research.
4. Protect confidentiality.

Avoiding Harmful Research

The goal of research is to discover knowledge not previously known or to verify existing data. In many instances, this can be done without ever having to inflict any undue stress, strain, or pain on respondents (that is, historical or survey research). Unfortunately, there are times when the research can be physically or emotionally harmful. The ethical approach is to avoid any such research regardless of how important its findings might be—*unless it can be shown that good from the information will far outweigh the harm* (an eventuality that is rare even in criminological research).

Being Objective

Biases can be detrimental to a research project. One such bias deals with objectivity. Assume that you do not like drinkers, that you perceive them as weak-willed and careless. Your research deals with individuals convicted of driving while intoxicated (DWI). You are interested in their reasons for doing so. The chances are good that if you allow your personal feelings against drinkers to guide you in your research, the results will be skewed, biased, and subjective. It is important, for good ethical research, to maintain objectivity. Of course, being objective is just one important characteristic of the ethical researcher.

Using Integrity

The last thing a researcher wants is for the results to not meet expectations. Sometimes, because of how important the research is perceived to be, there may be a tendency to manipulate the data and report the results in a manner that shows that the research was successful; that is, to put a positive spin on an otherwise negative result. This is especially possible when the research is evaluative and its results could influence additional funding for the program being evaluated. When faced with this dilemma, because of the desire not to jeopardize the program's future or to improve future chances for research, the researcher may not report the true findings. This is extremely unethical, but unfortunately, may be more commonplace than one would like to believe. The ethical researcher will accept the findings and report them as discovered.

Protecting Confidentiality

Undoubtedly, one of the biggest concerns in conducting research is the issue of confidentiality and/or privacy. As has been suggested,

> *privacy and confidentiality are two ethical issues that are crucial to social researchers who, by the very nature of their research, frequently request individuals to share with them their thoughts, attitudes, and experiences (Kimmel, 1988, p. 85).*

Because a good portion of criminal-justice and criminological research involves humans, chances are good that a particular study may uncover sensitive information in which others—nonresearchers—may have an interest. One such example would be conducting gang research in which street names and legal names are collected, perhaps along with identifying tattoos or scars, and voluntary statements of criminal history. Such details would be extremely valuable to a police agency. Ethically, that information must remain confidential.

Reasons for Confidentiality and Privacy

Overall, five reasons have been identified as to why confidentiality and privacy are important in research:

1. Disclosure of particularly embarrassing or sensitive information may present the respondent with a risk of psychological, social, or economic harm.
2. Sensitive information, if obtained solely for research purposes, is legally protected in situations where respondents' privacy rights are protected.
3. Long-term research may require data storage of information that can identify the participants.
4. The courts can subpoena data.
5. Respondents may be suspicious as to how the information is truly going to be used.

Privacy Protections

The bottom line is that confidentiality and privacy must be maintained. There are two methods of accomplishing this: physical protection and legal protection (Berg, 2004; Kimmel, 1988, 1996; Senese, 1997; Schutt, 2001).

Physical protection relates to setting up the data so that links cannot be made between identifying information and the respondents. Limiting the number of people who have access can also aid in protecting the data. Legal protection involves efforts to avoid official misuse (Kimmel, 1988). Researchers are aided in this protection by an amendment to the 1973 Omnibus Crime Control and Safe Streets Act, better known as the "Shield Law," which protects research findings from any administrative or judicial processes. Furthermore, as noted earlier, federally funded research, through such institutions as NIJ, have established their own regulations. Unfortunately, these guidelines do not completely protect the data, leaving researchers responsible for gathering information in a manner that will best protect the respondents.

By simply meeting the four suggested criteria, a researcher can avoid many ethical problems. However, perhaps the best way to avoid ethical problems is to conduct research using a method that will not compromise ethical standards—that is, research that is legal, relevant, and necessary.

■ Summary

The simple act of research, especially when it involves humans, creates a plethora of possible ethical dilemmas. Because ethics is important to professions, researchers need to be cognizant of several ethical considerations.

These include determining whether the topic itself is ethical, what harm or risk is involved to respondents, and issues of confidentiality and privacy. There are federal guidelines for protecting individuals' privacy and for obtaining their consent. In the university setting, these guidelines are often reinforced through an IRB. The key to ethical research is a professional approach. While some professions have created a code of ethics applicable to research, criminal justice and criminology are just now establishing such a code. However, there are four criteria that, when followed, alleviate the need for such a code: (1) avoid conducting harmful research, (2) be objective, (3) use integrity in conducting and reporting the research, and (4) protect confidentiality.

METHODOLOGICAL QUERIES

1. When conducting survey research, how important is informed consent? Confidentiality?

2. Is it necessary to have an ethical code that is geared specifically toward criminological and criminal-justice research?

3. You are asked to write a code of research ethics for criminology and criminal justice. What do you include in this code? Explain.

4. Write an informed consent for conducting a criminality study among college students.

REFERENCES

Adler, E. S., & Clark, R. (2003). *How it's done: An invitation to social research* (2nd ed.). Belmont, CA: Thomson/Wadsworth.

American Heritage Dictionary, 4th ed. 2001. New York: Dell Publishing.

Babbie, E. (2004). *The practice of social research* (10th ed.). Belmont, CA: Thomson/Wadsworth.

Berg, B. L. (2004). *Qualitative research methods for the social sciences* (5th ed.). Boston: Allyn and Bacon.

Dantzker, M. L., & Waters, J. E. (1999). Examining students' perceptions of policing: A pre- and post-comparison between students in criminal justice and non-criminal justice courses. In M. L. Dantzker, (Ed.), *Readings for research methods in criminology and criminal justice* (pp. 27–36). Woburn, MA: Butterworth-Heinemann.

Fitzgerald, J. D., & Cox, S. M. (2001). *Research methods and statistics in criminal justice: An introduction* (3rd ed.). Chicago: Nelson-Hall.

Golden, M. P., (Ed.). (1976). *The research experience*. Itasca, IL: F. E. Peacock.

Kaplan, A. (1963). *The conduct of inquiry*. New York: Harper and Row.

Kimmel, A. J. (1988). *Ethics and values in applied social research*. Thousand Oaks, CA: Sage.

Kimmel, A. J. (1996). *Ethical issues in behavioral research: A survey*. Cambridge, MA: Blackwell.

Schutt, R. K. (2001). *Investigating the social world: The process and practice of research* (3rd ed.). Thousand Oaks, CA: Pine Forge Press.

Senese, J. D. (1997). *Applied research methods in criminal justice*. Chicago: Nelson-Hall.

■ **Example of an IRB Submission**

Form I
Summary Cover Sheet
Protocol for Human Subjects in Research[a]

Please check off or provide details on the following (if not applicable, enter N/A)	√	Exemption Requested (see page 4)

Principal Investigator Name	M. L. Dantzker, Ph.D.	Faculty	√	Graduate Student
College/Department	Criminal Justice	Campus Mail SBS321	Phone 2967	

Project Title: Sexual Perceptions of College Students: Does Race, Ethnicity, or Degree Major Make a Difference?

Subjective Estimate of Risk to Subject:		Low		Moderate		High	√	None	
Gender of Subjects	Male		Female	√	Both	Age(s): 18–?	Total Participants (est.)	2,000	

	Source of Subjects		Subject Recruitment	
	Psychology Subject Pool		Direct Person-to-Person Contact	
√	Other UTPA Students		Telephone Solicitation	
	Community		Newspaper Ad[b]	
	Posted Notices[b]		Letter[b]	
	Prisons		Other (please describe)	
√	Other (please specify)—Students from other universities whose selection will be based on colleagues contacted by investigators			

Compensation[c]	Yes		No	√
Deception[d]	Yes		No	√
Location of Experiment	NOT APPLICABLE			

Invasive or Sensitive Procedures: Yes __ No √		Sensitive Subject Matter: Yes __ No √	
	Blood Samples	Urine Samples	Alcohol, Drug, Sex
	Physical Measurements (electrodes, etc.)	Stress Exercise	Depression/Suicide
	Psychological Inventory	Review of Medical Records	Learning Disability

continued

Form I *continued*

	rDNA		Other (specifiy)		Other (specify)

Use of Video__ Audiotapes__ (please indicate)				Provisions for Confidentiality/Anonymity	
Retained	Yes	No		Replies Coded	
Retained/Length of Time			√	Secure Storage	
Destroy/Erase	Yes	No	√	Anonymous Response	
Other (explain)				Confidential Response	
Use specified in consent form?	Yes	No			
Use/assess to tapes:					

Exact location where signed consent forms will be filed:	SBS 359 (locked file cabinet)
(Must be kept on file for 3 years after the completion of the project)	

UTPA IRB Workshop Completed	Date:
ORHP IRB Web-Based Training Completed	Date:

[a]Must include signature of committee chair on protocol	[b]Please attach
[c]Please attach conditions, schedule of payment	[d]If yes, attach a debriefing form

Federal Assurance   FWA00000805
Number # _____
UTPA IRB # _____
Reviewed by _____

REQUEST FOR EXEMPTION FROM FULL IRB REVIEW

Some research projects involving human subjects are exempt [45 CFR 46.110 (b) (1),] from full review by the IRB. See the attached sheet on research categories exempt from full IRB review.

Basis for Exemption [please refer to attached "Categories Exempt from Full IRB Review"]

_____Established Educational Setting/Normal Educational Practices (a letter of approval from a school official must be obtained before the study can be conducted; send copy to the IRB)

_____Use of educational anonymous tests (cognitive, diagnostic, aptitude, advancement; attach copy)

_____Survey or interview procedures [unless subjects might be identified or put at legal or personal risk, and unless survey or procedures deal with sensitive matters of personal behavior]

_____Observation of public behavior [unless subjects might be identified or put at legal or personal risk, and unless observations deal with sensitive matters of personal behavior]

_____Anonymous collection or study of existing documents, records, or pathological or diagnostic specimens

_____Taste and food-quality evolution and consumer-acceptance studies

Increasingly, the U.S. population is becoming culturally, linguistically, economically, and ethnically diverse. The research needs to make a concerted effort to ensure that research subjects reflect the population demographically, including those groups who traditionally have been underrepresented. However, it is recognized that the available pool of subjects may preclude having a balanced population. If you cannot use a diverse population in your research, you must justify why not.

Signature of Primary Investigator   _____   Date _____
                                        M. L. Dantzker, Ph.D.

Signature of Coinvestigator   _____   Date _____
                                        Russell Eisenman, Ph.D.

Department Head Signature   _____   Date _____
                                        Dan Dearth, Ph.D.

Institutional Review Board   Date _____
Signature

Form II
Protocol for Human Subjects
In Research

PART I

Project Title	Sexual Perceptions of College Students: Does Race, Ethnicity, or Degree Major Make a Difference?	

Primary Investigator   M. L. Dantzker, Ph.D.   Department: Criminal Justice

E-mail: mldantz@panam.edu   Campus Address: SBS321

Coinvestigator 1   Russell Eisenman, Ph.D.   Department: Psychology
E-mail: Campus Address:

Coinvestigator 2   Department:
E-mail: Campus Address:

Graduate Adviser   Department:
E-mail: Campus Address:

Department Head   Department:
E-mail: Campus Address:

PART II

We have read the Public Health Service Act as amended by the National Institutes of Health Revitalization Act of 1993 (Public Law 103-43, June 10, 1993—Code of Federal Regulations Title 45 CFR Part 46). Furthermore, we have read the Belmont Report ("Ethical Principles and Guidelines for the Protection of Human Subjects of Research") and subscribe to the principles it contains. We understand that we must keep a copy of Title 45 CFR Part 46 and the Belmont Report in our files along with this proposal. Included in this proposal where applicable are specific citations that relate to specific elements of 45 CFR Part 46. We have also completed the mandatory IRB tutorial sponsored by the University of Texas–Pan American Office of Sponsored Research Projects (see attached copies of Certificates of Completion). In view of this declaration, we present for the board's consideration the following information that will be explained to the subject about the proposed research.

PART III

SURVEY PROCEDURE:

The purpose of this research is to compare the sexual perceptions of college students by race, ethnicity, and declared major [Section 46.116 (a) (1) (ii)]. Approximately 2,000 college students (male and female), 18 years of age and above, will be asked to volunteer to complete a survey, "Sexual Perceptions of College Students" [Section 46.116 (a) (1) (i)]. Subjects will consist of college students enrolled during the fall 2002 semester in a variety of Criminal Justice and

Introduction to Psychology courses within the University of Texas–Pan American and at other designated universities.

The data-collection instrument is a 43-item questionnaire (see attached) developed by the investigators after a review of existing questionnaires and the literature. It is designed to solicit respondents' perceptions and beliefs regarding various facets of sexual activities and behaviors [Section 46.116 (a) (1) (iii)].

Due to the nature of the survey, there is no identifying information being sought. Rather than give respondents a separate informed consent form, which would offer a means of identifying them, there will be an "informed consent" statement at the top of the questionnaire.

> The following survey is being conducted strictly for research purposes. The researchers, who represent the disciplines of Criminal Justice and Psychology at the University of Texas–Pan American, are interested in today's college students' perceptions regarding certain sexual activities and behaviors. We are particularly interested in whether there are differences in perceptions by choice of major, race, and/or ethnicity. Participation in this survey is strictly voluntary, not required. The information sought is limited so that there is no way to identify the respondent. Your completion of the survey serves as your acceptance and willingness to participate. Responses will be kept in the strictest confidence and will be used only for research purposes. Your cooperation and participation are appreciated. Thank you.

The investigators and their representatives will read the statement out loud to the subjects as they follow along [Section 46.117]. Completing the questionnaire will signify consent. Subjects will then be asked to complete said questionnaire and, upon doing so, to return it to the monitoring representative. All completed questionnaires will then be returned to Dr. M. L. Dantzker for analysis.

PART IV

RISK AND BENEFITS TO SUBJECTS:

The health risks associated with this survey are nonexistent, as the only thing each subject will be doing is answering questions. Because there will be no identifying information, confidentiality is a given. However, all survey responses will eventually be locked in a cabinet in SBS 359 [Section 46.116 (a) (5)]. The purpose of this study is simply to compare the sexual perceptions of college students by race, ethnicity, and declared major. There are no direct benefits associated with this research investigation for each subject [Section 46.116 (a) (3)].

PART V

SOURCE OF SUBJECTS:

Subjects will be recruited from among students enrolled at the beginning of the fall 2002 semester in various Criminal Justice and Introduction to Psychology

continued

Form II *continued*

courses at the University of Texas–Pan American and at other participating universities. (The investigators will spend the next few months contacting colleagues at universities throughout the country in an attempt to enlist support and access to designated courses in an effort to establish a diverse, purposive sample of college students.) Subjects will be unpaid volunteers at least 18 years of age. Each participant is free to withdraw from the survey at any time without any penalty from the investigators or from cooperating instructors. Results from the survey will be confidential, and no names will be used that could identify any respondent(s).

SPECIAL NOTE:

To determine whether the final questionnaire meets all methodological requirements, the investigators plan to pretest the instrument this semester (spring 2002) by surveying the students in Dr. Dantzker's Criminal Justice Research Methods and Dr. Eisenman's Intro to Psychology.

PART VI

REQUIRED SIGNATURES FOR CURRENT INVESTIGATION:

Principal Investigator _____ Date _____
M. L. Dantzker, Ph.D.

Coinvestigator 1 _____ Date _____
Russell Eisenman, Ph.D.

Graduate Adviser _____ Date _____
Please Type Name Here

Department Head _____ Date _____
Dan Dearth, Ph.D.

Qualitative Research

Vignette 5-1   Must It Always Be a Question of Numbers?

As a student worker, you spend more time around the departmental office than you really care to, but this is how you earn that extra spending money. Furthermore, doing so can have its perks, such as becoming better acquainted with professors and learning more about criminal justice and criminology than you might have by just sitting in a classroom. There is also the downside, such as hearing a couple of professors arguing over what type of research is more acceptable, qualitative or quantitative. You have heard this debate on a couple of occasions, but you never really paid much attention before. Now that you are taking the research-methods course, however, the debate piques your interest.

The professor arguing in favor of quantitative research proclaims to be a sociocriminologist schooled in a strong theoretical, yet numbers-oriented, tradition. The other professor is a former practitioner whose doctorate is in criminal justice, but who claims to have come from a program that favored qualitative work. The debate, as usual, is about which form of research is more appropriate to criminal justice, especially as the field continues its drive toward being accepted as a pure social science. Both professors appear to be making reasonable arguments for their positions. Still, you are not sure who is right, if either. Perhaps it will become clearer after this debate has been discussed in your research-methods course.

Chapter Objectives

After studying this chapter, the student should be able to:

- Compare and contrast quantitative and qualitative research.
- Define qualitative research.
- Discuss the strengths and weaknesses of qualitative research.
- Explain how qualitative research differs from a literature review.
- Describe the types of field interviews and give examples.
- Describe the different roles that may be utilized in field observation.
- Describe ethnographic research.
- Describe sociometry.
- Describe historiography.
- Describe how a content analysis may be qualitative.

Because of criminal justice's long-standing image of being an applied social science, some of the criminal-justice research conducted and published has had detractors. This is the result primarily of what is perceived as the research's lack of statistical sophistication. This perception is central to the continuing debate over which is more "academic"-qualitative or quantitative research. Because the remainder of the text focuses on elements more commonly associated with quantitative research (although very applicable to qualitative research), this chapter offers a closer look at qualitative research.

Qualitative Versus Quantitative Research

In Chapter 1, it was briefly noted that the debate over qualitative versus quantitative research simply comes down to a question of "concepts as ideas or terms versus numerical values." Broadening this distinction in easy terms finds that quantitative research merely refers to counting and measuring items associated with the phenomena in question. Qualitative research focuses on meanings, concepts, definitions, characteristics, metaphors, symbols, and descriptions (Berg 2004). Based on these statements, one might easily understand why quantitative research appears more popular. However, is it always the better method to use?

In recent years, there has been a trend among scholarly journals to demand more quantitative than qualitative research. This preference is because qualitative research is often criticized as not being scientific (Berg, 2004; Crabtree & Miller, 1999; Denzin & Lincoln, 2005; Esterberg, 2002; Flick, 2002; Patton, 2002). Because we believe that both methods are appropriate and necessary to criminal justice and criminology, that debate will not be continued here. This view is not unique, as is demonstrated in the following:

> Qualitative and quantitative research can be complementary, together yielding better results than only one approach would. Furthermore,

qualitative data collected through observations can be used while planning quantitative research. Such observations can help define the research subject and indicate the issues that need further study (Eck & La Vigne, 1994, p. 5).

■ Qualitative Research Defined

Qualitative research is viewed as an examination and interpretation of observations as expressed by the researcher's words rather than by numerical assignments (Adler & Clark, 2003; Berg, 2004; Creswell, 2002; Maxwell, 2005; Silverman, 2000). Such analysis enables researchers to verbalize insights that quantifying of data would not permit. It also allows us to avoid the trap of "false precision," which frequently occurs when subjective numerical assignments are made. These quantifications are misleading in that they convey the impression of a precision that does not really exist.

■ Merits and Limitations of Qualitative Research

The insights gained from qualitative research and its usefulness in designing specific questions and analyses for individuals and groups make it invaluable in the study of criminal justice and criminology. However, the costs and time involved in such studies may not be logistically feasible (Flick, 2002; Silverman, 2000). One of the major complaints about qualitative research is that it takes too long to complete. Other complaints about qualitative research include the following:

1. *It requires clearer goals and cannot be statistically analyzed (Berg, 2004; Marshall & Rossman, 1999; Maxwell, 2005; Silverman, 2000).*

2. *It suffers from problems with reliability in that replication may prove quite difficult (Flick, 2002, Silverman, 2002).*

3. *Validity issues may arise from the inability to quantify the data (Creswell, 2002, Esterberg, 2002, Patton, 2002).*

■ What You Have Done Before

Before we proceed further, we should address the question that may be forming in your mind as you read about qualitative research. We have stressed that most, if not all, of the "research" that you have done in the past was not true research, but merely an extended literature review. Now we are telling you that research does not have to use numbers. Does this mean we were wrong and you have been doing research? Unless you have used the scientific method to structure your inquiry so as to yield results that logically extend from your analysis, you have not conducted qualitative research. A mere reciting of what others have done does not qualify as research. However, if you actually used the prior research to compare or assess an issue or event, you may have done genuine research.

The distinction we are making between true qualitative research and the literature-review "research" will become clearer after you review the various types of qualitative research that are available for use. The variety of methods available for conducting qualitative research include field interviews, focus groups, field observation, ethnography, sociometry, and historiography (Berg, 2004; Crabtree & Miller, 1999; Denzin & Lincoln, 2005; Marshall & Rossman, 1999; Maxwell, 2005; Silverman, 2000).

■ Types of Qualitative Research

Conducting qualitative research may be time-consuming, but because this type of research better reflects the actual being of something, the time factor becomes moot for the qualitative researcher. Therefore, the bigger issue becomes what method to employ. Obviously, this will depend on the goals of the research and on the source of the information being sought. When information is sought directly from individuals, the most common method to use is interviewing.

Field Interviewing

Simply put, interviewing is the asking of questions by one individual of another in order to obtain information. If the interview consists of specific questions for which designated responses may be chosen, this would qualify as quantitative research. (Quantitative interviews will be discussed in the next chapter.) Generally, even if a field interview is structured, the answers are open-ended. By this, we mean that the response given by the interviewee is recorded exactly as stated rather than assigned to a predetermined category.

There is no one agreed-upon way to conduct a field interview. Consensus could probably be found that one of the keys to successful interviewing is asking the right questions. A reflection on the questions would be based on the type of interview being conducted and the information sought. Although there may be debate as to what the different ways of interviewing are called, three types of interviews are possible: structured, semistructured, and unstructured.

Structured Interviews

A structured interview entails asking every respondent a list of preestablished, open-ended questions. As stated above, if the questions asked are closed-ended (respondents select from a choice of predetermined answers for which a numerical value can be assigned), this would qualify as quantitative survey research. The majority of structured interviews are quantitative in that they consist entirely or predominantly of closed-ended questions. Responses are recorded as given, and the interview pace is such that all the questions can be asked and responded to in a timely fashion, but neither the interviewer nor the respondent is rushed.

The following have been suggested as guidelines for conducting a structured interview. The interviewer should never:

- get involved in long explanations of the research;
- deviate from the study introduction, sequence of questions, or question wording;
- let another person interrupt the interview, or respond for the person being questioned;
- suggest, agree to, or disagree to, an answer;
- interpret the meaning of a question; or
- improvise (Fontana & Frey, 2005).

The structured interview is geared toward limiting errors and ensuring a consistency of order in the responses even though the responses themselves may vary. Still, there are factors that could cause problems that will eventually affect the outcome. Some errors include, but are not limited to, the respondent's behavior (for example, is the respondent being truthful, or saying only what he or she believes the interviewer wants to hear?), the setting of the interview (such as face-to-face or telephonic), the wording of the questions (such as using uncommon terms), and poor interviewer skills (for example, the interviewer changes the wording of a question or does not clearly enunciate).

Additionally, if an interviewer is not familiar with the respondent's background, culture, education, or other factors, this can be detrimental to the interview. For example:

> A researcher interested in gang membership decides to interview all juveniles arrested during a certain month without knowing anything about why any particular person was arrested or his or her life leading up to the arrest. This individual may find it very difficult to receive cooperation or truthful responses because his or her questions may not be appropriate; for example, asking every juvenile how long he or she has been in a gang assumes gang affiliation without actually knowing if it exists.

Overall, the structured interview can elicit rational, legitimate responses. Unfortunately, it does not consider the emotional aspect. This is where a semistructured interview might be more useful.

Semistructured Interviews

This type of interview primarily follows the same ideas or guidelines of a structured interview. The major difference is that in this type of interview, the interviewer can go beyond the responses for a broader understanding of the answers. This is known as "probing for more detail." Probing may consist of asking for more explanation of an answer than has been given or following up with an additional question or questions depending upon the answers given. Semistructured interviews are commonly used as a qualitative-research strategy.

Semistructured interviews allow for deeper probing into the answers given to structured, closed-ended questions. Still, there are limitations to this type of interview. If a researcher wants to really explore a topic through interviewing without having specific question boundaries, then the unstructured interview would best serve this purpose.

In order to study how academic researchers gain access to data, Flanyak (1999) used the qualitative-research method of in-depth interviewing, but in a semi-structured manner. This method provided a high response rate and allowed the interviewer to have personal contact with, and observation of, her subjects. Using an interview guide instrument permitted the researcher to maintain a general outline and framework of questions to ensure that specific topics were investigated, yet provided the researcher with the opportunity and discretion to explore or probe respondents for detail in specific areas.

Unstructured Interviews

The unstructured interview is far less rigid than either of the previous two methods. Seldom is a schedule kept or are there any predetermined possible answers. Often the questions are created as the interaction proceeds (Adler & Clark, 2003).

The most common form of unstructured interview makes use of open-ended (ethnographic or in-depth) questions. In many cases, this style of interview is done in conjunction with participant observation (Fontana & Frey, 2005). For example:

> To gain a better understanding of what police detectives find stressful, a researcher chose to spend several days with detectives from a particular police agency. While the primary role was to observe how detectives responded to certain situations or events, during "down times" (i.e., between calls, during meals, after the shift), the researcher was able to ask open-ended questions pertaining to what the detectives found stressful. One such question might be: "What do you find stressful about being a detective?"

Because of the nature of an unstructured interview, the researcher must be able to complete the following for the study to be successful:

- Gain access to the setting
- Understand the language and culture of respondents
- Decide how to present oneself
- Locate a contact or informant
- Gain the respondent's trust
- Establish rapport (Berg, 2004; Esterberg, 2002; Fontana & Frey, 2005; Maxwell, 2005; Silverman, 2000)

By meeting the above requirements, the researcher should be successful in his or her efforts.

Obviously, interviewing can be a tedious means of gaining data, especially if it is of the one-on-one variety. However, sometimes research requires interviewing more than one person at a time. This qualitative method is often called "focus groups" or "group interviewing" (Berg, 2004; Creswell, 2002; Fontana & Frey, 2005; Silverman, 2000).

Focus Groups

Perhaps the best way to define a focus group is that it is "the interviewing of several individuals in one setting." While not meant to replace individual interviews, focus groups have long been in use in marketing and politics (Fontana & Frey, 2005; Madriz, 2005). The focus group is basically an information-gathering method where the researcher-interviewer directs the interaction and inquiry. This can occur in either a structured (for example, pretesting a questionnaire) or unstructured (for example, brainstorming) manner. In either case, the researcher-interviewer must meet the same guidelines offered for conducting any interview. But why would someone use this method?

The use of focus groups has its advantages and disadvantages. The advantages include flexibility, stimulation, and limited expenses. The disadvantages include group culture, dominant responder, and topic sensitivity (Berg, 2004; Flick, 2002; Fontana & Frey, 2005; Maxwell, 2005; Patton, 2002). The focus group can be a useful qualitative method for gathering information and can be particularly interesting. However, there may be times when the researcher may wish to take part in the activities or just observe the subjects of the research in their natural setting, a method of research referred to as observational.

Field Observation (or Participant-Observer)

The type of observation is interesting because of the context in which it places the researcher. While this method of qualitative research has not received the same attention as interviewing, it is still a very viable tool, especially in criminal justice and criminology. Usually this manner of study has focused on only two modes: observer and participant-observer.

The observer method is where the researcher gathers information in the most unobtrusive fashion by simply watching the study subjects interact, preferably without their knowledge. With participant observation, the subjects not only are aware of the researcher, but also actually interact as the researcher takes an active role in activities under study. These two methods are quite fitting; however, to date, what still appears to be a more useful description of the options for this type research is the one offered by Senese (1997). His model includes four types: full participant, participant-researcher, researcher who participates, and the complete researcher.

The Full Participant

Sometimes it may be fitting, or perhaps even essential, that a researcher become part of the study. The full-participant method allows the researcher to carry out observational research, but in a "covert" manner (for example, to study the workings of a gang, the researcher takes an active role as a gang member, where other members are unaware of the research agenda). Of course, this method has some problems, such as the researcher's possibly facing ethical and moral dilemmas that could adversely affect the research if the wrong decision is made—for example, having to compromise one's beliefs, or even placing the researcher in legal jeopardy (such as being in a car during a drive-by shooting). To avoid ethical and moral dilemmas, a researcher may decide to move one step down and become a participant-researcher.

The Participant-Researcher

Because participating in the activities of the research subjects can offer insights and information not attainable through other forms of research, and to avoid dilemmas that come with full participation, the participant-research method can be a good option. In this method, the researcher participates in the activities of the research environment, but the research subjects know that the participant-observer is a researcher. (For example, in order to study the behavior of males in a reformatory, the researcher goes in and participates in all activities, but everyone knows that he or she is there collecting information.) The biggest drawback of this research method is that, because the subjects know the researcher's role, behaviors other than those being studied can be influenced. The subjects may not act as they would under unobserved conditions, either over- or underexaggerating their actions. This is known as "subject reactivity" to the research. Furthermore, by being part of the activities, the researcher can influence outcomes and behaviors that may not have existed without his or her presence. This, then, leads us to the third method of observation.

The Researcher Who Participates

Rather than taking part in activities, the researcher-who-participates method requires nothing more than observation by the researcher, whose status as a researcher is known to the research subjects. For example, to study whether a particular treatment offered to juveniles who have been incarcerated is working, the researcher enters the environment where his or her status as a researcher is known, but does nothing more than observe. While this method eliminates many of the problems of the previous two methods, the mere presence of the researcher who participates can still influence behavior and activities. How does one avoid this dilemma?

METHODOLOGICAL

LINKS

To determine who actually steals, Dabney, Hollinger, and Dugan (2004) conducted a covert observational study for which they used closed-circuit television. Initially (for the first six months of the study), their researchers were tasked to observe every third shopper who entered the store. Eventually, the protocol was redesigned to watch every third shopper who was dressed in a particular fashion. The researchers were also allowed some discretion to observe anyone who entered the store exhibiting specific behavioral cues.

The Complete Researcher

The way for a researcher to minimize the problems generally associated with observational-participatory research is to avoid all possible interaction with the research subjects. Data collection may involve "covert" methods of observation (for example, from some disguised vantage point, such as a guard tower in a maximum-security prison, or from the review of records). As you can imagine, the benefits that are gained by covert observation or assumption of a noninteracting role are countered by possible resentment and denial of access by those being observed.

Regardless of which form is used, observational research can be time-consuming and may not provide the results ultimately sought. Still, it can be a very interesting means for gathering data.

Despite the respective problems of observational research, it does provide a perspective that is often missed through quantitative research. Furthermore, it can be an important part of another form of qualitative research: ethnography.

Ethnographic Study

Ethnographic study or field research (ethnography) overlaps with field observation in that the researcher actually enters the environment under study, but does not necessarily take part in any activities. Although the defining of ethnographic study has been controversial (Berg, 2004; Silverman, 2002; Tedlock, 2005), it is a form of qualitative research in which the researcher looks at various sociological, psychological, and educational variables as they exist in the real social context (Crabtree & Miller, 1999; Creswell, 2002; Esterberg, 2002; Maxwell, 2005). It consists of several attributes, including the following:

1. *Exploration of the nature of particular social phenomena, rather than hypotheses testing*
2. *Primary use of "unstructured" data*
3. *Investigation of a limited number of cases*
4. *Data analyses that involve explicit interpretation, mainly in the form of verbal descriptions and explanations (Berg, 2004; Creswell, 2002; Flick, 2002; Maxwell, 2005; Patton, 2002; Silverman, 2000)*

Although not a particularly popular means of conducting research, ethnography, like observation, can provide insights not found through quantitative research. For example, the study of gang graffiti from a quantitative perspective might simply identify the differing types of symbols drawn and how many of each. However, an ethnographic study could provide what the symbols mean, why they have been placed where, and who is placing them. This information gives a different slant to the information than does the quantitative approach. One of the interesting aspects of ethnographic study is the possibility for the researcher to examine social interactions, which leads to another form of qualitative research: sociometry.

Sociometry

Sociometry is a technique by which the researcher can measure social dynamics or relational structures such as who likes whom (Berg, 2004; Denizen &

Lincoln, 2005). Information can be gathered through interviews or by observation, and will indicate who is chosen and the characteristics of those who do the choosing. With respect to criminal justice, a sociometric study might involve prosecutor–defense attorney relationships, where the researcher observes the interaction of prosecutors with defense attorneys, noting how each treats and is treated by the other and how that affects outcomes such as plea bargains. This study might show whether there is a hierarchy among lawyers or among potential defendants (the accused).

As with observation and ethnography, the researcher's presence, attitudes, biases, and other personal factors can influence the outcomes of sociometric research. Because the mere presence of the researcher can be problematic, a less obtrusive means of conducting qualitative research is available.

Historiography

Historiography (also known as historical/comparative research) (Berg, 2004) is basically the study of actions, events, and phenomena that have already occurred. This type of research often involves the study of documents and records that contain information about the topic under study. This type of study is generally inexpensive and unobtrusive. It can assist in determining why or how an event occurred and whether such an event could happen again. It is also a means by which researchers may compare and contrast events or phenomena that have already occurred. Historiography can be either qualitative or quantitative in nature depending on the materials being utilized and the focus of the research. Historians, as well as Marxist scholars, utilize this method.

Content Analysis

Like historical research, content analysis is the study of social artifacts in order to gain insights about an event or phenomenon. It differs from historical research in that the focus of content analysis is on the coverage of the event by the particular medium being evaluated (for example, books, magazines, television programs, news coverage, and so on), rather than on the event itself. Depending on how the research is conducted, this analysis may be either qualitative or quanti-

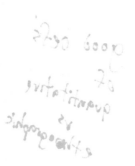

METHODOLOGICAL

LINKS

In an effort to examine any historical trends in the relationship between homicide and suicide rates, in particular the extent to which gender differences exist in this relationship, Batton (2004) conducted a time-series analysis on national-level data for the period 1960 to 2000. To conduct this study, Batton simply had to review data already in existence; thus, the study was unobtrusive and relatively inexpensive.

METHODOLOGICAL LINKS

Based on news stories aired by three different television stations, Maguire, Sandage, and Weatherby (1999) examined the development of citizen perceptions of policing. The researchers' main focus was on the types of stories being aired—that is, positive or negative. Similarly, Colomb and Damphouse (2004) examined newspaper coverage of hate crimes through a content analysis of such coverage throughout the 1990s.

tative in nature. Qualitative content analysis would emphasize verbal rather than statistical analysis of various forms of communication.

Whether it is qualitative or quantitative, the research can serve a purpose in criminal justice and criminology. Thus, the debate should not be over which is better, but over what should be studied. How the selection of research impacts upon the research design will be discussed in a later chapter.

■ Summary

There is a continuing debate between criminal-justice and criminology researchers as to what type of research is better, qualitative or quantitative. This chapter argues that the two types complement one another and have appropriate roles in related research. To that end, this chapter explores the nature of qualitative research by noting that it is the research of ideas and concepts, not of numbers. While there are many forms of qualitative research, the more popular ones include the following:

1. Field interviewing: structured, semistructured, and unstructured
2. Field observation: the full participant, the participant-researcher, the researcher who participates, and the complete researcher
3. Ethnography
4. Sociometry
5. Historiography
6. Content analysis

METHODOLOGICAL QUERIES

1. You are interested in interviewing probation officers about their jobs. For each type of interview structure, what are some questions you would ask?

2. There has been some discussion about implementing a Drug Awareness and Reduction Education program in the local elementary school. However, before this happens, a qualitative study of other programs has been ordered. What method would you suggest? Why?

3. To better understand the workings of a boot camp, you are asked to conduct an observational study. What form would you use, and why?

4. What method of qualitative research would you use to study: (1) police-dispatcher job satisfaction, (2) correctional officers' interaction with individuals awaiting trial compared to interaction with those who have been convicted, and (3) a particular judge's sentencing patterns? Explain how you would conduct each study.

5. How might ethnographic research be best used in criminal justice? In criminology?

REFERENCES

Adler, E. S., & Clark, R. (2003). *How it's done: An invitation to social research* (2nd ed.). Belmont, CA: Thomson/Wadsworth.

Batton, C. (2004). Gender differences in lethal violence: Historical trends in the relationship between homicide and suicide rates, 1960–2000. *Justice Quarterly, 21*(3), 423–461.

Berg, B. L. (2004). *Qualitative research methods for the social sciences* (5th ed.). Boston: Allyn and Bacon.

Colomb, W., & Damphouse, K. (2004). Examination of newspaper coverage of hate crimes: A moral panic perspective. *American Journal of Criminal Justice, 28*(2), 149–163.

Crabtree, B. F., & Miller, W. L. (Eds.). (1999). *Doing qualitative research.* Thousand Oaks, CA: Sage.

Creswell, J. W. (2002). *Research design: Qualitative, quantitative, and mixed methods approaches* (2nd ed.). Thousand Oaks, CA: Sage.

Dabney, D. A., Hollinger, R. C., & Dugan, L. (2004). Who actually steals? A study of covertly observed shoplifters. *Justice Quarterly, 21*(4), 693–728.

Denzin, N. K., & Lincoln, Y. S. (Eds.). (2005). *Handbook of qualitative research* (3rd ed.). Thousand Oaks, CA: Sage.

Eck, J. E., & La Vigne, N. G. (1994). *Using research: A primer for law enforcement managers* (2nd ed.). Washington, DC: Police Executive Research Forum.

Esterberg, K. G. (2002). *Qualitative methods in social research.* New York: McGraw-Hill Humanities.

Flanyak, C. M. (1999). Accessing data: Procedures, practices, and problems of academic researchers. In M. L. Dantzker, (Ed.), *Readings for research methods in criminology and criminal justice* (pp. 157–180). Woburn, MA: Butterworth-Heinemann.

Flick, U. (2002). *An introduction to qualitative research* (2nd ed.). Thousand Oaks, CA: Sage.

Fontana, A., & Frey, J. H. (2005). The interview: From structured questions to negotiated text. In N. K. Denzin & Y. S. Lincoln (Eds.), *Handbook of qualitative research* (3rd ed., pp. 645–672). Thousand Oaks, CA: Sage.

Madriz, E. (2005). Focus groups in feminist research. In N. K. Denzin & Y. S. Lincoln, *Handbook of qualitative research* (3rd ed., pp. 835–850). Thousand Oaks, CA: Sage.

Maguire, B., Sandage, D., & Weatherby, G. A. (1999). Television news coverage of the police: An exploratory study from a small town locale. *Journal of Contemporary Criminal Justice, 15*(2), 171–190.

Marshall, C., & Rossman, G. B. (1999). *Designing qualitative research* (3rd ed.). Thousand Oaks, CA: Sage.

Maxwell, J. A. (2005). *Qualitative research design: An interactive approach* (2nd ed.). Thousand Oaks, CA: Sage.

Patton, M. Q. (2002). *Qualitative evaluation and research methods* (3rd ed.). Thousand Oaks, CA: Sage.

Senese, J. D. (1997). *Applied research methods in criminal justice.* Chicago: Nelson-Hall.

Silverman, D. (2000). *Doing qualitative research: A practical handbook.* Thousand Oaks, CA: Sage.

Silverman, D., (Ed.) (2002). *Qualitative research: Theory, method, and practice* (3rd ed.). Thousand Oaks, CA: Sage.

Tedlock, B. (2005). Ethnography and ethnographic representation. In N. K. Denzin & Y. S. Lincoln (Eds.), *Handbook of qualitative research* (3rd ed., pp. 455–486). Thousand Oaks, CA: Sage.

6 Quantitative Research

Vignette 6-1   The Debate Over Numbers-Oriented Research Continues

Last week, you observed two faculty members in your department debating which form of research is better: qualitative or quantitative. The last time your methods course met, qualitative research was discussed. You are a little clearer as to the purpose and means of conducting qualitative research, but you find yourself still skeptical about its relevance over quantitative. Knowing that the next course topic is quantitative, you hope that this will finally make both sides clear. As you enter the classroom, you are handed a questionnaire by the instructor's assistant, who advises you that you are being asked to participate in the most important and most-often-used type of research in criminal justice: a survey. A quick review of the questionnaire finds that there are 20 questions with responses that are categorical or have a numeric choice. Now, normally, this might not make an impression on you, but the survey is being conducted by your current instructor, the same person who strongly supported qualitative research. Now you are really confused.

When the instructor finally comes into the classroom, you immediately offer a challenge as to why this type of research is being conducted. An answer, you are told, will be clearer by the end of this night's class.

After studying this chapter, the student should be able to:

- Define quantitative research.
- Define empiricism and discuss how it relates to quantitative research.
- Contrast the two types of causality.
- Identify and discuss the three criteria for causality.
- Contrast necessary and sufficient cause.
- Describe what is meant by false precision.
- Identify and explain the four levels of measurement.
- Recognize and describe the types of survey research.
- Explain the strengths and weaknesses of survey research.
- Describe field research and give an example.
- Discuss the types of unobtrusive research.
- Describe evaluation research.

Quantitative Research

As was stressed in Chapter 5, qualitative research is a valuable tool that provides many insights into the study of crime, criminality, and society's responses to crime. It is not only an excellent means of conducting primary research, but is also highly useful in complementing quantitative research. However, to be a complete criminological researcher, one must be able to move beyond qualitative research. Quantitative research is the means to do so.

Quantitative Research Defined

Quantitative research might best be defined as *describing and explaining observations of a phenomenon through numerical discourse* (Creswell, 2002; Nardi, 2002; Punch, 2005). This means that research is not based on a possibly subjective interpretation of the observations, but is (hopefully) a more objective analysis based on the numerical findings produced from observations.

Qualitative Versus Quantitative Research, Part II

In the previous chapter, we stated that quantitative research refers to counting and measuring items associated with the phenomena in question, whereas qualitative research focuses on meanings, concepts, definitions, characteristics, metaphors, symbols, and descriptions. Because of the potential for bias and the criticism that qualitative research is unscientific, the majority of criminal-justice-related research tends to be quantitative in nature. A quick review of the leading journals that publish criminal-justice and criminology research would support this assertion.

There are many issues that are not suitable for numerical assignments. To use an issue that is not suitable would be both inaccurate and misleading. Some of the more intense theoretical debates, such as the merits of the death penalty, are based on personal beliefs about human nature that are shaped by deep-seated religious, political, and moral convictions. As a result, perceptions of these frequently tend to be more influenced by emotion and ideology than by scientific study. This does not mean that quantitative research cannot be conducted, but to do so is difficult at best.

■ What You Have Not Done Before

As a developing researcher, you may feel that you have conducted qualitative research through the literature reviews and comparative/historical research that you have done for previous courses. If performed in a systematic and logical manner consistent with the scientific method, perhaps you have. But have you actually assigned numerical values, collected data utilizing that assignment, and then analyzed the results? Unless you have a strong background in math and science or have been fortunate enough to have been involved in an empirical-research project, chances are you have not. (For those who are still struggling with methods phobia, we define "fortunate" here as having benefited from the knowledge and insights of the experience rather than from the pleasure of the experience.) This is a deficiency that we hope to aid your instructor in correcting. As a college graduate who values and is capable of critical thinking and independent learning, you need to be able to conduct quantitative research. It will serve you not only in your academic career, but also in future work tasks or civic duties. You will be surprised to find how many things in life warrant "looking into." You will also find that in some ways, quantitative research is actually easier than qualitative research.

■ Empirical Observation

If you think back to your introductory course in criminology/criminal justice and/or your course in criminological theory, you have already received an introduction to empiricism. Cesare Lombroso, the founder of the positive school of criminology, used empiricism in his study of criminals. Earlier scholars (for example, Quetelet and Guerry in their independent area studies of crime rates in France) also used empirical techniques.

Empiricism requires using sensations and experiences (observations) to reach conclusions related to our daily life (Black, 1999; Punch, 2005). The use of the scientific method with its focus on causation rather than casual observation is what makes empiricism important. It is this emphasis on empiricism rather than idealism that is the basis upon which positive criminology is founded. Rather than just quoting an "eye for an eye," we can use empirical techniques to gather and evaluate data as to the effectiveness of correctional programs, or to decide which patrol strategy is more cost-effective, or to determine whether extralegal factors influence conviction rates. Quantitative research is based upon empiricism.

■ Causality

In applying empirical observation to criminal-justice research, we focus on causal relationships. Simply stated, what behaviors or events lead to other behaviors or events? When we try to answer that question, we seek to determine causality.

Idiographic and Nomothetic Causes

Idiographic refers to the concrete, the individual, the unique. Nomothetic, on the other hand, deals with the abstract, the general, the universal. Examining numerous explanations for why an event occurred is known as idiographic explanation. Historians and Marxist criminologists tend to use this method in their qualitative analyses. *Idiographic* causation may also be quantitative in that many causes may be compared and contrasted using numerical assignments (Nardi, 2002). When researchers focus on relatively few observations in order to provide a partial explanation for an event, this is known as nomothetic causation (Babbie, 2004).

Rather than trying to provide a total picture of every influence in a causal relationship, nomothetic explanation focuses on one factor or a few factors that could provide a general understanding of the phenomena being studied. Nomothetic explanations of causality are based on probabilities (which will be discussed in Chapter 9). It is this use of probability that enables us to make inferences based on a relatively few observations.

■ The Criteria for Causality

When attempting to determine if a causal relationship exists between the events or issues that we are studying, there are three criteria that we must observe:

1. *The independent variable, the variable providing the influence, must occur before the dependent variable, the variable that is being acted upon.*

2. *The relationship between the independent and dependent variable must be observable.*

3. *The apparent relationship is not explained by a third variable.* (Babbie, 2004; Black, 1999; Creswell, 2002; Nardi, 2002)

As an example, you see individual A struck by another person, B. Person A then falls down. Using the criteria for causality, you would conclude that the striking (independent variable) led to the falling (dependent variable). It occurred prior to the falling and was clearly related to what you witnessed. If no other event occurred—for example, a third variable, such as a blow having also been struck by Person C—then it is reasonable to assume that the criteria for causality have been met.

Necessary and Sufficient Cause

In investigating causality, we must meet the above criteria, but we do not have to demonstrate a perfect correlation. In probabilistic models, such as those used in most inferential research, we will often find exceptions to the rule. If a condition or event must occur in order for another event to take place, that is known as a necessary cause. For example, the female egg must be fertilized by a male sperm in order to start development of a fetus. The cause must be present in order for the effect to occur.

When the presence of a condition will ordinarily cause the effect to occur, this is known as a sufficient cause. The cause will usually create the effect, but will not always do so. Playing golf in a thunderstorm may not result in your being struck by lightning, but the conditions are sufficient for it to occur. In social-science research, we prefer to identify a necessary cause for an event, but to do so is often impossible. Instead, we are more likely to identify causes that are sufficient.

■ False Precision

We have discussed the issue of false precision earlier, but it warrants another visitation. When quantifying data, it is imperative that the numerical assignments are valid. If you arbitrarily assign numbers to variables without a logical reason for doing so, the numbers have no true meaning. This assignment is known as false precision. We have quantified a concept, but that assignment is subjective rather than objective. The precision that we claim does not really exist. In those cases, a qualitative analysis would be more appropriate.

■ Quantitative Measurement

On many occasions in our lives, we are confronted with some form of measurement. Based on our earlier definition of quantitative research, the term "measurement," as it is applied here to criminal-justice and criminological research, is viewed as *the assignment of numerical values or categorical labels to phenomena for the expressed purpose of quantifiable identification or analysis*. With respect to quantifying something, there is more than one means or level.

Levels of Measurement

What can often be a very confusing part of conducting quantitative research is determining what level of measurement to use. There are four levels from which to choose: nominal, ordinal, interval, and ratio. The level that is chosen will have an extremely important impact on how the data are collected and analyzed. Researchers can move down from a higher level of data to a lower level during data analysis, but they cannot move up to a higher level from a lower level. As we discuss the various levels of measurement, you will see why this is so.

Nominal-Level Data

The simplest level of measurement is the nominal level. At this level, measurement is categorical where each is mutually exclusive. There is neither a quantitative nor a statistical value assigned, except for the expressed need to describe the results or to code them for data analyses. Most often, nominal measures are used to represent independent variables that describe characteristics of the sample, but nominal measures may also be used to describe dependent variables (see **Box 6-1**).

Ordinal-Level Data

The second level of measurement is the ordinal level. This level moves beyond being merely categorical by assigning a rank or a placement of order to variables. Although, in using this level, numbers are assigned for ranking purposes (for example, 1-10), these numbers are not meant to explain—or are unable to explain—the response, but are viewed simply as demonstrative of where the respondent believes the item to fall. For example, in looking at the difference between the seriousness of criminal offenses—where murder is labeled as a 9, robbery a 5, and theft a 1—there is a four-unit difference between each, but again, we cannot explain what that difference truly represents.

Most often, ordinal measures are found in attitudinal surveys, perceptual surveys, quality-of-life studies, or service studies. **Box 6-2** offers a list of occupations that respondents could be asked to rank in order of how stressful they perceive each to be, from most stressful to least stressful. Although the respondents would write any number between 1 and 10, the listed order would tell us only what the

---

Box 6-1
Examples of Nominal Measures

Gender—Male, Female
Ethnicity—American, African, Hispanic, Asian
Religion—Catholic, Jewish, Protestant, Baptist
Education—High School, B.S., M.S., Ph.D.
Marital Status—Single, never married
   Single, divorced
   Married
   Widow/Widower
Criminal Offense—Murder, Sexual Assault, Robbery, Theft, Burglary
Sentence Disposition—Probation, Jail, Prison
Prison Security Level—Maximum, Medium, Minimum

Box 6-2
Ordinal Measures: Rank Order or Continuum Choice

Rank by level of stressfulness (most to least, 1–10)
_____Air-Traffic Controller
_____Psychiatrist
_____Police Officer
_____Inner-City Schoolteacher
_____Firefighter
_____Administrative Secretary
_____Emergency Room Nurse
_____Restaurant Server
_____Taxi Driver
_____Stockbroker

Choose the response that you feel is most appropriate.

Excellent	Good	Satisfactory	Fair	Poor
5	4	3	2	1

individuals perceive. There is no way to determine how much difference there is in the perceived stressfulness between each occupation. Despite being assigned numerical values and being useful in data analysis, ordinal-level data are limited in providing explanation.

Interval-Level Data

The third-highest level of measure is interval, which provides far better opportunity for explanation than data collected at the nominal and ordinal levels. Within interval data, there is an expected equality in the distance between choices on the continuum. This allows us to use more sophisticated techniques during data analysis.

Unlike ratio-level data (discussed below), there is no set zero or starting point for interval data. Since numbers assigned have an arbitrary beginning, the usefulness of the information may be limited. For example, the difference between an IQ of 135 and 150 is the same 15-unit difference as between 150 and 165. However, there is no distinction as to what the difference means. We can comment on the difference, but cannot explain what that difference means. To be able to do so would require ratio-level data.

Ratio-Level Data

The highest and most quantifiable level of measure is ratio. This level is characterized primarily by an absolute beginning point of zero, and the differences between each point are equal and can be explained. Two of the more common ratio measures are age and money. With respect to research, ratio measures can be collapsed into nominal or ordinal measures. Age and family income are often ratio-level, independent variables that, for analysis purposes, are collapsed into a nominal measure (for example, under 18, 18–25, 26–34, over 34; and under

$10,000, $10,000–$24,999, $25,000–$49,999, over $50,000). The benefits of collapsing ratio measures will be discussed in a later chapter.

Obviously, choosing a level of measurement is just one of the first steps in conducting quantitative research. Probably the most important step is deciding what type of method or design to use.

■ Types of Quantitative Research

There are a variety of designs available to the criminal-justice professional and criminologist for conducting quantitative research. Yet, despite all the possibilities, there is one form of research that is both a research method and a research tool: the survey. Because of its dual nature, it will be discussed briefly here as a quantitative-research design, and in Chapter 9 as a data-collection device.

Survey Research

The survey is one of the most popular research methods in criminal justice. The survey design is used when researchers are interested in the experiences, attitudes, perceptions, or beliefs of individuals, or when trying to determine the extent of a policy, procedure, or action among a specific group. Most often, a researcher will contact a sample of individuals presumed to have participated in a particular event, who belong to a certain group, or who are part of a specific audience having experienced similar events. Of the identified group, certain questions pertaining to the topic under study will be asked, either verbally or in written form. The solicited responses to the questions make up the data used to test the research hypothesis or hypotheses. The three primary survey methods are personal interview, mail questionnaire, and telephone survey.

Personal Interviews

Personal interviews are surveys that are administered by face-to-face discussions between the researcher and the survey respondent. Unstructured interviews in which the researcher's questions are developed during the conversation are qualitative and were discussed in Chapter 5. Structured interviews in which the researcher asks only open-ended questions would also be qualitative.

Interviews in which the researcher reads from a previously developed questionnaire to which responses are numerically assigned are quantitative. Such interviews may in fact be nothing more than the reading of a questionnaire that may have been mailed out to respondents. Personal interviews permit the researcher to obtain not only responses to the questions asked, but also permit probing on open-ended questions, as well as observation of the respondent's demeanor and nonverbal responses to the questions asked. Personal interviews are, however, more costly and time-consuming, as well as less safe than other strategies that do not bring researchers into physical contact with respondents.

Mail Questionnaires

Mail questionnaires are survey instruments that are mailed to selected respondents for them to complete on their own rather than being directly interviewed by the researcher. These questionnaires are much cheaper and safer to administer. In addition, they enable researchers to easily survey large numbers of people very quickly.

Mail questionnaires may be administered in four different ways. The questionnaire may be mailed with a request for it to be completed and then returned to the researcher by means of a self-addressed, stamped (or metered) envelope. Also, in this age of the computer, the questionnaire may be sent as an e-mail or an attached file, with a request to complete and e-mail back to the researcher.

To provide a more personal touch, the researcher may drop off the questionnaire in a face-to-face contact with the respondent, requesting that the questionnaire be mailed back to the researcher. Or, in a strategy designed to intimidate people into completing the questionnaire (which we do not recommend), the researcher may mail out the questionnaire and advise that he or she will come by at a later time to retrieve it. Either of the latter two strategies will greatly increase the time and costs involved in conducting the survey.

Telephone Surveys

The last form of survey is popular among pollsters. Telephone surveys are quick and easy to do, enabling the researcher to contact large numbers of people in an efficient manner. They are safe in that verbal abuse is about the worst that researchers can incur from their dealings with respondents. Telephone surveys may be more efficient in that they may utilize random-digit dialing to sample the population. They may also have the added advantage of actually inputting data into a computer as the surveyor asks the questions. The biggest disadvantage is that people who are sick of telephone solicitors will often refuse to participate. The various means of administering survey research will be explored in greater depth in Chapter 10.

Pros and Cons of Survey Research

There are numerous reasons why the survey design is popular:

1. It uses a carefully selected probability sample and a standardized questionnaire from which one can make descriptive assertions about any large population.

2. Survey research makes it feasible to use large samples.

3. This design offers more flexibility to the researcher in developing operational definitions based on actual observations.

4. It generally uses standardized questionnaires, which, from a measurement perspective, offer strength to the data because the same question is being asked of all respondents, thus requiring credence to the same response from a large number of respondents.

Yet, despite the positives, the survey design also has its share of negatives:

1. A standardized questionnaire is limited with respect to whether the questions are appropriate since it is designed for all respondents and not for a select group.

2. It can seldom allow for the development of the feel for the context in which respondents are thinking or acting.

METHODOLOGICAL

Standardized Field Sobriety Tests (SFSTs) were developed during the 1980s to enable traffic officers to accurately estimate drug and alcohol impairment. These SFSTs consist of Walk-and-Turn (WAT), One-Leg Stand (OLS), and Horizontal Gaze Nystagmus (HGN). Traffic officers in all 50 states have been trained to administer these tests to individuals suspected of impaired driving, and to numerically score drivers' performance on them. It has been claimed that the SFST test battery is valid for detection of low blood-alcohol concentrations (BACs), and that no other measures of observation offer greater validity for BACs of 0.08% and higher.

To study the legitimacy of these claims, Burns and Dioquino (1997) conducted field research in Pinellas County, Florida. Eight sheriff's deputies with years of experience in traffic control, each having made hundreds of arrests for driving under the influence (DUI) and all having extensive training in DUI enforcement, including certification in SFST, were selected to participate. A rigorous observation procedure was established in which officers, as well as observers assigned to each officer, carefully recorded the SFST scoring and the actual outcome of measured BACs. A total of 379 traffic stops were evaluated. In 313 cases, SFSTs were administered. Drivers refused to take breath tests in 57 of these cases. In 256 cases, a breath test was administered to verify the accuracy of the SFST. Based upon the use of SFSTs, the traffic officers were found to have an accuracy level of 97% in their arrest decisions.

3. Survey research is inflexible in that it typically mandates that no change occur throughout the research, thus often requiring a preliminary study to be conducted.

4. The survey tool is often subject to artificiality.

Even with the negatives, the survey design remains one of the most popular methods for conducting research. Furthermore, it is an extremely popular tool for collecting data. The issues involved in conducting survey research will be discussed in more detail in the following chapters.

Field Research

In Chapter 5, we discussed *ethnography* as a qualitative-research method. In that discussion, it was stated that such research may often be quantitative in nature. When structured interviews are used that permit closed-ended questions to be answered, this would become a personal interview as described above. *If field observations* were made (such as observing how many vehicles ran a certain stop sign in a given time period, or how many times members of the group being observed exhibited specific behaviors), allowing for numerical assignments, then this would be quantified field research. When quantified, field research becomes an even more valuable tool for criminological researchers.

METHODOLOGICAL
LINKS

As noted in Chapter 1, Metraux and Culhane (2004) examined the incidence of and interrelationships between shelter use and reincarceration. To accomplish this task, they used data from two administrative databases maintained by two public entities. Batton (2004) used national-level data to examine the historical trends in the relationship between homicide and suicide rates. Finally, Kingsnorth and Macintosh (2004), in a study of domestic violence, made use of data from more than 5,000 cases processed through a county district attorney's office.

Unobtrusive Research

As was mentioned in Chapter 5, unobtrusive research does not require the researcher to be directly involved with the subjects of his or her study. There is no observation or interaction with the individuals or groups involved because the data have already been gathered by someone else or the data are available in a format that does not require such interaction. Examples of quantitative unobtrusive research include analysis of existing data, historical/archival research, and content analysis.

Analysis of Existing Data

Analysis of existing data is a very efficient way to conduct criminal-justice-related research. The data have already been gathered by a governmental organization, a research foundation, or an independent researcher. Rather than gathering new data, the researcher obtains the existing data and reanalyzes them. This may include taking data from a prior study and reevaluating the data using a new method of analysis. Or it could involve the use of government-generated data such as Uniform Crime Reports or census data in a new research analysis.

Quantified Historical Research

Historical or archival research involves the review of prior research, documents, or social artifacts to gain insights about an event or era in history. The majority of these types of research are qualitative. However, much of this research can be quantified, and empirical assessments are becoming more common on the part of historians and neo-Marxist criminologists.

Quantified Content Analysis

Like historical research, content analysis is the study of social artifacts to gain insights about an event or phenomenon. It differs in that the focus is on the coverage of the event by the particular medium being evaluated (books, magazines, television programs, news coverage, and so on) rather than on the event. Depending on how the research is conducted, this may be either qualitative or

METHODOLOGICAL
LINKS

Recall that Gaarder, Rodrigues, and Zatz (2004) were interested in whether and how gender, race/ethnicity, and class influenced the perception of juvenile-court personnel with respect to girls. For this study, two methods were used. First, an unobtrusive method was used when the researchers examined official case-file narratives from court records. The second method was a semi-structured interview with juvenile-court probation officers.

quantitative in nature. Quantitative content analysis would emphasize statistical rather than verbal analysis of various forms of communication. Instead of reading to understand the general emphasis or nature of the communication, the researcher would either count the number of occurrences in which a topic or issue was presented, or numerically assess the presentations based upon a predetermined scale or ranking.

Evaluation Research

To this point, almost all the research designs discussed are used after an event, situation, or other unexplained phenomenon occurs, in which case we want to understand it better. They are designs that are quite useful to the academic researcher—but what about the practitioner who wants to know how something will work or what might occur when something not previously done is attempted? In particular, what about the manager or administrator who is interested in making a change that could have sweeping policy implications? Oftentimes the best type of research design for this situation is evaluation research.

Evaluation research is a quantified comparative-research design that assists in the development of new skills or approaches. It aids in the solving of problems with direct implications for the "real world." This type of research usually has a quasi-experimental perspective to it. For example:

> A police agency is debating whether to add a nonlethal weapon, a stun gun, to the equipment available to its officers. To see how these guns might work and to examine the outcome of their use, an action design would use a select group of officers who are issued stun guns for a set period of time. Each time a gun is used, a report must be filed, explaining the reasons for that use and the results of the incident. At the end of the experimental period, the reports are analyzed. Depending on the results, stun guns would be issued to all officers, to certain officers, or not at all.

Evaluation research is important for the criminal-justice practitioner-researcher because it assesses the merits of programs or policies being used (or under consideration for use) in the field. Whereas, more-basic research seeks to develop theoretical insights, and much applied research seeks to determine if a theory can actually be applied in the field, evaluation research allows practitioners to determine the costs and effectiveness of the program or project that is being or has been implemented. For this reason, evaluation research that studies existing programs is frequently referred to as program evaluation.

Combination Research

Each of the methods presented above is an excellent means of conducting quantitative research. However, you have even more strategies available to you. Frequently in criminological research, a combination of strategies is utilized. A research design is, in actuality, a combination of qualitative and quantitative research in that a serious review of the prior research is expected to have been conducted (qualitative), which then contributes to the development of the quantitative research. This is demonstrated in scholarly works in the problem statement and the literature review.

Combinations of different quantitative methods are also commonly used. They may include survey research and field observation, survey research and unobtrusive research, unobtrusive research and field observation, or a combination of all three.

■ Summary

This chapter explores quantitative research by noting that it is research based on the assignment and assessment of numbers. Quantitative research is based on empiricism. It uses causality and probability to describe and explain relationships among variables. In order to construct a proper quantitative design, the level of measurement (nominal, ordinal, interval, or ratio) must be considered.

Of the many forms of quantitative research, the more popular include the following:

1. Survey research: personal interviews, mail questionnaires, telephone surveys, and e-mail.
2. Field research (quantified field observation).
3. Quantified unobtrusive research: existing data, historical research, and content analysis.
4. Combination research, which uses a mixture of research methodologies.

Overall, quantitative research offers a perspective that contrasts with, yet can compare to, that discovered through qualitative research.

METHODOLOGICAL QUERIES

1. What level of measurement would you use for the following variables: gender, race, perceptions of stress, convicted felons, courts' sentences, and average prison stay for burglars?

2. For the following research queries, identify what type of research design you would use, and explain why.

   Stress among correctional officers

   Probation-officer caseloads

   Police-involved shootings

3. Why is causality an important issue?

4. What type of research should never or could never be conducted quantitatively?

5. When is necessary or sufficient cause not important in conducting research?

REFERENCES

Babbie, E. (2004). *The practice of social research* (10th ed.). Belmont, CA: Thomson/Wadsworth.

Batton, C. (2004). Gender differences in lethal violence: Historical trends in the relationship between homicide and suicide rates, 1960–2000. *Justice Quarterly, 21*(3), 423–461.

Black, T. R. (1999). *Doing quantitative research in the social sciences: An integrated approach to research design.* Thousand Oaks, CA: Sage.

Burns, M., & Dioquino, T. (1997). *A Florida validation study of the standardized field sobriety test battery.* Tallahassee: Florida Department of Transportation.

Creswell, J. W. (2002). *Research design: Qualitative, quantitative, and mixed methods approaches* (2nd ed.). Thousand Oaks, CA: Sage.

Gaarder, E., Rodrigues, N., & Zatz, M. S. (2004). Criers, liars, and manipulators: Probation officers' views of girls. *Justice Quarterly, 21*(3), 547–578.

Kingsnorth, R. F., & Macintosh, R. C. (2004). Domestic violence: Predictors of victim support for official action. *Justice Quarterly, 21*(2), 301–328.

Metraux, S., & Culhane, D. P. (2004). Homeless shelter use and reincarceration following prison release. *Criminology & Public Policy, 3*(2), 139–160.

Nardi, P. M. (2002). *Doing survey research: A guide to quantitative research methods.* Boston: Allyn and Bacon.

Punch, K. F. (2005). *Intro to social research: Quantitative and qualitative approaches.* Thousand Oaks, CA: Sage.

Procedures

II

Research Designs

Chapter Objectives

After studying this chapter, the student should be able to:

- Discuss the issues to consider in selecting a research design.
- Describe how a historical research design is conducted.
- Explain the merits of a descriptive research design.
- Discuss developmental or time-series research. List the various types of time-series designs.
- Compare and contrast longitudinal and cross-sectional research designs.
- Compare and contrast trend studies, cohort studies, and panel studies.
- Compare and contrast case studies with correlational and causal-comparative studies.
- Discuss the strengths and weaknesses of experimental and quasi-experimental designs.

■ Research Designs

In order to successfully complete any type of research, it is important to establish a feasible plan or blueprint: the research design. This plan responds primarily to the common five W's (who, what, where, when, and why) and the H (how) of investigation. Because the criminal-justice practitioner and the criminologist have a choice of research designs, it is important to be able to properly match the design to the desired outcomes. In selecting a research design, a number of issues should be weighed. It is recommended that an outline be created in order to ensure that all relevant issues have been considered. **Box 7-1** is an example of such an outline. The reader will note that most of these issues were discussed in previous chapters. The remainder will be covered in detail in later chapters.

This chapter discusses the more common forms of research designs applied to criminal justice and criminology. They include historical, descriptive, developmental, case, correlational, and causal-comparative. A brief mention will be made of experimental and quasi-experimental action designs. The main focus will be on what appears to be the most popular research design: survey research.

Historical

Probably one of the most debated topics in criminal justice and criminology is the deterrent effect of capital punishment. A common hypothesis for pro–capital punishment supporters is that the death penalty serves as a better deterrent for homicides than life imprisonment does. To study this hypothesis, a historical research design (sometimes referred to as records research design) would be appropriate.

Box 7-1
Issues to Consider in Selecting a Research Design

Purpose of Research
The purpose of the research project should be clearly indicative of what will be studied.

Prior Research
Review similar or relevant research. This will promote knowledge of the literature.

Theoretical Orientation
Describe the theoretical framework upon which the research is based.

Concept Definition
List the various concepts that have been developed and clarify their meanings.

Research Hypotheses
Develop the various hypotheses that will be evaluated in the research.

Unit of Analysis
Describe the particular objects, individuals, or entities that are being studied as elements of the population.

Data-Collection Techniques
Determine how the data are to be collected. Who will collect the data, who will be studied, and how will the collection be done?

Sampling Procedures
Sample type, sample size, as well as the specific procedures to be utilized

Instrument(s) Used
The nature of the measurement instrument or data-collection device that is used

Analytic Techniques
How the data will be processed and examined. What specific statistical procedures will be used?

Time Frame
The period of time covered by the study. This will include the time period examined by research questions as well as the amount of time spent in preparation, data collection, data analysis, and presentation.

Ethical Issues
Address any concerns as to the potential harm that might occur to participants. Also deal with any potential biases or conflicts of interest that could affect the study.

Historical designs allow the researcher to systematically and objectively reconstruct the past. This is accomplished through the collection, evaluation, verification, and synthesis of information, usually secondary data already existing in previously gathered records, to establish facts. The goal is to reach a defensible conclusion relating to the hypothesis. So, using the above hypothesis about

METHODOLOGICAL LINKS

To examine their hypothesis that "defendants convicted of killing white fe-males are significantly more likely to receive death sentences than killers of victims with other race-gender characteristics," Holcomb, Williams, and Demuth (2004) collected their data from Supplemental Homicide Reports for the years 1981–1997. In a similar design, Alpert, Dunham, and MacDonald (2004), look-ing at interactive police-citizen encounters that resulted in the use of force, took their data from the agency's use-of-force reports for a two-year period. Metraux and Culhane (2004) examined the incidence of and interrelationships between shelter use and reincarceration among a cohort of 48,424 people. Their findings suggested that more use of shelters limited reincarceration rates.

the death penalty, a historical design could include a study of homicide rates in the United States between 1950 and 1997. Although just studying the numbers might provide an interesting conclusion, the true historical study requires in-clusion of possible intervening factors, which in this case could include U.S. Supreme Court decisions, sentencing patterns, social episodes (for example, a war), and population growth. A successful historical study will consider all rel-evant information in order to provide proper conclusions.

The historical design is an economically efficient means for conducting re-search. Considering the vast array of available records related to criminal jus-tice, there is no shortage of possible research topics. A shortcoming of this design is the difficulty of expanding beyond what is documented; therefore, the scope of the research is limited. Researchers are restricted to the information in the files, and seldom have any means of following up or getting clarification of the available data. This shortcoming may render historical design unfit for your purpose. In addition, there is the old computer maxim of "garbage in, garbage out." Your research is only as good as the data that are contained in the records. If there is inaccurate information or missing data in the original, your research will suffer.

Descriptive

Assume that you want to know the composition of a particular jail population. A descriptive research design would be very appropriate because it focuses on the description of facts and characteristics of a given population, issue, policy, or any given area of interest in a systematic and accurate manner. Like the histori-cal design, a descriptive study can also rely on secondary or records data. It is also similar in that much historical research is descriptive in nature.

The information obtained in descriptive studies can provide insights not recognized in previously published research. It can also lead to the study's be-

METHODOLOGICAL
LINKS

As noted in Chapter 1, Vaughn, Del Carmen, Perfecto, and Charand (2004) conducted a purely descriptive study to provide an updated and expanded guide for authors of criminal-justice-related journals. This study offered potential researchers descriptive information about the various journals as a means of helping guide them toward possible publishing outlets.

coming inferential. An inferential study generalizes findings from a sample group and applies them to a larger population. However, descriptive-design findings are not always accurate or reliable because elements that are present in other parts of the population may not be present in the sample. Therefore, if one is going to make inferences from this type of study, they must be sure that the population is well represented within the sample studied. Referring back to the previous Methodological Link, Vaughn, Del Carmen, Perfecto, and Charand, in order to avoid a sampling issue, examined all the top refereed journals associated with criminal justice and criminology.

Both historical and descriptive research can be cost-effective and logistically easier to conduct than other designs. However, they present researchers with limitations as to what variables can be examined and the extent of the information available. They may also be more time-sensitive, which means that data may be available for only a certain time frame, and the information obtained may be limited in its usefulness. Thus, what if a researcher wants to control the information to be studied over a period of time that he or she regulates? The answer is to use a longitudinal design.

Developmental, or Time Series

Perhaps you are interested in following the activities of members from a rookie police class from graduation through its first five years of service. In particular, you are interested in turnover rate, promotions, injuries, accommodations and complaints, and their levels of job satisfaction. The best research design for this type of study is developmental, more commonly referred to as time-series studies. This type of research design allows for the investigation of specifically identified patterns and events, growth, and/or change over a specific amount of time. Unfortunately, this type of research can be very costly and time-consuming, so it is not readily used. There are several time-series designs that are available: cross-sectional studies, longitudinal studies, trend studies, cohort studies, and panel studies.

Cross-sectional Studies

The primary concept of the cross-sectional design is that it allows for a complete description of a single entity during a specific time frame. In this instance, an entity might include an individual, agency, community, or, in the case of the U.S. Census, an entire nation. These studies are best used as exploratory or descriptive research.

Longitudinal Studies

Where cross-sectional studies view events or phenomena at one time, longitudinal studies examine events over an extended period. For this reason, longitudinal studies are useful for explanation as well as for exploration and description. A majority of field-research projects tend to be longitudinal studies (Adler & Clark, 2003; Babbie, 2004; Creswell, 2002).

Trend Studies

Trend studies examine changes in a general population over time. For example, one might compare results from several census studies to determine what demographic changes have occurred in that population. Surveys might indicate that opinions on the death penalty fluctuate over time, depending upon social conditions not related to crime, as well as upon changes in the incidences of murder and the occasional occurrences of sensational murders.

Cohort Studies

Cohort studies are trend studies that focus on the changes that occur in specific subpopulations over time. Usually cohort studies employ age groupings. For example, in a famous criminological study, Wolfgang, Figlio, and Sellin (1972) examined delinquency among a cohort of juveniles. The findings from this study significantly impacted future research and practice in juvenile justice.

Panel Studies

Panel studies are similar to trend and cohort studies, except that they examine the same set of people each time. By utilizing the same individuals, couples, or

METHODOLOGICAL **LINKS**

An innovative differential police-response protocol offering citizens the option of problem solving with an officer over the telephone was developed. To determine citizen satisfaction with this program, a cross-sectional approach was employed. Because an evaluation-research component was built into this program, data collection was much easier. The particular data examined included perceived deputy demeanor, departmental problem-solving skills, and overall citizen satisfaction. The data analyses revealed that "most socio-demographic factors make no significant difference in the degree to which citizens are satisfied with problem-solving services offered by the department. The exception is found in age and education. Age makes a difference in the degree to which citizens are satisfied with the overall service received, and overall satisfaction from beginning to end of the problem-solving process is dependent on education but only for those receiving tele-policing service" (Fitzpatrick, 1999, p. 100).

METHODOLOGICAL

LINKS

Hunter and Wood (1994) were interested in the relationship between severity of sanction and unarmed assaults upon police officers. They obtained assault data on officers from all 50 states. They then compared this data with the sanctions applied for unarmed assaults on police officers within each respective state during 1991. Taking the assault rates in states that had felony sanctions for weaponless assault upon police officers, the researchers compared these rates with those in neighboring states during the years 1977 through 1991. This resulted in the longitudinal analysis of four groups of states. Analysis of results in these groupings did not reveal support for the hypothesis that more sanctions would decrease the incidence of weaponless assaults upon police officers.

groups, researchers are able to more precisely investigate the extent of changes and the events that influenced them. However, due to the effects of deaths, movements from the area, refusal to continue as subjects, and other factors that cause the sample to lose members, these studies are logistically difficult to continue over an extended period of time.

Case Studies

The case (sometimes referred to as case and field) research design allows for the intensive study of a given issue, policy, or group in its social context at one point in time, even though that period may span months or years (Adler & Clark, 2003; Babbie, 2004; Creswell, 2002). It includes close scrutiny of the background, current status, and relationships or interactions of the topic under study. Case studies often focus on a specific phenomenon, such as Willis, Mastrofski, and Weisburd's (2004) study of one police department's experiences with the use of COMPSTAT.

Case studies may also be longitudinal in that they sometimes observe repeated cases over a certain length of time. These observations are closely linked with the observing of potential independent variables that may be associated with changes in the dependent variables. There are three basic features to this design:

1. *Qualitative and/or quantitative descriptions of a variable over the extended period of time*

2. *Provides a context wherein the researcher can observe the changes in the variables*

3. *Can be used for developing measurement instruments and the testing of their reliability over time (Berg, 2004; Black, 1999; Creswell, 2002)*

Case research designs are not limited as to what can be studied. However, they can be costly and time-prohibitive, and may not provide an explanation for why the results turned out as they did. If one wants to know why something is occurring or has occurred, along with possible correlating factors, then a correlational design may be more appropriate.

Correlational

A popular research design is one that allows researchers to investigate how one factor may affect or influence another factor, or how the one factor correlates with another—the correlational design. In particular, this type of design focuses on how variations of one variable correspond with variations of other variables. An example might be a study of the level of education of police officers and promotion rates, arrest rates, or job satisfaction. The goal of this research design is to obtain correlational coefficients at a statistically significant difference.

Causal-Comparative

Why do men rape? Why do teens turn to gangs? Why do individuals become serial killers? To answer these types of questions, a causal-comparative (or ex post facto) design is useful. This design allows the researcher to examine relationships from a cause-and-effect perspective. This is done through the observation of an existing outcome or consequence and searching back through the data for plausible causal factors.

Each of the previously discussed designs can be found relatively frequently in the criminal-justice and criminological research. There are three other designs that could be used, but they are much more difficult to employ because of costs, logistics, and the fact that they cannot be easily applied to topics in criminal justice and criminology. They are the true experimental, quasi-experimental, and action designs.

True or Classic Experimental

Although it is most often used in the natural sciences, occasionally social scientists may attempt research requiring a true experimental design. This type of design allows for the investigation of possible cause-and-effect relationships where one or more experimental units will be exposed to one or more treatment conditions. The outcomes are then compared to the outcomes of one or more control groups that did not receive the treatment. This design includes three major components: (1) independent and dependent variables, (2) experimental and control groups, and (3) pre- and posttesting.

The primary advantages of the experimental design are the isolation of the experimental variation and its impact over time; individual experiments can be limited in scope and require little time, money, and number of subjects; and it is often possible to replicate the results. The major disadvantage is artificiality. Processes that occur in a controlled setting may not actually occur in the natural setting.

With respect to criminal justice and criminology, this type of research is often expensive and logistically difficult to perform. Probably one of the most difficult issues is obtaining consent when the research involves human test subjects. However, sometimes consent is easier to obtain if the experiment could prove useful to the subjects. For example, a new drug has been created that could suppress sexual desires. A group of convicted pedophiles are asked if they will participate in a study in which part of the group will receive the new drug while the other half are given a placebo. After a certain number of weeks, both groups are tested for sexual response to certain stimuli. The results are compared.

Another major problem in conducting true experimental research is the difficulty in being able to maintain and control the environment where the experiment is conducted. The environment in which criminal-justice and criminology research is conducted is often far from stable, and filled with possible interfering or intervening variables. As a result of the control and consent issues, along with costs and other logistical problems, it is rare to see a criminal-justice practitioner or criminologist conduct true experimental research. This has not stopped some efforts to conduct this form of research. Some examples found in criminal justice include the Kansas City Preventive Patrol Experiment, the Minneapolis Domestic Violence Study, and San Diego's one- versus two-person patrol units.

Reality dictates that few experimental research projects are possible in criminal justice and criminology. The limitations, however, can be addressed to some degree with a quasi-experimental design.

Quasi-Experimental

Unlike the true experimental design, where the researcher has almost complete control over relevant variables, the quasi-experimental design allows for the approximation of conditions similar to those of the true experiment. However, the quasi-experimental setting does not allow for control and/or manipulation of the relevant variables.

Although easier to implement than the true experimental design, the quasi-experimental design has its difficulties, too, which make it less appealing to most social scientists. The main problem lies in the interpretation of the results that is, being able to separate the effects of a treatment from the effects due to the initial inability to make comparisons between the average units in each treatment group. As with experimental designs, the quasi-experimental design is rare in theoretical criminological research. It is more commonly utilized in evaluation research (previously discussed in Chapter 6), to evaluate new approaches

METHODOLOGICAL

LINKS

To examine the level of citizen satisfaction with a telepolicing response, Fitzpatrick (1999) conducted research that combined case study (cross-sectional) with a quasi-experimental design. The research design used provided randomly selected citizens who had phoned the department for assistance, which provided the citizens with an opportunity to express feedback on their experiences with the department. The results from this group were then compared to a group of citizens who had received an in-person response.

in the criminal-justice system and to solve problems with direct application to justice-system operations.

Overall, there are a number of research designs to choose from. The design chosen will depend largely on what the researcher is seeking to discover, explain, or describe. Other considerations include economics, logistics, and time. Ultimately, the researcher must decide which design will allow for the best results.

■ Summary

Selecting a topic and creating the research question are just the beginning of conducting research. One of the most important steps becomes the choosing of an appropriate research design. While one of the most popular designs is survey research, which is also a means of collecting data in the other designs, there are a variety of other possible methods. These include the following:

1. Historical—reconstructing the past objectively and accurately, often in relation to the tenability of a hypothesis

2. Descriptive—systematically describing a situation or area of interest factually and accurately

3. Developmental—investigating patterns and sequences of growth and/or change as a function of time

4. Case—intensively studying the background, current status, and environmental interactions of a given social unit, such as individual, group, institution, or community

5. Correlational—investigating the extent to which variations in one factor correspond with variations in one or more other factors, based on correlation coefficients

6. Causal-comparative, or ex post facto—investigating possible cause-and-effect relationships by observing some existing consequence and searching back through the data for plausible causal factors

7. True experimental—investigating possible cause-and-effect relationships by exposing one or more experimental groups to one or more treatment conditions, and then comparing the results to one or more control groups not receiving the treatment (random assignment being essential)

8. Quasi-experimental—approximating the conditions of the true experiment in a setting that does not allow the control and/or manipulation of all relevant variables. The researcher must clearly understand what compromises exist in the internal and external validity of his design, and proceed within these limitations

The chosen design should best meet the needs of the research goals.

METHODOLOGICAL QUERIES

What type of research design would you use to study the following topics? Why?

1. Gang activity in prisons
2. Sentencing patterns of a particular court
3. The effect of a treatment program for drug users
4. Perceived job stress of police officers
5. Caseload of parole officers
6. The effect of a community-policing program on crime
7. Recidivism and first-time DUI/DWI offenders
8. Race and sentencing for drug offenses

REFERENCES

Adler, E. S., & Clark, R. (2003). *How it's done: An invitation to social research* (2nd ed.). Belmont, CA: Thomson/Wadsworth.

Alpert, G. P., Dunham, R. G., & MacDonald, J. M. (2004). Interactive police-citizen encounters that result in force. *Police Quarterly, 7*(4), 475–488.

Babbie, E. (2004). *The practice of social research* (10th ed.). Belmont, CA: Thomson/Wadsworth.

Berg, B. L. (2004). *Qualitative research methods for the social sciences* (5th ed.). Boston: Allyn and Bacon.

Black, T. R. (1999). *Doing quantitative research in the social sciences: An integrated approach to research design*. Thousand Oaks, CA: Sage.

Creswell, J. W. (2002). *Research design: Qualitative, quantitative, and mixed methods approaches* (2nd ed.). Thousand Oaks, CA: Sage.

Fitzpatrick, C. (1999). A survey of citizen perceptions of treatment and satisfaction with a telephone service option in a rural sheriff's department. In M. L. Dantzker (Ed.), *Readings for research methods in criminology and criminal justice* (pp. 99–122). Woburn, MA: Butterworth-Heinemann.

Holcomb, J. E., Williams, M. R., & Demuth, S. (2004). White female victims and death penalty disparity research. *Justice Quarterly, 21*(4), 877–902.

Hunter, R. D., & Wood, R. L. (1994). Impact of felony sanctions: An analysis of weaponless assaults upon American police. *American Journal of Police, XII*(1), 65–89.

Metraux, S. & Culhane, D. P. (2004). Homeless shelter use and reincarceration following prison release. *Criminology & Public Policy, 3*(2), 139–160.

Vaughn, M. S., Del Carmen, R. V., Perfecto, M., & Charand, K. X. (2004). Journals in criminal justice and criminology: An updated and expanded guide for authors. *Journal of Criminal Justice Education, 15*(1), 61–192.

Willis, J. J., Mastrofski, S. D., & Weisburd, D. (2004). COMPSTAT and bureaucracy: A case study of challenges and opportunities for change. *Justice Quarterly, 21*(3), 463–496.

Wolfgang, M. E., Figlio, R. M., & Sellin, T. (1972). *Delinquency in a birth cohort*. Chicago: University of Chicago Press.

8 Questionnaire Construction

Vignette 8-1   A Matter of the Right Questions

You are beginning to see some light at the end of the tunnel. The concept of conducting research is making sense. Maybe the senior project is not going to be so bad after all. Then you meet with your supervising professor. You were originally planning on using archival data to examine the type of crimes for which students at your university are most frequently arrested. You were planning to look at arrest records for the past five years. Your supervising professor approves of the topic, but not the approach. She seems to think it would be more interesting if you did a survey of self-reported criminal behavior. She believes there is probably more criminal activity among the students than what appears in arrest records, and it would be interesting to see what might be going undetected or unpunished. Furthermore, her position is that this type of research project will be helpful to you when you have to write a master's thesis and, should you pursue a Ph.D., a dissertation (both of which you have acknowledged as a possibility).

After some discussion, you reluctantly agree to pursue your research using a survey, which you decide to call "The College Students' Criminality Survey." Now the problem is, what questionnaire will you use? Your professor is encouraging you to design your own. It does not have to be fancy or something everyone will want to use, but it will still need to meet specific research criteria. So, once again you look toward your research-methods class for guidance.

Chapter Objectives

After studying this chapter, the student should be able to:

- Describe what is involved in listing the items you are interested in knowing about the group, concept, or phenomenon.
- Explain how to establish validity and reliability.
- Discuss why the wording in the questionnaire must be appropriate for the target audience.
- Explain why who should answer the questions should be clearly identifiable.
- Discuss why it is important to avoid asking any questions that are biased, leading, threatening, or double-barreled in nature.
- Explain why prior to construction, a decision must be made whether to use open-ended questions or closed-ended questions or a combination of the two.
- Discuss how the respondents may not have all the general information needed to complete the questionnaire.
- Explain why a questionnaire should be pretested whenever possible before it is officially used.
- Discuss why it is important to set up questions so that the responses are easily recognizable, whether the format is self-administered or interview.
- Explain why the questionnaire should be organized in a concise manner that will keep the interest of the respondent, encouraging him or her to complete the entire questionnaire.
- Define scales and explain their purpose. Identify the different types of scales available for use.
- Compare and contrast Thurstone Scales, Likert Scales, and Guttman Scales.

■ Questionnaire Development

When conducting survey research, a well-recognized research rule of thumb, or perhaps golden rule, is to use a questionnaire that has previously been developed and tested. The primary reason for this is that it eliminates the worries of validity and reliability, two major concerns of questionnaire development. However, an instrument may not exist for a particular research question—or, if it does exist, it may not meet the researcher's specific needs. Therefore, the researcher must resort to creating a research-specific questionnaire. For example, one of the author's research interests is job satisfaction among police officers. Several years ago, he decided to study this concept and its relationship to education. Although there were several job satisfaction-related questionnaires available, none of them appeared to be able to accomplish his research goals. Therefore, he created his own Police Job Satisfaction Survey (see Dantzker, 1993).

In creating a new survey instrument, there are several things to consider, including reliability and validity, and the level of measurement to use. Every textbook offers a different way to approach this task, but in the end, the basic elements are similar. To make understanding this task as easy as possible, a set of guidelines, offered in the manner of rules, is provided that can make questionnaire construction easier.

■ Rules for Questionnaire Construction

When possible, many of us would prefer not to follow rules, or at least would like to bend them to our satisfaction. The rules with which you are about to be presented do not have to be followed in a strict manner, but complete failure to follow them will lead to a failed questionnaire.

Rule One

Start with a list of all the items you are interested in knowing about the group, concept, or phenomenon.

How many times have you gone grocery shopping without a list? When that happens, it is common to end up with many things you did not want, and without things you really need. Questionnaire development should be approached with a "grocery list" mentality. List all the things you want to know, things you would like to know, and things that would be interesting to know about each item for which you are seeking information.

Consider the situation in the opening vignette. The student is interested in unreported criminal activity among college students. To collect this information, a questionnaire should be developed that will ask the respondents to provide certain identifying characteristics (the independent variables) along with their responses to questions about criminality (dependent variables). What is asked about the students will depend on what type of comparisons or analysis will be conducted. Assume that the researcher is interested in reported behavior by age, year in college, ethnicity/race, gender, and major. Therefore, questions pertaining to this information will be necessary. This information will also aid in describing the sample. Regardless of the nature of the sample, there are various formats of soliciting the desired information.

Listing the characteristics for the sample is the easier phase. Often researchers get into trouble because they fail to list everything they know or want to know about the subject. This failure could cause a shortage of very important data. The key is to decide what is of interest and what is needed. The questions will then take care of the rest, regardless of how they are asked, in statement form or as a question.

Regardless of which approach is used, the key is to ask all the questions or create all the statements believed necessary to obtain the information desired. You can always edit out data, but it is difficult to go back and get what was missed.

METHODOLOGICAL

LINKS

In Dantzker and Waters' (1999) study of students' perceptions of policing, the data for their sample were gathered in the following manner:

Gender: Male_____ Female_____

Race/Ethnicity: White_____ African-American_____ Hispanic_____
Other_____

Age: _____

Year in College: Freshman_____ Sophomore_____ Junior_____ Senior_____
Other_____

Major: _____ **Minor:** _____

Last four digits of Social Security number (for analysis purposes only)

FOR CRIMINAL-JUSTICE STUDENTS ONLY

Other than Intro to Criminal Justice, have you taken any other courses with a police component? Yes_____ No_____ If Yes, how many?_____

Employment Goal: Law Enforcement__ Probation__ Courts__
Corrections__ Law__ Other__

Are you related to a police officer? Yes___ No___ If Yes, what is the relationship?_____

Note the similarity in information, yet the differing format used in Ford and Williams' (1999) study of police and correctional officers' perception of a cultural-diversity course.

Personal Information

Sex: ( ) M   ( ) F   **Race:** ( ) American Indian   ( ) Hispanic   ( ) Asian
( ) White   ( ) Black   ( ) Other_____

Age: ( ) 18–21   ( ) 22–24   ( ) 25–29   ( ) 30–34   ( ) 35–39   ( ) 40–44
( ) 45–49   ( ) 50+

Number of Years in Policing/Corrections: _____   **Rank:** Patrol _____

Supervisor **Ed:** ( ) High School/GED   OR   ( ) 2-yr. A.A. degree
( ) 4-yr. B.S./B.A. degree   ( ) Grad school or Degree

In sum, Rule One suggests that prior to creating any questions or statements you make a list of desired information.

Rule Two

Be prepared to establish validity and reliability.

After the golden rule, using a questionnaire that has previously been developed and tested may actually be the next most critical rule for questionnaire construction. These two concepts will establish whether the data collected will be acceptable to others who may be interested in using your findings, or perhaps even in trying to replicate them.

METHODOLOGICAL LINKS

Dantzker (2003) used a variety of formats to obtain information from students regarding their perceptions of specific criminal-justice activities and their employment goals.

The following are potential situations you may have already experienced or may someday experience. Rank these situations, from 1 to 5, in terms of your level of fear of them (1 = most fearful of; 5 = least fearful of). No two items should be ranked the same.

_____ Stopped by a police officer for a traffic violation
_____ Being a victim of a violent crime
_____ Arrested for a crime you didn't commit
_____ Convicted of a crime you didn't commit
_____ Having an incompetent lawyer

(2) The reason I am majoring in Criminal Justice is because I want to work somewhere in the criminal-justice system. (Please circle your response.)

Strongly Agree	Agree	Not Sure	Disagree	Strongly Disagree
5	4	3	2	1

(3) With a degree in Criminal Justice, what type of starting salary do you expect to earn?

_____ (per year)

(4) In which area of Criminal Justice do you plan to seek long-term employment? (Choose only one area.)

_____Federal Law Enforcement*	_____Fed. Correctional Officer
_____State Police	_____State Correctional Officer
_____County Sheriff	_____Local Correctional Officer
_____Municipal Police	_____Fed. Probation/Parole
_____Private Police	_____State Probation/Parole
_____Other Police/Law Enforcement	_____Local Probation/Parole
_____Court Officer	_____Lawyer (Pros. or Def.)

_____I do not plan on employment in Criminal Justice

*If you selected federal law enforcement, what is the primary position you hope to attain: (Choose only one.)

_____Border Patrol	_____ Customs Agent	_____ INS Agent
_____DEA agent	_____ Treasury Agent	_____ U.S. Marshal
_____FBI Agent	_____ Secret Service	_____ IRS Agent
_____U.S. Postal Inspector	_____ Federal Police Officer	_____ Other

Validity refers to whether the questionnaire is in fact measuring what it claims to measure. That is, it is imperative that the questions or statements are a true measure of the topic under study. This requires that the researcher be able to determine and establish the questionnaire's validity, which can be accomplished through one or more of the following ways: face, content, construct, and criterion validity.

Face Validity

The simplest means of establishing validity is *face* validity. This requires the researcher to accept that the questionnaire is in fact measuring what he or she is attempting to measure—simply because the researcher believes this to be true. This is a very judgmental process, lacking empirical support and requiring the researcher to demonstrate why he or she believes that the questionnaire measures what is expected. For example, in creating the questionnaire to measure perceptions of policing by students, Dantzker and Waters (1999) offered face validity as the means of supporting the questionnaire's validity because the questionnaire yielded expected responses. The statements were developed based on one researcher's anecdotal and observational experiences. Although this is an acceptable means of validation, it is the least acceptable method because it is empirically weak.

Content Validity

The second form of validation, *content* validity, also suffers from being judgmental and usually nonempirical. Unlike face validity, where the belief in validity focuses on the questionnaire as a whole, content validity emphasizes each individual item's ability to measure the concept in question. Now, instead of simply supporting the complete questionnaire's ability to measure what is expected, the researcher must be able to explain why each item measures what is expected. Again, the responsibility falls to the researcher to support why it is believed that each item measures what is expected. For example, in a study of the perception of job satisfaction among police officers, one question may simply ask the respondent to indicate how satisfied he or she is with being a police officer. Although there is no empirical evidence to support this question, it can be argued that, because the goal is to measure perceived job satisfaction, directly asking someone how satisfied he or she is would be indicative of how he or she perceives his or her job-satisfaction level. Although this is an acceptable means of validation, relying solely on this method is not recommended.

Construct Validity

Although you are seeking to measure a particular phenomenon, there may be related concepts that are equally important to understanding the phenomenon in question. *Construct* validity (sometimes referred to as *concept* validity) seeks to demonstrate that the questions do actually measure what they have been designated to measure in relation to other variables. This method is interested in establishing the fit between the theoretical and operational aspects of the item. With respect to the job-satisfaction study, it was expected that individuals with a college degree would indicate a higher level of satisfaction with some items than would individuals without a college degree. If the responses to those particular questions support this, than you have established construct validity. However, if the responses from both groups indicate equal satisfaction, then the validity may be challenged. Construct validity can be reinforced through empirical measures.

Criterion Validity

Criterion, also called *pragmatic* or *empirical*, validation is concerned with the relationship between the questionnaire and its results. The assumption is that if the questionnaire is valid, a certain empirical relationship should exist between the data collected and other recognizable properties of the phenomenon. Most often, the evidence to support this is garnered from correlational measures consistent with the level of measure. The key requirement, however, is that a reliable and valid measure must already exist to make the comparison. To apply criterion validity to the previously mentioned job-satisfaction measure, one group of officers is given the job-satisfaction measure, which is then compared to the results of a reliable and validated job-stress measure (because it has been established that job stress is linked to job satisfaction). With the two sets of scores, a correlation coefficient can be computed, providing what is called the *validity coefficient*. The more common form of criterion validity is predictive validity, which rests upon the questionnaire's ability to accurately predict future conditions or responses.

There may be debates over the best type of validity. Failing to establish any type of validity will devalue your data. Obviously, the more ways you can establish validity, the better. Still, validity alone is not enough. It must be accompanied by reliability.

Everyone who lives in a climate that experiences extremely cold weather wants a car battery that will start the vehicle day in and day out. Perhaps the battery was purchased because of its reliability to do just that. When the vehicle does not start as expected, the battery is no longer considered reliable. A questionnaire has the same expectation: that it is reliable each time it is used. If the questionnaire is consistent over time and yields similar results each time it is employed, it is reliable. To further establish reliability, one must demonstrate stability and consistency.

Stability occurs when, under similar conditions, a respondent will provide the same answers to the same questions on a second testing. Consistency is determined when the set of questions is strongly related and is measuring the same concept. There are three standard ways to test reliability: test-and-retest (pretesting), split-half technique, and using multiple forms.

Pretesting is the most fundamental method, yet perhaps the most inconvenient in terms of time and money. The test-and-retest method requires distributing the questionnaire to the same population twice. If the results are the same, then reliability is accepted. Another method is to distribute the questionnaire to similar samples and look for consistent results between the samples.

A popular and widely used method is the split-half technique. Here, the questionnaire is divided into sections or halves. Both sections are given to the same group or among similar groups. A similarity of scores between both halves supports stability.

Using several variations or formats of the same questionnaire, the multiple-forms method can support stability. As with the previous methods, if scores on each format are similar, one can assume stability.

All these methods are acceptable; however, it is preferable to employ the test-and-retest method when possible. In addition, many statistical packages offer methods for statistical comparison by item-to-item and item-to-scale analyses, and the use of Cronbach's alpha, a commonly used reliability coefficient.

Overall, there are a number of ways to establish validity and reliability. Therefore, there is no reason to fail to meet Rule Two: being able to establish both validity and reliability.

Rule Three

The wording in the questionnaire must be appropriate for the target audience.

Everyone is required to complete questionnaires of one type or another at some point in their lives. Sometimes the questions are quite clear, and other times they may befuddle the respondent. When developing a questionnaire, the first guideline is to be sure to use language geared toward the target population. Obviously, you do not want to use words or phrases with which the respondent is not familiar. Otherwise, it can cause confusion and misunderstanding and probably lead to tainted data. For example, on the questionnaire for college students and criminal behavior, in a question about drug use, you would want to use the slang or more common usage rather than the scientific one.

Have you ever smoked cannabis? (Wrong)

Have you ever smoked marijuana? (Right)

Therefore, Rule Three suggests that the questions or statements be written in a manner that the target audience can understand.

Rule Four

Be sure that it is clearly identifiable who should answer the questions.

How many times have you received a questionnaire in the mail addressed to "Dear Occupant"—and upon opening the envelope, discovered that it was not clear who should be completing this questionnaire. At least it was not clear who should fill out which parts. Referring back to the Methodological Link demonstrating the identifying questions posed by Dantzker and Waters (1999), did you note that there was a section specifically for criminal-justice students? Anyone not majoring in criminal justice was to avoid answering those questions. All it takes is a simple statement advising who should complete which questions. Thus, for Rule Four, the idea is to be sure to clarify who fills out or responds to which questions.

Rule Five

Avoid asking any questions that are biased, leading, threatening, or double-barreled in nature.

"Does it not feel great to get high?" "How often do you get high, and do you enjoy it?" "Do you cheat on exams, and if you do, do you know you are only cheating yourself?" These kinds of questions are considered biased, double-barreled, or leading. The basic premise is this: do not create questions that cause confusion for the respondent as to how he or she should answer, and do not create questions that push toward a particular answer.

Questions or statements that confuse respondents can cause ambiguous responses. Questions that seek to "guide" the respondent can create blatantly false responses. In addition, the structure of the questionnaire may be such that preceding questions will influence the responses to later questions. If any of the above occurs, the findings will not be valid.

Ultimately, the questionnaire format and the wording of questions can influence responses. Be aware of that when responding to surveys conducted by ideological groups or organizations that hold particular positions on controversial issues (such as the opposing views of the Brady Campaign to Prevent Gun Violence and the National Rifle Association). Potential biases may also be observed among the questionnaires of scholars and students who are trying to support a favored hypothesis. If those administering a survey have an interest in or might benefit from the outcome of the survey, they may word the questions or structure the format so as to enhance the likelihood of desired responses. Be skeptical of survey findings by such individuals or groups.

Rule Six

Prior to construction, a decision must be made whether to use open-ended questions, closed-ended questions, or a combination of the two.

Because the goal of the questionnaire is to ascertain specific information related to the topic and to readily analyze this information, deciding on what type of questions should be asked is important. Open-ended questions can make data analyses somewhat more difficult, but can provide more-in-depth responses. On the other hand, well-constructed closed-ended questions can provide sufficient data that are more readily analyzable. The more popular method is to combine the types of questions in an effort to collect the most-pertinent information about the topic.

Examine **Box 8-1**. This questionnaire was created as a telephone survey to investigate a community's satisfaction with its police department. Observe how the questionnaire is composed of both closed- and open-ended questions. Notice how the open-ended questions are worded so that responses could be more readily coded for statistical analysis.

Rule Seven

Consider that the respondents may not have all the general information needed to complete the questionnaire.

Under any circumstances, making assumptions could be problematic. This is especially true in questionnaire development. It is a common error to believe that would-be respondents have all the information needed to answer the questionnaire. For example, several questions about drug and alcohol programs on campus might be asked in your College Students' Criminality Survey simply because it is assumed that all students are familiar with these programs. This assumption might result in few responses, causing another incorrect assumption about the results. To avoid this dilemma, always provide an "escape" response such as "Unknown" or "No Prior Knowledge." Refer back to **Box 8-1** and the use of the "Unable to Respond" choice.

Rule Eight

Whenever possible, pretest the questionnaire before it is officially used.

A reinforcement to Rule Two (stability), and one of the most difficult of the rules to follow, this rule is undoubtedly very legitimate and should be employed whenever possible. With the College Students' Criminality Survey example, after you have completed the first draft of the questionnaire, you might have members in one of your classes answer the questionnaire. By pretesting it, you can find errors in construction, language, or other flaws that may cause the data

Box 8-1

Questionnaire: Open- and Closed-ended Questions

This questionnaire was created as part of a proposal to evaluate a police agency. To date, it has neither been tested nor published elsewhere.

POLICE COMMUNITY TELEPHONE SURVEY

(1) Have you had any official contact (by telephone or in person) with any member of the XXXXX Police Department during the past 18 months?
_____Yes_____No

IF YES, what was the reason/circumstance?

_____ Traffic stop	_____ Traffic accident	_____ Victim of a crime
_____ Arrested	_____ Witness to accident	_____ Witness to a crime
_____ Informational	_____ Telephone contact	_____ Other

How would you rate the performance of the person you had contact with?

Unsatisfactory	Wholly Satisfactory	Less than Adequate	Completely Satisfactory	Unable to Respond
1	2	3	4	0
Providing Assistance		1 2 3 4 0		
Knowledge		1 2 3 4 0		
Courtesy		1 2 3 4 0		
Sensitivity		1 2 3 4 0		
Friendliness		1 2 3 4 0		
Handling of Situation		1 2 3 4 0		
Overall Conduct		1 2 3 4 0		

IF NO, what is your opinion, perception, or attitude of the XXXXX Police:

Unsatisfactory	Wholly Satisfactory	Less than Adequate	Completely Satisfactory	Unable to Respond
1	2	3	4	0
Providing Assistance		1 2 3 4 0		
Courtesy		1 2 3 4 0		
Sensitivity		1 2 3 4 0		
Friendliness		1 2 3 4 0		
Handling of Situation(s)		1 2 3 4 0		
Competence		1 2 3 4 0		
Attitude		1 2 3 4 0		
Behavior		1 2 3 4 0		
Traffic Enforcement		1 2 3 4 0		
Crime Prevention		1 2 3 4 0		
Enforcing Laws		1 2 3 4 0		
Solving Crimes		1 2 3 4 0		
Dealing with Citizens		1 2 3 4 0		
Dealing w/Arrested Persons		1 2 3 4 0		
Overall Performance		1 2 3 4 0		

(2) In your opinion, what is the main problem needing police attention in your neighborhood?

(continued)

Box 8-1
Questionnaire: Open- and Closed-ended Questions (cont.)

(3) In your opinion, what is the main problem needing police attention in the city of XXXXX?

(4) In your opinion, what is the BEST thing about the XXXXX Police?

(5) In your opinion, what is the WORST thing about the XXXXX Police?

(6) In your opinion, what is one change you would make that could improve the XXXXX Police?

For Analysis Purposes Only:

Gender _____Male _____Female

Race/Ethnicity _____Caucasian _____African-American _____Hispanic _____Asian _____Native American _____Other

Age _____18–29 _____30–49 _____50–65 _____Over 65

Employment _____Professional (i.e., doctor, lawyer, etc.) _____Education _____Retail Business _____Food Service _____Clerical _____Laborer _____Other

Education _____High School _____Some College _____Two-yr. Degree _____Four-yr. Degree _____Graduate Degree

In what area of the city do you live?
_____North _____South _____East _____West _____Central

THANK YOU FOR YOUR ASSISTANCE.

to be useless if not corrected. Keep in mind that this does not necessarily require anything more than a few individuals from the target population being willing to complete the questionnaire and provide you with feedback. While this process might take a little more time and effort, it is well worth it in the long term.

Rule Nine

Set up questions so that the responses are easily recognizable whether the format is self-administered or interview.

The fastest way to jeopardize research is through a questionnaire in which the respondents are not clear on how to respond. Be sure to provide adequate, clear instructions and establish recognizable means for responding. Also, try not to make the format too busy (hard to read due to squeezing too many questions onto a page). If at all possible, avoid using small print. Regardless of the format, it should be clear to respondents what you want them to do and how to accomplish it. Returning to both the Dantzker and Waters (1999) and the Ford and Williams (1999) questionnaires, specific instructions were provided, and the ways and means for answering are quite clear.

Rule Ten

The questionnaire should be organized in a concise manner that will keep the interest of the respondent, encouraging him or her to complete the entire questionnaire.

METHODOLOGICAL

LINKS

Dantzker and Waters
This survey was designed to examine students' perceptions of policing prior to taking, and then after completing, an introductory-level police course. Please read each statement and, without spending too much time "analyzing" the statement, indicate your level of agreement/disagreement using the scale provided. Thank you for your cooperation.

Strongly Disagree	Not Strongly	Not Sure	Agree	Strongly Agree
-2	-1	0	1	2

Question & Response Example:
Many individuals who become police officers want to help society.

-2	-1	0	1	2

Ford and Williams
Introduction: This study is being conducted by two professionals who work in the law-enforcement and correctional fields. We are conducting the survey to understand your reactions to the Human Diversity Training course that was required in the Academy for initial certification or in later retraining. While this survey is being distributed at your work site through the courtesy of your Chief/Director, it is not intended to be shown/used there. We would appreciate your help—and your honesty—about this course. You do not have to put your name on the survey; it is anonymous. The personal questions at the end of the survey may help us interpret differences in survey responses. Thank you for your time!

Question & Response Example:
How would you rate your understanding of other cultures prior to taking the course?
( ) Good   ( ) Fair   ( ) Poor

How often have you started a novel only to quit reading it after the first few chapters because it was boring? If you had continued to read, it might have become more pleasurable, but you had lost interest. This same concept is applicable to questionnaire development. If the beginning questions are not interesting and do not hold the respondents' attention, chances are that they may not complete the rest of the questions, which leaves you with missing data. Therefore, it is beneficial to have questions that may pique the respondents' interest both at the beginning and at the end.

In addition to asking interesting questions, brevity in the number of questions is important. If respondents see several pages of questions, they are less likely to begin the survey. While it is tempting to try to "cover everything," a clear and concise survey that consists of a few easy-to-read questions will receive more responses. While specialized questionnaires that target a specific population (one that has a vested interest in the subject matter) may be longer, we recommend that most surveys be kept to two pages of questions using normal-size type.

Rules and guidelines are fallible, but the ten rules offered for questionnaire construction, if followed, will certainly improve the chances of obtaining good, analyzable data. Still, keeping all the rules in mind might not be enough to prevent us from creating a poor questionnaire. Consequently, these rules are not the only thing that must be known to create a usable questionnaire. A key aspect in questionnaire construction is measurement.

■ Scales

A common element of survey research is the construction of scales. A scale can either be (1) a measurement device for responding to a question or statement, or (2) a compilation of statements or questions used to represent the concept studied. For example, in the previous Methodological Link, the responses to Dantzker and Waters' (1999) statement is a scale that ranges from −2 to +2. Each statement is a separate variable of perception. Putting all the statements from their questionnaire together (attaining a numerical result for responses to all statements) gave them what they refer to as the Student's Perceptions of Policing scale. Scales, as compilations, are particularly important and a relevant part of research for three primary reasons:

1. *They allow the collapsing of several variables into a single variable that produces a representative value, thus reducing the complexity of the data*

2. *They offer measures that are quantifiable and more open to precision and statistical manipulation*

3. *They can increase the measurement's reliability (Nachmias & Nachmias 2000; Nardi 2002; Punch 2005)*

To accomplish these things, a scale must fit the "Principle of Unidimensionality" (Nachmias & Nachmias, 2000). This principle suggests that the items making up the scale need to represent one dimension, befitting a continuum that is supposed to be reflective of only one concept. For example, if you are measuring job satisfaction, the scale should not be capable of measuring job stress, too. The representativeness of any scale will rely greatly on the level of measurement used.

Scaling Procedures

Ultimately, to conduct research, we are looking to complete a measurement. Yet what is the actual purpose of this measurement? We use measurement in research as a means of connecting phenomena with numbers for analytic purposes. Scaling is identified as a means of assisting in making the necessary and proper connections. Despite the existence of numerous scales, there will be times when the researcher must create his or her own. The key is to understand that you are trying to explain a phenomenon and that the scale must meet this criterion. There are two primary types of scaling procedures to choose from.

Arbitrary Scales

An arbitrary scale is designed to measure what the researcher believes it is measuring, and is based on face validity (discussed earlier) and professional judgment. Although this allows for the creation of many different scales, this mode is easily criticized for its lack of substantive support. Still, this type of scale does provide a viable starting point for exploratory research, even though it is the less recommended method of scaling.

Attitudinal Scales

More commonly found in criminal-justice and criminological research are the attitudinal scales. There are three primary types available: Thurstone, Likert, and Guttman (Nachmias & Nachmias, 2000; Nardi, 2002; Punch, 2005).

Thurstone Scales

The construction of a Thurstone scale relies on the use of others (sometimes referred to as "judges") to indicate what items they think best fit the concept. There are two methods for completing this task. The first method is paired comparisons. Here, the judges are provided several pairs of questions or statements and are asked to choose which most favorably fit the concept under study. The questions or statements picked most often by the judges become part of the questionnaire or compose the complete questionnaire. For example, which question would better fit the concept of job satisfaction:

1. I enjoy going to work every day.
2. Sometimes I am very tired when I get home from work.

The second method, and one more often used, is equal appearing intervals. For this method, the researcher will submit a list of questions or statements to the judges, who are then asked to give each a number. The number will depend on how large a scale is desired, indicating the strength of the question or statement to the concept. The researcher would then keep those items where judges were in the strongest agreement, and eliminate those with the weakest indicator scores. For example, in designing your College Students' Criminality Survey questionnaire, you want the questions to form a 15-point criminality scale. You submit 50 questions to judges, asking them to score each question from 1 (strongest indicator) to 15 (weakest indicator). The top 15 questions become your scale.

Consequently, Thurstone scaling is not very popular because of the time it takes for the judges to complete their tasks. Furthermore, since the judges have to be experts in the area of study, finding an adequate pool of qualified judges could also be problematic for the researcher.

Likert Scales

Probably the most commonly used method in attitudinal research is the Likert scale. This method generally makes use of a bipolar, five-point response range (typically, "Strongly Agree" to "Strongly Disagree"). Questions where all respondents provide similar responses are usually eliminated. The remaining questions are used to compose the scale.

Guttman Scales

The last method, the Guttman scale, requires that an attitudinal scale measure only one dimension or concept. The questions or statements must be progressive so that if the respondent answers positively to a question, he or she must respond the same to the following questions.

There are various other types of scaling procedures. However, because so few are used in criminal-justice and criminological research, they will not be discussed here. Furthermore, advanced statistical techniques, such as factor analysis and Cronbach's alpha, are much faster and simpler to use to determine a scale's composition. For example, the Student's Perceptions of Policing scale (Dantzker & Waters, 1999) was originally 20 items, before a factor analysis and Cronbach's alpha eliminated 6 items, thus resulting in the current 14-point scale. The question at this point might be, Why use scales at all?

There are three primary reasons for, or advantages to, using scales. First, a scale allows for a clearer and more precise measure of the concept than do individual items. Second, scales can be replicated and used as longitudinal measures. Finally, scales require more thought.

The disadvantages to scales are twofold: (1) concern as to whether true attitudes can be measured on a scale, and (2) the question of validity and reliability. Despite the shortcomings, overall, scales can be quite useful in measuring data, and should be used where and when it is appropriate and necessary.

■ Summary

To conduct research, data must be collected. Generally, this means that some type of tool (a questionnaire) must be available to assist in collecting the data. The golden rule is to try to use a questionnaire that has previously been tested. However, when that is not possible and a questionnaire must be constructed, following the suggested rules will help create an acceptable tool. These rules are:

1. Start with a list of all the items you are interested in knowing about the group, concept, or phenomenon
2. Be prepared to establish validity and reliability
3. The wording in the questionnaire must be appropriate for the targeted audience
4. Be sure that it is clearly identifiable as to who should answer the questions
5. Avoid asking any questions that are biased, leading, threatening, or double-barreled in nature
6. Prior to construction, a decision must be made whether to use open-ended questions or closed-ended questions or a combination of the two
7. Consider that the respondents may not have the general information needed to complete the questionnaire

8. Whenever possible, pretest the questionnaire before it is officially used

9. Set up questions so that the responses are easily recognizable whether the format is self-administered or interview

10. The questionnaire should be organized in a manner that will keep the interest of the respondent, encouraging him or her to complete the entire questionnaire

In addition to the rules, questionnaire development requires familiarity with issues such as reliability, validity, measurement level, and scales. Scales can be either arbitrary or attitudinal in nature. Three primary attitudinal scales are Thurstone, Likert, and Guttman. The most popular scale is Likert, which makes use of a bipolar set number of points.

METHODOLOGICAL QUERIES

Referring to the opening vignette,

1. What type of questionnaire would you develop to measure student criminality? Give some examples of the information you would seek.

2. What are some questions you would ask?

3. How would you develop the questions? Would you hope to create a scale? Why?

REFERENCES

Dantzker, M. L. (1993). Designing a measure of job satisfaction for policing: A research note. *Journal of Crime and Justice, 16*(2), 171–181.

Dantzker, M. L. (2003). Criminal justice: Why major, employment goals, and perceptions of situations—An exploratory examination among criminal justice students. *Police Forum, 13*(1), 1–4.

Dantzker, M. L., & Waters, J. E. (1999). Examining students' perceptions of policing—A pre- and post-comparison between students in criminal justice and non-criminal justice courses. In M. L. Dantzker (Ed.), *Readings for research methods in criminology and criminal justice* (pp. 27–36). Woburn, MA: Butterworth-Heinemann.

Ford, M., & Williams, L. (1999). Human/cultural diversity training for justice personnel. In M. L. Dantzker (Ed.), *Readings for research methods in criminology and criminal justice* (pp. 37–60). Woburn, MA: Butterworth-Heinemann.

Nachmias, D., & Nachmias, C. (2000). *Research methods in the social sciences* (6th ed.). New York: Worth.

Nardi, P. M. (2002). *Doing survey research: A guide to quantitative research methods*. Boston: Allyn and Bacon.

Punch, K. F. (2005). *Intro to social research: Quantitative and qualitative approaches*. Thousand Oaks, CA: Sage.

Sampling

Vignette 9-1   Would You Like to Sample . . . ?

Finally, it is the weekend, time to do some chores other than school. In particular, you would like a break from your research class and your pending project. It seems that more and more, everything you do has research-related implications, and you would like to get away. So the first thing you decide to do is some grocery shopping. Having shopped at the same store for a few years, you are quite familiar with where everything is, and you are quick to notice any unusual activities. Only now, for the first time, you pay some attention to the individuals at the end of each aisle offering samples of a product to shoppers. You decide to watch one of the "vendors" for a few minutes, taking note of who is being solicited to sample this particular product and who accepts. You observe that not everyone is offered the samples, and of those who are approached, not everyone accepts. You make the same observation of several of the other vendors.

Later that day, you are at the mall. While walking among the stores, you have observed several "vendors" attempting to get passersby to sample their goods. At one point, you are approached by an individual who asks if you could take a few minutes to participate in a marketing survey. After responding to a few personal questions, you are advised that you do not fit the demographics being sought, and are then thanked for your time. By the end of your shopping day, you realize that you have witnessed or have taken part in several "research" efforts where sampling was a very important component. Yet you wonder whether the sampling efforts you observed were appropriate and whether you could try the same methods for your research. Could you just stand out in the quad and stop every other student? Are there certain demographics you might need to screen for? Would this method be acceptable? Representative? Even on the weekend, you cannot escape thinking about your research project. However, while every phase is important, a poor job of sampling would make all other efforts useless. The question, then, is: What type of sample should you use?

Chapter Objectives

After studying this chapter, the student should be able to:

- Discuss the purpose of sampling in criminological research.
- Define what is meant by population, sampling frame, and sample. Describe their relationships. Give examples of each.
- Explain how probability theory enables the researcher to obtain representative samples.
- Identify and describe the various types of probability samples.
- Compare and contrast probability sampling with nonprobability sampling.
- Identify and discuss the various types of nonprobability samples.
- Explain the importance of sample size. Include confidence intervals, confidence levels, and sampling error in your discussion.
- Determine how many observations would be necessary to obtain a sample with an error tolerance of ± 3 at the 95 percent confidence level. Explain how many more observations you would add to this number and why you would do so.

■ Sampling

Conducting research requires the gathering of information about a specific concept, phenomenon, event, or group. Although there are some types of research that require gathering information about every element associated with the topic, a natural-science necessity, this is neither feasible nor necessary in the social sciences. In conducting criminal-justice and criminological research, the primary focus is usually on some specific population.

Recall from Chapter 2 that a population is the complete group or class from which information is to be gathered. For example, police officers, probation officers, and correctional officers are each a population. Again, although it would be great if every member of a population could provide the information sought, it is just not practical. Therefore, sampling the population is a necessity. Before one can begin to sample, the first step is to identify the group from which the sample will come, or what is referred to as the *sampling frame*. The sampling frame is simply that segment of the population from which a sample is chosen (Babbie, 2004; Nardi, 2002; Punch, 2005).

For example, keeping with the idea of the College Students' Criminality Survey (introduced in Chapter 8), it is obvious that college students are the population. However, it is impossible to survey all college students. Even surveying all the college students at one university could prove to be quite burdensome. Therefore, a sampling frame must be chosen. For discussion purposes, under the above circumstances, the sampling frame will be freshman students at the university.

Having identified the sampling frame, the next decision is to choose the type of sample to be used. Again, recall from Chapter 2 that a sample is a *group chosen from a target population to provide information sought*. That sample will either be of the *probability* or *nonprobability* nature. It is appropriate at this point to provide an overview of probability theory.

■ Probability Theory

A friend of ours frequently buys lottery tickets. On a number of occasions, individuals (usually people he does not know) have taken it upon themselves to inform our friend that "you are wasting your money. The odds of your being hit by lightning are better than of your winning the lottery." To which he honestly replies, "Thank you for your concern. I *have* been hit by lightning. This is more fun." The individuals who are warning our friend are statistically correct: his chance of winning the lottery is extremely small, and actually is less than his chance of being hit by lightning. However, since our friend doesn't really care if he wins (he amuses himself by checking the lottery results several days later, asserting that he is potentially a winner until he discovers otherwise), and since his investment averages only about two dollars per week, statistical probabilities don't mean much to him. Unfortunately, many people who wager far more than they can afford also disregard statistical probability. These individuals tend to either believe that "it is time for their luck to change," or that "God [or fate, depending on their religious orientation] will intervene in their lives." While we do not question the benevolence of a Supreme Being, we do feel that if God, or even luck, were to preordain such an event, the purchase of one lottery ticket would be adequate. If not preordained, the sincere gambler might want to seriously consider the statistical probability of success.

Probability theory is based on the concept that over time, there is a statistical order in which things occur. If you flip an unaltered coin 10 times, it is possible that it will land on heads 5 times and tails 5 times. However, it might land on heads 8 times and tails only 2. This is because each time the coin is flipped, it has an equal chance of being heads or tails. What happened previously has no influence on what will happen in the future. We cannot accurately predict what will happen on the next coin toss. Yet we can accurately assume that over a lengthy period of time, the number of heads and the number of tails will be about the same. This is the basis of statistical probability. Anything can happen, but over the long run, there will be a statistical order.

The knowledge that over time, things tend to adhere to a statistical order allows us to choose samples that are representative of a population in general. We cannot say in advance that a sample is representative, but we can follow a procedure that "should" lead to a representative sample's being selected. Because every number (representing people, items, or events) has the same chance of being chosen, most of the time the sample drawn will be representative. On occasion, it will not be.

■ Probability Sampling

The general goal when choosing a sample is *to obtain one that is representative of the target population*. By being representative, the results can be said to be applicable to the whole population, and would be similar no matter how many different samples were surveyed. Representation requires that every member in the population or the sampling frame have an equal chance of being selected for the sample. This is a probability sample. Four types of probability samples exist: simple random, stratified random, systematic, and cluster.

Simple Random Samples

As previously stated, a random sample is *one in which all members of a given population have the same chance of being selected*. Furthermore, the selection of each member must be independent from the selection of any other member (Adler & Clark, 2003; Babbie, 2004; Fitzgerald & Cox, 2001). To assist in selecting a random sample, a device known as a table of random numbers is often used (which can be found in almost every statistics book published). You select a numeral at random, and then use the subsequent numerals provided within the table until you have selected the appropriate number of population members needed. Today, using the computer to randomly generate a sample is becoming more popular. In either case, the researcher must have a complete list of every member of the sampling frame, which is one of the disadvantages of random sampling. Yet, even with this obstacle, random sampling is very popular, partly because it has become easier for researchers to obtain statistically acceptable random samples.

METHODOLOGICAL **LINKS**

Moriarty (1999) and Moriarty, Pelfrey, & Vasu (1999) made use of random sampling to conduct a telephone survey. The sampling element was telephone numbers belonging to a sampling frame of North Carolina's estimated phone households. The initial sample pool of telephone numbers was 35,000; however, only 16,800 numbers were necessary to generate the required sample size.

Son & Rome (2004) conducted a survey of citizens and police officers for the purpose of examining the prevalence and visibility of police misconduct. The citizen sample was obtained from random-digit-dialing telephone interviews. Similarly, Weitzer & Kubrin (2004) also used a telephone survey of residents through a random-digit-dialing program. As with the others, Wilson & Jasinski (2004), in their study of public satisfaction with the police in domestic-violence cases, used random-digit-dialing techniques from a sample of telephone households in the United States.

Stratified Random Samples

Chapter 2 defines a stratified sample as *one that has been chosen from a population that has been divided into subgroups called strata*. These strata are selected based on specified characteristics that the researcher wishes to ensure for inclusion in the study (Adler & Clark, 2003; Babbie, 2004; Fitzgerald & Cox, 2001). This type of sample requires the researcher to have knowledge of the sampling frame's demographic characteristics. These characteristics (selected variables) are then used to create the strata from which the sample is chosen. Depending on the interests or needs of the researcher, a proportionate selection will be made from each stratum (in a random manner), or else oversampling (disproportionate sampling) may be necessary.

Systematic Samples

The nature of systematic sampling has been debated; it has been discussed as both probability and nonprobability sampling. It is offered here as a probability sample because it includes random selection and initially allows inclusion of every member of the sampling frame. With a systematic sample, every nth item in the sampling frame is included in the sample. To begin selecting, the nth item is derived from a sampling interval established based on the ratio of the sample size to the population. A warning should be given when using systematic sampling. If you are sampling an organization, such as a police patrol division, ensure that your selection procedure (for example, every 20th officer) does not result in a rhythm with the organization's bureaucratic structure (Babbie, 2004) that would cause a particular type of individual (patrol-squad sergeant) to be selected each time. This would negate the purpose of such a sample.

Cluster Samples

The last of the probability-sampling methods is the cluster sample (also known as area probability sample). This sample consists of randomly selected groups rather than individuals. Basically, the population to be surveyed is divided into clusters (for example, census tracts). This is a multistage sample (sampling occurs two or more times) in which groups (clusters) are sampled initially (Fitzgerald & Cox, 2001; Nardi, 2002; Schutt, 2001). Subsequent subsamples of the clusters

METHODOLOGICAL LINKS

To obtain the second group of individuals (the police officers) for their study, Son & Rome (2004) used stratified sampling of police departments by size, then random selection of officers from within each agency. Engel & Calnon (2004) made use of a stratified multistage design in drawing a sample from data collected in a 1999 National Crime Victims Survey.

METHODOLOGICAL LINKS

To conduct her study of citizen perceptions of treatment and satisfaction with the telephone-service option in Larimer County, Colorado, Fitzpatrick (1999) made use of systematic random sampling. A comprehensive monthly listing of citizens who had called the department for help served as the sampling frame. Callers were then randomly selected by going through the sampling frame systematically, using a sampling interval based on a predetermined percentage of the population needed for inclusion in the study and the total size of the monthly population. For example, if the population for a given month was 200 callers, and the sample size needed was 10 percent of the population, then the sampling interval became the proportionate sample size multiplied by the monthly population total (that is, [.10][200] = 20 which is the minimum sample size needed; the sampling interval became 200/20 =10; therefore, every 10th element was selected until reaching the sample size of 20).

are then selected. This method is popular for national victimization or other national-interest topics. It is a particularly useful tool for political scientists.

Usually the researcher wants to make use of probability samples primarily because they are often more statistically stable. However, random sampling can be very expensive and logistically difficult to complete. Therefore, it is common to find nonprobability sampling in criminal-justice and criminological research.

■ Nonprobability Sampling

The major difference between probability and nonprobability sampling is that one provides the opportunity for all members of the sampling frame to be selected

METHODOLOGICAL LINKS

To examine the ethical and value orientation of criminal-justice students, Bjerregaard & Lord (2004) targeted the student body at a large university. Sample selection was based on cluster sampling of classes from which all the students in each of those classes were asked to complete a self-administered questionnaire.

while the other does not. This shortcoming of nonprobability sampling often leads to questions and concerns over the representativeness of the sample. However, when the sample produces the requisite information, representativeness is often not as much of a concern (although its limitations must still be noted). Furthermore, a nonprobability sample could be perceived as representative if enough characteristics of the target population exist in the sample. There are four types of nonprobability samples: purposive, quota, snowball, and convenience.

Purposive Samples

Among the nonprobability samples, the purposive sample appears to be the most popular. Based on the researcher's skill, judgment, and needs, an appropriate sample is selected (Black, 1999; Fitzgerald & Cox, 2001; Senese, 1997). When the subjects are selected in advance based on the researcher's view that they reflect normal or average scores, this process is sometimes referred to as *typical-case sampling*. If subgroups are sampled to permit comparisons among them, this technique is known as *stratified purposeful sampling* (Adler & Clark, 2003; Babbie, 2004; Black, 1999). A major factor of purposive sampling is accessibility to units or individuals that are part of the target population.

In all of the studies from the preceding Methodological Link, the researchers chose their samples because they believed that the samples best fit the needs of the study. The selection was based on the researchers' knowledge of the topic, the target populations, and accessibility. Although the samples may not have been representative, they did provide the requisite data to complete the studies. In most cases, because the purposive sample is not representative, findings cannot be generalized to complete populations. This does not mean that a purposive sample

METHODOLOGICAL **LINKS**

Ventura, Lambertt, Bryant, & Pasupuleti (2004) targeted all the students from one university, but randomly chose classes in an effort to attain a wide sample. Dantzker & Waters (1999) chose specific classes of students, both criminal justice and American government, to compose their sample of college students. Accessibility to these classes played a major role in their selection. Stevens (1999), to better study women, drugs, and criminality, made use of a group of women in a particular prison at which he was teaching. Cooper, McLearen, & Zapf (2004) used one police department for their study's sample. Gordon (1999) surveyed all the employees of three different institutions to examine the attitudes of correctional officers among the three different types of institutions. Finally, Ford & Williams' (1999) sample consisted only of those individuals who had taken the diversity class and were employed by two area police agencies and a local department of corrections.

METHODOLOGICAL LINKS

As previously noted, one of Dantzker's research interests is job satisfaction among police officers. In his studies of this subject, he has used purposive sampling, choosing police agencies he perceived as being representative of a "typical municipal police agency." Since he has surveyed only 14 agencies to date, one might easily suggest that only the job satisfaction for each agency could be discussed, and that the findings could not be applied to all police agencies. However, when the data from all the agencies are combined, he has a sample whose characteristics are quite similar to the police population in terms of gender, race, age, and educational composition, and thus, generalizing the findings is possible (Dantzker, 1997).

cannot be generalizable, but it must conform to some similar elements of the population. Yet, despite statistical concerns about the sample, purposive sampling can offer researchers a legitimate and acceptable means of collecting data.

Quota Samples

Recall from the opening vignette that one of the observations dealt with a marketing researcher who decided that the individual did not fit the sampling needs. These types of research efforts often rely on quota sampling. For this type of sample, the proportions are based on the researcher's judgment for inclusion. In other words, does the individual or unit fit the needs of the survey? Selection continues until enough individuals have been chosen to fill out the sample.

Assume that for the College Students' Criminality Survey, only second-semester freshman students at the university are being targeted. Since you have no means of identifying these individuals, you set up a booth in the student union where you stop students as they come by and inquire as to their status at the university. You survey only those who advise you that they are second-semester freshman students, and continue this approach until you have reached your desired sample size or your quota.

To ensure some level of representativeness by gender and race, you set your quota at a percentage equivalent to what the university claims to have in its population. For example, by gender, the university is 45 percent female and 55 percent male, and racially it is 43 percent white, 37 percent African-American, and 20 percent other.

Reaching some minimal level of representativeness requires you to continue selecting students until your quota sample appears to reflect the population of the university. Obviously, this can be a painstakingly long method and does not guarantee representation.

METHODOLOGICAL

LINKS

Flanyak (1999), conducting a qualitative, exploratory research study, utilized both snowball- and convenience-sampling methods. Through this means, she obtained 22 subjects for the study. While her sampling frame consisted of lists of Sociology and Criminal Justice Department faculty members in several universities in Illinois, it was as a result of initial interviews during a pilot study with respondents at her academic institution that other potential subjects were identified. Furthermore, other subjects were chosen from the faculty of her undergraduate institution to ensure a high response rate.

Snowball Samples

Although not a highly promoted form of quantitative sampling, snowball sampling is commonly used as a qualitative technique. The snowball sample begins with a person or persons who provide names of other persons for the sample. This sample type is most often seen used in exploratory studies where an appropriate target population is not readily identifiable, making a sampling frame more difficult to select, but not eliminating the existence of an identifiable sampling frame (Senese, 1997). Additionally, despite the issue of representation, snowball sampling requires the researcher to rely on the expertise of others to identify prospective units for the sample. Snowball sampling is frequently used in field research when the researcher must rely on introductions from group members in order to access other group members.

Obviously, the snowball method may lead to an elite sample that has no representative or generalizable attributes. Consequently, if the data address the research question, then these shortcomings are acceptable.

Convenience Sample

Undoubtedly, the last choice for a sample is the convenience sample or available-subjects sample. Here, there is no attempt to ensure any type of representativeness. Usually this sample is a very abstract representation of the population or target frame. Units or individuals are chosen simply because they were "in the right place at the right time."

Analysis of data from a convenience sample is extremely limited. The sample selected may or may not represent the population that is being studied. Therefore, generalizations that are made about the population cannot be considered to be valid (Adler & Clark, 2003; Punch, 2005). Because of this limitation, convenience samples are not useful for explanation or even for description beyond the sample surveyed. They are often useful as explorations upon which future research may be based.

METHODOLOGICAL

To study officer opinions on police misconduct, Hunter (1999) developed a survey instrument based on the findings of prior research on police ethics and misconduct. Before administering this survey to a sample of several hundred officers in the southeastern United States, he sought feedback from a convenience sampling of currently serving officers. One group consisted of officers on a patrol shift from a midsize metropolitan police agency. A second group was composed of officers taking college courses at a regional college. A third group was made up of officers in their final phase of training at a regional police academy. Findings from this convenience sample not only permitted Hunter to refine the questionnaire, but he was also able to gain insights as to how officers felt about different forms of police misconduct and a variety of proposed solutions aimed at curbing such behaviors. Obviously, the results were indicative only of this sample's opinions, and could not be construed to be representative of the opinions of officers outside the sample. However, as an exploratory study, it was quite useful.

The quality and quantity of the data are dependent on the sampling technique. Statistical support is stronger for probability samples. However, there are times when nonprobability samples are fruitful. Regardless of which type is used, an important element of each is the sample size.

■ Sample Size

The quality of a sample is considered to be dependent largely on its size (Adler & Clark, 2003; Babbie, 2004; Black, 1999; Nardi, 2002; Punch, 2005; Schutt, 2001). The belief is that the larger the sample, the more likely the data will more truly reflect the population. An interesting aspect about sample size seems to be that there is no set size that a sample should be. Usually the sample size is the result of several elements:

1. *How accurate the sample must be*
2. *Economic feasibility (how much you have to spend)*
3. *The availability of requisite variables (including any subcategories)*
4. *Accessibility to the target population (Adler & Clark, 2003; Babbie, 2004; Black, 1999; Nardi, 2002; Punch, 2005; Schutt, 2001; Senese, 1997)*

Confidence Levels

Deciding how large the sample should be requires an understanding of confidence intervals, which indicates a range of numbers (for example, ±15). Since a sam-

METHODOLOGICAL LINKS

> Moriarty (1999) made a total of 809 complete telephone interviews. Considering the size of the target population, her sample size represented a ±5 point margin of error with a 95 percent confidence level.

ple is merely an estimated reflection of the target population, a confidence interval suggests the accuracy of the estimate (Adler & Clark, 2003; Babbie, 2004; Black, 1999; Nardi, 2002; Punch, 2005; Schutt, 2001).

The smaller the confidence interval is, the more accurate the estimated sample. The estimated probability that a population parameter will fall within a given confidence interval is known as the confidence level (Adler & Clark, 2003; Babbie, 2004; Black, 1999; Nardi, 2002; Punch, 2005; Schutt, 2001). Thus, to reduce sampling error, the researcher would desire a smaller confidence interval. To do so, he or she would select a smaller confidence level. Consider **Box 9-1**, which offers an excerpt from a grant proposal in which job satisfaction of both sworn and nonsworn personnel in a municipal police agency is to be measured. Specifically, note the difference in confidence levels and the reasons why.

Sampling Formulas

The key aspect to selecting appropriate confidence levels is the sample size. As previously suggested, the larger the sample, the more accurate the estimate. Therefore, it would be beneficial to know just how large a sample is required to attain the best confidence level. There are several mathematical formulas to assist in determining sample size. Unless you are a good mathematician, it is suggested that preexisting tables or computer statistical packages be used to make that determination. Should those means not be available to you, in the following paragraphs we shall demonstrate how such a formula may be utilized.

A Commonly Used Sampling Formula

When you select a sample size, you are seeking to draw a large enough number of observations from the target population to ensure that the sample accurately represents that population. As was discussed above, the larger the sample size, the more likely that it will be representative. However, since the costs in time and money of sampling large numbers are prohibitive, we rely upon probability theory to estimate the proper sample size. We are guided in our selection by our knowledge of acceptable sample sizes. Generally, in social-science research, we seek a sample size that would, 95 times out of 100, vary by 5 percent or less from the population. In some cases, we may use less-stringent requirements; in others, we may wish to have (and be able to afford) a higher level of accuracy.

Box 9-1
Confidence-Level Example

FOR SWORN OFFICERS

(B) After the data from the surveys have been tabulated, interviews could then be held with a stratified random sample (by rank and assignment) of 50 officers. (The sample of 50 officers has been calculated to have a ± 3.65 confidence level, which is, statistically, a very good level. This would mean that if 56 percent of the officers interviewed indicated the same reason for satisfaction with a given item, then it would be safe to say that if all 167 officers were interviewed, the chances are that a confidence interval between 52 percent to 59 percent would give the same response.)

FOR NONSWORN EMPLOYEES

(B) After the data from the surveys have been tabulated, interviews could then be held with a random sample of 30 nonsworn employees. (The sample of 30 has been calculated to have a ±15.12 percent confidence level. This would mean that if 56 percent of the employees interviewed indicated the same reason for satisfaction with a given item, then it would be safe to say that if all 94 employees were interviewed, the chances are that between 41 percent and 71 percent would give the same response.) In the case of the nonsworn, a higher number could be interviewed, which would improve the confidence level, should the city so desire to spend the additional funds to complete these interviews. However, it is believed that the combination of the surveys and the interviews will be sufficient to offer reliable findings and recommendations.

In social-science research, confidence levels are very important, although they are rarely explained or identified. In many cases, readers are expected to accept that samples are statistically acceptable or are an accurate estimate of the target population. This does not mean that the findings should be ignored. It simply means that their application must be more conservative and judicious.

Assuming that we wish to have a sample of a large population that is at the 95 percent confidence level and has a sample error within 5 percent of the population, we could use the following formula:

$$n = \frac{(1.96)^2 \, [p \, (1 - p)]}{se}$$

where n = sample size needed

p = assumed population variance

se = standard error

1.96 = represents a normal curve z score value at a confidence level of 95 percent

For an error tolerance of 5 percent at the 95 percent confidence level, we would use 0.05 as the SE. The formula would then become:

$$n = \frac{(1.96)^2\,[0.5\,(1-.5\,)]}{0.05}$$

$n = 384.16$ which rounds up to $n = 385$.

Thus, we would find that a sample size of 385 would provide us with a sample that had an error tolerance of ± 5 percent at the 95 percent confidence level. If we wished to change confidence levels and/or error tolerance, we would then adapt the formula to do so. For example, if you wanted to ensure that your sample was representative, and had the money and time to do so, an error tolerance of ± 1 percent at the 99 percent confidence level would result in the following:

$$n = \frac{(4.2930175)^2[0.1\,(1-0.1)]}{.01}$$

$n = 16586.99$ or $16{,}587$

A Sampling-Size Selection Chart

Having read how the above formula was used to obtain the desired sample size, you may decide that you have no desire to ever do so. To save you from such an exercise, we have included a simple chart that will make sample-size selection much easier. Simply determine the confidence level and error tolerance that you desire in your survey sample, and then look it up in **Table 9-1**. The number indicated is how many observations from the study population that you would need to randomly select in order to have a representative sample.

Table 9-1 provides you with the sample size you will need based upon the error tolerance and confidence level desired. However, those are the numbers of observations needed in the sample. To ensure that those numbers are obtained, we recommend that you always oversample by 20 percent. If this isn't enough, you can always add more observations as long as they are randomly selected from the same population, and as long as any time differences do not affect responses. Remember, the sample must be selected randomly if it is to be representative of the population.

Table 9-1 Sample-Size Selection Chart

Error Tolerance	Confidence Levels (percent)	
(percent)	95%	99%
1	9,604	16,587
2	2,401	4,147
3	1,068	1,843
4	601	1,037
5	385	664

Source: Adapted from Richard L. Cole, *Introduction to Political Science and Policy Research* (New York: St. Martin's Press, 1996), 83.

■ Summary

Gaining data from a complete population is usually impossible. In most cases, research data are best obtainable through a sample. Before a sample is chosen, identifying the sampling frame is necessary. Having an identifiable sampling frame leads to a decision as to what type of sample to select: probability or nonprobability. Probability samples include random, stratified random, strata, and cluster sampling. Purposive, quota, snowball, and accidental are forms of nonprobability sampling.

Regardless of the type of sampling, there is a question of sample size. Although no magical number exists, confidence levels provide a statistical means for establishing legitimacy of the sample. The smaller the confidence interval, the more representative is the sample. As can be seen, careful thought should be given prior to choosing a sample type and a sample size.

METHODOLOGICAL QUERIES

Referring to the College Students' Criminality Survey,

1. Briefly describe how you could use each type of sample to conduct the survey.
2. What would be the best sample type? Why?
3. What size sample would you need?
4. Discuss the roles that confidence level and error tolerance would play.

REFERENCES

Adler, E. S., & Clark, R. (2003). *How it's done: An invitation to social research* (2nd ed.). Belmont, CA: Thomson/Wadsworth.

Babbie, E. (2004). *The practice of social research* (10th ed.). Belmont, CA: Thomson/Wadsworth.

Batton, C. (2004). Gender differences in lethal violence: Historical trends in the relationship between homicide and suicide rates, 1960–2000. *Justice Quarterly, 21*(3), 423–461.

Bjerregaard, B., & Lord, V. B. (2004). An examination of the ethical and value orientation of criminal justice students. *Police Quarterly, 7*(2), 262–284.

Black, T. R. (1999). *Doing quantitative research in the social sciences: An integrated approach to research design.* Thousand Oaks, CA: Sage.

Cole, R. L. (1996). *Introduction to political science and policy research.* New York: St. Martin's Press.

Cooper, V. G., McLearen, A. M., & Zapf, P. A. (2004). Dispositional decisions with the mentally ill: Police perceptions and characteristics. *Police Quarterly, 7*(3), 295–310.

Dantzker, M. L. (1997). Police officer job satisfaction: Does agency size make a difference? *Criminal Justice Policy Review, 8*(2–3), 309–322.

Dantzker, M. L., & Waters, J. E. (1999). Examining students' perceptions of policing—A pre- and post-comparison between students in criminal justice and non-criminal justice courses. In M. L. Dantzker (Ed.), *Readings for research methods in criminology and criminal justice* (pp. 27–36). Woburn, MA: Butterworth-Heinemann.

Engel, R.S., & Calnon, J. M. (2004). Examining the influence of drivers' characteristics during traffic stops with police: Results from a national survey. *Justice Quarterly, 21*(1), 49–90.

Fitzgerald, J. D., & Cox, S. M. (2001). *Research methods and statistics in criminal justice: An introduction* (3rd ed.). Chicago: Nelson-Hall.

Fitzpatrick, C. (1999). A survey of citizen perceptions of treatment and satisfaction with a telephone service option in a rural sheriff's department. In M. L. Dantzker (Ed.), *Readings for research methods in criminology and criminal justice* (pp. 99–122). Woburn, MA: Butterworth-Heinemann.

Flanyak, C. M. (1999). Accessing data: Procedures, practices, and problems of academic researchers. In M. L. Dantzker (Ed.), *Readings for research methods in criminology and criminal justice* (pp. 157–180). Woburn, MA: Butterworth-Heinemann.

Ford, M., & Williams, L. (1999). Human/cultural diversity training for justice personnel. In M. L. Dantzker (Ed.), *Readings for research methods in criminology and criminal justice* (pp. 37–60). Woburn, MA: Butterworth-Heinemann.

Gordon, J. (1999). Correctional officers' attitudes toward delinquents and delinquency: Does the type of institution make a difference? In M. L. Dantzker (Ed.), *Readings for research methods in criminology and criminal justice* (pp. 85–98). Woburn, MA: Butterworth-Heinemann.

Hunter, R. D. (1999). Officer opinions on police misconduct. *Journal of Contemporary Criminal Justice, 15*(2), 155–170.

Moriarty, L. J. (1999). The conceptualization and operationalization of the intervening dimensions of social disorganization. In M. L. Dantzker (Ed.), *Readings for research methods in criminology and criminal justice* (pp. 15–26). Woburn, MA: Butterworth-Heinemann.

Moriarty, L. J., Pelfrey, W. V., & Vasu, M. L. (1999). Measuring violent crime in North Carolina. In M. L. Dantzker (Ed.), *Readings for research methods in criminology and criminal justice* (pp.75–84). Woburn, MA: Butterworth-Heinemann.

Nardi, P.M. (2002). *Doing survey research: A guide to quantitative research methods.* Boston: Allyn and Bacon.

Punch, K. F. (2005). *Intro to social research: Quantitative and qualitative approaches.* Thousand Oaks, CA: Sage.

Schutt, R. K. (2001). *Investigating the social world: The process and practice of research* (3rd ed.). Thousand Oaks, CA: Pine Forge Press.

Senese, J. D. (1997). *Applied research methods in criminal justice.* Chicago: Nelson-Hall.

Son, I. S., & Rome, D. M. (2004). The prevalence and visibility of police misconduct: A survey of citizens and police officers. *Police Quarterly, 7*(2), 179–204.

Stevens, D. J. (1999). Women offenders, drug addiction, and crime. In M. L. Dantzker (Ed.), *Readings for research methods in criminology and criminal justice* (pp. 61–74). Woburn, MA: Butterworth-Heinemann.

Ventura, L. A., Lambertt, E. G., Bryant, M., & Pasupuleti, S. (2004). Differences in attitudes toward gays and lesbians among criminal justice and non-criminal justice majors. *American Journal of Criminal Justice, 28*(2), 165–179.

Weitzer, R., & Kubrin, C. E. (2004). Breaking news: How local TV news and real-world conditions affect fear of crime. *Justice Quarterly, 21*(3), 497–520.

Wilson, S., & Jasinski, J. L. (2004). Public satisfaction with the police in domestic violence cases: The importance of arrest, expectations, and involuntary consent. *American Journal of Criminal Justice, 28*(2), 235–254.

Data Collection

10

Vignette 10-1   Obtaining the Data

Despite the fact that the spring break is several months away, you learned the hard way that if you do not start planning early, you might end up spending your break in a wading pool in your backyard. So you and a few friends start discussing where to go. There are several possibilities, and so it is helpful to obtain information. The debate begins as to "how and where" to get the information. The "how" is always an interesting question. One person suggests that someone call travel agencies, another person suggests looking through travel sections of newspapers, and another says that letters of inquiry should be sent to the chambers of commerce of the prospective vacation sites. Each is a good idea, but they all seem to present a problem: none of the methods will provide all the required data, such as room availability and rates, airfares, special activities, and so forth.

While the discussion continues on the best way to collect the required information, your research-methods class comes to mind. You recognize that the current situation could be viewed as a form of a research problem, and therefore, if you follow the steps associated with conducting research, the answers will become clear. However, you have made it only up through designing the research effort. Collecting the data is the next part of the course.

Chapter Objectives

After studying this chapter, the student should be able to:

- Identify the four primary data-collection techniques that are available.
- Explain the strengths and weaknesses of mail surveys.
- Describe the strengths and weaknesses of self-administered surveys.
- Compare and contrast structured, unstructured, and in-depth interviews.
- Compare and contrast face-to-face and telephone interviews.
- Discuss the strengths and weaknesses of observational research.
- Explain the strengths and weaknesses of archival research.
- Describe the strengths and weaknesses of content analysis.
- Compare and contrast the advantages of survey, interview, observational, and unobtrusive research.
- Identify and explain the disadvantages of survey, interview, observational, and unobtrusive research.

Data Collection

One of the most crucial aspects of the research effort is the collection of the data. Improperly collected or incorrect data can delay, or even cause the cancellation of, the research effort. Therefore, before the researcher begins any type of data collection, he or she must be sure to choose the right data-collection technique. One of the best means of collecting data is through the experimental design, as previously noted, but this method is not very conducive to social-science research. However, there are other alternatives that are very effective and efficient, especially for the criminal-justice professional and criminologist. There are four primary data-collection techniques available: survey, interview, observation, and unobtrusive means. (Note that we have broken interviews out of survey research for discussion purposes in this chapter. But please keep in mind that interviews are usually considered to be a component of survey research.) This was evident in Chapter 8's discussion of questionnaire development. These research methods have been discussed in detail in previous chapters. Our focus in this chapter will be on the issues involved in data collection utilizing these strategies.

Survey Research

Probably the most frequently used method for data collection is the survey, despite the fact that the research may be formed around invalid assumptions (Glicken, 2003; Leedy & Ormond, 2005; Talarico, 1980). Although an excellent tool for gathering primary data, the survey is often misunderstood. It is quite useful in both descriptive and analytical studies. In criminal justice and criminology, some of the uses include measuring attitudes, fears, perceptions, and victimizations. There are two primary means for collecting data through surveys: interviews and self-completing questionnaires. A common means of distributing questionnaires is through the mail or by direct distribution. A more recent means of distributing surveys is through the Internet using e-mail or a specific Web-site link. Interviews can be conducted in person or via telephone.

Mail Surveys

Although there are many means available for conducting surveys, one of the most popular approaches is distributing surveys through the mail. This method allows for use of fairly large samples, broader area coverage, and minimized cost in terms of time and money. Additional advantages include avoiding the need for a field staff, eliminating the possible bias effect in interviews, allowing greater privacy to the respondents, placing fewer time constraints on the respondents so that more consideration can be given to the answers, and finally, the fact that the likelihood of a high percentage of returns improves the representativeness of the sample.

The mail-survey method is extremely advantageous, but it has numerous disadvantages, too. Probably one of the most frustrating disadvantages is the relative lack of response, or the nonresponse. As shown in the following methodological link, to combat the nonresponse problem, the researchers sent several follow-ups. Despite the fact that this will help increase the number of respondents, it also can add costs not part of the original research plan.

A second disadvantage is the possible differences that might exist between the respondents and nonrespondents. For example, what if only individuals who were pleased with the way their police agency performed its duties responded to a citizen's satisfaction survey?

METHODOLOGICAL **LINKS**

To examine violent crime in North Carolina, one of the data-collection tools used by Moriarty, Pelfry, & Vasu (1999) was a mail survey. The survey was sent to a random sample of 2,000 respondents selected from a roster of North Carolina licensed drivers. All 2,000 were sent a postcard notifying them that they would be receiving a survey approximately one week later.

Hass & Senjo (2004), to study the perceptions of effectiveness and the actual use of technology-based methods of instruction among California criminal-justice-related faculty, used a mail survey. After identifying 325 individuals who fit their study's criteria, surveys were sent to each. Three weeks later, the researchers sent a follow-up, and after the fourth week sent a third copy.

Although the findings would be very pleasing to the police agency and to city management, would they really be a true indication of citizen satisfaction?

Still another disadvantage depends on the type of survey sent. A lack of uniformity in responses could present problems when open-ended questions are used. Since each respondent will answer in a different manner (for example, by paragraph, by listing, or by a single word), this could make data compiling more difficult. In addition to the lack of uniformity is the problem that misinterpretation of the question could also create glitches in the data. Finally, slow return rates can delay the project. It took several weeks before the researchers in the previous Methodological Link example could move to the next phase of the study.

Obviously, the disadvantages of mail surveys can be disconcerting, but these disadvantages are not difficult to overcome. The key to this type of data collection is to attain the highest response rate possible. The follow-up is just one way. Other ways to increase response rates include the following:

1. *Offering some type of remuneration or "reward" for completing the survey. One popular method is to offer a cash incentive (for example, enclosing a dollar bill with the survey).*

2. *Appealing to the respondent's altruistic side. Advising the perspective respondent that his or her response would be extremely helpful in learning more about the subject of the research, and would be greatly appreciated.*

3. *Using an attractive and shortened format. Although this may sound silly, it is amazing how much more likely someone is to respond to a questionnaire that is eye-catching. This tends to show the respondent that some time and thought were given to this questionnaire, thus making it more likely to be completed than questionnaires with lackluster designs. Furthermore, a questionnaire with a short and simple format is likely to generate a better response than would a lengthy questionnaire.*

4. *Indicating that the survey is sponsored or endorsed by a recognizable entity. Respondents may be more encouraged to respond to a survey when they recognize and, hopefully, respect the entity supporting the research.*

5. *Personalizing the survey. Addressing the questionnaire to a specific person often adds more legitimacy to the research, as opposed to receiving something addressed to "Dear Occupant" or "Dear Resident".*

6. *The timing of the survey. When a survey is sent could be extremely important. For example, many individuals spent hours and hours watching the O. J. Simpson trial. Research geared toward public perceptions of the court process as observed in this trial probably would have received much better response immediately following the completion of the trial than if such a study were to be conducted today (Adler & Clark, 2003; Babbie, 2004; Fitzgerald & Cox, 2001; Glicken, 2003; Leedy & Ormond, 2005).*

Acceptable Mail-Survey Response Rates

The previous section discussed the frustration of dealing with low response rates, and provided recommendations for enhancing return rates. Perhaps the best way to cope with low return rates is (in addition to following the recommendations that were provided) to allow for them in your research design. As you may recall from Chapter 9, we recommend that you oversample in order to meet sample-size requirements. In mail surveys, the 20 percent oversampling rate may not be enough. Suggested response rates for mail surveys are:

> *40 percent within two weeks*
>
> *20 percent within two weeks of a follow-up letter*
>
> *10 percent within two weeks of the final contact (Babbie, 2004)*

Furthermore, it's been advised that response rates of 50 percent are adequate for analysis and reporting, that 60 percent is good, and that 70 percent is very good (Babbie, 2004; Fitzgerald & Cox, 2001; Leedy & Ormond, 2005). These numbers are consistent with our own experiences.

Note that based on the return rate indicated above, it may require several follow-ups to obtain a good, or even adequate, response rate. In the survey described in the Methodological Link that follows, strenuous efforts on the part of Moriarty, Pelfrey, & Vasu (1999), just short of badgering respondents, provided a 75 percent return rate. While this was an excellent rate overall, the researchers worked very hard to get it.

The response rate will vary depending on the type of survey (we have already discussed the importance of brevity and clarity) and the targeted respondents. Ordinary citizens are far less likely to respond to a general survey than are members of a constituent group being polled by an organization in which they hold membership. In some situations, a 100 percent response rate may be possible, but it is a rare occurrence. In all, a mail survey can be very effective and efficient.

E-mail

For many years, the three primary methods of conducting survey research were personal interview, mail questionnaire, and telephone survey. With the proliferation of technology, a more recent means of conducting survey research has been with a computer and the use of electronic mail (e-mail). Although the use of e-mail for conducting survey research has not become a staple in criminal-justice research (Mueller, Giacomazzi, & Wada, 2004), it does appear to be very popular in other arenas, especially education research (Heflich & Rice, 1999; Schaefer & Dillman, 1998; Sheehan, 1999; Zhang, 2000).

A review of available literature tends to support the growing interest in the use of e-mail to conduct surveys. While a majority of the literature appears to support and promote the use of e-mail, there do seem to be some cautionary trends with respect to using e-mail versus regular mail. These have included the following cautions:

> **1.** *Although e-mail saves time and money, e-mail surveys may not be as representative as regular mail.*

2. *Respondents may need more notice on e-mail availability and response requests.*

3. *Postal surveys were far superior to e-mail surveys with respect to return and response rates, and the decision to use e-mail surveys should be dependent upon issues such as cost, convenience, and timeliness.*

4. *Response rates were better for mail surveys than for the electronic surveys (Furlong, 1997; Mavis & Brocato, 1998; Meehan & Burns, 1997; Paolo, Bonaminio, Gibson, Partridge, & Kallail, 2000; Schaefer & Dillman, 1998; Underwood, Kim, & Matier, 2000).*

While it appears there is growing support for the use of e-mail to conduct surveys, the return rate remains questionable as to its viability.

Mailed or e-mailed surveys may be feasible under certain circumstances; there are also situations in which neither is feasible but the survey method is still necessary to complete the research. The most commonly used means of collecting data appears to be through self-administered surveys.

Self-Administered Surveys

Personal or telephone access to particular populations is becoming increasingly difficult for researchers. Some populations might need to be kept restricted (for example, prison inmates), while others wish to remain anonymous or do not want

METHODOLOGICAL

LINKS

The police department of a university in Texas was interested in seeing how the campus community perceived the services that the department provided. To complete this task, a short survey instrument was designed and distributed to faculty, staff, and students. For ease of distribution and analysis, the final survey instrument was kept to eight subject-matter questions and five demographic questions. At the time of the study (spring 2001), the university employed 2,692 full- and part-time faculty and staff. Among this group, only 1,128 had active e-mail accounts. This group was sent an e-mail, with the survey sent as an attachment, explaining the study and advising that completed surveys could be either e-mailed back or printed out and sent back through campus mail. One week later, a reminder e-mail with the survey attachment was sent again.

Of the 1,128 faculty and staff who received the e-mail survey request, 322 (28.5 percent) returned usable surveys. Among the 322 respondents, 34 (10.6 percent) sent the survey back via e-mail, with the rest being sent back through campus mail (Dantzker, 2001).

to allow personal contact with researchers (for example, police officers). However, these types of populations can offer vital data regarding numerous research topics. This is where the self-administered survey is applicable.

The self-administered survey is generally a written questionnaire that is distributed to the selected sample in a structured environment. Respondents are allowed to complete the survey within a given time period and then return it to the researcher, often through an emissary of the sample. The advantages to this method include targeting large samples, covering wide geographic areas, cost efficiency, ease of data processing, and the ability to address a wide variety of topics (Adler & Clark, 2003; Babbie, 2004; Creswell, 2002; Fitzgerald & Cox, 2001; Glicken, 2003; Leedy & Ormond, 2005).

The disadvantages to self-administered surveys include a low return rate, nonresponse to some questions, and misinterpretation or misunderstanding of the questions (Adler & Clark, 2003; Babbie, 2004; Creswell, 2002; Fitzgerald & Cox,

METHODOLOGICAL

 LINKS

The following studies used self-administered surveys to collect their data. Take note of the diversity of populations/samples and purposes for which they were surveyed:

Bjerregaard & Lord (2004), to examine the ethical and value orientation of criminal-justice students, surveyed all the students in each class chosen using cluster sampling of a student body at a large university.

Cooper, McLearen, & Zapf (2004) surveyed a single police agency to examine police perceptions in dealing with the mentally ill.

Dantzker & Waters (1999), to study students' perceptions of policing, had the survey instruments distributed by instructors to all students attending the first day of class in several courses, at several universities, where they were given approximately 15 to 20 minutes to complete the survey.

Ford & Williams (1999), to collect data about cultural-diversity training for police and correctional officers in Florida, distributed the survey at the officers' places of employment during a two-week period.

To examine correctional officers' attitudes toward delinquents and delinquency and whether the type of institution they worked in made a difference, Gordon (1999) surveyed all correctional staff members at three juvenile institutions.

Studying female offenders, Stevens (1999) distributed his survey to 68 women incarcerated in a high-custody prison in North Carolina. These women had all been part of a drug program at the prison.

Interested in the differences in attitudes toward gays and lesbian among students, Ventura, Lambertt, Bryant, & Pasupuleti (2004) surveyed a purposive sample of students from one university.

2001; Glicken, 2003; Leedy & Ormond, 2005). Disadvantages aside, self-administered surveys allow for greater diversity in criminal-justice and criminological research.

Overall, self-administered surveys offer economic and efficient means of collecting data. Still, this type of survey does not typically allow for in-depth responses or for the researcher to follow up on why a particular response was given. This is where interviewing is appropriate.

■ Interviews

For the purpose of this text, interviewing is viewed as *the interaction between two individuals where one of the individual's goals is to obtain recognizable responses to specific questions*. Interviewing is not an easy task, and often requires years of training in order for one to be reasonably good at it. This does not preclude many researchers from trying this method, however. There are three types of possible interviews: structured, unstructured, and in-depth. Each can be conducted in person or by telephone.

Structured Interviews

Probably the most used type of interview in criminal-justice research is the structured interview. This requires the use of closed-ended questions that every individual interviewed must be asked in the same order. Responses are set and can be checked off by the interviewer. The advantage to this type of interview is that it can be easily administered, has high response rates, and makes data processing much easier (Adler & Clark, 2003; Babbie, 2004; Fitzgerald & Cox, 2001; Glicken, 2003; Leedy & Ormond, 2005).

The interview, in reality, is a questionnaire that is being administered orally, with the interviewer completing the form for the respondent. Disadvantages include that it does not allow for further exploration of the responses attained, that it is time-consuming and costly, and that it can limit the types of responses given (Adler & Clark, 2003; Babbie, 2004; Fitzgerald & Cox, 2001; Glicken, 2003; Leedy & Ormond, 2005).

Unstructured Interviews

The unstructured interview offers respondents open-ended questions where no set response is provided. While this allows for more-in-depth responses, it is much more difficult to quantify the responses. This type of interview is also more susceptible to intervening or biasing elements. Unstructured interviews are, as discussed in previous chapters, often conducted in field research. They require a very experienced and disciplined interviewer in order to be successful.

In-depth Interviews

Finally, the in-depth interview can make use of both fixed and open-ended questions. The difference from the other types is that the in-depth interviewer can further explore why the response was given and can ask additional qualifying questions. The advantage to this method of interviewing is that a substantial amount of information can be obtained. The disadvantages include that it is time-consuming, requires small samples, and can limit the topics researched. Like the unstructured interview, this technique is best left to experienced researchers who are very familiar with the issue being studied as well as with how to conduct in-depth interviews.

Face-to-Face Interviews

In general, there are many advantages to using interviewing as a data-collection tool. However, these advantages differ slightly when the interview is completed face-to-face rather than by telephone. Face-to-face interviews provide contact between the researcher and the respondent. This contact can be positive reinforcement for participating in the research. Oftentimes simply receiving a questionnaire in the mail can be very sterile, and because of that lack of personal touch, would-be respondents may simply ignore the survey. The face-to-face interview can usually guarantee a higher response rate, too.

Another advantage to this type of interview is that any misunderstandings or confusion can be cleared up. This helps ensure that the responses are truer to the question. It also allows for the researcher to act as an observer, giving the interviewer the opportunity to focus on nonverbal cues. The other advantages to the face-to-face interview include being able to use audiovisual aids, to schedule additional interviews, to make use of language the respondent can relate to, and to exercise discretion.

Although the advantages clearly outweigh the disadvantages, they cannot be ignored. There are four basic disadvantages to face-to-face interviews:

1. *Extremely time-consuming and costly*
2. *Interviewer effect or bias*
3. *Interviewer error*
4. *The interviewer's skills or lack of them could be detrimental (Adler & Clark, 2003; Babbie, 2004; Fitzgerald & Cox, 2001; Glicken, 2003; Leedy & Ormond, 2005)*

METHODOLOGICAL LINKS

In order to study how academic researchers gain access to data, Flanyak (1999) used in-depth interviewing. This method provided her with a high response rate, and allowed her to have personal contact with her subjects and to observe them during the interview. To assist in conformity, she made use of an interview guide instrument, which provided her with the opportunity and discretion to explore or probe respondents for detail in specific areas. Each interview lasted from 45 to 75 minutes, with the longest being two hours in length. Follow-up interviews were completed as needed, and lasted approximately 15 minutes.

It is common for researchers to make use of graduate students to assist in conducting interviews. Unfortunately, few graduate students come equipped with the skills required to conduct a good interview. Failing to provide or to hone the necessary skills will negatively affect the data. Therefore, to avoid interviewer errors, it is important to properly train those who will be conducting the interview. Furthermore, interview results can be enhanced through the use of audio- and videotaping.

The face-to-face interview can be a very useful data-collection technique. However, there are times when it is not possible to conduct face-to-face interviews, but the interview method is still necessary. This is when the telephone survey is useful.

Telephone Surveys

The advantages of telephone surveying begin with being able to eliminate the need for a field staff. This type of survey can allow for the creation of a very small in-house staff. With this method, it is also easier to monitor interviewer bias; specifically, telephone surveying eliminates the possibility of sending any nonverbal cues. Although not common, long in-depth interviews could be completed via the telephone. Finally, the telephone interview is less expensive and can be quick. The disadvantages to the telephone interview include the following:

1. *Limiting of the scope of research*
2. *Difficulty in obtaining in-depth responses*
3. *Elimination from the sample parameters of anyone without a telephone*
4. *Possible high refusal rates (Adler & Clark, 2003; Babbie, 2004; Creswell, 2002; Fitzgerald & Cox, 2001; Glicken, 2003; Leedy & Ormond, 2005)*

■ Comparison of Survey Strategies

Essentially, there are five common ways to collect data through surveys: mail, e-mail, self-administered, personal interviews, and telephone interviewing. A comparison of similar criteria finds that there are advantages and disadvantages to each (see **Table 10-1**). Ultimately, it is up to the researcher to determine which might best meet the needs of the research topic. Furthermore, it is possible to combine methods. For example, Moriarty, Pelfrey, & Vasu (1999) made use of both mail and telephone surveys in their study of violent crime in North Carolina. Son & Rome (2004) employed both a telephone survey and a self-administered survey.

Even though combinations are possible, there are times when none of these methods are practical, and yet a survey technique may still be necessary to obtain the data. Survey data collecting, regardless of the means, is very popular. However, it is not always the most appropriate or the best means of collecting data. Therefore, other ways of collecting data must be available. As discussed in Chapters 5 and 6, there are several other methods.

Table 10-1 Comparison of Survey Methods					
Criteria	Mail	E-mail	Self-Administered	Personal Interview	Telephone Interview
Cost	Low	Low	Low	High	Moderate
Response Rates	Moderate	Moderate	High	High	High
Control	None	None	High	High	Moderate
Diverse Population	High	Moderate	High	Moderate	Moderate
In-depth Information	Low	Low	Moderate	High	Moderate
Timeliness	Slow	Moderate	Fast	Slow	Fast

■ Other Data-Collection Techniques

Assume that you want to understand the inner workings of a gang or how particular patrol techniques are affecting citizen satisfaction. You could probably conduct interviews or create a self-administered survey, but neither of these may be able to give you a complete picture because you may not know everything you need to ask. In some instances, observation is the best method for collecting data.

Observation/Field Research

Observation, as discussed in Chapters 5 and 6, can fall into one of four approaches: (1) the full participant, (2) the participant-researcher, (3) the researcher who participates, and (4) the complete researcher (Senese, 1997). Regardless of which approach is employed, observation allows the researcher to see firsthand how or why something works. It provides an opportunity to become aware of aspects unfamiliar to those who do not have firsthand experience. To conduct observational data collection, the researcher needs to do the following:

1. Decide where the observations are to be done
2. Decide on the focus of the observations
3. Determine when the observations will be conducted (Senese, 1997)

A choice of where observations are to be done may be quite limited. While the idea is to determine whether the observations should take place in public or in private, in many instances, that choice does not exist. For example, observing how incarcerated juveniles respond to a particular treatment program may be possible only in the institutional setting. However, if the program is provided to non-incarcerated juveniles, then the observations may take place in a public setting (for example, school). Regardless of the choice, it is still an important one. The wrong setting will generally mean an unsuccessful research venture.

What is it that we want to know? Deciding what aspect to observe is another important element. If we know absolutely nothing about a phenomenon or entity, we may end up observing everything about it. The researcher needs to have an idea of what aspects are to be studied and how to do so. If the research is quantitative, a checklist will need to be prepared in advance rather than relying on field notes (for an example, see **Figure 10-1**).

Finally, the period or time frame when the observations are to be conducted should be determined in order to provide the best possible opportunity of collecting the desired data. For example, in Memory's (1999) study, he had only 180 hours to make observations in six different jurisdictions. Therefore, he had to decide how many patrol shifts he would ride in each area. Furthermore, to get the greatest amount of diversity, he rode shifts that ended no later than 1:00 A.M. and did not start before 10:00 A.M.

Like survey research, observational research has its advantages and disadvantages. One of the greatest advantages is the direct collection of the data. Rather than having to rely on what others have seen, here the researcher relies only on his or her observations. However, that could also serve as a disadvantage due to researcher misinterpretation or not understanding what is seen. An extremely important facet is recording the observations either in field notes, with an audio recorder, or by video as quickly and as accurately as possible. This will also help reduce inaccuracy and inconsistency. It is further recommended that you tran-

On-Site Evaluation Form			
Store: _____			
Location: _____			
City (if applicable): _____			
County: _____			
Law Enforcement jurisdiction: _____			
Variable Score: 1	2	3	
1. Location of cashier:	Cent.	Side	____
2. Number of clerks:	Three	Two	One ____
3. Visibility within:	Good	Poor	____
4. Visibility from outside:	Good	Poor	____
5. Within two blocks of major street:	No	Yes	
6. Amount of vehicular traffic:	Heav.	Mod.	Light ____
7. Type of land use nearby:	Com.	Res.	Unused ____
8. Concealed access/escape:	No	Yes	____
9. Evening commercial activity nearby:	Yes	No	
10. Exterior well lighted:	Yes	No	____
11. Gas pumps:	Yes	No	____
12. Security devices in use:	Yes	No	____
13. Cash handling procedures:	Good	Poor	____
14. Hours of operation:	Day	6-12	24 hr ____

Figure 10-1 Checklist Example for a Quantitative Field Research Effort
Note that the checklist provides for either circling answers or edge coding as an aid in the later inputting of data. Also, the order of attributes: Yes No, No, Yes are reversed in some questions to ensure that the numerical coding 1, 2, or 3 is consistent with increasing vulnerability to robbery. Source: Hunter (1988).

METHODOLOGICAL LINKS

As part of a 1995 to 1996 study of implementation of community policing in five cities and one county in North Carolina, Memory (1999) rode along with community-policing and patrol officers in each jurisdiction. His goal was to attain firsthand knowledge of officers' attitudes and behaviors in their natural setting as they relate to the implementation of community policing. Considering all the different things one might observe while riding with police officers, without that specific focus, Memory might have ended up with all kinds of information, but not necessarily what he required in order to complete his research.

Along similar lines, Dabney, Hollinger, & Dugan (2004) had to change their sampling protocols after the first six months of their observational study of who shoplifts. During the first six months, they had discovered that a segment of those who came into this particular store didn't even shop, but went directly to some other service available, then left. The researchers also observed that shoplifters tended to dress in a particular fashion, so their new sampling protocol included every third shopper who was dressed in a particular way.

scribe your field notes as soon as possible afterward, while they are still fresh in your mind, to ensure that you can interpret your hurried handwriting and any abbreviations that were used. The fact that the research is being conducted in the phenomenon's natural environment is a bonus. Recall that a shortcoming of experiments is that the environment is controlled, perhaps biasing the results.

Observational research takes place in the real world, legitimizing the observations. "This is what actually happened," rather than "This is what should happen." Observational data collection, too, may not be used in all circumstances. What happens when a topic deals with a phenomenon that has already occurred and can no longer be observed or surveyed? What if you want to research a phenomenon without having to "disturb" anyone? This type of data collection would rely on using unobtrusive data.

Unobtrusive Data Collection

The last means for collecting data is through what are referred to as unobtrusive measures. These are any methods of data collection where the subjects of the research are completely unaware of being studied and where that study is not observational. It is a method that prevents the researcher from direct interaction or involvement with what is being studied. Two of the more commonly used types of unobtrusive data collection are the use of archival data (analyzing existing statistics and/or documents) and content analysis.

METHODOLOGICAL

The following studies made use of archival data. Note the various sources used.

Gaardner, Rodrigues, & Zatz (2004)—collected part of their data from official case-file narratives from court records

Holcomb, Williams, & Demuth (2004)—collected their data from Supplemental Homicide Reports through the FBI

Kingsnorth & Macintosh (2004)—made use of 5,272 cases processed through a county D.A.'s office

Liddick (1999)—used police records to look at the role of women in organized numbers gambling in New York City; these records offered an abundance of information

Metraux & Culhane (2004)—used administrative databases of two public entities to obtain their data

Warchol & Johnson (1999)—examined records kept by U.S. marshals to analyze federal asset forfeiture

Archival Data

In criminal justice and criminology, using official statistics or records is viewed as a form of archival collection. For example, one of the most common means of studying crime is through the use of the Uniform Crime Reports—UCR, published yearly by the Federal Bureau of Investigation (FBI). Data in the UCR are collected monthly from police agencies on a voluntary basis. Because the Uniform Crime Reports provide crime data from all over the country, and include arrest and offense information, a researcher could do an in-depth analysis of crime patterns or arrest characteristics without the arrestees or victims having any knowledge of the research in progress.

Another use of archival data is historical research. Rather than a quantitative analysis of existing statistics, historical study is generally a qualitative analysis of documents and prior research. Archival data are often found in two types of records, public and private. Public records include actuarial, political, judicial, and other governmental documents, as well as the mass media. Private records include diaries, letters, foundations, and autobiographies. One of the biggest problems with archival data is proving the authenticity of the data. Still, archival collection allows researchers to be less intrusive than with other means, and usually offers sufficient data to assess the phenomenon even though it can no longer be observed. One of the benefits of archival data is that there are many possible sources for information.

Regardless of what types of records are used, archival collection can offer the researcher a wide array of topics and data. The biggest problem to overcome is access.

METHODOLOGICAL LINKS

Colomb & Damphouse (2004), in an effort to determine if newspaper coverage of hate crimes leads to a moral panic, used content analysis. Their data were culled from newspaper coverage of hate crimes throughout the 1990s using the LexisNexis database.

To provide an updated and expanded guide for authors, Vaughn, Del Carmen, Perfecto, & Charand (2004) did a content analysis of criminal-justice-related journals. They also employed a self-administered survey.

Content Analysis

The other unobtrusive means that we will discuss is content analysis. This technique has been discussed in previous chapters and is a favorite strategy among researchers who wish to compare social events from different eras. Analysis of the contents of archival documents could be included in this research. Generally, the focus of the research is on publications and presentations (particularly media documents such as newspapers, magazines, and television programs). Depending on how the research is structured, the analysis may be qualitative or quantitative in nature.

METHODOLOGICAL LINKS

Dantzker (1994) conducted a content analysis of employment advertisements for police chiefs as found in *Police Chief* (1985–1993). Although a checklist form was not created, every advertisement was examined for the following information: population size that the police agency served, budget, number of sworn and nonsworn personnel, education requirement, required years of police experience, required years of police management experience, and any other additional requirements (such as graduation from the FBI National Academy). Once all this information was collected, it was then a matter of collapsing it into quantifiable categories for data entry and analyses.

There are a variety of means for collecting data. Ultimately, it is the task of the researcher to be able to properly choose one or more means that will provide the best access to the required data (see **Table 10-2**). Having provided the foundation of the concept of surveys, the next step is to understand and develop the primary survey instrument, the questionnaire.

Table 10-2	Data Collection Methods—Advantages and Disadvantages		
Survey	**Interview**	**Observation**	**Unobtrusive Means**
Advantages	**Advantages**	**Advantages**	**Advantages**
Wide variety of topics	Wide variety of topics	Actual observation of behaviors in natural setting	Wide variety of topics
Simple to administer	Can give complex answers	Better ability to link behavior to concept	Cost-effective Simple to administer
Cost-effective	Clarifications		
Anonymous	Increases response rate		Anonymous
			Comparable
Comparable	Can consider nonverbal cues		
Disadvantages	**Disadvantages**	**Disadvantages**	**Disadvantages**
Misinterpretation	Misinterpretation	Observer influence	Misinterpretation
Nonresponse to questions	Interviewer biases	Only current behaviors observable	Researcher biases
Low return rates	Costly		Limited by what has been done previously
		Costly	
Cannot clarify questions	Not all behavior is observable		Cannot clarify questions
Cannot expand answers			Cannot expand answers

When engaging in content analysis, we recommend that you try to create a quantifiable instrument to utilize. This requires serious thought about the issue that you are researching, as well as the creation of a code sheet or checklist to record observations on a daily, weekly, or yearly basis (depending on the nature of the research). A summary sheet or form that permits the code sheets to be easily totaled is also recommended. These summary forms can then be used to input data for analysis. However, a checklist, in and of itself, is not as important as having a list of those items you want to collect or observe.

■ Summary

Data collection can take many forms. The most popular method tends to be the survey. Surveys can be either self-administered or interviews. Self-administered surveys can be accomplished through direct distribution to respondents. Interviews can be conducted in person (face-to-face) or over the telephone. They may be structured, unstructured, or in-depth. Other means of collecting data include observation, archival, and through unobtrusive means.

METHODOLOGICAL QUERIES

Previously, you were asked to decide what type of research design you would use to study the following topics. Now, what form of data collection would you employ? Why?

1. Gang activity in prisons
2. Sentencing patterns of a particular court
3. The effect of a treatment program for drug users
4. Perceived job stress of police officers
5. Caseload of parole officers
6. The effect of a community-policing program on crime
7. Recidivism and first-time DUI offenders
8. Race and sentencing of drug offenders

REFERENCES

Adler, E. S., & Clark, R. (2003). *How it's done: An invitation to social research* (2nd ed.) Belmont, CA: Thomson/Wadsworth.

Babbie, E. (2004). *The practice of social research* (10th ed.). Belmont, CA: Thomson/Wadsworth.

Bjerregaard, B., & Lord, V. B. (2004). An examination of the ethical and value orientation of criminal justice students. *Police Quarterly, 7*(2), 262–284.

Colomb, W., & Damphouse, K. (2004). Examination of newspaper coverage of hate crimes: A moral panic perspective. *American Journal of Criminal Justice, 28*(2), 149–163.

Cooper, V. G., McLearen, A. M., & Zapf, P. A. (2004). Dispositional decisions with the mentally ill: Police perceptions and characteristics. *Police Quarterly, 7*(3), 295–310.

Creswell, J. W. (2002). *Research design: Qualitative, quantitative, and mixed methods approaches* (2nd ed.) Thousand Oaks, CA: Sage.

Dabney, D. A., Hollinger, R. C. & Dugan, L. (2004). Who actually steals? A study of covertly observed shoplifters. *Justice Quarterly, 21*(4), 693–728.

Dantzker, M. L. (1994). Requirements for the position of municipal police chief: A content analysis. *Police Studies, 17*(3), 33–42.

Dantzker, M. L. (2001). *Survey research via e-mail: Results from a study on perceptions of a university police department.* Paper presented at the annual conference of the Southwestern Criminal Justice Association, October, in San Antonio, Texas.

Dantzker, M. L., & Waters. J. E. (1999). Examining students' perceptions of policing—A pre- and post-comparison between students in criminal justice and noncriminal justice courses. In M. L. Dantzker (Ed.), *Readings for research methods in criminology and criminal justice* (pp. 27–36). Woburn, MA: Butterworth-Heinemann.

Chapter Resources

Fitzgerald, J. D., & Cox, S. M. (2001). *Research methods and statistics in criminal justice: An introduction* (3rd ed.). Chicago: Nelson-Hall.

Flanyak, C. M. (1999). Accessing data: Procedures, practices, and problems of academic researchers. In M. L. Dantzker (Ed.), *Readings for research methods in criminology and criminal justice* (pp. 157–180). Woburn, MA: Butterworth-Heinemann.

Ford, M., & Williams, L. (1999). Human/cultural diversity training for justice personnel. In M. L. Dantzker (Ed.), *Readings for research methods in criminology and criminal justice* (pp. 37–60). Woburn, MA: Butterworth-Heinemann.

Furlong, D. K. (1997). Between anecdote and science: Using e-mail to learn about student experiences. Paper presented at the 37th annual forum of the Association for Institutional Research, May 18–21, in Orlando, Florida.

Gaardner, E., Rodrigues, N., & Zatz, M. S. (2004). Criers, liars, and manipulators: Probation officers' views of girls. *Justice Quarterly, 21*(3), 547–578.

Glicken, M. D. (2003). *Social research: A simple guide*. Boston: Allyn and Bacon.

Gordon, J. (1999). Correctional officers' attitudes toward delinquents and delinquency: Does the type of institution make a difference? In M. L. Dantzker (Ed.), *Readings for research methods in criminology and criminal justice* (pp. 85–98). Woburn, MA: Butterworth-Heinemann.

Hass, S. M., & Senjo, S. R. (2004). Perceptions of effectiveness and the actual use of technology-based methods of instruction: A study of California criminal justice and crime-related faculty. *Journal of Criminal Justice Education, 15*(2), 263–285.

Heflich, D. A., & Rice, M. L. (1999). Online survey research: A venue for reflective conversation and professional development. Paper presented at the 10th annual conference of the Society for Information Technology & Teacher Education, February 28–March 4, in San Antonio, Texas.

Holcomb, J. E., Williams, M. R., & Demuth, S. (2004). White female victims and death penalty disparity research. *Justice Quarterly, 21*(4), 877–902.

Hunter, R. D. (1988). *The effects of environmental factors upon convenience store robbery in Florida*. Tallahassee: Florida Department of Legal Affairs.

Kingsnorth, R. F., & Macintosh, R. C. (2004). Domestic violence: Predictors of victim support for official action. *Justice Quarterly, 21*(2), 301–328.

Leedy, P. D., & Ormond, J. E. (2005). *Practical research: Planning and design* (8th ed.). Upper Saddle River, NJ: Pearson/Merrill Prentice Hall.

Liddick, D. R., Jr. (1999). Women as organized criminals: An examination of the numbers gambling industry in New York City. In M. L. Dantzker (Ed.), *Readings for research methods in criminology and criminal justice* (pp. 123–138). Woburn, MA: Butterworth-Heinemann.

Mavis, B. E., & Brocato, J. J. (1998). Postal surveys versus electronic mail surveys. *Evaluation & the Health Professions, 21*(3), 395–409.

Meehan, M. L., & Burns, R. C. (1997). E-mail survey of a listserv discussion group: Lessons learned from surveying an electronic network of learners. Paper presented at the annual meeting of the American Educational Research Association, March 24–28, in Chicago.

Memory, J. M. (1999). Some impressions from a qualitative study of implementation of community policing in North Carolina. In M. L. Dantzker (Ed.),

Readings for research methods in criminology and criminal justice (pp. 1–14). Woburn, MA: Butterworth-Heinemann.

Metraux, S., & Culhane, D. P. (2004). Homeless shelter use and reincarceration following prison release. *Criminology & Public Policy, 3*(2), 139–160.

Moriarty, L. J., Pelfrey, W. V., & Vasu, M. L. (1999). Measuring violent crime in North Carolina. In M. L. Dantzker (Ed.), *Readings for research methods in criminology and criminal justice* (pp. 75–84). Woburn, MA: Butterworth-Heinemann.

Mueller, D., Giacomazzi, A., & Wada, J. (2004). So how was your conference? Panel chairs' perceptions of the 2003 ACJS meeting in Boston. *Journal of Criminal Justice Education, 15*(2), 201–218.

Paolo, A. M., Bonaminio, G. A., Gibson, C., Partridge, T., & Kallail, K. (2000). Response rate comparisons of e-mail and mail-distributed student evaluations. *Teaching & Learning in Medicine, 12*(2), 81–85.

Schaefer, D. R., & Dillman, D. A. (1998). Development of a standard e-mail methodology. *Public Opinion Quarterly, 62*(3), 378–399.

Senese, J. D. (1997). *Applied research methods in criminal justice.* Chicago: Nelson-Hall.

Sheehan, K. B. (1999). Response variation in e-mail surveys: An exploration. *Journal of Advertising Research, 39*(4), 45–56.

Son, I. S., & Rome, D. M. (2004). The prevalence and visibility of police misconduct: A survey of citizens and police officers. *Police Quarterly, 7*(2), 179–204.

Stevens, D. J. (1999). Women offenders, drug addiction, and crime. In M. L. Dantzker (Ed.), *Readings for research methods in criminology and criminal justice* (pp. 61–74). Woburn, MA: Butterworth-Heinemann.

Talarico, S. M. (1980). *Criminal justice research: Approaches, problems, and policy.* Cincinnati, OH: Anderson.

Underwood, D., Kim, H., & Matier, M. (2000). To mail or to Web: Comparisons of survey response rates and respondent characteristics. Paper presented at the 40th annual forum of the Association of Institutional Research, May 21–24, in Cincinnati, Ohio.

Vaughn, M. S., Del Carmen, R. V., Perfecto, M., & Charand, K. X. (2004). Journals in criminal justice and criminology: An updated and expanded guide for authors. *Journal of Criminal Justice Education, 15*(1), 61–192.

Ventura, L. A., Lambertt, E. G., Bryant, M., & Pasupuleti, S. (2004). Differences in attitudes toward gays and lesbians among criminal justice and non-criminal justice majors. *American Journal of Criminal Justice, 28*(2), 165–179.

Warchol, G. L., & Johnson, B. R. (1999). A cross-sectional quantitative analysis of federal asset forfeiture. In M. L. Dantzker (Ed.), *Readings for research methods in criminology and criminal justice* (pp. 139–156). Woburn, MA: Butterworth-Heinemann.

Zhang, Y. (2000). Using the Internet for survey research: A case study. *Journal of the American Society for Information Science, 51*(1), pp. 57–68,

Final Steps

Data Processing and Analysis

Vignette 11-1   Now What Do I Do with All This Data?

Having just gotten out of your 11:00 A.M. class and needing to be at work by 1:00 P.M., you realize that you had better grab some lunch here at the university. So you head into the student union, where you run into some friends and all decide to have lunch together. There is one person there whom you do not know other than by sight, since he is a year behind you in the program. You are introduced, and he immediately begins to question you about the research-methods class. He is currently in the statistics class and is debating taking the methods course next semester. You suggest that he do just that because you made the mistake of waiting a year after taking statistics, a prerequisite, to take the methods course. Now you are getting close to having to start analyzing data, and you can barely recall what you learned in statistics. He suggests reviewing your statistics book, but you, in your infinite wisdom (or just the need for quick cash), sold the book back. He asks whether your methods text discusses statistics, because he recalls his statistics teacher's complaining about the lack of pure-statistics books for criminal justice and criminology. He added that until recently, the teacher had to use a combined methods/statistics text. Although you do not have your book with you, you recall that there was something about statistics in the text. You make yourself a mental note to check your syllabus and your text on the off chance that something on statistics is in it. You also wonder if your text has material in it on what you are supposed to do once the data are analyzed and it is time to write up the research project.

Chapter Objectives

After studying this chapter, the student should be able to:

- Identify and discuss the three stages of data processing.
- Describe what occurs during the data-coding process.
- Describe the data-cleaning process.
- Compare and contrast the different means of dealing with missing data.
- Explain why data may need to be recoded, and provide an example of how recoding may be done.
- Identify and describe the three types of data analysis.
- Recognize and explain the three types of statistical analysis.
- Present and discuss the four types of frequency distributions.
- Describe the various means of presenting data in addition to frequency tables.
- Identify and discuss the three measures of central tendency.
- Present and discuss the three measures of variability.
- Discuss what is meant by the terms skewness and kurtosis.

Data Processing and Analysis

To this point, you have been indoctrinated with a wealth of information on how to go about conducting research. The time has finally come to address what to do with those data once they are collected: processing and analysis.

Be aware that this chapter is not intended to teach you how to do statistical analyses; that is for another book and a different class. Instead, what this chapter provides is a general overview of the issues involved in processing and analyzing data, as well as an introduction to the terminology needed to communicate with whoever might be analyzing the data for you.

Data Processing

Will the results support the hypothesis or hypotheses? Has something new been discovered? Are these findings consistent with previous research? These are examples of questions one hopes to answer through the data analyses. Thus, the data have been collected and are ready to be analyzed—now what? The first task is to prepare the data for analysis, what is generally referred to as *data processing*. Data processing consists of data coding, data entry, and data cleaning.

Data Coding

Coding is simply assigning values to the data for statistical analyses. Not all data need to be coded. Quantitative data that are already in a numerical format can be left as is—such as age, or numerical responses to scales. Nonnumerical variables—such as gender, marital status, or race—however, need to be coded. How these are coded is up to the researcher, but it is common to use a standard numbering format.

It is usually easier for the researcher if the coding scheme is developed in advance. Precoding is when the coding scheme has been incorporated into the questionnaire or observational-checklist design. Such a design may enable the researcher to input data directly from the survey form rather than having to translate it to a code sheet. If the survey form has provided for edge coding, it is very easy to input data directly into the computer. (Refer back to **Figure 10-1**, the field research-checklist. Note how the form allows for edge coding, and how the data are run to have consistent responses—that is, they run in a logical format based upon knowledge of the subject so that during statistical analysis, positive and negative influences will be consistent in their directionality.)

During the coding process, qualitative data may also be converted into quantitative data. For example, an open-ended question about prior arrests may later be converted into numerical groupings based upon the number of arrests, type of offense, seriousness of the charges, conviction versus acquittal, or other logical groupings created by the researcher. Remember our earlier warning about false precision when doing such a conversion. Be certain that there is an explainable logic to your numerical assignments.

Ultimately, it is the researcher's decision to code the data in a manner that will be best for analyses. While part of this depends upon the computer statistics package you use, the coding should be clear. To ensure clarity, you should create codebooks or coding keys to show others (and remind yourself) exactly where the variables and attributes are located. The coding scheme for a survey document is often a one-page document referred to as the *codebook*. Recall in the previous chapter the study for the university police department regarding community perception. Its codebook showing the variables created and how they were coded is displayed in **Figure 11-1**.

Data Entry

Once the data are coded, they can then be entered into a computer-software program for analyses. **Figure 11-2** offers an example of coded data after they have been entered into a statistical program for analysis.

Coded-Data Example, Computer Entries

At various points in the text, it has been suggested that a computer can assist in conducting differing aspects of the research process. The same is true for the analysis portion. Today, there are a number of statistical-software packages available to researchers, such as *Excel*, *Quattro Pro*, *Statistical Package for the Social Sciences (SPSS)*, and *Statistical Analysis System (SAS)*. Each has its own quirks and specialties that require individuals to choose what best suits their needs and abilities.

Regardless of which software is chosen, each program allows for the entry, analyses, and storage of data. We recommend SPSS, which is now available for personal computers after years of having been accessible only through mainframes. We find that SPSS provides us with the ability to conduct almost every

LEGEND:

STRONGLY AGREE	AGREE	NO OPINION	DISAGREE	STRONGLY DISAGREE
5	4	3	2	1

The actual number circled---

(1) University Police Officers act **profess**ionally   5   4   3   2   1
(2) University Police Officers are **sensitive** to your needs
(3) I feel **safe** on campus
(4) University Police Officers treat people **fairly**
(5) University Police Officers are highly **visible**
(6) It is easy to contact the University Police (**easycont**)

(7) Have you ever had any personal contact with a University Police Officer? (**perscont**)   Yes=1 No=2

(8) If "YES" what type of contact was it? (place an x by all that apply)   None=0 Yes=1

_____   Request for **assist**ance
_____   **Witness** to a crime
_____   **Victim** of a crime
_____   Received a **ticket** for a moving violation
_____   Was **arrested**
_____   Vehicle problems (**vehprob**)
_____   Other (write in) _____

PERSONAL INFORMATION:

What is your **gender**?	Female 1	Male 2	
What is your **age** group?	Under 22	1	
	23–28	2	
	29–34	3	
	35–40	4	
	41–46	5	
	47–52	6	
	Over 52	7	
Status:	Faculty (Full-time)	1	
	Faculty (Part-time)	2	
	Staff (Full)	3	
	Staff (Part)	4	
	Student	5	

When are you most often on **campus**: Day   1   Night   2   Equally day and night   3

IF a student:

What is your Classification?	(**stuclass**)	Freshman	1
		Sophomore	2
		Junior	3
		Senior	4
		Graduate	5
What is your major?	(**stumajor**)	type in first 8 letters of major	

Figure 11-1 Data Codebook.

type of statistical technique we might require. It seems to be a common tool for many criminal-justice and criminological researchers. Before choosing any of the packages, the researcher should test several to see which is most comfortable to him or her. Once the choice has been made, it is simply a matter of learning how to use the software and being able to interpret the results. Most statistical packages not only have handbooks, but excellent tutorials as well.

001	97	23	17	1	1	1	2	0	2	2
002	88	26	14	1	1	2	2	0	2	2
003	94	25	12	2	1	2	1	3.7	2	2
004	87	27	14	1	1	2	1	4	2	2
005	87	27	12	2	1	2	1	5	2	2
006	93	30	16	2	1	2	1	4	2	2
007	94	23	13	2	1	1	2	0	2	2
008	94	22	14	2	1	2	2	0	2	2
009	99	32	13	2	2	2	2	0	2	2
010	98	22	12	2	1	1	2	0	2	2
011	98	40	18	1	1	2	1	4	2	2
012	98	21	15	1	1	1	2	0	2	2
013	97	23	12	1	1	1	2	0	2	2
014	97	26	14	1	1	2	2	0	2	2
015	94	24	15	1	1	2	2	0	2	2
016	94	21	12	1	1	1	1	1 mo	2	2
017	97	30	12	1	1	1	2	0	2	2
018	99	27	16	1	1	1	2	0	2	2
019	98	23	14	1	1	1	1	3	2	2
020	98	31	12	1	1	2	1	5	2	2
021	98	31	14	1	1	2	2	0	2	2
022	99	26	16	1	2	2	2	0	1	2
023	96	22	15	1	1	1	2	0	2	2
024	96	24	12	2	1	1	2	0	2	2
025	96	30	14	1	1	2	1	5	2	2
026	96	25	15	2	1	1	1	4	2	2
027	97	24	14	1	1	1	2	0	1	2
028	96	27	12	2	1	1	2	0	2	2
029	97	21	13	2	2	1	2	0	2	2

Figure 11-2 Coded Data Example, Computer Entries.

The key to data entry is accuracy. If possible, have a reliable person read the data to you as you enter the information into the computer so that you do not have to continuously switch your viewing from the code sheet to the computer screen. This will help prevent mistakes. However, you should still review what you have inputted to make certain that it is accurate.

Of course, the above assumes that you are entering the data yourself. With modern technology, this may not be the case. You may have obtained the information from existing sources, in which case it probably was provided on a computer disk. If the data are compatible with your statistical package, a great deal of time will be saved. If you conducted a telephone survey, you may have been able to enter the data directly into the computer as you asked the questions. Another shortcut is to use optical-scan sheets such as the Scantron sheets that you have used in taking multiple-choice exams. This permits the data to be entered directly from the sheets marked by the respondents. Regardless of which technique is utilized, the data will need to be cleaned.

Data Cleaning

Data cleaning is the preliminary analysis of your data (Babbie, 2004; Bachman & Peternoster, 2004; Fitzgerald & Cox, 2001). Here, you "clean" any mistakes that might have occurred during the initial recording of data or during data entry. As mentioned above, the first step is reviewing what you have entered for accuracy.

If you have a computer program that is programmed to check for errors, it will either beep at you or refuse to accept data that do not meet the coding requirements for that variable. This is automatic data cleaning. For example, assume that you have used a Likert scale where 1 = Strongly Agree, 2 = Agree, 3 = Neither Agree or Disagree, 4 = Disagree, and 5 = Strongly Disagree. You try to enter a 6 as a value, and the program beeps to alert you to the error.

Unfortunately, not all data-analysis programs have this automatic function. Therefore, cleaning must be done semimanually (for example, using SPSS)—that is, a frequency analysis is run on all the data. From the results, any incorrectly inputted value should be observable.

Another type of data cleaning is contingency cleaning. In this technique, your review of the data is expedited by the knowledge that certain responses should have been made only by certain individuals. Not all females would indicate having given birth to a child. But no males should have indicated such.

As you are reviewing the data, there will be certain questions that will logically lead to similar responses on following questions. If they do not, you need to review that particular questionnaire or form to check the accuracy of what was entered. The next step is determining what to do with missing data.

Missing Data

If you have collected a great deal of data, you will find that, despite your best efforts, you have "lost" some information. This may be due to an oversight in data entry (which can usually be easily corrected), or it may be because the respondents or recorders accidentally overlooked or deliberately chose not to answer a particular question. If missing data are the product of a data-entry error, this mistake may easily be corrected by obtaining the right information from the survey form or code sheet. If the mistake is due to oversight or intentional omission, there are a number of ways to deal with this missing information.

If the data have been left out on a single question, you may chose to input this information as a nonresponse. If you are not using 0 as a response, you may assign 0 as a value. Researchers frequently use 99 (assuming they are not using continuous variables in which 99 could be a response) to indicate missing data. This is, in our opinion, the preferred method of dealing with nonresponses.

Another option for dealing with nonresponses is to assume that the missing data are due to an oversight rather than an intentional omission. In this situation, you might look at the other responses to try to determine what the missing responses would most likely have been. For example, if, on related questions, a respondent had indicated support for strict law enforcement, you might assume a similar answer on the unanswered question. We include this solution because some researchers use it, but we do not recommend this solution because it can lead to challenges about the objectivity and validity of your analysis.

Yet another option is to exclude from your analysis the survey instrument containing the omission. If there are several nonresponses, that option may be appropriate. However, if only one or two questions in a survey are not answered, this solution can lead to the loss of worthwhile information.

If the instrument used is a Likert scale, the solution is simple. Classify the response as a "neither agree nor disagree" or "don't know" (depending upon how your scale is worded). This solution allows the data to be used without the fear of skewing the results.

Recoding Data

Although some data may be received in a numerical format (for example, age), sometimes, for purposes of analysis, these data are recoded to fit into groups. If you have gathered data such as income or age, you may find that you wish to use a simpler method of analysis such as cross-tabulations to examine their relationships. If you run a frequencies table (discussed later in this chapter), you would note that these categories are quite extensive. A comparison of age by income could result in a table that is lengthy and confusing. Assuming that age was presented in rows, and income in columns, if the people surveyed ranged from 20 years of age up to 70 years of age, and if their incomes ranged from $10,000 to $100,000, the resulting table would be enormous. Because each individual year of age would have to be represented, there would be 51 rows in our hypothetical table. Since there would likely be as many different incomes as there were respondents, we could end up with thousands of columns. Yet, by collapsing the categories into logical groupings, the data can be presented clearly and concisely (see **Table 11-1**). The resulting table could easily be collapsed even further if necessary. In collapsing data, please recall our earlier discussions of the different levels of measurement. Higher-level data (such as ratio or interval data) can

Table 11-1 Hypothetical Age by Income Comparison						
(Ordinal Data) **Age**	**20–29**	**30–39**	**40–49**	**50–59**	**60–69**	**70+**
Income						
$10,000 to $19,000	50	30	20	10	5	15
$20,000 to $29,000	100	80	50	30	50	80
$30,000 to $39,000	80	100	80	60	80	60
$40,000 to $49,000	50	100	160	120	100	80
$50,000 to $59,000	30	80	120	150	120	50
$60,000 to $69,000	20	50	100	120	100	40
$70,000 to $79,000	10	40	80	100	80	30
$80,000 to $89,000	5	30	60	80	60	20
$90,000 to $99,000	5	20	40	60	40	10
$100,000+	0	10	30	50	30	10

be collapsed down into lower-level data (such as ordinal or nominal data), but you cannot do the opposite and convert lower-level data to a higher-level.

■ Data Analysis

Now that we have entered our data, we may begin to analyze them. There are three types of data analysis: univariate, bivariate, and multivariate analysis. With univariate analysis, an examination of the case distribution is conducted one variable at a time (Babbie, 2004). The process by which this examination takes place is referred to as *descriptive statistics*. Descriptive statistics provide us with an understanding of the variable that we are investigating. Descriptive statistics will be discussed in detail later in this chapter.

Bivariate analysis occurs when the relationship between two variables is examined. This examination may be comparative or inferential, depending on the nature of the analysis. If we were exploring the relationship between the two variables, this would denote descriptive statistics, but since it also compares the two variables, the process becomes comparative statistics. Comparative statistics usually involve analysis of the attributes of the variables being examined in order to better describe the relationship between the two variables. If our hypothetical **Table 11-1** were real, it would be an example of comparative statistics. Comparative statistics will be discussed further in bivariate techniques in Chapter 12. An example will also be provided near the end of this chapter.

If one of the variables is identified as being dependent, and the other variable is identified as being independent, the analysis of their relationship becomes inferential. Inferential statistics simply mean that we are trying to not only describe the relationship, but also to use that knowledge to make predictions or inferences about the dependent variable based on the influence of the independent variable. You can see that bivariate analysis may be descriptive, comparative, or inferential in nature.

The final type of statistical analysis is multivariate analysis. Multivariate analysis is the examination of three or more variables. This technique is inferential in nature in that we have usually already conducted both descriptive and comparative statistical analyses (through univariate and bivariate analyses) of the data, and are now seeking to examine the relationships among several variables. From this examination, we try to develop explanations for the observed relationships. Inferential statistics will be covered in detail in Chapter 12.

Statistical Analysis

Statistics are data presented in a manner that best represents what it is the researcher wants to present. Statistical analyses might best be viewed as processes for solving problems (Bachman & Peternoster, 2004; Lurigio, Dantzker, Seng, & Sinacore, 1997; Vito & Blankenship, 2002). Statistics are used in criminal justice and criminology to help describe a variety of associated aspects such as crime rates, number of police officers, or prison populations. In addition, statistics can be used to make inferences about a phenomenon. As discussed in the preceding section, there are three types of statistics:

1. Descriptive, whose function is describing the data.

2. Comparative, whose function is to compare the attributes (or subgroups) of two variables.[1]

3. Inferential, whose function is to make an inference, estimation, or prediction about the data.

The remainder of this chapter focuses on providing an overview of the processes and terminology of descriptive statistics. We will not try to turn you into a statistician, but you should understand the basic principles so that you can comprehend the work of others and communicate with those who might be aiding you with statistical analysis of your own work.

■ Descriptive Statistics

When the researcher is interested in knowing selected characteristics about the sample, it requires some form of descriptive statistics. One of the most common descriptive statistics is the use of frequencies.

When data are first collected, they are referred to as raw data; that is, they are not neatly organized. A first step to organizing the data, after coding and entry, is through a frequency distribution, which simply indicates the number of times a particular score or characteristic occurs in the sample. This can be reported in whole numbers or in percentages. Frequencies are commonly used to describe sample characteristics.

Frequency Distributions

There are four types of frequency distributions: absolute, relative, cumulative, and cumulative relative (Bachman & Peternoster, 2004; Lurigio, Dantzker, Seng, & Sinacore, 1997; Vito & Blankenship, 2002). Each offers a statistically sound indication of the sample's composition. None is recommended over the others. Instead, we suggest that you select the one that appears to be the most desirable for reporting the data contained in your research.

Absolute frequency distributions simply display the data based on the numbers assigned. *Relative* frequency distributions are the percentage equivalent of absolute frequency distributions. When dealing with large numbers, it is usually much easier for the reader to interpret percentages than raw numbers. *Cumulative* frequency distributions enable the reader to see what the products of the grouping are in the frequencies table by adding the absolute frequency of each previous variable. *Cumulative relative* frequency distributions do the same as cumulative frequency distributions, but add relative frequencies rather than numbers. **Table 11-2** demonstrates how the four types of frequencies are related.

---

[1]We have categorized comparative statistics as a separate category, as do Lurigio, Dantzker, Seng, & Sinacore (1997). Most methods texts include comparative in their discussion of descriptive statistics. Comparative statistics exist in a gray area between descriptive and inferential statistics. We do not really care how you classify them as long as you understand what is involved.

Table 11-2	**Absolute, Relative, Cumulative, and Cumulative Relative Frequency Distributions of Crime Types from 20 Hypothetical Offense Reports**			
Type of Crime	**Absolute Frequency**	**Relative Frequency (%)**	**Cumulative Frequency**	**Cumulative Relative Frequency (%)**
Theft	6	30	6	30
Robbery	3	15	9	45
Auto Theft	4	20	13	65
Burglary	5	25	18	90
Assault	2	10	20	100
	$n = 20$	100		

Source: Lurigio, et al., (1997).

Displaying Frequencies

Frequencies, by whole numbers and/or percentages, in table form are just one means of describing data. Other means include pie charts, bar graphs, histograms and polygons, line charts, and maps. As demonstrated in **Figure 11-3** (a pie chart), the frequency percentages can be pictorially depicted simply. Such a display is clear and easily understood. Bar charts are also easily interpreted. They are used to display nominal- and ordinal-level data. **Figure 11-4** demonstrates a bar chart. Histograms are bar graphs that are used to display interval and ratio data. They indicate the continuous nature of the variable by drawing the lines adjacent to each other. **Figure 11-5** displays a histogram. Polygons display the same data as histograms, but use dots instead of bars. Lines are then drawn between the dots to reveal the shape of the distribution. **Figure 11-6** is an example of a frequency polygon.

In addition to the above frequency-presentation techniques, criminological researchers may also use line charts and maps. Line charts are polygons that demonstrate scores across time. As such, they are useful to reflect changes over time in the same dot-and-line format as frequency polygons. **Figure 11-7** demonstrates a line graph.

In addition to the tables, graphs, and charts discussed above, there are four other ways to describe the properties of the data: measures of central tendency, measures of variability, skewness, and kurtosis.

Measures of Central Tendency

Because frequencies can be quite cumbersome, researchers sometimes require a way to summarize the data in a simpler manner. Measures of central tendency are one way to summarize data. The three most common measures are the *mean*, *median*, and *mode*. The mean is the arithmetic average. The median is the midpoint, or the number that falls in the middle. The mode is the number that occurs most frequently. The mean is usually used as a measure of central tendency

METHODOLOGICAL

 **LINKS**

Several of the studies cited throughout this text make use of frequencies to either fully describe the samples or to describe a particular characteristic. The following descriptive data come from the analysis of the "Study on Perceptions of a University Police Department" survey (Dantzker, 2001).

Variable Sample, $n = 1296$	Strongly Agree	Agree	No Opinion	Disagree	Strongly Disagree
Professional	242 (18.9%)	562 (43.4%)	358 (27.9%)	89 (6.9%)	32 (2.5%)
Sensitive	147 (11.3%)	419 (32.7%)	506 (39.5%)	123 (9.6%)	87 (6.8%)
Safe	305 (23.7%)	641 (49.8%)	200 (15.5%)	96 (7.5%)	46 (3.6%)
Fairly	156 (12.2%)	465 (36.2%)	498 (38.8%)	90 (7.0%)	74 (5.8%)
Visible	214 (16.7%)	507 (39.5%)	218 (17.0%)	255 (19.9%)	90 (7.0%)
Easy	226 (17.6%)	500 (39.0%)	376 (29.3%)	113 (8.8%)	67 (5.2%)

(1) 62.3% of the sample agree or strongly agree that University Police Officers act professionally.   (Professional)

(2) 44.0% of the sample agree or strongly agree that University Police Officers are sensitive to individuals' need.   (Sensitive)

(3) 73.5% of the sample agree or strongly agree to feeling safe on campus.   (Safe)

(4) 48.4% of the sample agree or strongly agree that University Police Officers treat people fairly.   (Fairly)

(5) 56.2% of the sample agree or strongly agree that University Police Officers are highly visible.   (Visible)

(6) 56.6% of the sample agree or strongly agree that it is easy to contact the University Police.   (Easy)

(7) 52.8% (680) noted having had personal contact with a University Police Officer.
　　344 (26.5%) requested assistance
　　 20 (1.5%) were a witness to a crime
　　 37 (2.9%) claimed to have been a victim of a crime
　　154 (11.9%) received a ticket for a moving violation
　　 1 (.1%) was arrested
　　210 (16.2%) had vehicle problems
　　197 (15.2%) identified some other reason for the contact

Gender	Female 788 (61.2%) Male 500 (38.8%)
Age	Under 22 611 (47.5%) 23–28 324 (25.2%) 29–34 120 (9.3%) 35–40 76 (5.9%) 41–46 52 (4.0%) Over 46 102 (8.0%)
Status	Faculty 142 (11.3%) Staff 179 (14.2%) Student 934 (74.4%)
On campus	Day 881 (70.4%) Night 140 (11.2%) About equally day and night 230 (18.4)
Student Class	Freshmen 176 (13.6%) Soph 298 (29.4%) Junior 247 (24.4%) Senior 14 (14.5%) Graduate 144 (14.2%)

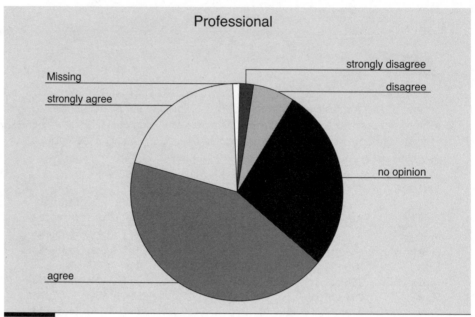

Figure 11-3 Pie Chart.

for interval- or ratio-level data. The median is used mostly for ordinal-level data. The mode is generally used for nominal-level data. **Figure 11-8** shows how the three measures are obtained.

Using a measure of central tendency allows the researcher to simplify the numbers in a summary manner. Despite the more simplistic nature of these measures, researchers should be familiar with their characteristics before using

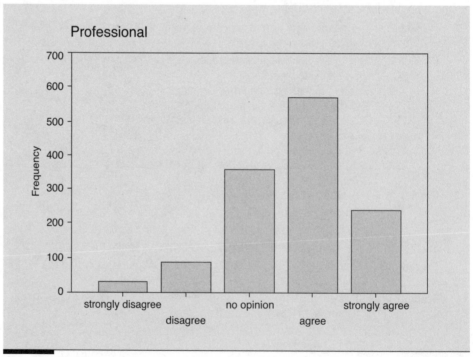

Figure 11-4 Bar Chart.

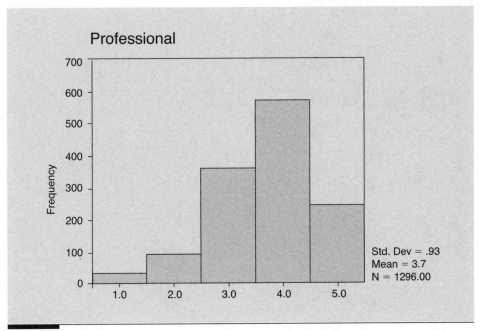

Figure 11-5 Histogram.

them. In addition, these measures are often used in conjunction with measures of variability.

Measures of Variability

Despite their similarities, all statistics are not the same. The difference that occurs among statistics is called variability. The three main measures are range,

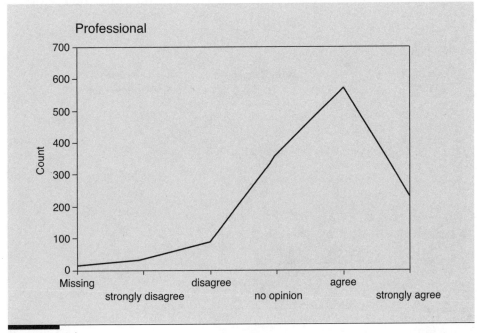

Figure 11-6 Polygon.

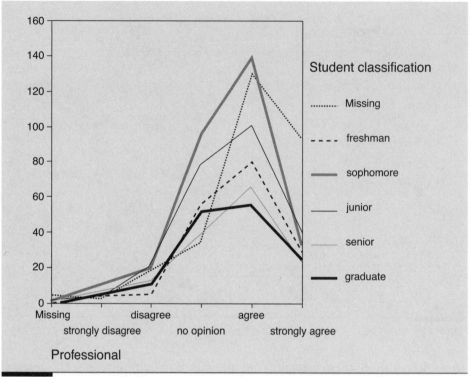

Figure 11-7 Line Graph.

variance, and standard deviation. The range is simply the difference between the highest and lowest scores. Variance is the difference between the scores and the mean. Standard deviation indicates how far from the mean the score actually is. To compute measures of dispersion, such as standard deviation, statisticians use z-scores. In this text, we will go no further into the use of this

---

Sample data $n = 100$

Years of College Completed	Number of Responses	Responses x Years of College
1	10	10
2	20	40
3	30	90
4	20	80
5	10	50
6	8	48
7	2	14
	100	332

Mean = average = 332/100 = 3.32 years of college
Mode = most frequent (30 responses) = 3 years of college
Median = midpoint = (30 responses are below 3 years, 40 responses above 3 years, 30 responses are within the 3 years grouping. The midpoint would be between the 20th and 21st respondents in the 3-year group.) = 3 years of college.

Figure 11-8 Measures of Central Tendency.

METHODOLOGICAL

LINKS

As with frequencies, several of the studies cited made use of both measures of central tendency and variability to help describe the data. **Tables 11-3** and **11-4** are examples.

methodology. If you need to calculate dispersion (variability) in your research, we recommend that you either take a course in statistics or consult with a statistician.

Skewness

In our discussion thus far, we have alluded to the distribution of the data and have depicted it somewhat in the figures that were displayed. Many of the statistical techniques that we discussed in this chapter (and which will influence our discussions of inferential statistics in Chapter 12) are based on the assumption of a normal distribution. A normal distribution may also be referred to as a normal, or bell, curve. By using polygons or line charts (discussed earlier) or scatterplots (which will be discussed in Chapter 12), researchers are able to see the distribution of their data. If it is a normal distribution, the researcher is able to use a broader range of statistical techniques. If it is a nonnormal (also known as nonparametric) distribution, the statistical techniques that may be used are more limited.

Table 11-3	**Measures of Central Tendency: From Stevens**			
Criminal Activities of Sample (n=68)				
Criminal Activities	*%[a]*	*Frequency[b]*	*Age*	*Range*
Shoplifting	65	very often	14	10–25
Prostitution	16	sometimes	15	12–23
Assault	4	seldom	15	13–21
Armed Robbery	3	seldom	16	14–15
Property Crimes	3	sometimes	13	12–15
Other	6	seldom	12	12–14
Murder	3	once	25	23–27

Source: Stevens, 1999.

[a]Percentages rounded.

[b]In discussing coding, it was intimated that all data are reported in numerical fashion. Obviously, this example shows how data can be reported nonnumerically despite the numerical orientation to the variable.

Table 11-4	Combination of Descriptive Measures: From Gordon	
Demographic Characteristics		
Variable	**Open-Security**	**Closed-Security**
Age		
Mean	34.08	37.35
Standard Deviation	12.00	13.06
Gender		
Male	18 (69%)	87 (69%)
Female	8 (31%)	40 (31%)
Race		
White	20 (77%)	68 (53%)
Nonwhite	6 (23%)	56 (44%)
Education		
Less than High School	0 (0%)	1 (1%)
High-School Graduate	6 (23%)	19 (15%)
Some College	8 (31%)	49 (39%)
Bachelor Degree	12 (46%)	42 (33%)
Graduate Degree	0 (0%)	16 (12%)
Length at Current Position (in months)		
Mean	31.23	63.36
Standard Deviation	29.98	80.26

Source: Gordon, 1999.

The measures that we have discussed previously (central tendency and variability) may be noted in the location of the center of the curve (central tendency) and in the spread of the curve (variability). They may also differ based on the symmetry of the curve. If one side has more values so as to cause the slope of that side to tail farther outward, the distribution is said to be skewed to that side. Skewness alerts the researcher to the presence of outliers. Such knowledge aids the statistician in conducting analysis of the data.

Kurtosis

Kurtosis is another distribution consideration that warrants some discussion. Kurtosis refers to the amount of smoothness or pointedness of the curve. A high, thin curve is described as being leptokurtic. A low, flat curve is platykurtic. Frankly, you will have little need of this knowledge except to recognize the terms if a statistician states that your data distribution exhibits such features.

These statistics, in tandem with measures of central tendency and variability, provide useful ways to describe the data. In general, descriptive statistics are used primarily to describe how the data are composed. However, describing the information is usually just a small portion of what we truly want to do with the data, which is to make inferences from them.

Comparative Statistics

As we mentioned earlier, descriptive statistics usually consist of univariate statistics that describe the data. Inferential statistics consist of ether bivariate or multivariate analyses of the relationships among variables. Between the two lie comparative statistics. Comparative statistics are often classified as being part of descriptive statistics because they tend to provide more insight about the nature of the variables than about their relationships with other variables. However, comparison of variable attributes, as indicated in **Table 11-4**, moves beyond simple description and begins the inferential process. Depiction of crime rates over time, noting the percentage of change in criminal activity, and trend analyses are all examples of comparative statistics. Depending upon the text that is utilized, such activities may be categorized as either descriptive or inferential statistics. In this text, we have chosen to discuss comparison as being within both.

Summary

Once the data collection has been accomplished, the next two phases in completing the research are data processing and data analysis. Since the data are often obtained in a raw manner, they must be coded for entry into a statistical-software program. Once the data have been entered, they must be cleaned to ensure accuracy and appropriateness for subsequent statistical analysis. At this point, missing data are dealt with, and recoding may also be required.

Univariate analysis is conducted to gain knowledge about the data prior to any bivariate and multivariate analyses. Descriptive statistics are then utilized. Description may involve the use of frequency-distribution tables, as well as charts and graphs. The researcher will also examine the data by using measures of central tendency and measures of variability. The data may be further assessed by reviewing the shape of the data distribution.

While the data are being examined, the analysis may progress from description to comparison of variables. This process links description to inferential statistics, which are discussed in the following chapter.

Chapter Resources

METHODOLOGICAL QUERIES

Based on the idea of the College Students' Criminality Survey:

1. What type of data will be required? Descriptive or inferential? Explain.
2. How will you report it? Describe the formats you might use to show the results.
3. One variable collected is raw age. Describe the differing ways you could report this variable.
4. What data will you simply describe? What data will you compare?

REFERENCES

Babbie, E. 2004. *The Practice of Social Research,* 10th ed. Belmont, CA: Thomson/Wadsworth.

Bachman, R., and R. Peternoster. 2004. *Statistics for Criminology and Criminal Justice,* 2d ed. Boston: McGraw-Hill.

Dantzker, M. L. 2001. "Survey Research via E-mail: Results from a Study on Perceptions of a University Police Department." Paper presented at the annual conference of the Southwestern Criminal Justice Association, October, in San Antonio, Texas.

Fitzgerald, J. D., and S. M. Cox. 2001. *Research Methods and Statistics in Criminal Justice: An Introduction,* 3d ed. Chicago: Nelson-Hall.

Gordon, J. (1999). Correctional officers' attitudes toward delinquents and delinquency: Does the type of institution make a difference? In M.L. Dantzker (Ed.), *Readings for Research Methods in Criminology and Criminal Justice,* pp. 85–98. Woburn, MA: Butterworth-Heinemann.

Lurigio, A., M. L. Dantzker, M. Seng, and J. Sinacore. 1997. *Criminal Justice Statistics: A Practical Approach.* Woburn, MA: Butterworth-Heinemann.

Stevens, D. J. 1999. "Women Offenders, Drug Addiction, and Crime." In M. L. Dantzker, ed., *Readings for Research Methods in Criminology and Criminal Justice,* pp. 61–74. Woburn, MA: Butterworth-Heinemann.

Vito, G. F., and M. B. Blankenship. 2002. *Statistical Analysis in Criminal Justice and Criminology.* Upper Saddle River, NJ: Prentice Hall.

Inferential Statistics

Vignette 12-1 Numerically Explaining Relationships

Consider that the College Students' Criminality Survey has been conducted. Let us assume we want to infer how much unreported or unfounded crime is actually happening on campus, and who is most likely to commit what types of offenses. The descriptive data might tell us that among the sample, there were 57 thefts, 14 burglaries, 2 sexual assaults, and a variety of drug- and alcohol-related offenses. Essentially, these numbers are telling us how much crime there was; however, they do not allow us to infer who is more likely to commit these crimes. The task of inferential statistics is to allow us to explain relationships and to predict future events based on that knowledge. A reminder: the type of inferential statistic used depends on the level of measurement used to gather the data.

Chapter Objectives

After studying this chapter, the student should be able to:

- Differentiate between descriptive, comparative, and inferential statistics.
- Discuss measures of association and provide examples.
- Explain what is meant by statistical significance and describe how tests of significance are used.
- Present and describe the commonly used comparative-statistics techniques.
- Discuss bivariate analysis and provide examples.
- Discuss multivariate statistics and provide an example of a multivariate technique for nominal- and ordinal-level data.
- Describe the various multivariate techniques for interval-level data.
- Explain what are meant by nonparametric techniques.

◼ Statistical Analysis

In the previous chapter, we discussed the three types of statistics. Descriptive statistics describe the data being analyzed. A variety of descriptive statistics were presented in Chapter 11. Comparative statistics, whose function is to compare the attributes of two variables, were also introduced. As you recall, we stated that comparative statistics are within a "gray area" that moves from description to inference. As such, comparative statistics are often classified as either descriptive or inferential rather than as a separate category. An example of how comparative statistics might be used for description was provided.

Inferential statistics were also defined in Chapter 11. The purpose of inferential statistics is to make inferences, estimations, or predictions about the data. In this chapter, we shall provide an overview of inferential statistics. How comparative statistics may be used to begin making inferences about the data will be demonstrated. We shall then present and discuss a variety of inferential techniques utilized by criminological researchers.

◼ An Overview of Inferential Statistics

Inferential statistics allow the researcher to develop inferences (predictions) about the data. If the sample is representative, these predictions may be extended to the population from which the data were drawn. Inferential statistics allow criminological researchers to conduct research that can be generalized to larger populations within society. When making inferences about data sets, researchers rely on measures of association to determine the strength of the relationship(s) between or among variables. Tests of significance are also used in order to discover whether the sample that was examined is representative of the population from which it was drawn.

Measures of Association

Measures of association are *the means by which researchers determine the strengths of relationships among the variables that are being studied* (Bachman & Peternoster, 2004; Fitzgerald & Cox, 2001; Vito & Blankenship, 2002). The measure of association that is used is dependent upon the type of analysis that is being conducted, the distribution of the data, and the level of data under analysis. There are many measures of association that are utilized within criminological research. Individual researchers may prefer to use different measures. However, some measures are considered to be standards. Lambda is commonly used for nominal-level data. Gamma is commonly used for ordinal-level research. Pearson's r and R^2 are commonly used for interval- and ratio-level data.

Typically, measures of association for nominal-level data tell researchers how strong the relationship is, but do not indicate directionality. A measure such as lambda runs from 0 (no relationship) to 1 (perfect relationship). A .00001 would indicate a very weak relationship. A 0.9999 would indicate an extremely strong relationship. Depending upon the measure used (some tend to be more powerful than others), the researcher would assess the relationship as being weak, moderate, or strong. For example, a lambda score of 0.5367 would indicate a moderate relationship, whereas a lambda score of 0.8249 would be an indicator of a relatively strong relationship. The researcher would have to assess the contingency table (cross-tabulations) to determine whether the relationship was positive or negative.

Measures of association for ordinal-level data tell the researcher both the strength of the relationship and the direction of the relationship. The ordinal measures range from -1 to $+1$. A zero (0) indicates no relationship, a negative one (-1) indicates a perfect negative relationship (as one variable increases, the other variable decreases), and a positive one $(+1)$ indicates a perfect positive relationship (as one variable increases, the other variable increases). A score of -0.8790 for the commonly used gamma indicates a strong negative relationship. A score of $+0.2358$ indicates a weak positive relationship. It should be noted that there are several other measures available for researchers to use—some of which have the advantage of being PRE (proportional reduction in error) measures that are more attractive to statisticians. We are merely providing the more commonly used measures. To review the advantages of other choices, we recommend that the reader consult with a statistician, take a statistics course, or consult a statistics text.

Measures of association for interval and ratio data are determined by the statistical technique that is used. For correlation, Pearson's r is the measure of association; for simple linear regression and multiple regression, R^2 is used. Other techniques use different measures. However, like ordinal measures, they range from -1 to $+1$. Different interval measures will be discussed within the various strategies presented.

Statistical Significance

Statistical significance is *how researchers determine whether their sample findings are representative of the population they are studying* (Bachman & Peternoster, 2004; Fitzgerald & Cox, 2001; Lurigio, Dantzker, Seng, & Sinacore, 1997; Vito & Blankenship, 2002). If you are using a complete enumeration (the entire population is studied, rather than just a sample from that population), then statistical significance is a moot point in that we already know that the population is accurately represented. However, complete enumerations are rare because very small populations limit generalizabilty, and large populations are too costly and time-consuming to study as a whole.

Statistical significance is based on probability sampling. Nomothetic explanations of causality are based on probabilities. It is this use of probability that enables us to make inferences based on a relatively few observations. Generally, social-science research desires a statistical significance of 0.05 or better. This means that we are 95 percent confident that our findings represent the population that was sampled. Before computers were readily accessible to researchers, the statistical significance of data was obtained by using calculators to laboriously figure mathematical equations. Today, thanks to statistical packages, this work is performed by the computers, which provide the significance in exacting detail.

■ Comparative Statistics

There are several comparative techniques available to criminal-justice researchers. The ones that we shall briefly discuss are crime rates, crime-specific rates, percentage change, and trend analyses.

Crime Rates

Crime rates are perhaps the most frequently presented data within criminal-justice and criminological research. These are nothing more than the number of crimes for an area (city, county, state, and so on) divided by the population for that area and then multiplied by 100,000. Crime rates for index crimes are commonly displayed in Uniform Crime Reports (UCR). An example of crime rates is displayed in **Table 12-1**. By viewing the rates presented in the following table, the reader may easily compare the rates of property crimes by household income.

Table 12-1 Crime Rates

**Estimated rate (per 1,000 households) of property victimization
By type of crime and characteristics of household, United States, 2003**

Characteristics of household	Total	Type of Property Crime		
		Burglary	Motor-vehicle theft	Theft
Household income				
Under $7,500	204.6	58.0	6.3	140.3
$7,500 to $14,999	167.7	42.2	7.3	118.3
$15,000 to $24,999	179.2	38.4	8.9	131.9
$25,000 to $34,999	180.7	35.3	12.3	133.1
$35,000 to $49,999	177.1	27.6	9.5	140.0
$50,000 to $74,999	168.1	24.9	8.4	134.7
$75,000 and over	176.4	20.8	11.9	143.7
Region				
Northeast	122.1	20.5	7.2	94.4
Midwest	160.2	32.5	6.9	120.9
South	160.5	32.2	7.8	120.4
West	207.4	30.6	15.2	161.6
Residence				
Urban	216.3	38.7	13.0	164.7
Suburban	144.8	24.0	9.3	111.6
Rural	136.6	30.5	4.0	102.1
Home ownership				
Owned	143.5	24.5	7.3	111.7
Rented	206.4	41.2	13.0	152.2

Source: U.S. Department of Justice, Bureau of Justice Statistics, *Criminal Victimization, 2003*, NCJ 205455 (Washington, DC: U.S. Department of Justice, September 2004), p 9, Table 8.

Crime-Specific Rates

Crime-specific rates differ from crime rates in that, within the computations, they use a base other than population. For example, we will use motor-vehicle theft. The number of registered automobiles in 2002 was 234,624,135. The estimated number of auto thefts was 1,246,096. Using the number of auto thefts divided by the number of autos multiplied by 100,000 produces an estimated auto-theft rate of 531 automobiles per 100,000. **Table 12-2** displays crime-specific rates as they apply to motor-vehicle theft in the United States from 1980 to 2002. This method can also be used to calculate victimization rates, arrest rates, and clearance rates.

Table 12-2	Crime-Specific Rates		
Motor-Vehicle Registrations and Thefts **United States, 1980–2002**			
	Number of motor-vehicle registrations	Estimated number of motor-vehicle thefts	Ratio of vehicles stolen to registered	Thefts per 100,000 registered
1980	161,614,294	1,131,700	1:143	700
1981	164,287,643	1,087,800	1:151	662
1982	165,298,024	1,062,400	1:156	643
1983	167,718,000	1,007,933	1:166	601
1984	169,446,281	1,032,165	1:164	609
1985	175,709,000	1,102,862	1:159	628
1986	181,890,000	1,224,137	1:149	673
1987	186,137,000	1,288,674	1:144	692
1988	183,930,000	1,432,916	1:128	779
1989	188,981,016	1,564,800	1:121	828
1990	194,502,000	1,635,907	1:119	841
1991	194,897,000	1,661,738	1:117	853
1992	193,775,000	1,610,834	1:120	831
1993	198,041,338	1,563,060	1:127	789
1994	201,763,492	1,539,287	1:131	763
1995	205,297,050	1,472,441	1:139	717
1996	210,236,393	1,394,238	1:151	663
1997	211,580,033	1,354,189	1:156	640
1998	215,496,003	1,242,781	1:173	577
1999	220,461,056	1,152,075	1:191	523
2000	225,821,241	1,160,002	1:195	514
2001	235,331,382	1,228,391	1:192	522
2002	234,624,135	1,246,096	1:188	531

Source: *Sourcebook of Criminal Justice Statistics,* (31st ed.) (Albany: State University of New York at Albany, 2003). Retrieved from www.albany.edu/sourcebook.

Percentage Change

Percentage-change statistics allow researchers to compare data over time and across jurisdictions. The computation for this is rather straightforward: subtract the earlier number from the later number, then divide the difference by the earlier number. This statistic allows us to determine whether there has been an increase or decrease in particular crimes. The bottom of **Table 12-3** demonstrates this statistic for index crimes in the United States for three different sets of years.

Trend Analyses

Trend analyses are yet another way of comparing differences over time. We may examine on a histogram how rates have increased for a particular offense, or we may use other means of determining how the data have changed. Trend analyses are quite useful in assessing the impact of preventive programs in criminal justice. Again we refer you to **Table 12-3**, which shows the estimated number of index crimes from 1994 to 2003. From this table, you can determine what trend(s) may have existed for these crimes during the reported time frame.

Table 12-3 Crime in the United States by Volume, Rate, and Percent Change, 1994–2003

Population	Violent crime				Property crime			
	Murder and non-negligent manslaughter	Forcible rape	Robbery	Aggravated assault	Property crime	Burglary	Larceny-theft	Motor vehicle theft
Population by year:	Number of Offenses							
1994–260,327,021	23,326	102,216	618,949	1,113,179	12,131,873	2,712,774	7,879,812	1,539,287
1995–262,803,276	21,606	97,470	580,509	1,099,207	12,063,935	2,593,784	7,997,710	1,472,441
1996–265,228,572	19,645	96,252	535,594	1,037,049	11,805,323	2,506,400	7,904,685	1,394,238
1997–267,783,607	18,208	96,153	498,534	1,023,201	11,558,475	2,460,526	7,743,760	1,354,189
1998–270,248,003	16,974	93,144	447,186	976,583	10,951,827	2,332,735	7,376,311	1,242,781
1999–272,690,813	15,522	89,411	409,371	911,740	10,208,334	2,100,739	6,955,520	1,152,075
2000–281,421,906	15,586	90,178	408,016	911,706	10,182,584	2,050,992	6,971,590	1,160,002
2001–285,317,559	16,037	90,863	423,557	909,023	10,437,189	2,116,531	7,092,267	1,228,391
2002–287,973,924	16,229	95,235	420,806	891,407	10,455,277	2,151,252	7,057,379	1,246,646
2003–290,809,777	16,503	93,433	413,402	857,921	10,435,523	2,153,464	7,021,588	1,260,471
Percent change, number of offenses:								
2003/2002	+1.7	−1.9	−1.8	−3.8	−0.2	+0.1	−0.5	+1.1
2003/1999	+6.3	+4.5	+1.0	−5.9	+2.2	+2.5	+0.9	+9.4
2003/1994	−29.3	−8.6	−33.2	−22.9	−14.0	−20.6	−10.9	−18.1

Source: Federal Bureau of Investigation, *Crime in the United States 2003*, Uniform Crime Reports (Washington, DC: FBI, 2004). Retrieved from www.fbi.gov/ucr/03cius.htm

Inferential Statistics

Due to the nature of inferential statistics, to do justice in explaining them requires a text of its own. Because it is not a goal of this text to teach statistics, further explanations are left for statistics courses, and only brief descriptions of selected statistics are offered.

Bivariate Analysis

Bivariate analysis is the examination of the relationship between two variables. Usually this involves attempting to determine how a dependent variable is influenced by an independent variable. The more commonly used bivariate techniques are cross-tabulations (contingency tables) and bivariate (simple linear) regression (Bachman & Peternoster, 2004; Fitzgerald & Cox, 2001; Lurigio, Dantzker, Seng, & Sinacore, 1997; Vito & Blankenship, 2002). In assessing the relationship between the two variables, we examine the contingency table or regression-scatterplot results, the measure of association (such as gamma or R^2), and the level of statistical significance (hopefully 0.05 or lower).

Contingency Tables

With nominal-level data, two popular statistical techniques are contingency tables (cross-tabulations) and chi-square, which is a common statistic for a contingency table. A contingency table is a set of interrelated cells. Each cell can display a variety of data (see **Table 12-4**). From these data, a chi-square statistic is available. Chi-square is one test of statistical significance. These techniques offer a statistical relationship from which one might make an inference.

Bivariate Regression

Bivariate regression, also known as simple linear regression, is based on the principle that over time, things tend to regress toward the mean. For example, if you were to measure the height of female students enrolled at your school, you would find that they would range from well above the average to well below the average height for women. Assuming a normal population, most of the heights would tend to cluster around the mean (average) height. A scatterplot of these heights would most likely enable a line to be drawn showing most heights to be near the mean height.

If you are using interval-level data, are dealing with a normal distribution (determined through earlier descriptive statistics), and have a linear relationship, this would be an appropriate procedure to see how an independent variable would predict the outcome of a dependent variable. We will not go into a description of the principles upon which simple linear regression is based. However, if you have a linear relationship, as X (the predictor variable) increases, so should Y (the dependent variable). Conversely, if a negative relationship exists (such as a crime-prevention strategy), as X (the strategy used) increases, Y (the specific crime targeted) will (hopefully) decrease.

Table 12-4 Example of Contingency/Cross-tabulations

Overall Job Satisfaction by Level of Education/Degree

OVERALL	Count Exp Val Row Pct Col Pct Tot Pct	EDUCATION				
		H.S. Diploma 1	Assoc. Deg. 2	Bach. Deg. 3	Master's Deg. 4	Row Total
	2	1	0	0	0	1
		.5	.2	.3	.0	2.3%
		100.0%	.0%	.0%	.0%	
		4.5%	.0%	.0%	.0%	
		2.3%	.0%	.0%	.0%	
Neutral	3	11	4	4	1	20
		10.2	4.2	5.1	.5	46.5%
		55.0%	20.0%	20.0%	5.0%	
		50.0%	44.4%	36.4%	100.0%	
		25.6%	9.3%	9.3%	2.3%	
	4	9	3	6	0	18
		9.2	3.8	4.6	.4	41.9%
		50.0%	16.7%	33.3%	.0%	
		40.9%	33.3%	54.5%	.0%	
		20.9%	7.0%	14.0%	.0%	
Extremely Satisfied	5	1	2	1	0	4
		2.0	.8	1.0	.1	9.3%
		25.0%	50.0%	25.0%	.0%	
		4.5%	22.2%	9.1%	.0%	
		2.3%	4.7%	2.3%	.0%	
Column Total		22 51.2%	9 20.9%	11 25.6%	1 2.3%	43 100%

Chi-Square	Value	DF	Significance
Pearson	5.12525	9	.82326
Likelihood Ratio	5.53040	9	.78584
Linear-by-Linear Association	.61069	1	.43453

Minimum Expected Frequency — .023

Cells with Expected Frequency < 5 – 13 of 16 (81.3%)

Approximate Statistic	Value	ASE1	Val/ASE0	Significance
Phi	.34524			.82326
Cramer's V	.19933			82326
Contingency Coefficient	.32634			.82326

■ Multivariate Analysis

Multivariate analysis is the examination of the relationship between or among three or more variables. Usually this involves attempting to determine how a dependent variable is influenced by several independent variables. This methodology offers more insights than does bivariate analysis, in that we are able to study the relationships among several variables at one time. The more commonly used multivariate techniques are correlation, multiple regression, Student's t-test, analysis of variance, discriminant analysis, probit regression, factor analysis, and path analysis (Bachman & Peternoster, 2004; Fitzgerald & Cox, 2001; Lurigio, Dantzker, Seng, & Sinacore, 1997; Vito & Blankenship, 2002).

In assessing the relationship between the multiple variables, we examine the correlation table, regression-scatterplot results, or other indicators (depending on the technique used); the measure of association (such as Pearson's r, R^2, Wilks' lambda, or other appropriate measure); as well as the level of statistical significance. We shall provide a number of multivariate examples in this chapter.

Student's t-Test

The Student's t-test is used to compare groups' means for a particular variable and hypothesis testing. Computing Student's t is a fairly complex process that contrasts expected outcomes with observed outcomes. The differences among the means of the variables are then assessed. The Student's t-test provides means for each variable by group, and then offers a statistic called the t-value, which indicates whether the relationship between the groups is statistically significant (see **Table 12-5**). As stressed earlier, we do not intend to teach you how to compute this measure, but rather, to inform you of what to look for in the work of others, and what to discuss with your statistician if you use this strategy. As seen in **Table 12-5**, the differences between the means are obvious. The t-values will not mean anything to you at this point, but will indicate the values used by the computer to calculate the significance (which should mean something to you by now).

Correlation

Correlation is a commonly used technique for evaluating interval- and ratio-level data. In our earlier discussion of bivariate regression, we talked about how relationships between two variables were examined based on the assumption of a linear relationship. In correlation, relationships are assessed based upon covariation. Covariation simply means that as changes occur in one variable, X, they will also change in another variable, Y. A positive correlation would reveal that as X values increase, Y values would also increase. Assessing correlations is based upon how the variation in one value corresponds to variation in the other value.

The means of assessing the correlation of interval-level data is Pearson's product-moment correlation. Pearson's r is used to determine the strength of the association among variables by dividing the covariance of X and Y by the product of the standard deviation of X and Y. You do not have to calculate these numbers; the computer does it for you. What you are interested in is the direction of r (recall that we are looking at a number between negative 1 and positive 1), the

Table 12-5	Student's T for Student's Perceptions of Policing Comparison of Selected Means Scores, by Time		
Variable	Mean (T1)	Mean (T2)	T-value
Primary Role	.554	−.458	5.49*
Level of Competency	−.747	−1.289	4.29*
Serve and Protect	−1.000	−.800	−1.27
Corrupt Act	−.598	−.390	−1.33
Strike a Minority	−.171	−.500	2.37*
Ignore Needs	−1.000	−1.060	.55
Preventing Crime	−.476	−.951	2.97*
Harass or Help	−1.374	−1.470	.96
Unknown Reaction	.482	.716	−1.65
Professionalism	.183	.598	−3.38*
Help Society	.627	.928	−1.84
Benefit of Doubt	.256	.646	−2.39*

$* = p < .05$

Note: T1 and T2 represent the distribution of the questionnaire. T1 was at the beginning of the semester, and T2 was the end of the semester.

Source: Dantzker & Ali-Jackson, (1998).

strength of r, and the significance of r. **Table 12-6** is an example of correlation in analyzing interval data.

Analysis of Variance

Analysis of variance, commonly referred to as ANOVA, is another means of examining interval-level data. Where correlation uses Pearson's r to determine the nature of relationships among variables, ANOVA uses something known as an F ratio to compare the means of groups. This technique helps avoid committing errors that might occur when using multiple t-tests (Iverson & Norpoth, 1987). ANOVA allows statisticians to determine significance by assessing the variability of group means. Therefore, this is a useful method for evaluating grouped data (such as the outcomes of correctional treatments on inmate groups). **Table 12-7** is an example of ANOVA findings.

Multiple Regression

Multiple (sometimes referred to by statisticians as ordinary least squares, or OLS) regression is yet another means of evaluating interval-level data. It is based upon the same assumptions as bivariate regression. However, instead of assessing the relationship between only two variables, multiple regression usually examines several variables at once. This popular technique enables researchers to look not only at how the independent variables predict the outcome of the dependent variable, but also at the relationships among the independent variables. Multiple regression builds on bivariate regression and correlation by examining partial correlations. In other words, it uses variance to assess the ability of an in-

Table 12-6 Correlation

Variable(s)	Incomp	Motto	Corrupt	College
Role				
Pearson's r	.119	.133	.058	−.145
Sig. (2-tailed)	.013	.006	.230	.003
N	439	435	437	413
Incomp				
Pearson's r	1.000	.346	.308	−.054
Sig. (2-tailed)		.000	.000	.277
N	440	436	438	414
Motto				
Pearson's r	.346	1.000	.349	−.085
Sig. (2-tailed)	.000		.000	.086
N	436	436	434	410
Corrupt				
Pearson's r	.308	.349	1.000	−.106
Sig. (2-tailed)	.000	.000		.032
N	438	434	438	412
College Years				
Pearson's r	−.054	−.085	−.106	1.000
Sig. (2-tailed)	.277	.086	.032	
N	414	410	412	414

dependent variable to predict the dependent variable. But multiple regression goes beyond this analysis by assessing variance among the independent variables (Kleinbaum, Kupper, Muller, & Nizam, 1998). The influence on total variation that additional variables cause on the prior variables is known as partial correlation. We are able to see how the variables interact, and we can use this knowledge to add or remove independent variables from the regression equation. Computers will do this for you in a process known as stepwise regression.

As in previous sections, you do not have to understand the process to be able to interpret multiple regression. You look for the same criteria as in bivariate regression. The direction of R^2, the strength of R^2, and the significance are important. Additionally, the relationships between the independent variables must be examined by reviewing their correlation coefficients. However, to determine whether to use multiple regression and how to deal with problems that may arise, you should consult with a statistician or someone experienced in using regression. An example of multiple-regression results is shown in **Table 12-8**.

Other Multivariate Techniques

In addition to the previous multivariate techniques, there are several others that are popular among criminologists. All of them require a solid understanding of the statistical procedures involved. Probit analysis (also referred to as probit regression

Table 12-7	Selected ANOVA Results from a Perceptions Study				
Value Label	Mean	Std Dev	Sum of Sq	d.f.	F
AVOID					
Springfield Acad	−1.3750	.5310	13.2500		
MA Regional Acad	−1.7500	.4935	9.5000	1	11.60*
CORRUPT					
Springfield Acad	−1.4375	.7693	27.8125		
MA Regional Acad	−1.4000	.9282	33.6000	1	.04
DRUGS					
Springfield Acad	.0625	1.4790	102.8125		
MA Regional Acad	.4500	1.4313	79.9000	1	1.54
EXPECTATIONS					
Springfield Acad	.1702	1.2036	66.6383		
MA Regional Acad	−.2500	1.0801	45.5000	1	2.89
HELP SOCIETY					
Springfield Acad	1.3750	.7889	29.2500		
MA Regional Acad	1.4000	.8412	27.6000	1	.02
IGNORE					
Springfield 1.3958	.8440	33.4792			
MA Regional Acad	−1.6500	.6222	15.1000	1	2.50

*p < .01

or just probit) is similar to, yet different from, multiple regression. It is in effect a cumulative-distribution-regression model that helps straighten out an S-shaped distribution (Montgomery, Peck, & Vining, 2001). It is also appropriate when you have interval independent variables but an ordinal-level dependent variable (Kleinbaum, Kupper, Muller, & Nizam, 1998; Montgomery, Peck, & Vining, 2001).

Logit analysis is also known as logit and logistic regression. Like probit analysis, it is a type of regression that may be used to deal with S-shaped distributions. Logistic analysis is a sophisticated technique used by statisticians when the cumulative distribution is logistic rather than normal as in probit analysis. Like regression, both logit and probit results are assessed using R^2 as the measure of association (Kleinbaum, Kupper, Muller, & Nizam, 1998; Montgomery, Peck, & Vining, 2001).

Discriminant analysis is a favorite technique of the authors. It is appropriate when you have interval independent variables and a nominal-level dependent variable. Where regression is based upon the ability of the independent variables to predict the dependent variable, discriminant analysis focuses upon the ability to classify observations to the nominal categories of the dependent variable based upon their values on a set of independent variables. The measure of association for discriminant analysis is Wilks' lambda.

Factor analysis also categorizes data. It is used to determine patterns among the variation of values of the variables being studied. Variables that are highly correlated are clustered together based upon computer-generated "factors" (Kim & Mueller, 1978). This is an extremely complex procedure that must later be in-

Table 12-8	Multiple Regression				
Regressions of County Population Against Crime and Arrests in Montgomery County, 1970–1990					
Variable	b0	b1	R2	F	Sig F
Part I Crimes	1,810.7	38.3	.50	18.7	.000
Part II Crimes	3,029.4	56.4	.29	7.8	.012
Total Crimes	4,840.1	94.7	.50	18.6	.000
Part I Arrests	3,177.5	2.6	40	12.6	.002
Part II Arrests	−1,059.8	11.9	.47	16.9	.001
Total Arrests	2,117.7	14.6	.60	28.0	.000
Source: Guynes & McEwen, (1998).					

terpreted by the researcher to determine whether the factor loadings have logical meaning.

Path analysis seeks to provide a graphic depiction of the causal relationships among the independent variables in order to explain their influences upon the dependent variable. Like factor analysis, it is a complex procedure that is best left to statisticians.

Nonparametric Techniques

When the distribution of the data is not normal, standard statistical techniques are usually not appropriate. In those cases, other procedures that are used include chi-square (based upon the statistic discussed earlier), nonparametric correlation, and nonlinear regression. The strategies used in nonparametric analysis are complex. The reader is advised to consult with a statistician in these circumstances. We mention these strategies here so that you will know that there are techniques that are available should you have data that are not in a normal distribution.

Summary

In this chapter, we have provided an overview of several statistical techniques that should aid the reader in understanding the research of others as well as in preparing their own. We do not claim to give you the knowledge needed for in-depth data interpretation (that is provided in statistics texts), but you should be able to grasp the principles involved in conducting inferential statistics. Today's reality is that researchers do not really need to be expert statisticians. Many statistical analyses can be completed through a variety of user-friendly software. Often all the researcher needs to do is be able to code and enter data, choose what statistical techniques should be run, interpret the results, and report their findings. To attain a better understanding of statistical analyses without a statistics course, we suggest that you read almost any criminal-justice or criminological study, focusing particularly on the statistics portion.

Chapter Resources

METHODOLOGICAL QUERIES

Based on the idea of the College Students' Criminality Survey:

1. Which statistical techniques would you use? Identify at least one descriptive, one comparative, and one inferential technique.
2. Which variables would you use for measures of association?
3. What might be the most statistically significant relationship you would want to find?
4. What tests of significance would you use?

REFERENCES

Bachman, R., & Peternoster, R. (2004). *Statistics for criminology and criminal justice* (2nd ed.). Boston: McGraw-Hill.

Dantzker, M. L., & Ali-Jackson, N. (1998). Examining students' perceptions of policing and the effect of completing a police-related course. In M. L. Dantzker, A. J. Lurigio, M. J. Seng, & J. M. Sinacore (Eds.), *Practical applications for criminal justice statistics* (pp. 195–210). Boston: Butterworth-Heinemann.

Federal Bureau of Investigation. (2004). *Crime in the United States 2003.* Uniform Crime Reports. Washington, D.C.: FBI. Retrieved from www.fbi.gov/ucr/03cius.htm.

Fitzgerald, J. D., & Cox, S. M. (2001). *Research methods and statistics in criminal justice: An introduction* (3rd ed.). Chicago: Nelson-Hall.

Guynes, R., & McEwen, T. (1998). Regression analysis applied to local correctional systems. In M. L. Dantzker, A. J. Lurigio, M. J. Seng, & J. M. Sinacore (Eds.), *Practical applications for criminal justice statistics* (pp. 149–168). Boston: Butterworth-Heinemann.

Iverson, G. R., & Norpoth, H. (1987). *Analysis of variance* (2nd ed.). Quantitative applications in the social sciences. Thousand Oaks, CA: Sage.

Kim, J., & Mueller, C. W. (1978). *Introduction to factor analysis: What it is and how to do it.* Quantitative applications in the social sciences. Thousand Oaks, CA: Sage.

Kleinbaum, D. G., Kupper, L. L., Muller, K. E., & Nizam, A. (1998). *Applied regression analysis and multivariate methods* (3rd ed.). Pacific Grove, CA: Brooks/ Cole.

Lurigio, A. J., Dantzker, M. L., Seng, M. J., & Sinacore, J. M. (1997). *Criminal justice statistics: A practical approach.* Boston: Butterworth-Heinemann.

Montgomery, D. C., Peck, E. A., & Vining, G. G. (2001). *Introduction to linear regression analysis* (3rd ed.) New York: John Wiley.

Sourcebook of Criminal Justice Statistics (31st ed.). (2003). Albany: State University of New York at Albany. Retrieved from www.albany.edu/sourcebook.

U.S. Department of Justice, Bureau of Justice Statistics, *Criminal Victimization, 2003,* NCJ 205455 (Washington, DC: U.S. Department of Justice, September 2004), p 9, Table 8.

Vito, G. F., & Blankenship, M. B. (2002). *Statistical analysis in criminal justice and criminology.* Upper Saddle River, NJ: Prentice Hall.

Writing the Research

13

Vignette 13-1   The End Is Near!!

The semester is winding down. Next semester will be here too soon, and it will be time to write your final project. Your research class has been quite helpful in preparing you to conduct your research, but you still are not quite sure how to write up the findings. Yes, you have read many articles, but how they were put together still eludes you. Hopefully, during the last few weeks of your course, how research is put on paper will become clearer.

Chapter Objectives

After studying this chapter, the student should be able to:

- Explain the purpose of the title page and describe its structure.
- Explain the purpose of the abstract and describe its contents.
- Explain the purpose of the introduction and describe its contents.
- Explain the purpose of the literature review and describe its contents.
- Explain the purpose of the methodology section and describe its contents.
- Explain the purpose of the results section and describe its contents.
- Explain the purpose of the conclusions section and describe its contents.
- Explain the purpose of the references and describe their structure.
- Explain the purpose of tables and figures and describe their contents.
- Explain the purpose of appendixes and describe their contents.

■ The Research Paper

The topic has been chosen, the design implemented, the questionnaire constructed, the data collected and analyzed, and now you think, "Here comes the hard part." For many people, students and scholars alike, conducting the research is seen as the easy or fun part, and would be great to do if it did not have to be written up. Our experiences suggest that students, in particular, really can "get into" the designing and collecting of the data, but then they fear the analyses and loathe having to provide a written explanation. However, since the written project is generally the required final goal, whether for fulfilling a course requirement or attempting to get published, it must be taken as seriously as the research itself. Furthermore, the transition from data to words is not as difficult as it may appear (Morgan, Reichert, & Harrison, 2002).

Because each of us has our own writing style, we will not begin to try to tell you how to go about writing. We will, however, suggest an order for your paper and what should be included. The basic order should be title page, abstract, introduction, methodology, results, conclusions, references, and appendixes. Within this chapter, we provide not only an overview of what should be included within each of the above, but also an APA (American Psychological Association) writing style example from a previously unpublished paper. (Note: Prior to writing the final paper, one should consult the most current writing manual of the style that will be used.)

The Title Page

The title of your research paper (article or thesis) should tell the reader in clear and concise terms what your research is about. Often, individuals who are perusing journals or article abstracts do not have (or will not take) the time to read the abstracts. The title is what draws their attention to your paper as possibly being of interest to them. The author's (or authors') identity and affiliation then follow. If the research has been funded by an external organization, then that is also indicated on the title page. The journal, organization, or instructor to whom the completed research is being submitted may have specific requirements as to how this page should be structured.

Sample Title Page

The State of COP Among Grant Recipients:
Results from a National Survey

M. L. Dantzker
Dept. of Criminal Justice
UTPA
Edinburg, TX 78539

Abstract

The abstract is the summary, or synopsis, of the information being presented in the paper, and it starts with the research title. The abstract presents the paper's major argument and describes the methods that were used. Note that this abstract is limited to one paragraph. Generally the abstract is between 100 and 150 words in length.

Sample Abstract

To gain a better understanding of the state of community-oriented policing in this country as it compared to a previous year, Macro International and the Police Executive Research Forum (PERF) teamed up on an NIJ grant to conduct a 1997 follow-up to a 1993 PERF study. The 1997 study focused on a sample of 2,000 police and sheriffs' agencies that had either participated in the 1993 study or were among agencies identified to have received some form of COP grant from the federal government. This paper examines one aspect from the questionnaire relating to the state of COP among the COP-grant recipients' sample.

The Introduction

This section will vary in length, depending on whether there is a page limit or on how much information is really available. Regardless of length, this section needs to establish the research problem, the literature that supports its existence, and the reason to research the problem. Furthermore, this section must report the research question(s) and hypothesis or hypotheses, and will usually briefly describe what was done and how.

The introduction and literature review may be contained within one section or may be broken into two sections. If these parts are separated, the researcher uses the introduction to introduce the reader to the topic and research question. Whether separated or not, this introductory paragraph should alert the reader as to what to expect from the paper. This is followed by the main portion or the literature review, where the writer offers a body of support for the research.

In some cases, there may be very little support; if so, that fact must be acknowledged. In other cases, the writer will have to decide how to limit the extensive amount of evidence that is available. Finally, the literature-review section should end with a summary paragraph that indicates what research is being reported and how it was accomplished.

Sample Introduction and Literature Review

Citizens have long been outspoken about the effectiveness of the police in controlling crime (Moore, Trojanowicz, & Kelling, 1988), and quick to criticize the handling of problems, crime related or social oriented, by the police (Dantzker, 1997). Police departments have been criticized for their inability to control crime and for their poor relationships with citizens. Throughout the decades, in response to these criticisms, attempts have been made to improve police response and effectiveness through a variety of innovations and reforms. In the 1970s, it was team policing; in the 1980s, it was patrol decentralization; and in the wave of the 1990s and upon entering the new millennium, it appears to be a community-based policing most often referred to as community-oriented policing (COP) (Dantzker, 1997).

Resulting primarily from the civil unrest of the 1960s, police agencies have searched for more than 20 years for ways to improve police-community relations (Carter & Radelet, 1999; Champion & Rush, 1997; Mayhall, Barker, & Hunter, 1995; Peak & Glensor, 1999; Trojanowicz & Bucqueroux, 1990; Trojanowicz, Hockwater, Sinclair, & Wriggelsworth, 1994; Trojanowicz, Kappeler, Gaines, & Bucqueroux, 1998.). Team policing and patrol decentralization attempted to bring policing and the community closer together by providing community sectors where a variety of police services were available. Both programs had a limited impact on community relations because they failed to seek assistance and input from an important element of the community, the citizens themselves (Alpert & Dunham, 1986; Bennett, 1998; Community Policing Consortium, 1994; Dantzker, 1994; Goldstein, 1990; Greene, 1989; Lurigio & Rosenbaum, 1997; Miller & Hess, 1994; Oliver, 1998a, 1998b; Skogan, 1998; Trojanowicz & Bucqueroux, 1990; Trojanowicz, Hockwater, Sinclair, & Wriggelsworth, 1994; Trojanowicz, Kappeler, Gaines, & Bucqueroux, 1998; Wycoff, 1995).

In more-recent times, police departments are being called upon to become more proactive and innovative in their patrol strategies (Brown, 1989; Friedmann, 1992; Rosenbaum, 1998; Sparrow, Moore, & Kennedy, 1990; Strecher, 1997; Watson, Stone, & DeLuca, 1998). Furthermore, these strategies require that police not only listen to the voices of citizens, but that police also seek out and request citizens to speak of the problems with policing and crime and to assist in seeking ways to combat these growing concerns—in particular, those problems that may eventually lead to crime (for example, community disorder) (Goldstein, 1990; Lurigio & Rosenbaum, 1997; Murphy, 1988; Pace, 1993; Trojanowicz & Carter, 1988). At one point, this drive for change led one scholar to note that "a quiet revolution" (Kelling, 1988) was occurring, reshaping how policing is performed in the United States. The catalyst of the revolution has become known as community-oriented policing (COP), and is no longer quiet but is taking the country by storm.

To rectify and remedy problems continues to be a challenge for many police departments. As noted by Brown (1989, p 1), "Like many other social institutions, American police departments are responding to rapid social change and emerging problems by rethinking their basic strategies." Furthermore, "regardless of how one experiences it, something is happening, and this something is an attempt to rethink and restructure the role of the police in society" (Rosenbaum 1998, p 3). The most current attempt to eliminate problems and restructure policing has been through projects or strategies falling under the rubric of "community policing." As noted by Trojanowicz &

Bucqueroux, (1994, p vii), "Community policing is being touted by some as the cure-all for the problems within and without the criminal justice system." According to Sparrow (1988, p 1):

> The concept of community policing envisages a police department striving for an absence of crime and disorder and concerned with, and sensitive to, the quality of life in the community. It perceives the community as an agent and partner in promoting security rather than as a passive audience.

Recent literature has noted that community policing appears to be improving the problems that have led to citizen criticism of the police, such as lack of citizen input, poor police-citizen interaction, and rising crime rates (Dewitt, 1992; Kennedy, 1993; Lurigio & Rosenbaum, 1997; McElroy, Cosgrove, & Sadd, 1993; Peak & Glensor, 1999; Skogan & Hartnett, 1997; Trojanowicz & Bucqueroux, 1994; Vardalis, 1992; Watson, Stone, & DeLuca, 1998; Wycoff, 1988; Wycoff & Skogan, 1993). Community policing also seems to be providing a variety of potential benefits to communities, such as an active voice in problem solving, improved police-citizen interactions, and a better understanding of what the police are doing, leading to enhanced police accountability ("Community Policing in the 1990s", 1992; Community Policing Consortium, 1994; Jiao, 1998; Kelling, Wasserman, & Williams, 1988; Kratcoski & Dukes, 1995; Murphy, 1988; Toch & Grant, 1991; Trojanowicz, Kappeler, Gaines, & Bucqueroux, 1998; Watson, Stone, & DeLuca, 1998).

As a result of the growing number of positive experiences community policing apparently is producing for both police and communities (Brodeur, 1998, DeWitt, 1992; Eggers & O'Leary, 1995; Hayeslip & Cordner, 1987; Jolin & Moose, 1997; McElroy, Cosgrove, & Sadd, 1993; Memory, 1999; Palmiotto & Donahue, 1995; Rosenbaum, 1994; Skolnick & Bayley, 1988), as well as the funding available from the federal government, an increasing number of police agencies seem to be looking toward community policing as an answer to their communities' problems. To assist in their implementation of COP, more and more police agencies are seeking funding through grants available from the federal government. This paper examines one aspect of COP-grant recipients through a sample available from a nationally conducted comparative study on the status of COP.

Methodology

Despite the relevance and importance of the introductory section, one should consider the methodology section the mainstay of the paper. The writer should discuss the hypothesis or hypotheses, the research design, and the data-gathering technique. This includes explaining the research population, the sampling frame, and the questionnaire or other method used to gather the data. It is within this section that the researcher can fully explain where, when, how, and why the data were attained and analyzed. The methodology section may be written up in one complete section, or it may be subdivided.

Sample Methodology

The original study from which the data reported here were taken was geared primarily toward comparing the general state of COP nationally from 1993 to 1997. However, part of the state of COP is related to funding. There are a growing number of police agencies that have turned to COP via grants from the federal government. In August 1994, Congress passed—and on September 13, 1994, President Clinton signed into law—the Violent Crime Control and Law Enforcement Act of 1994. This act lead to the creation of the Office of Community Oriented Policing Services (COPS), which currently oversees the distribution of more than $8 billion allocated to encourage and support the adaptation of COP. In particular, this office oversees grants to police agencies who have agreed to use the money to hire additional police officers or change current practices, with COP as the goal. To date, hundreds of police agencies have received a COP grant; as of May 12, 1999, more than 101,000 police officers had been hired as a result of these grants.

Types of Grants

To date, a variety of grant programs have been established to promote COP. The first of these grants—COPS: Phase I—were awarded in October 1994. This grant program provided funding to 392 state, municipal, county, and tribal police agencies to hire more than 2,700 new officers.

In November 1994, two new grant programs, COPS AHEAD and COPS FAST, were initiated. COPS AHEAD (Accelerated Hiring Education and Deployment) was an expedited hiring program for agencies servicing jurisdictions with a population of more than 50,000. The objective was for agencies who anticipated grant funding to begin hiring new officers immediately. Money to hire more than 4,100 officers was awarded. For the COPS FAST (Funding Accelerated for Smaller Towns) program, the concept was to help speed deployment of new officers to towns with populations of less than 50,000. Money awarded led to the hiring of more than 6,200 officers and deputies.

In December 1994, another new grant initiative became available: COPS MORE (Making Officer Redeployment Effective). These funds were to be used to acquire new technologies and equipment, to pay overtime, and to hire nonpolice personnel. The idea behind this initiative was to allow agencies to reassign officers in a manner that allowed them to spend more time on the streets "problem solving," instead of back at their desks doing paperwork.

By May 1995, another new grant initiative became available: *Troops to COPS*. This grant provided up to $5,000 to agencies that hire newly designated veterans. In June 1995, the COPS AHEAD and COPS FAST grants were replaced with the Universal Hiring Program (UHP). The UHP was designed to provide funding for additional officers devoted to community policing as supplemental to existing forces or for jurisdictions establishing a new agency.

In June 1996, the COPS Community Policing to Combat Domestic Violence program was created. This grant provided agencies with an opportunity to create innovative strategies through community policing to confront and combat domestic violence. Three hundred and thirty-six communities received a part of more than $46 million for this new strategy.

The last of the major grant initiatives associated with this study were the Problem-Solving Partnerships. More than $40 million was provided to police agencies to create cooperative efforts with community-based organizations to address crime and public-safety issues. Other grant initiatives that were available to agencies in 1997 were for establishing regional community-policing institutes, training, and antigang programs.

As part of the comparative study, a sample of recipients of COPS grants was surveyed too. This paper discusses selected findings from this particular sample.

The Sample

Initially, a random sample of 500 COPS grantees was selected. Gleaned from this initial 500 were those agencies that were in the comprehensive (original) sampling frame and those designated as "out of scope" (that is, agencies that employed fewer than five officers or had no patrol function). Through this process, 250 departments were surveyed, of which 177 (71 percent) responded. For these analyses, 62 agencies that were originally surveyed in 1993, and who also responded to the 1997 survey, were added to the 177, for a final random sample of 239 agencies who had been identified as receiving some form of COP grants.

Among the 239 agencies in the sample, 198 (83 percent) were municipal police agencies, and 41 (17 percent) were sheriffs' departments. Approximately one half of all the agencies employed between 5 and 24 sworn officers (n = 128, or 53 percent). The largest percentage (29 percent) indicated serving a town jurisdiction with a population greater than 2,500 (n = 68). As for the type of grants, the three most popular grants received were COPS FAST (n = 127), Universal Hiring (n = 110), and COPS MORE (n = 93). Finally, despite the larger number of municipal agencies in the sample, there was no statistical difference found between the two types of agencies and the type(s) of grants they received (see **Table 13-1**).

Table 13-1 Selected Sample Characteristics ($n = 239$)		
Agency Type	n	Percentage
Municipal	198	82.8
Sheriff	41	17.2
Sworn Officers		
5–24	128	53.6
25–49	52	21.9
50–99	27	11.3
100–499	29	12.1
500+	3	1.3
Jurisdiction Type		
Rural	24	10.0
Town (2,500+)	68	28.5
Mixed Town & Rural	50	20.9
Independent City (25,000+)	22	9.2
Suburb (in a metro area)	40	16.7
Unincorporated (metro area)	2	0.8
Metropolitan center	6	2.5
Combined city/county	14	5.9
Other	10	4.2
Missing	3	1.3
Type of Grant(s) received		
COPS FAST	127	51.4[a]
Universal Hiring Grant	110	46.0
COPS MORE	93	38.9
COPS AHEAD	22	9.2
Domestic Violence Initiative	16	6.7
Problem-Solving Partnerships	7	2.9
Phase 1	7	2.9

[a]Frequencies and percentages do not equal 239 for this variable because some agencies received more than one type of grant.

Results

Whether this is a separate section or part of the methodology is actually a matter of preference. Either way, in this section, the writer describes the sample's characteristics, the statistical techniques used, the results, and whether they supported the hypothesis or hypotheses. It is in this section that various tables, graphs, and charts are commonly used to describe the data.

Sample Results

The questionnaire used in the national study was composed of a series of 34 questions divided among nine sections. The data discussed here pertain to the section on organizational programs and practices.

The concept of COP advocates a complete acceptance and change within the police organization, not a piecemeal or programmatic approach. However, reality indicates that the programmatic approach is the more popular means of implementing COP. To support this stance, respondents were given 26 items thought to be either a practice or program associated with COP, and were asked to indicate whether the program or practice has been implemented by them. Twelve items perceived as the truest components of COP (versus police community relations) are examined. They are equally divided into three categories: Response to Needs, Organizational Commitment, and Expanding the Mandate.

Response to Needs

Whether it is "traditional" policing or "COP," a main concern is the response to calls for service and how this component can often detract an officer from accomplishing other tasks (such as problem solving). Therefore, two recognizable items of COP are classifying and prioritizing calls and creating alternative-response methods. Among the COP sample, 118 (49 percent) advised that they had implemented a system to classify and prioritize calls, thus increasing officers' time for other activities. Between the two types of agencies, there was no significant difference in implementing this system. Yet 102 (43 percent) claimed to have created alternative-response methods (for example, telephone reports or mail-in reports). Again, there was no significant difference between types of agencies.

To better understand what is needed and how well the police are fulfilling those needs, 118 (49 percent) of the agencies claim to give citizen surveys to determine community needs and priorities, while only 106 (44 percent) conduct citizen surveys to evaluate police service. As with the previous two items, no statistical differences were found by agency type (see **Table 13-2**).

Organizational Commitment

If COP has not become the direction of the whole agency, it is often found in some form of officer-oriented practice or program. According to the literature, among the more popular approaches is assigning or designating police as COP officers who are responsible for certain areas or activities. In this study, 147 (62 percent) of the respondents indicated that they had these specifically designated officers. One of the duties of COP officers is attending meetings with community groups on a regular basis; 159 (67 percent) claim that this is done. In both cases, there was no significant difference by type of agency.

Since a major element of COP is problem identification and resolution, it is important that COP officers be prepared for this task. Yet only a little more than half of the respondents (53 percent, n = 126) have implemented specific training for problem identification and

Table 13-2 Organizational Programs and Practices

Program or Practice		Implemented	Not Implemented	Cramer's V
Response to Needs				
Classification and prioritization of calls	Municipal	97(82%)[a]	70(80%)	
	Sheriff	21(18%)	17(20%)	.089
Alternative-response methods for calls	M	82(80%)	90(83%)	
	S	20(20%)	19(17%)	.093
Citizen surveys: needs and priorities	M	100(85%)	83(82%)	
	S	18(15%)	18(18%)	.086
Citizen surveys to evaluate police service	M	89(84%)	93(83%)	
	S	17(16%)	19(17%)	.080
Organizational Commitment				
Designating some officers as community or neighborhood officers	M	122(83%)	62(82%)	
	S	25(17%)	14(18%)	.032
Regularly scheduled meetings w/community groups	M	129(81%)	60(88%)	
	S	30(19%)	8(12%)	.103
Specific training for problem identification/ resolution	M	107(85%)	85(82%)	
	S	19(15%)	19(18%)	.094
Training for citizens in problem identification/resolution	M	61(80%)	127(86%)	
	S	15(20%)	21(14%)	.130
Expansion of Mandate				
Landlord/manager training programs	M	36(90%)	139(83%)	
	S	4(10%)	29(17%)	.124
Building-code enforcement	M	106(95%)	68(73%)	
	S	6(5%)	25(27%)	.305[b]
Use of other regulatory codes	M	119(88%)	65(78%)	
	S	16(12%)	18(22%)	.203[b]
Geographically based crime analysis	M	94(84%)	84(82%)	
	S	18(16%)	18(18%)	.077

[a]Column percentages.
[b]*Significant at the 0.01 level.

resolution. Furthermore, because citizens are supposed to be an important part of COP, they too should be able to identify and resolve problems. However, only 76 (32 percent) agencies had implemented training for citizens in problem identification or resolution. Again, there was no statistical differences by agency type (see **Table 13-2**).

Expanding the Mandate

For COP to be truly successful, it requires the use of many sources available to the police, including citizens who can have significant *impact because of their position in the community (for example, land-lords), various codes (such as building and regulatory), and crime analysis. This study found that only 40 (17 percent) agencies have implemented training programs for landlords and building managers in order maintenance and drug reduction; 112 (47 percent) make use of building-code enforcement as a means of helping remove crime po-tential—there was a statistical difference between agency types at .01, with municipal agencies indicating a much greater use of this practice; 135 (56 percent) use other regulatory codes to combat drugs and crimes, which was statistically significant at .01 between agen-cies; and 112 (47 percent) have implemented geographically based crime analysis (see Table 13-2).*

Conclusions

Usually the last section of the research paper is the conclusion(s). Generally this section is used to offer insights about the research—whether it did what was ex-pected, along with any possible problems. This section can also be used to dis-cuss implications of the research and to provide a forum for suggestions for future related research. Some authors choose to divide this information into two sec-tions: discussion and conclusions. There is no wrong or right here; it is simply a matter of preference.

Sample Conclusion

Accepting the position that the sample of COP-grant recipients is rep-resentative of all COP-grant recipients, the findings may be gener-alized. If so, these findings allow one to question what is really being funded—the COP concept, or approaches labeled "COP" for the purpose of obtaining funding. Obviously, this position is a mat-ter of perception. However, those who truly believe in and understand COP as it was developed through Goldstein, Trojanowicz, and oth-ers have grounds to question just how COP is being implemented and how the federal dollars are being spent. In contrast, those who are trying to implement COP may just as easily argue that how COP is being implemented is the most "realistic" way to do it—that is, through components, programs, or approaches rather than through a com-plete adoption and overhaul of traditional policing. The findings re-ported here, if nothing else, definitely provide a good foundation for future research and inquiry as to how COP is being implemented, particularly by those agencies receiving federal funding to do so.

References and/or Bibliography

Unless the topic has never been addressed in research prior to your project (a very unlikely event), there are always some sources that help to support the research. These sources are what help establish the literature review. When using other sources—whether quoting, paraphrasing, or simply as an outlet for affirming what is already known—each source should be recognized. Not only can this be done throughout the paper by various citation methods, but it must be done at the end in the form of a reference list or a bibliography. The format depends upon to whom the paper is being submitted (i.e., publication, instructor, organization). Failing to cite sources can lead to charges of plagiarism, something every writer should strive to avoid.

The majority of the papers written for criminal justice and criminology follow the APA style for reference citing in the text and at the end of the paper. Reviewing the introduction section, you will observe how two different formats are used. One is for paraphrasing or using someone else's ideas and giving credit (name[s] of the author[s], publication date), and the other for direct quotes (name[s] of the author[s], publication date, page number[s]). For the reference list, only those sources cited in the body of the text should be included. The information listed should include the name(s) of the author(s); the year of publication; the name of publication (if it is an article, the article title comes first, followed by the publication title); and, if a book, the city, state, and name of publisher (or, if a journal, the volume and issue number and the page number[s]).

Sample References

Alpert, G. P., & Dunham, R. G. (1986). Community policing. *Journal of Police Science and Administration, 14*(3), 212–222.

Bennett, T. (1998). Police and public involvement in the delivery of community policing. In J. P. Brodeur (Ed.), *How to recognize good policing: Problems and issues* (pp. 107–122). Thousand Oaks, CA: Sage.

Brodeur, J. P. (Ed.). (1998). *How to recognize good policing: Problems and issues.* Thousand Oaks, CA: Sage.

Brown, L. P. (1989). Community policing: A practical guide for police officials. *Perspectives on Policing, 12*(September).

Carter, D. L., & Radelet, L. A. (1999). *The police and the community* (6th ed.). Upper Saddle River, NJ: Prentice Hall.

Champion, D. J., & Rush, G. E. (1997). *Policing in the community.* Upper Saddle River, NJ: Prentice Hall.

Community Policing in the 1990's. (1992). *NIJ Journal, 225*(August) (pp 1–8).

Community Policing Consortium. (1994). *Understanding community policing: A framework for action.* Washington, DC: U.S. Department of Justice.

Dantzker, M. L. (1994). The future of municipal law enforcement is community-oriented policing: Suggestions for implementation. *Alternative Visions* (August), 3A–4A. First published in *Texas Police Journal, 42*(4), 15–17.

Dantzker, M. L. (1997). Job satisfaction and community policing: A preview of future research? *Police Chief, 64*(10), 97–99.

Dewitt, C. B. (1992). Community policing in Seattle: A model partnership between citizens and police. *Research in Brief* (August).

Eggers, W. D., & O'Leary, J. (1995). The beat generation: Community policing at its best. *Policy Review, 74*, 4–12.

Friedmann, R. R. (1992). *Community policing: Comparative perspectives and prospects.* New York: St. Martin's Press.

Goldstein, H. (1990). *Problem-oriented policing.* New York: McGraw-Hill.

Greene, J. R. (1989). Police officer job satisfaction and community perceptions: Implications for community-oriented policing. *Journal of Research in Crime and Delinquency, 26*(2), 168–183.

Hayeslip, D. W., Jr., & Cordner, G. W. (1987). The effects of community-oriented patrol on police officer attitudes. *American Journal of Police, 1*(1), 95–119.

Jiao, A. Y. (1998). Community policing in the eye of the beholder: Perceptions of the community-oriented model. In M. L. Dantzker, A. J. Lurigio, M. J. Seng, and J. M. Sinacore, *Practical applications for criminal justice statistics* (pp. 169–193). Woburn, MA: Butterworth-Heinemann.

Jolin, A., & Moose, C. A. (1997). Evaluating a domestic violence program in a community policing environment: Research implementation issues. *Crime and Delinquency, 43*(3), 279–297.

Kelling, G. L. (1988). Police and communities: The quiet revolution. *Perspectives on Policing, 1*(June).

Kelling, G. L., Wasserman, R., & Williams, H. (1988). Police accountability and community policing. *Perspectives on Policing, 7*(November).

Kennedy, D. M. (1993). The strategic management of police resources. *Perspectives on Policing, 14*(January).

Kratcoski, P. C., & Dukes, D. (Eds.). (1995). *Issues in community policing.* Cincinnati, OH: Anderson.

Lurigio, A. J., & Rosenbaum, D. P. (1997). Community policing: Major issues and unanswered questions. In M. L. Dantzker (Ed.), *Contemporary policing: Personnel, issues, and trends* (pp. 195–216). Woburn, MA: Butterworth-Heinemann.

Mayhall, P. D., Barker, T., & Hunter, R. D. (1995). *Police-community relations and the administration of justice* (4th ed.). Upper Saddle River, NJ: Prentice Hall.

McElroy, J. E., Cosgrove, C. A., & Sadd, S. (1993). *Community policing: The CPOP in New York.* Newbury Park, CA: Sage.

Memory, J. M. (1999). Some impressions from a qualitative study of implementation of community policing in North Carolina. In M. L. Dantzker (Ed.), *Readings for research methods in criminology and criminal justice* (pp. 1–14). Woburn, MA: Butterworth-Heinemann.

Miller, L. S., & Hess, K. M. (1994). *Community policing: Theory and practice.* St. Paul, MN: West.

Moore, M. H., Trojanowicz, R. C., & Kelling, G. L. (1988). Crime and policing. *Perspectives on Policing, 2*(June).

Murphy, C. (1988). Community problems, problem communities, and community policing in Toronto. *Journal of Research in Crime and Delinquency, 25*(4), 392–410.

Oliver, W. M. (1998a). *Community-oriented policing: A systematic approach to policing.* Upper Saddle River, NJ: Prentice Hall.

Oliver, W. M. (1998b). Moving beyond "police-community relations" and "the police and society": Community-oriented policing as an academic course. *Journal of Criminal Justice Education, 9*(2), 303–317.

Pace, D. F. (1993). *Community relations: Concepts.* Placerville, CA: Copperhouse.

Palmiotto, M. J., & Donahue, M. E. (1995). Evaluating community policing: Problems and prospects. *Police Studies, 18*(2), 33–53.

Peak, K. J., & Glensor, R. W. (1999). *Community policing and problem solving: Strategies and practices* (2nd ed.). Upper Saddle River, NJ: Prentice Hall.

Rosenbaum, D. P. (1998). The changing role of the police: Assessing the current transition to community policing. In J. P. Brodeur (Ed.), *How to recognize good policing: Problems and issues* (pp. 3–29). Thousand Oaks, CA: Sage.

Rosenbaum, D. P. (Ed.). (1994). *The challenge of community policing: Testing the promises.* Thousand Oaks, CA: Sage.

Skogan, W. G. (1998). Community participation and community policing. In J. P. Brodeur (Ed.), How to recognize good policing: Problems and issues (pp. 88–106). Thousand Oaks, CA: Sage.

Skogan, W. G., & Hartnett, S. M. (1997). *Community policing, Chicago style.* New York: Oxford University Press.

Skolnick, J. H., & Bayley, D. H. (1988). Community policing: Issues and practices around the world. Washington, DC: National Institute of Justice.

Sparrow, M. K. (1988). Implementing community policing. *Perspectives on Policing, 9*(November).

Sparrow, M. K., Moore, M., & Kennedy, D. M. (1990). *Beyond 911: A new era for policing.* New York: Basic Books.

Strecher, V. G. (1997). *Planning community policing: Goal specific cases and exercises.* Prospect Heights, IL: Waveland Press.

Toch, H., & Grant, J. D. (1991). *Police as problem solvers.* New York: Plenum Press.

Trojanowicz, R., & Belknap, J. (1986). *Community policing: Training issues.* Community Policing Series, no. 9. Flint, MI: National Neighborhood Foot Patrol Center.

Trojanowicz, R., & Bucqueroux, B. (1990). *Community policing: A contemporary perspective.* Cincinnati, OH: Anderson.

Trojanowicz, R., & Bucqueroux, B. (1994). *Community policing: How to get started.* Cincinnati, OH: Anderson.

Trojanowicz, R., & Carter, D. (1988). *The philosophy and role of community policing.* Community Policing Series, no. 13. Flint, MI: National Neighborhood Foot Patrol Center.

Trojanowicz, R., Hockwater, G., Sinclair, D., & Wriggelsworth, D. (1994). Extending community policing into corrections operations. *Corrections Today, 56*(2), 190–193.

Trojanowicz, R., Kappeler, V. E., Gaines, L. K., & Bucqueroux, B. (1998). *Community policing: A contemporary perspective* (2nd ed.). Cincinnati, OH: Anderson.

Vardalis, J. (1992). Prospects of community policing and converting police behavior. *Journal of Police and Criminal Psychology, 8*(2), 37–40.

Watson, E. M., Stone, A. R., & DeLuca, S. M. (1998). *Strategies for community policing.* Upper Saddle River, NJ: Prentice Hall.

Wycoff, M. A. (1988). The benefits of community policing: Evidence and conjecture. In J. R. Greene, & S. D. Mastrofski (Eds.), *Community policing: Rhetoric or reality* (pp. 103–120). New York: Praeger Press.

Wycoff, M. A. (1995). *Community policing strategies.* NIJ Research Preview. Washington, DC: U.S. Department of Justice.

Wycoff, M. A., & Skogan, W. G. (1993). *Community policing in Madison: Quality from the inside, out: An evaluation of implementation and impact.* Washington, DC: National Institute of Justice.

Special Note

The previous reference example did not use interviews, Web sources, or court cases. Since these are commonly found within the criminal-justice/criminology literature, we are providing a brief notation on how to cite each type.

How to reference an interview:

Interviews are considered a type of personal communication, and are referenced only within the body of the text, using the following format:

the interviewee's name (interview, date) or

the interviewee's name (personal communication, date)

How to reference a Web source:

The Internet is quickly becoming a popular tool for finding sources to support research. Perhaps the two most popular Internet sources are a Web site and an electronic journal. For citing a Web site, provide the specific Web address. For an Internet article that is printed in a "hard-copy" journal, you use the same format as for a journal article, except that you add {Electronic version} after the name of the article. For the article that is available only electronically, provide the name(s) of the author(s), the data, the title of the article, the name of the publication, the issue and/or volume number, the date retrieved, and the Web address from which the article was retrieved.

How to reference a court case:

Perhaps the easiest item to reference is a court case. The format is simply this:

Name v. Name, volume source page (court date).

Tables and Figures

Most likely, your research paper will include at least one table or figure. As previously noted, these items may be placed within the text, kept separate and noted where they should be inserted, or else they may be placed at the end of the paper. Regardless of their location, tables and figures need to be clear as to their content, and must be readily understandable.

Appendixes

This last section is not a requirement of every paper. However, it is often useful to include a copy of the questionnaire or other tools that should be shared but do not belong in the body of the paper. There are no limitations to the number of appendixes a paper may have, except for those established by the instructor or the journal.

■ Summary

Regardless of the fear or loathing one feels about writing up the research, this task is important. It may also be required. Formatting the paper in the manner suggested can make the process easier. Grammar and spelling are extremely important, along with using language that the intended audience can understand. Today, with the availability of various word-processing software, which often includes spelling and grammar checkers, this aspect of the writing should not be as difficult as in years past. Ultimately, the goal should be to submit the most efficiently written paper possible.

The objective of this chapter has been to demonstrate the research process through the act of writing up the research into a complete paper, divided into sections to better explain each part. Consequently, you should now have a much better understanding of research methods. We trust that you have found by this point that conducting and reporting research is not as intimidating as you perhaps had perceived it to be at the beginning of this text.

METHODOLOGICAL QUERIES

Based on the idea of the College Students' Criminality Survey:

1. Describe the elements you would include in the introduction, methodology, and conclusion(s). Would you need an appendix? If so, what would be in it?

2. Why do you think students fear writing research papers?

REFERENCES

Morgan, S. E., T. Reichert, and T. R. Harrison. 2002. *From Numbers to Words.* Boston: Allyn and Bacon.

14 Summing Up

Vignette 14-1 In a Nutshell!

Next week is finals. It has been an interesting semester, especially in your research-methods class. The information you have received will definitely assist you in the completion of your senior project. However, the more pressing matter is the final for the research course. You understand that it is comprehensive—and therefore, anything goes—but you obviously do not have the time or inclination to reread every chapter. Your notes are good, but you are not completely confident that you have everything you need to know. Suddenly you realize that 13 chapters of your book were covered during the course, but not the last one. So you decide to check out the last chapter with a hope that maybe it will be the study guide you were looking for. Here it is!!!

Chapter Objectives

After studying this chapter, the student should be able to:

- Present and discuss the issues involved in Research: What, Why, and How.
- Identify and describe the issues involved in The Language of Research.
- Present and discuss the issues involved in Getting Started.
- Recognize and explain the issues involved in Research Ethics.
- Present and discuss the issues involved in Qualitative Research.
- Recognize and explain the issues involved in Quantitative Research.
- Present and discuss the issues involved in Research Designs.
- Identify and describe the issues involved in Questionnaire Construction.

- Present and discuss the issues involved in Sampling.
- Explain the issues involved in Data Collection.
- Recognize and explain the issues involved in Data Processing and Analysis.
- Present and discuss the issues involved in Inferential Statistics.
- Present and discuss the issues involved in Writing the Research.

■ Summing Up

The purpose of this chapter is to provide an overview of the key elements of research discussed in the previous chapters of this text. Our intent is to help you see how all of the information provided earlier enables you to progress from the development of a possible research topic to the completion of a methodologically sound research paper. This should refresh your memory in preparation for a possible final examination in this course. In addition, it will aid as a reference for dealing with future research assignments.

■ Doing Criminological Research

Ordinary human inquiry may be flawed due to inaccurate observation, overgeneralization, selective observation, and illogical reasoning. The scientific method seeks to prevent the errors of casual inquiry by utilizing procedures that specify objectivity, logic, theoretical understanding, and knowledge of prior research in the development and use of a precise-measurement instrument designed to accurately record observations.

Types of Research

Research creates questions, but ultimately, regardless of the subject or topic under study, it is the goal of research to provide answers. Research may occur in one of four formats or types, as descriptive, explanatory, predictive, or intervening knowledge. Knowledge that is descriptive allows us to understand what something is. Explanatory research tries to tell us why something occurs (the causes behind it). Predictive research gives some foresight as to what may happen if something is implemented or tried. Intervening knowledge allows one to intercede before a problem or issue gets too difficult to address.

Steps in Research

Whether the research is applied or basic, qualitative or quantitative, the basic steps are applicable to each. There are five primary steps in conducting research:

1. *Identifying the Problem*: Identifying or determining the problem, issue, or policy to be studied is what sets the groundwork for the rest of the research.

2. *Research Design*: The research design is the "blueprint," which outlines how the research is conducted.

3. *Data Collection*: Regardless of the research design, data collection is a key component. A variety of methods exist. They include surveys, interviews, observations, and previously existing data.

4. *Data Analysis*: Proper analysis and interpretation of the data is integral to the research process.

5. *Reporting*: The last phase of any research project is the reporting of the findings. Regardless of the audience or the medium used, the findings must be coherent and understandable.

■ The Language of Research Theory

All criminal-justice practice is grounded in criminological theory. A theory is a statement that attempts to make sense of reality. Proving that a theory is valid is a common goal of criminological and criminal-justice researchers.

Conceptualization

Concepts are viewed as the beginning point for all research endeavors and are often very broad in nature. They are the bases of theories and serve as a means to communicate, introduce, classify, and build thoughts and ideas. To conduct research, the concept must first be taken from its conceptual or theoretical level to an observational level. This process is known as conceptualization.

Operationalization

Operationalization is describing how a concept is measured. This process is best described as the conversion of the abstract idea or notion into a measurable item. The primary focus of the operationalization process is the creation of variables and subsequently developing a measurement instrument to assess those variables. Variables are concepts that may be divided into two or more categories or groupings known as attributes.

Variables

A dependent variable is a factor that requires other factors to cause or influence change. Basically, the dependent variable is the outcome factor or that which is being predicted. The independent variable is the influential or the predictor factor. These are the variables believed to cause the change or outcome of the dependent variable, and are something the researcher can control.

Hypotheses

Once the concept has been operationalized into variables befitting the theory in question, most research focuses on testing the validity of a statement (or statements) called a hypothesis (or hypotheses). The hypothesis is a specific statement describing the expected relationship between the independent and dependent variables. There are three common types of hypotheses: research, null, and rival.

■ Sampling

A sample is a group chosen from within a target population to provide information sought. There are a number of sampling strategies that are available in criminological research. These include random sampling, stratified random sampling, cluster sampling, snowball sampling, and purposive sampling.

Validity

Validity is a term describing whether the employed measure accurately represents the concept it is meant to measure. There are four types of validity: face, content, construct, and criterion.

1. *Face Validity*: This is the simplest form of validity, and basically refers to whether the measuring device appears, on its face, to measure what the researcher wants to measure. This is primarily a judgmental decision.

2. *Content Validity*: Each item of the measuring device is examined to determine whether each element is measuring the concept in question.

3. *Construct Validity*: This validity inquires as to whether the measuring device does indeed measure what it has been designed to measure. It refers to the fit between theoretical and operational definition of the concept.

4. *Criterion (or Pragmatic) Validity*: This type of validity represents the degree to which the measure relates to an external criterion. It can be either concurrent (does the measure enhance the ability to assess the current characteristics of the concept under study?) or predictive (the ability to accurately foretell future events or conditions).

Reliability

Reliability refers to how consistent the measuring device would be over time. In other words, if the study is replicated, the measuring device provides consistent results. The two key components of reliability are stability and consistency. Stability means the ability to retain accuracy and resist change. Consistency is the ability to yield similar results when replicated.

■ Data

Data are simply pieces of information gathered from the sample. The information describes events, beliefs, characteristics, people, or other phenomena. This data may exist at one of four levels: nominal, ordinal, interval, or ratio.

Nominal Data

This data level is categorical based on some defined characteristic. The categories are exclusive and have no logical order. For example, gender is a nominal-level data form.

Ordinal Data

Like nominal data, ordinal data are categorical, but the characteristics of ordinal data may be rank-ordered. These data categories are also exclusive, but are scaled in a manner representative of the amount of characteristic in question, along some dimension. For example, types of prisons composed as minimum, medium, and maximum.

Interval Data

Categorical data for which there is a distinctive yet equal difference among the characteristics measured are interval data. The categories have order, and represent equal units on a scale with no set zero starting point (for example, the IQ of prisoners).

Ratio Data

This data type is ordered, has equal units of distance, and has a true zero starting point (for example, age, weight, income).

■ Getting Started

As with so many issues in life, often the hardest aspect of research is getting started. There are a number of issues involved in beginning criminological research. Proper preparation is vital to the successful completion of a research project.

Picking a Topic

Before the topic is chosen, one should consider the following:

1. What currently exists in the literature
2. Any gaps in theory or the current state of art
3. The feasibility of conducting the research
4. Whether there are any policy implications
5. Possible funding availability

Reviewing the Literature

Ultimately, the best way to begin a research effort is to focus on a particular issue, phenomenon, or problem that most interests the individual. In doing so, one must be sure to determine what the problem, issue, or phenomenon is, and one must then organize what is known about it. Once a literature search has been completed, the research question(s) can be formulated.

The Research Question

A well-worded research question should give a clear indication of the outcomes one might expect at the conclusion of the research. After establishing the research question(s), the researcher must next offer what specifically is going to be studied and the expected results. This is usually accomplished through statements or propositions referred to as hypotheses.

Hypotheses

A hypothesis is a specific statement describing the expected result or relationship between the independent and dependent variables. The three most common types are:

1. *The research hypothesis*: A statement of the expected relationship between variables offered in a positive manner
2. *The null hypothesis*: A statement that the relationship or difference being tested does not exist
3. *The rival hypothesis*: A statement offering an alternate explanation for the research findings

Variables

Variables are factors that can change or influence change. They result from the operationalization of a concept. The two types of variables are:

1. *The dependent variable(s)*: The factor(s) being influenced to change over which the researcher has no control. Basically, the dependent variable(s) is/are the outcome item(s) or what is being predicted.
2. *The independent variable(s)*: The factor(s) that will influence or predict the outcome of the dependent variable(s). This variable is something the researcher can control.

■ Research Ethics

Ethics was defined as doing what is morally and legally right in the conducting of research. This requires the researcher to be knowledgeable about what is being done; to use reasoning when making decisions; to be both intellectual and truthful in approach and reporting; and to consider the consequences—in particular, to be sure that the outcome of the research outweighs any negatives that might occur.

Ethical neutrality requires that the researchers' moral or ethical beliefs are not allowed to influence the gathering of data or the conclusions that are made from analyzing the data. Objectivity is striving to prevent personal ideology or prejudices from influencing the process. In addition to these concerns, the researcher must also ensure that their research concerns do not negatively impact upon the safety of others.

Ethical Concerns

Ethical concerns include the following:

1. *Harm to Others*: Physical harm most often can occur during experimental or applied types of research. Psychological harm might result through the type of information being gathered. Social harm may be inflicted if certain information gathered is released that should not have been released.

2. *Privacy Concerns*: Individuals in America have a basic right to privacy. In many cases, research efforts may violate that right. Ethically speaking, if a person does not want his or her life examined, then that right should be respected.

3. *Informed Consent*: Normally, this requires having the individual sign an "Informed Consent" form or for the instructions to indicate that the survey is completely anonymous, voluntary, and that the information is being used only for the purpose of research.

4. *Voluntary Participation*: Participation should be voluntary. If not, there must be valid reasons that can be given showing that the knowledge could not otherwise be reasonably obtained, and that no harm will come to the participants from their compulsory involvement. To ensure that informed consent is provided and to judge the value and ethical nature of the research, many universities have institutional review boards (IRBs).

5. *Deception*: Some types of research (particularly field research that requires the researcher to in essence "go undercover" in order to gain the knowledge that he or she is seeking) cannot be conducted if the subjects are aware that they are being studied. Such research is controversial and must be carefully thought out before it is undertaken.

Ethical Research Criteria

The following criteria should be followed to produce ethical research:

1. Avoid harmful research.
2. Be objective in designing, conducting, and evaluating your research.
3. Use integrity in the performance and reporting of the research.
4. Protect confidentiality.

■ Qualitative Research

Qualitative research is defined as the nonnumerical examination and interpretation of observations for the purpose of discovering underlying meanings and patterns of relationships. Such analysis enables researchers to verbalize insights that quantifying of data would not permit. It also allows us to avoid the trap of "false precision," which frequently occurs when subjective numerical assignments are made.

Types of Qualitative Research

Field Interviewing

Field interviewing consists of structured interviews, semistructured interviews, unstructured interviews, and focus groups. A structured interview entails the asking of preestablished, open-ended questions of every respondent. A semistructured interview goes beyond the responses given to the actual questions for a broader understanding of the answer. Unstructured interviews seldom keep to a schedule, nor are there usually any predetermined possible answers. Focus groups interview several individuals in one setting.

Field Observation (or Participant-Observer)

Field observation consists of observing individuals in their natural setting. The method of observation is determined by the role of the researcher. The full-participant method allows the researcher to carry out observational research, but does so in a "covert" manner. The participant-researcher participates in the activities of the research environment, but is known to the research subjects to be a researcher. The researcher-who-participates method requires nothing more than observation by the researcher, whose status as a researcher is known to the research subjects. The complete researcher avoids all possible interaction with the research subjects.

Ethnographic Study

Ethnographic study or field research overlaps with field observation in that the researcher actually enters the environment under study, but does not necessarily take part in any activities.

Sociometry

Sociometry is a technique by which the researcher can measure social dynamics or relational structures such as who likes whom. Information can be gathered through interviews or by observation, and will indicate who is chosen and the characteristics about those who do the choosing.

Historiography

Historiography (also known as historical/comparative research) is basically the study of actions, events, phenomena, and so forth that have already occurred. This type of research often involves the study of documents and records with information about the topic under study. Historiography can be either qualitative or quantitative in nature, depending on the materials being utilized and the focus of the research.

Content Analysis

Like historical research, content analysis is the study of social artifacts to gain insights about an event or phenomenon. It differs in that the focus is on the coverage of the event by the particular medium being evaluated rather than on the event. Depending upon how the research is conducted, this may be either qualitative or quantitative in nature.

■ Quantitative Research

Quantitative research was defined as the numerical representation and manipulation of observations for the purpose of describing and explaining the phenomena that those observations represent. It is based upon empiricism. The use of the scientific method, with its focus on causation rather than casual observation, is what makes empiricism important. It is this emphasis on empiricism rather than idealism that is the basis upon which positive criminology is founded.

Causality

In applying empirical observation to criminal-justice research, we focus on causal relationships. When we try to examine numerous explanations for why an event occurred, this is known as idiographic explanation. When researchers focus on a relatively few observations in order to provide a partial explanation for an event, this is known as nomothetic causation. Nomothetic explanations of causality are based on probabilities. It is this use of probability that enables us to make inferences based upon a relatively few observations.

The Criteria for Causality

The first criterion is that the independent variable (the variable that is providing the influence) must occur before the dependent variable (the variable that is being acted upon). The second criterion is that a relationship between the independent variable and the dependent variable must be observed. The third criterion is that the apparent relationship is not explained by a third variable.

Necessary and Sufficient Cause

In investigating causality, we must meet the above criteria, but we do not have to demonstrate a perfect correlation. If a condition or event must occur in order for another event to take place, that is known as a necessary cause. The cause must be present in order for the effect to occur. When the presence of a condition will ordinarily cause the effect to occur, this is known as a sufficient cause. The cause will usually create the effect, but will not always do so.

False Precision

When quantifying data, it is imperative that the numerical assignments are valid. If you arbitrarily assign numbers to variables without a logical reason for doing so, the numbers have no true meaning. This assignment is known as false precision. We have quantified a concept, but that assignment is subjective rather than objective. The precision that we claim does not really exist.

Types of Quantitative Research

Survey Research

One of the most popular research methods in criminal justice is the survey. The survey design is used when researchers are interested in the experiences, attitudes, perceptions, or beliefs of individuals, or when trying to determine the extent of a policy, procedure, or action among members of a specific group. Surveys may consist of personal interviews, mail and e-mail questionnaires, or telephone surveys.

Field Research

If field observations were made (such as observing how many vehicles ran a certain stop sign in a given time period, or how many times members of the group being observed exhibited specific behaviors) that allowed for numerical assignments, then this would be quantified field research.

Unobtrusive Research

Unobtrusive research is research that does not disturb or intrude into the lives of human subjects in order to obtain research information. Examples of quantitative unobtrusive research include analysis of existing data, historical research, and content analysis. In the analysis of existing data, the researcher obtains the existing information and reanalyzes it. Historical research and content analysis are conducted as discussed previously, but emphasize statistical rather than verbal analysis.

Evaluation Research

Evaluation research is a quantified comparative-research design that assists in the development of new skills or approaches. It aids in the solving of problems with direct implications to the "real world." This type of research usually has a quasi-experimental perspective to it. Evaluation research that studies existing programs is frequently referred to as program evaluation.

Combination Research

Combinations of different quantitative methods are commonly used. They may include the use of survey research and field observation, survey research and unobtrusive research, unobtrusive research and field observation, or a combination of all three.

■ Research Designs

There are a number of issues to consider in selecting a research design. These include the following:

1. *Purpose of Research*: The purpose of the research project. It should be clearly indicative of what will be studied.

2. *Prior Research*: Review similar or relevant research. This will promote knowledge of the literature.

3. *Theoretical Orientation*: Describe the theoretical framework upon which the research is based.

4. *Definition*: List the various concepts that have been developed and clarify their meanings.

5. *Research Hypotheses*: Develop the various hypotheses that will be evaluated in the research.

6. *Unit of Analysis*: Describe the particular objects, individuals, or entities that are being studied as elements of the population.

7. *Data-Collection Techniques*: Determine how the data are to be collected. Who will collect the data, who or what will be studied, and how will it be done?

8. *Sampling Procedures*: Sample type, sample size, as well as the specific procedures to be utilized.

9. *Instrument(s) Used*: The nature of the measurement instrument or data-collection device that is used.

10. *Analytic Techniques*: How the data will be processed and examined. What specific statistical procedures will be used?

11. *Time Frame*: The period of time covered by the study. This will include the time period examined by research questions, as well as the amount of time spent in preparation, data collection, data analysis, and presentation.

12. *Ethical Issues*: Will address any concerns as to the potential harm that could occur to participants. Will also deal with any potential biases or conflicts of interest that could impact upon the study.

Types of Design

There are a number of designs used by criminological researchers.

Historical

Historical designs allow the researcher to systematically and objectively reconstruct the past. This is accomplished through the collection, evaluation, verification, and synthesis of information, usually secondary data already existing in previously gathered records, in order to establish facts.

Descriptive

Descriptive research focuses on the describing of facts and characteristics of a given population, issue, policy, or any given area of interest in a systematic and accurate manner. Like the historical design, a descriptive study can also rely on secondary or records data.

Developmental or Time Series

This type of research design allows for the investigation of specifically identified patterns and events, growth, and/or change over a specific amount of time. There are several time-series designs that are available: cross-sectional studies, longitudinal studies, trend studies, cohort studies, and panel studies.

Cross-sectional Studies

The primary concept of the cross-sectional design is that it allows for a complete description of a single entity during a specific time frame.

Longitudinal Studies

Where cross-sectional studies view events or phenomena at one time, longitudinal studies examine events over an extended period. For this reason, longitudinal studies are useful for explanation as well as exploration and description.

Trend Studies

Trend studies examine changes in a general population over time. For example, one might compare results from several census studies to determine what demographic changes have occurred within that population.

Cohort Studies

Cohort studies are trend studies that focus upon the changes that occur in specific subpopulations over time. Usually cohort studies employ age groupings.

Panel Studies

Panel studies are similar to trend and cohort studies, except that they examine the same set of people each time. By utilizing the same individuals, couples, groups, and so forth, researchers are able to more precisely examine the extent of changes and the events that influenced them.

Case Studies

The case (sometimes referred to as case-and-field) research design allows for the intensive study of a given issue, policy, or group in its social context at one point in time, even though that period may span months or years. It includes close scrutiny of the background, current status, and relationships or interactions of the topic under study.

Correlational

One of the more popular research designs is one that allows researchers to investigate how one factor may affect or influence another factor, or how the one factor correlates with another. In particular, this type of design focuses on how variations of one variable correspond with variations of other variables.

Causal-Comparative

This design allows the researcher to examine relationships from a cause-and-effect perspective. This is done through the observation of an existing outcome or consequence, and through searching back through the data for plausible causal factors.

True, or Classic, Experimental

This type of design allows for the investigation of possible cause-and-effect relationships where one or more experimental units will be exposed to one or more treatment conditions. The outcomes are then compared to the outcomes of one or more control groups that did not receive the treatment. This design includes three major components: (1) independent and dependent variables, (2) experimental and control groups, and (3) pre- and post-testing.

Quasi-Experimental

Unlike the true experimental design, where the researcher has almost complete control over relevant variables, the quasi-experimental design allows for the approximation of conditions similar to the true experiment. However, the setting does not allow for control and/or manipulation of the relevant variables.

■ Questionnaire Construction

Whenever possible, use a questionnaire that has previously been developed and tested. The primary reason for this is because it eliminates the worries of validity and reliability, two major concerns of questionnaire development. In creating a new survey instrument, there are several aspects for consideration, including reliability and validity and the level of measurement to use.

Rules for Questionnaire Construction

1. Start with a list of all the items you are interested in knowing about the group, concept, or phenomenon.
2. Be prepared to establish validity and reliability.
3. The wording in the questionnaire must be appropriate for the target audience.
4. Be sure that it is clearly identifiable as to who should answer the questions.

5. Avoid asking any questions that are biased, leading, threatening, or double-barreled in nature.

6. Prior to construction, a decision must be made whether to use open- or closed-ended questions, or a combination.

7. Consider that the respondents may not have all the general information needed to complete the questionnaire.

8. Whenever possible, pretest the questionnaire before it is officially used.

9. Set up questions so that the responses are easily recognizable whether the questionnaire format is self-administered or interview.

10. The questionnaire should be organized in a concise manner that will keep the interest of the respondent, encouraging him or her to complete the entire questionnaire.

Scales

A common element of survey research is the construction of scales. A scale can be either the measurement device for a question or statement, or a compilation of statements or questions used to represent or acknowledge change. The items making up the scale need to represent one dimension befitting a continuum that is supposed to be reflective of only one concept. The representativeness of any scale will rely greatly on the level of measurement used.

Arbitrary Scales

This type of scale is designed to measure what the researcher believes the scale is measuring, and is based on face validity (discussed earlier) and professional judgment. While this allows for the creation of many different scales, the arbitrary type is easily criticized for its lack of substantive support.

Attitudinal Scales

More commonly found in criminal-justice and criminological research are the attitudinal scales. There are three primary types available: Thurstone, Likert, and Guttman.

1. *Thurstone Scales*: The construction of a Thurstone scale relies on the use of others (sometimes referred to as "judges") to indicate what items they think best fit the concept. There are two methods for completing this task. The first method is the "paired comparisons." Here, the judges are provided several pairs of questions or statements, and are asked to choose which most favorably fits the concept under study. The questions or statements picked most often by the judges become part of the questionnaire or compose the complete questionnaire.

2. *Likert Scales*: Probably the most commonly used method in attitudinal research is the Likert scale. This method generally makes use of a bipolar, five-point response range (that is, from "strongly agree" to "strongly disagree"). Questions to which all respondents provide similar responses are usually eliminated. The remaining questions are used to make up the scale.

3. *Guttman Scales*: The last type, the Guttman scale, requires that an attitudinal scale measure only one dimension or concept. The questions or statements must be progressive so that if the respondent answers positively to a question, he or she must respond the same to the following one.

■ Sampling

A population is the complete group or class from which information is to be gathered. A sample is a group chosen from within a target population to provide information sought.

Probability Theory

Probability theory is based on the concept that over time, there is a statistical order in which things occur. The knowledge that over time, things tend to adhere to a statistical order allows us to choose samples that are representative of a population in general.

Probability Sampling

The general goal when choosing a sample is to obtain one that is representative of the target population. Representation requires that every member in the population or the sampling frame have an equal chance of being selected for the sample. This is a probability sample. Four types of probability samples exist: simple random, stratified random, systematic, and cluster.

Simple Random Samples

A simple random sample is one in which all members of a given population have the same chance of being selected. Furthermore, the selection of each member must be independent from the selection of any other members.

Stratified Random Samples

These strata are selected based upon specified characteristics that the researcher wishes to ensure for inclusion within the study. This type of sample requires the researcher to have knowledge of the sampling frame's demographic characteristics. These characteristics (selected variables) are then used to create the strata from which the sample is chosen.

Systematic Samples

There seems to be some debate over this type of sampling. It includes random selection, and initially allows inclusion of every member of the sampling frame. With a systematic sample, every nth item in the sampling frame is included in the sample.

Cluster Samples

The last of the probability-sampling methods is the cluster sample (also known as area-probability sample). This sample consists of randomly selected groups rather than individuals. Basically, the population to be surveyed is divided into clusters. Subsequent subsamples of the clusters are then selected.

Nonprobability Sampling

The major difference between probability and nonprobability sampling is that one provides the opportunity for all members of the sampling frame to be selected while the other does not.

Purposive Samples

Among the nonprobability samples, the purposive sample appears to be the most popular. Based on the researcher's skill, judgment, and needs, an appropriate sample is selected. When the subjects are selected in advance based upon the researcher's view that they reflect normal or average scores, this is sometimes referred to as typical-case sampling. If subgroups are sampled to permit comparisons among them, this technique is known as stratified purposeful sampling.

Quota Samples

These types of research efforts often rely on quota sampling. For this type of sample, the proportions are based on the researcher's judgment for inclusion. Selection continues until enough individuals have been chosen to fill out the sample.

Snowball Samples

Although not a highly promoted form of quantitative sampling, snowball sampling is commonly used as a qualitative technique. The snowball sample begins with a person or persons who provide names of other people for the sample.

Convenience Sample

Undoubtedly the last choice for a sample is the convenience sample, or available-subjects sample. Here, there is no attempt to ensure any type of representativeness. Usually this sample is a very abstract representation of the population or target frame. Units or individuals are chosen simply because they were "in the right place at the right time." Convenience samples are often useful as explorations upon which future research may be based.

Sample Size

Usually the sample size is the result of several elements:

> **1.** How accurate the sample must be
>
> **2.** Economic feasibility (how much you have to spend)
>
> **3.** The availability of requisite variables (including any subcategories)
>
> **4.** Accessibility to the target population

Confidence Levels

Addressing how large the sample should be requires an understanding of confidence intervals. The smaller the confidence interval, the more accurate the estimated sample. The estimated probability that a population parameter will fall within a given confidence interval is known as the confidence level. Thus, to reduce sampling error, the researcher would desire a smaller confidence interval. To do so, he or she would select a smaller confidence level. Generally, in social-science research, we seek a sample size that would vary 95 times out of 100 by 5 percent or less from the population. A sampling formula and sample-size selection chart was provided in Chapter 9.

To ensure that the necessary numbers are obtained, we recommend that you always oversample by 20 percent. If this isn't enough, you can always add more observations as long as they are randomly selected from the same population, and as long as any time differences would not impact upon responses.

■ Data Collection

There are four primary data-collection techniques available: survey, interview (often classified in surveys), observation, and unobtrusive means.

Survey Research

Probably the most frequently used method for data collection is the survey. There are two primary means for collecting data through surveys: mail surveys and self-completing questionnaires. A common means of distributing questionnaires is through the mail or by direct distribution. A newer means of distribution is through e-mail.

Mail Surveys

This method allows for use of fairly large samples and broader area coverage, and the cost in terms of time and money can be kept to a minimum. Additional advantages include the fact that no field staff is required, that this method eliminates the bias effect possible in interviews, that it allows the respondents greater privacy, that it places fewer time constraints on the respondents so that more consideration can be given to the answers, and finally, that this method offers the chance of a high percentage of returns, thus improving the representativeness of the sample. The most frustrating disadvantage of mail surveys is the lack of responses.

Ways to increase response rates include offering some type of remuneration or "reward" for completing the survey, appealing to the respondent's altruistic side, using an attractive and shortened format, being able to indicate that the survey is sponsored or endorsed by a recognizable entity, personalizing the survey, and enhancing the timing of the survey.

E-mail

With the growing popularity of the computer and the Internet, e-mail is becoming a natural means for quickly distributing surveys to a broad geographic area and diverse population. Although many questions arise as to its strength for garnering large enough samples, this method will continue to be an increasingly popular means of distributing and collecting data.

Self-Administered Surveys

The self-administered survey is generally a written questionnaire that is distributed to the selected sample in a structured environment. Respondents are allowed to complete the survey in a given time period and then return it to the researcher, often through an emissary of the sample.

Interviews

There are several types of interviews that may be utilized in criminological research.

1. *Structured Interviews*: Probably the most used type of interview in criminal-justice research is the structured interview. This requires the use of closed-ended questions that every individual interviewed must be asked in the same order. Responses are set and can be checked off by the interviewer.

It is, in reality, a questionnaire that is being administered orally, with the interviewer completing the form for the respondent.

2. *Unstructured Interviews*: The unstructured interview offers respondents open-ended questions where no set response is provided. While this allows for more-in-depth responses, it is much more difficult to quantify the responses.

3. *In-depth Interviews*: The in-depth interview can make use of both fixed and open-ended questions. The difference from the others is that the interviewer can further explore why the response was given and could ask additional qualifying questions.

4. *Face-to-Face Interviews*: Face-to-face interviews provide contact between the researcher and the respondent. This contact can be positive reinforcement for participating in the research. Oftentimes simply receiving a questionnaire in the mail can be very sterile and, because of that lack of personal touch, might cause would-be respondents to simply ignore the survey.

Telephone Surveys

The advantages of telephone surveying begin with being able to eliminate a field staff and get by with only a very small in-house staff. This method also makes it easier to monitor interviewer bias; specifically, it eliminates the sending of any nonverbal cues. In addition, the telephone interview is less expensive and very quick.

Observation/Field Research

Like survey research, observational research has its advantages and disadvantages. One of the best advantages is the direct collection of the data. Rather than having to rely on what others have seen, the field researcher relies only on his or her personal observations.

Unobtrusive Data Collection

The last means for collecting data is through unobtrusive measures. These are any methods of data collection where the subjects of the research are completely unaware of being studied, and where that study is not observational. Two of the more commonly used types of unobtrusive data collection have been discussed previously in this chapter. They are content analysis and the use of archival data (analyzing existing statistics and/or documents).

Data Processing and Analysis

Data processing consists of data coding, data entry, and data cleaning. Coding is simply assigning values to the data for statistical analyses. Once the data have been coded, they can then be entered into a computer-software program for analysis. The key to data entry is accuracy. Data cleaning is the preliminary analysis of your data. Here, you "clean" any mistakes that might have occurred during the initial recording of data or during data entry.

Dealing with Missing Data

There are a number of ways to deal with missing information. If the data have been left out on a single question, you may chose to input this as a nonresponse.

Another option is to assume that the missing data are due to an oversight rather than an intentional omission. Yet another option is to exclude from your analysis the survey instrument containing the omission. If the instrument used is a Likert scale, the response may be classified as "neither agree nor disagree" or "don't know" (depending upon how your scale is worded).

Recoding Data

By collapsing the categories into logical groupings, the data can be presented clearly and concisely. If necessary, the resulting table could easily be collapsed even more. In collapsing data, please recall our earlier discussions of the different levels of measurement. Higher-level data (such as ratio or interval data) can be collapsed down into lower-level data (such as ordinal or nominal data), but you cannot do the opposite and convert lower-level data to a higher level.

Data Analysis

There are three types of data analysis: univariate, bivariate, and multivariate. Univariate analysis is the examination of the distribution of cases on only one variable at a time. Bivariate analysis is when the relationship between two variables is examined. Multivariate analysis is the examination of three or more variables. This technique is inferential in nature in that we have usually already conducted both descriptive and comparative statistical analyses (through univariate and bivariate analyses) of the data and are now seeking to examine the relationships among several variables.

Statistical Analysis
There are three types of statistics:

1. *Descriptive*: The function of which is describing the data
2. *Comparative*: The function of which is compare the attributes (or subgroups) of two variables
3. *Inferential*: The function of which is to make an inference, estimation, or prediction about the data

Frequency Distributions
There are four types of frequency distributions with which you should be familiar: absolute, relative, cumulative, and cumulative relative. The most common are absolute frequency distributions, which display the raw numbers, and relative frequency distributions, which convert the numbers into percentages for easier interpretation by readers.

Displaying Frequencies
Frequencies, by whole numbers and/or percentages in table form, are just one means of describing the data. Other means include pie charts, bar graphs, histograms and polygons, line charts, and maps.

Other Ways to Describe the Data
In addition to frequency distributions, the researcher may describe the properties of the data through measures of central tendency, measures of variability, skewness, and kurtosis.

1. *Measures of Central Tendency*: The three most common measures of central tendency are the mean, the median, and the mode. The mean is the arithmetic average. The median is the midpoint. The mode is the most frequently occurring number. The uses of measures of central tendency and how to compute them were discussed in detail in Chapter 11.

2. *Measures of Variability*: The three main measures of variability are range, variance, and standard deviation. The range is simply the difference between the highest and lowest scores. Variance is the difference between the scores and the mean. Standard deviation indicates how far from the mean the score actually is.

3. *Skewness and Kurtosis*: By using polygons, line charts, or scatterplots, researchers are able to see the distribution of their data. If it is a normal distribution, the researcher is able to use a broader range of statistical techniques. If it is a nonnormal (also known as nonparametric) distribution, the statistical techniques that may be used are more limited. Skewness alerts the researcher to the presence of outliers. Kurtosis refers to the amount of smoothness or pointedness of the curve. Such knowledge aids statisticians in conducting their analyses of the data.

Inferential Statistics

Inferential statistics allow the researcher to develop inferences (predictions) about the data. By using statistical analyses, researchers are able to make estimations or predictions about the data. If the sample is representative, these predictions may be extended to the population from which the data were drawn. Inferential statistics allow criminological researchers to conduct research that can be generalized to larger populations within society.

Measures of Association

Measures of association are the means by which researchers are able to determine the strengths of relationships among the variables that are being studied. The measure of association that is used is dependent upon the type of analysis that is being conducted, the distribution of the data, and the data level that is used. There are many measures of association that are utilized in criminological research. Individual researchers may prefer to use different measures. However, there are some measures that are considered to be standards. Lambda is commonly used for nominal-level data. Gamma is commonly used for ordinal-level research. Pearson's r and R^2 are commonly used for interval- and ratio-level data.

Statistical Significance

Statistical significance is how researchers determine whether their sample findings are representative of the population that they are studying. If you are using a complete enumeration (the entire population is studied rather than just a sample from that population), then statistical significance is a moot point in that we already know that the population is accurately represented. However, complete enumerations are rare in that very small populations limit generalizabilty, and large populations are too costly and time-consuming to study as a whole. Statistical significance is based upon probability sampling. Generally, social-science research desires a statistical significance of .05 or better. This means that we are 95 percent confident that our findings represent the population that was sampled. As seen in Chapter 12, determining statistical significance varies depending upon the statistical procedures that are used.

Bivariate Analysis

Bivariate analysis is the examination of the relationship between two variables. Usually this involves attempting to determine how a dependent variable is influenced by an independent variable. The more commonly used bivariate techniques are cross-tabulations (contingency tables), chi-square, and bivariate (simple linear) regression. In assessing the relationship between the two variables, we examine the contingency table or the regression-scatterplot results, the measure of association (such as gamma or R^2), and the level of statistical significance (hopefully 0.05 or lower).

Multivariate Analysis

Multivariate analysis is the examination of the relationship between or among three or more variables. Usually this involves attempting to determine how a dependent variable is influenced by several independent variables. This methodology offers more insights than bivariate analysis in that we are able to study the relationships among several variables at one time. The more commonly used multivariate techniques are correlation, multiple regression, Student's t-test, analysis of variance (ANOVA), discriminant analysis, probit regression, factor analysis, and path analysis. In assessing the relationship between the multiple variables, we examine the correlation table, regression-scatterplot results, or other indicators (depending on the technique used); the measure of association (such as Pearson's r, R^2, Wilks' lambda, or other appropriate measure); as well as the level of statistical significance.

Nonparametric Techniques

When the distribution of the data is not normal, standard statistical techniques are usually not appropriate. In those cases, other procedures that are used include chi-square, nonparametric correlation, and nonlinear regression. As noted in Chapter 12, the reader is advised to consult with a statistician in these circumstances.

■ Writing the Research

In Chapter 13, a research-paper example was provided. The outline recommended in that chapter is as follows:

1. *The Title Page*: The title of your research paper (or article or thesis) should tell the reader in clear and concise terms what your research is about.

2. *Abstract*: The abstract is the summary or synopsis of the information being presented in the paper. It starts with the research title. The abstract presents the paper's major argument and describes the methods that were used.

3. *The Introduction*: This section establishes the research problem, the literature that supports its existence, and the reason to research the problem.

In addition, this section reports the research question or questions and the hypothesis or hypotheses, and briefly describes what was done.

4. *Methodology*: The methodology section is the mainstay of the paper. The writer should discuss the hypothesis or hypotheses, the research design, and the data-gathering technique. This includes explaining the research population, the sampling frame, and the questionnaire or other method used to gather the data. It is in this section that the researcher can fully explain where, when, how, and why the data were attained and analyzed.

5. *Results*: In this section, the writer describes the sample's characteristics, the statistical techniques used, the results, and whether they supported the hypothesis or hypotheses. It is within this section that various tables, graphs, and charts are commonly used to describe the data.

6. *Conclusions*: Usually the last section of the research paper is the conclusion or conclusions. Generally this section is used to offer insights about the research, whether it did what was expected, and possible problems. This section can also be used to discuss implications of the research and to provide a forum for suggestions for future related research.

7. *References*: When using other sources—whether quoting, paraphrasing, or simply as an outlet for affirming what is already known—the source should be recognized. This is done throughout the paper by various citation methods. The complete list of references, or bibliography, is provided at the end of the paper. The format depends upon to whom the paper is being submitted. The majority of the papers written for criminal justice and criminology will follow the APA style for reference citing in the text and at the end of the paper.

8. *Tables and Figures*: Tables and figures are included in research papers to aid the author in presenting and explaining information. Regardless of their location, tables and figures need to be clear as to their content and readily understandable.

9. *Appendixes*: It is often useful to include a copy of the questionnaire or other tools that need to be shared but just do not belong in the body of the paper. There are no limitations to the number of appendixes a paper could have, except for those established by the instructor or the journal.

■ Summary Statement

In this chapter, we have summarized those issues from the text that we thought important enough to warrant repetition. It is our hope that this text has provided you with the knowledge and insights necessary for successfully understanding and conducting research in criminal justice and/or criminology. We wish you the very best in your future research endeavors.

Index